RACIAL

AND ETHNIC

DIVERSITY

Asians, Blacks, Hispanics, Native Americans, and Whites

7th
EDITION

RACIAL
AND ETHNIC
DIVERSITY

Asians, Blacks, Hispanics, Native Americans, and Whites

New Strategist Press, LLC
Amityville, New York

New Strategist Press, LLC
P.O. Box 635, Amityville, New York 11701
800/848-0842; 631/608-8795
www.newstrategist.com

ISBN 978-1-940308-01-2 (paper)

Printed in the United States of America

Table of Contents

Chapter 6. Non-Hispanic Whites

Chapter 7. Total Population

List of Tables

Chapter 3. Asians

Education

Health

Housing

Income

Population

Spending

Wealth

Chapter 5. Hispanics

Education

Health

Chapter 6. Non-Hispanic Whites

Education

Health

Housing

Chapter 7. Total Population

Education

Health

Housing

Introduction

Demographic change is slow and steady, but not always. In the United States today, the racial and ethnic composition of the population is changing rapidly—fast enough to surprise census takers in 2010 and to be felt in neighborhoods, schools, and communities across the country. A number of factors are behind our rapidly growing diversity including immigration, higher fertility rates among blacks and Hispanics, and the more fluid racial categories introduced in 2000.

The 2000 census was the first in modern history to allow respondents to place themselves in more than one racial category. The results of that census documented the enormous complexity of racial and Hispanic-origin identities in the United States. Following the 2000 census, the government's many surveys adopted the new racial definitions and kept us well informed about the changing demographics of the population—or so we thought until the 2010 census surprised us. It counted 3 million fewer non-Hispanic whites than the Census Bureau had estimated. Our population was changing even faster than the government's number crunchers had suspected.

As we work our way through the second decade of the 21st century, something has changed in the United States. We have crossed a threshold from what will be to what is—we are now the multicultural nation that had been forecast for so many decades. More than 100 million Americans are Hispanic, African American, or Asian. Minorities account for more than one-third of the population and can determine the success or failure of everything from marketing plans to political campaigns. Hispanics are the largest minority. Asians are the most-affluent segment of the population—more so than non-Hispanic whites. Most African Americans are middle class, having made significant gains in education and earning power over the past few decades. Each of these growing segments of the population is of vital importance to policymakers and businesspeople searching for success.

The seventh edition of *Racial and Ethnic Diversity: Asians, Blacks, Hispanics, Native Americans, and Whites* reveals what you need to know about the multicultural United States. It is a family portrait of the new America. It is a reference tool that profiles the social and economic wellbeing of each racial and Hispanic origin group. *Racial and Ethnic Diversity* provides an all-important look at our demographics, revealing patterns of change that can no longer be ignored. The future has arrived.

In addition to detailed estimates and projections of the U.S. population by race and Hispanic origin, the seventh edition of *Racial and Ethnic Diversity* includes an Attitudes chapter that reveals what blacks, Hispanics, and non-Hispanic whites think about a range of issues from the American Dream to gay marriage. It presents the latest housing, income, labor force, and living arrangement data on American Indians, Asians, blacks, Hispanics, and non-Hispanic whites. This edition of *Racial and Ethnic Diversity* includes 2011 household spending data by race and Hispanic origin. It includes state and metropolitan area data for each race and Hispanic origin group, with numbers from the invaluable American Community Survey—which has replaced the census long form. Results from the 2011 American Time Use Survey are also included in these pages, profiling the similarities and differences in how people allocate their time by race and Hispanic origin.

Understanding the demographics, lifestyles, and attitudes of racial and ethnic groups is of vital importance to researchers and policymakers. *Racial and Ethnic Diversity* provides the key to understanding both the similarities and differences among non-Hispanic whites, blacks, Hispanics, Asians, and American Indians. Whenever possible, the tables in *Racial and Ethnic Diversity* include data that allow researchers to compare characteristics across racial groups.

There's no doubt Americans are more alike than different, and *Racial and Ethnic Diversity* documents our many similarities. But there are also important differences among racial and ethnic groups that, if not taken into account, can derail public policy efforts and business strategies. The living arrangements of Hispanics differ from those of non-Hispanic whites or blacks, for example, and those differences affect not only political attitudes but also consumer behavior. The educational level of Asians distinguishes them from other minorities. The educational and occupational gains made by African Americans over the past few decades are contrary to media portrayals and popular perception, but they are of utmost importance to policymakers and business leaders.

Racial and Ethnic Diversity is as complete and up-to-date as possible given the constraints of the data. In a perfect world, the tabulations for each racial and ethnic group would be identical, but this is impossible because the government does not collect some types of information for smaller racial and ethnic groups. There are no spending or wealth data for American Indians, for example. The sample size of the General Social Survey is not large enough to include reliable attitudinal data for Asians. Despite these limitations, the scope of data provided in the seventh edition of *Racial and Ethnic Diversity* provides not only a comprehensive portrait of each major racial group and Hispanics but also insightful comparisons among groups.

Racial Classification

The 2000 census transformed racial classification in the United States. The census allowed Americans, for the first time in modern history, to identify themselves as belonging to more than one racial group. This made the analysis of racial and ethnic diversity more complex—and more rewarding—than ever before. The 2010 census followed the same classification system, and most government surveys do as well.

Here's how it works. Three terms are used to distinguish one group from another. The "race alone" population consists of people who identify themselves as being of only one race. The "race in combination" population consists of people who identify themselves as being of more than one race, such as white and black. The "race, alone or in combination" population includes both those who identify themselves as being of one race and those who identify themselves as being of more than one race. For example, the "black, alone or in combination" population includes those who say they are black alone and those who say they are black and white and those who say they are black, white, and Asian, and so on.

While the new classification system is a goldmine for researchers, the numbers no longer add up. This may frustrate some, but it provides a more accurate picture of each racial group than the previous methodology, which required the multiracial to align with only one race. Under the new scheme, however, tables showing the "race alone" population exclude the multiracial. Tables showing the "race in combination" population count some people more than once. To make matters even more complex, Hispanics are considered an ethnic group rather than a race and can be American Indian, Asian, black, or white. In addition, the non-Hispanic white category is a combination of race and ethnicity. Non-Hispanic whites are those who identify their race as white alone and who are not Hispanic. Keep these factors in mind as you examine the numbers.

Whenever possible, the tables in *Racial and Ethnic Diversity* show the "race alone or in combination" populations. We prefer this classification because it includes everyone who identifies with a particular racial group and does not exclude the multiracial. American Indians are the only exception. Because it is a point of pride for many in the United States to claim having American Indian ancestry, the "American Indian alone or in combination" population is too diluted by American Indian wannabes for meaningful analysis. Therefore, in this reference, the American Indian numbers shown include only those who identify themselves as American Indian alone. Another caveat: In some tables, the "race alone or in combination" population figures are unavailable. In these cases, the "race alone" population is shown. Racial classifications are noted at the bottom of each table. Some data sources, however, do not specify their racial classifications.

How to Use This Book

Racial and Ethnic Diversity is designed for easy use. It is divided into seven sections. The first section, Attitudes, shows what African Americans, Hispanics, and non-Hispanic whites think about a broad range of issues, based on the 2012 General Social Survey. Sections two through six are devoted to the major racial and ethnic groups: American Indians, Asians, Blacks, Hispanics, and Non-Hispanic Whites. A seventh section provides comparative information for the Total Population if total figures do not appear in individual race/Hispanic tables.

In each of the race/Hispanic sections, nine chapters are arranged alphabetically: Education, Health, Housing, Income, Labor Force, Living Arrangements, Population, Spending, and Wealth. Each chapter includes introductory text describing the most-important trends for the race/Hispanic group. There are no wealth or spending chapters for American Indians because data are unavailable. Within chapters, identically structured tables appear for each race/Hispanic group. If a table is structured differently, it is because equivalent data were unavailable.

The Total Population section allows readers to compare a group's numbers with those for the nation as a whole. If total population statistics appear within an individual racial/Hispanic table, however, a repetition of the same statistics is usually omitted from the Total Population chapter.

Most of the tables in *Racial and Ethnic Diversity* are based on data collected by the federal government, in particular the Census Bureau, the Bureau of Labor Statistics, the National Center for Education Statistics, and the National Center for Health Statistics. The federal government continues to be the best source of up-to-date, reliable information on the changing characteristics of Americans.

Several government surveys are of particular importance to *Racial and Ethnic Diversity*. One is the Census Bureau's Current Population Survey. The CPS is a nationally representative survey of the civilian noninstitutional population aged 15 or older. The Census Bureau takes it monthly, collecting information from 60,000 households on employment and unemployment. Each year, the March survey includes a demographic supplement that is the source of most national data on the characteristics of Americans, such as their educational attainment, living arrangements, and incomes. CPS data appear in many tables of this book.

The American Community Survey is another important source of data for *Racial and Ethnic Diversity*. The ACS is an ongoing nationwide survey of 250,000 households per month, providing detailed demographic data at the community level. Designed to replace the census long-form questionnaire, the ACS includes more than 60 questions that formerly appeared on the long form, such as language spoken at home, income, and education. ACS data are available for the nation, regions, states, counties, metropolitan areas, and places. Many of the tables in the American Indian section are from the American Community Survey.

The Consumer Expenditure Survey is the data source for the Spending chapters. Sponsored by the Bureau of Labor Statistics, the CEX is an ongoing study of the day-to-day spending of American households. The data collected by the survey are used to update prices for the Consumer Price Index. The CEX includes an interview survey and a diary survey administered to two separate, nationally representative samples. The average spending figures shown in the Spending chapters of this book are the integrated data from both the diary and interview components of the survey. For the interview survey, about 7,500 consumer units are interviewed on a rotating panel basis each quarter for five consecutive quarters. For the diary survey, another 7,500 consumer units keep weekly diaries of spending for two consecutive weeks. Spending data are unavailable for American Indians.

Most of the data in the Attitudes chapter are from the 2012 General Social Survey, a biennial survey of the attitudes of Americans taken by the University of Chicago's National Opinion Research Center. NORC conducts the GSS through face-to-face interviews with an independently drawn, representative sample of 1,500 to 3,000 noninstitutionalized people aged 18 or older who live in the United States.

While the government collected most of the data in *Racial and Ethnic Diversity*, the tables published here are not simple reproductions of the government's spreadsheets—as is the case in many reference books. Instead, New Strategist's editors spent hundreds of hours scouring web sites, compiling numbers into meaningful statistics, and creating tables with calculations that reveal trends. Researchers who want more information can use the source listed at the bottom of each table to locate the original data. The book contains a comprehensive table list to help readers locate the information they need. For a more detailed search, use the index at the back of the book. Also at the back of the book is the glossary, which defines most of the terms commonly used in the tables and text and describes the many surveys from which the data come.

Since we published the first edition of *Racial and Ethnic Diversity*, the Internet has reshaped the reference industry. The government's detailed demographic data, once published in printed reports, are now available almost exclusively online. The government's web sites, which house enormous spreadsheets of data, are of great value to researchers with the time to search for, download, and analyze information themselves. But the shift from printed reports to databases on the Internet has outsourced demographic analysis to the market researcher, student, or library patron sitting at a keyboard. In short, despite the abundance of data available on the Internet, it has become more time-consuming than ever to get no-nonsense answers to questions about the ever-changing demographics of the American population. In *Racial and Ethnic Diversity*, New Strategist has done the work for you, showing trends, producing indexes and other calculations, and providing analysis.

Racial and Ethnic Diversity has the answers. Thumbing through its pages, you can gain more insight into the multicultural dynamics of the U.S. population than you could by spending all afternoon surfing databases on the Internet. By having *Racial and Ethnic Diversity* on your bookshelf, you can get answers to your questions faster than you can online. For even more convenience, download *Racial and Ethnic Diversity* to your computer to access the Excel version of each table in the book.

Racial and Ethnic Diversity is a reference tool that will help you discover the many ways Americans are the same—and different. You will gain a critical understanding of the multicultural nation we are today.

CHAPTER 1

Attitudes

Different Perspectives on Many Issues

The attitudes of Americans differ by race and Hispanic origin, although not as much as incomes, wealth, and education. Regardless of race or Hispanic origin, most adults are at least moderately religious, are at least "pretty happy," think hard work is more important than luck in getting ahead, and believe their family income is average or higher.

But the outlook of blacks and Hispanics is much more positive than the outlook of non-Hispanic whites. Only 46 percent of non-Hispanic whites believe families like theirs have the opportunity to improve their standard of living in the United States. In contrast, a much larger 71 to 73 percent of blacks and Hispanics feel that way.

Despite their greater optimism, blacks and Hispanics are less trusting than non-Hispanic whites. Thirty-nine percent of non-Hispanic whites say most people can be trusted versus only 16 to 18 percent of blacks and Hispanics.

Blacks are more likely than Hispanics or non-Hispanic whites to identify themselves as "very religious," with 30 percent doing so. This compares with only 17 percent of non-Hispanic whites and 13 percent of Hispanics. Blacks are more likely than non-Hispanic whites or Hispanics to regard the Bible as the actual word of God—56 versus 26 and 35 percent, respectively. Perhaps as a consequence, only 47 percent of blacks believe in evolution compared with 57 percent of non-Hispanic whites and 53 percent of Hispanics.

Blacks are far less likely than Hispanics or non-Hispanic whites to support gay marriage. Only 43 percent of blacks are in support versus half of non-Hispanic whites and 52 percent of Hispanics.

More than 80 percent of blacks regard themselves as Democrats versus 46 percent of Hispanics and 39 percent of non-Hispanic whites. In the 2012 presidential election, for the first time, the black voting rate surpassed the non-Hispanic white rate.

Blacks and Hispanics are less trusting of others

(percent of people aged 18 or older who say most people can be trusted, by race and Hispanic origin, 2012)

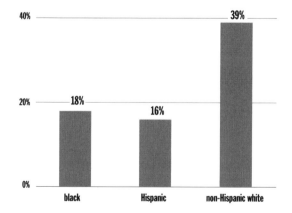

Table 1.1 General Happiness, 2012

"Taken all together, how would you say things are these days—would you say that you are very happy, pretty happy, or not too happy?"

(percent of people aged 18 or older responding by race and Hispanic origin, 2012)

	very happy	pretty happy	not too happy
Total people	**32.9%**	**54.2%**	**12.9%**
Black	23.3	57.5	19.2
Hispanic	27.7	57.3	15.0
Non-Hispanic white	35.8	52.7	11.5

Source: Survey Documentation and Analysis, Computer-assisted Survey Methods Program, University of California, Berkeley, General Social Survey, 1972–2012 Cumulative Data Files, Internet site http://sda.berkeley.edu/cgi-bin/hsda?harcsda+gss12; calculations by New Strategist

Table 1.2 Happiness of Marriage, 2012

"Taking all things together, how would you describe your marriage?"

(percent of people aged 18 or older responding by race and Hispanic origin, 2012)

	very happy	pretty happy	not too happy
Total married people	**65.4%**	**32.2%**	**2.3%**
Black	49.0	44.6	6.4
Hispanic	60.7	36.2	3.1
Non-Hispanic white	67.6	30.6	1.8

Source: Survey Documentation and Analysis, Computer-assisted Survey Methods Program, University of California, Berkeley, General Social Survey, 1972–2012 Cumulative Data Files, Internet site http://sda.berkeley.edu/cgi-bin/hsda?harcsda+gss12; calculations by New Strategist

Table 1.3 Life Exciting or Dull, 2012

"In general, do you find life exciting, pretty routine, or dull?"

(percent of people aged 18 or older responding by race and Hispanic origin, 2012)

	exciting	pretty routine	dull
Total people	**52.7%**	**42.6%**	**4.7%**
Black	47.6	45.7	6.7
Hispanic	61.5	35.2	3.3
Non-Hispanic white	51.3	43.6	5.0

Source: Survey Documentation and Analysis, Computer-assisted Survey Methods Program, University of California, Berkeley, General Social Survey, 1972–2012 Cumulative Data Files, Internet site http://sda.berkeley.edu/cgi-bin/hsda?harcsda+gss12; calculations by New Strategist

Table 1.4 Trust in Others, 2012

"Generally speaking, would you say that most people can be trusted or that you can't be too careful in life?"

(percent of people aged 18 or older responding by race and Hispanic origin, 2012)

	can trust	cannot trust	depends
Total people	**32.2%**	**64.2%**	**3.7%**
Black	17.6	78.8	3.6
Hispanic	15.8	82.4	1.8
Non-Hispanic white	39.0	56.8	4.2

Source: Survey Documentation and Analysis, Computer-assisted Survey Methods Program, University of California, Berkeley, General Social Survey, 1972–2012 Cumulative Data Files, Internet site http://sda.berkeley.edu/cgi-bin/hsda?harcsda+gss12; calculations by New Strategist

Table 1.5 How People Get Ahead, 2012

"Some people say that people get ahead by their own hard work;
others say that lucky breaks or help from other people are more important.
Which do you think is most important?"

(percent of people aged 18 or older responding by race and Hispanic origin, 2012)

	hard work	both equally	luck
Total people	**69.9%**	**20.1%**	**10.0%**
Black	70.3	19.5	10.2
Hispanic	76.4	11.3	12.4
Non-Hispanic white	68.9	21.7	9.4

Source: Survey Documentation and Analysis, Computer-assisted Survey Methods Program, University of California, Berkeley, General Social Survey, 1972–2012 Cumulative Data Files, Internet site http://sda.berkeley.edu/cgi-bin/hsda?harcsda+gss12; calculations by New Strategist

Table 1.6 Geographic Mobility Since Age 16, 2012

"When you were 16 years old, were you living
in this same (city/town/county)?"

(percent of people aged 18 or older responding by race and Hispanic origin, 2012)

	same city	same state, different city	different state
Total people	**39.5%**	**23.8%**	**36.6%**
Black	51.4	18.2	30.4
Hispanic	34.0	17.0	48.9
Non-Hispanic white	38.5	28.2	33.4

Source: Survey Documentation and Analysis, Computer-assisted Survey Methods Program, University of California, Berkeley, General Social Survey, 1972–2012 Cumulative Data Files, Internet site http://sda.berkeley.edu/cgi-bin/hsda?harcsda+gss12; calculations by New Strategist

Table 1.7 Social Class Membership, 2012

"If you were asked to use one of four names for your social class, which
would you say you belong in: the lower class, the working class,
the middle class, or the upper class?"

(percent of people aged 18 or older responding by race and Hispanic origin, 2012)

	lower	working	middle	upper
Total people	**8.4%**	**44.3%**	**43.7%**	**3.6%**
Black	12.4	51.0	33.7	3.0
Hispanic	7.7	64.3	26.1	1.9
Non-Hispanic white	7.9	38.2	49.5	4.4

*Source: Survey Documentation and Analysis, Computer-assisted Survey Methods Program, University of California, Berkeley,
General Social Survey, 1972–2012 Cumulative Data Files, Internet site http://sda.berkeley.edu/cgi-bin/hsda?harcsda+gss12;
calculations by New Strategist*

Table 1.8 Family Income Relative to Others, 2012

"Compared with American families in general, would you say your family
income is far below average, below average, average,
above average, or far above average?"

(percent of people aged 18 or older responding by race and Hispanic origin, 2012)

	far below average	below average	average	above average	far above average
Total people	**6.8%**	**25.9%**	**45.5%**	**19.0%**	**2.7%**
Black	9.0	29.9	45.5	12.5	3.1
Hispanic	8.6	35.6	43.3	10.9	1.7
Non-Hispanic white	6.1	23.6	44.3	23.0	3.0

*Source: Survey Documentation and Analysis, Computer-assisted Survey Methods Program, University of California, Berkeley,
General Social Survey, 1972–2012 Cumulative Data Files, Internet site http://sda.berkeley.edu/cgi-bin/hsda?harcsda+gss12;
calculations by New Strategist*

Table 1.9 Satisfaction with Financial Situation, 2012

"We are interested in how people are getting along financially these days.
So far as you and your family are concerned, would you say that you
are pretty well satisfied with your present financial situation,
more or less satisfied, or not satisfied at all?"

(percent of people aged 18 or older responding by race and Hispanic origin, 2012)

	satisfied	more or less satisfied	not at all sarisfied
Total people	**27.0%**	**45.0%**	**28.0%**
Black	22.0	39.0	39.0
Hispanic	18.3	52.2	29.5
Non-Hispanic white	30.3	43.5	26.2

Source: Survey Documentation and Analysis, Computer-assisted Survey Methods Program, University of California, Berkeley, General Social Survey, 1972–2012 Cumulative Data Files, Internet site http://sda.berkeley.edu/cgi-bin/hsda?harcsda+gss12; calculations by New Strategist

Table 1.10 Change in Financial Situation, 2012

"During the last few years, has your financial situation been
getting better, worse, or has it stayed the same?"

(percent of people aged 18 or older responding by race and Hispanic origin, 2012)

	better	worse	stayed same
Total people	**28.2%**	**30.2%**	**41.6%**
Black	29.1	27.5	43.4
Hispanic	29.6	30.0	40.4
Non-Hispanic white	28.0	31.5	40.5

Source: Survey Documentation and Analysis, Computer-assisted Survey Methods Program, University of California, Berkeley, General Social Survey, 1972–2012 Cumulative Data Files, Internet site http://sda.berkeley.edu/cgi-bin/hsda?harcsda+gss12; calculations by New Strategist

Table 1.11 Parents' Standard of Living, 2012

"Compared to your parents when they were the age you are now, do you
think your own standard of living now is much better, somewhat better,
about the same, somewhat worse, or much worse than theirs was?"

(percent of people aged 18 or older responding by race and Hispanic origin, 2012)

	much better	somewhat better	about the same	somewhat worse	much worse
Total people	**33.5%**	**28.6%**	**21.2%**	**12.0%**	**4.6%**
Black	35.7	33.2	19.0	8.9	3.3
Hispanic	45.1	27.0	14.3	10.9	2.8
Non-Hispanic white	28.9	27.8	24.5	13.7	5.1

Source: Survey Documentation and Analysis, Computer-assisted Survey Methods Program, University of California, Berkeley, General Social Survey, 1972–2012 Cumulative Data Files, Internet site http://sda.berkeley.edu/cgi-bin/hsda?harcsda+gss12; calculations by New Strategist

Table 1.12 Standard of Living Will Improve, 2012

"The way things are in America, people like me and my family have a
good chance of improving our standard of living.
Do you agree or disagree?"

(percent of people aged 18 or older responding by race and Hispanic origin, 2012)

	strongly agree	agree	neither	disagree	strongly disagree
Total people	**14.1%**	**40.7%**	**17.9%**	**23.4%**	**4.0%**
Black	19.1	52.1	9.7	17.1	2.0
Hispanic	25.6	47.5	17.7	5.7	3.4
Non-Hispanic white	9.2	36.5	19.9	29.6	4.8

Source: Survey Documentation and Analysis, Computer-assisted Survey Methods Program, University of California, Berkeley, General Social Survey, 1972–2012 Cumulative Data Files, Internet site http://sda.berkeley.edu/cgi-bin/hsda?harcsda+gss12; calculations by New Strategist

Table 1.13 Children's Standard of Living, 2012

"When your children are at the age you are now, do you think their standard of living will be much better, somewhat better, about the same, somewhat worse, or much worse than yours is now?"

(percent of people aged 18 or older with children responding by race and Hispanic origin, 2012)

	much better	somewhat better	about the same	somewhat worse	much worse
Total people with children	**31.4%**	**25.6%**	**20.5%**	**16.3%**	**6.2%**
Black	50.5	22.9	8.9	10.7	6.9
Hispanic	47.3	25.3	14.8	9.5	3.1
Non-Hispanic white	21.6	25.9	25.6	20.0	6.9

Source: Survey Documentation and Analysis, Computer-assisted Survey Methods Program, University of California, Berkeley, General Social Survey, 1972–2012 Cumulative Data Files, Internet site http://sda.berkeley.edu/cgi-bin/hsda?harcsda+gss12; calculations by New Strategist

Table 1.14 Ideal Number of Children, 2012

"What do you think is the ideal number of children for a family to have?"

(percent of people aged 18 or older responding by race and Hispanic origin, 2012)

	none	one	two	three	four or more	as many as want
Total people	**0.8%**	**2.6%**	**46.8%**	**27.8%**	**11.3%**	**10.7%**
Black	1.1	0.7	35.7	34.3	20.9	7.3
Hispanic	0.0	5.0	35.7	43.2	11.6	4.6
Non-Hispanic white	0.9	2.6	50.6	24.6	8.6	12.6

Source: Survey Documentation and Analysis, Computer-assisted Survey Methods Program, University of California, Berkeley, General Social Survey, 1972–2012 Cumulative Data Files, Internet site http://sda.berkeley.edu/cgi-bin/hsda?harcsda+gss12; calculations by New Strategist

Table 1.15 Better for Man to Work, Woman to Tend Home, 2012

"Do you strongly agree, agree, disagree, or strongly disagree with the
statement: It is much better for everyone involved if the man
is the achiever outside the home and the woman takes
care of the home and family?"

(percent of people aged 18 or older responding by race and Hispanic origin, 2012)

	strongly agree	agree	disagree	strongly disagree
Total people	**6.5%**	**25.2%**	**48.3%**	**20.0%**
Black	5.2	24.7	46.9	23.2
Hispanic	7.3	31.4	47.7	13.5
Non-Hispanic white	5.8	23.8	48.5	21.8

Source: Survey Documentation and Analysis, Computer-assisted Survey Methods Program, University of California, Berkeley, General Social Survey, 1972–2012 Cumulative Data Files, Internet site http://sda.berkeley.edu/cgi-bin/hsda?harcsda+gss12; calculations by New Strategist

Table 1.16 Working Mother's Relationship with Children, 2012

"Do you strongly agree, agree, disagree, or strongly disagree with the
statement: A working mother can establish just as warm and secure a
relationship with her children as a mother who does not work?"

(percent of people aged 18 or older responding by race and Hispanic origin, 2012)

	strongly agree	agree	disagree	strongly disagree
Total people	**25.0%**	**46.7%**	**23.1%**	**5.2%**
Black	30.8	42.0	23.1	4.1
Hispanic	14.0	42.5	34.8	8.8
Non-Hispanic white	27.0	49.2	19.8	4.0

Source: Survey Documentation and Analysis, Computer-assisted Survey Methods Program, University of California, Berkeley, General Social Survey, 1972–2012 Cumulative Data Files, Internet site http://sda.berkeley.edu/cgi-bin/hsda?harcsda+gss12; calculations by New Strategist

Table 1.17 Should Government Help the Sick, 2012

"Some people think that it is the responsibility of the government in Washington to see to it that people have help in paying for doctors and hospital bills; they are at point 1. Others think that these matters are not the responsibility of the federal government and that people should take care of these things themselves; they are at point 5. Where would you place yourself on this scale?"

(percent of people aged 18 or older responding by race and Hispanic origin, 2012)

	1 government should help	2	3 agree with both	4	5 people should help themselves
Total people	**28.4%**	**18.1%**	**31.4%**	**12.4%**	**9.7%**
Black	44.8	17.4	30.4	2.0	5.4
Hispanic	33.3	14.9	34.6	8.3	9.0
Non-Hispanic white	23.8	19.5	30.2	15.5	10.9

Source: Survey Documentation and Analysis, Computer-assisted Survey Methods Program, University of California, Berkeley, General Social Survey, 1972–2012 Cumulative Data Files, Internet site http://sda.berkeley.edu/cgi-bin/hsda?harcsda+gss12; calculations by New Strategist

Table 1.18 Attitude toward Science, 2012

"Do you strongly agree, agree, disagree, or strongly disagree with the statement: Science makes our way of life change too fast?"

(percent of people aged 18 or older responding by race and Hispanic origin, 2012)

	strongly agree	agree	disagree	strongly disagree
Total people	**9.8%**	**33.7%**	**52.5%**	**4.0%**
Black	15.8	28.6	50.1	5.5
Hispanic	17.8	48.7	30.5	3.0
Non-Hispanic white	6.3	30.2	59.3	4.3

Source: Survey Documentation and Analysis, Computer-assisted Survey Methods Program, University of California, Berkeley, General Social Survey, 1972–2012 Cumulative Data Files, Internet site http://sda.berkeley.edu/cgi-bin/hsda?harcsda+gss12; calculations by New Strategist

Table 1.19 Attitude toward Evolution, 2012

"True or false: Human beings, as we know them today,
developed from earlier species of animals?"

(percent of people aged 18 or older responding by race and Hispanic origin, 2012)

	true	false
Total people	**55.8%**	**44.2%**
Black	46.9	53.1
Hispanic	53.3	46.7
Non-Hispanic white	57.4	42.6

Source: Survey Documentation and Analysis, Computer-assisted Survey Methods Program, University of California, Berkeley, General Social Survey, 1972–2012 Cumulative Data Files, Internet site http://sda.berkeley.edu/cgi-bin/hsda?harcsda+gss12; calculations by New Strategist

Table 1.20 Religious Preference, 2012

"What is your religious preference?"

(percent of people aged 18 or older responding by race and Hispanic origin, 2012)

	Protestant	Catholic	none	Jewish	Moslem/ Islam	Hinduism	Buddhism	other
Total people	**44.3%**	**24.2%**	**19.7%**	**1.5%**	**1.1%**	**0.5%**	**0.4%**	**8.3%**
Black	65.9	6.8	17.1	0.6	2.0	0.0	0.1	7.5
Hispanic	21.0	56.9	15.7	0.0	0.0	0.0	0.0	6.4
Non-Hispanic white	47.3	20.9	21.2	2.0	0.5	0.0	0.2	7.9

Source: Survey Documentation and Analysis, Computer-assisted Survey Methods Program, University of California, Berkeley, General Social Survey, 1972–2012 Cumulative Data Files, Internet site http://sda.berkeley.edu/cgi-bin/hsda?harcsda+gss12; calculations by New Strategist

Table 1.21 Degree of Religiosity, 2012

"To what extent do you consider yourself a religious person?"

(percent of people aged 18 or older responding by race and Hispanic origin, 2012)

	very religious	moderately religious	slightly religious	not religious
Total people	**18.8%**	**39.5%**	**21.6%**	**20.1%**
Black	30.1	47.4	13.7	8.8
Hispanic	12.6	42.4	30.8	14.2
Non-Hispanic white	17.0	38.1	21.2	23.8

Source: Survey Documentation and Analysis, Computer-assisted Survey Methods Program, University of California, Berkeley, General Social Survey, 1972–2012 Cumulative Data Files, Internet site http://sda.berkeley.edu/cgi-bin/hsda?harcsda+gss12; calculations by New Strategist

Table 1.22 Confidence in the Existence of God, 2012

"Which statement comes closest to expressing what you believe about God: 1) I don't believe in God. 2) I don't know whether there is a God and I don't believe there is any way to find out. 3) I don't believe in a personal God, but I do believe in a Higher Power of some kind. 4) I find myself believing in God some of the time, but not at others. 5) While I have doubts, I feel that I do believe in God. 6) I know God really exists and I have no doubts about it?"

(percent of people aged 18 or older responding by race and Hispanic origin, 2012)

	1 don't believe	2 no way to find out	3 higher power	4 believe sometimes	5 believe but doubts	6 know God exists
Total people	**3.1%**	**5.6%**	**11.6%**	**4.2%**	**16.5%**	**59.1%**
Black	0.7	2.2	3.2	1.2	10.8	81.8
Hispanic	2.2	5.3	7.8	2.1	15.6	67.0
Non-Hispanic white	3.8	6.4	14.0	5.1	18.3	52.4

Source: Survey Documentation and Analysis, Computer-assisted Survey Methods Program, University of California, Berkeley, General Social Survey, 1972–2012 Cumulative Data Files, Internet site http://sda.berkeley.edu/cgi-bin/hsda?harcsda+gss12; calculations by New Strategist

Table 1.23 Attendance at Religious Services, 2012

"How often do you attend religious services?"

(percent of people aged 18 or older responding by race and Hispanic origin, 2012)

	more than once a week	every week	nearly every week	two or three times a month	once a month	several times a year	once a year	less than once a year	never
Total people	**6.5%**	**19.7%**	**4.0%**	**8.9%**	**6.8%**	**10.8%**	**13.0%**	**5.0%**	**25.3%**
Black	12.4	19.3	6.2	17.1	8.0	11.9	9.4	2.5	13.2
Hispanic	4.4	23.4	3.9	8.1	13.7	12.9	9.8	4.2	19.7
Non-Hispanic white	5.8	18.5	3.8	7.6	4.9	10.2	14.0	5.8	29.5

Source: Survey Documentation and Analysis, Computer-assisted Survey Methods Program, University of California, Berkeley, General Social Survey, 1972–2012 Cumulative Data Files, Internet site http://sda.berkeley.edu/cgi-bin/hsda?harcsda+gss12; calculations by New Strategist

Table 1.24 Belief in the Bible, 2012

"Which of these statements comes closest to describing your feelings about the Bible? 1) The Bible is the actual word of God and is to be taken literally, word for word; 2) The Bible is the inspired word of God but not everything in it should be taken literally, word for word; 3) The Bible is an ancient book of fables, legends, history, and moral precepts recorded by men."

(percent of people aged 18 or older responding by race and Hispanic origin, 2012)

	word of God	inspired word	book of fables	other
Total people	**32.1%**	**44.6%**	**21.8%**	**1.5%**
Black	55.8	35.1	8.6	0.5
Hispanic	34.5	45.5	18.6	1.4
Non-Hispanic white	26.4	47.3	24.7	1.5

Source: Survey Documentation and Analysis, Computer-assisted Survey Methods Program, University of California, Berkeley, General Social Survey, 1972–2012 Cumulative Data Files, Internet site http://sda.berkeley.edu/cgi-bin/hsda?harcsda+gss12; calculations by New Strategist

Table 1.25 Spend Evening with Relatives, 2012

"How often do you spend a social evening with relatives?"

(percent of people aged 18 or older responding by race and Hispanic origin, 2012)

	almost daily	several times a week	several times a month	once a month	several times a year	once a year	never
Total people	**13.6%**	**23.5%**	**22.4%**	**13.6%**	**15.8%**	**6.7%**	**4.4%**
Black	19.0	28.9	16.8	11.1	12.1	4.7	7.3
Hispanic	16.4	20.6	19.8	15.8	9.4	12.7	5.3
Non-Hispanic white	10.2	23.4	24.3	13.8	18.6	6.0	3.7

Source: Survey Documentation and Analysis, Computer-assisted Survey Methods Program, University of California, Berkeley, General Social Survey, 1972–2012 Cumulative Data Files, Internet site http://sda.berkeley.edu/cgi-bin/hsda?harcsda+gss12; calculations by New Strategist

Table 1.26 Spend Evening with Friends, 2012

"How often do you spend a social evening with friends who live outside the neighborhood?"

(percent of people aged 18 or older responding by race and Hispanic origin, 2012)

	almost daily	several times a week	several times a month	once a month	several times a year	once a year	never
Total people	**4.5%**	**19.6%**	**21.0%**	**21.0%**	**16.2%**	**8.3%**	**9.5%**
Black	5.3	18.7	27.0	20.0	10.0	5.5	13.6
Hispanic	5.6	22.2	13.0	15.7	14.0	12.7	16.8
Non-Hispanic white	4.3	19.5	21.3	21.6	18.5	7.7	7.0

Source: Survey Documentation and Analysis, Computer-assisted Survey Methods Program, University of California, Berkeley, General Social Survey, 1972–2012 Cumulative Data Files, Internet site http://sda.berkeley.edu/cgi-bin/hsda?harcsda+gss12; calculations by New Strategist

Table 1.27 Premarital Sex, 2012

"If a man and woman have sex relations before marriage,
do you think it is always wrong, almost always wrong,
wrong only sometimes, or not wrong at all?"

(percent of people aged 18 or older responding by race and Hispanic origin, 2012)

	always wrong	almost always wrong	sometimes wrong	not wrong at all
Total people	**21.9%**	**5.1%**	**15.5%**	**57.5%**
Black	26.5	5.5	14.1	53.9
Hispanic	26.5	7.8	12.0	53.7
Non-Hispanic white	21.1	4.7	15.3	58.9

Source: Survey Documentation and Analysis, Computer-assisted Survey Methods Program, University of California, Berkeley, General Social Survey, 1972–2012 Cumulative Data Files, Internet site http://sda.berkeley.edu/cgi-bin/hsda?harcsda+gss12; calculations by New Strategist

Table 1.28 Homosexual Relations, 2012

"What about sexual relations between two adults of the same sex?"

(percent of people aged 18 or older responding by race and Hispanic origin, 2012)

	always wrong	almost always wrong	sometimes wrong	not wrong at all
Total people	**45.7%**	**2.9%**	**7.7%**	**43.8%**
Black	61.4	1.8	7.3	29.5
Hispanic	45.6	6.0	7.0	41.3
Non-Hispanic white	42.1	2.3	7.3	48.4

Source: Survey Documentation and Analysis, Computer-assisted Survey Methods Program, University of California, Berkeley, General Social Survey, 1972–2012 Cumulative Data Files, Internet site http://sda.berkeley.edu/cgi-bin/hsda?harcsda+gss12; calculations by New Strategist

Table 1.29 Legality of Gay Marriage, 2012

"Do you agree or disagree? Homosexual couples should
have the right to marry one another."

(percent of people aged 18 or older responding by race and Hispanic origin, 2012)

	agree	neither agree nor disagree	disagree
Total people	**48.9%**	**12.0%**	**39.1%**
Black	43.4	13.0	43.6
Hispanic	51.8	16.0	32.2
Non-Hispanic white	50.1	9.5	40.4

Source: Survey Documentation and Analysis, Computer-assisted Survey Methods Program, University of California, Berkeley, General Social Survey, 1972–2012 Cumulative Data Files, Internet site http://sda.berkeley.edu/cgi-bin/hsda?harcsda+gss12; calculations by New Strategist

Table 1.30 Main Source of Information about Events in the News, 2012

"We are interested in how people get information about events in the news. Where do you get most of your information about current news events?"

(percent of people aged 18 or older responding by race and Hispanic origin, 2012)

	TV	Internet	newspapers	radio	family, friends and colleagues	magazines	other
Total people	47.9%	30.0%	12.4%	4.7%	3.6%	0.6%	0.8%
Black	60.0	15.8	20.5	1.8	0.6	0.0	1.3
Hispanic	59.3	24.7	7.2	2.6	5.6	0.5	0.1
Non-Hispanic white	44.4	31.7	12.1	6.0	4.2	0.9	0.7

Source: Survey Documentation and Analysis, Computer-assisted Survey Methods Program, University of California, Berkeley, General Social Survey, 1972–2012 Cumulative Data Files, Internet site http://sda.berkeley.edu/cgi-bin/hsda?harcsda+gss12; calculations by New Strategist

Table 1.31 Political Leanings, 2012

"We hear a lot of talk these days about liberals and conservatives. On a seven-point scale from extremely liberal (1) to extremely conservative (7), where would you place yourself?"

(percent of people aged 18 or older responding by race and Hispanic origin, 2012)

	1 extremely liberal	2 liberal	3 slightly liberal	4 moderate	5 slightly conservative	6 conservative	7 extremely conservative
Total people	4.0%	11.8%	11.2%	38.5%	15.4%	15.5%	3.7%
Black	6.1	10.1	13.6	46.2	10.7	10.2	3.1
Hispanic	4.6	11.8	10.8	41.0	12.7	12.5	6.7
Non-Hispanic white	3.2	12.0	11.1	35.5	16.7	18.0	3.5

Source: Survey Documentation and Analysis, Computer-assisted Survey Methods Program, University of California, Berkeley, General Social Survey, 1972–2012 Cumulative Data Files, Internet site http://sda.berkeley.edu/cgi-bin/hsda?harcsda+gss12; calculations by New Strategist

Table 1.32 Political Party Affiliation, 2012

"Generally speaking, do you usually think of yourself as a Republican, Democrat, Independent, or what?"

(percent of people aged 18 or older responding by race and Hispanic origin, 2012)

	strong Democrat	not strong Democrat	independent, near Democrat	independent	independent, near Republican	not strong Republican	strong Republican	other party
Total people	**16.7%**	**17.0%**	**12.4%**	**19.8%**	**8.2%**	**13.7%**	**9.8%**	**2.3%**
Black	45.1	22.5	13.1	13.7	2.2	0.7	1.2	1.4
Hispanic	10.8	22.5	12.3	31.5	7.0	10.1	5.3	0.6
Non-Hispanic white	11.7	14.6	12.3	17.5	10.0	18.0	12.9	3.1

Source: Survey Documentation and Analysis, Computer-assisted Survey Methods Program, University of California, Berkeley, General Social Survey, 1972–2012 Cumulative Data Files, Internet site http://sda.berkeley.edu/cgi-bin/hsda?harcsda+gss12; calculations by New Strategist

Table 1.33 Favor or Oppose Death Penalty for Murder, 2012

"Do you favor or oppose the death penalty for persons convicted of murder?"

(percent of people aged 18 or older responding by race and Hispanic origin, 2012)

	favor	oppose
Total people	**65.1%**	**34.9%**
Black	47.9	52.1
Hispanic	55.8	44.2
Non-Hispanic white	71.1	28.9

Source: Survey Documentation and Analysis, Computer-assisted Survey Methods Program, University of California, Berkeley, General Social Survey, 1972–2012 Cumulative Data Files, Internet site http://sda.berkeley.edu/cgi-bin/hsda?harcsda+gss12; calculations by New Strategist

Table 1.34 Favor or Oppose Gun Permits, 2012

"Would you favor or oppose a law which would require a person to obtain
a police permit before he or she could buy a gun?"

(percent of people aged 18 or older responding by race and Hispanic origin, 2012)

	favor	oppose
Total people	**73.7%**	**26.3%**
Black	82.9	17.1
Hispanic	72.2	27.8
Non-Hispanic white	72.2	27.8

Source: Survey Documentation and Analysis, Computer-assisted Survey Methods Program, University of California, Berkeley, General Social Survey, 1972–2012 Cumulative Data Files, Internet site http://sda.berkeley.edu/cgi-bin/hsda?harcsda+gss12; calculations by New Strategist

Table 1.35 Voting Rate in Presidential Elections by Race and Hispanic Origin, 1992 to 2012

(percent of citizens aged 18 or older who reported voting in presidential elections by race and Hispanic origin, and index of race-and-Hispanic-origin group to total, 1992 to 2012)

	total	Asian	black	Hispanic	non-Hispanic white
2012	61.8%	47.9%	65.9%	48.0%	64.1%
2008	63.6	47.6	64.7	49.9	66.1
2004	63.8	44.6	59.9	47.2	67.1
2000	59.5	43.4	56.8	45.1	61.8
1996	58.4	45.0	53.0	44.0	60.7
1992	67.7	53.9	59.2	51.6	70.2

INDEX OF RACE AND HISPANIC ORIGIN GROUP TO TOTAL

2012	100	78	107	78	104
2008	100	75	102	78	104
2004	100	70	94	74	105
2000	100	73	95	76	104
1996	100	77	91	75	104
1992	100	80	87	76	104

Note: Asians and blacks are those who identify themselves as being of the race alone and those who identify themselves as being of the race in combination with other races. Non-Hispanic whites are those who identify themselves as being white alone and not Hispanic. The index is calculated by dividing the race-and-Hispanic-origin group voting rate by the total voting rate and multiplying by 100.
Source: Bureau of the Census, Voting and Registration, Internet site http://www.census.gov/hhes/www/socdemo/voting/index .html; calculations by New Strategist

Table 1.36 Voting Rate in Congressional Elections by Race and Hispanic Origin, 1990 to 2010

(percent of citizens aged 18 or older who reported voting in congressional elections by race and Hispanic origin, and index of race-and-Hispanic-origin group to total, 1990 to 2010)

	total	Asian	black	Hispanic	non-Hispanic white
2010	45.5%	30.8%	43.5%	31.2%	48.6%
2006	47.8	32.4	41.0	32.3	51.6
2002	46.1	31.2	42.3	30.4	49.1
1998	45.3	32.4	41.8	32.8	47.4
1994	48.4	39.4	38.9	34.0	51.0
1990	49.3	40.0	42.4	36.0	51.4

INDEX OF RACE AND HISPANIC ORIGIN GROUP TO TOTAL

	total	Asian	black	Hispanic	non-Hispanic white
2010	100	68	96	69	107
2006	100	68	86	68	108
2002	100	68	92	66	107
1998	100	72	92	72	105
1994	100	81	80	70	105
1990	100	81	86	73	104

Note: Asians and blacks are those who identify themselves as being of the race alone and those who identify themselves as being of the race in combination with other races. Non-Hispanic whites are those who identify themselves as being white alone and not Hispanic. The index is calculated by dividing the race-and-Hispanic-origin group voting rate by the total voting rate and multiplying by 100.
Source: Bureau of the Census, Voting and Registration, Internet site http://www.census.gov/hhes/www/socdemo/voting/index .html; calculations by New Strategist

Table 1.37 Voters by Age, Race, and Hispanic Origin, 2012

(number and percent distribution of people who reported voting in the presidential election by age, race, and Hispanic origin, 2012; numbers in thousands)

	total	Asian	black	Hispanic	non-Hispanic white
Total voters	**132,948**	**4,331**	**18,558**	**11,188**	**98,041**
Aged 18 to 24	11,353	408	2,306	1,677	6,933
Aged 25 to 44	39,942	1,652	6,595	4,365	27,216
Aged 45 to 64	52,013	1,522	6,890	3,609	39,507
Aged 65 or older	29,641	748	2,767	1,537	24,385
Total voters	**100.0%**	**3.3%**	**14.0%**	**8.4%**	**73.7%**
Aged 18 to 24	100.0	3.6	20.3	14.8	61.1
Aged 25 to 44	100.0	4.1	16.5	10.9	68.1
Aged 45 to 64	100.0	2.9	13.2	6.9	76.0
Aged 65 or older	100.0	2.5	9.3	5.2	82.3

Note: Asians and blacks are those who identify themselves as being of the race alone and those who identify themselves as being of the race in combination with other races. Non-Hispanic whites are those who identify themselves as being white alone and not Hispanic.
Source: Bureau of the Census, Voting and Registration, Internet site http://www.census.gov/hhes/www/socdemo/voting/index .html; calculations by New Strategist

2

American Indians

■ Numbering 2.9 million, American Indians and Alaska Natives (race alone) are one of the smallest minorities in the United States, accounting for just 0.9 percent of the population.

■ Forty-five percent of American Indians aged 25 or older have at least some college experience, and 13 percent are college graduates.

■ Only 43 percent of American Indians say their health is "very good" or "excellent," far below the 60 percent of all Americans who rate their health highly.

■ The 51 percent majority of American Indian households own their home, a homeownership rate that exceeds the rate of blacks or Hispanics.

■ The median income of American Indian households stood at $36,779 in 2006–10, well below the $51,914 median for all households.

■ American Indians are less likely than the average worker to be managers or professionals and more likely to be service workers.

■ Married couples head only 40 percent of American Indian households.

■ American Indians and Alaska Natives account for 15 percent of Alaska's population. In New Mexico, Oklahoma, and South Dakota, they are at least 8 percent of the population.

Note: There are no spending or wealth data for American Indians.

American Indians account for less than 1 percent of the U.S. population

(percent distribution of people by race and Hispanic origin, 2010)

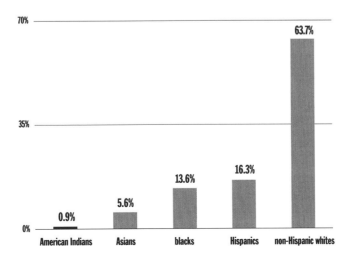

Nearly 45 Percent of American Indians Have Attended College for One or More Years

Forty-five percent of American Indians aged 25 or older have at least some college experience, and 13 percent have a bachelor's degree—a figure that is as high as 17 percent in the Northeast.

American Indians account for 0.7 percent of the nation's college students. More than 19,000 American Indians earned a degree in 2010–11, with nearly 5,000 earning a bachelor's degree.

■ The educational attainment of American Indians would rise if college were more affordable.

Seventy-seven percent of American Indians are high school graduates

(percent of American Indians aged 25 or older by educational attainment, 2006–10)

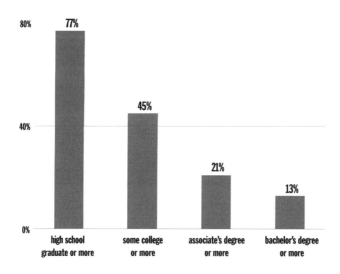

Table 2.1 Educational Attainment of American Indians, 2006–10

(number and percent distribution of American Indians aged 25 or older by educational attainment, 2006–10; numbers in thousands)

	number	percent distribution
Total American Indians	**1,446**	**100.0%**
Not a high school graduate	338	23.4
High school graduate only	458	31.7
Some college, no degree	349	24.2
Associate's degree	112	7.7
Bachelor's degree	126	8.7
Graduate degree	63	4.4
High school graduate or more	1,107	76.6
Some college or more	650	44.9
Associate's degree or more	300	20.8
Bachelor's degree or more	188	13.0

Note: American Indians include Alaska Natives. The American Indian and Alaska Native population are those who identify themselves as being of the race alone.
Source: Bureau of the Census, 2006–10 American Community Survey, Internet site http://factfinder2.census.gov/faces/nav/jsf/pages/index.xhtml; calculations by New Strategist

Table 2.2 Educational Attainment of American Indians by Region, 2006–10

(number and percent of American Indians aged 25 or older by educational attainment and region, 2006–10; numbers in thousands)

	total	Northeast	Midwest	South	West
Total American Indians	**1,446**	**90**	**226**	**444**	**685**
Not a high school graduate	338	22	44	105	168
High school graduate only	458	29	74	139	216
Some college, no degree	349	18	58	101	173
Associate's degree	112	7	20	32	53
Bachelor's degree	126	9	21	45	51
Graduate degree	63	6	10	22	24
High school graduate or more	76.6%	75.9%	80.5%	76.5%	75.5%
Some college or more	44.9	44.0	47.8	45.2	44.0
Associate's degree or more	20.8	24.4	22.2	22.5	18.7
Bachelor's degree or more	13.0	16.7	13.6	15.2	11.0

Note: American Indians include Alaska Natives. The American Indian and Alaska Native population are those who identify themselves as being of the race alone.
Source: Bureau of the Census, 2006–10 American Community Survey, Internet site http://factfinder2.census.gov/faces/nav/jsf/pages/index.xhtml; calculations by New Strategist

Table 2.3 **School Enrollment of American Indians, 2006–10**

(total number of people aged 3 or older enrolled in school, number of American Indians enrolled, and American Indian share of total, by level of enrollment, 2006–10; numbers in thousands)

		American Indian	
	total	number	share of total
Total enrolled in school	**80,939**	**751**	**0.9%**
Nursery school or preschool	4,924	44	0.9
Kindergarten	4,114	40	1.0
Grades 1 to 8	32,579	325	1.0
Grades 9 to 12	17,532	182	1.0
College, undergraduate	17,942	142	0.8
Graduate or professional school	3,848	19	0.5

Note: American Indians include Alaska Natives. The American Indian and Alaska Native population are those who identify themselves as being of the race alone.
Source: Bureau of the Census, 2006–10 American Community Survey, Internet site http://factfinder2.census.gov/faces/nav/jsf/pages/index.xhtml; calculations by New Strategist

Table 2.4 **College Enrollment of American Indians, 2006–10**

(total number of people aged 15 or older enrolled in college, number of American Indians enrolled, and American Indian share of total, by age, 2006–10; numbers in thousands)

		American Indian	
	total	number	share of total
Total enrolled in college	**21,790**	**160**	**0.7%**
Aged 18 to 24	12,672	80	0.6
Aged 25 to 34	4,964	39	0.8
Aged 35 or older	4,154	41	1.0

Note: American Indians include Alaska Natives. The American Indian and Alaska Native population are those who identify themselves as being of the race alone.
Source: Bureau of the Census, 2006–2010 American Community Survey, Internet site http://factfinder2.census.gov/faces/nav/jsf/pages/index.xhtml

Table 2.5 Degrees Earned by American Indians, 2010–11

(total number of degrees conferred and number and percent earned by American Indians, 2010–11)

| | total | American Indian | |
		number	share of total
Total degrees	**3,552,640**	**19,373**	**0.5%**
Associate's degrees	942,327	10,173	1.1
Bachelor's degrees	1,715,913	4,798	0.3
Master's degrees	730,635	3,948	0.5
Doctoral and first-professional degrees	163,765	454	0.3

Note: American Indians include Alaska Natives.
Source: National Center for Education Statistics, Digest of Education Statistics 2012, Internet site http://nces.ed.gov/programs/digest/2012menu_tables.asp; calculations by New Strategist

Health of American Indians Is below Average

Fewer than half (43 percent) of American Indians aged 18 or older say their health is "very good" or "excellent," far below the 60 percent of all American adults who rate their health highly. Twenty-one percent of American Indians say their health is only "fair" or "poor," a much higher share than the 13 percent in fair or poor health among the population as a whole. Smoking may be one factor behind the poor health of American Indians, who are 40 percent more likely than average to smoke. More than two-thirds of American Indians are overweight.

The 46,536 births to American Indian women in 2011 accounted for only 1 percent of all U.S. births. But American Indians, including Aleuts and Eskimos, account for 25 percent of births in Alaska, 18 percent in South Dakota, 13 percent in New Mexico, and 12 percent in Montana.

The most-common health conditions among American Indians are chronic joint symptoms or arthritis, lower back pain, and hypertension. One in four American Indian adults has not seen a doctor for more than a year. Twenty-one percent of American Indians have difficulties in physical functioning, and 10 percent say they would find it "very difficult" or impossible to walk a quarter of a mile. Heart disease and cancer are the two leading causes of death among American Indians, but they account for only 37 percent of Indian deaths versus 48 percent of deaths among all Americans. Accidents and diabetes are much more likely causes of death among American Indians than among the U.S. population as a whole.

■ Many of the health problems of American Indians are common in populations where poverty is widespread.

Fewer than half of American Indians say their health is very good or excellent

(percent distribution of American Indians aged 18 or older by self-reported health status, 2011)

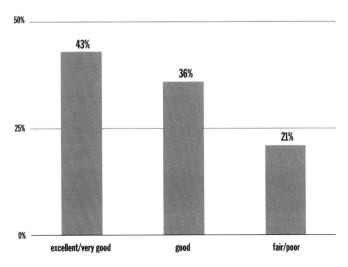

Table 2.6 Health Status of Total People and American Indians, 2011

(number and percent distribution of total people and American Indians aged 18 or older by self-reported health status, and index of American Indian to total, 2011; numbers in thousands)

	total		American Indian		index, American Indian to total
	number	percent distribution	number	percent distribution	
Total people	**231,376**	**100.0%**	**1,980**	**100.0%**	–
Excellent/very good	139,424	60.3	858	43.3	72
Good	60,973	26.4	714	36.1	137
Fair/poor	30,856	13.3	408	20.6	155

Note: American Indians are those who identify themselves as being American Indian or Alaska Native alone. Numbers may not add to total because "unknown" is not shown. The index is calculated by dividing the American Indian percentage by the total percentage and multiplying by 100. "–" means not applicable.
Source: National Center for Health Statistics, Summary Health Statistics for U.S. Adults: National Health Interview Survey, 2011, Vital and Health Statistics, Series 10, No. 256, 2012, Internet site http://www.cdc.gov/nchs/nhis.htm; calculations by New Strategist

Table 2.7 Weight Status of Total People and American Indians, 2011

(number and percent distribution of total people and American Indians aged 18 or older by body mass index based on self-reported height and weight, and index of American Indian to total, 2011; numbers in thousands)

	total		American Indian		index, American Indian to total
	number	percent distribution	number	percent distribution	
Total people	**231,376**	**100.0%**	**1,980**	**100.0%**	–
Underweight	3,549	1.5	–	–	–
Healthy weight	79,984	34.6	515	26.0	75
Overweight, total	141,072	61.0	1,345	67.9	111
Overweight, but not obese	77,586	33.5	577	29.1	87
Obese	63,486	27.4	768	38.8	141

Note: "Overweight" is defined as a body mass index of 25 or higher. "Obese" is defined as a body mass index of 30 or higher. Body mass index is calculated by dividing weight in kilograms by height in meters squared. American Indians are those who identify themselves as being American Indian or Alaska Native alone. Numbers may not add to total because "unknown" is not shown. The index is calculated by dividing the American Indian percentage by the total percentage and multiplying by 100. "–" means not applicable or sample is too small to make a reliable estimate.
Source: National Center for Health Statistics, Summary Health Statistics for U.S. Adults: National Health Interview Survey, 2011, Vital and Health Statistics, Series 10, No. 256, 2012, Internet site http://www.cdc.gov/nchs/nhis.htm; calculations by New Strategist

Table 2.8 Drinking Status of Total People and American Indians, 2011

(number and percent distribution of total people and American Indians aged 18 or older by drinking status, and index of American Indian to total, 2011; numbers in thousands)

	total		American Indian		index, American Indian to total
	number	percent distribution	number	percent distribution	
Total people	**231,376**	**100.0%**	**1,980**	**100.0%**	–
Lifetime abstainer	45,367	19.6	418	21.1	108
Former drinker	33,663	14.5	404	20.4	140
Current drinker	148,970	64.4	1,072	54.1	84
Infrequent	31,158	13.5	221	11.2	83
Regular	117,812	50.9	851	43.0	84

Note: "Lifetime abstainers" have had fewer than 12 drinks in lifetime. "Former drinkers" have had 12 or more drinks in lifetime, none in past year. "Current infrequent drinkers" have had 12 or more drinks in lifetime and fewer than 12 drinks in past year. "Current regular drinkers" have had 12 or more drinks in lifetime and at least 12 drinks in past year. American Indians are those who identify themselves as being American Indian or Alaska Native alone. Numbers may not add to total because "unknown" is not shown. The index is calculated by dividing the American Indian percentage by the total percentage and multiplying by 100. "–" means not applicable.
Source: National Center for Health Statistics, Summary Health Statistics for U.S. Adults: National Health Interview Survey, 2011, Vital and Health Statistics, Series 10, No. 256, 2012, Internet site http://www.cdc.gov/nchs/nhis.htm; calculations by New Strategist

Table 2.9 Smoking Status of Total People and American Indians, 2011

(number and percent distribution of total people and American Indians aged 18 or older by smoking status, and index of American Indian to total, 2011; numbers in thousands)

	total		American Indian		index, American Indian to total
	number	percent distribution	number	percent distribution	
Total people	**231,376**	**100.0%**	**1,980**	**100.0%**	–
Never smoked	136,528	59.0	1,124	56.8	96
Former smoker	50,416	21.8	324	16.4	75
Current smoker	43,821	18.9	525	26.5	140

Note: "Never smoked" means fewer than 100 cigarettes in lifetime. "Former smokers" have smoked 100 or more cigarettes in lifetime but did not smoke at time of interview. "Current smokers" have smoked at least 100 cigarettes in lifetime and currently smoke. American Indians are those who identify themselves as being American Indian or Alaska Native alone. Numbers may not add to total because "unknown" is not shown. The index is calculated by dividing the American Indian percentage by the total percentage and multiplying by 100. "–" means not applicable.
Source: National Center for Health Statistics, Summary Health Statistics for U.S. Adults: National Health Interview Survey, 2011, Vital and Health Statistics, Series 10, No. 256, 2012, Internet site http://www.cdc.gov/nchs/nhis.htm; calculations by New Strategist

Table 2.10 Births to Total and American Indian Women by Age, 2011

(total number of births, number and percent distribution of births to American Indians, and American Indian share of total, by age, 2011)

		American Indian		
	total	number	percent distribution	share of total
Total births	**3,953,593**	**46,536**	**100.0%**	**1.2%**
Under age 15	3,974	95	0.2	2.4
Aged 15 to 19	329,797	6,818	14.7	2.1
Aged 20 to 24	925,213	15,610	33.5	1.7
Aged 25 to 29	1,127,592	12,500	26.9	1.1
Aged 30 to 34	986,661	7,401	15.9	0.8
Aged 35 to 39	463,815	3,305	7.1	0.7
Aged 40 to 44	108,891	774	1.7	0.7
Aged 45 to 54	7,651	32	0.1	0.4

Note: American Indians include Alaska Natives.
Source: National Center for Health Statistics, Births: Preliminary Data for 2011, National Vital Statistics Report, Vol. 61, No. 5, 2012, Internet site http://www.cdc.gov/nchs/births.htm; calculations by New Strategist

Table 2.11 Births to American Indian Women by Age and Marital Status, 2010

(total number of births to American Indians, number of births to unmarried American Indians, and unmarried share of total, by age, 2010)

		unmarried	
	total	number	share of total
Births to American Indians	**46,760**	**30,670**	**65.6%**
Under age 15	100	100	100.0
Aged 15 to 19	7,408	6,744	91.0
Aged 20 to 24	15,743	11,686	74.2
Aged 25 to 29	12,225	6,867	56.2
Aged 30 to 34	7,311	3,528	48.3
Aged 35 to 39	3,212	1,402	43.6
Aged 40 or older	761	343	45.1

Note: American Indians include Alaska Natives.
Source: National Center for Health Statistics, Births: Final Data for 2010, National Vital Statistics Reports, Vol. 61, No. 1, 2012, Internet site http://www.cdc.gov/nchs/births.htm; calculations by New Strategist

Table 2.12 Births to Total and American Indian Women by Birth Order, 2011

(total number of births, number and percent distribution of births to American Indians, and American Indian share of total, by age, 2011)

	total	American Indian		
		number	percent distribution	share of total
Total births	**3,953,593**	**46,536**	**100.0%**	**1.2%**
First child	1,577,344	16,575	35.6	1.1
Second child	1,239,136	12,474	26.8	1.0
Third child	648,124	8,217	17.7	1.3
Fourth or later child	458,777	9,043	19.4	2.0

Note: American Indians include Alaska Natives. Numbers do not add to total because "not stated" is not shown.
Source: National Center for Health Statistics, Births: Preliminary Data for 2011, National Vital Statistics Report, Vol. 61, No. 5, 2012, Internet site http://www.cdc.gov/nchs/births.htm; calculations by New Strategist

Table 2.13 Births to Total and American Indian Women by State, 2011

(total number of births, number and percent distribution of births to American Indians, and American Indian share of total, by state, 2011)

| | total | American Indian | | |
		number	percent distribution	share of total
Total births	3,953,593	46,536	100.0%	1.2%
Alabama	59,347	196	0.4	0.3
Alaska	11,455	2,842	6.1	24.8
Arizona	85,543	5,989	12.9	7.0
Arkansas	38,713	280	0.6	0.7
California	502,118	3,461	7.4	0.7
Colorado	65,055	675	1.5	1.0
Connecticut	37,280	255	0.5	0.7
Delaware	11,257	23	0.0	0.2
District of Columbia	9,314	20	0.0	0.2
Florida	213,344	435	0.9	0.2
Georgia	132,488	339	0.7	0.3
Hawaii	18,957	80	0.2	0.4
Idaho	22,305	414	0.9	1.9
Illinois	161,312	218	0.5	0.1
Indiana	83,702	157	0.3	0.2
Iowa	38,213	266	0.6	0.7
Kansas	39,642	380	0.8	1.0
Kentucky	55,377	86	0.2	0.2
Louisiana	61,889	381	0.8	0.6
Maine	12,704	112	0.2	0.9
Maryland	73,086	205	0.4	0.3
Massachusetts	73,225	279	0.6	0.4
Michigan	114,004	793	1.7	0.7
Minnesota	68,411	1,540	3.3	2.3
Mississippi	39,856	282	0.6	0.7
Missouri	76,117	395	0.8	0.5
Montana	12,069	1,486	3.2	12.3
Nebraska	25,720	514	1.1	2.0
Nevada	35,295	468	1.0	1.3
New Hampshire	12,852	23	0.0	0.2
New Jersey	105,886	182	0.4	0.2
New Mexico	27,289	3,615	7.8	13.2
New York	241,290	1183	2.5	0.5
North Carolina	120,385	1,982	4.3	1.6
North Dakota	9,527	1,036	2.2	10.9
Ohio	137,916	273	0.6	0.2
Oklahoma	52,274	6,186	13.3	11.8

| | total | American Indian | | |
		number	percent distribution	share of total
Oregon	45,157	873	1.9%	1.9%
Pennsylvania	143,148	383	0.8	0.3
Rhode Island	10,960	149	0.3	1.4
South Carolina	57,368	241	0.5	0.4
South Dakota	11,849	2,094	4.5	17.7
Tennessee	79,588	234	0.5	0.3
Texas	377,449	1,106	2.4	0.3
Utah	51,223	770	1.7	1.5
Vermont	6,078	17	0.0	0.3
Virginia	102,648	121	0.3	0.1
Washington	86,976	2,234	4.8	2.6
West Virginia	20,720	19	0.0	0.1
Wisconsin	67,811	975	2.1	1.4
Wyoming	7,398	268	0.6	3.6

Note: American Indians include Alaska Natives.
Source: National Center for Health Statistics, Births: Preliminary Data for 2011, National Vital Statistics Report, Vol. 61, No. 5, 2012, Internet site http://www.cdc.gov/nchs/births.htm; calculations by New Strategist

Table 2.14 Health Insurance Coverage of Total People and American Indians under Age 65, 2011

(percent distribution of total people and American Indians under age 65 by health insurance coverage status, 2011; numbers in thousands)

	total		American Indian		index, American Indian to total
	number	percent distribution	number	percent distribution	
Total people under age 65	**266,181**	**100.0%**	**2,527**	**100.0%**	–
With health insurance	218,502	82.1	1,642	65.0	79
Private insurance	163,116	61.3	842	33.3	54
Medicaid	45,534	17.1	694	27.5	161
Other	9,852	3.7	106	4.2	113
Uninsured	45,376	17.0	854	33.8	198

Note: American Indians are those who identify themselves as being American Indian or Alaska Native alone. Numbers may not add to total because "unknown" is not shown. The index is calculated by dividing the American Indian percentage by the total percentage and multiplying by 100. "–" means not applicable.
Source: National Center for Health Statistics, Summary Health Statistics for the U.S. Population: National Health Interview Survey, 2011, Vital and Health Statistics, Series 10, No. 255, 2012, Internet site http://www.cdc.gov/nchs/nhis.htm; calculations by New Strategist

Table 2.15 Health Conditions among Total People and American Indians Aged 18 or Older, 2011

(number of total people and American Indians aged 18 or older with selected health conditions, percent of American Indians with condition, and American Indian share of total with condition, 2011; numbers in thousands)

| | total | American Indian | | |
		number	percent with condition	share of total
TOTAL PEOPLE	**231,376**	**1,980**	**100.0%**	**0.9%**
Selected circulatory diseases				
Heart disease, all types	26,485	249	12.6	0.9
Coronary	15,300	137	6.9	0.9
Hypertension	5?,959	505	25.5	0.9
Stroke	6,171	90	4.5	1.5
Selected respiratory conditions				
Emphysema	4,680	90	4.5	1.9
Asthma, ever	29,041	390	19.7	1.3
Asthma, still	18,869	279	14.1	1.5
Hay fever	16,869	96	4.8	0.6
Sinusitis	29,611	223	11.3	0.8
Chronic bronchitis	10,071	111	5.6	1.1
Selected types of cancer				
Any cancer	19,025	89	4.5	0.5
Other selected diseases and conditions				
Diabetes	20,589	267	13.5	1.3
Ulcers	15,502	166	8.4	1.1
Kidney disease	4,381	49	2.5	1.1
Liver disease	3,016	60	3.0	2.0
Arthritis	53,782	527	26.6	1.0
Chronic joint symptoms	68,749	661	33.4	1.0
Migraines or severe headaches	37,904	426	21.5	1.1
Pain in neck	35,798	326	16.5	0.9
Pain in lower back	66,917	612	30.9	0.9
Pain in face or jaw	11,436	127	6.4	1.1
Selected sensory problems				
Hearing	37,122	311	15.7	0.8
Vision	21,232	297	15.0	1.4
Absence of all natural teeth	18,038	265	13.4	1.5

Note: The conditions shown are those that have ever been diagnosed by a doctor, except as noted. Hay fever, sinusitis, and chronic bronchitis have been diagnosed in the past 12 months. Kidney and liver disease have been diagnosed in the past 12 months and exclude kidney stones, bladder infections, and incontinence. Chronic joint symptoms are shown if respondent had pain, aching, or stiffness in or around a joint (excluding back and neck) and the condition began more than three months ago. Migraines, pain in neck, lower back, face, or jaw are shown only if pain lasted a whole day or more. American Indians are those who identify themselves as being of the race alone.

Source: National Center for Health Statistics, Summary Health Statistics for U.S. Adults: National Health Interview Survey, 2011, Vital and Health Statistics, Series 10, No. 256, 2012, Internet site http://www.cdc.gov/nchs/nhis.htm; calculations by New Strategist

Table 2.16 Health Conditions among Total and American Indian Children, 2011

(number of total people and American Indians under age 18 with selected health conditions, percent of American Indians with condition, and American Indian share of total, 2011; numbers in thousands)

	total	American Indian number	American Indian percent with condition	American Indian share of total
Total children	**74,518**	**873**	**100.0%**	**1.2%**
Ever told have asthma	10,463	134	15.3	1.3
Still have asthma	7,074	69	7.9	1.0
Hay fever in past 12 months	6,711	86	9.9	1.3
Respiratory allergies in past 12 months	8,269	63	7.2	0.8
Food allergies in past 12 months	4,126	52	6.0	1.3
Skin allergies in past 12 months	9,516	84	9.6	0.9
Prescription medication taken regularly for at least three months	10,019	106	12.1	1.1
Learning disability*	4,660	61	7.0	1.3
Attention deficit hyperactivity disorder*	5,240	71	8.1	1.4

* Diagnosed by a school representative or health professional; data exclude children under age 3.
Note: American Indians are those who identify themselves as being American Indian or Alaska Native alone.
Source: National Center for Health Statistics, Summary Health Statistics for U.S. Children: National Health Interview Survey, 2011, Vital and Health Statistics, Series 10, No. 254, 2012, Internet site http://www.cdc.gov/nchs/nhis.htm

Table 2.17 Health Care Office Visits by Total People and American Indians, 2011

(number of total people and American Indians aged 18 or older by visits to a health care provider in the past 12 months, percent distribution of American Indians by number of visits, and American Indian share of total, 2011; numbers in thousands)

	total	American Indian number	American Indian percent distribution	American Indian share of total
Total people	**231,376**	**1,980**	**100.0%**	**0.9%**
No visits	43,578	493	24.9	1.1
One visit	39,552	295	14.9	0.7
Two to three visits	59,226	559	28.2	0.9
Four to nine visits	55,721	406	20.5	0.7
10 or more visits	30,822	188	9.5	0.6

Note: Health care visits exclude overnight hospitalizations, visits to emergency rooms, home visits, dental visits, and telephone calls. American Indians include Alaska Natives and are those who identify themselves as being of the race alone. Numbers may not add to total because "unknown" is not shown.
Source: National Center for Health Statistics, Summary Health Statistics for U.S. Adults: National Health Interview Survey, 2011, Vital and Health Statistics, Series 10, No. 256, 2012, Internet site http://www.cdc.gov/nchs/nhis.htm; calculations by New Strategist

Table 2.18 Difficulties in Physical Functioning among Total People and American Indians, 2011

(number of total people and American Indians aged 18 or older, with difficulties in physical functioning, percent of American Indians with difficulty, and American Indian share of total, by type of difficulty, 2011; numbers in thousands)

| | | American Indian | | |
	total	number	percent	share of total
TOTAL PEOPLE	**231,376**	**1,980**	**100.0%**	**0.9%**
Total with any physical difficulty	**37,368**	**415**	**21.0**	**1.1**
Walk quarter of a mile	17,597	205	10.4	1.2
Climb 10 steps without resting	12,887	190	9.6	1.5
Stand for two hours	22,369	273	13.8	1.2
Sit for two hours	7,724	106	5.4	1.4
Stoop, bend, or kneel	21,677	240	12.1	1.1
Reach over head	6,550	99	5.0	1.5
Grasp or handle small objects	4,329	47	2.4	1.1
Lift or carry 10 pounds	10,677	167	8.4	1.6
Push or pull large objects	15,998	212	10.7	1.3

Note: Respondents were classified as having difficulty if they responded "very difficult" or "can't do at all." American Indians are those who identify themselves as being American Indian or Alaska Native alone.
Source: National Center for Health Statistics, Summary Health Statistics for U.S. Adults: National Health Interview Survey, 2011, Vital and Health Statistics, Series 10, No. 256, 2012, Internet site http://www.cdc.gov/nchs/nhis.htm; calculations by New Strategist

Table 2.19 AIDS Cases among Total People and American Indians, through December 2009

(number of total AIDS cases diagnosed, number and percent distribution among American Indians, and American Indian share of total, by sex, through December 2009)

| | | American Indian | | |
	total	number	percent distribution	share of total
Total diagnosed with AIDS	**1,108,611**	**3,699**	**100.0%**	**0.3%**
Males aged 13 or older	878,366	2,879	77.8	0.3
Females aged 13 or older	220,795	789	21.3	0.4
Children under age 13	9,448	31	0.8	0.3

Note: American Indians include Alaska Natives.
Source: National Center for Health Statistics, Health United States 2011, Internet site http://www.cdc.gov/nchs/hus.htm; calculations by New Strategist

Table 2.20 Leading Causes of Death among American Indians, 2009

(number and percent distribution of deaths to American Indians accounted for by the 10 leading causes of death among American Indians, 2009)

		number	percent distribution
Total American Indian deaths		**14,960**	**100.0%**
1.	Diseases of the heart (1)	2,764	18.5
2.	Malignant neoplasms (cancer) (2)	2,710	18.1
3.	Accidents (unintentional injuries) (5)	1,733	11.6
4.	Diabetes mellitus (7)	786	5.3
5.	Chronic liver disease and cirrhosis	714	4.8
6.	Chronic lower respiratory disease (3)	610	4.1
7.	Cerebrovascular diseases (4)	561	3.8
8.	Suicide (10)	429	2.9
9.	Influenza and pneumonia (8)	402	2.7
10.	Nephritis, nephrotic syndrome, and nephrosis (9)	307	2.1
	All other causes	3,944	26.4

Note: Number in parentheses shows rank for all Americans if the cause of death is in top 10. American Indians include Alaska Natives.
Source: National Center for Health Statistics, Deaths: Leading Causes for 2009, National Vital Statistics Report, Vol. 61, No. 7, 2012, Internet site http://www.cdc.gov/nchs/deaths.htm; calculations by New Strategist

American Indians: Housing

Most American Indians Own Their Home

The homeownership rate among American Indian households stood at just over 51 percent in 2012, according to the Census Bureau's Housing Vacancies and Homeownership Survey. The 2010 census had found a homeownership rate of 54 percent. By region, the homeownership rate of American Indians is below 50 percent only in the Northeast.

American Indian homeowners report a median home value of $116,400, well below the median of $188,400 for all homeowners. The 58 percent majority of American Indian homeowners have a mortgage. Among those who do, median monthly housing costs are $1,215.

■ Thirteen percent of American Indian households do not own a vehicle, a much larger share than the 9 percent of all households without a vehicle.

American Indian homeownership is lowest in the Northeast

(percent of American Indian households that own their home, by region, 2010)

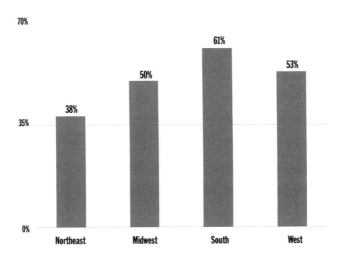

Table 2.21 Total and American Indian Homeownership Rate, 2000 to 2012

(homeownership rate of total and American Indian households and index of American Indian to total, 2000 to 2012; percentage point change for selected years)

	total households	American Indian households	index, American Indian to total
2012	65.4%	51.1%	78
2011	66.1	53.5	81
2010	66.9	52.3	78
2009	67.4	56.2	83
2008	67.8	56.5	83
2007	68.1	56.9	84
2006	68.8	58.2	85
2005	68.9	58.2	84
2004	69.0	55.6	81
2003	68.3	54.3	80
2002	67.9	54.0	80
2001	67.8	55.4	82
2000	67.4	56.2	83

PERCENTAGE POINT CHANGE

2004 to 2012	–3.6	–4.5	–
2000 to 2012	–2.0	–5.1	–

Note: American Indians are those who identify themselves as being of the race alone. The index is calculated by dividing the American Indian homeownership rate by the total rate and multiplying by 100. "–" means not applicable.
Source: Bureau of the Census, Housing Vacancies and Homeownership, Internet site http://www.census.gov/housing/hvs/; calculations by New Strategist

Table 2.22 American Indian Homeownership Status by Age of Householder, 2010

(number and percent of American Indian households by homeownership status and age of householder, 2010; numbers in thousands)

	total	owner		renter	
		number	percent	number	percent
Total American Indian households	**940**	**510**	**54.2%**	**430**	**45.8%**
Under age 25	57	11	19.3	46	80.7
Aged 25 to 34	167	59	35.3	108	64.7
Aged 35 to 44	194	99	51.0	95	49.0
Aged 45 to 54	220	132	60.1	88	39.9
Aged 55 to 64	164	110	66.8	54	33.2
Aged 65 or older	137	99	72.0	38	28.0

Note: American Indians include Alaska Natives. The American Indian and Alaska Native population are those who identify themselves as being of the race alone.
Source: Bureau of the Census, 2010 Census, American Factfinder, Internet site http://factfinder2.census.gov/faces/nav/jsf/pages/index.xhtml; calculations by New Strategist

Table 2.23 Total and American Indian Homeowners by Age of Householder, 2010

(number of total homeowners, number and percent distribution of American Indian homeowners, and American Indian share of total, by age of householder, 2010; numbers in thousands)

	total	American Indians		
		number	percent distribution	share of total
Total homeowners	**75,986**	**510**	**100.0%**	**0.7%**
Under age 25	870	11	2.2	1.3
Aged 25 to 34	7,547	59	11.6	0.8
Aged 35 to 44	13,256	99	19.4	0.7
Aged 45 to 54	17,804	132	25.9	0.7
Aged 55 to 64	16,503	110	21.5	0.7
Aged 65 or older	20,007	99	19.4	0.5

Source: Bureau of the Census, American Housing Survey for the United States: 2011, Internet site http://www.census.gov/housing/ahs/index.html; calculations by New Strategist

Table 2.24 Total and American Indian Renters by Age of Householder, 2010

(number of total renters, number and percent distribution of American Indian renters, and American Indian share of total, by age of householder, 2010; numbers in thousands)

	total	American Indian number	American Indian percent distribution	American Indian share of total
Total renters	**40,730**	**430**	**100.0%**	**1.1%**
Under age 25	4,531	46	10.8	1.0
Aged 25 to 34	10,410	108	25.1	1.0
Aged 35 to 44	8,035	95	22.2	1.2
Aged 45 to 54	7,103	88	20.4	1.2
Aged 55 to 64	4,838	54	12.7	1.1
Aged 65 or older	5,813	38	8.9	0.7

Note: American Indians include Alaska Natives. The American Indian and Alaska Native population are those who identify themselves as being of the race alone.
Source: Bureau of the Census, 2010 Census, Internet site http://factfinder2.census.gov/faces/nav/jsf/pages/index.xhtml; calculations by New Strategist

Table 2.25 American Indian Homeownership Status by Household Type, 2010

(number and percent of American Indian households by household type and homeownership status, 2010; numbers in thousands)

	total	owner number	owner percent	renter number	renter percent
Total American Indian households	**940**	**510**	**54.2%**	**430**	**45.8%**
Family households	661	390	58.9	272	41.1
Married couples	377	264	70.0	113	30.0
Female-headed family, no spouse present	201	86	42.5	116	57.5
Male-headed family, no spouse present	83	40	48.3	43	51.7
Nonfamily households	278	120	43.1	158	56.9
Female householder	129	56	43.5	73	56.5
Living alone	101	46	45.4	55	54.6
Male householder	149	64	42.7	85	57.3
Living alone	112	50	44.9	62	55.1

Note: American Indians include Alaska Natives. The American Indian and Alaska Native population are those who identify themselves as being of the race alone.
Source: Bureau of the Census, 2010 Census, Internet site http://factfinder2.census.gov/faces/nav/jsf/pages/index.xhtml; calculations by New Strategist

Table 2.26 Total and American Indian Homeowners by Household Type, 2010

(number of total homeowners, number and percent distribution of American Indian homeowners, and American Indian share of total, by household type, 2010; numbers in thousands)

	total	American Indian number	percent distribution	share of total
Total homeowners	**75,986**	**6,368**	**100.0%**	**8.4%**
Family households	56,206	390	76.5	0.7
Married couples	45,801	264	51.8	0.6
Female-headed family, no spouse present	7,278	86	16.8	1.2
Male-headed family, no spouse present	3,127	40	7.9	1.3
Nonfamily households	19,780	120	23.5	0.6
Female householder	11,053	56	11.0	0.5
Living alone	9,625	46	9.0	0.5
Male householder	8,727	64	12.5	0.7
Living alone	6,828	50	9.9	0.7

Note: American Indians include Alaska Natives. The American Indian and Alaska Native population are those who identify themselves as being of the race alone.
Source: Bureau of the Census, 2010 Census, Internet site http://factfinder2.census.gov/faces/nav/jsf/pages/index.xhtml; calculations by New Strategist

Table 2.27 Total and American Indian Renters by Household Type, 2010

(number of total renters, number and percent distribution of American Indian renters, and American Indian share of total, by household type, 2010; numbers in thousands)

	total	American Indian number	American Indian percent distribution	American Indian share of total
Total renters	**40,730**	**430**	**100.0%**	**1.1%**
Family households	21,332	272	63.2	1.3
Married couples	10,710	113	26.2	1.1
Female-headed family, no spouse present	7,972	116	26.9	1.5
Male-headed family, no spouse present	2,651	43	10.0	1.6
Nonfamily households	19,398	158	36.8	0.8
Female householder	9,666	73	17.0	0.8
Living alone	7,673	55	12.8	0.7
Male householder	9,732	85	19.9	0.9
Living alone	7,078	62	14.3	0.9

Note: American Indians include Alaska Natives. The American Indian and Alaska Native population are those who identify themselves as being of the race alone.
Source: Bureau of the Census, 2010 Census, Internet site http://factfinder2.census.gov/faces/nav/jsf/pages/index.xhtml; calculations by New Strategist

Table 2.28 American Indian Homeownership Status by Region, 2010

(number and percent of American Indian households by homeownership status and region, 2010; numbers in thousands)

	total	owners		renters	
		number	share of total	number	share of total
Total American Indian households	**940**	**510**	**54.2%**	**430**	**45.8%**
Northeast	70	27	38.2	43	61.8
Midwest	149	74	50.0	75	50.0
South	316	193	61.2	122	38.8
West	405	215	53.1	190	46.9

Note: American Indians include Alaska Natives. The American Indian and Alaska Native population are those who identify themselves as being of the race alone.
Source: Bureau of the Census, 2010 Census, Internet site http://factfinder2.census.gov/faces/nav/jsf/pages/index.xhtml; calculations by New Strategist

Table 2.29 Total and American Indian Homeowners by Region, 2010

(number of total homeowners, number and percent distribution of American Indian homeowners, and American Indian share of total, by region, 2010; numbers in thousands)

	total	American Indian		
		number	percent distribution	share of total
Total homeowners	**75,986**	**510**	**100.0%**	**0.7%**
Northeast	13,203	27	5.2	0.2
Midwest	18,147	74	14.6	0.4
South	29,100	193	37.9	0.7
West	15,536	215	42.2	1.4

Note: American Indians include Alaska Natives. The American Indian and Alaska Native population are those who identify themselves as being of the race alone.
Source: Bureau of the Census, 2010 Census, Internet site http://factfinder2.census.gov/faces/nav/jsf/pages/index.xhtml; calculations by New Strategist

Table 2.30 Total and American Indian Renters by Region, 2010

(number of total renters, number and percent distribution of American Indian renters, and American Indian share of total, by region, 2010; numbers in thousands)

	total	American Indian		
		number	percent distribution	share of total
Total renters	**40,730**	**430**	**100.0%**	**0.7%**
Northeast	8,013	43	10.0	0.5
Midwest	8,069	75	17.3	0.9
South	14,510	122	28.5	0.8
West	10,139	190	44.2	1.9

Note: American Indians include Alaska Natives. The American Indian and Alaska Native population are those who identify themselves as being of the race alone.
Source: Bureau of the Census, 2010 Census, Internet site http://factfinder2.census.gov/faces/nav/jsf/pages/index.xhtml; calculations by New Strategist

Table 2.31 **Characteristics of Total and American Indian Occupied Housing Units, 2006–10**

(number of total and American Indian occupied housing units, and percent distribution by selected characteristics, 2006–10; numbers in thousands)

	total		American Indian	
	number	percent distribution	number	percent distribution
TOTAL OCCUPIED HOUSING UNITS	**114,236**	**100.0%**	**804**	**100.0%**
Year householder moved into unit				
Total households	**114,236**	**100.0**	**804**	**100.0**
2005 or later	39,766	34.8	309	38.5
2000 to 2004	26,517	23.2	179	22.3
1990 to 1999	23,883	20.9	165	20.5
1980 to 1989	10,804	9.5	79	9.8
1970 to 1979	7,147	6.3	46	5.7
Before 1970	6,120	5.4	26	3.2
Vehicles available				
Total households	**114,236**	**100.0**	**804**	**100.0**
None	10,113	8.9	107	13.3
One or more	104,123	91.1	697	86.7
House heating fuel				
Total households	**114,236**	**100.0**	**804**	**100.0**
Utility gas	57,018	49.9	313	38.9
Bottled gas	6,146	5.4	88	11.0
Electricity	39,066	34.2	273	33.9
Fuel oil or kerosene	8,073	7.1	44	5.4
Coal or coke	135	0.1	1	0.2
Wood	2,250	2.0	70	8.7
Solar energy	38	0.0	0	0.1
Other fuel	483	0.4	7	0.8
No heating fuel used	1,025	0.9	8	1.0
TOTAL OWNER-OCCUPIED HOMES	**76,090**	**100.0**	**442**	**100.0**
Housing units with a mortgage	51,697	67.9	258	58.4
Housing units without a mortgage	24,393	32.1	184	41.6
Median value of home	$188,400	–	$116,400	–
Median monthly owner costs with a mortgage	1,524	–	1,215	–
Median monthly owner costs without a mortgage	431	–	294	–
TOTAL RENTER-OCCUPIED HOMES	**38,146**	**100.0**	**362**	**100.0**
Occupied units paying rent	35,274	92.5	323	89.4
Median rent	$841	–	$702	–

Source: Bureau of the Census, 2006–10 American Community Survey, Internet site http://factfinder2.census.gov/faces/nav/jsf/ pages/index.xhtml; calculations by New Strategist

Table 2.32 Geographic Mobility of American Indians in the Past Year, 2006–10

(total number of American Indians aged 1 or older, and percent distribution by mobility status in the past year, 2006–10; numbers in thousands)

	number	percent distribution
Total American Indians	**2,441**	**100.0%**
Same house (nonmovers)	1,979	81.1
Total movers	462	18.9
Different house in the United States	449	18.4
Same county	275	11.2
Different county, same state	107	4.4
Different state	68	2.8
Abroad	13	0.5

Note: American Indians include Alaska Natives.. The American Indian and Alaska Native population are those who identify themselves as being of the race alone.
Source: Bureau of the Census, 2006–10 American Community Survey, Internet site http://factfinder2.census.gov/faces/nav/jsf/pages/index.xhtml; calculations by New Strategist

American Indians Have Below-Average Incomes

The median annual income of the nation's 803,954 American Indian households stood at $36,779 in 2006–10, according to the American Community Survey. This figure is well below the $51,914 median income of all households during those years.

American Indian median household income peaks among householders aged 45 to 64, at just over $42,000. American Indian men who work full-time had median earnings of $35,920 in 2006–10, only 77 percent as high as the median of all men who work full-time. American Indian women who work full-time had median earnings of $30,198, an amount 16 percent below the median for all women who work full-time.

Among American Indian families, 22.1 percent were poor in 2006–10. The poverty rate ranges from a low of 11.6 percent among American Indian married couples to a high of 40.3 percent among American Indian female-headed families. By age, American Indian children are most likely to be poor with a poverty rate of 33.3 percent.

■ American Indian households have below-average incomes because a relatively small share are headed by married couples, the most-affluent household type.

The median income of American Indian households is only 71 percent as high as the national median

(median income of total and American Indian households, 2006–10)

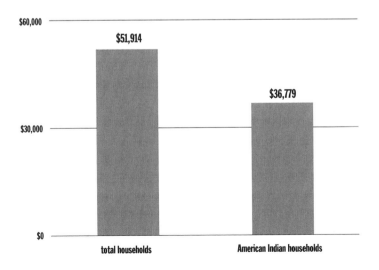

Table 2.33 Total and American Indian Household Income, 2006–2010

(number of total households, number and percent distribution of American Indian households, and American Indian share of total, by household income, 2006–10)

	total	American Indian number	percent distribution	share of total
Total households	**114,235,996**	**803,954**	**100.0%**	**0.7%**
Under $10,000	8,274,388	107,503	13.4	1.3
$10,000 to $14,999	6,294,748	65,428	8.1	1.0
$15,000 to $19,999	6,107,790	57,120	7.1	0.9
$20,000 to $24,999	6,232,948	55,648	6.9	0.9
$25,000 to $29,999	5,973,676	50,867	6.3	0.9
$30,000 to $34,999	6,070,164	49,008	6.1	0.8
$35,000 to $39,999	5,586,881	43,582	5.4	0.8
$40,000 to $44,999	5,608,270	42,027	5.2	0.7
$45,000 to $49,999	4,937,751	35,353	4.4	0.7
$50,000 to $59,999	9,421,693	62,612	7.8	0.7
$60,000 to $69,999	11,780,018	70,644	8.8	0.6
$70,000 to $99,999	14,097,295	76,136	9.5	0.5
$100,000 to $124,999	8,947,140	40,049	5.0	0.4
$125,000 to $149,999	5,118,616	20,250	2.5	0.4
$150,000 to $199,999	4,993,775	15,771	2.0	0.3
$200,000 or more	4,790,843	11,956	1.5	0.2
Median income	$51,914	$36,779	–	–

Note: American Indians include Alaska Natives. The American Indian and Alaska Native population are those who identify themselves as being of the race alone.
Source: Bureau of the Census, 2006–10 American Community Survey, Internet site http://factfinder2.census.gov/faces/nav/jsf/pages/index.xhtml; calculations by New Strategist

Table 2.34 American Indian Household Income by Age of Householder, 2006–10

(number and percent distribution of American Indian households by household income and age of householder, 2006–10)

	total	under 25	25 to 44	45 to 64	65 or older
Total American Indian households	**803,954**	**50,339**	**315,070**	**327,465**	**111,080**
$10,000 to $14,999	65,428	5,226	20,886	23,092	16,224
$15,000 to $19,999	57,120	4,673	19,707	20,069	12,671
$20,000 to $24,999	55,648	5,468	21,525	18,706	9,949
$25,000 to $29,999	50,867	4,750	20,700	17,551	7,866
$30,000 to $34,999	49,008	3,384	21,275	17,838	6,511
$35,000 to $39,999	43,582	3,043	18,389	16,978	5,172
$40,000 to $44,999	42,027	2,633	17,771	16,951	4,672
$45,000 to $49,999	35,353	1,646	15,501	14,126	4,080
$50,000 to $59,999	62,612	2,839	26,872	26,214	6,687
$60,000 to $69,999	70,644	2,436	30,481	31,512	6,215
$70,000 to $99,999	76,136	1,723	32,443	35,233	6,737
$100,000 to $124,999	40,049	604	16,424	20,175	2,846
$125,000 to $149,999	20,250	322	7,451	10,807	1,670
$150,000 to $199,999	15,771	129	5,293	9,102	1,247
$200,000 or more	11,956	270	3,865	6,811	1,010
Median income	$36,779	$23,730	$39,593	$42,090	$24,535

PERCENT DISTRIBUTION BY INCOME

Total American Indian households	**100.0%**	**100.0%**	**100.0%**	**100.0%**	**100.0%**
Under $10,000	13.4	22.2	11.6	12.9	15.8
$10,000 to $14,999	8.1	10.4	6.6	7.1	14.6
$15,000 to $19,999	7.1	9.3	6.3	6.1	11.4
$20,000 to $24,999	6.9	10.9	6.8	5.7	9.0
$25,000 to $29,999	6.3	9.4	6.6	5.4	7.1
$30,000 to $34,999	6.1	6.7	6.8	5.4	5.9
$35,000 to $39,999	5.4	6.0	5.8	5.2	4.7
$40,000 to $44,999	5.2	5.2	5.6	5.2	4.2
$45,000 to $49,999	4.4	3.3	4.9	4.3	3.7
$50,000 to $59,999	7.8	5.6	8.5	8.0	6.0
$60,000 to $69,999	8.8	4.8	9.7	9.6	5.6
$70,000 to $99,999	9.5	3.4	10.3	10.8	6.1
$100,000 to $124,999	5.0	1.2	5.2	6.2	2.6
$125,000 to $149,999	2.5	0.6	2.4	3.3	1.5
$150,000 to $199,999	2.0	0.3	1.7	2.8	1.1
$200,000 or more	1.5	0.5	1.2	2.1	0.9

Note: American Indians include Alaska Natives. The American Indian and Alaska Native population are those who identify themselves as being of the race alone.
Source: Bureau of the Census, 2006–10 American Community Survey, Internet site http://factfinder2.census.gov/faces/nav/jsf/pages/index.xhtml; calculations by New Strategist

Table 2.35 Earnings of American Indians Working Full-Time by Sex, 2006–10

(number and percent distribution of American Indians aged 16 or older working full-time, year-round by earnings, median earnings, and percent working full-time, by sex, 2006–10)

	men	women
Total American Indians working full-time	**337,582**	**282,265**
Under $5,000	2,419	1828
$5,000 to $7,499	3,724	3,407
$7,500 to $9,999	3,733	4,960
$10,000 to $12,499	9,325	11,767
$12,500 to $14,999	9,911	12,547
$15,000 to $17,499	16,308	17,990
$17,500 to $19,999	13,368	15,917
$20,000 to $22,499	21,742	22,657
$22,500 to $24,999	14,693	16,140
$25,000 to $29,999	33,269	32,252
$30,000 to $34,999	34,833	34,098
$35,000 to $39,999	25,982	23,776
$40,000 to $44,999	28,849	20,470
$45,000 to $49,999	17,593	12,751
$50,000 to $54,999	20,428	12,738
$55,000 to $64,999	24,247	14,234
$65,000 to $74,999	17,275	8,742
$75,000 to $99,999	20,976	10,753
$100,000 or more	18,907	5,238
Median earnings	$35,920	$30,198
Percent working full-time	37.4%	30.3%

	men	women
PERCENT DISTRIBUTION BY EARNINGS		
Total American Indians working full-time	**100.0%**	**100.0%**
Under $5,000	0.7	0.6
$5,000 to $7,499	1.1	1.2
$7,500 to $9,999	1.1	1.8
$10,000 to $12,499	2.8	4.2
$12,500 to $14,999	2.9	4.4
$15,000 to $17,499	4.8	6.4
$17,500 to $19,999	4.0	5.6
$20,000 to $22,499	6.4	8.0
$22,500 to $24,999	4.4	5.7
$25,000 to $29,999	9.9	11.4
$30,000 to $34,999	10.3	12.1
$35,000 to $39,999	7.7	8.4
$40,000 to $44,999	8.5	7.3
$45,000 to $49,999	5.2	4.5
$50,000 to $54,999	6.1	4.5
$55,000 to $64,999	7.2	5.0
$65,000 to $74,999	5.1	3.1
$75,000 to $99,999	6.2	3.8
$100,000 or more	5.6	1.9

Note: American Indians include Alaska Natives. The American Indian and Alaska Native population are those who identify themselves as being of the race alone.
Source: Bureau of the Census, 2006–10 American Community Survey, Internet site http://factfinder2.census.gov/faces/nav/jsf/ pages/index.xhtml; calculations by New Strategist

Table 2.36 Earnings of Total People and American Indians, 2006–10

(median earnings of total people and American Indians aged 16 or older by sex and work status, and index of American Indian earnings to total, 2006–10)

	total	American Indian	index, American Indian earnings to total
Total people aged 16 or older	**$29,701**	**$21,510**	**72**
Men	35,201	24,513	70
Worked full-time, year-round	46,478	35,920	77
Women	24,139	19,115	79
Worked full-time, year-round	36,040	30,198	84

Note: American Indians include Alaska Natives. The American Indian and Alaska Native population are those who identify themselves as being of the race alone.
Source: Bureau of the Census, 2006–10 American Community Survey, Internet site http://factfinder2.census.gov/faces/nav/jsf/pages/index.xhtml; calculations by New Strategist

Table 2.37 American Indian Families in Poverty, 2006–10

(number and percent of American Indian families with income below poverty level by family type and presence of children under age 18 at home, 2006–10)

	total	with children
NUMBER IN POVERTY		
Total American Indian families	**122,958**	**100,454**
Married couples	37,492	26,226
Female householder, no spouse present	68,200	60,154
Male householder, no spouse present	17,266	14,074
PERCENT IN POVERTY		
Total American Indian families	**22.1%**	**29.4%**
Married couples	11.6	15.3
Female householder, no spouse present	40.3	47.2
Male householder, no spouse present	26.9	33.6

Note: American Indians include Alaska Natives. The American Indian and Alaska Native population are those who identify themselves as being of the race alone.
Source: Bureau of the Census, 2006–10 American Community Survey, Internet site http://factfinder2.census.gov/faces/nav/jsf/pages/index.xhtml; calculations by New Strategist

Table 2.38 Poverty Status of American Indians by Sex and Age, 2006–10

(total number of American Indians, and number and percent below poverty level by sex and age, 2006–10)

		in poverty	
	total	number	percent
Total American Indians	**2,390,948**	**631,614**	**26.4%**
Under age 18	716,251	238,827	33.3
Aged 18 to 24	275,210	85,500	31.1
Aged 25 to 34	330,453	84,655	25.6
Aged 35 to 44	338,031	76,460	22.6
Aged 45 to 54	337,877	69,428	20.5
Aged 55 to 64	225,132	43,821	19.5
Aged 65 to 74	108,099	19,835	18.3
Aged 75 or older	59,895	13,088	21.9
American Indian females	**1,223,108**	**344,719**	**28.2**
Under age 18	352,621	118,412	33.6
Aged 18 to 24	135,652	46,900	34.6
Aged 25 to 34	168,990	50,179	29.7
Aged 35 to 44	175,059	44,110	25.2
Aged 45 to 54	178,878	38,360	21.4
Aged 55 to 64	117,743	25,143	21.4
Aged 65 to 74	58,223	12,367	21.2
Aged 75 or older	35,942	9,248	25.7
American Indian males	**1,167,840**	**286,895**	**24.6**
Under age 18	363,630	120,415	33.1
Aged 18 to 24	139,558	38,600	27.7
Aged 25 to 34	161,463	34,476	21.4
Aged 35 to 44	162,972	32,350	19.9
Aged 45 to 54	158,999	31,068	19.5
Aged 55 to 64	107,389	18,678	17.4
Aged 65 to 74	49,876	7,468	15.0
Aged 75 or older	23,953	3,840	16.0

Note: American Indians include Alaska Natives. The American Indian and Alaska Native population are those who identify themselves as being of the race alone.
Source: Bureau of the Census, 2006–10 American Community Survey, Internet site http://factfinder2.census.gov/faces/nav/jsf/pages/index.xhtml; calculations by New Strategist

Twenty-five Percent of American Indian Workers Are Managers or Professionals

The 947,000 employed American Indians account for only 0.7 percent of the nation's workers. American Indians are less likely than the average worker to be employed as managers or professionals (25 versus 35 percent) and more likely to be employed as service workers (23 versus 17 percent).

Overall, 63 percent of American Indian men and 57 percent of American Indian women were in the labor force in 2006–10. The unemployment rate among American Indians exceeds 10 percent in most age groups.

■ American Indians are less educated than the average American and more likely to be employed in service occupations, which accounts for their below-average incomes.

Most American Indian women are in the labor force

(percent of American Indians aged 16 or older in the labor force, by sex, 2006–10)

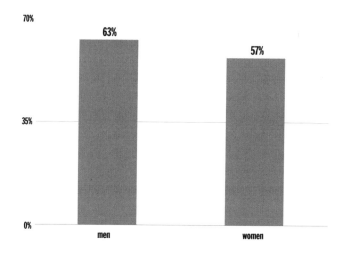

Table 2.39 Employment Status of American Indians by Sex and Age, 2006–10

(total number of American Indians aged 16 or older, and number in the civilian labor force by sex, age, and employment status, 2006–10; numbers in thousands)

		civilian labor force			unemployed	
	total	total	percent of population	employed	number	percent of labor force
Total American Indians	**1,836**	**1,100**	**59.9%**	**947**	**153**	**13.9%**
Aged 16 to 19	186	66	35.5	44	22	33.5
Aged 20 to 24	204	135	66.4	106	30	21.8
Aged 25 to 34	346	251	72.3	216	35	14.0
Aged 35 to 44	351	260	74.0	229	31	11.8
Aged 45 to 54	346	240	69.4	216	24	10.1
Aged 55 to 64	228	121	53.2	112	9	7.7
Aged 65 or older	173	27	15.3	24	2	7.8
American Indian men	**903**	**569**	**63.0**	**482**	**87**	**15.2**
Aged 16 to 19	96	34	35.1	22	12	35.5
Aged 20 to 24	105	72	68.2	55	17	23.8
Aged 25 to 34	175	133	76.3	113	20	15.2
Aged 35 to 44	174	134	76.8	117	17	12.5
Aged 45 to 54	166	121	72.9	107	14	11.4
Aged 55 to 64	110	61	55.7	56	5	8.8
Aged 65 or older	76	14	17.9	12	1	9.3
American Indian women	**933**	**531**	**57.0**	**465**	**66**	**12.5**
Aged 16 to 19	90	32	35.9	22	10	31.4
Aged 20 to 24	99	64	64.5	51	12	19.5
Aged 25 to 34	172	117	68.3	103	15	12.5
Aged 35 to 44	177	126	71.2	112	14	10.9
Aged 45 to 54	180	119	66.2	109	11	8.8
Aged 55 to 64	118	60	50.8	56	4	6.6
Aged 65 or older	97	13	13.2	12	1	6.1

Note: American Indians include Alaska Natives. The American Indian and Alaska Native population are those who identify themselves as being of the race alone.
Source: Bureau of the Census, 2006–10 American Community Survey, Internet site http://factfinder2.census.gov/faces/nav/jsf/pages/index.xhtml

Table 2.40 American Indian Workers by Occupation, 2006–10

(total number of employed aged 16 or older in the civilian labor force, number and percent distribution of employed American Indians, and American Indian share of total, by occupation, 2006–10; numbers in thousands)

	total	American Indian number	percent distribution	share of total
TOTAL EMPLOYED	**141,833**	**947**	**100.0%**	**0.7%**
Management, business, science, and arts occupations	**50,035**	**241**	**25.4**	**0.5**
Management, business, and financial occupations	20,239	95	10.0	0.5
Management occupations	13,679	67	7.1	0.5
Business and financial operations occupations	6,560	28	3.0	0.4
Computer, engineering, and science occupations	7,330	28	2.9	0.4
Computer and mathematical occupations	3,435	11	1.2	0.3
Architecture and engineering occupations	2,698	11	1.1	0.4
Life, physical, and social science occupations	1,198	6	0.6	0.5
Education, legal, community service, arts, and media occupations	15,041	84	8.9	0.6
Community and social service occupations	2,312	19	2.0	0.8
Legal occupations	1,643	7	0.7	0.4
Education, training, and library occupations	8,436	48	5.0	0.6
Arts, design, entertainment, sports and media occupations	2,650	11	1.2	0.4
Health care practitioners and technical occupations	7,424	34	3.5	0.5
Health diagnosing and treating practitioners and other technical occupations	5,050	18	2.0	0.4
Health technologists and technicians	2,374	15	1.6	0.6

	total	American Indian		
		number	percent distribution	share of total
Service occupations	**24,281**	**222**	**23.4%**	**0.9%**
Health care support occupations	3,275	29	3.0	0.9
Protective service occupations	3,092	29	3.0	0.9
Fire fighting and prevention, and other protective service workers including supervisors	1,691	18	1.9	1.0
Law enforcement workers including supervisors	1,400	11	1.2	0.8
Food preparation and serving related occupations	7,677	65	6.8	0.8
Building and grounds cleaning and maintenance occupations	5,493	57	6.0	1.0
Personal care and service occupations	4,744	43	4.6	0.9
Sales and office occupations	**36,000**	**219**	**23.1**	**0.6**
Sales and related occupations	15,908	86	9.0	0.5
Office and administrative support occupations	20,093	133	14.1	0.7
Natural resources, construction, and maintenance occupations	**13,940**	**131**	**13.8**	**0.9**
Farming, fishing, and forestry occupations	1,011	14	1.4	1.3
Construction and extraction occupations	8,135	84	8.8	1.0
Installation, maintenance, and repair occupations	4,793	34	3.6	0.7
Production, transportation, and material moving occupations	**17,577**	**134**	**14.2**	**0.8**
Production occupations	8,913	66	7.0	0.7
Transportation occupations	5,089	37	3.9	0.7
Material moving occupations	3,576	31	3.2	0.9

Note: American Indians include Alaska Natives. The American Indian and Alaska Native population are those who identify themselves as being of the race alone.
Source: Bureau of the Census, 2006–10 American Community Survey, Internet site http://factfinder2.census.gov/faces/nav/jsf/pages/index.xhtml

Married Couples Head Fewer than Half of American Indian Households

Married couples account for only 40 percent of households headed by American Indians, according to the 2010 census. Among all households, married couples account for about half the total.

Female-headed families are a substantial 21 percent of American Indian households, much higher than the female-headed family share of households nationwide. People who live alone account for 23 percent of American Indian households, somewhat smaller than their share nationally.

Thirty-six percent of American Indian households include children under age 18. Among American Indian married couples, a 48 percent minority includes children. The majority of female- and male-headed families have children at home.

Forty percent of American Indian men are currently married. Among American Indian women, the figure is 38 percent. Eleven percent of American Indian men and 15 percent of American Indian women are currently divorced.

■ The large share of families headed by women without a spouse results in lower incomes and higher poverty rates for American Indians.

Female-headed families account for one in five American Indian households

(percent distribution of American Indian households by household type, 2010)

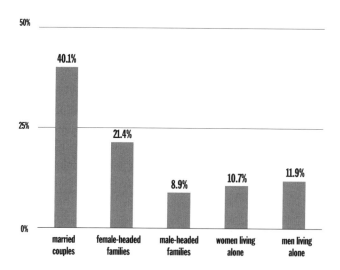

Table 2.41 American Indian Households by Age of Householder, 2010

(number of total households, number and percent distribution of American Indian households, and American Indian share of total, by age of householder, 2010)

	total	American Indian		
		number	percent distribution	share of total
Total households	**116,716,292**	**939,707**	**100.0%**	**0.8%**
Under age 25	5,400,799	57,404	6.1	1.1
Aged 25 to 34	17,957,375	166,957	17.8	0.9
Aged 35 to 44	21,290,880	194,324	20.7	0.9
Aged 45 to 54	24,907,064	219,584	23.4	0.9
Aged 55 to 64	21,340,338	164,024	17.5	0.8
Aged 65 or older	25,819,836	137,414	14.6	0.5

Note: American Indians include Alaska Natives. The American Indian and Alaska Native population are those who identify themselves as being of the race alone.
Source: Bureau of the Census, 2010 Census, American Factfinder, Internet site http://factfinder2.census.gov/faces/nav/jsf/pages/index.xhtml; calculations by New Strategist

Table 2.42 American Indian Households by Household Type, 2010

(number of total households, number and percent distribution of American Indian households, and American Indian share of total, by household type, 2010)

	total	American Indian		
		number	percent distribution	share of total
TOTAL HOUSEHOLDS	**116,716,292**	**939,707**	**100.0%**	**0.8%**
Family households	**77,538,296**	**661,386**	**70.4**	**0.9**
Married couples	56,510,377	376,727	40.1	0.7
Female householder, no spouse present	15,250,349	201,493	21.4	1.3
Male householder, no spouse present	5,777,570	83,166	8.9	1.4
Nonfamily households	**39,177,996**	**278,321**	**29.6**	**0.7**
Female householder	20,718,743	129,211	13.8	0.6
Living alone	17,298,615	100,566	10.7	0.6
Male householder	18,459,253	149,110	15.9	0.8
Living alone	13,906,294	111,983	11.9	0.8

Note: American Indians include Alaska Natives. The American Indian and Alaska Native population are those who identify themselves as being of the race alone.
Source: Bureau of the Census, 2010 Census, American Factfinder, Internet site http://factfinder2.census.gov/faces/nav/jsf/pages/index.xhtml; calculations by New Strategist

Table 2.43 American Indian Households by Type of Household and Presence of Children, 2010

(number and percent distribution of American Indian households by type of household and presence of own children under age 18, 2010)

	number	percent distribution
Total American Indian households	**939,707**	**100.0%**
American Indian households with children	340,942	36.3
Married couples	376,727	100.0
With children under age 18	182,627	48.5
Without children under age 18	194,100	51.5
Female householder, no spouse present	201,493	100.0
With children under age 18	115,394	57.3
Without children under age 18	86,099	42.7
Male householder, no spouse present	83,166	100.0
With children under age 18	42,921	51.6
Without children under age 18	40,245	48.4

Source: Bureau of the Census, Current Population Survey Annual Social and Economic Supplement, Internet site http://www .census.gov/hhes/www/income/data/incpovhlth/2011/index.html; calculations by New Strategist

Table 2.44 Marital Status of American Indians by Sex, 2006–10

(number and percent distribution of American Indians aged 15 or older by current marital status and sex, 2006–10)

	men		women	
	number	percent distribution	number	percent distribution
Total American Indians	**925,578**	**100.0%**	**954,362**	**100.0%**
Never married	409,175	43.2	351,354	35.1
Married	386,825	39.9	401,462	38.2
Divorced	106,719	11.4	132,200	14.9
Widowed	22,859	2.7	69,346	7.9

Note: American Indians include Alaska Natives. The American Indian and Alaska Native population are those who identify themselves as being of the race alone.
Source: Bureau of the Census, 2006–2010 American Community Survey, American Factfinder Internet site http://factfinder2 .census.gov/faces/nav/jsf/pages/index.xhtml; calculations by New Strategist

Nearly 3 Million Identify Themselves as American Indian Alone

Many American Indians are of mixed race. In 2010, 2.9 million people identified their race as American Indian alone (the term American Indian also refers to Alaska Natives), and almost as many—2.3 million—identified themselves as American Indian and some other race. More than one in five people who identified themselves as American Indian alone also said they were Hispanic. Among American Indians who identified themselves as belonging to just one tribe in 2010, Navajo was the largest.

Forty-six percent of American Indians live in the West, and another 32 percent live in the South. California is home to 12 percent of American Indians. American Indians account for 15 percent of Alaska's population, the largest share among the 50 states. In New Mexico and Oklahoma, American Indians are 9 percent of the population. By metropolitan area, American Indians account for the largest share of the population in Farmington, New Mexico (37 percent) and Flagstaff, Arizona (27 percent).

■ American Indians are a tiny minority of the U.S. population, increasingly dwarfed by Hispanics, blacks, and Asians.

American Indians are a tiny share of the population in every region

(American Indian and Alaska Native alone share of population by region, 2010)

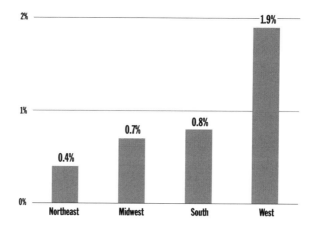

Table 2.45 American Indians by Racial Identification, 2000 and 2010

(total number of people, and number and percent distribution of American Indians by racial identification, 2000 and 2010; percent change, 2000–10)

	2010		2000		percent change 2000–10
	number	percent distribution	number	percent distribution	
Total people	**308,745,538**	**100.0%**	**281,421,906**	**100.0%**	**9.7%**
American Indian alone or in combination with one or more other races	**5,220,579**	**1.7**	**4,225,058**	**1.5**	**23.6**
American Indian alone	2,932,248	0.9	2,475,956	0.9	18.4
American Indian in combination	2,288,331	0.7	1,749,102	0.6	30.8

Note: American Indians include Alaska Natives.
Source: Bureau of the Census, An Overview: Race and Hispanic Origin and the 2010 Census, 2010 Census Briefs, Internet site http://www.census.gov/2010census/data/2010-census-briefs.php; calculations by New Strategist

Table 2.46 American Indians by Hispanic Origin, 2010

(number and percent distribution of American Indians by Hispanic origin and racial identification, 2010)

	American Indian alone or in combination		American Indian alone	
	number	percent distribution	number	percent distribution
Total American Indians	**5,220,579**	**100.0%**	**2,932,248**	**100.0%**
Not Hispanic	4,029,675	77.2	2,247,098	76.6
Hispanic	1,190,904	22.8	685,150	23.4

Note: American Indians include Alaska Natives.
Source: Bureau of the Census, An Overview: Race and Hispanic Origin and the 2010 Census, 2010 Census Briefs, Internet site http://www.census.gov/2010census/data/2010-census-briefs.php; calculations by New Strategist

Table 2.47 American Indians and Alaska Natives by Tribe, 2010

(number and percent distribution of people identifying themselves as American Indian or Alaska Native alone by tribe-alone identification, 2010)

	number	percent distribution
Total American Indians and Alaska Natives alone	**2,932,248**	**100.0%**
One tribal group specified	2,034,255	69.4
American Indians alone specifying one tribal group	**1,935,363**	**100.0**
Apache	63,193	3.3
Arapahoe	8,014	0.4
Blackfeet	27,279	1.4
Canadian and French American Indian	6,433	0.3
Central American Indian	15,882	0.8
Cherokee	284,247	14.7
Cheyenne	11,375	0.6
Chickasaw	27,973	1.4
Chippewa	112,757	5.8
Choctaw	103,910	5.4
Colville	8,114	0.4
Comanche	12,284	0.6
Cree	2,211	0.1
Creek	48,352	2.5
Crow	10,332	0.5
Delaware	7,843	0.4
Hopi	12,580	0.7
Houma	8,169	0.4
Iroquois	40,570	2.1
Kiowa	9,437	0.5
Lumbee	62,306	3.2
Menominee	8,374	0.4
Mexican American Indian	121,221	6.3
Navajo	286,731	14.8
Osage	8,938	0.5
Ottawa	7,272	0.4
Palute	9,340	0.5
Pima	22,040	1.1
Potawatomi	20,412	1.1
Pueblo	49,695	2.6
Puget Sound Salish	14,320	0.7
Seminole	14,080	0.7
Shoshone	7,852	0.4
Sioux	112,176	5.8

	number	percent distribution
South American Indian	20,901	1.1%
Spanish American Indian	13,460	0.7
Tohono O'Odham	19,522	1.0
Ute	7,435	0.4
Yakama	8,786	0.5
Yaqui	21,679	1.1
Yuman	7,727	0.4
Other American Indian tribe	270,141	14.0
Alaska Native alone specifying one tribal group	**98,892**	**100.0**
Alaskan Athabascan	15,623	15.8
Aleut	11,920	12.1
Inupiat	24,859	25.1
Tlingit–Haida	15,256	15.4
Tsimshian	2,307	2.3
Yup'ik	28,927	29.3

Note: American Indians are those who identify themselves as American Indian or Alaska Native alone. Tribes shown are for those identifying themselves as belonging to the tribe alone.
Source: Bureau of the Census, The American Indian and Alaska Native Population: 2010, 2010 Census Brief, Internet site http://www.census.gov/2010census/data/2010-census-briefs.php; calculations by New Strategist

Table 2.48 American Indians by Age, 2000 and 2010

(number of American Indians by age, 2000 and 2010; percent change, 2000–10)

	2010	2000	percent change 2000–10
Total American Indians	**2,932,248**	**2,475,956**	**18.4%**
Under age 5	244,615	213,052	14.8
Aged 5 to 9	243,259	239,007	1.8
Aged 10 to 14	245,049	245,677	–0.3
Aged 15 to 19	263,805	232,351	13.5
Aged 20 to 24	240,716	198,010	21.6
Aged 25 to 29	221,654	186,689	18.7
Aged 30 to 34	202,928	186,072	9.1
Aged 35 to 39	196,017	202,013	–3.0
Aged 40 to 44	194,713	189,201	2.9
Aged 45 to 49	207,857	159,422	30.4
Aged 50 to 54	191,893	128,303	49.6
Aged 55 to 59	154,320	90,531	70.5
Aged 60 to 64	118,362	67,189	76.2
Aged 65 to 69	79,079	49,463	59.9
Aged 70 to 74	53,926	36,434	48.0
Aged 75 to 79	35,268	25,608	37.7
Aged 80 to 84	21,963	14,646	50.0
Aged 85 or older	16,824	12,288	36.9
Aged 18 to 24	349,072	287,785	21.3
Aged 18 or older	2,043,876	1,635,644	25.0
Aged 65 or older	207,060	138,439	49.6

Note: American Indians are those who identify themselves as being American Indian or Alaska Native alone.
Source: Bureau of the Census, 2000 Census and 2010 Census, Internet site http://factfinder2.census.gov/faces/nav/jsf/pages/index.xhtml; calculations by New Strategist

Table 2.49 American Indian Share of Total Population by Age, 2010

(total number of people, number and percent distribution of American Indians, and American Indian share of total, by age, 2010)

		American Indian		
	total	number	percent distribution	share of total
Total people	**308,745,538**	**2,932,248**	**100.0%**	**0.9%**
Under age 5	20,201,362	244,615	8.3	1.2
Aged 5 to 9	20,348,657	243,259	8.3	1.2
Aged 10 to 14	20,677,194	245,049	8.4	1.2
Aged 15 to 19	22,040,343	263,805	9.0	1.2
Aged 20 to 24	21,585,999	240,716	8.2	1.1
Aged 25 to 29	21,101,849	221,654	7.6	1.1
Aged 30 to 34	19,962,099	202,928	6.9	1.0
Aged 35 to 39	20,179,642	196,017	6.7	1.0
Aged 40 to 44	20,890,964	194,713	6.6	0.9
Aged 45 to 49	22,708,591	207,857	7.1	0.9
Aged 50 to 54	22,298,125	191,893	6.5	0.9
Aged 55 to 59	19,664,805	154,320	5.3	0.8
Aged 60 to 64	16,817,924	118,362	4.0	0.7
Aged 65 to 69	12,435,263	79,079	2.7	0.6
Aged 70 to 74	9,278,166	53,926	1.8	0.6
Aged 75 to 79	7,317,795	35,268	1.2	0.5
Aged 80 to 84	5,743,327	21,963	0.7	0.4
Aged 85 or older	5,493,433	16,824	0.6	0.3
Aged 18 to 24	30,672,088	349,072	11.9	1.1
Aged 18 or older	234,564,071	2,043,876	69.7	0.9
Aged 65 or older	40,267,984	207,060	7.1	0.5

Note: American Indians are those who identify themselves as being American Indian or Alaska Native alone.
Source: Bureau of the Census, 2010 Census, Internet site http://factfinder2.census.gov/faces/nav/jsf/pages/index.xhtml; calculations by New Strategist

Table 2.50 American Indians by Age and Sex, 2010

(number of American Indians by age and sex, and sex ratio by age, 2010)

	total	females	males	sex ratio
Total American Indians	**2,932,248**	**1,468,909**	**1,463,339**	**100**
Under age 5	244,615	120,863	123,752	102
Aged 5 to 9	243,259	119,761	123,498	103
Aged 10 to 14	245,049	120,455	124,594	103
Aged 15 to 19	263,805	128,143	135,662	106
Aged 20 to 24	240,716	116,263	124,453	107
Aged 25 to 29	221,654	108,619	113,035	104
Aged 30 to 34	202,928	99,930	102,998	103
Aged 35 to 39	196,017	97,438	98,579	101
Aged 40 to 44	194,713	97,348	97,365	100
Aged 45 to 49	207,857	105,557	102,300	97
Aged 50 to 54	191,893	99,173	92,720	93
Aged 55 to 59	154,320	79,903	74,417	93
Aged 60 to 64	118,362	60,866	57,496	94
Aged 65 to 69	79,079	41,251	37,828	92
Aged 70 to 74	53,926	29,098	24,828	85
Aged 75 to 79	35,268	20,046	15,222	76
Aged 80 to 84	21,963	13,076	8,887	68
Aged 85 or older	16,824	11,119	5,705	51
Aged 18 to 24	349,072	168,357	180,715	107
Aged 18 or older	2,043,876	1,031,781	1,012,095	98
Aged 65 or older	207,060	114,590	92,470	81

Note: American Indians are those who identify themselves as being American Indian or Alaska Native alone. The sex ratio is the number of males divided by the number of females multiplied by 100.
Source: Bureau of the Census, 2010 Census, Internet site http://factfinder2.census.gov/faces/nav/jsf/pages/index.xhtml; calculations by New Strategist

Table 2.51 American Indians by Region, 2000 and 2010

(number of American Indians by region, 2000 and 2010; percent change, 2000–10)

	2010	2000	percent change 2000–10
Total American Indians	**2,932,248**	**2,475,956**	**18.4%**
Northeast	212,864	162,558	30.9
Midwest	458,611	399,490	14.8
South	923,783	725,919	27.3
West	1,336,990	1,187,989	12.5

Note: American Indians are those who identify themselves as being American Indian or Alaska Native alone. Total American Indians in 2000 do not match the 2000 total in some of the other tables because this figure has not been adjusted to eliminate the "some other race" category that was included in the census.
Source: Bureau of the Census, The American Indian and Alaska Native Population: 2010, 2010 Census Brief, Internet site http://www.census.gov/2010census/data/2010-census-briefs.php; calculations by New Strategist

Table 2.52 American Indian Share of the Total Population by Region, 2010

(total number of people, number and percent distribution of American Indians, and American Indian share of total, by region, 2010)

	total	American Indian		
		number	percent distribution	share of total
Total people	**308,745,538**	**2,932,248**	**100.0%**	**0.9%**
Northeast	55,317,240	212,864	7.3	0.4
Midwest	66,927,001	458,611	15.6	0.7
South	114,555,744	923,783	31.5	0.8
West	71,945,553	1,336,990	45.6	1.9

Note: American Indians are those who identify themselves as being American Indian or Alaska Native alone.
Source: Bureau of the Census, The American Indian and Alaska Native Population: 2010, 2010 Census Brief, Internet site http://www.census.gov/2010census/data/2010-census-briefs.php; calculations by New Strategist

Table 2.53 American Indians by State, 2000 and 2010

(number of American Indians by state, 2000 and 2010; percent change, 2000–10)

	2010	2000	percent change 2000–10
Total American Indians	**2,932,248**	**2,475,956**	**18.4%**
Alabama	28,218	22,430	25.8
Alaska	104,871	98,043	7.0
Arizona	296,529	255,879	15.9
Arkansas	22,248	17,808	24.9
California	362,801	333,346	8.8
Colorado	56,010	44,241	26.6
Connecticut	11,256	9,639	16.8
Delaware	4,181	2,731	53.1
District of Columbia	2,079	1,713	21.4
Florida	71,458	53,541	33.5
Georgia	32,151	21,737	47.9
Hawaii	4,164	3,535	17.8
Idaho	21,441	17,645	21.5
Illinois	43,963	31,006	41.8
Indiana	18,462	15,815	16.7
Iowa	11,084	8,989	23.3
Kansas	28,150	24,936	12.9
Kentucky	10,120	8,616	17.5
Louisiana	30,579	25,477	20.0
Maine	8,568	7,098	20.7
Maryland	20,420	15,423	32.4
Massachusetts	18,850	15,015	25.5
Michigan	62,007	58,479	6.0
Minnesota	60,916	54,967	10.8
Mississippi	15,030	11,652	29.0
Missouri	27,376	25,076	9.2
Montana	62,555	56,068	11.6
Nebraska	18,427	14,896	23.7
Nevada	32,062	26,420	21.4
New Hampshire	3,150	2,964	6.3
New Jersey	29,026	19,492	48.9
New Mexico	193,222	173,483	11.4
New York	106,906	82,461	29.6
North Carolina	122,110	99,551	22.7
North Dakota	36,591	31,329	16.8
Ohio	25,292	24,486	3.3
Oklahoma	321,687	273,230	17.7

	2010	2000	percent change 2000–10
Pennsylvania	26,843	18,348	46.3%
Rhode Island	6,058	5,121	18.3
South Carolina	19,524	13,718	42.3
South Dakota	71,817	62,283	15.3
Tennessee	19,994	15,152	32.0
Texas	170,972	118,362	44.4
Utah	32,927	29,684	10.9
Vermont	2,207	2,420	8.8
Virginia	29,225	21,172	38.0
Washington	103,869	93,301	11.3
West Virginia	3,787	3,606	5.0
Wisconsin	54,526	47,228	15.5
Wyoming	13,336	11,133	19.8

Note: American Indians are those who identify themselves as being American Indian or Alaska Native alone.
Source: Bureau of the Census, The American Indian and Alaska Native Population: 2010, 2010 Census Brief, Internet site http://www.census.gov/2010census/data/2010-census-briefs.php; calculations by New Strategist

Table 2.54 American Indian Share of Total Population by State, 2010

(total number of people, number and percent distribution of American Indians, and American Indian share of total, by state, 2010)

	total	American Indian number	percent distribution	share of total
Total people	**308,745,538**	**2,932,248**	**100.0%**	**0.9%**
Alabama	4,779,736	28,218	1.0	0.6
Alaska	710,231	104,871	3.6	14.8
Arizona	6,392,017	296,529	10.1	4.6
Arkansas	2,915,918	22,248	0.8	0.8
California	37,253,956	362,801	12.4	1.0
Colorado	5,029,196	56,010	1.9	1.1
Connecticut	3,574,097	11,256	0.4	0.3
Delaware	897,934	4,181	0.1	0.5
District of Columbia	601,723	2,079	0.1	0.3
Florida	18,801,310	71,458	2.4	0.4
Georgia	9,687,653	32,151	1.1	0.3
Hawaii	1,360,301	4,164	0.1	0.3
Idaho	1,567,582	21,441	0.7	1.4
Illinois	12,830,632	43,963	1.5	0.3
Indiana	6,483,802	18,462	0.6	0.3
Iowa	3,046,355	11,084	0.4	0.4
Kansas	2,853,118	28,150	1.0	1.0
Kentucky	4,339,367	10,120	0.3	0.2
Louisiana	4,533,372	30,579	1.0	0.7
Maine	1,328,361	8,568	0.3	0.6
Maryland	5,773,552	20,420	0.7	0.4
Massachusetts	6,547,629	18,850	0.6	0.3
Michigan	9,883,640	62,007	2.1	0.6
Minnesota	5,303,925	60,916	2.1	1.1
Mississippi	2,967,297	15,030	0.5	0.5
Missouri	5,988,927	27,376	0.9	0.5
Montana	989,415	62,555	2.1	6.3
Nebraska	1,826,341	18,427	0.6	1.0
Nevada	2,700,551	32,062	1.1	1.2
New Hampshire	1,316,470	3,150	0.1	0.2
New Jersey	8,791,894	29,026	1.0	0.3
New Mexico	2,059,179	193,222	6.6	9.4
New York	19,378,102	106,906	3.6	0.6
North Carolina	9,535,483	122,110	4.2	1.3
North Dakota	672,591	36,591	1.2	5.4
Ohio	11,536,504	25,292	0.9	0.2
Oklahoma	3,751,351	321,687	11.0	8.6

	total	American Indian		
		number	percent distribution	share of total
Oregon	3,831,074	53,203	1.8%	1.4%
Pennsylvania	12,702,379	26,843	0.9	0.2
Rhode Island	1,052,567	6,058	0.2	0.6
South Carolina	4,625,364	19,524	0.7	0.4
South Dakota	814,180	71,817	2.4	8.8
Tennessee	6,346,105	19,994	0.7	0.3
Texas	25,145,561	170,972	5.8	0.7
Utah	2,763,885	32,927	1.1	1.2
Vermont	625,741	2,207	0.1	0.4
Virginia	8,001,024	29,225	1.0	0.4
Washington	6,724,540	103,869	3.5	1.5
West Virginia	1,852,994	3,787	0.1	0.2
Wisconsin	5,686,986	54,526	1.9	1.0
Wyoming	563,626	13,336	0.5	2.4

Note: American Indians are those who identify themselves as being American Indian or Alaska Native alone.
Source: Bureau of the Census, The American Indian and Alaska Native Population: 2010, 2010 Census Brief, Internet site http://www.census.gov/2010census/data/2010-census-briefs.php; calculations by New Strategist

Table 2.55 American Indians by Metropolitan Area, 2010

(total number of people, number of American Indians, and American Indian share of total, for selected metropolitan areas, 2010)

	total population	American Indian number	American Indian share of total
Abilene, TX	165,252	1,084	0.7%
Akron, OH	703,200	1,311	0.2
Albany, GA	157,308	368	0.2
Albany–Schenectady–Troy, NY	870,716	2,072	0.2
Albuquerque, NM	887,077	51,987	5.9
Alexandria, LA	153,922	1,263	0.8
Allentown–Bethlehem–Easton, PA–NJ	821,173	2,166	0.3
Altoona, PA	127,089	143	0.1
Amarillo, TX	249,881	1,908	0.8
Ames, IA	89,542	163	0.2
Anchorage, AK	380,821	28,031	7.4
Anderson, IN	131,636	320	0.2
Anderson, SC	187,126	478	0.3
Ann Arbor, MI	344,791	1,174	0.3
Anniston–Oxford, AL	118,572	540	0.5
Appleton, WI	225,666	3,185	1.4
Asheville, NC	424,858	1,748	0.4
Athens–Clarke County, GA	192,541	405	0.2
Atlanta–Sandy Springs–Marietta, GA	5,268,860	17,963	0.3
Atlantic City–Hammonton, NJ	274,549	1,050	0.4
Auburn–Opelika, AL	140,247	445	0.3
Augusta–Richmond County, GA–SC	556,877	1,941	0.3
Austin–Round Rock–San Marcos, TX	1,716,289	13,452	0.8
Bakersfield–Delano, CA	839,631	12,676	1.5
Baltimore–Towson, MD	2,710,489	8,517	0.3
Bangor, ME	153,923	1,809	1.2
Barnstable Town, MA	215,888	1,324	0.6
Baton Rouge, LA	802,484	2,194	0.3
Battle Creek, MI	136,146	831	0.6
Bay City, MI	107,771	564	0.5
Beaumont–Port Arthur, TX	388,745	2,024	0.5
Bellingham, WA	201,140	5,683	2.8
Bend, OR	157,733	1,449	0.9
Billings, MT	158,050	5,965	3.8
Binghamton, NY	251,725	482	0.2
Birmingham–Hoover, AL	1,128,047	3,351	0.3
Bismarck, ND	108,779	4,393	4.0
Blacksburg–Christiansburg–Radford, VA	162,958	322	0.2

	total population	American Indian	
		number	share of total
Bloomington, IN	192,714	521	0.3%
Bloomington–Normal, IL	169,572	383	0.2
Boise City–Nampa, ID	616,561	5,282	0.9
Boston–Cambridge–Quincy, MA–NH	4,552,402	11,338	0.2
Boulder, CO	294,567	1,832	0.6
Bowling Green, KY	125,953	352	0.3
Bremerton–Silverdale, WA	251,133	4,040	1.6
Bridgeport–Stamford–Norwalk, CT	916,829	2,384	0.3
Brownsville–Harlingen, TX	406,220	1,688	0.4
Brunswick, GA	112,370	343	0.3
Buffalo–Niagara Falls, NY	1,135,509	8,193	0.7
Burlington, NC	151,131	1,020	0.7
Burlington–South Burlington, VT	211,261	980	0.5
Canton–Massillon, OH	404,422	1,038	0.3
Cape Coral–Fort Myers, FL	618,754	2,193	0.4
Cape Girardeau–Jackson, MO–IL	96,275	289	0.3
Carson City, NV	55,274	1,306	2.4
Casper, WY	75,450	781	1.0
Cedar Rapids, IA	257,940	659	0.3
Champaign–Urbana, IL	231,891	611	0.3
Charleston, WV	304,284	606	0.2
Charleston–North Charleston–Summerville, SC	664,607	3,039	0.5
Charlotte–Gastonia–Rock Hill, NC–SC	1,758,038	8,684	0.5
Charlottesville, VA	201,559	508	0.3
Chattanooga, TN–GA	528,143	1,800	0.3
Cheyenne, WY	91,738	878	1.0
Chicago–Joliet–Naperville, IL–IN–WI	9,461,105	36,525	0.4
Chico, CA	220,000	4,395	2.0
Cincinnati–Middletown, OH–KY–IN	2,130,151	4,105	0.2
Clarksville, TN–KY	273,949	1,530	0.6
Cleveland, TN	115,788	394	0.3
Cleveland–Elyria–Mentor, OH	2,077,240	4,056	0.2
Coeur d'Alene, ID	138,494	1,781	1.3
College Station–Bryan, TX	228,660	1,068	0.5
Colorado Springs, CO	645,613	6,159	1.0
Columbia, MO	172,786	671	0.4
Columbia, SC	767,598	2,746	0.4
Columbus, GA–AL	294,865	1,183	0.4
Columbus, IN	76,794	209	0.3
Columbus, OH	1,836,536	4,252	0.2
Corpus Christi, TX	428,185	2,685	0.6
Corvallis, OR	85,579	627	0.7

	total population	American Indian	
		number	share of total
Crestview–Fort Walton Beach–Destin, FL	180,822	1,068	0.6%
Cumberland, MD–WV	103,299	148	0.1
Dallas–Fort Worth–Arlington, TX	6,371,773	43,390	0.7
Dalton, GA	142,227	817	0.6
Danville, IL	81,625	191	0.2
Danville, VA	106,561	226	0.2
Davenport–Moline–Rock Island, IA–IL	379,690	1,001	0.3
Dayton, OH	841,502	1,951	0.2
Decatur, AL	153,829	2,995	1.9
Decatur, IL	110,768	226	0.2
Deltona–Daytona Beach–Ormond Beach, FL	494,593	1,778	0.4
Denver–Aurora–Broomfield, CO	2,543,482	25,169	1.0
Des Moines–West Des Moines, IA	569,633	1,670	0.3
Detroit–Warren–Livonia, MI	4,296,250	14,852	0.3
Dothan, AL	145,639	727	0.5
Dover, DE	162,310	1,043	0.6
Dubuque, IA	93,653	178	0.2
Duluth, MN–WI	279,771	7,431	2.7
Durham–Chapel Hill, NC	504,357	2,519	0.5
Eau Claire, WI	161,151	781	0.5
El Centro, CA	174,528	3,059	1.8
Elizabethtown, KY	119,736	578	0.5
Elkhart–Goshen, IN	197,559	747	0.4
Elmira, NY	88,830	233	0.3
El Paso, TX	800,647	6,007	0.8
Erie, PA	280,566	566	0.2
Eugene–Springfield, OR	351,715	4,070	1.2
Evansville, IN–KY	358,676	767	0.2
Fairbanks, AK	97,581	6,879	7.0
Fargo, ND–MN	208,777	2,630	1.3
Farmington, NM	130,044	47,640	36.6
Fayetteville, NC	366,383	9,652	2.6
Fayetteville–Springdale–Rogers, AR–MO	463,204	6,997	1.5
Flagstaff, AZ	134,421	36,714	27.3
Flint, MI	425,790	2,252	0.5
Florence, SC	205,566	658	0.3
Florence–Muscle Shoals, AL	147,137	605	0.4
Fond du Lac, WI	101,633	471	0.5
Fort Collins–Loveland, CO	299,630	2,206	0.7
Fort Smith, AR–OK	298,592	18,943	6.3
Fort Wayne, IN	416,257	1,414	0.3
Fresno, CA	930,450	15,649	1.7

	total population	American Indian	
		number	share of total
Gadsden, AL	104,430	448	0.4%
Gainesville, FL	264,275	856	0.3
Gainesville, GA	179,684	811	0.5
Glens Falls, NY	128,923	272	0.2
Goldsboro, NC	122,623	481	0.4
Grand Forks, ND–MN	98,461	2,110	2.1
Grand Junction, CO	146,723	1,554	1.1
Grand Rapids–Wyoming, MI	774,160	3,989	0.5
Great Falls, MT	81,327	3,487	4.3
Greeley, CO	252,825	2,817	1.1
Green Bay, WI	306,241	7,259	2.4
Greensboro–High Point, NC	723,801	3,891	0.5
Greenville, NC	189,510	736	0.4
Greenville–Mauldin–Easley, SC	636,986	1,784	0.3
Gulfport–Biloxi, MS	248,820	1,166	0.5
Hagerstown–Martinsburg, MD–WV	269,140	655	0.2
Hanford–Corcoran, CA	152,982	2,562	1.7
Harrisburg–Carlisle, PA	549,475	1,013	0.2
Harrisonburg, VA	125,228	336	0.3
Hartford–West Hartford–East Hartford, CT	1,212,381	2,904	0.2
Hattiesburg, MS	142,842	345	0.2
Hickory–Lenoir–Morganton, NC	365,497	1,169	0.3
Hinesville–Fort Stewart, GA	77,917	449	0.6
Holland–Grand Haven, MI	263,801	1,141	0.4
Honolulu, HI	953,207	2,438	0.3
Hot Springs, AR	96,024	587	0.6
Houma–Bayou Cane–Thibodaux, LA	208,178	9,050	4.3
Houston–Sugar Land–Baytown, TX	5,946,800	38,236	0.6
Huntington–Ashland, WV–KY–OH	287,702	654	0.2
Huntsville, AL	417,593	3,098	0.7
Idaho Falls, ID	130,374	993	0.8
Indianapolis–Carmel, IN	1,756,241	4,738	0.3
Iowa City, IA	152,586	343	0.2
Ithaca, NY	101,564	360	0.4
Jackson, MI	160,248	592	0.4
Jackson, MS	539,057	907	0.2
Jackson, TN	115,425	256	0.2
Jacksonville, FL	1,345,596	5,219	0.4
Jacksonville, NC	177,772	1,238	0.7
Janesville, WI	160,331	516	0.3
Jefferson City, MO	149,807	545	0.4
Johnson City, TN	198,716	538	0.3

	total population	American Indian	
		number	share of total
Johnstown, PA	143,679	147	0.1%
Jonesboro, AR	121,026	401	0.3
Joplin, MO	175,518	3,117	1.8
Kalamazoo–Portage, MI	326,589	1,728	0.5
Kankakee–Bradley, IL	113,449	286	0.3
Kansas City, MO–KS	2,035,334	10,437	0.5
Kennewick–Pasco–Richland, WA	253,340	2,105	0.8
Killeen–Temple–Fort Hood, TX	405,300	3,312	0.8
Kingsport–Bristol–Bristol, TN–VA	309,544	738	0.2
Kingston, NY	182,493	597	0.3
Knoxville, TN	698,030	2,115	0.3
Kokomo, IN	98,688	309	0.3
La Crosse, WI–MN	133,665	526	0.4
Lafayette, IN	201,789	502	0.2
Lafayette, LA	273,738	968	0.4
Lake Charles, LA	199,607	934	0.5
Lake Havasu City–Kingman, AZ	200,186	4,500	2.2
Lakeland–Winter Haven, FL	602,095	2,706	0.4
Lancaster, PA	519,445	1,195	0.2
Lansing–East Lansing, MI	464,036	2,345	0.5
Laredo, TX	250,304	1,006	0.4
Las Cruces, NM	209,233	3,147	1.5
Las Vegas–Paradise, NV	1,951,269	14,422	0.7
Lawrence, KS	110,826	2,951	2.7
Lawton, OK	124,098	7,266	5.9
Lebanon, PA	133,568	250	0.2
Lewiston, ID–WA	60,888	2,508	4.1
Lewiston–Auburn, ME	107,702	409	0.4
Lexington–Fayette, KY	472,099	1,138	0.2
Lima, OH	106,331	207	0.2
Lincoln, NE	302,157	2,193	0.7
Little Rock–North Little Rock–Conway, AR	699,757	3,265	0.5
Logan, UT–ID	125,442	743	0.6
Longview, TX	214,369	1,277	0.6
Longview, WA	102,410	1,570	1.5
Los Angeles–Long Beach–Santa Ana, CA	12,828,837	90,960	0.7
Louisville/Jefferson County, KY–IN	1,283,566	3,233	0.3
Lubbock, TX	284,890	2,075	0.7
Lynchburg, VA	252,634	904	0.4
Macon, GA	232,293	550	0.2
Madera–Chowchilla, CA	150,865	4,136	2.7

	total population	American Indian	
		number	share of total
Madison, WI	568,593	2,043	0.4%
Manchester–Nashua, NH	400,721	961	0.2
Manhattan, KS	127,081	940	0.7
Mankato–North Mankato, MN	96,740	277	0.3
Mansfield, OH	124,475	240	0.2
McAllen–Edinburg–Mission, TX	774,769	2,589	0.3
Medford, OR	203,206	2,386	1.2
Memphis, TN–MS–AR	1,316,100	3,360	0.3
Merced, CA	255,793	3,473	1.4
Miami–Fort Lauderdale–Pompano Beach, FL	5,564,635	16,108	0.3
Michigan City–La Porte, IN	111,467	306	0.3
Midland, TX	136,872	1,013	0.7
Milwaukee–Waukesha–West Allis, WI	1,555,908	8,483	0.5
Minneapolis–St. Paul–Bloomington, MN–WI	3,279,833	22,726	0.7
Missoula, MT	109,299	2,872	2.6
Mobile, AL	412,992	3,681	0.9
Modesto, CA	514,453	5,902	1.1
Monroe, LA	176,441	439	0.2
Monroe, MI	152,021	467	0.3
Montgomery, AL	374,536	1,131	0.3
Morgantown, WV	129,709	208	0.2
Morristown, TN	136,608	425	0.3
Mount Vernon–Anacortes, WA	116,901	2,516	2.2
Muncie, IN	117,671	302	0.3
Muskegon–Norton Shores, MI	172,188	1,407	0.8
Myrtle Beach–North Myrtle Beach–Conway, SC	269,291	1,279	0.5
Napa, CA	136,484	1,058	0.8
Naples–Marco Island, FL	321,520	1,123	0.3
Nashville–Davidson–Murfreesboro–Franklin, TN	1,589,934	5,182	0.3
New Haven–Milford, CT	862,477	2,497	0.3
New Orleans–Metairie–Kenner, LA	1,167,764	5,192	0.4
New York–Northern New Jersey–Long Island, NY–NJ–PA	18,897,109	92,632	0.5
Niles–Benton Harbor, MI	156,813	834	0.5
North Port–Bradenton–Sarasota, FL	702,281	1,989	0.3
Norwich–New London, CT	274,055	2,505	0.9
Ocala, FL	331,298	1,309	0.4
Ocean City, NJ	97,265	205	0.2
Odessa, TX	137,130	1,351	1.0
Ogden–Clearfield, UT	547,184	3,344	0.6
Oklahoma City, OK	1,252,987	51,303	4.1

	total population	American Indian	
		number	share of total
Olympia, WA	252,264	3,515	1.4%
Omaha–Council Bluffs, NE–IA	865,350	5,177	0.6
Orlando–Kissimmee–Sanford, FL	2,134,411	8,842	0.4
Oshkosh–Neenah, WI	166,994	1,036	0.6
Owensboro, KY	114,752	175	0.2
Oxnard–Thousand Oaks–Ventura, CA	823,318	8,068	1.0
Palm Bay–Melbourne–Titusville, FL	543,376	2,118	0.4
Palm Coast, FL	95,696	267	0.3
Panama City–Lynn Haven–Panama City Beach, FL	168,852	1,153	0.7
Parkersburg–Marietta–Vienna, WV–OH	162,056	346	0.2
Pascagoula, MS	162,246	634	0.4
Pensacol–Ferry Pass–Brent, FL	448,991	3,929	0.9
Peoria, IL	379,186	997	0.3
Philadelphia–Camden–Wilmington, PA–NJ–DE–MD	5,965,343	16,340	0.3
Phoenix–Mesa–Glendale, AZ	4,192,887	99,278	2.4
Pine Bluff, AR	100,258	274	0.3
Pittsburgh, PA	2,356,285	2,908	0.1
Pittsfield, MA	131,219	251	0.2
Pocatello, ID	90,656	2,798	3.1
Portland–South Portland–Biddeford, ME	514,098	1,631	0.3
Portland–Vancouver–Hillsboro, OR–WA	2,226,009	20,857	0.9
Port St. Lucie, FL	424,107	1,963	0.5
Poughkeepsie–Newburgh–Middletown, NY	670,301	2,641	0.4
Prescott, AZ	211,033	3,549	1.7
Providence–New Bedford–Fall River, RI–MA	1,600,852	8,178	0.5
Provo–Orem, UT	526,810	3,164	0.6
Pueblo, CO	159,063	3,055	1.9
Punta Gorda, FL	159,978	417	0.3
Racine, WI	195,408	781	0.4
Raleigh–Cary, NC	1,130,490	5,771	0.5
Rapid City, SD	126,382	10,345	8.2
Reading, PA	411,442	1,285	0.3
Redding, CA	177,223	4,950	2.8
Reno–Sparks, NV	425,417	7,273	1.7
Richmond, VA	1,258,251	5,480	0.4
Riverside–San Bernardino–Ontario, CA	4,224,851	46,399	1.1
Roanoke, VA	308,707	727	0.2
Rochester, MN	186,011	445	0.2
Rochester, NY	1,054,323	3,104	0.3
Rockford, IL	349,431	1,163	0.3
Rocky Mount, NC	152,392	826	0.5
Rome, GA	96,317	344	0.4

	total population	American Indian	
		number	share of total
Sacramento–Arden–Arcade–Roseville, CA	2,149,127	21,603	1.0%
Saginaw–Saginaw Township North, MI	200,169	877	0.4
St. Cloud, MN	189,093	632	0.3
St. George, UT	138,115	1,869	1.4
St. Joseph, MO–KS	127,329	585	0.5
St. Louis, MO–IL	2,812,896	6,811	0.2
Salem, OR	390,738	6,575	1.7
Salinas, CA	415,057	5,464	1.3
Salisbury, MD	125,203	321	0.3
Salt Lake City, UT	1,124,197	9,842	0.9
San Angelo, TX	111,823	884	0.8
San Antonio–New Braunfels, TX	2,142,508	17,322	0.8
San Diego–Carlsbad–San Marcos, CA	3,095,313	26,340	0.9
Sandusky, OH	77,079	232	0.3
San Francisco–Oakland–Fremont, CA	4,335,391	24,774	0.6
San Jose–Sunnyvale–Santa Clara, CA	1,836,911	13,855	0.8
San Luis Obispo–Paso Robles, CA	269,637	2,536	0.9
Santa Barbara–Santa Maria–Goleta, CA	423,895	5,485	1.3
Santa Cruz–Watsonville, CA	262,382	2,253	0.9
Santa Fe, NM	144,170	4,486	3.1
Santa Rosa–Petaluma, CA	483,878	6,489	1.3
Savannah, GA	347,611	945	0.3
Scranton–Wilkes–Barre, PA	563,631	942	0.2
Seattle–Tacoma–Bellevue, WA	3,439,809	36,819	1.1
Sebastian–Vero Beach, FL	138,028	408	0.3
Sheboygan, WI	115,507	444	0.4
Sherman–Denison, TX	120,877	1,835	1.5
Shreveport–Bossier City, LA	398,604	1,937	0.5
Sioux City, IA–NE–SD	143,577	2,923	2.0
Sioux Falls, SD	228,261	4,514	2.0
South Bend–Mishawaka, IN–MI	319,224	1,534	0.5
Spartanburg, SC	284,307	764	0.3
Spokane, WA	471,221	7,295	1.5
Springfield, IL	210,170	426	0.2
Springfield, MA	692,942	2,413	0.3
Springfield, MO	436,712	2,930	0.7
Springfield, OH	138,333	351	0.3
State College, PA	153,990	191	0.1
Steubenville–Weirton, OH–WV	124,454	156	0.1
Stockton, CA	685,306	7,196	1.1
Sumter, SC	107,456	389	0.4
Syracuse, NY	662,577	4,862	0.7

	total population	American Indian	
		number	share of total
Tallahassee, FL	367,413	1,140	0.3%
Tampa–St. Petersburg–Clearwater, FL	2,783,243	9,930	0.4
Terre Haute, IN	172,425	518	0.3
Texarkana, TX–Texarkana, AR	136,027	987	0.7
Toledo, OH	651,429	1,826	0.3
Topeka, KS	233,870	3,572	1.5
Trenton–Ewing, NJ	366,513	1,194	0.3
Tucson, AZ	980,263	32,605	3.3
Tulsa, OK	937,478	77,388	8.3
Tuscaloosa, AL	219,461	568	0.3
Tyler, TX	209,714	1,141	0.5
Utica–Rome, NY	299,397	762	0.3
Valdosta, GA	139,588	590	0.4
Vallejo–Fairfield, CA	413,344	3,212	0.8
Victoria, TX	115,384	657	0.6
Vineland–Millville–Bridgeton, NJ	156,898	1,746	1.1
Virginia Beach–Norfolk–Newport News, VA–NC	1,671,683	6,828	0.4
Visalia–Porterville, CA	442,179	6,993	1.6
Waco, TX	234,906	1,473	0.6
Warner Robins, GA	139,900	475	0.3
Washington–Arlington–Alexandria, DC–VA–MD–WV	5,582,170	22,791	0.4
Waterloo–Cedar Falls, IA	167,819	317	0.2
Wausau, WI	134,063	634	0.5
Wenatchee–East Wenatchee, WA	110,884	1,105	1.0
Wheeling, WV–OH	147,950	197	0.1
Wichita, KS	623,061	6,908	1.1
Wichita Falls, TX	151,306	1,577	1.0
Williamsport, PA	116,111	217	0.2
Wilmington, NC	362,315	2,057	0.6
Winchester, VA–WV	128,472	377	0.3
Winston–Salem, NC	477,717	1,841	0.4
Worcester, MA	798,552	1,976	0.2
Yakima, WA	243,231	10,568	4.3
York–Hanover, PA	434,972	942	0.2
Youngstown–Warren–Boardman, OH–PA	565,773	1,007	0.2
Yuba City, CA	166,892	3,040	1.8
Yuma, AZ	195,751	3,056	1.6

Note: American Indians are those who identify themselves as being American Indian or Alaska Native alone.
Source: Bureau of the Census, 2010 Census, Internet site http://factfinder2.census.gov/faces/nav/jsf/pages/index.xhtml; calculations by New Strategist

3

Asians

■ The Asian population (race alone or in combination) numbered 18 million in 2011, 52 percent larger than in 2000. Despite this rapid growth, only 5.8 percent of Americans are Asian.

■ Asians are far better educated than the population as a whole. Half the Asians aged 25 or older have a bachelor's degree versus 31 percent of the total population.

■ Asians are the only racial or ethnic group in which the majority has a healthy weight. Only 39 percent of Asians are overweight.

■ The $64,995 median income of Asian households in 2011 was 30 percent greater than the all-household median and higher than that of any other racial or ethnic group.

■ Fully 48 percent of Asian workers are employed in managerial or professional occupations— the largest share among racial and ethnic groups.

■ Asian households are much more likely than the average household to be headed by married couples—60 versus 49 percent.

■ Forty-six percent of Asians live in the West, where they account for 12 percent of the population. California is home to 32 percent of the nation's Asian population.

■ Asian households spent an average of $60,136 in 2011, a substantial 21 percent more than the average household.

■ The median net worth of Asian households was $89,339 in 2011, 30 percent higher than the $68,828 net worth of the average household.

Asians account for nearly 6 percent of the U.S. population

(percent distribution of people by race and Hispanic origin, 2011)

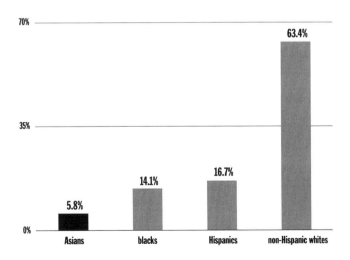

Asians Are Better Educated than the Average American

Asians are much more likely to be college graduates than the population as a whole. In 2012, half of Asians aged 25 or older had a bachelor's degree versus 31 percent of the total population. Nineteen percent of Asians had an advanced degree, much higher than the 11 percent among all Americans aged 25 or older.

Not surprisingly, Asians are more likely than the average person to be enrolled in school. While 48 percent of all Americans aged 20 to 21 are students, for example, the figure is a much higher 77 percent among Asians in the age group. Forty-one percent of Asians aged 22 to 24 are still in school versus 27 percent of all Americans in the age group. More than 1.2 million Asians were enrolled in college in 2011, representing 6 percent of total enrollment.

Asians earned 7 percent of bachelor's degrees in 2010–11. They earned 6 percent of master's degrees and 10 percent of doctoral and first-professional degrees.

■ The educational level of Asians is higher than that of the average American in part because many are immigrants with professional jobs.

Half of Asians aged 25 or older have a bachelor's degree

(percent of Asians aged 25 or older by educational attainment, 2012)

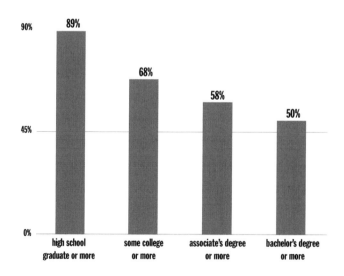

Table 3.1 Educational Attainment of Asians by Age, 2012

(number and percent distribution of Asians aged 25 or older by educational attainment and age, 2012; numbers in thousands)

	total	25 to 34	35 to 44	45 to 54	55 to 64	65 or older
Total Asians	**11,400**	**2,944**	**2,798**	**2,320**	**1,757**	**1,581**
Not a high school graduate	1,251	159	228	220	235	412
High school graduate only	2,354	432	461	563	469	430
Some college, no degree	1,228	393	262	244	182	146
Associate's degree	817	237	168	195	129	87
Bachelor's degree	3,542	1,089	931	705	502	315
Master's degree	1,545	471	538	270	166	100
Professional degree	304	101	73	46	32	52
Doctoral degree	356	64	137	77	43	37
High school graduate or more	10,146	2,787	2,570	2,100	1,523	1,167
Some college or more	7,792	2,355	2,109	1,537	1,054	737
Associate's degree or more	6,564	1,962	1,847	1,293	872	591
Bachelor's degree or more	5,747	1,725	1,679	1,098	743	504

PERCENT DISTRIBUTION

	total	25 to 34	35 to 44	45 to 54	55 to 64	65 or older
Total Asians	**100.0%**	**100.0%**	**100.0%**	**100.0%**	**100.0%**	**100.0%**
Not a high school graduate	11.0	5.4	8.1	9.5	13.4	26.1
High school graduate only	20.6	14.7	16.5	24.3	26.7	27.2
Some college, no degree	10.8	13.3	9.4	10.5	10.4	9.2
Associate's degree	7.2	8.1	6.0	8.4	7.3	5.5
Bachelor's degree	31.1	37.0	33.3	30.4	28.6	19.9
Master's degree	13.6	16.0	19.2	11.6	9.4	6.3
Professional degree	2.7	3.4	2.6	2.0	1.8	3.3
Doctoral degree	3.1	2.2	4.9	3.3	2.4	2.3
High school graduate or more	89.0	94.7	91.9	90.5	86.7	73.8
Some college or more	68.4	80.0	75.4	66.3	60.0	46.6
Associate's degree or more	57.6	66.6	66.0	55.7	49.6	37.4
Bachelor's degree or more	50.4	58.6	60.0	47.3	42.3	31.9

Note: Asians are those who identify themselves as being of the race alone and those who identify themselves as being of the race in combination with other races.
Source: Bureau of the Census, Educational Attainment in the United States: 2012, Internet site http://www.census.gov/hhes/socdemo/education/data/cps/2012/tables.html; calculations by New Strategist

Table 3.2 Educational Attainment of Asian Men by Age, 2012

(number and percent distribution of Asian men aged 25 or older by educational attainment and age, 2012; numbers in thousands)

	total	25 to 34	35 to 44	45 to 54	55 to 64	65 or older
Total Asian men	**5,269**	**1,403**	**1,304**	**1,102**	**779**	**681**
Not a high school graduate	501	71	101	100	92	138
High school graduate only	1,020	222	203	255	178	162
Some college, no degree	605	191	127	126	84	77
Associate's degree	371	124	69	88	54	36
Bachelor's degree	1,602	494	411	303	237	156
Master's degree	783	220	271	155	85	51
Professional degree	168	53	37	23	17	39
Doctoral degree	219	27	85	49	33	25
High school graduate or more	4,768	1,331	1,203	999	688	546
Some college or more	3,748	1,109	1,000	744	510	384
Associate's degree or more	3,143	918	873	618	426	307
Bachelor's degree or more	2,772	794	804	530	372	271

PERCENT DISTRIBUTION

	total	25 to 34	35 to 44	45 to 54	55 to 64	65 or older
Total Asian men	**100.0%**	**100.0%**	**100.0%**	**100.0%**	**100.0%**	**100.0%**
Not a high school graduate	9.5	5.1	7.7	9.1	11.8	20.3
High school graduate only	19.4	15.8	15.6	23.1	22.8	23.8
Some college, no degree	11.5	13.6	9.7	11.4	10.8	11.3
Associate's degree	7.0	8.8	5.3	8.0	6.9	5.3
Bachelor's degree	30.4	35.2	31.5	27.5	30.4	22.9
Master's degree	14.9	15.7	20.8	14.1	10.9	7.5
Professional degree	3.2	3.8	2.8	2.1	2.2	5.7
Doctoral degree	4.2	1.9	6.5	4.4	4.2	3.7
High school graduate or more	90.5	94.9	92.3	90.7	88.3	80.2
Some college or more	71.1	79.0	76.7	67.5	65.5	56.4
Associate's degree or more	59.7	65.4	66.9	56.1	54.7	45.1
Bachelor's degree or more	52.6	56.6	61.7	48.1	47.8	39.8

Note: Asians are those who identify themselves as being of the race alone and those who identify themselves as being of the race in combination with other races.
Source: Bureau of the Census, Educational Attainment in the United States: 2012, Internet site http://www.census.gov/hhes/ socdemo/education/data/cps/2012/tables.html; calculations by New Strategist

Table 3.3 Educational Attainment of Asian Women by Age, 2012

(number and percent distribution of Asian women aged 25 or older by educational attainment and age, 2012; numbers in thousands)

	total	25 to 34	35 to 44	45 to 54	55 to 64	65 or older
Total Asian women	**6,131**	**1,542**	**1,494**	**1,217**	**978**	**900**
Not a high school graduate	751	88	127	117	141	277
High school graduate only	1,334	210	258	307	290	269
Some college, no degree	623	203	135	118	98	69
Associate's degree	446	112	101	108	75	49
Bachelor's degree	1,941	594	520	402	265	159
Master's degree	763	251	267	115	81	49
Professional degree	136	48	35	22	16	14
Doctoral degree	138	37	51	28	10	12
High school graduate or more	5,381	1,455	1,367	1,100	835	621
Some college or more	4,047	1,245	1,109	793	545	352
Associate's degree or more	3,424	1,042	974	675	447	283
Bachelor's degree or more	2,978	930	873	567	372	234

PERCENT DISTRIBUTION

	total	25 to 34	35 to 44	45 to 54	55 to 64	65 or older
Total Asian women	**100.0%**	**100.0%**	**100.0%**	**100.0%**	**100.0%**	**100.0%**
Not a high school graduate	12.2	5.7	8.5	9.6	14.4	30.8
High school graduate only	21.8	13.6	17.3	25.2	29.7	29.9
Some college, no degree	10.2	13.2	9.0	9.7	10.0	7.7
Associate's degree	7.3	7.3	6.8	8.9	7.7	5.4
Bachelor's degree	31.7	38.5	34.8	33.0	27.1	17.7
Master's degree	12.4	16.3	17.9	9.4	8.3	5.4
Professional degree	2.2	3.1	2.3	1.8	1.6	1.6
Doctoral degree	2.3	2.4	3.4	2.3	1.0	1.3
High school graduate or more	87.8	94.4	91.5	90.4	85.4	69.0
Some college or more	66.0	80.7	74.2	65.2	55.7	39.1
Associate's degree or more	55.8	67.6	65.2	55.5	45.7	31.4
Bachelor's degree or more	48.6	60.3	58.4	46.6	38.0	26.0

Note: Asians are those who identify themselves as being of the race alone and those who identify themselves as being of the race in combination with other races.
Source: Bureau of the Census, Educational Attainment in the United States: 2012, Internet site http://www.census.gov/hhes/socdemo/education/data/cps/2012/tables.html; calculations by New Strategist

Table 3.4 Educational Attainment of Asians by Region, 2006–10

(number of Asians aged 25 or older and percent by educational attainment, by region, 2006–10; numbers in thousands)

	total	Northeast	Midwest	South	West
Total Asians, number	**10,271**	**2,068**	**1,118**	**2,171**	**4,913**
Not a high school graduate	1,424	345	136	282	661
High school graduate only	1,698	333	158	357	850
Some college, no degree	1,373	178	130	272	793
Associate's degree	707	109	63	134	402
Bachelor's degree	3,038	619	332	620	1,467
Graduate degree	2,030	484	299	507	741
High school graduate or more	86.1%	83.3%	87.8%	87.0%	86.5%
Some college or more	69.6	67.2	73.7	70.6	69.2
Associate's degree or more	56.2	58.6	62.1	58.0	53.1
Bachelor's degree or more	49.3	53.3	56.5	51.9	44.9

Note: Asians are those who identify themselves as being of the race alone and those who identify themselves as being of the race in combination with other races.
Source: Bureau of the Census, 2006–10 American Community Survey, Internet site http://factfinder2.census.gov/faces/nav/jsf/pages/index.xhtml; calculations by New Strategist

Table 3.5 School Enrollment of Asians, 2011

(total number of people aged 3 or older enrolled in school, number of Asians enrolled, and Asian share of total, by age, October 2011; numbers in thousands)

		Asian	
	total	number	share of total
Total aged 3 or older	**79,043**	**4,571**	**5.8%**
Aged 3 to 4	4,597	267	5.8
Aged 5 to 6	8,009	476	5.9
Aged 7 to 9	12,319	716	5.8
Aged 10 to 13	15,941	885	5.6
Aged 14 to 15	7,825	395	5.0
Aged 16 to 17	7,906	419	5.3
Aged 18 to 19	6,017	321	5.3
Aged 20 to 21	4,618	338	7.3
Aged 22 to 24	3,961	247	6.2
Aged 25 to 29	3,139	220	7.0
Aged 30 to 34	1,571	121	7.7
Aged 35 to 44	1,688	123	7.3
Aged 45 to 54	1,012	23	2.3
Aged 55 or older	438	19	4.3

Note: Asians are those who identify themselves as being of the race alone and those who identify themselves as being of the race in combination with other races.
Source: Bureau of the Census, School Enrollment, CPS October 2011—Detailed Tables, Internet site http://www.census.gov/ hhes/school/data/cps/2011/tables.html; calculations by New Strategist

Table 3.6 School Enrollment of Asians by Age and Sex, 2011

(number and percent of Asians aged 3 or older enrolled in school, by age and sex, October 2011; numbers in thousands)

	total		female		male	
	number	percent	number	percent	number	percent
Total Asians enrolled	**4,571**	**29.7%**	**2,285**	**28.7%**	**2,286**	**30.7%**
Aged 3 to 4	267	55.4	128	54.9	139	55.9
Aged 5 to 6	476	96.6	232	95.7	244	97.4
Aged 7 to 9	716	97.9	366	98.5	350	97.3
Aged 10 to 13	885	97.4	429	96.2	456	98.6
Aged 14 to 15	395	98.2	195	97.9	200	98.6
Aged 16 to 17	419	97.6	218	98.3	201	96.9
Aged 18 to 19	321	80.4	143	77.1	178	83.3
Aged 20 to 21	338	77.1	170	74.8	168	79.5
Aged 22 to 24	247	41.4	121	44.0	126	39.1
Aged 25 to 29	220	17.2	110	17.4	110	17.0
Aged 30 to 34	121	9.1	61	8.7	60	9.5
Aged 35 to 44	123	4.7	87	6.4	36	2.9
Aged 45 to 54	23	1.1	14	1.3	9	0.9
Aged 55 or older	19	0.6	10	0.6	9	0.6

Note: Asians are those who identify themselves as being of the race alone and those who identify themselves as being of the race in combination with other races.
Source: Bureau of the Census, School Enrollment, CPS October 2011—Detailed Tables, Internet site http://www.census.gov/hhes/school/data/cps/2011/tables.html; calculations by New Strategist

Table 3.7 Asian College Enrollment Rate, 2003 to 2011

(percentage of total people and Asians aged 16 to 24 who graduated from high school in the previous 12 months and were enrolled in college as of October, and index of Asian to total, 2003 to 2011; percentage point change in enrollment rate for selected years)

	total	Asian	index, Asian to total
2011	68.2%	86.1%	126
2010	68.1	84.7	124
2009	70.1	92.1	131
2008	68.6	88.4	129
2007	67.2	88.8	132
2006	66.0	82.3	125
2005	68.6	86.7	126
2004	66.7	75.6	113
2003	63.9	84.1	132

PERCENTAGE POINT CHANGE

2003 to 2011	4.3	2.0	–

Note: Asians are those who identify themselves as being of the race alone. The index is calculated by dividing the Asian figure by the total figure and multiplying by 100. "–" means not applicable.
Source: National Center for Education Statistics, Digest of Education Statistics 2012, Internet site ces.ed.gov/programs/ digest/2012menu_tables.asp; calculations by New Strategist

Table 3.8 College Enrollment of Asians by Age, 2011

(total number of people aged 15 or older enrolled in college, number of Asians enrolled, and Asian share of total, by age, 2011; numbers in thousands)

	total	Asian number	Asian share of total
Total enrolled in college	**20,397**	**1,204**	**5.9%**
Under age 20	4,446	261	5.9
Aged 20 to 21	4,460	279	6.3
Aged 22 to 24	3,869	228	5.9
Aged 25 to 29	3,066	189	6.2
Aged 30 or older	4,559	245	5.4

Note: Asians are those who identify themselves as being of the race alone.
Source: Bureau of the Census, School Enrollment, CPS October 2011—Detailed Tables, Internet site http://www.census.gov/ hhes/school/data/cps/2011/tables.html; calculations by New Strategist

Table 3.9 College Enrollment of Asians by Type of School and Sex, 2011

(number and percent distribution of Asians aged 15 or older enrolled in college by type of school and sex, and female share of total, 2011; numbers in thousands)

	total		men		women		
	number	percent distribution	number	percent distribution	number	percent distribution	share of total
Total Asians enrolled	**1,204**	**100.0%**	**567**	**100.0%**	**637**	**100.0%**	**52.9%**
Two-year undergraduate program	219	18.2	94	16.6	124	19.5	56.6
Four-year undergraduate program	635	52.7	326	57.5	309	48.5	48.7
Graduate school	351	29.2	148	26.1	203	31.9	57.8

Note: Asians are those who identify themselves as being of the race alone.
Source: Bureau of the Census, School Enrollment, CPS October 2011—Detailed Tables, Internet site http://www.census.gov/hhes/school/data/cps/2011/tables.html; calculations by New Strategist

Table 3.10 Associate's Degrees Earned by Asians by Field of Study, 2010–11

(total number of associate's degrees conferred and number and percent earned by Asians, by field of study, 2010–11)

	total	earned by Asians number	share of total
Total associate's degrees	**942,327**	**45,876**	**4.9%**
Agriculture and natural resources	6,425	54	0.8
Architecture and related programs	569	53	9.3
Area, ethnic, and cultural studies	209	4	1.9
Biological and biomedical sciences	3,245	480	14.8
Business	139,986	7,701	5.5
Communication, journalism, and related programs	3,051	153	5.0
Communications technologies	4,209	134	3.2
Computer and information sciences	37,677	1,747	4.6
Construction trades	5,402	83	1.5
Education	20,459	416	2.0
Engineering	2,825	229	8.1
Engineering technologies	35,521	1,187	3.3
English language and literature/letters	2,019	161	8.0
Family and consumer sciences	8,532	336	3.9
Foreign languages and literatures	1,876	62	3.3
Health professions and related sciences	201,831	9,524	4.7
Homeland security, law enforcement, and firefighting	44,923	1,039	2.3
Legal professions and studies	11,620	322	2.8
Liberal arts and sciences, general studies, and humanities	306,670	14,728	4.8
Library science	160	3	1.9
Mathematics and statistics	1,644	256	15.6
Mechanic and repair technologies	19,969	685	3.4
Military technologies	856	47	5.5
Multi/interdisciplinary studies	23,729	2,775	11.7
Parks, recreation, leisure, and fitness	2,366	88	3.7
Philosophy and religion	283	25	8.8
Physical sciences	5,078	524	10.3
Precision production trades	3,254	79	2.4
Psychology	3,866	204	5.3
Public administration and social services	7,472	132	1.8
Social sciences and history	12,767	1,261	9.9
Theology and religious vocations	758	13	1.7
Transportation and material moving	1,697	94	5.5
Visual and performing arts	21,379	1,277	6.0

Note: Asians include Pacific Islanders.
Source: National Center for Education Statistics, Digest of Education Statistics 2012, Internet site http://nces.ed.gov/programs/digest/2012menu_tables.asp; calculations by New Strategist

Table 3.11 Bachelor's Degrees Earned by Asians by Field of Study, 2010–11

(total number of bachelor's degrees conferred and number and percent earned by Asians, by field of study, 2010–11)

	total	earned by Asians number	earned by Asians share of total
Total bachelor's degrees	**1,715,913**	**116,794**	**6.8%**
Agriculture and natural resources	28,623	1,080	3.8
Architecture and related programs	9,832	857	8.7
Area, ethnic, and cultural studies	9,100	943	10.4
Biological and biomedical sciences	90,003	15,008	16.7
Business	365,093	26,583	7.3
Communication, journalism, and related programs	83,274	3,492	4.2
Communications technologies	4,858	257	5.3
Computer and information sciences	43,072	3,804	8.8
Construction trades	328	5	1.5
Education	103,992	1,843	1.8
Engineering	76,376	9,220	12.1
Engineering technologies	16,187	694	4.3
English language and literature/letters	52,744	2,367	4.5
Family and consumer sciences	22,444	1,132	5.0
Foreign languages, literatures, and linguistics	21,706	1,297	6.0
Health professions and related sciences	143,430	9,506	6.6
Homeland security, law enforcement, and firefighting	47,602	1,225	2.6
Legal professions and studies	4,429	211	4.8
Liberal arts and sciences, general studies, and humanities	46,727	1,552	3.3
Library science	96	3	0.0
Mathematics and statistics	17,182	1,822	10.6
Mechanic and repair technologies	226	13	5.8
Military technologies	64	0	0.0
Multi/interdisciplinary studies	42,228	2,557	6.1
Parks, recreation, leisure, and fitness	35,924	1,246	3.5
Philosophy and religion	12,836	660	5.1
Physical sciences	24,712	2,491	10.1
Precision production trades	43	5	11.6
Psychology	100,893	6,583	6.5
Public administration and social services	26,774	876	3.3
Social sciences and history	177,144	13,261	7.5
Theology and religious vocations	9,074	215	2.4
Transportation and material moving	4,941	206	4.2
Visual and performing arts	93,956	5,780	6.2

Note: Asians include Pacific Islanders.
Source: National Center for Education Statistics, Digest of Education Statistics 2012, Internet site http://nces.ed.gov/programs/ digest/2012menu_tables.asp; calculations by New Strategist

Table 3.12 Master's Degrees Earned by Asians by Field of Study, 2010–11

(total number of master's degrees conferred and number and percent earned by Asians, by field of study, 2010–11)

		earned by Asians	
	total	number	share of total
Total master's degrees	**730,635**	**43,728**	**6.0%**
Agriculture and natural resources	5,773	233	4.0
Architecture and related programs	7,788	549	7.0
Area, ethnic, and cultural studies	1,914	115	6.0
Biological and biomedical sciences	11,327	1,464	12.9
Business	187,213	15,378	8.2
Communication, journalism, and related programs	8,303	365	4.4
Communications technologies	502	27	5.4
Computer and information sciences	19,446	1,926	9.9
Education	185,009	5,002	2.7
Engineering	38,719	4,102	10.6
Engineering technologies	4,515	373	8.3
English language and literature/letters	9,476	347	3.7
Family and consumer sciences	2,918	77	2.6
Foreign languages, literatures, and linguistics	3,727	166	4.5
Health professions and related sciences	75,579	5,823	7.7
Homeland security, law enforcement, and firefighting	7,433	197	2.7
Legal professions and studies	6,300	365	5.8
Liberal arts and sciences, general studies, and humanities	3,971	187	4.7
Library science	7,727	284	3.7
Mathematics and statistics	5,843	521	8.9
Multi/interdisciplinary studies	6,748	374	5.5
Parks, recreation, leisure, and fitness	6,553	174	2.7
Philosophy and religion	1,833	54	2.9
Physical sciences	6,386	404	6.3
Precision production trades	5	0	0.0
Psychology	25,051	979	3.9
Public administration and social services	38,634	1,654	4.3
Social sciences and history	21,084	1,020	4.8
Theology and religious vocations	13,191	648	4.9
Transportation and material moving	1,390	41	2.9
Visual and performing arts	16,277	879	5.4

Note: Asians include Pacific Islanders.
Source: National Center for Education Statistics, Digest of Education Statistics 2012, Internet site http://nces.ed.gov/programs/digest/2012menu_tables.asp; calculations by New Strategist

Table 3.13 Doctoral and First-Professional Degrees Earned by Asians by Field of Study, 2010–11

(total number of doctoral and first-professional degrees conferred and number and percent earned by Asians, by field of study, 2010–11)

		earned by Asians	
	total	number	share of total
Total doctoral and first-professional degrees	**163,765**	**17,078**	**10.4%**
Agriculture and natural resources	1,246	40	3.2
Architecture and related programs	205	41	20.0
Area, ethnic, and cultural studies	278	27	9.7
Biological and biomedical sciences	7,693	688	8.9
Business	2,286	148	6.5
Communication, journalism, and related programs	577	17	2.9
Communications technologies	1	0	0.0
Computer and information sciences	1,588	146	9.2
Education	9,623	326	3.4
Engineering	8,369	644	7.7
Engineering technologies	56	3	5.4
English language and literature/letters	1,344	50	3.7
Family and consumer sciences	320	11	3.4
Foreign languages, literatures, and linguistics	1,158	48	4.1
Health professions and related sciences	60,153	9,933	16.5
Homeland security, law enforcement, and firefighting	131	5	3.8
Legal professions and studies	44,877	3,686	8.2
Liberal arts and sciences, general studies, and humanities	95	5	5.3
Library science	50	1	2.0
Mathematics and statistics	1,586	98	6.2
Multi/interdisciplinary studies	660	38	5.8
Parks, recreation, leisure, and fitness	257	6	2.3
Philosophy and religion	805	23	2.9
Physical sciences	5,295	272	5.1
Psychology	5,851	300	5.1
Public administration and social services	851	45	5.3
Social sciences and history	4,390	202	4.6
Theology and religious vocations	2,374	167	7.0
Visual and performing arts	1,646	108	6.6

Note: Asians include Pacific Islanders.
Source: National Center for Education Statistics, Digest of Education Statistics 2012, Internet site http://nces.ed.gov/programs/digest/2012menu_tables.asp; calculations by New Strategist

Few Asians Are Overweight

Asians are the only racial or ethnic group in which those with a healthy weight (neither over- nor underweight) are in the majority. Fifty-six percent of Asians are at a healthy weight, while only 39 percent are overweight. Among all Americans, 61 percent are overweight. Sixty-two percent of Asians report being in "very good" or "excellent" health. Just 10 percent smoke cigarettes.

Nearly 254,000 babies were born to Asian women in 2011, or 6 percent of all babies born that year. In Hawaii, nearly two-thirds of births were to Asians in 2011. In California, the figure was 14 percent.

Eighty-four percent of Asians were covered by some type of health insurance in 2011, most having employment-based coverage. Only 10 percent of Asian adults have difficulties in physical functioning, far below the 16 percent rate for the total population. The leading causes of death among Asians, cancer and heart disease, accounted for just over 50 percent of Asian deaths in 2009.

■ The Asian health advantage may diminish if poorly educated immigrants become a larger share of the Asian population.

Sixteen percent of Asians do not have health insurance

(percent distribution of Asians by health insurance coverage status, 2011)

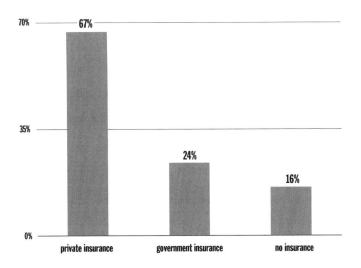

Table 3.14 Health Status of Total People and Asians, 2011

(number and percent distribution of total people and Asians aged 18 or older by self-reported health status, and index of Asian to total, 2011; numbers in thousands)

	total		Asian		index,
	number	percent distribution	number	percent distribution	Asian to total
Total people	**231,376**	**100.0%**	**11,468**	**100.0%**	–
Excellent/very good	139,424	60.3	7,116	62.1	103
Good	60,973	26.4	3,101	27.0	103
Fair/poor	30,856	13.3	1,251	10.9	82

Note: Asians are those who identify themselves as being Asian alone. Numbers may not add to total because "unknown" is not shown. The index is calculated by dividing the Asian percentage by the total percentage and multiplying by 100. "–" means not applicable.
Source: National Center for Health Statistics, Summary Health Statistics for U.S. Adults: National Health Interview Survey, 2011, Vital and Health Statistics, Series 10, No. 256, 2012, Internet site http://www.cdc.gov/nchs/nhis.htm; calculations by New Strategist

Table 3.15 Weight Status of Total People and Asians, 2011

(number and percent distribution of total people and Asians aged 18 or older by body mass index based on self-reported height and weight, and index of Asian to total, 2011; numbers in thousands)

	total		Asian		index,
	number	percent distribution	number	percent distribution	Asian to total
Total people	**231,376**	**100.0%**	**11,468**	**100.0%**	–
Underweight	3,549	1.5	457	4.0	260
Healthy weight	79,984	34.6	6,384	55.7	161
Overweight, total	141,072	61.0	4,429	38.6	63
Overweight, but not obese	77,586	33.5	3,377	29.4	88
Obese	63,486	27.4	1,052	9.2	33

Note: "Overweight" is defined as a body mass index of 25 or higher. "Obese" is defined as a body mass index of 30 or higher. Body mass index is calculated by dividing weight in kilograms by height in meters squared. Asians are those who identify themselves as being Asian alone. Numbers may not add to total because "unknown" is not shown. The index is calculated by dividing the Asian percentage by the total percentage and multiplying by 100. "–" means not applicable.
Source: National Center for Health Statistics, Summary Health Statistics for U.S. Adults: National Health Interview Survey, 2011, Vital and Health Statistics, Series 10, No. 256, 2012, Internet site http://www.cdc.gov/nchs/nhis.htm; calculations by New Strategist

Table 3.16 Drinking Status of Total People and Asians, 2011

(number and percent distribution of total people and Asians aged 18 or older by drinking status, and index of Asian to total, 2011; numbers in thousands)

	total		Asian		index, Asian to total
	number	percent distribution	number	percent distribution	
Total people	**231,376**	**100.0%**	**11,468**	**100.0%**	–
Lifetime abstainer	45,367	19.6	4,868	42.4	216
Former drinker	33,663	14.5	1,121	9.8	67
Current drinker	148,970	64.4	5,366	46.8	73
Infrequent	31,158	13.5	1,410	12.3	91
Regular	117,812	50.9	3,956	34.5	68

Note: "Lifetime abstainers" have had fewer than 12 drinks in lifetime. "Former drinkers" have had 12 or more drinks in lifetime, none in past year. "Current infrequent drinkers" have had 12 or more drinks in lifetime and fewer than 12 drinks in past year. "Current regular drinkers" have had 12 or more drinks in lifetime and at least 12 drinks in past year. Asians are those who identify themselves as being Asian alone. Numbers may not add to total because "unknown" is not shown. The index is calculated by dividing the Asian percentage by the total percentage and multiplying by 100. "–" means not applicable.
Source: National Center for Health Statistics, Summary Health Statistics for U.S. Adults: National Health Interview Survey, 2011, Vital and Health Statistics, Series 10, No. 256, 2012, Internet site http://www.cdc.gov/nchs/nhis.htm; calculations by New Strategist

Table 3.17 Smoking Status of Total People and Asians, 2011

(number and percent distribution of total people and Asians aged 18 or older by smoking status, and index of Asian to total, 2011; numbers in thousands)

	total		Asian		index, Asian to total
	number	percent distribution	number	percent distribution	
Total people	**231,376**	**100.0%**	**11,468**	**100.0%**	–
Never smoked	136,528	59.0	8,769	76.5	130
Former smoker	50,416	21.8	1,543	13.5	62
Current smoker	43,821	18.9	1,139	9.9	52

Note: "Never smoked" means fewer than 100 cigarettes in lifetime. "Former smokers" have smoked 100 or more cigarettes in lifetime but did not smoke at time of interview. "Current smokers" have smoked at least 100 cigarettes in lifetime and currently smoke. Asians are those who identify themselves as being Asian alone. Numbers may not add to total because "unknown" is not shown. The index is calculated by dividing the Asian percentage by the total percentage and multiplying by 100. "–" means not applicable.
Source: National Center for Health Statistics, Summary Health Statistics for U.S. Adults: National Health Interview Survey, 2011, Vital and Health Statistics, Series 10, No. 256, 2012, Internet site http://www.cdc.gov/nchs/nhis.htm; calculations by New Strategist

Table 3.18 Births to Total and Asian Women by Age, 2011

(total number of births, number and percent distribution of births to Asians, and Asian share of total, by age, 2011)

	total	Asian number	Asian percent distribution	Asian share of total
Total births	**3,953,593**	**253,864**	**100.0%**	**6.4%**
Under age 15	3,974	66	0.0	1.7
Aged 15 to 19	329,797	5,721	2.3	1.7
Aged 20 to 24	925,213	27,796	10.9	3.0
Aged 25 to 29	1,127,592	70,404	27.7	6.2
Aged 30 to 34	986,661	88,621	34.9	9.0
Aged 35 to 39	463,815	49,495	19.5	10.7
Aged 40 to 44	108,891	10,950	4.3	10.1
Aged 45 to 54	7,651	812	0.3	10.6

Note: Asians include Pacific Islanders.
Source: National Center for Health Statistics, Births: Preliminary Data for 2011, National Vital Statistics Report, Vol. 61, No. 5, 2012, Internet site http://www.cdc.gov/nchs/births.htm; calculations by New Strategist

Table 3.19 Births to Asian Women by Age and Marital Status, 2010

(total number of births to Asians, number of births to unmarried Asians, and unmarried share of total, by age, 2010)

	total	unmarried number	unmarried share of total
Births to Asians	**246,886**	**42,069**	**17.0%**
Under age 15	49	47	95.9
Aged 15 to 19	6,262	5,069	80.9
Aged 20 to 24	27,733	12,498	45.1
Aged 25 to 29	68,378	11,886	17.4
Aged 30 to 34	85,293	7,291	8.5
Aged 35 to 39	48,089	3,987	8.3
Aged 40 or older	11,082	1,291	11.6

Note: Asians include Pacific Islanders.
Source: National Center for Health Statistics, Births: Final Data for 2010, National Vital Statistics Reports, Vol. 61, No. 1, 2012, Internet site http://www.cdc.gov/nchs/births.htm; calculations by New Strategist

Table 3.20 Births to Total and Asian Women by Birth Order, 2011

(total number of births, number and percent distribution of births to Asians, and Asian share of total, by birth order, 2011)

	total	Asian number	percent distribution	share of total
Total births	**3,953,593**	**253,864**	**100.0%**	**6.4%**
First child	1,577,344	113,759	44.8	7.2
Second child	1,239,136	90,154	35.5	7.3
Third child	648,124	31,439	12.4	4.9
Fourth or later child	458,777	16,819	6.6	3.7

Note: Asians include Pacific Islanders. Numbers do not add to total because "not stated" is not shown.
Source: National Center for Health Statistics, Births: Preliminary Data for 2011, National Vital Statistics Report, Vol. 61, No. 5, 2012, Internet site http://www.cdc.gov/nchs/births.htm; calculations by New Strategist

Table 3.21 Births to Total and Asian Women by State, 2011

(total number of births, number and percent distribution of births to Asians, and Asian share of total, by state, 2011)

	total	Asian number	Asian percent distribution	Asian share of total
Total births	**3,953,593**	**253,864**	**100.0%**	**6.4%**
Alabama	59,347	1,016	0.4	1.7
Alaska	11,455	1,040	0.4	9.1
Arizona	85,543	3,553	1.4	4.2
Arkansas	38,713	755	0.3	2.0
California	502,118	70,418	27.7	14.0
Colorado	65,055	2,546	1.0	3.9
Connecticut	37,280	2,289	0.9	6.1
Delaware	11,257	552	0.2	4.9
District of Columbia	9,314	560	0.2	6.0
Florida	213,344	7,291	2.9	3.4
Georgia	132,488	6,200	2.4	4.7
Hawaii	18,957	12,247	4.8	64.6
Idaho	22,305	440	0.2	2.0
Illinois	161,312	9,727	3.8	6.0
Indiana	83,702	2,021	0.8	2.4
Iowa	38,213	1,208	0.5	3.2
Kansas	39,642	1,342	0.5	3.4
Kentucky	55,377	1,195	0.5	2.2
Louisiana	61,889	1,340	0.5	2.2
Maine	12,704	212	0.1	1.7
Maryland	73,086	5,722	2.3	7.8
Massachusetts	73,225	6,211	2.4	8.5
Michigan	114,004	3,991	1.6	3.5
Minnesota	68,411	5,115	2.0	7.5
Mississippi	39,856	427	0.2	1.1
Missouri	76,117	2,007	0.8	2.6
Montana	12,069	143	0.1	1.2
Nebraska	25,720	723	0.3	2.8
Nevada	35,295	2,980	1.2	8.4
New Hampshire	12,852	515	0.2	4.0
New Jersey	105,886	11,853	4.7	11.2
New Mexico	27,289	525	0.2	1.9
New York	241,290	24,794	9.8	10.3
North Carolina	120,385	5,164	2.0	4.3
North Dakota	9,527	172	0.1	1.8
Ohio	137,916	3,509	1.4	2.5
Oklahoma	52,274	1,474	0.6	2.8

	total	Asian		
		number	percent distribution	share of total
Oregon	45,157	2,687	1.1%	6.0%
Pennsylvania	143,148	6,290	2.5	4.4
Rhode Island	10,960	597	0.2	5.4
South Carolina	57,368	1,205	0.5	2.1
South Dakota	11,849	230	0.1	1.9
Tennessee	79,588	1,933	0.8	2.4
Texas	377,449	17,289	6.8	4.6
Utah	51,223	1,683	0.7	3.3
Vermont	6,078	158	0.1	2.6
Virginia	102,648	7,643	3.0	7.4
Washington	86,976	9,444	3.7	10.9
West Virginia	20,720	185	0.1	0.9
Wisconsin	67,811	3,141	1.2	4.6
Wyoming	7,398	102	0.0	1.4

Note: Asians include Pacific Islanders.
Source: National Center for Health Statistics, Births: Preliminary Data for 2011, National Vital Statistics Report, Vol. 61, No. 5, 2012, Internet site http://www.cdc.gov/nchs/births.htm; calculations by New Strategist

Table 3.22 Health Insurance Coverage of Asians by Age, 2011

(number and percent distribution of Asians by age and health insurance coverage status, 2011; numbers in thousands)

	total	with health insurance coverage during year			not covered at any time during the year
		total	private	government	
Total Asians	**17,821**	**14,933**	**11,990**	**4,192**	**2,888**
Under age 18	4,580	4,203	3,259	1,279	378
Aged 18 to 24	1,841	1,391	1,197	260	450
Aged 25 to 34	2,944	2,229	2,016	311	715
Aged 35 to 44	2,798	2,310	2,086	321	488
Aged 45 to 54	2,319	1,908	1,669	319	412
Aged 55 to 64	1,757	1,375	1,140	320	381
Aged 65 or older	1,581	1,516	624	1,382	65

PERCENT DISTRIBUTION BY COVERAGE STATUS

	total	with health insurance coverage during year			not covered at any time during the year
		total	private	government	
Total Asians	**100.0%**	**83.8%**	**67.3%**	**23.5%**	**16.2%**
Under age 18	100.0	91.8	71.2	27.9	8.3
Aged 18 to 24	100.0	75.6	65.0	14.1	24.4
Aged 25 to 34	100.0	75.7	68.5	10.6	24.3
Aged 35 to 44	100.0	82.6	74.6	11.5	17.4
Aged 45 to 54	100.0	82.3	72.0	13.8	17.8
Aged 55 to 64	100.0	78.3	64.9	18.2	21.7
Aged 65 or older	100.0	95.9	39.5	87.4	4.1

Note: Asians are those who identify themselves as being of the race alone and those who identify themselves as being of the race in combination with other races. Numbers do not add to total because some people have more than one type of health insurance.
Source: Bureau of the Census, Health Insurance, Internet site http://www.census.gov/hhes/www/cpstables/032012/health/toc.htm; calculations by New Strategist

Table 3.23 Asians with Private Health Insurance Coverage by Age, 2011

(number and percent distribution of Asians by age and private health insurance coverage status, 2011; numbers in thousands)

	total	with private health insurance			
		total	employment-based		direct purchase
			total	own	
Total Asians	**17,821**	**11,990**	**10,559**	**4,777**	**1,627**
Under age 18	4,580	3,259	3,040	20	307
Aged 18 to 24	1,841	1,197	819	206	236
Aged 25 to 34	2,944	2,016	1,810	1,308	256
Aged 35 to 44	2,798	2,086	1,933	1,256	206
Aged 45 to 54	2,319	1,669	1,498	1,006	248
Aged 55 to 64	1,757	1,140	1,013	703	166
Aged 65 or older	1,581	624	447	277	209

PERCENT DISTRIBUTION BY COVERAGE STATUS

Total Asians	**100.0%**	**67.3%**	**59.3%**	**26.8%**	**9.1%**
Under age 18	100.0	71.2	66.4	0.4	6.7
Aged 18 to 24	100.0	65.0	44.5	11.2	12.8
Aged 25 to 34	100.0	68.5	61.5	44.4	8.7
Aged 35 to 44	100.0	74.6	69.1	44.9	7.4
Aged 45 to 54	100.0	72.0	64.6	43.4	10.7
Aged 55 to 64	100.0	64.9	57.7	40.0	9.4
Aged 65 or older	100.0	39.5	28.3	17.5	13.2

Note: Asians are those who identify themselves as being of the race alone and those who identify themselves as being of the race in combination with other races. Numbers do not add to total because some people have more than one type of health insurance.
Source: Bureau of the Census, Health Insurance, Internet site http://www.census.gov/hhes/www/cpstables/032012/health/toc .htm; calculations by New Strategist

Table 3.24 Asians with Government Health Insurance Coverage by Age, 2011

(number and percent distribution of Asians by age and government health insurance coverage status, 2011; numbers in thousands)

		with government health insurance			
	total	total	Medicaid	Medicare	military
Total Asians	**17,821**	**4,192**	**2,549**	**1,611**	**627**
Under age 18	4,580	1,279	1077	17	208
Aged 18 to 24	1,841	260	224	9	36
Aged 25 to 34	2,944	311	218	20	85
Aged 35 to 44	2,798	321	235	31	78
Aged 45 to 54	2,319	319	229	59	61
Aged 55 to 64	1,757	320	183	110	68
Aged 65 or older	1,581	1,382	383	1,364	91

PERCENT DISTRIBUTION BY COVERAGE STATUS

Total Asians	**100.0%**	**23.5%**	**14.3%**	**9.0%**	**3.5%**
Under age 18	100.0	27.9	23.5	0.4	4.5
Aged 18 to 24	100.0	14.1	12.2	0.5	2.0
Aged 25 to 34	100.0	10.6	7.4	0.7	2.9
Aged 35 to 44	100.0	11.5	8.4	1.1	2.8
Aged 45 to 54	100.0	13.8	9.9	2.5	2.6
Aged 55 to 64	100.0	18.2	10.4	6.3	3.9
Aged 65 or older	100.0	87.4	24.2	86.3	5.8

Note: Asians are those who identify themselves as being of the race alone and those who identify themselves as being of the race in combination with other races. Numbers do not add to total because some people have more than one type of health insurance.
Source: Bureau of the Census, Health Insurance, Internet site http://www.census.gov/hhes/www/cpstables/032012/health/toc .htm; calculations by New Strategist

Table 3.25 Health Conditions among Total People and Asians Aged 18 or Older, 2011

(number of total people and Asians aged 18 or older with selected health conditions, percent of Asians with condition, and Asian share of total with condition, 2011; numbers in thousands)

	total	Asian number	Asian percent with condition	Asian share of total
TOTAL PEOPLE	231,376	11,468	100.0%	5.0%
Selected circulatory diseases				
Heart disease, all types	26,485	748	6.5	2.8
Coronary	15,300	421	3.7	2.8
Hypertension	58,959	1,975	17.2	3.3
Stroke	6,171	268	2.3	4.3
Selected respiratory conditions				
Emphysema	4,680	97	0.8	2.1
Asthma, ever	29,041	917	8.0	3.2
Asthma, still	18,869	568	5.0	3.0
Hay fever	16,869	743	6.5	4.4
Sinusitis	29,611	727	6.3	2.5
Chronic bronchitis	10,071	225	2.0	2.2
Selected types of cancer				
Any cancer	19,025	343	3.0	1.8
Breast cancer	3,221	88	0.8	2.7
Cervical cancer	1,188	21	0.2	1.8
Prostate cancer	2,280	37	0.3	1.6
Other selected diseases and conditions				
Diabetes	20,589	910	7.9	4.4
Ulcers	15,502	550	4.8	3.5
Kidney disease	4,381	141	1.2	3.2
Liver disease	3,016	188	1.6	6.2
Arthritis	53,782	1,306	11.4	2.4
Chronic joint symptoms	68,749	1,909	16.6	2.8
Migraines or severe headaches	37,904	1,292	11.3	3.4
Pain in neck	35,798	1,197	10.4	3.3
Pain in lower back	66,917	2,237	19.5	3.3
Pain in face or jaw	11,436	241	2.1	2.1
Selected sensory problems				
Hearing	37,122	954	8.3	2.6
Vision	21,232	695	6.1	3.3
Absence of all natural teeth	18,038	633	5.5	3.5

Note: The conditions shown are those that have ever been diagnosed by a doctor, except as noted. Hay fever, sinusitis, and chronic bronchitis have been diagnosed in the past 12 months. Kidney and liver disease have been diagnosed in the past 12 months and exclude kidney stones, bladder infections, and incontinence. Chronic joint symptoms are shown if respondent had pain, aching, or stiffness in or around a joint (excluding back and neck) and the condition began more than three months ago. Migraines, pain in neck, lower back, face, or jaw are shown only if pain lasted a whole day or more. Asians are those who identify themselves as being of the race alone.
Source: National Center for Health Statistics, Summary Health Statistics for U.S. Adults: National Health Interview Survey, 2011, Vital and Health Statistics, Series 10, No. 256, 2012, Internet site http://www.cdc.gov/nchs/nhis.htm; calculations by New Strategist

Table 3.26 Health Conditions among Total and Asian Children, 2011

(number of total people and Asians under age 18 with selected health conditions, percent of Asians with condition, and Asian share of total, 2011; numbers in thousands)

		Asian		
	total	number	percent with condition	share of total
Total children	**74,518**	**3,455**	**100.0%**	**4.6%**
Ever told have asthma	10,463	419	12.1	4.0
Still have asthma	7,074	240	6.9	3.4
Hay fever in past 12 months	6,711	347	10.0	5.2
Respiratory allergies in past 12 months	8,269	228	6.6	2.8
Food allergies in past 12 months	4,126	244	7.1	5.9
Skin allergies in past 12 months	9,516	463	13.4	4.9
Prescription medication taken regularly for at least three months	10,019	230	6.7	2.3
Learning disability*	4,660	147	4.3	3.2
Attention deficit hyperactivity disorder*	5,240	81	2.3	1.5

* Diagnosed by a school representative or health professional; data exclude children under age 3.
Note: Asians are those who identify themselves as being of the race alone.
Source: National Center for Health Statistics, Summary Health Statistics for U.S. Children: National Health Interview Survey, 2011, Vital and Health Statistics, Series 10, No. 254, 2012, Internet site http://www.cdc.gov/nchs/nhis.htm

Table 3.27 Health Care Office Visits by Total People and Asians, 2011

(number of total people and Asians aged 18 or older by visits to a health care provider in the past 12 months, percent distribution of Asians by number of visits, and Asian share of total, 2011; numbers in thousands)

		Asian		
	total	number	percent distribution	share of total
Total people	**231,376**	**11,468**	**100.0%**	**5.0%**
No visits	43,578	2,827	20.2	6.5
One visit	39,552	2,379	17.0	6.0
Two to three visits	59,226	2,882	26.4	4.9
Four to nine visits	55,721	2,371	22.4	4.3
10 or more visits	30,822	902	12.7	2.9

Note: Health care visits exclude overnight hospitalizations, visits to emergency rooms, home visits, dental visits, and telephone calls. Asians are those who identify themselves as being of the race alone. Numbers may not add to total because "unknown" is not shown.
Source: National Center for Health Statistics, Summary Health Statistics for U.S. Adults: National Health Interview Survey, 2011, Vital and Health Statistics, Series 10, No. 256, 2012, Internet site http://www.cdc.gov/nchs/nhis.htm; calculations by New Strategist

Table 3.28 Difficulties in Physical Functioning among Total People and Asians, 2011

(number of total people and Asians aged 18 or older, number with difficulties in physical functioning, percentage of Asians with difficulty, and Asian share of total, by type of difficulty, 2011; numbers in thousands)

		Asian		
	total	number	percent	share of total
TOTAL PEOPLE	**231,376**	**11,468**	**100.0%**	**5.0%**
Total with any physical difficulty	**37,368**	**1,054**	**10.1**	**2.8**
Walk quarter of a mile	17,597	394	4.0	2.2
Climb 10 steps without resting	12,887	306	3.1	2.4
Stand for two hours	22,369	593	5.9	2.7
Sit for two hours	7,724	191	1.8	2.5
Stoop, bend, or kneel	21,677	504	5.0	2.3
Reach over head	6,550	206	2.1	3.1
Grasp or handle small objects	4,329	118	1.2	2.7
Lift or carry 10 pounds	10,677	441	4.3	4.1
Push or pull large objects	15,998	552	5.4	3.5

Note: Respondents were classified as having difficulties if they responded "very difficult" or "can't do at all." Asians are those who identify themselves as being Asian alone.
Source: National Center for Health Statistics, Summary Health Statistics for U.S. Adults: National Health Interview Survey, 2011, Vital and Health Statistics, Series 10, No. 256, 2012, Internet site http://www.cdc.gov/nchs/nhis.htm; calculations by New Strategist

Table 3.29 AIDS Cases among Total People and Asians, through December 2009

(number of total AIDS cases diagnosed, number and percent distribution among Asians, and Asian share of total, by sex, through December 2009)

		Asian		
	total	number	percent distribution	share of total
Total diagnosed with AIDS	**1,108,611**	**8,324**	**100.0%**	**0.8%**
Males aged 13 or older	878,366	7,068	84.9	0.8
Females aged 13 or older	220,795	1,208	14.5	0.5
Children under age 13	9,448	48	0.6	0.5

Note: Asians include Pacific Islanders.
Source: National Center for Health Statistics, Health United States 2011, Internet site http://www.cdc.gov/nchs/hus.htm; calculations by New Strategist

Table 3.30 Leading Causes of Death among Asians, 2009

(number and percent distribution of deaths to Asians accounted for by the 10 leading causes of death among Asians, 2009)

		number	percent distribution
Total Asian deaths		**49,225**	**100.0%**
1.	Malignant neoplasms (cancer) (2)	13,274	27.0
2.	Diseases of the heart (1)	11,375	23.1
3.	Cerebrovascular diseases (4)	3,639	7.4
4.	Accidents (unintentional injuries) (5)	2,044	4.2
5.	Diabetes mellitus (7)	1,846	3.8
6.	Influenza and pneumonia (8)	1,568	3.2
7.	Chronic lower respiratory disease (3)	1,480	3.0
8.	Nephritis, nephrotic syndrome, and nephrosis (9)	1,062	2.2
9.	Alzheimer's disease (6)	1,024	2.1
10.	Suicide (10)	971	2.0
	All other causes	10,942	22.2

Note: Number in parentheses shows rank for all Americans if the cause of death is in top 10. Asians include Pacific Islanders.
Source: National Center for Health Statistics, Deaths: Leading Causes for 2009, National Vital Statistics Report, Vol. 61, No. 7, 2012, Internet site http://www.cdc.gov/nchs/deaths.htm; calculations by New Strategist

Asians: Housing

More than Half of Asian Households Own Their Home

Asian households are less likely than the average household to own a home. In 2012, 57 percent of Asian households owned their home versus 65 percent of all households. Although Asians are less likely than average to own a home, they are more likely to do so than blacks or Hispanics. The majority of Asian households own their home in every region.

Asian homeowners report that their homes are worth a median of $368,800, according to the American Community Survey. This value is far higher than the $188,400 median for all homeowners. More than three out of four Asian homeowners have a mortgage. Among those who do, median monthly housing costs are $2,260, a much higher sum than the median of $1,524 for all homeowners with a mortgage. Asian renters pay a median monthly rent of $1,056, more than the $841 monthly rent of the average renter.

■ Asians are more likely to be homeowners than blacks or Hispanics because they are better educated and earn higher incomes.

Asian homeownership is highest in the South

(percent of Asian households that own their home, by region, 2011)

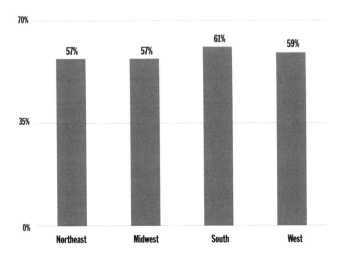

Table 3.31 Total and Asian Homeownership Rate, 2000 to 2012

(homeownership rate of total and Asian households and index of Asian to total, 2000 to 2012; percentage point change for selected years)

	total households	Asian households	index, Asian to total
2012	65.4%	56.6%	87
2011	66.1	58.0	88
2010	66.9	58.9	88
2009	67.4	59.3	88
2008	67.8	59.5	88
2007	68.1	60.0	88
2006	68.8	60.8	88
2005	68.9	60.1	87
2004	69.0	59.8	87
2003	68.3	56.3	82
2002	67.9	54.6	80
2001	67.8	53.9	79
2000	67.4	52.8	78

PERCENTAGE POINT CHANGE

2004 to 2012	−3.6	−3.2	–
2000 to 2012	−2.0	3.8	–

Note: Asians include Native Hawaiians and Pacific Islanders and are those who identify themselves as being of the race alone. The index is calculated by dividing the Asian homeownership rate by the total rate and multiplying by 100. "–" means not applicable.
Source: Bureau of the Census, Housing Vacancies and Homeownership, Internet site http://www.census.gov/housing/hvs/; calculations by New Strategist

Table 3.32 Asian Homeownership Status by Age of Householder, 2010

(number and percent of Asian households by age of householder and homeownership status, 2010; numbers in thousands)

	total	owner number	owner percent	renter number	renter percent
Total Asian households	**5,223**	**2,994**	**57.3%**	**2,229**	**42.7%**
Under age 25	271	33	12.2	238	87.8
Aged 25 to 34	1,083	377	34.8	707	65.3
Aged 35 to 44	1,284	786	61.2	497	38.7
Aged 45 to 54	1,117	777	69.6	340	30.4
Aged 55 to 64	790	578	73.2	211	26.7
Aged 65 to 74	404	283	70.0	121	30.0
Aged 75 or older	274	159	58.0	115	42.0

Note: Asians are those who identify themselves as being of the race alone and those who identify themselves as being of the race in combination with other races.
Source: Bureau of the Census, 2010 Census, Internet site http://factfinder2.census.gov/faces/nav/jsf/pages/index.xhtml; calculations by New Strategist

Table 3.33 Total and Asian Homeowners by Age of Householder, 2010

(number of total homeowners, number and percent distribution of Asian homeowners, and Asian share of total, by age of householder, 2010; numbers in thousands)

	total	Asian number	Asian percent distribution	share of total
Total homeowners	**75,986**	**2,994**	**100.0%**	**3.9%**
Under age 25	870	33	1.1	3.8
Aged 25 to 34	7,547	377	12.6	5.0
Aged 35 to 44	13,256	786	26.3	5.9
Aged 45 to 54	17,804	777	26.0	4.4
Aged 55 to 64	16,503	578	19.3	3.5
Aged 65 to 74	10,834	283	9.5	2.6
Aged 75 or older	9,173	159	5.3	1.7

Note: Asians are those who identify themselves as being of the race alone and those who identify themselves as being of the race in combination with other races.
Source: Bureau of the Census, 2010 Census, Internet site http://factfinder2.census.gov/faces/nav/jsf/pages/index.xhtml; calculations by New Strategist

Table 3.34 Total and Asian Renters by Age of Householder, 2010

(number of total renters, number and percent distribution of Asian renters, and Asian share of total, by age of householder, 2010; numbers in thousands)

		Asian		
	total	number	percent distribution	share of total
Total renters	**40,730**	**2,229**	**100.0%**	**5.5%**
Under age 25	4,531	238	10.7	5.3
Aged 25 to 34	10,410	707	31.7	6.8
Aged 35 to 44	8,035	497	22.3	6.2
Aged 45 to 54	7,103	340	15.3	4.8
Aged 55 to 64	4,838	211	9.5	4.4
Aged 65 to 74	2,670	121	5.4	4.5
Aged 75 or older	3,143	115	5.2	3.7

Note: Asians are those who identify themselves as being of the race alone and those who identify themselves as being of the race in combination with other races.
Source: Bureau of the Census, 2010 Census, Internet site http://factfinder2.census.gov/faces/nav/jsf/pages/index.xhtml; calculations by New Strategist

Table 3.35 Asian Homeownership Status by Household Type, 2010

(number and percent of Asian households by household type and homeownership status, 2010; numbers in thousands)

		owner		renter	
	total	number	percent	number	percent
Total Asian households	**5,223**	**2,994**	**57.3%**	**2,229**	**42.7%**
Family households	3,819	2,514	65.8	1,305	34.2
Married couples	3,043	2,102	69.1	941	30.9
Female-headed family, no spouse present	523	275	52.7	247	47.3
Male-headed family, no spouse present	253	137	53.9	117	46.1
Nonfamily households	1,404	480	34.2	924	65.8
Female householder	707	265	37.6	441	62.4
Living alone	530	217	41.0	313	59.0
Male householder	697	214	30.7	483	69.3
Living alone	477	161	33.8	316	66.2

Note: Asians are those who identify themselves as being of the race alone and those who identify themselves as being of the race in combination with other races.
Source: Bureau of the Census, 2010 Census, Internet site http://factfinder2.census.gov/faces/nav/jsf/pages/index.xhtml; calculations by New Strategist

Table 3.36 Total and Asian Homeowners by Household Type, 2010

(number of total homeowners, number and percent distribution of Asian homeowners, and Asian share of total, by household type, 2010; numbers in thousands)

		Asian		
	total	number	percent distribution	share of total
Total homeowners	**75,986**	**2,994**	**100.0%**	**3.9%**
Family households	56,206	2,514	84.0	4.5
Married couples	45,801	2,102	70.2	4.6
Female-headed family, no spouse present	7,278	275	9.2	3.8
Male-headed family, no spouse present	3,127	137	4.6	4.4
Nonfamily households	19,780	480	16.0	2.4
Female householder	11,053	265	8.9	2.4
Living alone	9,625	217	7.3	2.3
Male householder	8,727	214	7.2	2.5
Living alone	6,828	161	5.4	2.4

Note: Asians are those who identify themselves as being of the race alone and those who identify themselves as being of the race in combination with other races.
Source: Bureau of the Census, 2010 Census, Internet site http://factfinder2.census.gov/faces/nav/jsf/pages/index.xhtml; calculations by New Strategist

Table 3.37 Total and Asian Renters by Household Type, 2010

(number of total renters, number and percent distribution of Asian renters, and Asian share of total, by household type, 2010; numbers in thousands)

	total	Asian number	Asian percent distribution	Asian share of total
Total renters	**40,730**	**2,229**	**100.0%**	**5.5%**
Family households	21,332	1,305	58.5	6.1
Married couples	10,710	941	42.2	8.8
Female-headed family, no spouse present	7,972	247	11.1	3.1
Male-headed family, no spouse present	2,651	117	5.2	4.4
Nonfamily households	19,398	924	41.5	4.8
Female householder	9,666	441	19.8	4.6
Living alone	7,673	313	14.0	4.1
Male householder	9,732	483	21.7	5.0
Living alone	7,078	316	14.2	4.5

Note: Asians are those who identify themselves as being of the race alone and those who identify themselves as being of the race in combination with other races.
Source: Bureau of the Census, 2010 Census, Internet site http://factfinder2.census.gov/faces/nav/jsf/pages/index.xhtml; calculations by New Strategist

Table 3.38 Asian Homeownership Status by Region, 2011

(number and percent of Asian households by homeownership status and region, 2011; numbers in thousands)

	total	owners		renters	
		number	share of total	number	share of total
Total Asian households	**4,620**	**2,714**	**58.7%**	**1,907**	**41.3%**
Northeast	1,019	580	56.9	439	43.1
Midwest	547	313	57.2	234	42.8
South	908	558	61.5	350	38.5
West	2,146	1,262	58.8	884	41.2

Note: Asians are those who identify themselves as being of the race alone.
Source: Bureau of the Census, American Housing Survey for the United States: 2011, Internet site http://www.census.gov/ housing/ahs/index.html; calculations by New Strategist

Table 3.39 Total and Asian Homeowners by Region, 2011

(number of total homeowners, number and percent distribution of Asian homeowners, and Asian share of total, by region, 2011; numbers in thousands)

	total	Asian		
		number	percent distribution	share of total
Total homeowners	**76,091**	**2,714**	**100.0%**	**3.6%**
Northeast	13,480	580	21.4	4.3
Midwest	18,032	313	11.5	1.7
South	29,119	558	20.6	1.9
West	15,460	1,262	46.5	8.2

Note: Asians are those who identify themselves as being of the race alone.
Source: Bureau of the Census, American Housing Survey for the United States: 2011, Internet site http://www.census.gov/ housing/ahs/index.html; calculations by New Strategist

Table 3.40 Total and Asian Renters by Region, 2011

(number of total renters, number and percent distribution of Asian renters, and Asian share of total, by region, 2011; numbers in thousands)

	total	Asian number	Asian percent distribution	Asian share of total
Total renters	**38,816**	**1,907**	**100.0%**	**4.9%**
Northeast	7,585	439	23.0	5.8
Midwest	7,650	234	12.3	3.1
South	13,465	350	18.4	2.6
West	10,115	884	46.4	8.7

Note: Asians are those who identify themselves as being of the race alone.
Source: Bureau of the Census, American Housing Survey for the United States: 2011, Internet site http://www.census.gov/housing/ahs/index.html; calculations by New Strategist

Table 3.41 Characteristics of Total and Asian Occupied Housing Units, 2006–10

(number of total and Asian occupied housing units, and percent distribution by selected characteristics, 2006–10; numbers in thousands)

	total		Asian	
	number	percent distribution	number	percent distribution
TOTAL OCCUPIED HOUSING UNITS	**114,236**	**100.0%**	**4,903**	**100.0%**
Year householder moved into unit				
Total households	**114,236**	**100.0**	**4,903**	**100.0**
2005 or later	39,766	34.8	2,198	44.8
2000 to 2004	26,517	23.2	1,272	25.9
1990 to 1999	23,883	20.9	873	17.8
1980 to 1989	10,804	9.5	339	6.9
1970 to 1979	7,147	6.3	146	3.0
Before 1970	6,120	5.4	75	1.5
Vehicles available				
Total households	**114,236**	**100.0**	**4,903**	**100.0**
None	10,113	8.9	543	11.1
One or more	104,123	91.1	4,360	88.9
House heating fuel				
Total households	**114,236**	**100.0**	**4,903**	**100.0**
Utility gas	57,018	49.9	2,880	58.7
Bottled gas	6,146	5.4	94	1.9
Electricity	39,066	34.2	1,547	31.6
Fuel oil or kerosene	8,073	7.1	191	3.9
Coal or coke	135	0.1	1	0.0
Wood	2,250	2.0	10	0.2
Solar energy	38	0.0	5	0.1
Other fuel	483	0.4	12	0.2
No heating fuel used	1,025	0.9	163	3.3
TOTAL OWNER-OCCUPIED HOMES	**76,090**	**100.0**	**2,877**	**100.0**
Housing units with a mortgage	51,697	67.9	2,255	78.4
Housing units without a mortgage	24,393	32.1	622	21.6
Median value of home	$188,400	–	$368,800	–
Median monthly owner costs with a mortgage	1,524	–	2,260	–
Median monthly owner costs without a mortgage	431	–	552	–
TOTAL RENTER-OCCUPIED HOMES	**38,146**	**100.0**	**2,026**	**100.0**
Occupied units paying rent	35,274	92.5	1,952	96.3
Median rent	$841	–	$1,056	–

Note: Asians are those who identify themselves as being of the race alone and those who identify themselves as being of the race in combination with other races. "–" means not applicable.
Source: Bureau of the Census, 2006–10 American Community Survey, Internet site http://factfinder2.census.gov/faces/nav/jsf/pages/index.xhtml; calculations by New Strategist

Table 3.42 Geographic Mobility of Asians by Age, 2011–12

(total number of Asians aged 1 or older, and number and percent who moved between March 2011 and March 2012, by age and type of move; numbers in thousands)

	total	same house (nonmovers)	total movers	same county	different county, same state	different state total	same region	different region	movers from abroad
Total Asians	17,572	15,303	2,269	1,101	387	425	190	235	356
Aged 1 to 4	1,081	905	176	75	28	49	26	23	25
Aged 5 to 9	1,345	1,209	136	66	22	32	16	16	15
Aged 10 to 14	1,172	1,069	103	50	27	15	2	13	11
Aged 15 to 17	734	676	58	24	10	7	1	6	17
Aged 18 to 19	464	402	62	33	12	4	0	4	13
Aged 20 to 24	1,377	1,000	377	194	38	49	22	27	96
Aged 25 to 29	1,467	1,047	420	200	58	92	58	34	70
Aged 30 to 34	1,477	1,217	260	126	27	72	30	42	34
Aged 35 to 39	1,458	1,265	193	94	35	41	6	35	24
Aged 40 to 44	1,340	1,233	107	47	31	15	7	8	14
Aged 45 to 49	1,198	1,074	124	66	24	17	0	17	17
Aged 50 to 54	1,122	1,043	79	33	29	6	3	3	10
Aged 55 to 59	969	910	59	31	18	5	5	0	5
Aged 60 to 61	340	330	10	2	2	2	2	0	4
Aged 62 to 64	448	424	24	16	6	0	0	0	2
Aged 65 or older	1,581	1,499	82	44	20	16	10	6	0

PERCENT DISTRIBUTION BY MOBILITY STATUS

Total Asians	100.0%	87.1%	12.9%	6.3%	2.2%	2.4%	1.1%	1.3%	2.0%
Aged 1 to 4	100.0	83.7	16.3	6.9	2.6	4.5	2.4	2.1	2.3
Aged 5 to 9	100.0	89.9	10.1	4.9	1.6	2.4	1.2	1.2	1.1
Aged 10 to 14	100.0	91.2	8.8	4.3	2.3	1.3	0.2	1.1	0.9
Aged 15 to 17	100.0	92.1	7.9	3.3	1.4	1.0	0.1	0.8	2.3
Aged 18 to 19	100.0	86.6	13.4	7.1	2.6	0.9	0.0	0.9	2.8
Aged 20 to 24	100.0	72.6	27.4	14.1	2.8	3.6	1.6	2.0	7.0
Aged 25 to 29	100.0	71.4	28.6	13.6	4.0	6.3	4.0	2.3	4.8
Aged 30 to 34	100.0	82.4	17.6	8.5	1.8	4.9	2.0	2.8	2.3
Aged 35 to 39	100.0	86.8	13.2	6.4	2.4	2.8	0.4	2.4	1.6
Aged 40 to 44	100.0	92.0	8.0	3.5	2.3	1.1	0.5	0.6	1.0
Aged 45 to 49	100.0	89.6	10.4	5.5	2.0	1.4	0.0	1.4	1.4
Aged 50 to 54	100.0	93.0	7.0	2.9	2.6	0.5	0.3	0.3	0.9
Aged 55 to 59	100.0	93.9	6.1	3.2	1.9	0.5	0.5	0.0	0.5
Aged 60 to 61	100.0	97.1	2.9	0.6	0.6	0.6	0.6	0.0	1.2
Aged 62 to 64	100.0	94.6	5.4	3.6	1.3	0.0	0.0	0.0	0.4
Aged 65 or older	100.0	94.8	5.2	2.8	1.3	1.0	0.6	0.4	0.0

Note: Asians are those who identify themselves as being of the race alone and those who identify themselves as being of the race in combination with other races.
Source: Bureau of the Census, Geographic Mobility: 2011 to 2012, Internet site http://www.census.gov/hhes/migration/data/cps/cps2012.html; calculations by New Strategist

Table 3.43 Reasons for Moving among Asian Movers, 2011–12

(number and percent distribution of Asian movers by main reason for move, 2011–12; numbers in thousands)

	number	percent distribution
Total Asian movers	2,269	100.0%
FAMILY REASONS	494	21.8
Change in marital status	95	4.2
To establish own household	151	6.7
Other family reason	248	10.9
EMPLOYMENT REASONS	665	29.3
New job or job transfer	374	16.5
To look for work or lost job	50	2.2
To be closer to work, easier commute	156	6.9
Retired	22	1.0
Other job-related reason	63	2.8
HOUSING REASONS	1,014	44.7
Wanted own home, not rent	132	5.8
Wanted new or better home/apartment	288	12.7
Wanted better neighborhood, less crime	58	2.6
Wanted cheaper housing	145	6.4
Foreclosure, eviction	26	1.1
Other housing reason	365	16.1
OTHER REASONS	94	4.1
To attend or leave college	49	2.2
Change of climate	0	0.0
Health reasons	14	0.6
Natural disaster	2	0.1
Other reason	29	1.3

Note: Asians are those who identify themselves as being of the race alone and those who identify themselves as being of the race in combination with other races.
Source: Bureau of the Census, Geographic Mobility: 2011 to 2012, Internet site http://www.census.gov/hhes/migration/data/cps/cps2012.html; calculations by New Strategist

Asians Have the Highest Incomes

The $64,995 median income of Asian households in 2011 was 30 percent greater than the all-household average and higher than that of any other racial or ethnic group. Since 2000, Asian households have lost ground, their median income declining by a substantial 11 percent after adjusting for inflation. During those years, the average household saw its median income decline by a slightly smaller 9 percent.

Among Asian households, median income peaks at more than $80,000 for householders aged 35 to 54. By household type, Asian married couples have the highest median—$81,842 in 2011. Nearly 31 percent of Asian households had incomes of $100,000 or more in 2011.

Among full-time workers, the median earnings of Asian men and women rose 3 percent between 2000 and 2011, after adjusting for inflation. Between 2007 and 2011, however, the median earnings of Asian men fell slightly (down 0.1 percent) and the earnings of Asian women fell by a much larger 6 percent.

Asians are less likely to be poor than blacks or Hispanics, but more likely to be poor than non-Hispanic whites. The poverty rate of Asian married couples stood at 7.7 percent in 2011. Among Asian female-headed families, the poverty rate was 21.4 percent, much higher than the 14.0 percent poverty rate among Asian male-headed families.

■ Asian households have higher incomes than black, Hispanic, and non-Hispanic white households because Asians are much better educated and their households include more earners.

Asian household income fell more than average between 2000 and 2011

(percent change in total and Asian median household income, 2000 to 2011; in 2011 dollars)

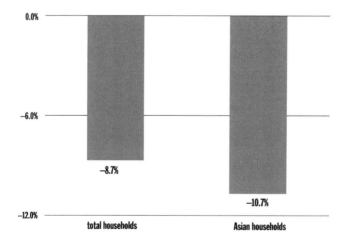

total households	−8.7%
Asian households	−10.7%

Table 3.44 Median Income of Total and Asian Households, 1990 to 2011

(median income of total and Asian households, and index of Asian to total, 1990 to 2011; percent change in median for selected years; in 2011 dollars)

	total households	Asian households	index, Asian to total
2011	$50,054	$64,995	130
2010	50,830	65,531	129
2009	52,195	68,234	131
2008	52,546	68,491	130
2007	54,489	71,458	131
2006	53,768	71,281	133
2005	53,371	70,332	132
2004	52,788	68,404	130
2003	52,973	67,579	128
2002	53,019	65,366	123
2001	53,646	68,137	127
2000	54,841	72,821	133
1999	54,932	68,787	125
1998	53,582	64,265	120
1997	51,704	63,222	122
1996	50,661	61,772	122
1995	49,935	59,516	119
1994	48,418	60,751	125
1993	47,884	58,775	123
1992	48,117	59,371	123
1991	48,516	58,699	121
1990	49,950	64,142	128

Percent change

2007 to 2011	−8.1%	−9.0%	–
2000 to 2011	−8.7	−10.7	–
1990 to 2011	0.2	1.3	–

Note: Beginning in 2002, Asians are those who identify themselves as being of the race alone and those who identify themselves as being of the race in combination with other races. The index is calculated by dividing the Asian median by the total median and multiplying by 100. "–" means not applicable.
Source: Bureau of the Census, Current Population Surveys, Annual Social and Economic Supplement, Internet site http://www .census.gov/hhes/www/income/data/historical/household/index.html; calculations by New Strategist

Table 3.45 Asian Household Income by Age of Householder, 2011

(number and percent distribution of Asian households by household income and age of householder, 2011; households in thousands as of 2012)

							65 or older		
	total	15 to 24	25 to 34	35 to 44	45 to 54	55 to 64	total	65 to 74	75 or older
Asian households	**5,705**	**407**	**1,249**	**1,324**	**1,138**	**855**	**731**	**424**	**308**
Under $5,000	248	89	47	26	23	28	35	18	17
$5,000 to $9,999	142	21	30	20	20	17	35	14	22
$10,000 to $14,999	222	26	27	32	34	30	74	29	45
$15,000 to $19,999	247	34	48	43	25	37	59	33	26
$20,000 to $24,999	262	29	62	47	49	33	42	21	21
$25,000 to $29,999	210	18	41	25	43	35	47	17	30
$30,000 to $34,999	258	25	74	56	44	18	40	22	18
$35,000 to $39,999	245	30	48	36	45	43	42	28	14
$40,000 to $44,999	194	12	41	49	29	26	37	20	17
$45,000 to $49,999	200	6	36	51	50	29	27	18	9
$50,000 to $54,999	236	20	50	49	47	43	28	16	12
$55,000 to $59,999	171	11	47	41	24	29	20	13	7
$60,000 to $64,999	218	29	54	60	24	31	21	17	4
$65,000 to $69,999	184	7	37	40	35	37	27	22	5
$70,000 to $74,999	175	4	40	49	34	30	19	11	7
$75,000 to $79,999	159	6	45	33	42	23	10	8	2
$80,000 to $84,999	194	3	63	48	39	29	11	11	0
$85,000 to $89,999	136	0	36	32	33	19	15	6	9
$90,000 to $94,999	124	1	34	30	32	21	6	4	2
$95,000 to $99,999	116	5	15	43	29	16	9	5	5
$100,000 to $124,999	606	19	138	169	146	90	47	36	10
$125,000 to $149,999	380	4	84	89	101	70	31	22	9
$150,000 to $174,999	218	4	49	60	50	43	13	7	6
$175,000 to $199,999	154	0	33	45	40	24	13	8	5
$200,000 or more	403	4	73	150	99	53	23	19	5
Median income	$64,995	$25,855	$67,721	$80,265	$80,138	$68,636	$38,938	$48,340	$28,969

PERCENT DISTRIBUTION

							65 or older		
Asian households	**100.0%**	**100.0%**	**100.0%**	**100.0%**	**100.0%**	**100.0%**	**100.0%**	**100.0%**	**100.0%**
Under $25,000	19.6	48.9	17.1	12.7	13.3	17.0	33.5	27.1	42.5
$25,000 to $49,999	19.4	22.4	19.2	16.4	18.5	17.7	26.4	24.8	28.6
$50,000 to $74,999	17.2	17.4	18.3	18.1	14.4	19.9	15.7	18.6	11.4
$75,000 to $99,999	12.8	3.7	15.5	14.0	15.4	12.6	7.0	8.0	5.8
$100,000 or more	30.9	7.6	30.2	38.7	38.3	32.7	17.4	21.7	11.4

Note: Asians are those who identify themselves as being of the race alone and those who identify themselves as being of the race in combination with other races.
Source: Bureau of the Census, 2012 Current Population Survey, Internet site http://www.census.gov/hhes/www/income/data/incpovhlth/2011/dtables.html; calculations by New Strategist

Table 3.46 Asian Household Income by Household Type, 2011

(number and percent distribution of Asian households by household income and household type, 2011; households in thousands as of 2012)

| | total | family households | | | nonfamily households | | | |
| | | married couples | female hh, no spouse present | male hh, no spouse present | female householder | | male householder | |
					total	living alone	total	living alone
Asian households	**5,705**	**3,435**	**573**	**334**	**685**	**534**	**677**	**480**
Under $5,000	248	54	37	8	74	50	75	44
$5,000 to $9,999	142	31	18	3	56	52	35	31
$10,000 to $14,999	222	72	28	12	64	54	45	39
$15,000 to $19,999	247	98	38	17	38	37	56	51
$20,000 to $24,999	262	124	24	32	33	33	50	45
$25,000 to $29,999	210	99	29	20	40	35	22	21
$30,000 to $34,999	258	105	39	15	57	48	42	25
$35,000 to $39,999	245	136	30	14	41	37	23	17
$40,000 to $44,999	194	101	27	6	31	24	30	19
$45,000 to $49,999	200	125	39	7	12	10	17	13
$50,000 to $54,999	236	143	23	16	27	17	28	20
$55,000 to $59,999	171	105	17	20	18	11	11	11
$60,000 to $64,999	218	115	20	20	35	29	28	26
$65,000 to $69,999	184	133	20	7	13	9	11	4
$70,000 to $74,999	175	115	19	12	20	17	10	8
$75,000 to $79,999	159	101	12	10	21	15	16	12
$80,000 to $84,999	194	125	13	8	17	4	31	22
$85,000 to $89,999	136	113	8	7	4	3	5	5
$90,000 to $94,999	124	79	11	3	16	12	15	11
$95,000 to $99,999	116	85	12	8	8	7	3	2
$100,000 to $124,999	608	433	52	35	30	19	58	31
$125,000 to $149,999	381	291	24	31	9	3	26	8
$150,000 to $174,999	218	175	13	13	6	4	11	2
$175,000 to $199,999	154	127	11	4	1	1	11	3
$200,000 or more	403	351	12	6	14	3	20	11
Median income	$64,995	$81,842	$47,171	$59,645	$32,571	$30,584	$37,496	$31,093

PERCENT DISTRIBUTION

Asian households	**100.0%**	**100.0%**	**100.0%**	**100.0%**	**100.0%**	**100.0%**	**100.0%**	**100.0%**
Under $25,000	19.6	11.0	25.1	21.4	38.7	42.2	38.5	43.9
$25,000 to $49,999	19.4	16.4	28.7	18.7	26.4	28.9	19.7	19.7
$50,000 to $74,999	17.3	17.8	17.3	22.2	16.6	15.4	13.0	14.5
$75,000 to $99,999	12.8	14.7	9.6	10.7	9.6	7.9	10.3	10.8
$100,000 or more	30.9	40.1	19.4	27.0	8.7	5.7	18.6	11.1

Note: Asians are those who identify themselves as being of the race alone and those who identify themselves as being of the race in combination with other races. "hh" stands for householder.
Source: Bureau of the Census, 2012 Current Population Survey, Internet site http://www.census.gov/hhes/www/income/data/ incpovhlth/2011/dtables.html; calculations by New Strategist

Table 3.47 Income of Asian Men by Age, 2011

(number and percent distribution of Asian men aged 15 or older by income and age, 2011; median income of men with income and of men working full-time, year-round; percent working full-time, year-round; men in thousands as of 2012)

	total	under 25	25 to 34	35 to 44	45 to 54	55 to 64	65 or older
TOTAL ASIAN MEN	6,578	1,310	1,403	1,305	1,102	778	681
Without income	1,022	650	158	64	81	38	31
With income	5,556	660	1,245	1,240	1,022	740	650
Under $5,000	397	187	63	37	34	34	42
$5,000 to $9,999	479	161	77	35	43	59	106
$10,000 to $14,999	394	75	60	60	52	59	88
$15,000 to $19,999	396	50	92	67	58	63	66
$20,000 to $24,999	451	66	106	78	80	57	63
$25,000 to $29,999	266	27	68	40	51	34	47
$30,000 to $34,999	332	27	81	68	60	56	40
$35,000 to $39,999	257	11	101	58	34	33	20
$40,000 to $44,999	211	8	51	52	50	32	19
$45,000 to $49,999	196	6	51	52	42	23	22
$50,000 to $54,999	246	13	77	54	56	30	17
$55,000 to $59,999	149	1	25	48	38	22	16
$60,000 to $64,999	201	9	49	73	31	21	17
$65,000 to $69,999	100	0	37	19	24	15	5
$70,000 to $74,999	160	2	36	56	29	31	6
$75,000 to $79,999	129	0	41	32	35	11	10
$80,000 to $84,999	158	2	32	66	38	17	3
$85,000 to $89,999	76	0	24	17	23	8	4
$90,000 to $94,999	99	2	21	30	22	19	4
$95,000 to $99,999	81	4	14	25	21	11	5
$100,000 or more	776	9	140	273	200	105	48
MEDIAN INCOME							
Men with income	$35,835	$9,278	$37,841	$56,248	$50,304	$36,100	$21,757
Working full-time	56,088	27,870	51,164	62,329	58,078	55,625	56,479
Percent full-time	52.2%	12.1%	61.3%	76.7%	73.4%	61.6%	18.6%
PERCENT DISTRIBUTION							
TOTAL ASIAN MEN	100.0%	100.0%	100.0%	100.0%	100.0%	100.0%	100.0%
Without income	15.5	49.6	11.2	4.9	7.3	4.9	4.5
With income	84.5	50.4	88.8	95.1	92.7	95.1	95.5
Under $15,000	19.3	32.3	14.2	10.1	11.6	19.5	34.7
$15,000 to $24,999	12.9	8.8	14.1	11.1	12.6	15.5	19.0
$25,000 to $34,999	9.1	4.1	10.6	8.3	10.1	11.5	12.7
$35,000 to $49,999	10.1	1.9	14.4	12.4	11.5	11.3	8.9
$50,000 to $74,999	13.0	1.9	16.0	19.2	16.1	15.2	9.0
$75,000 or more	20.1	1.3	19.4	34.0	30.8	22.0	11.1

Note: Asians are those who identify themselves as being of the race alone and those who identify themselves as being of the race in combination with other races.
Source: Bureau of the Census, 2012 Current Population Survey Annual Social and Economic Supplement, Internet site http:// www.census.gov/hhes/www/cpstables/032012/perinc/toc.htm; calculations by New Strategist

Table 3.48 Income of Asian Women by Age, 2011

(number and percent distribution of Asian women aged 15 or older by income and age, 2011; median income of women with income and of women working full-time, year-round; percent working full-time, year-round; women in thousands as of 2012)

	total	under 25	25 to 34	35 to 44	45 to 54	55 to 64	65 or older
TOTAL ASIAN WOMEN	**7,397**	**1,265**	**1,542**	**1,494**	**1,217**	**978**	**900**
Without income	**1,576**	**551**	**334**	**246**	**179**	**162**	**104**
With income	**5,820**	**714**	**1,208**	**1,248**	**1,038**	**816**	**796**
Under $5,000	844	267	135	173	109	94	66
$5,000 to $9,999	738	142	101	77	77	88	254
$10,000 to $14,999	601	100	75	103	84	74	164
$15,000 to $19,999	466	49	87	102	95	65	68
$20,000 to $24,999	489	42	109	91	97	99	52
$25,000 to $29,999	351	21	94	71	72	52	41
$30,000 to $34,999	359	25	102	79	82	48	23
$35,000 to $39,999	254	14	59	61	58	34	27
$40,000 to $44,999	261	19	78	63	53	33	14
$45,000 to $49,999	171	13	48	31	44	22	12
$50,000 to $54,999	192	3	58	46	35	33	16
$55,000 to $59,999	98	7	25	24	16	15	11
$60,000 to $64,999	153	5	41	37	29	32	8
$65,000 to $69,999	74	0	22	23	11	18	1
$70,000 to $74,999	85	0	27	20	16	14	7
$75,000 to $79,999	102	0	21	34	28	12	7
$80,000 to $84,999	87	0	20	31	15	18	4
$85,000 to $89,999	45	0	10	20	10	3	2
$90,000 to $94,999	59	0	15	18	12	12	2
$95,000 to $99,999	28	0	2	12	10	2	2
$100,000 or more	364	7	77	131	87	48	14
MEDIAN INCOME							
Women with income	$22,013	$7,622	$30,083	$30,303	$28,601	$24,232	$12,050
Working full-time	41,687	26,983	43,979	47,839	40,579	40,618	–
Percent full-time	35.2%	9.5%	43.2%	48.4%	51.0%	42.2%	6.9%
PERCENT DISTRIBUTION							
TOTAL ASIAN WOMEN	**100.0%**	**100.0%**	**100.0%**	**100.0%**	**100.0%**	**100.0%**	**100.0%**
Without income	**21.3**	**43.6**	**21.7**	**16.5**	**14.7**	**16.6**	**11.6**
With income	**78.7**	**56.4**	**78.3**	**83.5**	**85.3**	**83.4**	**88.4**
Under $15,000	29.5	40.2	20.2	23.7	22.2	26.1	53.8
$15,000 to $24,999	12.9	7.2	12.7	12.9	15.8	16.8	13.3
$25,000 to $34,999	9.6	3.6	12.8	10.0	12.6	10.2	7.1
$35,000 to $49,999	9.3	3.6	12.1	10.4	12.8	9.1	6.0
$50,000 to $74,999	8.1	1.2	11.2	10.1	8.8	11.5	4.8
$75,000 or more	9.3	0.5	9.4	16.5	13.2	9.7	3.4

Note: Asians are those who identify themselves as being of the race alone and those who identify themselves as being of the race in combination with other races. "–" means sample is too small to make a reliable estimate.
Source: Bureau of the Census, 2012 Current Population Survey Annual Social and Economic Supplement, Internet site http:// www.census.gov/hhes/www/cpstables/032012/perinc/toc.htm; calculations by New Strategist

Table 3.49 Median Earnings of Asians Working Full-Time by Sex, 1990 to 2011

(median earnings of Asians working full-time, year-round by sex; index of Asian to total population median earnings, and Asian women's earnings as a percent of Asian men's earnings, 1990 to 2011; percent change in earnings for selected years; in 2011 dollars)

	Asian men			Asian women		women's earnings as a percent of men's earnings
	earnings	index		earnings	index	
2011	$54,750	114		$41,035	111	74.9%
2010	53,075	107		42,426	111	79.9
2009	54,148	110		44,430	117	82.1
2008	53,446	110		44,068	118	82.5
2007	54,810	112		43,686	115	79.7
2006	57,032	121		44,092	122	77.3
2005	54,265	114		41,452	113	76.4
2004	54,459	112		42,746	115	78.5
2003	55,147	111		39,678	106	71.9
2002	52,184	106		39,331	104	75.4
2001	53,169	109		38,982	105	73.3
2000	52,968	109		39,802	111	75.1
1999	49,797	101		38,566	109	77.4
1998	47,992	99		37,300	105	77.7
1997	48,458	103		38,816	111	80.1
1996	49,177	107		36,477	108	74.2
1995	46,268	100		36,455	111	78.8
1994	48,113	104		36,695	110	76.3
1993	47,365	102		37,314	112	78.8
1992	47,938	101		35,812	107	74.7
1991	48,569	103		34,099	103	70.2
1990	44,649	97		35,572	108	79.7

	percent change		percent change		percentage point change	
2007 to 2011	−0.1%	–	−6.1%	–	−4.8	
2000 to 2011	3.4	–	3.1	–	−0.2	
1990 to 2011	22.6	–	15.4	–	−4.7	

Note: Beginning in 2002, Asians are those who identify themselves as being of the race alone and those who identify themselves as being of the race in combination with other races. The Asian/total indexes are calculated by dividing the median earnings of Asian men and women by the median earnings of total men and women and multiplying by 100. "–" means not applicable.
Source: Bureau of the Census, Current Population Survey, Historical Tables, Internet site http://www.census.gov/hhes/www/income/data/historical/people/; calculations by New Strategist

Table 3.50 Median Earnings of Asians Working Full-Time by Education and Sex, 2011

(median earnings of Asians aged 25 or older working full-time, year-round, by educational attainment and sex, and Asian women's earnings as a percent of Asian men's earnings, 2011)

	men	women	women's earnings as a percent of men's earnings
Total Asians	**$56,370**	**$41,733**	**74.0%**
Less than 9th grade	25,768	–	–
9th to 12th grade, no diploma	31,663	20,882	66.0
High school graduate	32,896	26,877	81.7
Some college, no degree	40,058	33,856	84.5
Associate's degree	48,090	41,259	85.8
Bachelor's degree or more	75,988	56,678	74.6
Bachelor's degree or more	71,778	51,942	72.4
Bachelor's degree	62,700	49,833	79.5
Master's degree	90,720	70,970	78.2
Professional degree	120,699	112,002	92.8
Doctoral degree	90,786	76,604	84.4

Note: "–" means sample is too small to make a reliable estimate.
Source: Bureau of the Census, 2012 Current Population Survey Annual Social and Economic Supplement, Internet site http://www.census.gov/hhes/www/cpstables/032012/perinc/toc.htm; calculations by New Strategist

Table 3.51 Poverty Status of Asian Married Couples, 2002 to 2011

(total number of Asian married couples, and number and percent below poverty level by presence of children under age 18 at home, 2002 to 2011; percent change in numbers and percentage point change in rates for selected years; married couples in thousands as of March the following year)

		in poverty	
	total	number	percent
Total Asian married couples			
2011	3,440	265	7.7%
2010	3,210	232	7.2
2009	2,987	239	8.0
2008	2,932	254	8.7
2007	2,760	187	6.8
2006	2,858	183	6.4
2005	2,692	201	7.5
2004	2,634	150	5.7
2003	2,576	203	7.9
2002	2,344	137	5.9

	percent change		percentage point change
2007 to 2011	24.6%	41.7%	0.9
2002 to 2011	46.8	93.4	1.8

		in poverty	
	total	number	percent
Asian married couples with children			
2011	1,845	168	9.1%
2010	1,746	140	8.0
2009	1,698	153	9.0
2008	1,601	141	8.8
2007	1,536	109	7.1
2006	1,595	116	7.3
2005	1,504	121	8.1
2004	1,527	97	6.3
2003	1,514	121	8.0
2002	1,368	94	6.9

	percent change		percentage point change
2007 to 2011	20.1%	54.1%	2.0
2002 to 2011	34.9	78.7	2.2

Note: Asians are those who identify themselves as being of the race alone and those who identify themselves as being of the race in combination with other races.
Source: Bureau of the Census, Current Population Surveys, Historical Poverty Tables, Internet site http://www.census.gov/hhes/www/poverty/data/historical/families.html; calculations by New Strategist

Table 3.52 Poverty Status of Asian Female-Headed Families, 2002 to 2011

(total number of Asian female-headed families, and number and percent below poverty level by presence of children under age 18 at home, 2002 to 2011; percent change in numbers and percentage point change in rates for selected years; families in thousands as of March the following year)

		in poverty	
	total	number	percent
Total Asian female-headed families			
2011	573	122	21.4%
2010	556	115	20.7
2009	481	87	18.0
2008	457	76	16.5
2007	452	77	17.0
2006	392	61	15.6
2005	415	83	20.0
2004	387	54	14.0
2003	378	89	23.5
2002	354	51	14.3

	percent change		percentage point change
2007 to 2011	26.8%	58.4%	4.4
2002 to 2011	61.9	139.2	7.1

		in poverty	
	total	number	percent
Asian female-headed families with children			
2011	306	92	30.1%
2010	320	93	29.1
2009	274	64	23.4
2008	243	52	21.4
2007	235	65	27.8
2006	194	46	23.8
2005	221	54	24.3
2004	218	43	19.5
2003	235	66	28.2
2002	188	39	21.0

	percent change		percentage point change
2007 to 2011	30.2%	41.5%	2.3
2002 to 2011	62.8	135.9	9.1

Note: Asians are those who identify themselves as being of the race alone and those who identify themselves as being of the race in combination with other races.
Source: Bureau of the Census, Current Population Surveys, Historical Poverty Tables, Internet site http://www.census.gov/hhes/www/poverty/data/historical/families.html; calculations by New Strategist

Table 3.53 Poverty Status of Asian Male-Headed Families, 2002 to 2011

(total number of Asian male-headed families, and number and percent below poverty level by presence of children under age 18 at home, 2002 to 2011; percent change in numbers and percentage point change in rates for selected years; families in thousands as of March the following year)

		in poverty	
	total	number	percent
Total Asian male-headed families			
2011	334	47	14.0%
2010	328	32	9.7
2009	273	34	12.3
2008	255	26	10.1
2007	242	17	7.0
2006	239	27	11.4
2005	251	22	8.8
2004	262	39	14.8
2003	241	28	11.8
2002	241	30	12.6

	percent change		percentage point change
2007 to 2011	38.0%	176.5%	3.9
2002 to 2011	38.6	56.7	2.2

		in poverty	
	total	number	percent
Asian male-headed families with children			
2011	120	27	22.6%
2010	103	11	10.7
2009	100	21	20.7
2008	89	11	12.5
2007	85	4	5.1
2006	83	16	19.2
2005	91	14	15.5
2004	100	15	15.4
2003	82	12	15.2
2002	86	18	21.1

	percent change		percentage point change
2007 to 2011	41.2%	575.0%	17.5
2002 to 2011	41.5	75.0	22.6

Note: Asians are those who identify themselves as being of the race alone and those who identify themselves as being of the race in combination with other races.
Source: Bureau of the Census, Current Population Surveys, Historical Poverty Tables, Internet site http://www.census.gov/hhes/ www/poverty/data/historical/families.html; calculations by New Strategist

Table 3.54 Poverty Status of Asians by Sex and Age, 2011

(total number of Asians, and number and percent below poverty level by sex and age, 2011; people in thousands as of 2012)

	total	in poverty number	in poverty percent
Total Asians	**17,813**	**2,189**	**12.3%**
Under age 18	4,572	607	13.3
Aged 18 to 24	1,841	420	22.8
Aged 25 to 34	2,944	347	11.8
Aged 35 to 44	2,798	265	9.5
Aged 45 to 54	2,319	217	9.3
Aged 55 to 59	969	65	6.8
Aged 60 to 64	788	83	10.5
Aged 65 or older	1,581	185	11.7
Asian females	**9,326**	**1,151**	**12.3%**
Under age 18	2,290	292	12.8
Aged 18 to 24	905	222	24.5
Aged 25 to 34	1,542	177	11.5
Aged 35 to 44	1,494	150	10.0
Aged 45 to 54	1,217	105	8.6
Aged 55 to 59	552	42	7.6
Aged 60 to 64	426	42	10.0
Aged 65 or older	900	121	13.4
Asian males	**8,487**	**1,038**	**12.2%**
Under age 18	2,282	315	13.8
Aged 18 to 24	936	198	21.2
Aged 25 to 34	1,403	170	12.1
Aged 35 to 44	1,305	115	8.8
Aged 45 to 54	1,102	112	10.1
Aged 55 to 59	417	24	5.7
Aged 60 to 64	362	41	11.2
Aged 65 or older	681	64	9.4

Note: Asians are those who identify themselves as being of the race alone and those who identify themselves as being of the race in combination with other races.
Source: Bureau of the Census, 2012 Current Population Survey, Internet site http://www.census.gov/hhes/www/cpstables/032012/pov/toc.htm; calculations by New Strategist

Nearly Half of Asian Workers Are Managers or Professionals

Eight million Asians aged 16 or older were in the civilian labor force in 2012. Seventy-two percent of Asian men and 57 percent of Asian women are in the labor force.

Fully 48 percent of Asian workers are employed in managerial or professional occupations—the largest share among all racial and ethnic groups. Although Asians account for only 5 percent of the nation's employed, they account for 29 percent of software developers, 22 percent of medical scientists, and 18 percent of physicians. Among Asians in the labor force, fully 58 percent have a bachelor's degree.

Forty-seven percent of Asian households have two or more earners. Among Asian couples, the 51 percent majority are dual earners. Asian workers are twice as likely as the average worker to use public transportation to get to work.

Between 2010 and 2020, the number of Asian workers will expand by 30 percent. Despite this rapid growth, the Asian share of the labor force will rise from only 4.7 to 5.7 percent during those years.

■ Asian incomes are well above average because so many Asian households are headed by two-earner couples.

Most Asian women are in the labor force

(percent of Asians aged 16 or older in the labor force, by sex, 2012)

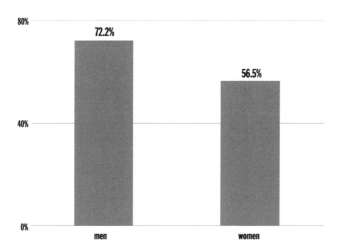

Table 3.55 Labor Force Participation Rate of Asians by Age and Sex, 2012

(percent of Asians aged 16 or older in the civilian labor force, by age and sex, 2012)

	total	men	women
Total Asians	**63.9%**	**72.2%**	**56.5%**
Aged 16 to 19	20.1	18.7	21.7
Aged 20 to 24	52.8	57.0	48.7
Aged 25 to 29	74.5	83.5	66.3
Aged 30 to 34	78.7	91.1	67.7
Aged 35 to 39	80.4	93.2	69.0
Aged 40 to 44	81.4	91.5	72.7
Aged 45 to 49	82.1	92.3	73.1
Aged 50 to 54	80.2	88.6	72.9
Aged 55 to 59	75.6	84.5	68.6
Aged 60 to 64	56.2	64.9	48.9
Aged 65 or older	18.3	23.9	13.9
Aged 65 to 69	31.0	36.8	26.1
Aged 70 to 74	19.1	26.5	12.9
Aged 75 or older	6.3	9.2	4.3

Note: The civilian labor force equals the number of employed plus the number of unemployed.
Source: Bureau of Labor Statistics, Labor Force Statistics from the Current Population Survey, Internet site http://www.bls.gov/cps/tables.htm#empstat

Table 3.56 Employment Status of Asians by Sex and Age, 2012

(number and percent of Asians aged 16 or older in the civilian labor force by sex, age, and employment status, 2012; numbers in thousands)

	civilian noninstitutional population	civilian labor force			unemployed	
		total	percent of population	employed	number	percent of labor force
Total Asians	**12,815**	**8,188**	**63.9%**	**7,705**	**483**	**5.9%**
Aged 16 to 19	802	162	20.1	128	34	20.8
Aged 20 to 24	1,151	608	52.8	544	64	10.5
Aged 25 to 34	2,699	2,067	76.6	1,956	111	5.4
Aged 35 to 44	2,632	2,129	80.9	2,038	90	4.2
Aged 45 to 54	2,195	1,782	81.2	1,684	98	5.5
Aged 55 to 64	1,719	1,144	66.5	1,071	73	6.4
Aged 65 or older	1,617	296	18.3	283	12	4.2
Asian men	**6,000**	**4,334**	**72.2**	**4,085**	**249**	**5.8**
Aged 16 to 19	411	77	18.7	59	18	22.8
Aged 20 to 24	576	328	57.0	295	34	10.2
Aged 25 to 34	1,279	1,117	87.3	1,066	51	4.6
Aged 35 to 44	1,228	1,135	92.4	1,090	44	3.9
Aged 45 to 54	1,024	928	90.6	871	57	6.1
Aged 55 to 64	772	580	75.2	543	38	6.5
Aged 65 or older	708	170	23.9	161	8	4.9
Asian women	**6,815**	**3,853**	**56.5**	**3,620**	**234**	**6.1**
Aged 16 to 19	391	85	21.7	69	16	19.0
Aged 20 to 24	575	280	48.7	250	31	10.9
Aged 25 to 34	1,419	950	67.0	890	60	6.3
Aged 35 to 44	1,404	994	70.8	948	46	4.7
Aged 45 to 54	1,171	855	73.0	813	41	4.9
Aged 55 to 64	947	563	59.5	528	35	6.3
Aged 65 or older	909	126	13.9	122	4	3.2

Note: The civilian labor force equals the number of the employed plus the number of the unemployed. The civilian population equals the number in the labor force plus the number not in the labor force.
Source: Bureau of Labor Statistics, Labor Force Statistics from the Current Population Survey, Internet site http://www.bls.gov/cps/tables.htm#empstat

Table 3.57 Asian Workers by Occupation, 2012

(total number of employed persons aged 16 or older in the civilian labor force, number and percent distribution of employed Asians, and Asian share of total, by occupation, 2012; numbers in thousands)

	total	Asian number	Asian percent distribution	Asian share of total
TOTAL EMPLOYED	**142,469**	**7,705**	**100.0%**	**5.4%**
Management, professional and related occupations	**54,043**	**3,735**	**48.5**	**6.9**
Management, business, and financial operations	22,678	1,305	16.9	5.8
Management occupations	16,042	814	10.6	5.1
Business and financial operations occupations	6,636	491	6.4	7.4
Professional and related occupations	31,365	2,431	31.6	7.8
Computer and mathematical occupations	3,816	666	8.6	17.5
Architecture and engineering occupations	2,846	308	4.0	10.8
Life, physical, and social science occupations	1,316	130	1.7	9.9
Community and social services occupations	2,265	71	0.9	3.1
Legal occupations	1,786	70	0.9	3.9
Education, training, and library occupations	8,543	368	4.8	4.3
Arts, design, entertainment, sports, and media occupations	2,814	145	1.9	5.2
Health care practitioner and technical occupations	7,977	671	8.7	8.4
Service occupations	**25,459**	**1,415**	**18.4**	**5.6**
Health care support occupations	3,496	156	2.0	4.5
Protective service occupations	3,096	83	1.1	2.7
Food preparation and serving related occupations	8,018	495	6.4	6.2
Building and grounds cleaning and maintenance occupations	5,591	184	2.4	3.3
Personal care and service occupations	5,258	497	6.5	9.5
Sales and office occupations	**33,152**	**1,564**	**20.3**	**4.7**
Sales and related occupations	15,457	815	10.6	5.3
Office and administrative support occupations	17,695	749	9.7	4.2
Natural resources, construction, and maintenance occupations	**12,821**	**274**	**3.6**	**2.1**
Farming, fishing, and forestry occupations	994	18	0.2	1.8
Construction and extraction occupations	7,005	110	1.4	1.6
Installation, maintenance, and repair occupations	4,821	146	1.9	3.0
Production, transportation, and material moving occupations	**16,994**	**716**	**9.3**	**4.2**
Production occupations	8,455	488	6.3	5.8
Transportation and material moving occupations	8,540	229	3.0	2.7

Source: Bureau of Labor Statistics, Labor Force Statistics from the Current Population Survey, Internet site http://www.bls.gov/cps/tables.htm#empstat

Table 3.58 Asian Workers by Detailed Occupation, 2012

(total number of employed workers aged 16 or older and percent Asian, by detailed occupation, 2012; numbers in thousands)

	total employed	Asian, share of total
TOTAL EMPLOYED AGED 16 OR OLDER	**142,469**	**5.4%**
Management, professional, and related occupations	**54,043**	**6.9**
Management, business, and financial operations occupations	22,678	5.8
Management occupations	16,042	5.1
Chief executives	1,513	4.2
General and operations managers	1,064	4.7
Legislators	11	–
Advertising and promotions managers	77	4.3
Marketing and sales managers	967	6.0
Public relations and fundraising managers	58	3.4
Administrative services managers	144	4.4
Computer and information systems managers	605	14.5
Financial managers	1,228	5.7
Compensation and benefits managers	15	–
Human resources managers	224	2.4
Training and development managers	36	–
Industrial production managers	261	5.1
Purchasing managers	218	4.6
Transportation, storage, and distribution managers	287	3.3
Farmers, ranchers, and other agricultural managers	944	1.2
Construction managers	983	2.2
Education administrators	811	2.2
Architectural and engineering managers	120	7.7
Food service managers	1,085	9.5
Funeral service managers	13	–
Gaming managers	26	–
Lodging managers	154	13.9
Medical and health services managers	585	5.1
Natural sciences managers	18	–
Postmasters and mail superintendents	39	–
Property, real estate, and community association managers	644	3.4
Social and community service managers	315	3.7
Emergency management directors	6	–
Managers, all other	3,594	5.0
Business and financial operations occupations	6,636	7.4
Agents and business managers of artists, performers, and athletes	47	–
Buyers and purchasing agents, farm products	13	–
Wholesale and retail buyers, except farm products	198	7.7

	total employed	Asian, share of total
Purchasing agents, except wholesale, retail, and farm products	261	4.4%
Claims adjusters, appraisers, examiners, and investigators	323	3.1
Compliance officers	199	3.3
Cost estimators	114	2.0
Human resources workers	603	4.4
Compensation, benefits, and job analysis specialists	71	4.2
Training and development specialists	126	0.8
Logisticians	94	2.2
Management analysts	773	8.8
Meeting, convention, and event planners	127	4.2
Fundraisers	86	4.6
Market research analysts and marketing specialists	219	9.1
Business operations specialists, all other	251	5.6
Accountants and auditors	1,765	12.0
Appraisers and assessors of real estate	93	2.7
Budget analysts	55	8.7
Credit analysts	30	–
Financial analysts	89	9.0
Personal financial advisors	378	6.2
Insurance underwriters	103	0.7
Financial examiners	14	–
Credit counselors and loan officers	333	6.0
Tax examiners and collectors, and revenue agents	82	11.5
Tax preparers	107	7.1
Financial specialists, all other	82	8.4
Professional and related occupations	31,365	7.8
Computer and mathematical occupations	3,816	17.5
Computer and information research scientists	29	–
Computer systems analysts	499	15.8
Information security analysts	52	14.2
Computer programmers	480	17.3
Software developers, applications and systems software	1,084	29.4
Web developers	190	8.0
Computer support specialists	476	7.7
Database administrators	101	10.0
Network and computer systems administrators	226	11.0
Computer network architects	127	14.6
Computer occupations, all other	341	11.7
Actuaries	26	–
Mathematicians	4	–
Operations research analysts	130	9.3
Statisticians	47	–
Miscellaneous mathematical science occupations	3	–

	total employed	Asian, share of total
Architecture and engineering occupations	2,846	10.8%
Architects, except naval	195	6.2
Surveyors, cartographers, and photogrammetrists	51	5.4
Aerospace engineers	119	13.4
Agricultural engineers	4	–
Biomedical engineers	10	–
Chemical engineers	71	9.3
Civil engineers	358	9.0
Computer hardware engineers	91	20.8
Electrical and electronics engineers	335	16.6
Environmental engineers	43	–
Industrial engineers, including health and safety	197	9.6
Marine engineers and naval architects	8	–
Materials engineers	40	–
Mechanical engineers	288	12.3
Mining and geological engineers, including mining safety engineers	9	–
Nuclear engineers	11	–
Petroleum engineers	38	–
Engineers, all other	359	15.4
Drafters	149	7.7
Engineering technicians, except drafters	395	5.0
Surveying and mapping technicians	77	2.5
Life, physical, and social science occupations	1,316	9.9
Agricultural and food scientists	42	–
Biological scientists	101	11.7
Conservation scientists and foresters	25	–
Medical scientists	136	22.4
Astronomers and physicists	25	–
Atmospheric and space scientists	15	–
Chemists and materials scientists	105	9.2
Environmental scientists and geoscientists	105	1.3
Physical scientists, all other	154	20.4
Economists	26	–
Survey researchers	2	–
Psychologists	178	3.9
Sociologists	7	–
Urban and regional planners	28	–
Miscellaneous social scientists and related workers	57	5.5
Agricultural and food science technicians	32	–
Biological technicians	19	–
Chemical technicians	70	4.8
Geological and petroleum technicians	21	–
Nuclear technicians	3	–

	total employed	Asian, share of total
Social science research assistants	3	–
Miscellaneous life, physical, and social science technicians	160	14.4%
Community and social service occupations	2,265	3.2
Counselors	661	2.9
Social workers	734	3.1
Probation officers and correctional treatment specialists	88	1.3
Social and human service assistants	151	3.8
Miscellaneous community and social service specialists, including health educators and community health workers	94	2.4
Clergy	408	4.2
Directors, religious activities and education	61	2.1
Religious workers, all other	69	2.8
Legal occupations	1,786	3.9
Lawyers	1,061	4.3
Judicial law clerks	17	–
Judges, magistrates, and other judicial workers	67	0.7
Paralegals and legal assistants	418	4.6
Miscellaneous legal support workers	223	1.4
Education, training, and library occupations	8,543	4.3
Postsecondary teachers	1,350	11.3
Preschool and kindergarten teachers	678	4.2
Elementary and middle school teachers	2,838	2.1
Secondary school teachers	1,127	3.1
Special education teachers	366	1.1
Other teachers and instructors	860	5.9
Archivists, curators, and museum technicians	46	–
Librarians	181	2.5
Library technicians	45	–
Teacher assistants	898	2.7
Other education, training, and library workers	153	2.5
Arts, design, entertainment, sports, and media occupations	2,814	5.2
Artists and related workers	212	9.3
Designers	756	5.9
Actors	37	–
Producers and directors	121	3.3
Athletes, coaches, umpires, and related workers	267	1.4
Dancers and choreographers	21	–
Musicians, singers, and related workers	203	2.8
Entertainers and performers, sports and related workers, all other	41	–
Announcers	50	8.3
News analysts, reporters and correspondents	82	6.1
Public relations specialists	155	5.8
Editors	159	3.2

	total employed	Asian, share of total
Technical writers	58	6.7%
Writers and authors	208	4.2
Miscellaneous media and communication workers	98	15.0
Broadcast and sound engineering technicians and radio operators	108	1.6
Photographers	178	4.3
Television, video, and motion picture camera operators and editors	57	5.6
Media and communication equipment workers, all other	2	–
Health care practitioners and technical occupations	7,977	8.4
Chiropractors	58	3.5
Dentists	167	10.6
Dietitians and nutritionists	116	5.1
Optometrists	33	–
Pharmacists	286	18.5
Physicians and surgeons	911	18.1
Physician assistants	108	9.0
Podiatrists	9	–
Audiologists	14	–
Occupational therapists	118	4.0
Physical therapists	211	9.1
Radiation therapists	14	–
Recreational therapists	13	–
Respiratory therapists	111	5.6
Speech-language pathologists	146	1.7
Exercise physiologists	2	–
Therapists, all other	148	2.9
Veterinarians	85	1.3
Registered nurses	2,875	7.3
Nurse anesthetists	27	–
Nurse midwives	3	–
Nurse practitioners	103	4.6
Health diagnosing and treating practitioners, all other	23	–
Clinical laboratory technologists and technicians	319	14.0
Dental hygienists	163	5.6
Diagnostic related technologists and technicians	308	4.1
Emergency medical technicians and paramedics	172	1.6
Health practitioner support technologists and technicians	544	5.9
Licensed practical and licensed vocational nurses	531	5.1
Medical records and health information technicians	90	4.3
Opticians, dispensing	54	3.8
Miscellaneous health technologists and technicians	140	11.0
Other health care practitioners and technical occupations	75	3.1

	total employed	Asian, share of total
Service occupations	**25,459**	**5.6%**
Health care support occupations	3,496	4.5
Nursing, psychiatric, and home health aides	2,119	4.6
Occupational therapy assistants and aides	18	–
Physical therapist assistants and aides	66	3.6
Massage therapists	158	7.7
Dental assistants	274	3.6
Medical assistants	429	3.8
Medical transcriptionists	55	0.3
Pharmacy aides	45	–
Veterinary assistants and laboratory animal caretakers	47	–
Phlebotomists	119	4.8
Miscellaneous health care support occupations, including medical equipment preparers	166	4.0
Protective service occupations	3,096	2.7
First-line supervisors of correctional officers	46	–
First-line supervisors of police and detectives	112	4.4
First-line supervisors of fire fighting and prevention workers	64	0.0
First-line supervisors of protective service workers, all other	93	0.4
Firefighters	295	1.1
Fire inspectors	18	–
Bailiffs, correctional officers, and jailers	371	1.1
Detectives and criminal investigators	160	3.5
Fish and game wardens	7	–
Parking enforcement workers	4	–
Police and sheriff's patrol officers	657	3.1
Transit and railroad police	3	–
Animal control workers	11	–
Private detectives and investigators	103	2.2
Security guards and gaming surveillance officers	903	4.1
Crossing guards	61	1.8
Transportation security screeners	25	–
Lifeguards and other recreational, and all other protective service workers	162	1.2
Food preparation and serving related occupations	8,018	6.2
Chefs and head cooks	403	14.2
First-line supervisors of food preparation and serving workers	552	4.0
Cooks	1,970	6.0
Food preparation workers	868	5.7
Bartenders	412	3.5
Combined food preparation and serving workers, including fast food	343	3.1
Counter attendants, cafeteria, food concession, and coffee shop	233	4.8

	total employed	Asian, share of total
Waiters and waitresses	2,124	7.1%
Food servers, nonrestaurant	217	6.4
Dining room and cafeteria attendants and bartender helpers	359	5.5
Dishwashers	271	5.5
Hosts and hostesses, restaurant, lounge, and coffee shop	260	5.4
Food preparation and serving related workers, all other	6	–
Building and grounds cleaning and maintenance occupations	5,591	3.3
First-line supervisors of housekeeping and janitorial workers	277	3.3
First-line supervisors of landscaping, lawn service, and groundskeeping workers	281	1.1
Janitors and building cleaners	2,205	3.6
Maids and housekeeping cleaners	1,457	4.8
Pest control workers	73	0.1
Grounds maintenance workers	1,298	1.7
Personal care and service occupations	5,258	9.5
First-line supervisors of gaming workers	146	9.2
First-line supervisors of personal service workers	246	19.8
Animal trainers	44	–
Nonfarm animal caretakers	179	1.8
Gaming services workers	106	24.3
Motion picture projectionists	2	–
Ushers, lobby attendants, and ticket takers	43	–
Miscellaneous entertainment attendants and related workers	180	5.1
Embalmers and funeral attendants	16	–
Morticians, undertakers, and funeral directors	38	–
Barbers	109	2.5
Hairdressers, hairstylists, and cosmetologists	785	6.5
Miscellaneous personal appearance workers	300	59.6
Baggage porters, bellhops, and concierges	68	13.1
Tour and travel guides	51	7.1
Child care workers	1,314	3.3
Personal care aides	1,071	7.9
Recreation and fitness workers	406	4.5
Residential advisors	58	1.4
Personal care and service workers, all other	95	3.3
Sales and office occupations	**33,152**	**4.7**
Sales and related occupations	15,457	5.3
First-line supervisors of retail sales workers	3,237	5.9
First-line supervisors of nonretail sales workers	1,151	5.0
Cashiers	3,275	7.3
Counter and rental clerks	139	5.2
Parts salespersons	106	4.1
Retail salespersons	3,341	4.4
Advertising sales agents	230	2.3

	total employed	Asian, share of total
Insurance sales agents	540	1.8%
Securities, commodities, and financial services sales agents	280	8.3
Travel agents	73	9.3
Sales representatives, services, all other	457	3.7
Sales representatives, wholesale and manufacturing	1,277	3.7
Models, demonstrators, and product promoters	65	4.0
Real estate brokers and sales agents	761	4.7
Sales engineers	27	–
Telemarketers	97	1.1
Door-to-door sales workers, news and street vendors, and related workers	198	3.8
Sales and related workers, all other	204	4.7
Office and administrative support occupations	17,695	4.2
First-line supervisors of office and administrative support workers	1,416	3.5
Switchboard operators, including answering service	35	–
Telephone operators	42	–
Communications equipment operators, all other	9	–
Bill and account collectors	206	3.6
Billing and posting clerks	475	4.0
Bookkeeping, accounting, and auditing clerks	1,268	5.0
Gaming cage workers	8	–
Payroll and timekeeping clerks	155	4.6
Procurement clerks	27	–
Tellers	380	5.7
Financial clerks, all other	52	4.1
Brokerage clerks	5	–
Correspondence clerks	6	–
Court, municipal, and license clerks	85	1.2
Credit authorizers, checkers, and clerks	43	–
Customer service representatives	1,956	4.2
Eligibility interviewers, government programs	92	2.1
File clerks	292	4.6
Hotel, motel, and resort desk clerks	110	6.3
Interviewers, except eligibility and loan	135	6.0
Library assistants, clerical	97	3.2
Loan interviewers and clerks	144	4.0
New accounts clerks	26	–
Order clerks	104	4.1
Human resources assistants, except payroll and timekeeping	132	1.9
Receptionists and information clerks	1,237	4.3
Reservation and transportation ticket agents and travel clerks	117	10.9
Information and record clerks, all other	104	2.5
Cargo and freight agents	25	–
Couriers and messengers	213	2.4

	total employed	Asian, share of total
Dispatchers	277	2.3%
Meter readers, utilities	29	–
Postal service clerks	148	9.5
Postal service mail carriers	318	6.7
Postal service mail sorters, processors, and processing machine operators	66	12.7
Production, planning, and expediting clerks	272	3.2
Shipping, receiving, and traffic clerks	527	3.6
Stock clerks and order fillers	1,453	4.5
Weighers, measurers, checkers, and samplers, recordkeeping	74	2.8
Secretaries and administrative assistants	2,904	3.2
Computer operators	102	6.5
Data entry keyers	337	5.1
Word processors and typists	119	2.8
Desktop publishers	3	–
Insurance claims and policy processing clerks	230	3.6
Mail clerks and mail machine operators, except postal service	81	10.6
Office clerks, general	1,103	5.0
Office machine operators, except computer	46	–
Proofreaders and copy markers	10	–
Statistical assistants	32	–
Office and administrative support workers, all other	570	3.9
Natural resources, construction, and maintenance occupations	**12,821**	**2.1**
Farming, fishing, and forestry occupations	994	1.8
First-line supervisors of farming, fishing, and forestry workers	50	4.2
Agricultural inspectors	16	–
Animal breeders	6	–
Graders and sorters, agricultural products	118	2.1
Miscellaneous agricultural workers	711	1.5
Fishers and related fishing workers	33	–
Hunters and trappers	2	–
Forest and conservation workers	9	–
Logging workers	49	–
Construction and extraction occupations	7,005	1.6
First-line supervisors of construction trades and extraction workers	634	1.3
Boilermakers	23	–
Brickmasons, blockmasons, and stonemasons	122	0.3
Carpenters	1,223	1.9
Carpet, floor, and tile installers and finishers	150	0.4
Cement masons, concrete finishers, and terrazzo workers	68	3.1
Construction laborers	1,387	2.0
Paving, surfacing, and tamping equipment operators	23	–
Pile-driver operators	4	–
Operating engineers and other construction equipment operators	348	0.2

	total employed	Asian, share of total
Drywall installers, ceiling tile installers, and tapers	129	0.0%
Electricians	692	2.3
Glaziers	46	–
Insulation workers	44	–
Painters, construction and maintenance	485	2.0
Paperhangers	7	–
Pipelayers, plumbers, pipefitters, and steamfitters	534	1.5
Plasterers and stucco masons	18	–
Reinforcing iron and rebar workers	8	–
Roofers	196	0.5
Sheet metal workers	123	1.7
Structural iron and steel workers	65	0.0
Solar photovoltaic installers	7	–
Helpers, construction trades	53	1.3
Construction and building inspectors	118	2.1
Elevator installers and repairers	29	–
Fence erectors	33	–
Hazardous materials removal workers	38	–
Highway maintenance workers	108	0.1
Rail-track laying and maintenance equipment operators	10	–
Septic tank servicers and sewer pipe cleaners	8	–
Miscellaneous construction and related workers	32	–
Derrick, rotary drill, and service unit operators, oil, gas, and mining	37	–
Earth drillers, except oil and gas	35	–
Explosives workers, ordnance handling experts, and blasters	8	–
Mining machine operators	65	0.0
Roof bolters, mining	3	–
Roustabouts, oil and gas	14	–
Helpers—extraction workers	5	–
Other extraction workers	75	1.0
Installation, maintenance, and repair occupations	4,821	3.0
First-line supervisors of mechanics, installers, and repairers	292	1.0
Computer, automated teller, and office machine repairers	296	7.2
Radio and telecommunications equipment installers and repairers	158	3.2
Avionics technicians	14	–
Electric motor, power tool, and related repairers	37	–
Electrical and electronics installers and repairers, transportation equipment	5	–
Electrical and electronics repairers, industrial and utility	12	–
Electronic equipment installers and repairers, motor vehicles	18	–
Electronic home entertainment equipment installers and repairers	50	4.3
Security and fire alarm systems installers	41	–
Aircraft mechanics and service technicians	153	5.4
Automotive body and related repairers	140	2.3

	total employed	Asian, share of total
Automotive glass installers and repairers	22	–
Automotive service technicians and mechanics	867	4.7%
Bus and truck mechanics and diesel engine specialists	316	1.3
Heavy vehicle and mobile equipment service technicians and mechanics	194	2.0
Small engine mechanics	56	0.2
Miscellaneous vehicle and mobile equipment mechanics, installers, and repairers	87	0.0
Control and valve installers and repairers	27	–
Heating, air conditioning, and refrigeration mechanics and installers	340	3.2
Home appliance repairers	47	–
Industrial and refractory machinery mechanics	454	2.9
Maintenance and repair workers, general	442	3.2
Maintenance workers, machinery	28	–
Millwrights	53	1.4
Electrical power-line installers and repairers	110	0.3
Telecommunications line installers and repairers	177	1.9
Precision instrument and equipment repairers	60	1.1
Wind turbine service technicians	3	–
Coin, vending, and amusement machine servicers and repairers	33	–
Commercial divers	3	–
Locksmiths and safe repairers	31	–
Manufactured building and mobile home installers	5	–
Riggers	13	–
Signal and track switch repairers	5	–
Helpers—installation, maintenance, and repair workers	30	–
Other installation, maintenance, and repair workers	205	1.4
Production, transportation, and material moving occupations	**16,994**	**4.2**
Production occupations	8,455	5.8
First-line supervisors of production and operating workers	808	5.8
Aircraft structure, surfaces, rigging, and systems assemblers	23	–
Electrical, electronics, and electromechanical assemblers	166	16.3
Engine and other machine assemblers	32	–
Structural metal fabricators and fitters	25	–
Miscellaneous assemblers and fabricators	919	6.9
Bakers	199	5.1
Butchers and other meat, poultry, and fish processing workers	311	7.9
Food and tobacco roasting, baking, and drying machine operators and tenders	11	–
Food batchmakers	84	5.7
Food cooking machine operators and tenders	14	–
Food processing workers, all other	117	5.9
Computer control programmers and operators	67	3.3
Extruding and drawing machine setters, operators, and tenders, metal and plastic	10	–
Forging machine setters, operators, and tenders, metal and plastic	10	–
Rolling machine setters, operators, and tenders, metal and plastic	8	–

	total employed	Asian, share of total
Cutting, punching, and press machine setters, operators, and tenders, metal and plastic	87	3.3%
Drilling and boring machine tool setters, operators, and tenders, metal and plastic	3	–
Grinding, lapping, polishing, and buffing machine tool setters, operators, and tenders, metal and plastic	54	0.7
Lathe and turning machine tool setters, operators, and tenders, metal and plastic	17	–
Milling and planing machine setters, operators, and tenders, metal and plastic	3	–
Machinists	397	4.9
Metal furnace operators, tenders, pourers, and casters	17	–
Model makers and patternmakers, metal and plastic	11	–
Molders and molding machine setters, operators, and tenders, metal and plastic	37	–
Multiple machine tool setters, operators, and tenders, metal and plastic	5	–
Tool and die makers	56	5.6
Welding, soldering, and brazing workers	593	2.6
Heat treating equipment setters, operators, and tenders, metal and plastic	4	–
Layout workers, metal and plastic	4	–
Plating and coating machine setters, operators, and tenders, metal and plastic	18	–
Tool grinders, filers, and sharpeners	3	–
Metal workers and plastic workers, all other	375	6.6
Prepress technicians and workers	33	–
Printing press operators	201	3.4
Print binding and finishing workers	22	–
Laundry and dry-cleaning workers	185	10.3
Pressers, textile, garment, and related materials	54	3.5
Sewing machine operators	166	11.4
Shoe and leather workers and repairers	11	–
Shoe machine operators and tenders	11	–
Tailors, dressmakers, and sewers	86	19.5
Textile bleaching and dyeing machine operators and tenders	5	–
Textile cutting machine setters, operators, and tenders	12	–
Textile knitting and weaving machine setters, operators, and tenders	7	–
Textile winding, twisting, and drawing out machine setters, operators, and tenders	14	–
Extruding and forming machine setters, operators, and tenders, synthetic and glass fibers	1	–
Fabric and apparel patternmakers	3	–
Upholsterers	34	–
Textile, apparel, and furnishings workers, all other	14	–
Cabinetmakers and bench carpenters	45	–
Furniture finishers	7	–
Model makers and patternmakers, wood	0	–
Sawing machine setters, operators, and tenders, wood	30	–
Woodworking machine setters, operators, and tenders, except sawing	21	–
Woodworkers, all other	21	–
Power plant operators, distributors, and dispatchers	44	–

	total employed	Asian, share of total
Stationary engineers and boiler operators	121	4.3%
Water and wastewater treatment plant and system operators	72	1.7
Miscellaneous plant and system operators	39	–
Chemical processing machine setters, operators, and tenders	68	0.8
Crushing, grinding, polishing, mixing, and blending workers	100	6.8
Cutting workers	67	3.5
Extruding, forming, pressing, and compacting machine setters, operators, and tenders	45	–
Furnace, kiln, oven, drier, and kettle operators and tenders	16	–
Inspectors, testers, sorters, samplers, and weighers	689	6.7
Jewelers and precious stone and metal workers	46	–
Medical, dental, and ophthalmic laboratory technicians	95	8.9
Packaging and filling machine operators and tenders	261	8.8
Painting workers	150	4.3
Photographic process workers and processing machine operators	55	4.9
Semiconductor processors	4	–
Adhesive bonding machine operators and tenders	9	–
Cleaning, washing, and metal pickling equipment operators and tenders	7	–
Cooling and freezing equipment operators and tenders	2	–
Etchers and engravers	6	–
Molders, shapers, and casters, except metal and plastic	41	–
Paper goods machine setters, operators, and tenders	35	–
Tire builders	19	–
Helpers—production workers	59	2.9
Production workers, all other	933	4.0
Transportation and material moving occupations	8,540	2.7
Supervisors of transportation and material moving workers	200	4.4
Aircraft pilots and flight engineers	129	2.5
Air traffic controllers and airfield operations specialists	44	–
Flight attendants	88	5.9
Ambulance drivers and attendants, except emergency medical technicians	20	–
Bus drivers	558	2.3
Driver/sales workers and truck drivers	3,201	1.6
Taxi drivers and chauffeurs	336	13.8
Motor vehicle operators, all other	63	1.4
Locomotive engineers and operators	41	–
Railroad brake, signal, and switch operators	10	–
Railroad conductors and yardmasters	52	0.7
Subway, streetcar, and other rail transportation workers	11	–
Sailors and marine oilers	16	–
Ship and boat captains and operators	37	–
Ship engineers	7	–
Bridge and lock tenders	7	–
Parking lot attendants	81	5.3

	total employed	Asian, share of total
Automotive and watercraft service attendants	94	5.2%
Transportation inspectors	36	–
Transportation attendants, except flight attendants	38	–
Other transportation workers	17	–
Conveyor operators and tenders	4	–
Crane and tower operators	62	0.9
Dredge, excavating, and loading machine operators	42	–
Hoist and winch operators	5	–
Industrial truck and tractor operators	537	1.6
Cleaners of vehicles and equipment	315	2.7
Laborers and freight, stock, and material movers, hand	1,849	2.5
Machine feeders and offbearers	27	–
Packers and packagers, hand	431	3.5
Pumping station operators	25	–
Refuse and recyclable material collectors	106	1.4
Mine shuttle car operators	1	–
Tank car, truck, and ship loaders	4	–
Material moving workers, all other	45	–

Note: "–" means sample is too small to make a reliable estimate.
Source: Bureau of Labor Statistics, Labor Force Statistics from the Current Population Survey, Internet site http://www.bls.gov/cps/tables.htm#empstat; calculations by New Strategist

Table 3.59 Asian Workers by Industry, 2012

(total number of employed people aged 16 or older in the civilian labor force; number and percent distribution of employed Asians, and Asian share of total, by industry, 2012; numbers in thousands)

	total	Asian number	Asian percent distribution	Asian share of total
Total employed	**142,469**	**7,705**	**100.0%**	**5.4%**
Agriculture, forestry, fishing, and hunting	2,186	32	0.4	1.5
Mining	957	13	0.2	1.4
Construction	8,964	169	2.2	1.9
Manufacturing	14,686	912	11.8	6.2
Durable goods	9,244	614	8.0	6.6
Nondurable goods	5,443	298	3.9	5.5
Wholesale/retail trade	19,876	1,014	13.2	5.1
Wholesale trade	3,694	184	2.4	5.0
Retail trade	16,182	830	10.8	5.1
Transportation and utilities	7,271	282	3.7	3.9
Information	2,971	184	2.4	6.2
Financial activities	9,590	552	7.2	5.8
Professional and business services	16,539	1,143	14.8	6.9
Educational and health services	32,350	1,700	22.1	5.3
Leisure and hospitality	13,193	875	11.4	6.6
Other services	7,168	554	7.2	7.7
Other services, except private households	6,430	521	6.8	8.1
Private households	738	33	0.4	4.5
Public administration	6,717	275	3.6	4.1

Source: Bureau of Labor Statistics, Labor Force Statistics from the Current Population Survey, Internet site http://www.bls.gov/cps/tables.htm#empstat

Table 3.60 Asian Workers by Full-Time and Part-Time Status, 2012

(number and percent distribution of employed Asians aged 16 or older by employment status and sex, 2012; numbers in thousands)

	total	men	women
Total employed Asians	**7,434**	**3,968**	**3,466**
Worked full-time	5,903	3,368	2,535
Worked part-time	1,531	599	931
For economic reasons	348	158	190
PERCENT DISTRIBUTION			
Total employed Asians	**100.0%**	**100.0%**	**100.0%**
Worked full-time	79.4	84.9	73.1
Worked part-time	20.6	15.1	26.9
For economic reasons	4.7	4.0	5.5

Note: Part-time work is less than 35 hours per week. Part-time workers exclude those who usually work full-time but who worked less than 35 hours in the previous week because of vacation, holidays, child care problems, weather issues, and other temporary, noneconomic reasons. "Economic reasons" means a worker's hours have been reduced or workers cannot find full-time employment.
Source: Bureau of Labor Statistics, Labor Force Statistics from the Current Population Survey, Internet site http://www.bls.gov/cps/tables.htm#empstat

Table 3.61 Asian Workers by Educational Attainment, 2012

(number of total people and Asians aged 25 or older in the civilian labor force, Asian labor force participation rate, distribution of Asians in labor force, and Asian share of total labor force, by educational attainment, 2012; numbers in thousands)

	total labor force	Asian labor force			
		number	participation rate	percent distribution	share of total
Total aged 25 or older	**133,690**	**7,418**	**68.3%**	**100.0%**	**5.5%**
Not a high school graduate	11,328	516	44.3	7.0	4.6
High school graduate only	36,772	1,290	60.4	17.4	3.5
Some college	22,685	769	69.2	10.4	3.4
Associate's degree	14,675	544	71.8	7.3	3.7
Bachelor's degree or more	48,230	4,299	75.5	58.0	8.9

Source: Bureau of Labor Statistics, Labor Force Statistics from the Current Population Survey, Internet site http://www.bls.gov/cps/tables.htm#empstat

Table 3.62 Asian Workers by Job Tenure, 2012

(percent distribution of total and Asian wage and salary workers aged 16 or older by tenure with current employer, and index of Asian to total, 2012)

	total	Asian	index, Asian to total
Total workers	**100.0%**	**100.0%**	**100**
One year or less	21.1	21.1	100
13 months to 23 months	6.3	6.6	105
Two years	4.9	5.3	108
Three to four years	16.6	20.5	123
Five to nine years	21.8	23.8	109
10 to 14 years	12.5	11.3	90
15 to 19 years	6.1	4.8	79
20 or more years	10.6	6.6	62

Note: The index is calculated by dividing the Asian figure by the total figure and multiplying by 100.
Source: Bureau of Labor Statistics, Employee Tenure, Internet site http://www.bls.gov/news.release/tenure.toc.htm; calculations by New Strategist

Table 3.63 Asian Households by Number of Earners, 2012

(number of total households, number and percent distribution of Asian households and Asian share of total, by number of earners per household, 2012; number of households in thousands)

		Asian		
	total	number	percent distribution	share of total
Total households	**121,084**	**5,705**	**100.0%**	**4.7%**
No earners	28,569	795	13.9	2.8
One earner	45,578	2,242	39.3	4.9
Two or more earners	46,938	2,668	46.8	5.7
Two earners	37,943	2,082	36.5	5.5
Three earners	6,905	424	7.4	6.1
Four or more earners	2,089	161	2.8	7.7
Average number of earners per household	1.28	1.48	–	–

Note: Asians are those who identify themselves as being of the race alone and those who identify themselves as being of the race in combination with other races. "–" means not applicable.
Source: Bureau of the Census, 2012 Current Population Survey, Annual Social and Economic Supplement, Internet site http://www.census.gov/hhes/www/cpstables/032012/hhinc/toc.htm; calculations by New Strategist

Table 3.64 Labor Force Status of Asian Married Couples, 2012

(number and percent distribution of Asian married couples by age of householder and labor force status of husband and wife, 2012; numbers in thousands)

	total	husband and/or wife in labor force			neither husband nor wife in labor force
		husband and wife	husband only	wife only	
Total Asian couples	**3,810**	**1,951**	**1,092**	**292**	**476**
Under age 25	41	21	18	0	2
Aged 25 to 29	238	96	116	10	15
Aged 30 to 34	468	259	176	21	11
Aged 35 to 39	529	309	191	26	3
Aged 40 to 44	473	286	156	22	10
Aged 45 to 54	897	575	235	47	40
Aged 55 to 64	664	345	141	106	72
Aged 65 to 74	336	52	50	49	186
Aged 75 or older	165	7	10	10	138
Total Asian couples	**100.0%**	**51.2%**	**28.7%**	**7.7%**	**12.5%**
Under age 25	100.0	51.2	43.9	0.0	4.9
Aged 25 to 29	100.0	40.3	48.7	4.2	6.3
Aged 30 to 34	100.0	55.3	37.6	4.5	2.4
Aged 35 to 39	100.0	58.4	36.1	4.9	0.6
Aged 40 to 44	100.0	60.5	33.0	4.7	2.1
Aged 45 to 54	100.0	64.1	26.2	5.2	4.5
Aged 55 to 64	100.0	52.0	21.2	16.0	10.8
Aged 65 to 74	100.0	15.5	14.9	14.6	55.4
Aged 75 or older	100.0	4.2	6.1	6.1	83.6

Note: Asians are those who identify themselves as being of the race alone and those who identify themselves as being of the race in combination with other races.
Source: Bureau of the Census, America's Families and Living Arrangements: 2012, Internet site http://www.census.gov/hhes/ families/data/cps2012.html; calculations by New Strategist

Table 3.65 Asian Minimum Wage Workers by Sex, 2011

(number of total and Asian employed wage and salary workers, number of total and Asian wage and salary workers paid hourly rates at or below minimum wage and Asian share of total, by sex, 2011; numbers in thousands)

			workers paid at or below minimum wage		
	total paid hourly rates	percent distribution	number	percent distribution	share of total
Total workers aged 16 or older	**73,926**	**100.0%**	**3,828**	**100.0%**	**5.2%**
Asian workers aged 16 or older	3,037	4.1	99	2.6	3.3
Asian men	1,425	1.9	41	1.1	2.9
Asian women	1,612	2.2	58	1.5	3.6

Source: Bureau of Labor Statistics, Characteristics of Minimum Wage Workers: 2011, Internet site http://www.bls.gov/cps/ minwage2011tbls.htm; calculations by New Strategist

Table 3.66 Union Representation of Asian Workers by Sex, 2012

(number of employed Asian wage and salary workers aged 16 or older, number and percent represented by unions, median weekly earnings of those working full-time by union representation status, and index of union median to average median, by sex, 2012; number in thousands)

	total	men	women
Total employed Asians	**6,953**	**3,650**	**3,303**
Number represented by unions	758	369	388
Percent represented by unions	10.9%	10.1%	11.7%
Median weekly earnings of Asian full-time workers	**$920**	**$1,055**	**$770**
Represented by unions	986	1,022	951
Not represented by unions	907	1,062	747
Index, median weekly earnings of Asian workers represented by unions to average Asian worker	**107**	**97**	**124**

Note: Workers represented by unions are either members of a labor union or workers who report no union affiliation but whose jobs are covered by a union or an employee association contract. The index is calculated by dividing median weekly earnings of workers represented by unions by median weekly earnings of the average Asian worker and multiplying by 100.
Source: Bureau of Labor Statistics, Labor Force Statistics from the Current Population Survey, Internet site http://www.bls.gov/ cps/tables.htm#empstat

Table 3.67 Commuting Patterns of Asian Workers, 2011

(number of total and Asian workers aged 16 or older, percent distribution by means of transportation to work, and index of Asian to total, 2011; numbers in thousands)

	total	Asian	index
Total workers aged 16 or older, number	**138,270**	**8,041**	–
Total workers aged 16 or older, percent	**100.0%**	**100.0%**	–
Drove alone in car, truck, or van	76.4	66.9	88
Carpooled in car, truck, or van	9.7	13.4	138
Public transportation (excluding taxicab)	5.0	10.1	202
Walked	2.8	4.1	146
Other means	1.7	1.7	100
Worked at home	4.3	3.7	86
Average travel time to work (minutes)	25.5	28.1	110

Note: Asians are those who identify themselves as being of the race alone and those who identify themselves as being of the race in combination with other races. The index is calculated by dividing Asian figure by total figure and multiplying by 100. "–" means not applicable.
Source: Census Bureau, 2011 American Community Survey, Internet site http://factfinder2.census.gov/faces/nav/jsf/pages/index .xhtml; calculations by New Strategist

Table 3.68 Asian Labor Force Projections, 2010 and 2020

(number and percent of Asians aged 16 or older in the civilian labor force by sex, 2010 and 2020; percent change in number and percentage point change in rate, 2010–20; numbers in thousands)

NUMBER	2010	2020	percent change
Total Asians in labor force	**7,248**	**9,430**	**30.1%**
Asian men	3,893	4,968	27.6
Asian women	3,355	4,462	33.0

PARTICIPATION RATE	2010	2020	percentage point change
Total Asians in labor force	**64.7%**	**63.1%**	**–1.6**
Asian men	73.2	71.0	–2.2
Asian women	57.0	56.1	–0.9

Note: Asians are those who identify themselves as being of the race alone.
Source: Bureau of Labor Statistics, Labor Force Projections to 2020: A More Slowly Growing Workforce, Monthly Labor Review, January 2012, Internet site http://www.bls.gov/opub/mlr/2012/01/home.htm

Table 3.69 Asian Share of Labor Force, 2010 and 2020

(total people and Asians aged 16 or older in the civilian labor force, and Asian share of total, 2010 and 2020; numbers in thousands)

	2010			2020		
	total	Asian	Asian share of total	total	Asian	Asian share of total
Total labor force	**153,889**	**7,248**	**4.7%**	**164,360**	**9,430**	**5.7%**
Men	81,985	3,893	4.7	87,128	4,968	5.7
Women	71,904	3,355	4.7	77,232	4,462	5.8

Note: Asians are those who identify themselves as being of the race alone.
Source: Bureau of Labor Statistics, Labor Force Projections to 2020: A More Slowly Growing Workforce, Monthly Labor Review, January 2012, Internet site http://www.bls.gov/opub/mlr/2012/01/home.htm

Most Asian Households Are Headed by Married Couples

Asians were the heads of 5.7 million of the nation's 121 million households, or 4.7 percent of the total in 2012. Asian households are much more likely than the average household to be headed by married couples—60 versus 49 percent, according to the Census Bureau's 2012 Current Population Survey.

Asian children are much more likely than the average American child to live with both parents. Seventy-six percent of Asian children under age 18 live with married, biological parents. In comparison, a much smaller 58 percent of children nationwide live with their biological, married parents. Thirty-six percent of Asian households include children under age 18. Among Asian married couples, 51 percent have children living with them.

Many Asians are immigrants trying to establish themselves in the United States, which explains why Asian households are larger than average. The average Asian household is home to 2.96 people compared with 2.55 people in the average household.

Divorce is relatively uncommon among Asian men and women. Only 8 percent of Asian men have ever divorced, the proportion peaking at 17 percent among men in their fifties. Among Asian women, only 11 percent have ever divorced, with a peak of 19 percent among women aged 40 to 49.

■ Because many Asians are immigrants from countries with traditional family values, married couples are more common in Asian households than in the average household.

Few Asian households are female-headed families

(percent distribution of Asian households by household type, 2012)

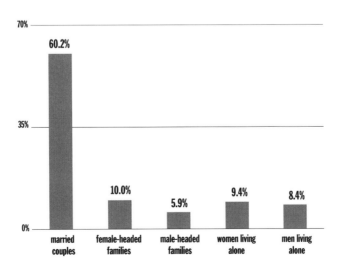

Table 3.70 Asian Households by Age of Householder, 2012

(number of total households, number and percent distribution of Asian households, and Asian share of total, by age of householder, 2012, numbers in thousands)

	total	Asian		
		number	percent distribution	share of total
Total households	**121,084**	**5,705**	**100.0%**	**4.7%**
Under age 25	6,180	407	7.1	6.6
Aged 25 to 29	9,208	554	9.7	6.0
Aged 30 to 34	10,638	695	12.2	6.5
Aged 35 to 39	10,111	717	12.6	7.1
Aged 40 to 44	11,129	607	10.6	5.5
Aged 45 to 49	11,763	629	11.0	5.3
Aged 50 to 54	12,433	509	8.9	4.1
Aged 55 to 59	12,037	466	8.2	3.9
Aged 60 to 64	10,742	389	6.8	3.6
Aged 65 or older	26,843	731	12.8	2.7

Note: Asians are those who identify themselves as being of the race alone and those who identify themselves as being of the race in combination with other races.
Source: Bureau of the Census, 2012 Current Population Survey, Internet site http://www.census.gov/hhes/www/income/data/incpovhlth/2011/dtables.html; calculations by New Strategist

Table 3.71 Asian Households by Household Type, 2012

(number of total households, number and percent distribution of Asian households, and Asian share of total, by type of household, 2012, numbers in thousands)

		Asian		
	total	number	percent distribution	share of total
TOTAL HOUSEHOLDS	**121,084**	**5,705**	**100.0%**	**4.7%**
Family households	**80,506**	**4,342**	**76.1**	**5.4**
Married couples	58,949	3,435	60.2	5.8
With children under age 18	25,114	1,842	32.3	7.3
Female householders, no spouse present	15,669	573	10.0	3.7
With children under age 18	10,380	306	5.4	2.9
Male householders, no spouse present	5,888	334	5.9	5.7
With children under age 18	2,982	120	2.1	4.0
Nonfamily households	**40,578**	**1,362**	**23.9**	**3.4**
Female householders	21,383	685	12.0	3.2
Living alone	18,354	534	9.4	2.9
Male householders	19,195	677	11.9	3.5
Living alone	14,835	480	8.4	3.2

Note: Asians are those who identify themselves as being of the race alone and those who identify themselves as being of the race in combination with other races.
Source: Bureau of the Census, 2012 Current Population Survey, Internet site http://www.census.gov/hhes/www/income/data/incpovhlth/2011/dtables.html; calculations by New Strategist

Table 3.72 Asian Households by Age of Householder and Household Type, 2012

(number and percent distribution of households by age of householder and type of household, 2012; numbers in thousands)

| | | family households | | | nonfamily households | | | |
| | | | | | female-headed | | male-headed | |
	total	married couples	female householder, no spouse present	male householder, no spouse present	total	living alone	total	living alone
Total Asian households	**5,705**	**3,435**	**573**	**334**	**685**	**534**	**677**	**480**
Under age 25	407	26	68	81	115	47	117	65
Aged 25 to 34	1,249	641	99	114	154	104	242	151
Aged 35 to 44	1,324	947	134	50	90	75	103	84
Aged 45 to 54	1,138	813	120	43	76	73	86	69
Aged 55 to 64	855	581	87	40	72	62	75	58
Aged 65 or older	731	427	66	7	178	173	54	52

PERCENT DISTRIBUTION BY HOUSEHOLD TYPE

Total Asian households	**100.0%**	**60.2%**	**10.0%**	**5.9%**	**12.0%**	**9.4%**	**11.9%**	**8.4%**
Under age 25	100.0	6.4	16.7	19.9	28.3	11.5	28.7	16.0
Aged 25 to 34	100.0	51.3	7.9	9.1	12.3	8.3	19.4	12.1
Aged 35 to 44	100.0	71.5	10.1	3.8	6.8	5.7	7.8	6.3
Aged 45 to 54	100.0	71.4	10.5	3.8	6.7	6.4	7.6	6.1
Aged 55 to 64	100.0	68.0	10.2	4.7	8.4	7.3	8.8	6.8
Aged 65 or older	100.0	58.4	9.0	1.0	24.4	23.7	7.4	7.1

PERCENT DISTRIBUTION BY AGE

Total Asian households	**100.0%**	**100.0%**	**100.0%**	**100.0%**	**100.0%**	**100.0%**	**100.0%**	**100.0%**
Under age 25	7.1	0.8	11.9	24.3	16.8	8.8	17.3	13.5
Aged 25 to 34	21.9	18.7	17.3	34.1	22.5	19.5	35.7	31.5
Aged 35 to 44	23.2	27.6	23.4	15.0	13.1	14.0	15.2	17.5
Aged 45 to 54	19.9	23.7	20.9	12.9	11.1	13.7	12.7	14.4
Aged 55 to 64	15.0	16.9	15.2	12.0	10.5	11.6	11.1	12.1
Aged 65 or older	12.8	12.4	11.5	2.1	26.0	32.4	8.0	10.8

Note: Asians are those who identify themselves as being Asian alone and those who identify themselves as being Asian in combination with other races.
Source: Bureau of the Census, 2012 Current Population Survey, Internet site http://www.census.gov/hhes/www/income/data/ incpovhlth/2011/dtables.html; calculations by New Strategist

Table 3.73 Asian Households by Size, 2012

(number of total households, number and percent distribution of Asian households, and Asian share of total, by household size, 2012; number of households in thousands)

		Asian		
	total	number	percent distribution	share of total
Total households	**121,084**	**5,705**	**100.0%**	**4.7%**
One person	33,188	1,013	17.8	3.1
Two people	40,983	1,592	27.9	3.9
Three people	19,241	1,173	20.6	6.1
Four people	16,049	1,166	20.4	7.3
Five people	7,271	452	7.9	6.2
Six people	2,734	166	2.9	6.1
Seven or more people	1,617	143	2.5	8.9
Average number of persons per household	2.55	2.96	–	–

Note: Asians are those who identify themselves as being Asian alone and those who identify themselves as being Asian in combination with other races. "–" means not applicable.
Source: Bureau of the Census, Current Population Survey Annual Social and Economic Supplement, Internet site http://www.census.gov/hhes/www/income/dinctabs.html; calculations by New Strategist

Table 3.74 Asian Households by Region, 2012

(number of total households, number and percent distribution of Asian households and Asian share of total, by region, 2012; numbers in thousands)

| | total | Asian | | |
		number	percent distribution	share of total
Total households	**121,084**	**5,705**	**100.0%**	**4.7%**
Northeast	21,774	1,168	20.5	5.4
Midwest	26,865	676	11.8	2.5
South	45,604	1,303	22.8	2.9
West	26,840	2,558	44.8	9.5

Note: Asians include those who identify themselves as being Asian alone and those who identify themselves as being Asian in combination with other races.
Source: Bureau of the Census, Current Population Survey Annual Social and Economic Supplement, Internet site http://www .census.gov/hhes/www/income/dinctabs.html; calculations by New Strategist

Table 3.75 Asian Households by Metropolitan Status, 2012

(number of total households, number and percent distribution of Asian households and Asian share of total, by metropolitan status, 2012; numbers in thousands)

| | total | Asian | | |
		number	percent distribution	share of total
Total households	**121,084**	**5,705**	**100.0%**	**4.7%**
Inside metropolitan areas	101,526	5,537	97.1	5.5
Inside principal cities	40,616	2,932	51.4	7.2
Outside principal cities	60,910	2,605	45.7	4.3
Outside metropolitan areas	19,558	167	2.9	0.9

Note: Asians are those who identify themselves as being Asian alone and those who identify themselves as being Asian in combination with other races.
Source: Bureau of the Census, Current Population Survey Annual Social and Economic Supplement, Internet site http://www .census.gov/hhes/www/income/dinctabs.html; calculations by New Strategist

Table 3.76 Asians Living Alone by Sex and Age, 2012

(total number of Asians aged 15 or older, number and percent living alone, and percent distribution of Asians living alone, by sex and age, 2012; numbers in thousands)

		living alone		
	total	number	percent distribution	share of total
Total Asians	**13,975**	**1,014**	**100.0%**	**7.3%**
Under age 25	2,575	112	11.0	4.3
Aged 25 to 34	2,944	255	25.1	8.7
Aged 35 to 44	2,798	159	15.7	5.7
Aged 45 to 54	2,319	142	14.0	6.1
Aged 55 to 64	1,757	120	11.8	6.8
Aged 65 to 74	958	95	9.4	9.9
Aged 75 or older	623	130	12.8	20.9
Asian men	**6,578**	**480**	**100.0**	**7.3**
Under age 25	1,310	65	13.5	5.0
Aged 25 to 34	1,403	151	31.5	10.8
Aged 35 to 44	1,305	84	17.5	6.4
Aged 45 to 54	1,102	69	14.4	6.3
Aged 55 to 64	778	58	12.1	7.5
Aged 65 to 74	439	23	4.8	5.2
Aged 75 or older	242	29	6.0	12.0
Asian women	**7,397**	**534**	**100.0**	**7.2**
Under age 25	1,265	47	8.8	3.7
Aged 25 to 34	1,542	104	19.5	6.7
Aged 35 to 44	1,494	75	14.0	5.0
Aged 45 to 54	1,217	73	13.7	6.0
Aged 55 to 64	978	62	11.6	6.3
Aged 65 to 74	519	72	13.5	13.9
Aged 75 or older	381	101	18.9	26.5

Note: Asians are those who identify themselves as being Asian alone and those who identify themselves as being Asian in combination with other races.
Source: Bureau of the Census, Current Population Survey Annual Social and Economic Supplement, Internet site http://www .census.gov/hhes/www/income/dinctabs.html; calculations by New Strategist

Table 3.77 Asian Households by Age of Householder, Type of Household, and Presence of Children, 2012

(number and percent distribution of Asian households by age of householder, type of household, and presence of own children under age 18, 2012; numbers in thousands)

	all households		married couples		female-headed families		male-headed families	
	total	with children	total	with children	total	with children	total	with children
Total Asian households	**5,705**	**2,070**	**3,435**	**1,758**	**573**	**239**	**334**	**73**
Under age 25	407	41	26	14	68	18	81	9
Aged 25 to 29	554	119	207	97	46	14	66	8
Aged 30 to 34	695	336	434	289	53	38	47	9
Aged 35 to 39	717	486	507	421	71	56	22	9
Aged 40 to 44	607	428	440	368	63	47	28	13
Aged 45 to 49	629	392	433	333	82	42	26	17
Aged 50 to 54	509	161	380	147	37	9	17	5
Aged 55 to 64	855	93	581	79	87	11	40	3
Aged 65 or older	731	11	427	9	66	2	7	0

PERCENT OF HOUSEHOLDS WITH CHILDREN BY TYPE

Total Asian households	**100.0%**	**36.3%**	**100.0%**	**51.2%**	**100.0%**	**41.7%**	**100.0%**	**21.9%**
Under age 25	100.0	10.1	100.0	53.8	100.0	26.5	100.0	11.1
Aged 25 to 29	100.0	21.5	100.0	46.9	100.0	30.4	100.0	12.1
Aged 30 to 34	100.0	48.3	100.0	66.6	100.0	71.7	100.0	19.1
Aged 35 to 39	100.0	67.8	100.0	83.0	100.0	78.9	100.0	40.9
Aged 40 to 44	100.0	70.5	100.0	83.6	100.0	74.6	100.0	46.4
Aged 45 to 49	100.0	62.3	100.0	76.9	100.0	51.2	100.0	65.4
Aged 50 to 54	100.0	31.6	100.0	38.7	100.0	24.3	100.0	29.4
Aged 55 to 64	100.0	10.9	100.0	13.6	100.0	12.6	100.0	7.5
Aged 65 or older	100.0	1.5	100.0	2.1	100.0	3.0	100.0	0.0

Note: Asians are those who identify themselves as being Asian alone and those who identify themselves as being Asian in combination with other races.
Source: Bureau of the Census, Current Population Survey Annual Social and Economic Supplement, America's Families and Living Arrangements: 2012, Internet site http://www.census.gov/hhes/families/data/cps2012.html; calculations by New Strategist

Table 3.78 Living Arrangements of Asian Children, 2012

(number and percent distribution of Asian children under age 18 by living arrangement, 2012; numbers in thousands)

	number	percent distribution
ASIAN CHILDREN	**4,542**	**100.0%**
Living with two parents	**3,785**	**83.3**
Married parents	3,657	80.5
Unmarried parents	129	2.8
Biological mother and father	3,554	78.2
Married parents	3,431	75.5
Biological mother and stepfather	73	1.6
Biological father and stepmother	29	0.6
Biological mother and adoptive father	10	0.2
Biological father and adoptive mother	2	0.0
Adoptive mother and father	109	2.4
Other	8	0.2
Living with one parent	**662**	**14.6**
Mother only	548	12.1
Father only	114	2.5
Living with no parents	**95**	**2.1**
Grandparents	29	0.6
Other	66	1.5
At least one biological parent	**4,290**	**94.5**
At least one stepparent	**121**	**2.7**
At least one adoptive parent	**150**	**3.3**

Note: Asians are those who identify themselves as being of the race alone and those who identify themselves as being of the race in combination with other races.
Source: Bureau of the Census, Current Population Survey Annual Social and Economic Supplement, America's Families and Living Arrangements: 2012, Detailed Tables, Internet site http://www.census.gov/hhes/families/data/cps2012.html; calculations by New Strategist

Table 3.79 Marital Status of Asian Men by Age, 2012

(number and percent distribution of Asian men aged 18 or older by age and marital status, 2012; numbers in thousands)

	total	never married	married, spouse present	married, spouse absent	separated	divorced	widowed
Total Asian men	**6,200**	**2,043**	**3,648**	**182**	**49**	**214**	**64**
Aged 18 to 19	226	219	2	2	3	0	0
Aged 20 to 24	709	673	23	8	2	3	0
Aged 25 to 29	717	527	165	13	6	6	0
Aged 30 to 34	686	247	388	29	2	19	0
Aged 35 to 39	692	98	532	23	7	32	0
Aged 40 to 44	612	97	450	32	6	29	0
Aged 45 to 49	553	60	432	15	6	34	6
Aged 50 to 54	545	39	451	17	7	28	4
Aged 55 to 64	778	71	618	31	6	44	8
Aged 65 to 74	439	5	396	12	3	13	10
Aged 75 to 84	191	6	155	1	0	7	23
Aged 85 or older	51	1	37	0	0	0	13
Total Asian men	**100.0%**	**33.0%**	**58.8%**	**2.9%**	**0.8%**	**3.5%**	**1.0%**
Aged 18 to 19	100.0	96.9	0.9	0.9	1.3	0.0	0.0
Aged 20 to 24	100.0	94.9	3.2	1.1	0.3	0.4	0.0
Aged 25 to 29	100.0	73.5	23.0	1.8	0.8	0.8	0.0
Aged 30 to 34	100.0	36.0	56.6	4.2	0.3	2.8	0.0
Aged 35 to 39	100.0	14.2	76.9	3.3	1.0	4.6	0.0
Aged 40 to 44	100.0	15.8	73.5	5.2	1.0	4.7	0.0
Aged 45 to 49	100.0	10.8	78.1	2.7	1.1	6.1	1.1
Aged 50 to 54	100.0	7.2	82.8	3.1	1.3	5.1	0.7
Aged 55 to 64	100.0	9.1	79.4	4.0	0.8	5.7	1.0
Aged 65 to 74	100.0	1.1	90.2	2.7	0.7	3.0	2.3
Aged 75 to 84	100.0	3.1	81.2	0.5	0.0	3.7	12.0
Aged 85 or older	100.0	2.0	72.5	0.0	0.0	0.0	25.5

Note: Asians are those who identify themselves as being Asian alone and those who identify themselves as being Asian in combination with other races.
Source: Bureau of the Census, Current Population Survey Annual Social and Economic Supplement, America's Families and Living Arrangements: 2012, Internet site http://www.census.gov/hhes/families/data/cps2012.html; calculations by New Strategist

Table 3.80 Marital Status of Asian Women by Age, 2012

(number and percent distribution of Asian women aged 18 or older by age and current marital status, 2012; numbers in thousands)

	total	never married	married, spouse present	married, spouse absent	separated	divorced	widowed
Total Asian women	**7,028**	**1,733**	**4,135**	**241**	**94**	**395**	**430**
Aged 18 to 19	235	226	5	4	0	0	0
Aged 20 to 24	664	565	78	9	3	7	2
Aged 25 to 29	751	375	344	16	5	10	2
Aged 30 to 34	791	182	548	24	15	23	0
Aged 35 to 39	765	115	548	30	17	49	6
Aged 40 to 44	726	69	568	22	13	41	13
Aged 45 to 49	645	62	467	24	8	66	18
Aged 50 to 54	572	45	424	38	10	37	18
Aged 55 to 64	978	55	722	34	9	90	69
Aged 65 to 74	519	24	299	18	8	52	118
Aged 75 to 84	293	13	117	15	4	17	127
Aged 85 or older	89	3	14	7	3	3	58
Total Asian women	**100.0%**	**24.7%**	**58.8%**	**3.4%**	**1.3%**	**5.6%**	**6.1%**
Aged 18 to 19	100.0	96.2	2.1	1.7	0.0	0.0	0.0
Aged 20 to 24	100.0	85.1	11.7	1.4	0.5	1.1	0.3
Aged 25 to 29	100.0	49.9	45.8	2.1	0.7	1.3	0.3
Aged 30 to 34	100.0	23.0	69.3	3.0	1.9	2.9	0.0
Aged 35 to 39	100.0	15.0	71.6	3.9	2.2	6.4	0.8
Aged 40 to 44	100.0	9.5	78.2	3.0	1.8	5.6	1.8
Aged 45 to 49	100.0	9.6	72.4	3.7	1.2	10.2	2.8
Aged 50 to 54	100.0	7.9	74.1	6.6	1.7	6.5	3.1
Aged 55 to 64	100.0	5.6	73.8	3.5	0.9	9.2	7.1
Aged 65 to 74	100.0	4.6	57.6	3.5	1.5	10.0	22.7
Aged 75 to 84	100.0	4.4	39.9	5.1	1.4	5.8	43.3
Aged 85 or older	100.0	3.4	15.7	7.9	3.4	3.4	65.2

Note: Asians are those who identify themselves as being Asian alone and those who identify themselves as being Asian in combination with other races.
Source: Bureau of the Census, Current Population Survey Annual Social and Economic Supplement, America's Families and Living Arrangements: 2012, Internet site http://www.census.gov/hhes/families/data/cps2012.html; calculations by New Strategist

Table 3.81 Marital History of Asian Men by Age, 2009

(number of Asian men aged 15 or older and percent distribution by marital history and age, 2009; numbers in thousands)

	total	15–19	20–24	25–29	30–34	35–39	40–49	50–59	60–69	70+
TOTAL ASIAN MEN, NUMBER	4,352	369	334	505	440	488	940	608	387	281
TOTAL ASIAN MEN, PERCENT	100.0%	100.0%	100.0%	100.0%	100.0%	100.0%	100.0%	100.0%	100.0%	100.0%
Never married	33.0	97.1	94.8	70.9	30.6	17.1	13.7	6.4	0.0	5.8
Ever married	67.0	2.9	5.2	29.1	69.4	82.9	86.3	93.6	100.0	94.2
Married once	62.4	1.9	5.2	27.6	68.8	77.0	80.0	84.6	90.7	91.2
Still married	55.8	1.6	4.2	26.3	67.5	71.8	72.4	74.1	75.5	74.0
Married twice	4.3	0.9	0.0	1.5	0.6	5.2	6.0	9.0	7.3	3.0
Still married	3.7	0.0	0.0	0.7	0.6	5.2	5.5	7.4	7.3	1.9
Married three or more times	0.3	0.0	0.0	0.0	0.0	0.7	0.4	0.0	2.0	0.0
Still married	0.2	0.0	0.0	0.0	0.0	0.7	0.0	0.0	1.4	0.0
Ever divorced	8.2	0.9	0.0	1.5	1.8	10.7	11.3	17.3	14.2	6.3
Currently divorced	4.4	0.9	0.0	0.8	1.2	4.7	6.1	9.5	7.3	5.0
Ever widowed	2.1	0.0	0.0	0.9	0.0	0.0	1.0	1.6	7.8	13.7
Currently widowed	1.7	0.0	0.0	0.9	0.0	0.0	0.6	1.6	5.4	12.0

Note: Asians are those who identify themselves as being of the race alone.
Source: Bureau of the Census, Number, Timing, and Duration of Marriages and Divorces: 2009, Detailed Tables, Internet site http://www.census.gov/hhes/socdemo/marriage/data/sipp/index.html

Table 3.82 Marital History of Asian Women by Age, 2009

(number of Asian women aged 15 or older and percent distribution by marital history and age, 2009; numbers in thousands)

	total	15–19	20–24	25–29	30–34	35–39	40–49	50–59	60–69	70+
TOTAL ASIAN WOMEN, NUMBER	4,919	364	347	492	549	565	957	794	443	408
TOTAL ASIAN WOMEN, PERCENT	100.0%	100.0%	100.0%	100.0%	100.0%	100.0%	100.0%	100.0%	100.0%	100.0%
Never married	23.8	96.5	85.2	51.6	11.8	10.2	6.6	5.8	7.1	1.3
Ever married	76.2	3.5	14.8	48.4	88.2	89.8	93.4	94.2	92.9	98.7
Married once	69.2	3.5	14.8	48.4	84.6	86.2	80.1	83.4	81.7	88.3
Still married	57.2	3.5	13.6	46.8	78.8	76.7	69.6	70.6	61.4	39.1
Married twice	6.4	0.0	0.0	0.0	3.0	3.3	12.0	10.1	10.2	9.6
Still married	5.0	0.0	0.0	0.0	3.0	2.8	11.4	7.0	7.7	4.0
Married three or more times	0.6	0.0	0.0	0.0	0.6	0.4	1.2	0.7	1.0	0.9
Still married	0.5	0.0	0.0	0.0	0.6	0.4	1.2	0.3	1.0	0.0
Ever divorced	11.1	0.0	0.7	0.6	6.9	11.9	19.2	17.4	14.8	11.2
Currently divorced	5.6	0.0	0.7	0.6	4.3	8.7	6.8	10.0	6.5	6.2
Ever widowed	7.1	0.0	0.0	0.0	1.3	0.6	1.7	5.5	17.2	49.9
Currently widowed	6.5	0.0	0.0	0.0	0.3	0.6	1.5	4.7	15.3	47.4

Note: Asians are those who identify themselves as being of the race alone.
Source: Bureau of the Census, Number, Timing, and Duration of Marriages and Divorces: 2009, Detailed Tables, Internet site http://www.census.gov/hhes/socdemo/marriage/data/sipp/index.html

Asian Population Numbers 18 Million

The number of Asians grew 52 percent between 2000 and 2011, increasing from 12 to 18 million—a figure that includes those who identify themselves as being Asian alone and those who identify themselves as being Asian in combination with one or more other races. Despite the rapid growth of Asians, they account for just 5.8 percent of the total U.S. population and are greatly outnumbered by Hispanics and blacks.

Behind the growth of the Asian population is immigration. Immigrants from the Asian world region accounted for 43 percent of all immigrants to the United States in 2011, the largest numbers coming from China, India, and the Philippines. Nearly 3 million U.S. residents speak Chinese at home, and more than 1 million each speak Tagalog, Vietnamese, or Korean.

Forty-six percent of Asians live in the West, where they account for 12 percent of the population. California is home to 32 percent of the nation's Asian population, where they account for 15 percent of the state's population. Los Angeles has more Asians (2.1 million) than any other metropolitan area, but Asians account for a larger share of the San Francisco metropolitan area population—26 percent in San Francisco versus 16 percent in Los Angeles. One-third of the population of the San Jose metropolitan area is Asian.

The American Time Use Survey reveals interesting findings about how Asians spend their time. Compared with the average person, Asians spend 15 percent more time at work, 48 percent more time in educational activities, and 95 percent more time using computers for leisure.

■ The Asian population is much larger in some areas than others, but the Asian influence on American culture can be felt throughout the nation.

Asians are a substantial share of the population in the West

(Asian share of population by region, 2011)

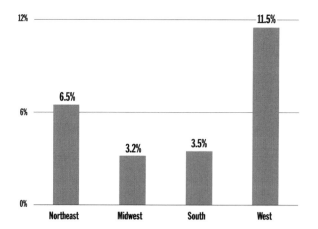

Table 3.83 Asians by Racial Identification, 2000 and 2010

(total number of people, and number and percent distribution of Asians by racial identification, 2000 and 2010; percent change, 2000–10)

	2010		2000		percent change 2000–10
	number	percent distribution	number	percent distribution	
Total people	**308,745,538**	**100.0%**	**281,421,906**	**100.0%**	**9.7%**
Asian alone or in combination with one or more other races	**17,320,856**	**5.6**	**12,006,894**	**4.3**	**44.3**
Asian alone	14,674,252	4.8	10,242,998	3.6	43.3
Asian in combination	2,646,604	0.9	1,763,896	0.6	50.0

Source: Bureau of the Census, An Overview: Race and Hispanic Origin and the 2010 Census, 2010 Census Briefs, Internet site http://www.census.gov/2010census/data/2010-census-briefs.php; calculations by New Strategist

Table 3.84 Asians by Hispanic Origin, 2010

(number and percent distribution of Asians by Hispanic origin and racial identification, 2010)

	Asian alone or in combination		Asian alone	
	number	percent distribution	number	percent distribution
Total Asians	**17,320,856**	**100.0%**	**14,674,252**	**100.0%**
Not Hispanic	16,722,710	96.5	14,465,124	98.6
Hispanic	598,146	3.5	209,128	1.4

Source: Bureau of the Census, An Overview: Race and Hispanic Origin and the 2010 Census, 2010 Census Briefs, Internet site http://www.census.gov/2010census/data/2010-census-briefs.php; calculations by New Strategist

Table 3.85 Asians Ranked by Ethnic Group, 2011

(number and percent distribution of people identifying themselves as Asian alone by ethnic group alone identification, 2011)

	number	percent distribution
Total Asians alone	**15,020,419**	**100.0%**
Chinese (except Taiwanese)	3,361,879	22.4
Asian Indian	2,908,204	19.4
Filipino	2,538,325	16.9
Vietnamese	1,669,447	11.1
Korean	1,449,876	9.7
Japanese	756,898	5.0
Pakistani	351,049	2.3
Cambodian	253,830	1.7
Hmong	241,308	1.6
Thai	189,889	1.3
Laotian	186,013	1.2
Taiwanese	158,271	1.1
Bangladeshi	140,153	0.9
Burmese	95,990	0.6
Nepalese	73,358	0.5
Indonesian	71,110	0.5
Sri Lankan	44,742	0.3
Malaysian	15,048	0.1
Mongolian	11,126	0.1
Bhutanese	9,978	0.1
Okinawan	2,245	0.0
Other ethnicity	132,560	0.9
Two or more ethnicities	359,120	2.4

Source: Bureau of the Census, 2011 American Community Survey, Internet site http://factfinder2.census.gov/faces/nav/jsf/pages/index.xhtml; calculations by New Strategist

Table 3.86 Asians by Age, 2000 to 2011

(number of Asians by age, 2000 to 2011; percent change, 2000–11)

	2011	2010	2000	percent change 2000–11
Total Asians	**18,205,898**	**17,320,856**	**12,006,894**	**51.6%**
Under age 5	1,382,588	1,316,614	930,047	48.7
Aged 5 to 9	1,345,572	1,284,504	908,462	48.1
Aged 10 to 14	1,249,814	1,183,975	883,594	41.4
Aged 15 to 19	1,243,851	1,228,860	926,392	34.3
Aged 20 to 24	1,407,387	1,333,493	972,071	44.8
Aged 25 to 29	1,496,962	1,433,444	1,127,360	32.8
Aged 30 to 34	1,484,221	1,411,567	1,072,489	38.4
Aged 35 to 39	1,485,466	1,445,044	1,023,667	45.1
Aged 40 to 44	1,370,357	1,279,149	946,015	44.9
Aged 45 to 49	1,234,863	1,188,028	826,430	49.4
Aged 50 to 54	1,117,182	1,076,192	682,390	63.7
Aged 55 to 59	976,196	916,286	471,213	107.2
Aged 60 to 64	806,014	740,411	371,569	116.9
Aged 65 to 69	549,622	508,364	296,358	85.5
Aged 70 to 74	406,742	378,904	237,557	71.2
Aged 75 to 79	287,787	268,859	168,244	71.1
Aged 80 to 84	194,838	180,327	95,060	105.0
Aged 85 or older	166,436	146,835	67,976	144.8
Aged 18 to 24	1,915,138	1,853,758	1,361,042	40.7
Aged 18 or older	13,491,824	12,827,168	8,747,370	54.2
Aged 65 or older	1,605,425	1,483,289	865,195	85.6

Note: Asians are those who identify themselves as being of the race alone and those who identify themselves as being of the race in combination with other races.
Source: Bureau of the Census, 2000 Census, 2010 Census, and Population Estimates, Internet site http://www.census.gov/ popest/index.html; calculations by New Strategist

Table 3.87 Asian Share of Total Population by Age, 2011

(total number of people, number of Asians, and Asian share of total, by age, 2011)

	total	Asian number	share of total
Total people	**311,591,917**	**18,205,898**	**5.8%**
Under age 5	20,162,058	1,382,588	6.9
Aged 5 to 9	20,334,196	1,345,572	6.6
Aged 10 to 14	20,704,852	1,249,814	6.0
Aged 15 to 19	21,644,043	1,243,851	5.7
Aged 20 to 24	22,153,832	1,407,387	6.4
Aged 25 to 29	21,279,794	1,496,962	7.0
Aged 30 to 34	20,510,704	1,484,221	7.2
Aged 35 to 39	19,594,309	1,485,466	7.6
Aged 40 to 44	21,033,645	1,370,357	6.5
Aged 45 to 49	22,158,005	1,234,863	5.6
Aged 50 to 54	22,560,198	1,117,182	5.0
Aged 55 to 59	20,255,548	976,196	4.8
Aged 60 to 64	17,806,592	806,014	4.5
Aged 65 to 69	12,873,788	549,622	4.3
Aged 70 to 74	9,607,950	406,742	4.2
Aged 75 to 79	7,388,687	287,787	3.9
Aged 80 to 84	5,786,543	194,838	3.4
Aged 85 or older	5,737,173	166,436	2.9
Aged 18 to 24	31,064,709	1,915,138	6.2
Aged 18 or older	237,657,645	13,491,824	5.7
Aged 65 or older	41,394,141	1,605,425	3.9

Note: Asians are those who identify themselves as being of the race alone and those who identify themselves as being of the race in combination with other races.
Source: Bureau of the Census, Population Estimates, Internet site http://www.census.gov/popest/index.html; calculations by New Strategist

Table 3.88 Asians by Age and Sex, 2011

(number of Asians by age and sex, and sex ratio by age, 2011)

	total	females	males	sex ratio
Total Asians	**18,205,898**	**9,480,263**	**8,725,635**	**92**
Under age 5	1,382,588	677,878	704,710	104
Aged 5 to 9	1,345,572	668,181	677,391	101
Aged 10 to 14	1,249,814	618,735	631,079	102
Aged 15 to 19	1,243,851	609,256	634,595	104
Aged 20 to 24	1,407,387	697,301	710,086	102
Aged 25 to 29	1,496,962	775,148	721,814	93
Aged 30 to 34	1,484,221	789,198	695,023	88
Aged 35 to 39	1,485,466	784,475	700,991	89
Aged 40 to 44	1,370,357	725,718	644,639	89
Aged 45 to 49	1,234,863	652,549	582,314	89
Aged 50 to 54	1,117,182	596,907	520,275	87
Aged 55 to 59	976,196	531,076	445,120	84
Aged 60 to 64	806,014	444,383	361,631	81
Aged 65 to 69	549,622	300,551	249,071	83
Aged 70 to 74	406,742	222,007	184,735	83
Aged 75 to 79	287,787	164,387	123,400	75
Aged 80 to 84	194,838	117,653	77,185	66
Aged 85 or older	166,436	104,860	61,576	59
Aged 18 to 24	1,915,138	945,374	969,764	103
Aged 18 or older	13,491,824	7,154,286	6,337,538	89
Aged 65 or older	1,605,425	909,458	695,967	77

Note: Asians are those who identify themselves as being of the race alone and those who identify themselves as being of the race in combination with other races. The sex ratio is the number of males divided by the number of females multiplied by 100.
Source: Bureau of the Census, Population Estimates, Internet site http://www.census.gov/popest/index.html; calculations by New Strategist

Table 3.89 Asian Population Projections, 2012 to 2050

(number of Asians by age, and Asian share of total population, 2012 to 2050, percent and percentage point change, 2012–50; numbers in thousands)

NUMBER	2012	2020	2030	2040	2050	percent change 2012–50
Total Asians	**18,647**	**22,384**	**27,482**	**32,876**	**38,407**	**106.0%**
Under age 5	1,414	1,664	1,912	2,238	2,558	80.9
Aged 5 to 9	1,378	1,602	1,878	2,169	2,505	81.7
Aged 10 to 14	1,270	1,489	1,817	2,079	2,409	89.8
Aged 15 to 19	1,247	1,447	1,750	2,036	2,329	86.8
Aged 20 to 24	1,430	1,474	1,788	2,136	2,403	68.0
Aged 25 to 29	1,514	1,689	1,964	2,309	2,604	72.0
Aged 30 to 34	1,535	1,825	2,009	2,367	2,725	77.6
Aged 35 to 39	1,493	1,779	2,053	2,359	2,710	81.5
Aged 40 to 44	1,436	1,627	2,036	2,241	2,601	81.2
Aged 45 to 49	1,252	1,571	1,893	2,181	2,487	98.7
Aged 50 to 54	1,137	1,360	1,676	2,088	2,295	101.9
Aged 55 to 59	1,012	1,221	1,575	1,897	2,187	116.0
Aged 60 to 64	836	1,086	1,339	1,649	2,055	145.9
Aged 65 or older	1,694	2,550	3,792	5,126	6,539	286.0

SHARE OF TOTAL POPULATION	2012	2020	2030	2040	2050	percentage point change 2012–50
Total Asians	**5.9%**	**6.7%**	**7.7%**	**8.7%**	**9.6%**	**3.7**
Under age 5	7.0	7.6	8.6	9.7	10.6	3.6
Aged 5 to 9	6.7	7.5	8.4	9.5	10.4	3.7
Aged 10 to 14	6.2	7.2	8.1	9.1	10.2	4.0
Aged 15 to 19	5.8	7.0	8.0	8.8	9.9	4.0
Aged 20 to 24	6.3	6.8	8.2	9.0	9.8	3.5
Aged 25 to 29	7.1	7.2	8.6	9.6	10.2	3.1
Aged 30 to 34	7.3	8.0	8.6	9.9	10.5	3.2
Aged 35 to 39	7.7	8.1	8.4	9.8	10.6	3.0
Aged 40 to 44	6.8	8.0	8.7	9.3	10.5	3.7
Aged 45 to 49	5.8	7.9	8.6	8.9	10.3	4.5
Aged 50 to 54	5.0	6.6	8.3	9.0	9.6	4.6
Aged 55 to 59	4.9	5.6	8.1	8.9	9.1	4.2
Aged 60 to 64	4.7	5.2	6.9	8.6	9.2	4.5
Aged 65 or older	3.9	4.6	5.2	6.4	7.8	3.9

Note: Asians are those who identify themselves as being of the race alone and those who identify themselves as being of the race in combination with other races.
Source: Bureau of the Census, Population Projections, Internet site http://www.census.gov/population/projections/; calculations by New Strategist

Table 3.90 Asians by Region, 2000 to 2011

(number of Asians by region, 2000 to 2011; percent change, 2000–11)

	2011	2010	2000	percent change 2000–11
Total Asians	**18,205,898**	**17,320,856**	**11,898,828**	**53.0%**
Northeast	3,595,059	3,428,624	2,368,297	51.8
Midwest	2,145,357	2,053,971	1,392,938	54.0
South	4,066,102	3,835,242	2,267,094	79.4
West	8,399,380	8,003,019	5,870,499	43.1

Note: Asians are those who identify themselves as being of the race alone and those who identify themselves as being of the race in combination with other races. Total Asians in 2000 do not match the 2000 total in some of the other tables because this figure has not been adjusted to eliminate the "some other race" category that was included in the census.
Source: Bureau of the Census, 2000 Census, 2010 Census, and Population Estimates, Internet site http://www.census.gov/popest/index.html; calculations by New Strategist

Table 3.91 Asian Share of the Total Population by Region, 2011

(total number of people, number and percent distribution of Asians, and Asian share of total, by region, 2011)

	total	Asian number	Asian percent distribution	Asian share of total
Total people	**311,587,816**	**18,205,898**	**100.0%**	**5.8%**
Northeast	55,597,646	3,595,059	19.7	6.5
Midwest	67,145,089	2,145,357	11.8	3.2
South	116,022,230	4,066,102	22.3	3.5
West	72,822,851	8,399,380	46.1	11.5

Note: Asians are those who identify themselves as being of the race alone and those who identify themselves as being of the race in combination with other races.
Source: Bureau of the Census, Population Estimates, Internet site http://www.census.gov/popest/index.html; calculations by New Strategist

Table 3.92 Asians by State, 2000 to 2011

(number of Asians by state, 2000 to 2011; percent change, 2000–11)

	2011	2010	2000	percent change 2000–11
Total Asians	**18,205,898**	**17,320,856**	**11,898,828**	**53.0%**
Alabama	70,956	67,036	39,458	79.8
Alaska	53,036	50,402	32,686	62.3
Arizona	251,161	230,907	118,672	111.6
Arkansas	48,698	44,943	25,401	91.7
California	5,838,176	5,556,592	4,155,685	40.5
Colorado	198,705	185,589	120,779	64.5
Connecticut	165,265	157,088	95,368	73.3
Delaware	35,379	33,701	18,944	86.8
District of Columbia	29,183	26,857	17,956	62.5
Florida	608,552	573,083	333,013	82.7
Georgia	385,074	365,497	199,812	92.7
Hawaii	784,626	780,968	703,232	11.6
Idaho	32,415	29,698	17,390	86.4
Illinois	695,365	668,694	473,649	46.8
Indiana	134,439	126,750	72,839	84.6
Iowa	68,364	64,512	43,119	58.5
Kansas	88,331	83,930	56,049	57.6
Kentucky	65,356	62,029	37,062	76.3
Louisiana	89,333	84,335	64,350	38.8
Maine	19,174	18,333	11,827	62.1
Maryland	387,746	370,044	238,408	62.6
Massachusetts	414,998	394,211	264,814	56.7
Michigan	301,732	289,607	208,329	44.8
Minnesota	257,910	247,132	162,414	58.8
Mississippi	35,038	32,560	23,281	50.5
Missouri	128,893	123,571	76,210	69.1
Montana	11,424	10,482	7,101	60.9
Nebraska	43,388	40,561	26,809	61.8
Nevada	257,171	242,916	112,456	128.7
New Hampshire	35,945	34,522	19,219	87.0
New Jersey	827,714	795,163	524,356	57.9
New Mexico	45,111	40,456	26,619	69.5
New York	1,661,271	1,579,494	1,169,200	42.1
North Carolina	270,023	252,585	136,212	98.2
North Dakota	9,758	9,193	4,967	96.5
Ohio	247,270	238,292	159,776	54.8
Oklahoma	90,029	84,170	58,723	53.3
Oregon	198,140	186,281	127,339	55.6

	2011	2010	2000	percent change 2000–11
Pennsylvania	420,938	402,587	248,601	69.3%
Rhode Island	38,703	36,763	28,290	36.8
South Carolina	81,322	75,674	44,931	81.0
South Dakota	11,077	10,216	6,009	84.3
Tennessee	119,791	113,398	68,918	73.8
Texas	1,183,436	1,110,666	644,193	83.7
Utah	85,240	77,748	48,692	75.1
Vermont	11,051	10,463	6,622	66.9
Virginia	548,663	522,199	304,559	80.1
Washington	636,734	604,251	395,741	60.9
West Virginia	17,523	16,465	11,873	47.6
Wisconsin	158,830	151,513	102,768	54.6
Wyoming	7,441	6,729	4,107	81.2

Note: Asians are those who identify themselves as being of the race alone and those who identify themselves as being of the race in combination with other races. Total Asians in 2000 do not match the 2000 total in some of the other tables because this figure has not been adjusted to eliminate the "some other race" category that was included in the census.
Source: Bureau of the Census, 2000 Census, 2010 Census, and Population Estimates, Internet site http://www.census.gov/popest/index.html; calculations by New Strategist

Table 3.93 Asian Share of Total Population by State, 2011

(total number of people, number and percent distribution of Asians, and Asian share of total, by state, 2011)

	total	Asian number	percent distribution	share of total
Total people	**311,587,816**	**18,205,898**	**100.0%**	**5.8%**
Alabama	4,802,740	70,956	0.4	1.5
Alaska	722,718	53,036	0.3	7.3
Arizona	6,482,505	251,161	1.4	3.9
Arkansas	2,937,979	48,698	0.3	1.7
California	37,691,912	5,838,176	32.1	15.5
Colorado	5,116,796	198,705	1.1	3.9
Connecticut	3,580,709	165,265	0.9	4.6
Delaware	907,135	35,379	0.2	3.9
District of Columbia	617,996	29,183	0.2	4.7
Florida	19,057,542	608,552	3.3	3.2
Georgia	9,815,210	385,074	2.1	3.9
Hawaii	1,374,810	784,626	4.3	57.1
Idaho	1,584,985	32,415	0.2	2.0
Illinois	12,869,257	695,365	3.8	5.4
Indiana	6,516,922	134,439	0.7	2.1
Iowa	3,062,309	68,364	0.4	2.2
Kansas	2,871,238	88,331	0.5	3.1
Kentucky	4,369,356	65,356	0.4	1.5
Louisiana	4,574,836	89,333	0.5	2.0
Maine	1,328,188	19,174	0.1	1.4
Maryland	5,828,289	387,746	2.1	6.7
Massachusetts	6,587,536	414,998	2.3	6.3
Michigan	9,876,187	301,732	1.7	3.1
Minnesota	5,344,861	257,910	1.4	4.8
Mississippi	2,978,512	35,038	0.2	1.2
Missouri	6,010,688	128,893	0.7	2.1
Montana	998,199	11,424	0.1	1.1
Nebraska	1,842,641	43,388	0.2	2.4
Nevada	2,723,322	257,171	1.4	9.4
New Hampshire	1,318,194	35,945	0.2	2.7
New Jersey	8,821,155	827,714	4.5	9.4
New Mexico	2,082,224	45,111	0.2	2.2
New York	19,465,197	1,661,271	9.1	8.5
North Carolina	9,656,401	270,023	1.5	2.8
North Dakota	683,932	9,758	0.1	1.4
Ohio	11,544,951	247,270	1.4	2.1
Oklahoma	3,791,508	90,029	0.5	2.4

| | total | Asian | | |
		number	percent distribution	share of total
Oregon	3,871,859	198,140	1.1%	5.1%
Pennsylvania	12,742,886	420,938	2.3	3.3
Rhode Island	1,051,302	38,703	0.2	3.7
South Carolina	4,679,230	81,322	0.4	1.7
South Dakota	824,082	11,077	0.1	1.3
Tennessee	6,403,353	119,791	0.7	1.9
Texas	25,674,681	1,183,436	6.5	4.6
Utah	2,817,222	85,240	0.5	3.0
Vermont	626,431	11,051	0.1	1.8
Virginia	8,096,604	548,663	3.0	6.8
Washington	6,830,038	636,734	3.5	9.3
West Virginia	1,855,364	17,523	0.1	0.9
Wisconsin	5,711,767	158,830	0.9	2.8
Wyoming	568,158	7,441	0.0	1.3

Note: Asians are those who identify themselves as being of the race alone and those who identify themselves as being of the race in combination with other races.
Source: Bureau of the Census, Population Estimates, Internet site http://www.census.gov/popest/index.html; calculations by New Strategist

Table 3.94 Number of Asians by State and Ethnicity, 2010

(number of Asians by state and ethnicity, 2010)

	total	Chinese	Asian Indian	Filipino	Vietnamese	Korean	Japanese	other Asian
Total Asians	**14,674,252**	**3,294,615**	**2,712,757**	**2,523,103**	**1,546,997**	**1,398,586**	**814,452**	**2,383,742**
Alabama	51,219	9,999	12,251	4,612	7,336	7,197	3,234	6,590
Alaska	36,021	2,003	648	20,415	1,288	4,058	1,484	6,125
Arizona	166,663	35,584	33,458	32,695	21,802	14,444	10,375	18,305
Arkansas	33,327	4,214	6,080	3,977	5,012	3,231	1,311	9,502
California	4,747,252	1,232,805	496,350	1,188,036	567,833	441,438	294,382	526,408
Colorado	133,134	25,147	17,029	13,444	21,755	22,015	12,077	21,667
Connecticut	129,904	29,776	44,715	12,225	9,708	9,156	3,533	20,791
Delaware	27,914	6,470	11,396	3,857	1,687	1,365	632	2,507
District of Columbia	20,323	5,737	4,849	2,405	1,824	2,141	891	2,476
Florida	444,584	68,657	126,708	85,074	62,704	27,174	13,926	60,341
Georgia	296,986	43,243	87,759	18,952	46,150	52,074	8,185	40,623
Hawaii	525,848	57,150	2,041	189,943	10,244	24,556	192,028	49,886
Idaho	17,939	3,365	2,156	2,575	1,742	1,855	2,987	3,259
Illinois	571,537	105,055	183,051	113,762	25,062	62,536	19,267	62,804
Indiana	96,189	23,318	24,384	10,960	7,348	9,731	4,835	15,613
Iowa	50,363	8,936	9,059	3,559	10,832	6,520	1,347	10,110
Kansas	66,119	12,045	14,044	5,271	13,402	5,470	1,672	14,215
Kentucky	45,604	8,779	10,842	5,473	5,245	4,660	4,913	5,692
Louisiana	67,210	10,103	9,123	5,777	28,173	3,022	2,020	8,992
Maine	13,432	3,162	1,901	1,829	2,157	1,437	586	2,360
Maryland	304,574	68,266	76,617	41,722	24,703	48,142	7,493	37,631
Massachusetts	335,906	123,561	68,956	13,247	42,919	22,202	9,037	55,984
Michigan	242,886	45,454	80,803	22,867	19,015	24,598	13,442	36,707
Minnesota	204,202	23,015	31,357	8,581	24,125	16,582	4,295	96,247
Mississippi	24,691	4,851	4,826	3,826	5,972	1,790	0	3,426
Missouri	92,147	20,021	21,634	10,453	14,938	10,516	3,063	11,522
Montana	6,091	1,040	0	1,391	0	959	714	1,987
Nebraska	29,624	5,522	5,431	2,749	7,705	2,919	1,711	3,587
Nevada	183,979	30,348	8,637	93,120	9,178	12,164	11,465	19,067
New Hampshire	27,754	6,558	8,962	1,787	2,786	2,093	832	4,736
New Jersey	697,788	133,583	279,275	112,111	23,676	87,873	14,734	46,536
New Mexico	27,463	6,060	3,778	4,439	4,840	2,197	2,619	3,530
New York	1,392,380	563,695	341,134	110,379	34,805	136,211	40,796	165,360
North Carolina	194,993	31,529	52,534	18,610	26,286	19,307	6,604	40,123
North Dakota	6,132	1,494	984	713	784	0	0	2,157
Ohio	186,464	42,458	60,559	17,971	14,611	15,122	9,777	25,966
Oklahoma	61,581	8,827	10,348	6,164	16,927	5,652	2,291	11,372
Oregon	135,518	29,225	13,676	15,721	27,389	16,055	13,448	20,004
Pennsylvania	332,435	78,547	100,269	21,054	40,923	38,676	6,593	46,373
Rhode Island	30,991	7,635	3,659	3,716	1,239	2,461	0	12,281

	total	Chinese	Asian Indian	Filipino	Vietnamese	Korean	Japanese	other Asian
South Carolina	54,288	9,471	12,690	9,426	6,384	4,468	2,774	9,075
South Dakota	7,126	1,170	723	1,095	1,363	946	0	1,829
Tennessee	87,257	15,777	19,693	9,263	9,376	10,264	4,449	18,435
Texas	904,831	153,386	230,842	100,262	204,999	64,351	19,460	131,531
Utah	53,046	11,902	5,011	5,675	6,869	5,944	6,830	10,815
Vermont	7,396	1,792	1,379	0	1,214	901	378	1,732
Virginia	416,549	60,272	96,091	64,588	53,542	70,670	10,527	60,859
Washington	457,771	93,112	52,187	86,650	63,678	61,777	38,065	62,302
West Virginia	11,482	2,415	2,949	1,889	986	857	749	1,637
Wisconsin	122,442	17,219	19,909	7,834	4,461	8,809	2,621	61,589
Wyoming	4,138	862	0	959	0	0	0	2,317

Note: Asians are those who identify themselves as being of the race alone. Asian ethnic groups are Asians alone who identify themselves as belonging to the ethnic group alone.
Source: Bureau of the Census, 2010 Census, Internet site http://factfinder2.census.gov/faces/nav/jsf/pages/index.xhtml; calculations by New Strategist

Table 3.95 Distribution of Asians by State and Ethnicity, 2010

(percent distribution of Asians by state and ethnicity, 2010)

	total	Chinese	Asian Indian	Filipino	Vietnamese	Korean	Japanese	other Asian
Total Asians	**100.0%**	**22.5%**	**18.5%**	**17.2%**	**10.5%**	**9.5%**	**5.6%**	**16.2%**
Alabama	100.0	19.5	23.9	9.0	14.3	14.1	6.3	12.9
Alaska	100.0	5.6	1.8	56.7	3.6	11.3	4.1	17.0
Arizona	100.0	21.4	20.1	19.6	13.1	8.7	6.2	11.0
Arkansas	100.0	12.6	18.2	11.9	15.0	9.7	3.9	28.5
California	100.0	26.0	10.5	25.0	12.0	9.3	6.2	11.1
Colorado	100.0	18.9	12.8	10.1	16.3	16.5	9.1	16.3
Connecticut	100.0	22.9	34.4	9.4	7.5	7.0	2.7	16.0
Delaware	100.0	23.2	40.8	13.8	6.0	4.9	2.3	9.0
District of Columbia	100.0	28.2	23.9	11.8	9.0	10.5	4.4	12.2
Florida	100.0	15.4	28.5	19.1	14.1	6.1	3.1	13.6
Georgia	100.0	14.6	29.5	6.4	15.5	17.5	2.8	13.7
Hawaii	100.0	10.9	0.4	36.1	1.9	4.7	36.5	9.5
Idaho	100.0	18.8	12.0	14.4	9.7	10.3	16.7	18.2
Illinois	100.0	18.4	32.0	19.9	4.4	10.9	3.4	11.0
Indiana	100.0	24.2	25.4	11.4	7.6	10.1	5.0	16.2
Iowa	100.0	17.7	18.0	7.1	21.5	12.9	2.7	20.1
Kansas	100.0	18.2	21.2	8.0	20.3	8.3	2.5	21.5
Kentucky	100.0	19.3	23.8	12.0	11.5	10.2	10.8	12.5
Louisiana	100.0	15.0	13.6	8.6	41.9	4.5	3.0	13.4
Maine	100.0	23.5	14.2	13.6	16.1	10.7	4.4	17.6
Maryland	100.0	22.4	25.2	13.7	8.1	15.8	2.5	12.4
Massachusetts	100.0	36.8	20.5	3.9	12.8	6.6	2.7	16.7
Michigan	100.0	18.7	33.3	9.4	7.8	10.1	5.5	15.1
Minnesota	100.0	11.3	15.4	4.2	11.8	8.1	2.1	47.1
Mississippi	100.0	19.6	19.5	15.5	24.2	7.2	0.0	13.9
Missouri	100.0	21.7	23.5	11.3	16.2	11.4	3.3	12.5
Montana	100.0	17.1	0.0	22.8	0.0	15.7	11.7	32.6
Nebraska	100.0	18.6	18.3	9.3	26.0	9.9	5.8	12.1
Nevada	100.0	16.5	4.7	50.6	5.0	6.6	6.2	10.4
New Hampshire	100.0	23.6	32.3	6.4	10.0	7.5	3.0	17.1
New Jersey	100.0	19.1	40.0	16.1	3.4	12.6	2.1	6.7
New Mexico	100.0	22.1	13.8	16.2	17.6	8.0	9.5	12.9
New York	100.0	40.5	24.5	7.9	2.5	9.8	2.9	11.9
North Carolina	100.0	16.2	26.9	9.5	13.5	9.9	3.4	20.6
North Dakota	100.0	24.4	16.0	11.6	12.8	0.0	0.0	35.2
Ohio	100.0	22.8	32.5	9.6	7.8	8.1	5.2	13.9
Oklahoma	100.0	14.3	16.8	10.0	27.5	9.2	3.7	18.5
Oregon	100.0	21.6	10.1	11.6	20.2	11.8	9.9	14.8
Pennsylvania	100.0	23.6	30.2	6.3	12.3	11.6	2.0	13.9
Rhode Island	100.0	24.6	11.8	12.0	4.0	7.9	0.0	39.6
South Carolina	100.0	17.4	23.4	17.4	11.8	8.2	5.1	16.7

	total	Chinese	Asian Indian	Filipino	Vietnamese	Korean	Japanese	other Asian
South Dakota	100.0%	16.4%	10.1%	15.4%	19.1%	13.3%	0.0%	25.7%
Tennessee	100.0	18.1	22.6	10.6	10.7	11.8	5.1	21.1
Texas	100.0	17.0	25.5	11.1	22.7	7.1	2.2	14.5
Utah	100.0	22.4	9.4	10.7	12.9	11.2	12.9	20.4
Vermont	100.0	24.2	18.6	0.0	16.4	12.2	5.1	23.4
Virginia	100.0	14.5	23.1	15.5	12.9	17.0	2.5	14.6
Washington	100.0	20.3	11.4	18.9	13.9	13.5	8.3	13.6
West Virginia	100.0	21.0	25.7	16.5	8.6	7.5	6.5	14.3
Wisconsin	100.0	14.1	16.3	6.4	3.6	7.2	2.1	50.3
Wyoming	100.0	20.8	0.0	23.2	0.0	0.0	0.0	56.0

Note: Asians are those who identify themselves as being of the race alone. Asian ethnic groups are Asians alone who identify themselves as belonging to the ethnic group alone.
Source: Bureau of the Census, 2010 Census, Internet site http://factfinder2.census.gov/faces/nav/jsf/pages/index.xhtml; calculations by New Strategist

Table 3.96 Asians by Metropolitan Area, 2010

(total number of people, number of Asians, and Asian share of total, for selected metropolitan areas, 2010)

	total population	Asian number	Asian share of total
Abilene, TX	165,252	3,162	1.9%
Akron, OH	703,200	17,195	2.4
Albany, GA	157,308	1,925	1.2
Albany–Schenectady–Troy, NY	870,716	32,758	3.8
Albuquerque, NM	887,077	25,267	2.8
Alexandria, LA	153,922	2,099	1.4
Allentown–Bethlehem–Easton, PA–NJ	821,173	24,459	3.0
Altoona, PA	127,089	982	0.8
Amarillo, TX	249,881	7,452	3.0
Ames, IA	89,542	5,991	6.7
Anchorage, AK	380,821	32,157	8.4
Anderson, IN	131,636	851	0.6
Anderson, SC	187,126	1,816	1.0
Ann Arbor, MI	344,791	31,250	9.1
Anniston–Oxford, AL	118,572	1,222	1.0
Appleton, WI	225,666	7,010	3.1
Asheville, NC	424,858	4,964	1.2
Athens–Clarke County, GA	192,541	7,258	3.8
Atlanta–Sandy Springs–Marietta, GA	5,268,860	287,942	5.5
Atlantic City–Hammonton, NJ	274,549	22,835	8.3
Auburn–Opelika, AL	140,247	4,323	3.1
Augusta–Richmond County, GA–SC	556,877	12,993	2.3
Austin–Round Rock–San Marcos, TX	1,716,289	97,923	5.7
Bakersfield–Delano, CA	839,631	43,382	5.2
Baltimore–Towson, MD	2,710,489	144,797	5.3
Bangor, ME	153,923	1,875	1.2
Barnstable Town, MA	215,888	3,062	1.4
Baton Rouge, LA	802,484	16,574	2.1
Battle Creek, MI	136,146	2,705	2.0
Bay City, MI	107,771	806	0.7
Beaumont–Port Arthur, TX	388,745	10,898	2.8
Bellingham, WA	201,140	10,030	5.0
Bend, OR	157,733	2,617	1.7
Billings, MT	158,050	1,620	1.0
Binghamton, NY	251,725	8,668	3.4
Birmingham–Hoover, AL	1,128,047	16,773	1.5
Bismarck, ND	108,779	699	0.6
Blacksburg–Christiansburg–Radford, VA	162,958	6,669	4.1

	total population	Asian	
		number	share of total
Bloomington, IN	192,714	8,743	4.5%
Bloomington–Normal, IL	169,572	8,232	4.9
Boise City–Nampa, ID	616,561	16,845	2.7
Boston–Cambridge–Quincy, MA–NH	4,552,402	329,091	7.2
Boulder, CO	294,567	15,569	5.3
Bowling Green, KY	125,953	3,652	2.9
Bremerton–Silverdale, WA	251,133	18,799	7.5
Bridgeport–Stamford–Norwalk, CT	916,829	48,431	5.3
Brownsville–Harlingen, TX	406,220	3,351	0.8
Brunswick, GA	112,370	1,339	1.2
Buffalo–Niagara Falls, NY	1,135,509	30,031	2.6
Burlington, NC	151,131	2,294	1.5
Burlington–South Burlington, VT	211,261	5,833	2.8
Canton–Massillon, OH	404,422	3,842	0.9
Cape Coral–Fort Myers, FL	618,754	10,995	1.8
Cape Girardeau–Jackson, MO–IL	96,275	1,201	1.2
Carson City, NV	55,274	1,641	3.0
Casper, WY	75,450	793	1.1
Cedar Rapids, IA	257,940	5,079	2.0
Champaign–Urbana, IL	231,891	20,152	8.7
Charleston, WV	304,284	3,179	1.0
Charleston–North Charleston–Summerville, SC	664,607	14,744	2.2
Charlotte–Gastonia–Rock Hill, NC–SC	1,758,038	63,932	3.6
Charlottesville, VA	201,559	9,452	4.7
Chattanooga, TN–GA	528,143	8,741	1.7
Cheyenne, WY	91,738	1,631	1.8
Chicago–Joliet–Naperville, IL–IN–WI	9,461,105	603,113	6.4
Chico, CA	220,000	11,480	5.2
Cincinnati–Middletown, OH–KY–IN	2,130,151	49,539	2.3
Clarksville, TN–KY	273,949	7,260	2.7
Cleveland, TN	115,788	1,107	1.0
Cleveland–Elyria–Mentor, OH	2,077,240	49,448	2.4
Coeur d'Alene, ID	138,494	1,796	1.3
College Station–Bryan, TX	228,660	11,552	5.1
Colorado Springs, CO	645,613	27,437	4.2
Columbia, MO	172,786	7,305	4.2
Columbia, SC	767,598	16,223	2.1
Columbus, GA–AL	294,865	7,050	2.4
Columbus, IN	76,794	2,846	3.7
Columbus, OH	1,836,536	68,444	3.7
Corpus Christi, TX	428,185	8,646	2.0
Corvallis, OR	85,579	5,776	6.7

	total population	Asian number	Asian share of total
Crestview–Fort Walton Beach–Destin, FL	180,822	8,319	4.6%
Cumberland, MD–WV	103,299	873	0.8
Dallas–Fort Worth–Arlington, TX	6,371,773	385,286	6.0
Dalton, GA	142,227	1,794	1.3
Danville, IL	81,625	742	0.9
Danville, VA	106,561	773	0.7
Davenport–Moline–Rock Island, IA–IL	379,690	7,416	2.0
Dayton, OH	841,502	19,954	2.4
Decatur, AL	153,829	1,061	0.7
Decatur, IL	110,768	1,424	1.3
Deltona–Daytona Beach–Ormond Beach, FL	494,593	9,750	2.0
Denver–Aurora–Broomfield, CO	2,543,482	119,177	4.7
Des Moines–West Des Moines, IA	569,633	20,319	3.6
Detroit–Warren–Livonia, MI	4,296,250	169,250	3.9
Dothan, AL	145,639	1,308	0.9
Dover, DE	162,310	4,521	2.8
Dubuque, IA	93,653	1,162	1.2
Duluth, MN–WI	279,771	3,299	1.2
Durham–Chapel Hill, NC	504,357	25,417	5.0
Eau Claire, WI	161,151	4,655	2.9
El Centro, CA	174,528	4,194	2.4
Elizabethtown, KY	119,736	3,199	2.7
Elkhart–Goshen, IN	197,559	2,597	1.3
Elmira, NY	88,830	1,334	1.5
El Paso, TX	800,647	12,286	1.5
Erie, PA	280,566	3,992	1.4
Eugene–Springfield, OR	351,715	12,484	3.5
Evansville, IN–KY	358,676	4,489	1.3
Fairbanks, AK	97,581	4,159	4.3
Fargo, ND–MN	208,777	5,411	2.6
Farmington, NM	130,044	863	0.7
Fayetteville, NC	366,383	11,810	3.2
Fayetteville–Springdale–Rogers, AR–MO	463,204	13,201	2.8
Flagstaff, AZ	134,421	2,734	2.0
Flint, MI	425,790	5,502	1.3
Florence, SC	205,566	2,225	1.1
Florence–Muscle Shoals, AL	147,137	1,157	0.8
Fond du Lac, WI	101,633	1,400	1.4
Fort Collins–Loveland, CO	299,630	8,210	2.7
Fort Smith, AR–OK	298,592	7,856	2.6
Fort Wayne, IN	416,257	11,763	2.8
Fresno, CA	930,450	101,134	10.9

	total population	Asian	
		number	share of total
Gadsden, AL	104,430	846	0.8%
Gainesville, FL	264,275	15,595	5.9
Gainesville, GA	179,684	3,791	2.1
Glens Falls, NY	128,923	986	0.8
Goldsboro, NC	122,623	2,186	1.8
Grand Forks, ND–MN	98,461	2,018	2.0
Grand Junction, CO	146,723	1,844	1.3
Grand Rapids–Wyoming, MI	774,160	18,283	2.4
Great Falls, MT	81,327	1,273	1.6
Greeley, CO	252,825	4,476	1.8
Green Bay, WI	306,241	7,873	2.6
Greensboro–High Point, NC	723,801	23,987	3.3
Greenville, NC	189,510	3,538	1.9
Greenville–Mauldin–Easley, SC	636,986	13,344	2.1
Gulfport–Biloxi, MS	248,820	7,459	3.0
Hagerstown–Martinsburg, MD–WV	269,140	4,078	1.5
Hanford–Corcoran, CA	152,982	7,735	5.1
Harrisburg–Carlisle, PA	549,475	18,589	3.4
Harrisonburg, VA	125,228	2,855	2.3
Hartford–West Hartford–East Hartford, CT	1,212,381	54,602	4.5
Hattiesburg, MS	142,842	1,461	1.0
Hickory–Lenoir–Morganton, NC	365,497	10,212	2.8
Hinesville–Fort Stewart, GA	77,917	2,211	2.8
Holland–Grand Haven, MI	263,801	8,194	3.1
Honolulu, HI	953,207	590,926	62.0
Hot Springs, AR	96,024	991	1.0
Houma–Bayou Cane–Thibodaux, LA	208,178	2,244	1.1
Houston–Sugar Land–Baytown, TX	5,946,800	429,689	7.2
Huntington–Ashland, WV–KY–OH	287,702	2,236	0.8
Huntsville, AL	417,593	11,692	2.8
Idaho Falls, ID	130,374	1,578	1.2
Indianapolis–Carmel, IN	1,756,241	48,478	2.8
Iowa City, IA	152,586	7,996	5.2
Ithaca, NY	101,564	9,963	9.8
Jackson, MI	160,248	1,524	1.0
Jackson, MS	539,057	6,684	1.2
Jackson, TN	115,425	1,253	1.1
Jacksonville, FL	1,345,596	58,029	4.3
Jacksonville, NC	177,772	5,757	3.2
Janesville, WI	160,331	2,211	1.4
Jefferson City, MO	149,807	1,670	1.1
Johnson City, TN	198,716	2,153	1.1

	total population	Asian number	share of total
Johnstown, PA	143,679	962	0.7%
Jonesboro, AR	121,026	1,388	1.1
Joplin, MO	175,518	2,488	1.4
Kalamazoo–Portage, MI	326,589	7,363	2.3
Kankakee–Bradley, IL	113,449	1,365	1.2
Kansas City, MO–KS	2,035,334	58,046	2.9
Kennewick–Pasco–Richland, WA	253,340	8,169	3.2
Killeen–Temple–Fort Hood, TX	405,300	15,822	3.9
Kingsport–Bristol–Bristol, TN–VA	309,544	1,997	0.6
Kingston, NY	182,493	4,029	2.2
Knoxville, TN	698,030	12,504	1.8
Kokomo, IN	98,688	1,108	1.1
La Crosse, WI–MN	133,665	5,409	4.0
Lafayette, IN	201,789	11,950	5.9
Lafayette, LA	273,738	4,470	1.6
Lake Charles, LA	199,607	2,637	1.3
Lake Havasu City–Kingman, AZ	200,186	3,221	1.6
Lakeland–Winter Haven, FL	602,095	12,263	2.0
Lancaster, PA	519,445	11,613	2.2
Lansing–East Lansing, MI	464,036	20,472	4.4
Laredo, TX	250,304	1,831	0.7
Las Cruces, NM	209,233	3,272	1.6
Las Vegas–Paradise, NV	1,951,269	207,775	10.6
Lawrence, KS	110,826	5,187	4.7
Lawton, OK	124,098	4,588	3.7
Lebanon, PA	133,568	1,887	1.4
Lewiston, ID–WA	60,888	668	1.1
Lewiston–Auburn, ME	107,702	1,186	1.1
Lexington–Fayette, KY	472,099	13,028	2.8
Lima, OH	106,331	1,043	1.0
Lincoln, NE	302,157	11,835	3.9
Little Rock–North Little Rock–Conway, AR	699,757	13,156	1.9
Logan, UT–ID	125,442	2,811	2.2
Longview, TX	214,369	2,220	1.0
Longview, WA	102,410	2,267	2.2
Los Angeles–Long Beach–Santa Ana, CA	12,828,837	2,095,708	16.3
Louisville/Jefferson County, KY–IN	1,283,566	25,247	2.0
Lubbock, TX	284,890	7,007	2.5
Lynchburg, VA	252,634	4,052	1.6
Macon, GA	232,293	3,665	1.6
Madera–Chowchilla, CA	150,865	3,832	2.5
Madison, WI	568,593	27,316	4.8

	total population	Asian	
		number	share of total
Manchester–Nashua, NH	400,721	15,179	3.8%
Manhattan, KS	127,081	5,905	4.6
Mankato–North Mankato, MN	96,740	2,129	2.2
Mansfield, OH	124,475	1,097	0.9
McAllen–Edinburg–Mission, TX	774,769	8,621	1.1
Medford, OR	203,206	3,914	1.9
Memphis, TN–MS–AR	1,316,100	29,146	2.2
Merced, CA	255,793	21,902	8.6
Miami–Fort Lauderdale–Pompano Beach, FL	5,564,635	158,400	2.8
Michigan City–La Porte, IN	111,467	883	0.8
Midland, TX	136,872	2,083	1.5
Milwaukee–Waukesha–West Allis, WI	1,555,908	53,746	3.5
Minneapolis–St. Paul–Bloomington, MN–WI	3,279,833	213,786	6.5
Missoula, MT	109,299	1,925	1.8
Mobile, AL	412,992	8,868	2.1
Modesto, CA	514,453	34,573	6.7
Monroe, LA	176,441	1,886	1.1
Monroe, MI	152,021	1,187	0.8
Montgomery, AL	374,536	7,149	1.9
Morgantown, WV	129,709	3,516	2.7
Morristown, TN	136,608	942	0.7
Mount Vernon–Anacortes, WA	116,901	3,006	2.6
Muncie, IN	117,671	1,577	1.3
Muskegon–Norton Shores, MI	172,188	1,478	0.9
Myrtle Beach–North Myrtle Beach–Conway, SC	269,291	3,799	1.4
Napa, CA	136,484	11,116	8.1
Naples–Marco Island, FL	321,520	4,711	1.5
Nashville–Davidson–Murfreesboro–Franklin, TN	1,589,934	44,411	2.8
New Haven–Milford, CT	862,477	34,892	4.0
New Orleans–Metairie–Kenner, LA	1,167,764	36,965	3.2
New York–Northern New Jersey–Long Island, NY–NJ–PA	18,897,109	2,060,331	10.9
Niles–Benton Harbor, MI	156,813	3,196	2.0
North Port–Bradenton–Sarasota, FL	702,281	12,754	1.8
Norwich–New London, CT	274,055	13,715	5.0
Ocala, FL	331,298	5,594	1.7
Ocean City, NJ	97,265	1,130	1.2
Odessa, TX	137,130	1,371	1.0
Ogden–Clearfield, UT	547,184	13,457	2.5
Oklahoma City, OK	1,252,987	43,911	3.5
Olympia, WA	252,264	18,261	7.2
Omaha–Council Bluffs, NE–IA	865,350	23,188	2.7

	total population	Asian	
		number	share of total
Orlando–Kissimmee–Sanford, FL	2,134,411	102,875	4.8%
Oshkosh–Neenah, WI	166,994	4,434	2.7
Owensboro, KY	114,752	924	0.8
Oxnard–Thousand Oaks–Ventura, CA	823,318	69,252	8.4
Palm Bay–Melbourne–Titusville, FL	543,376	15,771	2.9
Palm Coast, FL	95,696	2,530	2.6
Panama City–Lynn Haven–Panama City Beach, FL	168,852	4,970	2.9
Parkersburg–Marietta–Vienna, WV–OH	162,056	1,169	0.7
Pascagoula, MS	162,246	3,817	2.4
Pensacola–Ferry Pass–Brent, FL	448,991	15,630	3.5
Peoria, IL	379,186	8,546	2.3
Philadelphia–Camden–Wilmington, PA–NJ–DE–MD	5,965,343	333,116	5.6
Phoenix–Mesa–Glendale, AZ	4,192,887	176,895	4.2
Pine Bluff, AR	100,258	763	0.8
Pittsburgh, PA	2,356,285	48,898	2.1
Pittsfield, MA	131,219	2,164	1.6
Pocatello, ID	90,656	1,685	1.9
Portland–South Portland–Biddeford, ME	514,098	10,676	2.1
Portland–Vancouver–Hillsboro, OR–WA	2,226,009	161,325	7.2
Port St. Lucie, FL	424,107	7,790	1.8
Poughkeepsie–Newburgh–Middletown, NY	670,301	23,500	3.5
Prescott, AZ	211,033	2,791	1.3
Providence–New Bedford–Fall River, RI–MA	1,600,852	49,160	3.1
Provo–Orem, UT	526,810	11,801	2.2
Pueblo, CO	159,063	2,025	1.3
Punta Gorda, FL	159,978	2,497	1.6
Racine, WI	195,408	2,708	1.4
Raleigh–Cary, NC	1,130,490	57,737	5.1
Rapid City, SD	126,382	1,957	1.5
Reading, PA	411,442	6,861	1.7
Redding, CA	177,223	5,928	3.3
Reno–Sparks, NV	425,417	27,796	6.5
Richmond, VA	1,258,251	46,848	3.7
Riverside–San Bernardino–Ontario, CA	4,224,851	316,252	7.5
Roanoke, VA	308,707	6,055	2.0
Rochester, MN	186,011	9,359	5.0
Rochester, NY	1,054,323	32,143	3.0
Rockford, IL	349,431	9,229	2.6
Rocky Mount, NC	152,392	1,134	0.7
Rome, GA	96,317	1,535	1.6
Sacramento–Arden–Arcade–Roseville, CA	2,149,127	308,127	14.3
Saginaw–Saginaw Township North, MI	200,169	2,634	1.3

	total population	Asian	
		number	share of total
St. Cloud, MN	189,093	4,202	2.2%
St. George, UT	138,115	1,742	1.3
St. Joseph, MO–KS	127,329	1,148	0.9
St. Louis, MO–IL	2,812,896	73,955	2.6
Salem, OR	390,738	10,982	2.8
Salinas, CA	415,057	33,552	8.1
Salisbury, MD	125,203	3,190	2.5
Salt Lake City, UT	1,124,197	44,775	4.0
San Angelo, TX	111,823	1,725	1.5
San Antonio–New Braunfels, TX	2,142,508	61,824	2.9
San Diego–Carlsbad–San Marcos, CA	3,095,313	407,984	13.2
Sandusky, OH	77,079	606	0.8
San Francisco–Oakland–Fremont, CA	4,335,391	1,128,215	26.0
San Jose–Sunnyvale–Santa Clara, CA	1,836,911	620,507	33.8
San Luis Obispo–Paso Robles, CA	269,637	12,159	4.5
Santa Barbara–Santa Maria–Goleta, CA	423,895	27,475	6.5
Santa Cruz–Watsonville, CA	262,382	15,683	6.0
Santa Fe, NM	144,170	2,418	1.7
Santa Rosa–Petaluma, CA	483,878	25,180	5.2
Savannah, GA	347,611	9,298	2.7
Scranton–Wilkes–Barre, PA	563,631	8,505	1.5
Seattle–Tacoma–Bellevue, WA	3,439,809	476,716	13.9
Sebastian–Vero Beach, FL	138,028	2,096	1.5
Sheboygan, WI	115,507	5,732	5.0
Sherman–Denison, TX	120,877	1,441	1.2
Shreveport–Bossier City, LA	398,604	6,229	1.6
Sioux City, IA–NE–SD	143,577	3,803	2.6
Sioux Falls, SD	228,261	3,886	1.7
South Bend–Mishawaka, IN–MI	319,224	6,819	2.1
Spartanburg, SC	284,307	6,639	2.3
Spokane, WA	471,221	15,267	3.2
Springfield, IL	210,170	4,018	1.9
Springfield, MA	692,942	21,006	3.0
Springfield, MO	436,712	6,857	1.6
Springfield, OH	138,333	1,294	0.9
State College, PA	153,990	9,030	5.9
Steubenville–Weirton, OH–WV	124,454	703	0.6
Stockton, CA	685,306	116,818	17.0
Sumter, SC	107,456	1,769	1.6
Syracuse, NY	662,577	18,654	2.8
Tallahassee, FL	367,413	10,479	2.9
Tampa–St. Petersburg–Clearwater, FL	2,783,243	100,023	3.6

	total population	Asian number	Asian share of total
Terre Haute, IN	172,425	2,391	1.4%
Texarkana, TX–Texarkana, AR	136,027	1,246	0.9
Toledo, OH	651,429	11,721	1.8
Topeka, KS	233,870	3,245	1.4
Trenton–Ewing, NJ	366,513	35,838	9.8
Tucson, AZ	980,263	35,148	3.6
Tulsa, OK	937,478	21,011	2.2
Tuscaloosa, AL	219,461	2,870	1.3
Tyler, TX	209,714	3,195	1.5
Utica–Rome, NY	299,397	7,879	2.6
Valdosta, GA	139,588	2,514	1.8
Vallejo–Fairfield, CA	413,344	74,750	18.1
Victoria, TX	115,384	2,163	1.9
Vineland–Millville–Bridgeton, NJ	156,898	2,496	1.6
Virginia Beach–Norfolk–Newport News, VA–NC	1,671,683	77,572	4.6
Visalia–Porterville, CA	442,179	18,948	4.3
Waco, TX	234,906	4,169	1.8
Warner Robins, GA	139,900	4,689	3.4
Washington–Arlington–Alexandria, DC–VA–MD–WV	5,582,170	596,729	10.7
Waterloo–Cedar Falls, IA	167,819	2,546	1.5
Wausau, WI	134,063	7,738	5.8
Wenatchee–East Wenatchee, WA	110,884	1,477	1.3
Wheeling, WV–OH	147,950	999	0.7
Wichita, KS	623,061	25,369	4.1
Wichita Falls, TX	151,306	3,624	2.4
Williamsport, PA	116,111	900	0.8
Wilmington, NC	362,315	4,634	1.3
Winchester, VA–WV	128,472	2,121	1.7
Winston–Salem, NC	477,717	8,606	1.8
Worcester, MA	798,552	36,340	4.6
Yakima, WA	243,231	4,157	1.7
York–Hanover, PA	434,972	7,005	1.6
Youngstown–Warren–Boardman, OH–PA	565,773	4,801	0.8
Yuba City, CA	166,892	21,698	13.0
Yuma, AZ	195,751	3,671	1.9

Note: Asians are those who identify themselves as being of the race alone and those who identify themselves as being of the race in combination with other races.
Source: Bureau of the Census, 2010 Census, Internet site http://factfinder2.census.gov/faces/nav/jsf/pages/index.xhtml; calculations by New Strategist

Table 3.97 Immigrants from Asian Countries, 2011

(total number of immigrants admitted for legal permanent residence, and number and percent distribution of immigrants from Asia, by country of birth, 2011)

	number	percent distribution
Total immigrants	**1,062,040**	**100.0%**
Immigrants from Asia	451,593	42.5
Immigrants from Asia	**451,593**	**100.0**
Afghanistan	1,648	0.4
Armenia	2,983	0.7
Azerbaijan	728	0.2
Bahrain	119	0.0
Bangladesh	16,707	3.7
Bhutan	10,137	2.2
Brunei	25	0.0
Burma	16,518	3.7
Cambodia	2,745	0.6
China, People's Republic	87,016	19.3
Cyprus	101	0.0
Georgia	1,490	0.3
Hong Kong	2,306	0.5
India	69,013	15.3
Indonesia	2,856	0.6
Iran	14,822	3.3
Iraq	21,133	4.7
Israel	3,826	0.8
Japan	6,161	1.4
Jordan	3,876	0.9
Kazakhstan	1,235	0.3
Korea, North	36	0.0
Korea, South	22,824	5.1
Kosovo	670	0.1
Kuwait	973	0.2
Kyrgyzstan	542	0.1
Laos	956	0.2
Lebanon	3,295	0.7
Macau	130	0.0
Malaysia	2,273	0.5
Mongolia	774	0.2
Nepal	10,166	2.3
Oman	60	0.0
Pakistan	15,546	3.4
Philippines	57,011	12.6

	number	percent distribution
Qatar	193	0.0%
Saudi Arabia	1,396	0.3
Singapore	690	0.2
Sri Lanka	2,053	0.5
Syria	2,785	0.6
Taiwan	6,154	1.4
Tajikistan	382	0.1
Thailand	9,962	2.2
Turkey	4,403	1.0
Turkmenistan	260	0.1
United Arab Emirates	707	0.2
Uzbekistan	5,056	1.1
Vietnam	34,157	7.6
Yemen	3,361	0.7

Note: Immigrants are those granted legal permanent residence in the United States. They either arrive in the United States with immigrant visas issued abroad or adjust their status in the United States from temporary to permanent residence.
Source: Department of Homeland Security, 2011 Yearbook of Immigration Statistics, Internet site http://www.dhs.gov/yearbook-immigration-statistics

Table 3.98 People Who Speak Selected Asian Languages at Home, by State, 2009–11

(total number of people aged 5 or older, and number and percent who speak selected Asian languages at home, by state, 2009–11; Asian languages shown are those with at least 1 million at-home speakers)

	total people aged 5 or older	speak Chinese at home		speak Tagalog at home		speak Vietnamese at home		speak Korean at home	
		number	percent	number	percent	number	percent	number	percent
United States	288,553,996	2,815,395	1.0%	1,588,644	0.6%	1,371,147	0.5%	1,135,873	0.4%
Alabama	4,477,927	8,862	0.2	3,143	0.1	6,039	0.1	7,466	0.2
Alaska	658,127	1,483	0.2	13,718	2.1	1,108	0.2	4,336	0.7
Arizona	5,956,673	27,708	0.5	19,840	0.3	20,808	0.3	11,953	0.2
Arkansas	2,721,294	3,984	0.1	2,737	0.1	4,348	0.2	1,685	0.1
California	34,793,018	1,036,832	3.0	758,528	2.2	505,181	1.5	374,923	1.1
Colorado	4,702,519	18,110	0.4	7,925	0.2	20,062	0.4	16,449	0.3
Connecticut	3,372,311	25,417	0.8	8,896	0.3	7,594	0.2	5,947	0.2
Delaware	843,743	5,653	0.7	2,336	0.3	865	0.1	1,515	0.2
District of Columbia	571,129	3,836	0.7	1,145	0.2	965	0.2	1,358	0.2
Florida	17,774,767	55,269	0.3	57,540	0.3	57,545	0.3	19,030	0.1
Georgia	9,033,746	43,475	0.5	10,756	0.1	42,159	0.5	46,307	0.5
Hawaii	1,273,878	33,343	2.6	56,115	4.4	8,315	0.7	18,055	1.4
Idaho	1,449,701	3,336	0.2	1,494	0.1	787	0.1	1,428	0.1
Illinois	12,003,172	93,322	0.8	79,731	0.7	21,902	0.2	51,010	0.4
Indiana	6,057,433	22,056	0.4	5,421	0.1	4,789	0.1	7,111	0.1
Iowa	2,848,477	8,727	0.3	2,212	0.1	7,566	0.3	3,711	0.1
Kansas	2,651,027	10,909	0.4	3,600	0.1	12,519	0.5	3,423	0.1
Kentucky	4,063,448	6,853	0.2	2,894	0.1	5,239	0.1	2,925	0.1
Louisiana	4,223,687	9,133	0.2	4,285	0.1	26,598	0.6	2,488	0.1
Maine	1,260,061	2,492	0.2	1,361	0.1	1,538	0.1	1,155	0.1
Maryland	5,416,438	58,155	1.1	32,094	0.6	23,278	0.4	39,037	0.7
Massachusetts	6,187,386	102,945	1.7	8,792	0.1	41,397	0.7	16,044	0.3
Michigan	9,292,971	38,755	0.4	16,933	0.2	14,805	0.2	15,793	0.2
Minnesota	4,959,424	20,333	0.4	5,822	0.1	20,227	0.4	5,657	0.1
Mississippi	2,759,514	4,018	0.1	2,440	0.1	7,006	0.3	1,429	0.1
Missouri	5,602,736	18,115	0.3	7,021	0.1	12,132	0.2	6,651	0.1
Montana	930,061	777	0.1	810	0.1	0	0.0	518	0.1
Nebraska	1,697,746	3,640	0.2	1,874	0.1	7,007	0.4	1,046	0.1
Nevada	2,516,454	27,585	1.1	66,930	2.7	7,534	0.3	9,754	0.4
New Hampshire	1,247,618	4,389	0.4	1,021	0.1	2,180	0.2	1,477	0.1
New Jersey	8,253,094	112,057	1.4	77,905	0.9	21,476	0.3	79,408	1.0
New Mexico	1,917,278	4,302	0.2	2,011	0.1	3,290	0.2	1,458	0.1
New York	18,233,396	509,606	2.8	79,577	0.4	22,483	0.1	115,594	0.6
North Carolina	8,926,372	27,178	0.3	10,987	0.1	21,697	0.2	16,326	0.2
North Dakota	630,522	1,215	0.2	363	0.1	795	0.1	271	0.0
Ohio	10,821,383	38,301	0.4	11,900	0.1	11,621	0.1	11,782	0.1
Oklahoma	3,493,183	7,690	0.2	3,465	0.1	14,647	0.4	3,930	0.1
Oregon	3,603,503	26,306	0.7	8,385	0.2	25,782	0.7	10,183	0.3
Pennsylvania	11,982,323	68,666	0.6	14,791	0.1	36,998	0.3	29,500	0.2
Rhode Island	995,269	6,033	0.6	2,106	0.2	791	0.1	1,246	0.1
South Carolina	4,333,308	8,677	0.2	6,268	0.1	5,809	0.1	4,321	0.1

	total people aged 5 or older	speak Chinese at home		speak Tagalog at home		speak Vietnamese at home		speak Korean at home	
		number	percent	number	percent	number	percent	number	percent
South Dakota	757,925	1,096	0.1%	656	0.1%	746	0.1%	728	0.1%
Tennessee	5,949,415	13,052	0.2	5,894	0.1	9,652	0.2	8,547	0.1
Texas	23,304,988	133,825	0.6	70,177	0.3	188,188	0.8	54,963	0.2
Utah	2,509,875	10,549	0.4	4,124	0.2	6,962	0.3	4,865	0.2
Vermont	594,196	1,685	0.3	360	0.1	1,314	0.2	418	0.1
Virginia	7,508,820	48,075	0.6	42,448	0.6	46,525	0.6	59,267	0.8
Washington	6,307,524	80,415	1.3	53,531	0.8	57,548	0.9	48,140	0.8
West Virginia	1,749,410	2,254	0.1	975	0.1	894	0.1	1,114	0.1
Wisconsin	5,335,726	14,901	0.3	5,307	0.1	2,436	0.0	4,131	0.1
Wyoming	515,858	578	0.1	506	0.1	92	0.0	225	0.0

Note: Data for Wyoming are an ACS 5-year estimate, 2007–2011.
Source: Bureau of the Census, 2009–11 American Community Survey 3-Year Estimates, Internet site Internet site http://factfinder2.census.gov/faces/nav/jsf/pages/index.xhtml; calculations by New Strategist

Table 3.99 Time Use of Total Asians, 2011

(average hours per day spent in primary activities by total people and Asians aged 15 or older, and index of Asian to total, by type of activity, 2011)

	total people	total Asians	index, Asian to total
Total, all activities	**24.00 hrs.**	**24.00 hrs.**	**100**
Personal care activities	9.47	9.32	98
Sleeping	8.71	8.59	99
Grooming	0.69	0.68	99
Household activities	1.78	1.52	85
Housework	0.58	0.42	72
Food preparation and cleanup	0.56	0.74	132
Lawn, garden, and houseplants	0.19	0.10	53
Animals and pets	0.09	0.04	44
Household management	0.18	0.18	100
Caring for and helping household members	0.43	0.51	119
Caring for and helping household children	0.34	0.42	124
Caring for and helping people in other households	0.15	0.14	93
Working and work-related activities	3.29	3.79	115
Educational activities	0.44	0.65	148
Consumer purchases	0.37	0.35	95
Eating and drinking	1.12	1.36	121
Socializing, relaxing, and leisure	4.65	4.02	86
Socializing and communicating	0.61	0.54	89
Watching television	2.75	2.09	76
Playing games (including computer games)	0.22	0.17	77
Computer use for leisure	0.22	0.43	195
Reading	0.30	0.29	97
Sports, exercise, and recreation	0.34	0.38	112
Religious and spiritual activities	0.15	0.17	113
Volunteering	0.15	0.11	73
Telephone calls	0.10	0.12	120
Traveling	1.21	1.27	105

Note: Hours per day do not add to 24.00 because not all activities are shown. Primary activities are those respondents identified as their main activity. Other activities done simultaneously are not included. The index is calculated by dividing time use of Asians by time use of the average person and multiplying by 100.
Source: Bureau of Labor Statistics, unpublished tables from the American Time Use Survey, Internet site http://www.bls.gov/tus/home.htm; calculations by New Strategist

Table 3.100 Time Use of Asian Men, 2011

(average hours per day spent in primary activities by total and Asian men aged 15 or older, and index of Asian to total, by type of activity, 2011)

	total men	Asian men	index, Asian to total
Total, all activities	**24.00 hrs.**	**24.00 hrs.**	**100**
Personal care activities	9.23	9.16	99
Sleeping	8.62	8.49	98
Grooming	0.56	0.61	109
Household activities	1.36	0.78	57
Housework	0.27	0.14	52
Food preparation and cleanup	0.31	0.28	90
Lawn, garden, and houseplants	0.26	0.11	42
Animals and pets	0.08	0.04	50
Household management	0.15	0.14	93
Caring for and helping household members	0.27	0.38	141
Caring for and helping household children	0.21	0.31	148
Caring for and helping people in other households	0.15	0.06	40
Working and work-related activities	3.89	4.61	119
Educational activities	0.46	0.73	159
Consumer purchases	0.31	0.34	110
Eating and drinking	1.16	1.33	115
Socializing, relaxing, and leisure	4.88	4.24	87
Socializing and communicating	0.57	0.54	95
Watching television	2.99	2.27	76
Playing games (including computer games)	0.28	0.22	79
Computer use for leisure	0.26	0.51	196
Reading	0.24	0.29	121
Sports, exercise, and recreation	0.43	0.45	105
Religious and spiritual activities	0.12	0.12	100
Volunteering	0.13	–	–
Telephone calls	0.06	0.12	200
Traveling	1.25	1.31	105

Note: Hours per day do not add to 24.00 because not all activities are shown. Primary activities are those respondents identified as their main activity. Other activities done simultaneously are not included. The index is calculated by dividing time use of Asian men by time use of the average man and multiplying by 100. "–" means sample is too small to make a reliable estimate. Source: Bureau of Labor Statistics, unpublished tables from the American Time Use Survey, Internet site http://www.bls.gov/tus/home.htm; calculations by New Strategist

Table 3.101 Time Use of Asian Women, 2011

(average hours per day spent in primary activities by total and Asian women aged 15 or older, and index of Asian to total, by type of activity, 2011)

	total women	Asian women	index, Asian to total
Total, all activities	**24.00 hrs.**	**24.00 hrs.**	**100**
Personal care activities	9.71	9.48	98
Sleeping	8.80	8.69	99
Grooming	0.82	0.75	91
Household activities	2.18	2.24	103
Housework	0.87	0.69	79
Food preparation and cleanup	0.79	1.18	149
Lawn, garden, and houseplants	0.13	0.09	69
Animals and pets	0.10	0.03	30
Household management	0.21	0.21	100
Caring for and helping household members	0.58	0.63	109
Caring for and helping household children	0.47	0.53	113
Caring for and helping people in other households	0.13	–	–
Working and work-related activities	2.73	3.01	110
Educational activities	0.42	–	–
Consumer purchases	0.43	0.36	84
Eating and drinking	1.09	1.38	127
Socializing, relaxing, and leisure	4.43	3.81	86
Socializing and communicating	0.66	0.54	82
Watching television	2.52	1.91	76
Playing games (including computer games)	0.16	–	–
Computer use for leisure	0.18	0.36	200
Reading	0.35	0.29	83
Sports, exercise, and recreation	0.25	0.31	124
Religious and spiritual activities	0.19	0.21	111
Volunteering	0.16	0.18	113
Telephone calls	0.13	0.12	92
Traveling	1.16	1.24	107

Note: Hours per day do not add to 24.00 because not all activities are shown. Primary activities are those respondents identified as their main activity. Other activities done simultaneously are not included. The index is calculated by dividing time use of Asian women by time use of the average woman and multiplying by 100. "–" means sample is too small to make a reliable estimate.
Source: Bureau of Labor Statistics, unpublished tables from the American Time Use Survey, Internet site http://www.bls.gov/tus/home.htm; calculations by New Strategist

Table 3.102 Time Use of Asians by Sex, 2011

(average hours per day spent in primary activities by Asian men and women aged 15 or older, and index of Asian women to men, by type of activity, 2011)

	Asian men	Asian women	index, women's time to men's
Total, all activities	**24.00 hrs.**	**24.00 hrs.**	**100**
Personal care activities	9.16	9.48	103
Sleeping	8.49	8.69	102
Grooming	0.61	0.75	123
Household activities	0.78	2.24	287
Housework	0.14	0.69	493
Food preparation and cleanup	0.28	1.18	421
Lawn, garden, and houseplants	0.11	0.09	82
Animals and pets	0.04	0.03	75
Household management	0.14	0.21	150
Caring for and helping household members	0.38	0.63	166
Caring for and helping household children	0.31	0.53	171
Caring for and helping people in other households	0.06	–	–
Working and work-related activities	4.61	3.01	65
Educational activities	0.73	–	–
Consumer purchases	0.34	0.36	106
Eating and drinking	1.33	1.38	104
Socializing, relaxing, and leisure	4.24	3.81	90
Watching television	2.27	1.91	84
Playing games (including computer games)	0.22	–	–
Computer use for leisure	0.51	0.36	71
Reading	0.29	0.29	100
Sports, exercise, and recreation	0.45	0.31	69
Religious and spiritual activities	0.12	0.21	175
Volunteering	–	0.18	–
Telephone calls	0.12	0.12	100
Traveling	1.31	1.24	95

Note: Hours per day do not add to 24.00 because not all activities are shown. Primary activities are those respondents identified as their main activity. Other activities done simultaneously are not included. The index is calculated by dividing time use of Asian women by time use of Asian men and multiplying by 100. "–" means sample is too small to make a reliable estimate. Source: Bureau of Labor Statistics, unpublished tables from the American Time Use Survey, Internet site http://www.bls.gov/tus/ home.htm; calculations by New Strategist

Asian Households Spend the Most

Households headed by Asians spend more than those headed by blacks, Hispanics, or non-Hispanic whites. The nation's 5 million Asian households spent an average of $60,136 in 2011—21 percent more than the $49,705 spent by the average household.

Reasons for the higher spending of Asians include their larger household size (2.7 people per household versus an average of 2.5) and their high level of education. The Asian investment in education is revealed in these statistics. Asian households spend more than double the average on education and account for a disproportionate 8.9 percent of the market. Asians spend more than three times the average on fish and seafood and nearly three times the average on public transportation (which includes airfares). They spend only two-thirds of the average on alcoholic beverages.

■ Asian spending is above average because many Asians households have two or more earners, which boosts incomes.

Asian households spend 21 percent more than the average household

(average annual spending of total and Asian consumer units, 2011)

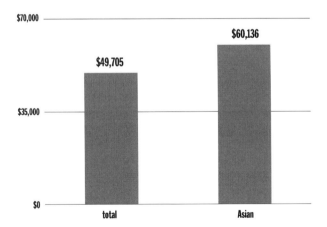

Table 3.103 Spending of Households Headed by Asians, 2011

(average annual spending of total consumer units, and average annual, indexed, and market share of spending of consumer units headed by Asians, by product and service category, 2011)

	total consumer units	Asian consumer units average spending	indexed spending	market share
Number of consumer units (000s)	122,287	5,048	–	4.1%
Average number of persons per consumer unit	2.5	2.7	–	–
Average annual spending	**$49,705**	**$60,136**	**121**	**5.0%**
FOOD	**6,458**	**8,163**	**126**	**5.2**
Food at home	**3,838**	**4,439**	**116**	**4.8**
Cereals and bakery products	531	618	116	4.8
Cereals and cereal products	175	265	151	6.3
Bakery products	356	353	99	4.1
Meats, poultry, fish, and eggs	832	1,094	131	5.4
Beef	223	201	90	3.7
Pork	162	210	130	5.4
Other meats	123	92	75	3.1
Poultry	154	186	121	5.0
Fish and seafood	121	327	270	11.2
Eggs	50	77	154	6.4
Dairy products	407	337	83	3.4
Fresh milk and cream	150	161	107	4.4
Other dairy products	257	175	68	2.8
Fruits and vegetables	715	1,059	148	6.1
Fresh fruits	247	392	159	6.6
Fresh vegetables	224	415	185	7.6
Processed fruits	116	111	96	4.0
Processed vegetables	128	139	109	4.5
Other food at home	1,353	1,332	98	4.1
Sugar and other sweets	144	157	109	4.5
Fats and oils	110	115	105	4.3
Miscellaneous foods	690	678	98	4.1
Nonalcoholic beverages	361	324	90	3.7
Food prepared by consumer unit on trips	48	57	119	4.9
Food away from home	**2,620**	**3,724**	**142**	**5.9**
ALCOHOLIC BEVERAGES	**456**	**311**	**68**	**2.8**
HOUSING	**16,803**	**20,834**	**124**	**5.1**
Shelter	**9,825**	**14,269**	**145**	**6.0**
Owned dwellings	6,148	8,209	134	5.5
Mortgage interest and charges	3,184	4,348	137	5.6
Property taxes	1,845	2,523	137	5.6
Maintenance, repair, insurance, other expenses	1,120	1,338	119	4.9

	total consumer units	Asian consumer units		
		average spending	indexed spending	market share
Rented dwellings	$3,029	$4,843	160	6.6%
Other lodging	648	1,217	188	7.8
Utilities, fuels, and public services	**3,727**	**3,279**	**88**	**3.6**
Natural gas	420	436	104	4.3
Electricity	1,423	1,035	73	3.0
Fuel oil and other fuels	157	62	39	1.6
Telephone	1,226	1,229	100	4.1
Water and other public services	501	517	103	4.3
Household services	**1,122**	**1,593**	**142**	**5.9**
Personal services	398	808	203	8.4
Other household services	724	785	108	4.5
Housekeeping supplies	**615**	**393**	**64**	**2.6**
Laundry and cleaning supplies	145	108	74	3.1
Other household products	340	211	62	2.6
Postage and stationery	130	74	57	2.3
Household furnishings and equipment	**1,514**	**1,300**	**86**	**3.5**
Household textiles	109	69	63	2.6
Furniture	358	381	106	4.4
Floor coverings	20	11	55	2.3
Major appliances	194	153	79	3.3
Small appliances, misc. housewares	89	83	93	3.8
Miscellaneous household equipment	744	603	81	3.3
APPAREL AND RELATED SERVICES	**1,740**	**2,324**	**134**	**5.5**
Men and boys	**404**	**603**	**149**	**6.2**
Men, aged 16 or older	324	503	155	6.4
Boys, aged 2 to 15	80	100	125	5.2
Women and girls	**721**	**911**	**126**	**5.2**
Women, aged 16 or older	604	761	126	5.2
Girls, aged 2 to 15	117	150	128	5.3
Children under age 2	**68**	**109**	**160**	**6.6**
Footwear	**321**	**342**	**107**	**4.4**
Other apparel products and services	**226**	**359**	**159**	**6.6**
TRANSPORTATION	**8,293**	**10,281**	**124**	**5.1**
Vehicle purchases	**2,669**	**3,450**	**129**	**5.3**
Cars and trucks, new	1,265	2,342	185	7.6
Cars and trucks, used	1,339	1,100	82	3.4
Other vehicles	64	8	13	0.5
Gasoline and motor oil	**2,655**	**2,283**	**86**	**3.5**
Other vehicle expenses	**2,454**	**3,075**	**125**	**5.2**
Vehicle finance charges	233	168	72	3.0
Maintenance and repairs	805	717	89	3.7
Vehicle insurance	983	1,608	164	6.8
Vehicle rentals, leases, licenses, other charges	433	582	134	5.5
Public transportation	**516**	**1,473**	**285**	**11.8**

	total consumer units	Asian consumer units		
		average spending	indexed spending	market share
HEALTH CARE	**$3,313**	**$2,919**	**88**	**3.6%**
Health insurance	1,922	1,882	98	4.0
Medical services	768	667	87	3.6
Drugs	489	285	58	2.4
Medical supplies	134	84	63	2.6
ENTERTAINMENT	**2,572**	**2,301**	**89**	**3.7**
Fees and admissions	594	768	129	5.3
Audio and visual equipment and services	977	868	89	3.7
Pets, toys, and playground equipment	631	269	43	1.8
Other entertainment products and services	370	396	107	4.4
PERSONAL CARE PRODUCTS AND SERVICES	**634**	**602**	**95**	**3.9**
READING	**115**	**111**	**97**	**4.0**
EDUCATION	**1,051**	**2,267**	**216**	**8.9**
TOBACCO PRODUCTS AND SMOKING SUPPLIES	**351**	**152**	**43**	**1.8**
MISCELLANEOUS	**775**	**696**	**90**	**3.7**
CASH CONTRIBUTIONS	**1,721**	**1,405**	**82**	**3.4**
PERSONAL INSURANCE AND PENSIONS	**5,424**	**7,771**	**143**	**5.9**
Life and other personal insurance	317	337	106	4.4
Pensions and Social Security	5,106	7,434	146	6.0
PERSONAL TAXES	**2,012**	**3,894**	**194**	**8.0**
Federal income taxes	1,370	3,032	221	9.1
State and local income taxes	505	728	144	6.0
Other taxes	136	134	99	4.1
GIFTS FOR PEOPLE IN OTHER HOUSEHOLDS	**1,037**	**1,120**	**108**	**4.5**

Definitions: The index compares Asian to average consumer unit spending by dividing Asian spending by average spending in each category and multiplying by 100. An index of 125 means Asian spending is 25 percent above average, while an index of 75 means Asian spending is 25 percent below average. The market share is the percentage of total spending on a product or service category accounted for by consumer units headed by Asians.
Note: The Bureau of Labor Statistics uses consumer unit rather than household as the sampling unit in the Consumer Expenditure Survey. For the definition of consumer unit, see the glossary. Spending by category does not add to total spending because gift spending is also included in the preceding product and service categories and personal taxes are not included in the total. "–" means not applicable or sample is too small to make a reliable estimate.
Source: Bureau of Labor Statistics, 2011 Consumer Expenditure Survey, Internet site http://www.bls.gov/cex/; calculations by New Strategist

Asian Households Are Wealthier than Average

The median net worth (assets minus debts) of Asian households was $89,339 in 2011, well above the $68,828 net worth of the average American household. Although the net worth of Asian households is above average, it fell by a steep 49 percent between 2005 and 2011, after adjusting for inflation. This decline exceeded the 36 percent loss for the average household during those years, according to the Census Bureau's Survey of Income and Program Participation.

Asians are more likely than the average household to own most assets. They are 11 percent more likely to have a savings account, 15 percent more likely to own stocks, and 19 percent more likely to have a 401(k) account. But they are less likely than the average household to be homeowners (59 versus 65 percent). Among Asian homeowners, however, home equity is far above average—$120,000 versus $80,000.

Asian households are slightly more likely than the average household to be in debt (72 versus 69 percent). Their home-secured debt (mortgage) is 62 percent above average, largely because many Asians live in California, where housing prices are higher than average.

■ Seventy-two percent of Asians aged 65 or older receive income from Social Security, 23 percent from earnings, and 20 percent from pensions.

The net worth of Asians is well above average

(median net worth of total and Asian households, 2011)

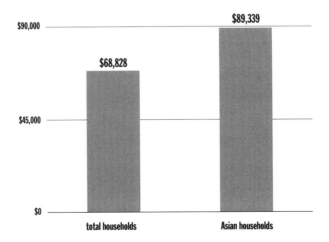

Table 3.104 Median Household Net Worth of Total and Asian Households, 2005 and 2011

(median net worth of total and Asian households, 2005 and 2011; percent change, 2005–11; in 2011 dollars)

	2011	2005	percent change 2005–11
Total households	**$68,828**	**$107,344**	**–35.9%**
Asian households	89,339	175,890	–49.2

Note: Asians are those who identify themselves as being Asian alone.
Source: Census Bureau, Wealth and Asset Ownership, Survey of Income and Program Participation, Internet site http://www
.census.gov/people/wealth/; calculations by New Strategist

Table 3.105 Distribution of Total and Asian Households by Net Worth, 2011

(number of total and Asian households, median net worth of total and Asian households, and percent distribution of total and Asian households by net worth, 2011)

	total households	Asian households number	Asian households index
Number of households	**118,689,091**	**3,939,591**	**–**
Median net worth	**$68,828**	**$89,339**	**130**

DISTRIBUTION OF HOUSEHOLDS BY NET WORTH

	total households	Asian households number	Asian households index
Total households	**100.0%**	**100.0%**	**–**
Zero or negative	18.1	15.4	85
$1 to $4,999	9.1	9.0	99
$5,000 to $9,999	4.8	5.5	115
$10,000 to $24,999	6.6	6.6	100
$25,000 to $49,999	6.9	7.2	104
$50,000 to $99,999	10.4	8.2	79
$100,000 to $249,999	17.9	17.0	95
$250,000 to $499,999	12.6	13.8	110
$500,000 or more	13.5	17.3	128

Note: Asians are those who identify themselves as being Asian alone. The index is calculated by dividing the Asian figure by the total figure and multiplying by 100. "–" means not applicable.
Source: Census Bureau, Wealth and Asset Ownership, Survey of Income and Program Participation, Internet site http://www
.census.gov/people/wealth/; calculations by New Strategist

Table 3.106 Percent of Total and Asian Households Owning Assets, 2011

(percent of total and Asian households owning selected assets, and index of Asian to total, 2011)

	total households	Asian households	
PERCENT WITH ASSET		percent	index
Interest earning asset at financial institution	69.8%	77.7%	111
Regular checking account	29.0	35.8	123
Stocks and mutal fund shares	19.6	22.6	115
Own business	13.8	15.2	110
Motor vehicles	84.7	84.2	99
Own home	65.3	58.7	90
Rental property	5.5	7.0	127
IRA or KEOGH account	28.9	31.5	109
401(k) and thrift savings	42.1	50.0	119

Note: Asians are those who identify themselves as being Asian alone. The index is calculated by dividing the Asian figure by the total figure and multiplying by 100.
Source: Census Bureau, Wealth and Asset Ownership, Survey of Income and Program Participation, Internet site http://www .census.gov/people/wealth/; calculations by New Strategist

Table 3.107 Median Value or Equity of Assets Owned by Total and Asian Households, 2011

(median value or equity of assets owned by total and Asian households, and index of Asian to total, 2011)

	total households	Asian households	
MEDIAN VALUE OF ASSETS		median	index
Interest earning asset at financial institution	$2,450	$4,500	184
Regular checking account	600	900	150
Stocks and mutal fund shares	20,000	19,000	95
Own business (equity)	8,000	6,000	75
Motor vehicles (equity)	6,824	7,839	115
Own home (equity)	80,000	120,000	150
Rental property (equity)	180,000	130,000	72
IRA or KEOGH account	34,000	26,000	76
401(k) and thrift savings	30,000	38,000	127

Note: Asians are those who identify themselves as being Asian alone. The index is calculated by dividing the Asian figure by the total figure and multiplying by 100.
Source: Census Bureau, Wealth and Asset Ownership, Survey of Income and Program Participation, Internet site http://www .census.gov/people/wealth/; calculations by New Strategist

Table 3.108 Asset Ownership of Asian Households, 2005 and 2011

(percent of Asian households owning financial assets, 2005 and 2011; percentage point change, 2005–11)

PERCENT OWNING ASSET	2011	2005	percentage point change
Interest earning asset at financial institution	77.7%	77.1%	0.6
Regular checking account	35.8	36.6	–0.8
Stocks and mutal fund shares	22.6	29.3	–6.7
Own business	15.2	15.5	–0.3
Motor vehicles	84.2	82.5	1.7
Own home	58.7	60.1	–1.4
Rental property	7.0	5.8	1.2
IRA or KEOGH account	31.5	33.2	–1.7
401(k) and thrift savings	50.0	46.7	3.3

Note: Asians are those who identify themselves as being Asian alone.
Source: Census Bureau, Wealth and Asset Ownership, Survey of Income and Program Participation, Internet site http://www
.census.gov/people/wealth/; calculations by New Strategist

Table 3.109 Median Value or Equity of Assets Owned by Asian Households, 2005 and 2011

(median value or equity of assets owned by Asian households, 2005 and 2011; percent change, 2005–11; in 2011 dollars)

MEDIAN VALUE OF ASSETS	2011	2005	percent change
Interest earning asset at financial institution	$4,500	$7,256	–38.0%
Regular checking account	900	1,152	–21.9
Stocks and mutal fund shares	19,000	22,459	–15.4
Own business (equity)	6,000	11,518	–47.9
Motor vehicles (equity)	7,839	8,293	–5.5
Own home (equity)	120,000	230,352	–47.9
Rental property (equity)	130,000	–	–
IRA or KEOGH account	26,000	25,327	2.7
401(k) and thrift savings	38,000	32,249	17.8

Note: Asians are those who identify themselves as being Asian alone. "–" means sample is too small to make a reliable estimate.
Source: Census Bureau, Wealth and Asset Ownership, Survey of Income and Program Participation, Internet site http://www
.census.gov/people/wealth/; calculations by New Strategist

Table 3.110 **Percent of Total and Asian Households with Debt, 2011**

(percent of total and Asian households with debt, and index of Asian to total, 2011)

	total households	Asian households	
		percent	index
PERCENT WITH DEBT			
Total debt	**69.0%**	**72.2%**	**105**
Secured debt	55.3	57.0	103
Home debt	40.5	43.8	108
Business debt	4.1	3.7	90
Vehicle debt	30.4	27.5	90
Unsecured debt	46.2	45.2	98
Credit card debt	38.3	40.4	105
Loans	6.8	5.0	74
Other debt	18.6	14.5	78

Note: "Other debt" includes student loans. Asians are those who identify themselves as being Asian alone. The index is calculated by dividing the Asian figure by the total figure and multiplying by 100.
Source: Census Bureau, Wealth and Asset Ownership, Survey of Income and Program Participation, Internet site http://www .census.gov/people/wealth/; calculations by New Strategist

Table 3.111 **Median Debt of Total and Asian Households, 2011**

(median amount of debt for total and Asian households with debt, and index of Asian to total, 2011)

	total households	Asian households	
		median	index
MEDIAN DEBT			
Total debt	**$70,000**	**$108,000**	**154**
Secured debt	91,000	160,000	176
Home debt	117,000	190,000	162
Business debt	25,000	–	–
Vehicle debt	10,000	11,000	110
Unsecured debt	7,000	7,000	100
Credit card debt	3,500	4,000	114
Loans	7,000	–	–
Other debt	10,000	14,000	140

Note: "Other debt" includes student loans. Asians are those who identify themselves as being Asian alone. The index is calculated by dividing the Asian figure by the total figure and multiplying by 100. "–" means sample is too small to make a reliable estimate.
Source: Census Bureau, Wealth and Asset Ownership, Survey of Income and Program Participation, Internet site http://www .census.gov/people/wealth/; calculations by New Strategist

Table 3.112 Total People and Asians Aged 65 or Older Receiving Income by Source, 2011

(number of total people and Asians aged 65 or older receiving income, percent of Asians receiving income, and Asian share of total, 2011; ranked by number of total people receiving type of income; people in thousands as of 2012)

	total people receiving income	Asians receiving income		
		number	percent	Asian share of total
Total people aged 65 or older	**40,195**	**1,446**	**100.0%**	**3.6%**
Social Security	35,169	1,039	71.9	3.0
Interest	19,862	597	41.3	3.0
Retirement income	14,325	335	23.2	2.3
Pension income	12,460	295	20.4	2.4
Earnings	8,648	329	22.8	3.8
Dividends	7,584	209	14.5	2.8
Rents, royalties, estates, or trusts	3,103	91	6.3	2.9
Survivor benefits	1,859	32	2.2	1.7
Veteran's benefits	1,299	23	1.6	1.8
SSI (Supplemental Security Income)	1,297	203	14.0	15.7

Note: Asians are those who identify themselves as being of the race alone and those who identify themselves as being of the race in combination with other races.

Source: Bureau of the Census, 2012 Current Population Survey Annual Social and Economic Supplement, Internet site http://www.census.gov/hhes/www/cpstables/032012/perinc/toc.htm; calculations by New Strategist

Table 3.113 Median Income of Total People and Asians Aged 65 or Older by Source, 2011

(median income received by total people and Asians aged 65 or older and index of Asian to total, by type of income, 2011)

	median income for total people receiving income	median income for Asians receiving income	index, Asian to total
Total people aged 65 or older	**$19,939**	**$15,060**	**76**
Social Security	13,376	11,768	88
Interest	1,590	1,573	99
Retirement income	12,282	13,443	109
Pension income	12,458	12,704	102
Earnings	24,893	30,197	121
Dividends	2,023	1,976	98
Rents, royalties, estates, or trusts	3,855	6,941	180
Survivor benefits	7,913	–	–
Veteran's benefits	8,770	–	–
SSI (Supplemental Security Income)	5,322	6,756	127

Note: Asians are those who identify themselves as being of the race alone and those who identify themselves as being of the race in combination with other races. The index is calculated by dividing the Asian figure by the total figure and multiplying by 100. "–" means sample is too small to make a reliable estimate.
Source: Bureau of the Census, 2012 Current Population Survey Annual Social and Economic Supplement, Internet site http:// www.census.gov/hhes/www/cpstables/032012/perinc/toc.htm; calculations by New Strategist

4

Blacks

■ The African American population numbered 44 million in 2011, accounting for a substantial 14 percent of the U.S. population.

■ More than half of blacks aged 25 or older have at least some college experience and 21 percent have a bachelor's degree.

■ Only 50 percent of African American adults say they are in "very good" or "excellent" health, less than the 60 percent share among the total population.

■ Forty-four percent of the nation's black households owned their home in 2012.

■ The $32,366 median income of black households in 2011 was 12 percent less than in 2007, after adjusting for inflation. Behind the decline was job loss caused by the Great Recession.

■ The 30 percent of African Americans employed as managers or professionals account for 9 percent of workers in those occupations.

■ African American households are diverse. Married couples head 28 percent of black households, while female-headed families account for another 28 percent.

■ More than half of blacks (54 percent) live in the South, where they account for 21 percent of the population.

■ The average African American household spent $36,644 in 2011. Blacks spend more than average on fish and seafood, footwear, and children's clothes, among other items.

■ At just $6,314 in 2011, the median net worth of black households is less than one-tenth of the $68,828 median net worth of the average household.

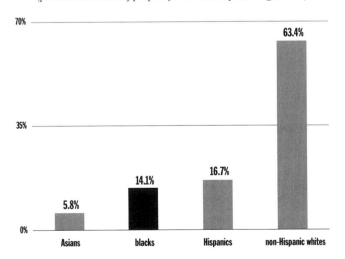

African Americans account for 14 percent of the U.S. population

(percent distribution of people by race and Hispanic origin, 2011)

More than Half of Blacks Have Attended College for One or More Years

Fifty-one percent of blacks aged 25 or older have at least some college experience, and 21 percent are college graduates. While these figures are lower than the shares among Asians and non-Hispanic whites, they are far above those of Hispanics. The educational attainment of blacks is rising as younger generations with more schooling replace the older, less-educated population. Among blacks aged 25 to 34, the 58 percent majority has college experience and 23 percent are college graduates.

A growing proportion of blacks are enrolling in college. The 67 percent majority of black high school graduates go to college within one year of graduating from high school, up from 55 percent in 2000. The 3.1 million blacks enrolled in college in 2011 accounted for 15 percent of the nation's college students. The majority of black college students are enrolled in four-year schools.

Blacks earned 14 percent of associate's degrees awarded in 2010–11. They earned 10 percent of bachelor's degrees, 11 percent of master's degrees, and 7 percent of doctoral and first-professional degrees.

■ The proportion of blacks with a college education will continue to climb, but only if college remains affordable for the middle class.

One in five blacks aged 25 or older has a bachelor's degree

(percent of blacks aged 25 or older by educational attainment, 2012)

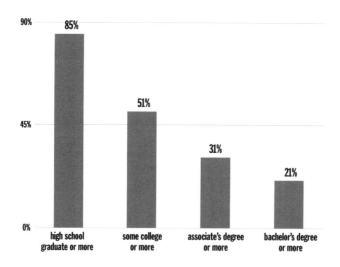

Table 4.1 Educational Attainment of Blacks by Age, 2012

(number and percent distribution of blacks aged 25 or older by educational attainment and age, 2012; numbers in thousands)

	total	25 to 34	35 to 44	45 to 54	55 to 64	65 or older
Total blacks	**24,713**	**5,775**	**5,325**	**5,637**	**4,259**	**3,717**
Not a high school graduate	3,684	692	530	715	619	1,133
High school graduate only	8,359	1,749	1,758	2,067	1,519	1,265
Some college, no degree	5,037	1,459	1,158	1,101	851	469
Associate's degree	2,350	549	595	565	393	249
Bachelor's degree	3,417	987	802	779	524	325
Master's degree	1,410	264	368	307	264	206
Professional degree	226	48	65	46	42	25
Doctoral degree	229	30	50	58	47	44
High school graduate or more	21,028	5,086	4,796	4,923	3,640	2,583
Some college or more	12,669	3,337	3,038	2,856	2,121	1,318
Associate's degree or more	7,632	1,878	1,880	1,755	1,270	849
Bachelor's degree or more	5,282	1,329	1,285	1,190	877	600

PERCENT DISTRIBUTION

	total	25 to 34	35 to 44	45 to 54	55 to 64	65 or older
Total blacks	**100.0%**	**100.0%**	**100.0%**	**100.0%**	**100.0%**	**100.0%**
Not a high school graduate	14.9	12.0	10.0	12.7	14.5	30.5
High school graduate only	33.8	30.3	33.0	36.7	35.7	34.0
Some college, no degree	20.4	25.3	21.7	19.5	20.0	12.6
Associate's degree	9.5	9.5	11.2	10.0	9.2	6.7
Bachelor's degree	13.8	17.1	15.1	13.8	12.3	8.7
Master's degree	5.7	4.6	6.9	5.4	6.2	5.5
Professional degree	0.9	0.8	1.2	0.8	1.0	0.7
Doctoral degree	0.9	0.5	0.9	1.0	1.1	1.2
High school graduate or more	85.1	88.1	90.1	87.3	85.5	69.5
Some college or more	51.3	57.8	57.1	50.7	49.8	35.5
Associate's degree or more	30.9	32.5	35.3	31.1	29.8	22.8
Bachelor's degree or more	21.4	23.0	24.1	21.1	20.6	16.1

Note: Blacks are those who identify themselves as being of the race alone and those who identify themselves as being of the race in combination with other races.
Source: Bureau of the Census, Educational Attainment in the United States: 2012, Internet site http://www.census.gov/hhes/socdemo/education/data/cps/2012/tables.html; calculations by New Strategist

Table 4.2 Educational Attainment of Black Men by Age, 2012

(number and percent distribution of black men aged 25 or older by educational attainment and age, 2012; numbers in thousands)

	total	25 to 34	35 to 44	45 to 54	55 to 64	65 or older
Total black men	**10,993**	**2,642**	**2,404**	**2,582**	**1,872**	**1,493**
Not a high school graduate	1,703	345	259	327	303	471
High school graduate only	3,984	829	926	1,036	715	479
Some college, no degree	2,297	722	507	504	361	204
Associate's degree	870	222	189	209	151	97
Bachelor's degree	1,442	416	345	334	207	140
Master's degree	467	79	127	115	90	57
Professional degree	105	15	25	27	17	20
Doctoral degree	124	14	24	29	29	27
High school graduate or more	9,289	2,297	2,143	2,254	1,570	1,024
Some college or more	5,305	1,468	1,217	1,218	855	545
Associate's degree or more	3,008	746	710	714	494	341
Bachelor's degree or more	2,138	524	521	505	343	244

PERCENT DISTRIBUTION

	total	25 to 34	35 to 44	45 to 54	55 to 64	65 or older
Total black men	**100.0%**	**100.0%**	**100.0%**	**100.0%**	**100.0%**	**100.0%**
Not a high school graduate	15.5	13.1	10.8	12.7	16.2	31.5
High school graduate only	36.2	31.4	38.5	40.1	38.2	32.1
Some college, no degree	20.9	27.3	21.1	19.5	19.3	13.7
Associate's degree	7.9	8.4	7.9	8.1	8.1	6.5
Bachelor's degree	13.1	15.7	14.4	12.9	11.1	9.4
Master's degree	4.2	3.0	5.3	4.5	4.8	3.8
Professional degree	1.0	0.6	1.0	1.0	0.9	1.3
Doctoral degree	1.1	0.5	1.0	1.1	1.5	1.8
High school graduate or more	84.5	86.9	89.1	87.3	83.9	68.6
Some college or more	48.3	55.6	50.6	47.2	45.7	36.5
Associate's degree or more	27.4	28.2	29.5	27.7	26.4	22.8
Bachelor's degree or more	19.4	19.8	21.7	19.6	18.3	16.3

Note: Blacks are those who identify themselves as being of the race alone and those who identify themselves as being of the race in combination with other races.
Source: Bureau of the Census, Educational Attainment in the United States: 2012, Internet site http://www.census.gov/hhes/socdemo/education/data/cps/2012/tables.html; calculations by New Strategist

Table 4.3 Educational Attainment of Black Women by Age, 2012

(number and percent distribution of black women aged 25 or older by educational attainment and age, 2012; numbers in thousands)

	total	25 to 34	35 to 44	45 to 54	55 to 64	65 or older
Total black women	**13,720**	**3,133**	**2,921**	**3,055**	**2,387**	**2,225**
Not a high school graduate	1,982	347	269	388	316	663
High school graduate only	4,375	920	832	1,031	805	787
Some college, no degree	2,740	737	651	597	491	266
Associate's degree	1,480	326	405	356	242	152
Bachelor's degree	1,975	571	457	444	317	185
Master's degree	943	185	241	193	175	150
Professional degree	121	32	40	18	25	5
Doctoral degree	105	15	27	28	17	17
High school graduate or more	11,739	2,786	2,653	2,667	2,072	1,562
Some college or more	7,364	1,866	1,821	1,636	1,267	775
Associate's degree or more	4,624	1,129	1,170	1,039	776	509
Bachelor's degree or more	3,144	803	765	683	534	357

PERCENT DISTRIBUTION

	total	25 to 34	35 to 44	45 to 54	55 to 64	65 or older
Total black women	**100.0%**	**100.0%**	**100.0%**	**100.0%**	**100.0%**	**100.0%**
Not a high school graduate	14.4	11.1	9.2	12.7	13.2	29.8
High school graduate only	31.9	29.4	28.5	33.7	33.7	35.4
Some college, no degree	20.0	23.5	22.3	19.5	20.6	12.0
Associate's degree	10.8	10.4	13.9	11.7	10.1	6.8
Bachelor's degree	14.4	18.2	15.6	14.5	13.3	8.3
Master's degree	6.9	5.9	8.3	6.3	7.3	6.7
Professional degree	0.9	1.0	1.4	0.6	1.0	0.2
Doctoral degree	0.8	0.5	0.9	0.9	0.7	0.8
High school graduate or more	85.6	88.9	90.8	87.3	86.8	70.2
Some college or more	53.7	59.6	62.3	53.6	53.1	34.8
Associate's degree or more	33.7	36.0	40.1	34.0	32.5	22.9
Bachelor's degree or more	22.9	25.6	26.2	22.4	22.4	16.0

Note: Blacks are those who identify themselves as being of the race alone and those who identify themselves as being of the race in combination with other races.
Source: Bureau of the Census, Educational Attainment in the United States: 2012, Internet site http://www.census.gov/hhes/ socdemo/education/data/cps/2012/tables.html; calculations by New Strategist

Table 4.4 Educational Attainment of Blacks by Region, 2006–10

(number of blacks aged 25 or older and percent by educational attainment, by region, 2006–10; numbers in thousands)

	total	Northeast	Midwest	South	West
Total blacks, number	**23,534**	**4,113**	**4,138**	**13,060**	**2,223**
Not a high school graduate	4,468	785	763	2,638	283
High school graduate only	7,553	1,364	1,311	4,307	570
Some college, no degree	5,538	846	1,085	2,942	666
Associate's degree	1,753	316	305	909	222
Bachelor's degree	2,761	521	433	1,493	315
Graduate degree	1,461	281	241	771	167
High school graduate or more	81.0%	80.9%	81.6%	79.8%	87.3%
Some college or more	48.9	47.7	49.9	46.8	61.6
Associate's degree or more	25.4	27.2	23.7	24.3	31.7
Bachelor's degree or more	17.9	19.5	16.3	17.3	21.7

Note: Blacks are those who identify themselves as being of the race alone and those who identify themselves as being of the race in combination with other races.
Source: Bureau of the Census, 2006–10 American Community Survey, Internet site http://factfinder2.census.gov/faces/nav/jsf/pages/index.xhtml; calculations by New Strategist

Table 4.5 School Enrollment of Blacks, 2011

(total number of people aged 3 or older enrolled in school, number of blacks enrolled, and black share of total, by age, October 2011; numbers in thousands)

	total	black number	share of total
Total aged 3 or older	**79,043**	**13,288**	**16.8%**
Aged 3 to 4	4,597	880	19.1
Aged 5 to 6	8,009	1,329	16.6
Aged 7 to 9	12,319	2,088	16.9
Aged 10 to 13	15,941	2,607	16.4
Aged 14 to 15	7,825	1,278	16.3
Aged 16 to 17	7,906	1,301	16.5
Aged 18 to 19	6,017	1023	17.0
Aged 20 to 21	4,618	566	12.3
Aged 22 to 24	3,961	638	16.1
Aged 25 to 29	3,139	549	17.5
Aged 30 to 34	1,571	329	20.9
Aged 35 to 44	1,688	395	23.4
Aged 45 to 54	1,012	206	20.4
Aged 55 or older	438	98	22.4

Note: Blacks are those who identify themselves as being of the race alone and those who identify themselves as being of the race in combination with other races.
Source: Bureau of the Census, School Enrollment, CPS October 2011—Detailed Tables, Internet site http://www.census.gov/ hhes/school/data/cps/2011/tables.html; calculations by New Strategist

Table 4.6 School Enrollment of Blacks by Age and Sex, 2011

(number and percent of blacks aged 3 or older enrolled in school, by age and sex, October 2011; numbers in thousands)

	total		female		male	
	number	percent	number	percent	number	percent
Total blacks enrolled	**13,288**	**33.6%**	**6,963**	**32.8%**	**6,325**	**34.5%**
Aged 3 to 4	880	53.9	456	55.0	423	52.8
Aged 5 to 6	1,329	92.1	589	91.3	740	92.8
Aged 7 to 9	2,088	97.3	1,076	97.2	1,012	97.5
Aged 10 to 13	2,607	98.5	1,283	98.4	1,324	98.6
Aged 14 to 15	1,278	98.7	649	99.4	629	97.9
Aged 16 to 17	1,301	96.0	660	97.5	641	94.5
Aged 18 to 19	1023	74.1	535	76.5	488	71.6
Aged 20 to 21	566	41.8	290	45.0	276	38.9
Aged 22 to 24	638	31.0	368	31.7	270	30.0
Aged 25 to 29	549	18.1	346	21.7	203	14.1
Aged 30 to 34	329	11.3	226	14.4	102	7.7
Aged 35 to 44	395	7.7	263	9.1	132	5.8
Aged 45 to 54	206	3.7	159	5.3	47	1.8
Aged 55 or older	98	1.3	62	1.4	36	1.1

Note: Blacks are those who identify themselves as being of the race alone and those who identify themselves as being of the race in combination with other races.
Source: Bureau of the Census, School Enrollment, CPS October 2011—Detailed Tables, Internet site http://www.census.gov/ hhes/school/data/cps/2011/tables.html; calculations by New Strategist

Table 4.7 Black College Enrollment Rate, 2000 to 2011

(percentage of total people and blacks aged 16 to 24 who graduated from high school in the previous 12 months and were enrolled in college as of October, and index of black to total, 2000 to 2011; percentage point change in enrollment rate for selected years)

	total	black	index, black to total
2011	68.2%	67.1%	98
2010	68.1	62.0	91
2009	70.1	69.5	99
2008	68.6	55.7	81
2007	67.2	55.7	83
2006	66.0	55.5	84
2005	68.6	55.7	81
2004	66.7	62.5	94
2003	63.9	57.5	90
2002	65.2	59.4	91
2001	61.8	55.0	89
2000	63.3	54.9	87

PERCENTAGE POINT CHANGE

2000 to 2011	4.9	12.2	–

Note: Blacks are those who identify themselves as being of the race alone. The index is calculated by dividing the black figure by the total figure and multiplying by 100. "–" means not applicable.
Source: National Center for Education Statistics, Digest of Education Statistics 2012, Internet site ces.ed.gov/programs/digest/2012menu_tables.asp; calculations by New Strategist

Table 4.8 College Enrollment of Blacks by Age, 2011

(total number of people aged 15 or older enrolled in college, number of blacks enrolled, and black share of total, by age, 2011; numbers in thousands)

		black	
	total	number	share of total
Total enrolled in college	**20,397**	**3,146**	**15.4%**
Under age 20	4,446	617	13.9
Aged 20 to 21	4,460	490	11.0
Aged 22 to 24	3,869	568	14.7
Aged 25 to 29	3,066	512	16.7
Aged 30 or older	4,559	955	20.9

Note: Blacks are those who identify themselves as being of the race alone.
Source: Bureau of the Census, School Enrollment, CPS October 2011—Detailed Tables, Internet site http://www.census.gov/hhes/school/data/cps/2011/tables.html; calculations by New Strategist

Table 4.9 College Enrollment of Blacks by Type of School and Sex, 2011

(number and percent distribution of blacks aged 15 or older enrolled in college by type of school and sex, and female share of total, 2011; numbers in thousands)

	total		men		women		
	number	percent distribution	number	percent distribution	number	percent distribution	share of total
Total blacks enrolled	**3,146**	**100.0%**	**1,212**	**100.0%**	**1,934**	**100.0%**	**61.5%**
Two-year undergraduate program	1,021	32.5	356	29.4	667	34.5	65.3
Four-year undergraduate program	1,577	50.1	660	54.5	917	47.4	58.1
Graduate school	549	17.5	197	16.3	351	18.1	63.9

Note: Blacks are those who identify themselves as being of the race alone.
Source: Bureau of the Census, School Enrollment, CPS October 2011—Detailed Tables, Internet site http://www.census.gov/hhes/school/data/cps/2011/tables.html; calculations by New Strategist

Table 4.10 Associate's Degrees Earned by Blacks by Field of Study, 2010–11

(total number of associate's degrees conferred and number and percent earned by non-Hispanic blacks, by field of study, 2010–11)

		earned by blacks	
	total	number	share of total
Total associate's degrees	**942,327**	**128,703**	**13.7%**
Agriculture and natural resources	6,425	56	0.9
Architecture and related programs	569	24	4.2
Area, ethnic, and cultural studies	209	24	11.5
Biological and biomedical sciences	3,245	281	8.7
Business	139,986	23,901	17.1
Communication, journalism, and related programs	3,051	286	9.4
Communications technologies	4,209	535	12.7
Computer and information sciences	37,677	5,911	15.7
Construction trades	5,402	518	9.6
Education	20,459	2,948	14.4
Engineering	2,825	187	6.6
Engineering technologies	35,521	4,296	12.1
English language and literature/letters	2,019	244	12.1
Family and consumer sciences	8,532	1,893	22.2
Foreign languages and literatures	1,876	84	4.5
Health professions and related sciences	201,831	28,024	13.9
Homeland security, law enforcement, and firefighting	44,923	7,667	17.1
Legal professions and studies	11,620	1,967	16.9
Liberal arts and sciences, general studies, and humanities	306,670	37,996	12.4
Library science	160	5	3.1
Mathematics and statistics	1,644	103	6.3
Mechanic and repair technologies	19,969	2,077	10.4
Military technologies	856	96	11.2
Multi/interdisciplinary studies	23,729	2,111	8.9
Parks, recreation, leisure, and fitness	2,366	350	14.8
Philosophy and religion	283	47	16.6
Physical sciences	5,078	618	12.2
Precision production trades	3,254	153	4.7
Psychology	3,866	334	8.6
Public administration and social services	7,472	2,181	29.2
Social sciences and history	12,767	1,464	11.5
Theology and religious vocations	758	167	22.0
Transportation and material moving	1,697	126	7.4
Visual and performing arts	21,379	2,029	9.5

Source: National Center for Education Statistics, Digest of Education Statistics 2012, Internet site http://nces.ed.gov/programs/digest/2012menu_tables.asp; calculations by New Strategist

Table 4.11 Bachelor's Degrees Earned by Blacks by Field of Study, 2010–11

(total number of bachelor's degrees conferred and number and percent earned by non-Hispanic blacks, by field of study, 2010–11)

	total	earned by blacks number	share of total
Total bachelor's degrees	**1,715,913**	**173,017**	**10.1%**
Agriculture and natural resources	28,623	811	2.8
Architecture and related programs	9,832	493	5.0
Area, ethnic, and cultural studies	9,100	1,447	15.9
Biological and biomedical sciences	90,003	6,885	7.6
Business	365,093	42,572	11.7
Communication, journalism, and related programs	83,274	8,761	10.5
Communications technologies	4,858	519	10.7
Computer and information sciences	43,072	4,914	11.4
Construction trades	328	8	2.4
Education	103,992	7,115	6.8
Engineering	76,376	3,245	4.2
Engineering technologies	16,187	1,506	9.3
English language and literature/letters	52,744	3,942	7.5
Family and consumer sciences	22,444	2,623	11.7
Foreign languages, literatures, and linguistics	21,706	922	4.2
Health professions and related sciences	143,430	17,119	11.9
Homeland security, law enforcement, and firefighting	47,602	9,687	20.3
Legal professions and studies	4,429	787	17.8
Liberal arts and sciences, general studies, and humanities	46,727	6,853	14.7
Library science	96	3	3.1
Mathematics and statistics	17,182	840	4.9
Mechanic and repair technologies	226	13	5.8
Military technologies	64	16	25.0
Multi/interdisciplinary studies	42,228	4,375	10.4
Parks, recreation, leisure, and fitness	35,924	3,548	9.9
Philosophy and religion	12,836	963	7.5
Physical sciences	24,712	1,329	5.4
Precision production trades	43	0	0.0
Psychology	100,893	12,397	12.3
Public administration and social services	26,774	6,093	22.8
Social sciences and history	177,144	16,682	9.4
Theology and religious vocations	9,074	585	6.4
Transportation and material moving	4,941	285	5.8
Visual and performing arts	93,956	5,679	6.0

Source: National Center for Education Statistics, Digest of Education Statistics 2012, Internet site http://nces.ed.gov/programs/ digest/2012menu_tables.asp; calculations by New Strategist

Table 4.12 Master's Degrees Earned by Blacks by Field of Study, 2010–11

(total number of master's degrees conferred and number and percent earned by non-Hispanic blacks, by field of study, 2010–11)

		earned by blacks	
	total	number	share of total
Total master's degrees	**730,635**	**80,706**	**11.0%**
Agriculture and natural resources	5,773	218	3.8
Architecture and related programs	7,788	336	4.3
Area, ethnic, and cultural studies	1,914	213	11.1
Biological and biomedical sciences	11,327	691	6.1
Business	187,213	26,712	14.3
Communication, journalism, and related programs	8,303	868	10.5
Communications technologies	502	46	9.2
Computer and information sciences	19,446	1,417	7.3
Education	185,009	19,816	10.7
Engineering	38,719	1,139	2.9
Engineering technologies	4,515	372	8.2
English language and literature/letters	9,476	462	4.9
Family and consumer sciences	2,918	412	14.1
Foreign languages, literatures, and linguistics	3,727	79	2.1
Health professions and related sciences	75,579	8,452	11.2
Homeland security, law enforcement, and firefighting	7,433	1,715	23.1
Legal professions and studies	6,300	386	6.1
Liberal arts and sciences, general studies, and humanities	3,971	378	9.5
Library science	7,727	381	4.9
Mathematics and statistics	5,843	171	2.9
Multi/interdisciplinary studies	6,748	543	8.0
Parks, recreation, leisure, and fitness	6,553	631	9.6
Philosophy and religion	1,833	121	6.6
Physical sciences	6,386	185	2.9
Precision production trades	5	0	0.0
Psychology	25,051	3,425	13.7
Public administration and social services	38,634	7,344	19.0
Social sciences and history	21,084	1,404	6.7
Theology and religious vocations	13,191	1,817	13.8
Transportation and material moving	1,390	92	6.6
Visual and performing arts	16,277	880	5.4

Source: National Center for Education Statistics, Digest of Education Statistics 2012, Internet site http://nces.ed.gov/programs/digest/2012menu_tables.asp; calculations by New Strategist

Table 4.13 Doctoral and First-Professional Degrees Earned by Blacks by Field of Study, 2010–11

(total number of doctoral and first-professional degrees conferred and number and percent earned by non-Hispanic blacks, by field of study, 2010–11)

	total	earned by blacks	
		number	share of total
Total doctoral and first-professional degrees	**163,765**	**10,925**	**6.7%**
Agriculture and natural resources	1,246	25	2.0
Architecture and related programs	205	8	3.9
Area, ethnic, and cultural studies	278	38	13.7
Biological and biomedical sciences	7,693	285	3.7
Business	2,286	338	14.8
Communication, journalism, and related programs	577	36	6.2
Communications technologies	1	0	0.0
Computer and information sciences	1,588	41	2.6
Education	9,623	1,743	18.1
Engineering	8,369	155	1.9
Engineering technologies	56	1	1.8
English language and literature/letters	1,344	59	4.4
Family and consumer sciences	320	30	9.4
Foreign languages, literatures, and linguistics	1,158	23	2.0
Health professions and related sciences	60,153	3,480	5.8
Homeland security, law enforcement, and firefighting	131	16	12.2
Legal professions and studies	44,877	3,207	7.1
Liberal arts and sciences, general studies, and humanities	95	4	4.2
Library science	50	1	2.0
Mathematics and statistics	1,586	25	1.6
Multi/interdisciplinary studies	660	71	10.8
Parks, recreation, leisure, and fitness	257	19	7.4
Philosophy and religion	805	54	6.7
Physical sciences	5,295	100	1.9
Psychology	5,851	430	7.3
Public administration and social services	851	145	17.0
Social sciences and history	4,390	194	4.4
Theology and religious vocations	2,374	362	15.2
Visual and performing arts	1,646	35	2.1

Source: National Center for Education Statistics, Digest of Education Statistics 2012, Internet site http://nces.ed.gov/programs/digest/2012menu_tables.asp; calculations by New Strategist

Most Blacks Say Their Health Is Very Good or Excellent

Slightly more than 50 percent of blacks say they are in "very good" or "excellent" health, according to the National Center for Health Statistics. This compares with a larger 60 percent of the total population who rate their health so highly. Nineteen percent of blacks say they are in "fair" or "poor" health, well above the 13 percent of the total population who feel that way.

More than 70 percent of black adults are overweight. About one in five blacks is a current smoker, and 40 percent drink alcohol regularly.

Non-Hispanic black women gave birth to more than 583,000 babies in 2011, accounting for 15 percent of all babies born that year. Seventy-three percent of black babies are born to unmarried women, the highest proportion among racial and ethnic groups. Blacks account for the majority of births in the District of Columbia, 43 percent of births in Mississippi, and about one-third of births in Georgia, Louisiana, Maryland, and South Carolina.

Only 44 percent of blacks were covered by employment-based health insurance in 2011, lower than the 55 percent share among the total population. Twenty percent of blacks aged 18 or older have physical difficulties, slightly greater than the 16 percent share among all adults.

Heart disease and cancer are the two leading causes of death among blacks, just as they are for the population as a whole. But AIDS ranks 10th as a cause of death among blacks while it is not among the top 10 causes for the total population. Blacks account for 42 percent of all AIDS cases diagnosed through 2009.

■ While blacks have made substantial gains in income and education over the past few decades, their health status is lagging.

Nearly one in five blacks does not have health insurance

(percent distribution of blacks by health insurance coverage status, 2011)

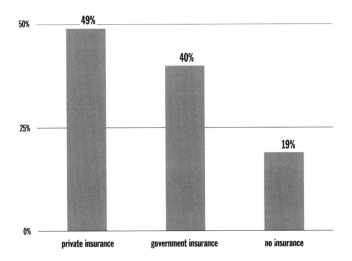

Table 4.14 Health Status of Total People and Blacks, 2011

(number and percent distribution of total people and blacks aged 18 or older by self-reported health status, and index of black to total, 2011; numbers in thousands)

	total		black		index, black to total
	number	percent distribution	number	percent distribution	
Total people	**231,376**	**100.0%**	**27,666**	**100.0%**	–
Excellent/very good	139,424	60.3	13,960	50.5	84
Good	60,973	26.4	8,472	30.6	116
Fair/poor	30,856	13.3	5,226	18.9	142

Note: Blacks are those who identify themselves as being black alone. Numbers may not add to total because "unknown" is not shown. The index is calculated by dividing the black percentage by the total percentage and multiplying by 100. "–" means not applicable.
Source: National Center for Health Statistics, Summary Health Statistics for U.S. Adults: National Health Interview Survey, 2011, Vital and Health Statistics, Series 10, No. 256, 2012, Internet site http://www.cdc.gov/nchs/nhis.htm; calculations by New Strategist

Table 4.15 Weight of Blacks by Age and Sex, 2007–10

(average weight in pounds of non-Hispanic blacks aged 20 or older by age and sex, 2007–10)

	men	women
Total blacks	**199.4 lbs.**	**187.9 lbs.**
Aged 20 to 39	198.1	186.2
Aged 40 to 59	203.1	194.7
Aged 60 or older	193.6	177.8

Note: Data are based on measured weight of a sample of the civilian noninstitutionalized population.
Source: National Center for Health Statistics, Anthropometric Reference Data for Children and Adults: United States, 2007–2010, National Health Statistics Reports, Series 11, Number 252, 2012, Internet site http://www.cdc.gov/nchs/nhanes.htm

Table 4.16 Weight Status of Total People and Blacks, 2011

(number and percent distribution of total people and blacks aged 18 or older by body mass index based on self-reported height and weight, and index of black to total, 2011; numbers in thousands)

	total		black		index, black to total
	number	percent distribution	number	percent distribution	
Total people	**231,376**	**100.0%**	**27,666**	**100.0%**	–
Underweight	3,549	1.5	264	1.0	62
Healthy weight	79,984	34.6	7,028	25.4	73
Overweight, total	141,072	61.0	19,522	70.6	116
Overweight, but not obese	77,586	33.5	9,036	32.7	97
Obese	63,486	27.4	10,486	37.9	138

Note: "Overweight" is defined as a body mass index of 25 or higher. "Obese" is defined as a body mass index of 30 or higher. Body mass index is calculated by dividing weight in kilograms by height in meters squared. Blacks are those who identify themselves as being black alone. Numbers may not add to total because "unknown" is not shown. The index is calculated by dividing the black percentage by the total percentage and multiplying by 100. "–" means not applicable.
Source: National Center for Health Statistics, Summary Health Statistics for U.S. Adults: National Health Interview Survey, 2011, Vital and Health Statistics, Series 10, No. 256, 2012, Internet site http://www.cdc.gov/nchs/nhis.htm; calculations by New Strategist

Table 4.17 Weight of Total and Black High School Students by Sex, 2011

(percent of total and black 9th to 12th graders by weight status and sex, 2011)

	total	black
MALES		
Measured as overweight*	31.2%	30.5%
Described themselves as overweight	23.9	18.2
Were trying to lose weight	31.6	26.6
FEMALES		
Measured as overweight*	25.2	38.2
Described themselves as overweight	34.8	35.4
Were trying to lose weight	61.2	55.2

* Students were classified as overweight if they were at or above the 85th percentile for body mass index, by age and sex, based on 2000 CDC growth charts.
Source: Centers for Disease Control and Prevention, Youth Risk Behavior Surveillance–United States, 2011, Mortality and Morbidity Weekly Report, Vol. 61, No. 4, June 8, 2012; Internet site http://www.cdc.gov/HealthyYouth/yrbs/index.htm

Table 4.18 Drinking Status of Total People and Blacks, 2011

(number and percent distribution of total people and blacks aged 18 or older by drinking status, and index of black to total, 2011; numbers in thousands)

	total		black		index, black to total
	number	percent distribution	number	percent distribution	
Total people	**231,376**	**100.0%**	**27,666**	**100.0%**	–
Lifetime abstainer	45,367	19.6	7,898	28.5	146
Former drinker	33,663	14.5	4,291	15.5	107
Current drinker	148,970	64.4	14,992	54.2	84
Infrequent	31,158	13.5	4,020	14.5	108
Regular	117,812	50.9	10,972	39.7	78

Note: "Lifetime abstainers" have had fewer than 12 drinks in lifetime. "Former drinkers" have had 12 or more drinks in lifetime, none in past year. "Current infrequent drinkers" have had 12 or more drinks in lifetime and fewer than 12 drinks in past year. "Current regular drinkers" have had 12 or more drinks in lifetime and at least 12 drinks in past year. Blacks are those who identify themselves as being black alone. Numbers may not add to total because "unknown" is not shown. The index is calculated by dividing the black percentage by the total percentage and multiplying by 100. "–" means not applicable.
Source: National Center for Health Statistics, Summary Health Statistics for U.S. Adults: National Health Interview Survey, 2011, Vital and Health Statistics, Series 10, No. 256, 2012, Internet site http://www.cdc.gov/nchs/nhis.htm; calculations by New Strategist

Table 4.19 Smoking Status of Total People and Blacks, 2011

(number and percent distribution of total people and blacks aged 18 or older by smoking status, and index of black to total, 2011; numbers in thousands)

	total		black		index, black to total
	number	percent distribution	number	percent distribution	
Total people	**231,376**	**100.0%**	**11,468**	**100.0%**	–
Never smoked	136,528	59.0	18,308	66.2	112
Former smoker	50,416	21.8	3,970	14.3	66
Current smoker	43,821	18.9	5,271	19.1	101

Note: "Never smoked" means fewer than 100 cigarettes in lifetime. "Former smokers" have smoked 100 or more cigarettes in lifetime but did not smoke at time of interview. "Current smokers" have smoked at least 100 cigarettes in lifetime and currently smoke. Blacks are those who identify themselves as being black alone. Numbers may not add to total because "unknown" is not shown. The index is calculated by dividing the black percentage by the total percentage and multiplying by 100. "–" means not applicable.
Source: National Center for Health Statistics, Summary Health Statistics for U.S. Adults: National Health Interview Survey, 2011, Vital and Health Statistics, Series 10, No. 256, 2012, Internet site http://www.cdc.gov/nchs/nhis.htm; calculations by New Strategist

Table 4.20 Births to Total and Non-Hispanic Black Women by Age, 2011

(total number of births, number and percent distribution of births to non-Hispanic blacks, and black share of total, by age, 2011)

	total	non-Hispanic black		
		number	percent distribution	share of total
Total births	**3,953,593**	**583,079**	**100.0%**	**14.7%**
Under age 15	3,974	1,379	0.2	34.7
Aged 15 to 19	329,797	78,637	13.5	23.8
Aged 20 to 24	925,213	186,443	32.0	20.2
Aged 25 to 29	1,127,592	147,886	25.4	13.1
Aged 30 to 34	986,661	104,460	17.9	10.6
Aged 35 to 39	463,815	50,305	8.6	10.8
Aged 40 to 44	108,891	12,960	2.2	11.9
Aged 45 to 54	7,651	1,008	0.2	13.2

Source: National Center for Health Statistics, Births: Preliminary Data for 2011, National Vital Statistics Report, Vol. 61, No. 5, 2012, Internet site http://www.cdc.gov/nchs/births.htm; calculations by New Strategist

Table 4.21 Births to Non-Hispanic Black Women by Age and Marital Status, 2010

(total number of births to non-Hispanic blacks, number of births to unmarried blacks, and unmarried share of total, by age, 2010)

	total	unmarried	
		number	share of total
Births to blacks	**589,808**	**427,687**	**72.5%**
Under age 15	1,573	1,571	99.9
Aged 15 to 19	88,329	86,250	97.6
Aged 20 to 24	187,981	164,547	87.5
Aged 25 to 29	147,684	98,495	66.7
Aged 30 to 34	100,765	50,558	50.2
Aged 35 to 39	49,742	20,831	41.9
Aged 40 or older	13,734	5,435	39.6

Source: National Center for Health Statistics, Births: Final Data for 2010, National Vital Statistics Reports, Vol. 61, No. 1, 2012, Internet site http://www.cdc.gov/nchs/births.htm; calculations by New Strategist

Table 4.22 Births to Total and Non-Hispanic Black Women by Birth Order, 2011

(total number of births, number and percent distribution of births to non-Hispanic blacks, and black share of total, by birth order, 2011)

	total	non-Hispanic black number	percent distribution	share of total
Total births	**3,953,593**	**583,079**	**100.0%**	**14.7%**
First child	1,577,344	225,254	38.6	14.3
Second child	1,239,136	162,896	27.9	13.1
Third child	648,124	97,485	16.7	15.0
Fourth or later child	458,777	88,510	15.2	19.3

Note: Numbers do not add to total because "not stated" is not shown.
Source: National Center for Health Statistics, Births: Preliminary Data for 2011, National Vital Statistics Report, Vol. 61, No. 5, 2012, Internet site http://www.cdc.gov/nchs/births.htm; calculations by New Strategist

Table 4.23 Births to Total and Non-Hispanic Black Women by State, 2011

(total number of births, number and percent distribution of births to non-Hispanic blacks, and black share of total, by state, 2011)

	total	non-Hispanic black		
		number	percent distribution	share of total
Total births	**3,953,593**	**583,079**	**100.0%**	**14.7%**
Alabama	59,347	17,983	3.1	30.3
Alaska	11,455	437	0.1	3.8
Arizona	85,543	4,083	0.7	4.8
Arkansas	38,713	7,231	1.2	18.7
California	502,118	29,901	5.1	6.0
Colorado	65,055	3,054	0.5	4.7
Connecticut	37,280	4,777	0.8	12.8
Delaware	11,257	3,031	0.5	26.9
District of Columbia	9,314	4,817	0.8	51.7
Florida	213,344	49,070	8.4	23.0
Georgia	132,488	44,667	7.7	33.7
Hawaii	18,957	508	0.1	2.7
Idaho	22,305	192	0.0	0.9
Illinois	161,312	27,183	4.7	16.9
Indiana	83,702	9,831	1.7	11.7
Iowa	38,213	1,844	0.3	4.8
Kansas	39,642	2,934	0.5	7.4
Kentucky	55,377	5,202	0.9	9.4
Louisiana	61,889	23,607	4.0	38.1
Maine	12,704	395	0.1	3.1
Maryland	73,086	23,844	4.1	32.6
Massachusetts	73,225	7,887	1.4	10.8
Michigan	114,004	21,774	3.7	19.1
Minnesota	68,411	6,473	1.1	9.5
Mississippi	39,856	17,302	3.0	43.4
Missouri	76,117	11,435	2.0	15.0
Montana	12,069	75	0.0	0.6
Nebraska	25,720	1,708	0.3	6.6
Nevada	35,295	3,695	0.6	10.5
New Hampshire	12,852	235	0.0	1.8
New Jersey	105,886	16,049	2.8	15.2
New Mexico	27,289	473	0.1	1.7
New York	241,290	39,158	6.7	16.2
North Carolina	120,385	28,598	4.9	23.8
North Dakota	9,527	218	0.0	2.3
Ohio	137,916	22,836	3.9	16.6
Oklahoma	52,274	4,815	0.8	9.2

		non-Hispanic black		
	total	number	percent distribution	share of total
Oregon	45,157	1,170	0.2%	2.6%
Pennsylvania	143,148	21,024	3.6	14.7
Rhode Island	10,960	961	0.2	8.8
South Carolina	57,368	18,283	3.1	31.9
South Dakota	11,849	266	0.0	2.2
Tennessee	79,588	16,557	2.8	20.8
Texas	377,449	43,211	7.4	11.4
Utah	51,223	568	0.1	1.1
Vermont	6,078	89	0.0	1.5
Virginia	102,648	21,942	3.8	21.4
Washington	86,976	4,303	0.7	4.9
West Virginia	20,720	724	0.1	3.5
Wisconsin	67,811	6,593	1.1	9.7
Wyoming	7,398	65	0.0	0.9

Source: National Center for Health Statistics, Births: Preliminary Data for 2011, National Vital Statistics Report, Vol. 61, No. 5, 2012, Internet site http://www.cdc.gov/nchs/births.htm; calculations by New Strategist

Table 4.24 Health Insurance Coverage of Blacks by Age, 2011

(number and percent distribution of blacks by age and health insurance coverage status, 2011; numbers in thousands)

	total	with health insurance coverage during year			not covered at any time during the year
		total	private	government	
Total blacks	**42,750**	**34,567**	**21,151**	**17,208**	**8,183**
Under age 18	13,070	11,772	5,659	7,253	1,298
Aged 18 to 24	4,967	3,459	2,291	1,444	1,508
Aged 25 to 34	5,775	3,808	2,785	1,183	1,967
Aged 35 to 44	5,325	4,110	3,225	1,117	1,215
Aged 45 to 54	5,637	4,343	3,279	1,395	1,293
Aged 55 to 64	4,258	3,463	2,367	1,417	795
Aged 65 or older	3,718	3,612	1,545	3,398	106

PERCENT DISTRIBUTION BY COVERAGE STATUS

	total	with health insurance coverage during year			not covered at any time during the year
		total	private	government	
Total blacks	**100.0%**	**80.9%**	**49.5%**	**40.3%**	**19.1%**
Under age 18	100.0	90.1	43.3	55.5	9.9
Aged 18 to 24	100.0	69.6	46.1	29.1	30.4
Aged 25 to 34	100.0	65.9	48.2	20.5	34.1
Aged 35 to 44	100.0	77.2	60.6	21.0	22.8
Aged 45 to 54	100.0	77.0	58.2	24.7	22.9
Aged 55 to 64	100.0	81.3	55.6	33.3	18.7
Aged 65 or older	100.0	97.1	41.6	91.4	2.9

Note: Blacks are those who identify themselves as being of the race alone and those who identify themselves as being of the race in combination with other races. Numbers do not add to total because some people have more than one type of health insurance.
Source: Bureau of the Census, Health Insurance, Internet site http://www.census.gov/hhes/www/cpstables/032012/health/toc .htm; calculations by New Strategist

Table 4.25 Blacks with Private Health Insurance Coverage by Age, 2011

(number and percent distribution of blacks by age and private health insurance coverage status, 2011; numbers in thousands)

| | | with private health insurance | | | |
| | | total | employment-based | | direct purchase |
	total	total	total	own	
Total blacks	**42,750**	**21,151**	**18,986**	**10,127**	**2,232**
Under age 18	13,070	5,659	5,227	41	460
Aged 18 to 24	4,967	2,291	1,853	492	186
Aged 25 to 34	5,775	2,785	2,569	2,056	218
Aged 35 to 44	5,325	3,225	3,016	2,428	257
Aged 45 to 54	5,637	3,279	3,056	2,445	320
Aged 55 to 64	4,258	2,367	2,168	1,757	258
Aged 65 or older	3,718	1,545	1098	909	533

PERCENT DISTRIBUTION BY COVERAGE STATUS

Total blacks	**100.0%**	**49.5%**	**44.4%**	**23.7%**	**5.2%**
Under age 18	100.0	43.3	40.0	0.3	3.5
Aged 18 to 24	100.0	46.1	37.3	9.9	3.7
Aged 25 to 34	100.0	48.2	44.5	35.6	3.8
Aged 35 to 44	100.0	60.6	56.6	45.6	4.8
Aged 45 to 54	100.0	58.2	54.2	43.4	5.7
Aged 55 to 64	100.0	55.6	50.9	41.3	6.1
Aged 65 or older	100.0	41.6	29.5	24.4	14.3

Note: Blacks are those who identify themselves as being of the race alone and those who identify themselves as being of the race in combination with other races. Numbers do not add to total because some people have more than one type of health insurance.
Source: Bureau of the Census, Health Insurance, Internet site http://www.census.gov/hhes/www/cpstables/032012/health/toc .htm; calculations by New Strategist

Table 4.26 Blacks with Government Health Insurance Coverage by Age, 2011

(number and percent distribution of blacks by age and government health insurance coverage status, 2011; numbers in thousands)

	total	with government health insurance			
		total	Medicaid	Medicare	military
Total blacks	**42,750**	**17,208**	**12,240**	**5,109**	**1,867**
Under age 18	13,070	7,253	6,852	176	471
Aged 18 to 24	4,967	1,444	1244	70	183
Aged 25 to 34	5,775	1,183	1012	128	135
Aged 35 to 44	5,325	1,117	859	221	173
Aged 45 to 54	5,637	1,395	865	404	324
Aged 55 to 64	4,258	1,417	733	737	292
Aged 65 or older	3,718	3,398	674	3,373	290

PERCENT DISTRIBUTION BY COVERAGE STATUS

	total	with government health insurance			
		total	Medicaid	Medicare	military
Total blacks	**100.0%**	**40.3%**	**28.6%**	**12.0%**	**4.4%**
Under age 18	100.0	55.5	52.4	1.3	3.6
Aged 18 to 24	100.0	29.1	25.0	1.4	3.7
Aged 25 to 34	100.0	20.5	17.5	2.2	2.3
Aged 35 to 44	100.0	21.0	16.1	4.2	3.2
Aged 45 to 54	100.0	24.7	15.3	7.2	5.7
Aged 55 to 64	100.0	33.3	17.2	17.3	6.9
Aged 65 or older	100.0	91.4	18.1	90.7	7.8

Note: Blacks are those who identify themselves as being of the race alone and those who identify themselves as being of the race in combination with other races. Numbers do not add to total because some people have more than one type of health insurance.
Source: Bureau of the Census, Health Insurance, Internet site http://www.census.gov/hhes/www/cpstables/032012/health/toc .htm; calculations by New Strategist

Table 4.27 Health Conditions among Total People and Blacks Aged 18 or Older, 2011

(number of total people and blacks aged 18 or older with selected health conditions, percent of blacks with condition, and black share of total with condition, 2011; numbers in thousands)

	total	black number	black percent with condition	black share of total
TOTAL PEOPLE	**231,376**	**27,666**	**100.0%**	**12.0%**
Selected circulatory diseases				
Heart disease, all types	26,485	2,789	10.1	10.5
Coronary	15,300	1,770	6.4	11.6
Hypertension	58,959	8,820	31.9	15.0
Stroke	6,171	1,129	4.1	18.3
Selected respiratory conditions				
Emphysema	4,680	496	1.8	10.6
Asthma, ever	29,041	4,201	15.2	14.5
Asthma, still	18,869	2,698	9.8	14.3
Hay fever	16,869	1,531	5.5	9.1
Sinusitis	29,611	3,378	12.2	11.4
Chronic bronchitis	10,071	1,358	4.9	13.5
Selected types of cancer				
Any cancer	19,025	1,251	4.5	6.6
Breast cancer	3,221	285	1.0	8.8
Cervical cancer	1,188	55	0.2	4.6
Prostate cancer	2,280	295	1.1	12.9
Other selected diseases and conditions				
Diabetes	20,589	3,226	11.7	15.7
Ulcers	15,502	1,672	6.0	10.8
Kidney disease	4,381	689	2.5	15.7
Liver disease	3,016	333	1.2	11.0
Arthritis	53,782	5,953	21.5	11.1
Chronic joint symptoms	68,749	7,619	27.5	11.1
Migraines or severe headaches	37,904	4,858	17.6	12.8
Pain in neck	35,798	3,603	13.0	10.1
Pain in lower back	66,917	7,634	27.6	11.4
Pain in face or jaw	11,436	1,278	4.6	11.2
Selected sensory problems				
Hearing	37,122	2,579	9.3	6.9
Vision	21,232	2,949	10.7	13.9
Absence of all natural teeth	18,038	2,357	8.5	13.1

Note: The conditions shown are those that have ever been diagnosed by a doctor, except as noted. Hay fever, sinusitis, and chronic bronchitis have been diagnosed in the past 12 months. Kidney and liver disease have been diagnosed in the past 12 months and exclude kidney stones, bladder infections, and incontinence. Chronic joint symptoms are shown if respondent had pain, aching, or stiffness in or around a joint (excluding back and neck) and the condition began more than three months ago. Migraines, pain in neck, lower back, face, or jaw are shown only if pain lasted a whole day or more. Blacks are those who identify themselves as being of the race alone.
Source: National Center for Health Statistics, Summary Health Statistics for U.S. Adults: National Health Interview Survey, 2011, Vital and Health Statistics, Series 10, No. 256, 2012, Internet site http://www.cdc.gov/nchs/nhis.htm; calculations by New Strategist

Table 4.28 Health Conditions among Total and Black Children, 2011

(number of total people and blacks under age 18 with selected health conditions, percent of blacks with condition, and black share of total, 2011; numbers in thousands)

	total	black number	black percent with condition	black share of total
Total children	**74,518**	**10,990**	**100.0%**	**14.7%**
Ever told have asthma	10,463	2,282	20.8	21.8
Still have asthma	7,074	1,804	16.4	25.5
Hay fever in past 12 months	6,711	761	6.9	11.3
Respiratory allergies in past 12 months	8,269	1,342	12.2	16.2
Food allergies in past 12 months	4,126	717	6.5	17.4
Skin allergies in past 12 months	9,516	1,885	17.2	19.8
Prescription medication taken regularly for at least three months	10,019	1,712	15.6	17.1
Learning disability*	4,660	783	7.1	16.8
Attention deficit hyperactivity disorder*	5,240	792	7.2	15.1

* Diagnosed by a school representative or health professional; data exclude children under age 3.
Note: Blacks are those who identify themselves as being of the race alone.
Source: National Center for Health Statistics, Summary Health Statistics for U.S. Children: National Health Interview Survey, 2011, Vital and Health Statistics, Series 10, No. 254, 2012, Internet site http://www.cdc.gov/nchs/nhis.htm

Table 4.29 Health Care Office Visits by Total People and Blacks, 2011

(number of total people and blacks aged 18 or older by visits to a health care provider in the past 12 months, percent distribution of blacks by number of visits, and black share of total, 2011; numbers in thousands)

	total	black number	black percent distribution	black share of total
Total people	**231,376**	**27,666**	**100.0%**	**12.0%**
No visits	43,578	5,584	20.2	12.8
One visit	39,552	4,698	17.0	11.9
Two to three visits	59,226	7,293	26.4	12.3
Four to nine visits	55,721	6,202	22.4	11.1
10 or more visits	30,822	3,502	12.7	11.4

Note: Health care visits exclude overnight hospitalizations, visits to emergency rooms, home visits, dental visits, and telephone calls. Blacks are those who identify themselves as being of the race alone. Numbers may not add to total because "unknown" is not shown.
Source: National Center for Health Statistics, Summary Health Statistics for U.S. Adults: National Health Interview Survey, 2011, Vital and Health Statistics, Series 10, No. 256, 2012, Internet site http://www.cdc.gov/nchs/nhis.htm; calculations by New Strategist

Table 4.30 Difficulties in Physical Functioning among Total People and Blacks, 2011

(number of total people and blacks aged 18 or older, number with difficulties in physical functioning, percentage of blacks with difficulty, and black share of total, by type of difficulty, 2011; numbers in thousands)

	total	black number	black percent	black share of total
TOTAL PEOPLE	**231,376**	**27,666**	**100.0%**	**12.0%**
Total with any physical difficulty	**37,368**	**5,131**	**19.7**	**13.7**
Walk quarter of a mile	17,597	2,626	10.4	14.9
Climb 10 steps without resting	12,887	1,968	7.8	15.3
Stand for two hours	22,369	3,073	11.9	13.7
Sit for two hours	7,724	1,129	4.2	14.6
Stoop, bend, or kneel	21,677	2,849	11.0	13.1
Reach over head	6,550	852	3.4	13.0
Grasp or handle small objects	4,329	550	2.1	12.7
Lift or carry 10 pounds	10,677	1,835	7.3	17.2
Push or pull large objects	15,998	2,376	9.3	14.9

Note: Respondents were classified as having difficulties if they responded "very difficult" or "can't do at all." Blacks are those who identify themselves as being black alone.
Source: National Center for Health Statistics, Summary Health Statistics for U.S. Adults: National Health Interview Survey, 2011, Vital and Health Statistics, Series 10, No. 256, 2012, Internet site http://www.cdc.gov/nchs/nhis.htm; calculations by New Strategist

Table 4.31 AIDS Cases among Total People and Blacks, through December 2009

(number of total AIDS cases diagnosed, number and percent distribution among blacks, and black share of total, by sex, through December 2009)

	total	black number	black percent distribution	black share of total
Total diagnosed with AIDS	**1,108,611**	**466,349**	**100.0%**	**42.1%**
Males aged 13 or older	878,366	323,872	69.4	36.9
Females aged 13 or older	220,795	136,690	29.3	61.9
Children under age 13	9,448	5,787	1.2	61.3

Source: National Center for Health Statistics, Health United States 2011, Internet site http://www.cdc.gov/nchs/hus.htm; calculations by New Strategist

Table 4.32 Leading Causes of Death among Blacks, 2009

(number and percent distribution of deaths to blacks accounted for by the 10 leading causes of death among blacks, 2009)

		number	percent distribution
Total black deaths		**286,623**	**100.0%**
1.	Diseases of the heart (1)	69,687	24.3
2.	Malignant neoplasms (cancer) (2)	64,649	22.6
3.	Cerebrovascular diseases (4)	15,878	5.5
4.	Accidents (unintentional injuries) (5)	12,074	4.2
5.	Diabetes mellitus (7)	11,960	4.2
6.	Nephritis, nephrotic syndrome, and nephrosis (9)	8,808	3.1
7.	Chronic lower respiratory disease (3)	8,530	3.0
8.	Homicide	7,874	2.7
9.	Septicemia	6,179	2.2
10.	Human immunodeficiency virus infection	5,377	1.9
	All other causes	75,607	26.4

Note: Number in parentheses shows rank for all Americans if the cause of death is in top 10.
Source: National Center for Health Statistics, Deaths: Leading Causes for 2009, National Vital Statistics Report, Vol. 61, No. 7, 2012, Internet site http://www.cdc.gov/nchs/deaths.htm; calculations by New Strategist

Table 4.33 Life Expectancy of Total People and Blacks by Sex, 2011

(average number of years of life remaining for total people and blacks at birth and age 65 by sex, and index of black life expectancy to total, 2011)

	total people	blacks	index, black to total
AT BIRTH			
Total	**78.7 yrs.**	**75.3 yrs.**	**96**
Female	81.1	78.2	96
Male	76.3	72.1	94
AT AGE 65			
Total	**19.2**	**18.0**	**94**
Female	20.4	19.4	95
Male	17.8	16.1	90

Note: The index is calculated by dividing black life expectancy by total life expectancy and multiplying by 100.
Source: National Center for Health Statistics, Deaths: Preliminary Data for 2011, National Vital Statistics Report, Vol. 61, No. 6, 2012, Internet site http://www.cdc.gov/nchs/deaths.htm; calculations by New Strategist

Most Black Households in the South Own Their Home

Forty-four percent of the nation's black households own their home. This compares with a much higher homeownership rate of 65 percent for all households. The 67 percent majority of black married couples own a home, as do most black householders aged 45 or older. Fifty-one percent of black households in the South are homeowners, while only 33 percent of those in the West own their home.

The 79 percent majority of black homeowners live in a single-family detached house. The homes owned by blacks had a reported median value of $139,400, according to the 2006–10 American Community Survey, well below the $188,400 median of all homeowners.

Sixteen percent of blacks moved between 2011 and 2012, a higher mobility rate than the 12 percent for the population as a whole. Among black movers, the primary reason for moving was to find a new or better home or apartment.

■ Because so many black households are female-headed families, one of the household types least likely to own a home, black homeownership is well below average.

Black homeownership is lowest in the West

(percent of black households that own their home, by region, 2011)

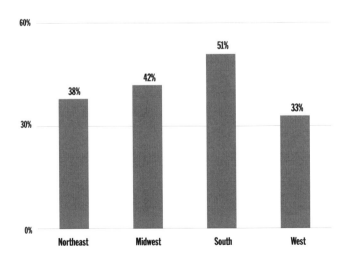

Table 4.34 Total and Black Homeownership Rate, 2000 to 2012

(homeownership rate of total and black households and index of black to total, 2000 to 2012; percentage point change for selected years)

	total households	black households	index, black to total
2012	65.4%	43.9%	67
2011	66.1	44.9	68
2010	66.9	45.4	68
2009	67.4	46.2	69
2008	67.8	47.4	70
2007	68.1	47.2	69
2006	68.8	47.9	70
2005	68.9	48.2	70
2004	69.0	49.1	71
2003	68.3	48.1	70
2002	67.9	47.4	70
2001	67.8	47.7	70
2000	67.4	47.2	70

PERCENTAGE POINT CHANGE

2004 to 2012	–3.6	–5.2	–
2000 to 2012	–2.0	–3.3	–

Note: Blacks are those who identify themselves as being of the race alone. The index is calculated by dividing the black homeownership rate by the total rate and multiplying by 100. "–" means not applicable.
Source: Bureau of the Census, Housing Vacancies and Homeownership, Internet site http://www.census.gov/housing/hvs/; calculations by New Strategist

Table 4.35 Black Homeownership Status by Age of Householder, 2011

(number and percent of black households by age of householder and homeownership status, 2011; numbers in thousands)

	total	owner		renter	
		number	percent	number	percent
Total black households	**14,694**	**6,662**	**45.3%**	**8,033**	**54.7%**
Under age 25	815	46	5.6	769	94.4
Aged 25 to 29	1,242	190	15.3	1,052	84.7
Aged 30 to 34	1,527	398	26.1	1,128	73.9
Aged 35 to 44	2,956	1,231	41.6	1,725	58.4
Aged 45 to 54	3,197	1,680	52.5	1,517	47.5
Aged 55 to 64	2,530	1,489	58.9	1,041	41.1
Aged 65 to 74	1,434	915	63.8	519	36.2
Aged 75 or older	995	713	71.7	282	28.3

Note: Blacks are those who identify themselves as being of the race alone.
Source: Bureau of the Census, American Housing Survey for the United States: 2011, Internet site http://www.census.gov/housing/ahs/index.html; calculations by New Strategist

Table 4.36 Total and Black Homeowners by Age of Householder, 2011

(number of total homeowners, number and percent distribution of black homeowners, and black share of total, by age of householder, 2011; numbers in thousands)

	total	black		
		number	percent distribution	share of total
Total homeowners	**76,091**	**6,662**	**100.0%**	**8.8%**
Under age 25	830	46	0.7	5.5
Aged 25 to 29	3,136	190	2.9	6.1
Aged 30 to 34	5,391	398	6.0	7.4
Aged 35 to 44	12,847	1,231	18.5	9.6
Aged 45 to 54	16,994	1,680	25.2	9.9
Aged 55 to 64	16,643	1,489	22.4	8.9
Aged 65 to 74	10,802	915	13.7	8.5
Aged 75 or older	9,448	713	10.7	7.5

Note: Blacks are those who identify themselves as being of the race alone.
Source: Bureau of the Census, American Housing Survey for the United States: 2011, Internet site http://www.census.gov/housing/ahs/index.html; calculations by New Strategist

Table 4.37 Total and Black Renters by Age of Householder, 2011

(number of total renters, number and percent distribution of black renters, and black share of total, by age of householder, 2011; numbers in thousands)

| | | black | | |
	total	number	percent distribution	share of total
Total renters	**38,816**	**8,033**	**100.0%**	**20.7%**
Under age 25	4,568	769	9.6	16.8
Aged 25 to 29	5,610	1,052	13.1	18.8
Aged 30 to 34	5,343	1,128	14.0	21.1
Aged 35 to 44	7,600	1,725	21.5	22.7
Aged 45 to 54	6,422	1,517	18.9	23.6
Aged 55 to 64	4,466	1,041	13.0	23.3
Aged 65 to 74	2,366	519	6.5	21.9
Aged 75 or older	2,442	282	3.5	11.5

Note: Blacks are those who identify themselves as being of the race alone.
Source: Bureau of the Census, American Housing Survey for the United States: 2011, Internet site http://www.census.gov/housing/ahs/index.html; calculations by New Strategist

Table 4.38 Black Homeownership Status by Household Type, 2010

(number and percent of black households by household type and homeownership status, 2010; numbers in thousands)

| | | owner | | renter | |
	total	number	percent	number	percent
Total black households	**14,722**	**6,479**	**44.0%**	**8,243**	**56.0%**
Family households	9,558	4,741	49.6	4,817	50.4
Married couples	4,200	2,834	67.5	1,367	32.5
Female-headed family, no spouse present	4,422	1,512	34.2	2,910	65.8
Male-headed family, no spouse present	935	395	42.3	540	57.7
Nonfamily households	5,165	1,738	33.7	3,427	66.3
Female householder	2,804	1,024	36.5	1,780	63.5
Living alone	2,433	918	37.7	1,516	62.3
Male householder	2,360	714	30.3	1,646	69.7
Living alone	1,922	598	31.1	1,324	68.9

Note: Blacks are those who identify themselves as being of the race alone and those who identify themselves as being of the race in combination with other races.
Source: Bureau of the Census, 2010 Census, Internet site http://factfinder2.census.gov/faces/nav/jsf/pages/index.xhtml; calculations by New Strategist

Table 4.39 Total and Black Homeowners by Household Type, 2010

(number of total homeowners, number and percent distribution of black homeowners, and black share of total, by household type, 2010; numbers in thousands)

	total	black number	black percent distribution	black share of total
Total homeowners	**75,986**	**6,479**	**100.0%**	**8.5%**
Family households	56,206	4,741	73.2	8.4
Married couples	45,801	2,834	43.7	6.2
Female-headed family, no spouse present	7,278	1,512	23.3	20.8
Male-headed family, no spouse present	3,127	395	6.1	12.6
Nonfamily households	19,780	1,738	26.8	8.8
Female householder	11,053	1,024	15.8	9.3
Living alone	9,625	918	14.2	9.5
Male householder	8,727	714	11.0	8.2
Living alone	6,828	598	9.2	8.8

Note: Blacks are those who identify themselves as being of the race alone and those who identify themselves as being of the race in combination with other races.
Source: Bureau of the Census, 2010 Census, Internet site http://factfinder2.census.gov/faces/nav/jsf/pages/index.xhtml; calculations by New Strategist

Table 4.40 Total and Black Renters by Household Type, 2010

(number of total renters, number and percent distribution of black renters, and black share of total, by household type, 2010; numbers in thousands)

		black		
	total	number	percent distribution	share of total
Total renters	**40,730**	**8,243**	**100.0%**	**20.2%**
Family households	21,332	4,817	58.4	22.6
Married couples	10,710	1,367	16.6	12.8
Female-headed family, no spouse present	7,972	2,910	35.3	36.5
Male-headed family, no spouse present	2,651	540	6.6	20.4
Nonfamily households	19,398	3,427	41.6	17.7
Female householder	9,666	1,780	21.6	18.4
Living alone	7,673	1,516	18.4	19.8
Male householder	9,732	1,646	20.0	16.9
Living alone	7,078	1,324	16.1	18.7

Note: Blacks are those who identify themselves as being of the race alone and those who identify themselves as being of the race in combination with other races.
Source: Bureau of the Census, 2010 Census, Internet site http://factfinder2.census.gov/faces/nav/jsf/pages/index.xhtml; calculations by New Strategist

Table 4.41 Black Homeownership Status by Region, 2011

(number and percent of black households by homeownership status and region, 2011; numbers in thousands)

	total	owners		renters	
		number	share of total	number	share of total
Total black households	**14,694**	**6,662**	**45.3%**	**8,033**	**54.7%**
Northeast	2,510	963	38.4	1,547	61.6
Midwest	2,659	1,111	41.8	1,549	58.3
South	8,144	4,135	50.8	4,009	49.2
West	1,381	453	32.8	928	67.2

Note: Blacks are those who identify themselves as being of the race alone.
Source: Bureau of the Census, American Housing Survey for the United States: 2011, Internet site http://www.census.gov/housing/ahs/index.html; calculations by New Strategist

Table 4.42 Total and Black Homeowners by Region, 2011

(number of total homeowners, number and percent distribution of black homeowners, and black share of total, by region, 2011; numbers in thousands)

	total	black		
		number	percent distribution	share of total
Total homeowners	**76,091**	**6,662**	**100.0%**	**8.8%**
Northeast	13,480	963	14.5	7.1
Midwest	18,032	1,111	16.7	6.2
South	29,119	4,135	62.1	14.2
West	15,460	453	6.8	2.9

Note: Blacks are those who identify themselves as being of the race alone.
Source: Bureau of the Census, American Housing Survey for the United States: 2011, Internet site http://www.census.gov/housing/ahs/index.html; calculations by New Strategist

Table 4.43 Total and Black Renters by Region, 2011

(number of total renters, number and percent distribution of black renters, and black share of total, by region, 2011; numbers in thousands)

	total	black number	black percent distribution	black share of total
Total renters	**38,816**	**8,033**	**100.0%**	**20.7%**
Northeast	7,585	1,547	19.3	20.4
Midwest	7,650	1,549	19.3	20.2
South	13,465	4,009	49.9	29.8
West	10,115	928	11.6	9.2

Note: Blacks are those who identify themselves as being of the race alone.
Source: Bureau of the Census, American Housing Survey for the United States: 2011, Internet site http://www.census.gov/housing/ahs/index.html; calculations by New Strategist

Table 4.44 Characteristics of Total and Black Occupied Housing Units, 2006–10

(number of total and black occupied housing units, and percent distribution by selected characteristics, 2006–10; numbers in thousands)

	total		black	
	number	percent distribution	number	percent distribution
TOTAL OCCUPIED HOUSING UNITS	**114,236**	**100.0%**	**14,103**	**100.0%**
Year householder moved into unit				
Total households	**114,236**	**100.0**	**14,103**	**100.0**
2005 or later	39,766	34.8	6,032	42.8
2000 to 2004	26,517	23.2	3,141	22.3
1990 to 1999	23,883	20.9	2,476	17.6
1980 to 1989	10,804	9.5	1,026	7.3
1970 to 1979	7,147	6.3	822	5.8
Before 1970	6,120	5.4	605	4.3
Vehicles available				
Total households	**114,236**	**100.0**	**14,103**	**100.0**
None	10,113	8.9	2,785	19.7
One or more	104,123	91.1	11,318	80.3
House heating fuel				
Total households	**114,236**	**100.0**	**14,103**	**100.0**
Utility gas	57,018	49.9	6,969	49.4
Bottled gas	6,146	5.4	430	3.0
Electricity	39,066	34.2	5,822	41.3
Fuel oil or kerosene	8,073	7.1	706	5.0
Coal or coke	135	0.1	3	0.0
Wood	2,250	2.0	49	0.3
Solar energy	38	0.0	3	0.0
Other fuel	483	0.4	39	0.3
No heating fuel used	1,025	0.9	83	0.6
TOTAL OWNER-OCCUPIED HOMES	**76,090**	**100.0**	**6,434**	**100.0**
Housing units with a mortgage	51,697	67.9	4,802	74.6
Housing units without a mortgage	24,393	32.1	1,632	25.4
Median value of home	$188,400	–	$139,400	–
Median monthly owner costs with a mortgage	1,524	–	1,405	–
Median monthly owner costs without a mortgage	431	–	393	–
TOTAL RENTER-OCCUPIED HOMES	**38,146**	**100.0**	**7,669**	**100.0**
Occupied units paying rent	35,274	92.5	7,363	96.0
Median rent	$841	–	$794	–

Note: Blacks are those who identify themselves as being of the race alone and those who identify themselves as being of the race in combination with other races.
Source: Bureau of the Census, 2006–10 American Community Survey, Internet site http://factfinder2.census.gov/faces/nav/jsf/ pages/index.xhtml; calculations by New Strategist

Table 4.45 Characteristics of Housing Units Occupied by Black Homeowners, 2011

(number and percent distribution of housing units occupied by black homeowners by selected characteristics, 2011; numbers in thousands)

	number	percent distribution
Total black homeowners	6,662	100.0%
UNITS IN STRUCTURE		
Total black homeowners	6,662	100.0
One, detached	5,235	78.6
One, attached	599	9.0
Two to four	194	2.9
Five to nine	39	0.6
10 to 19	54	0.8
20 to 49	22	0.3
50 or more	45	0.7
Mobile home or trailer	474	7.1
Median square footage of unit*	1,700	–
NUMBER OF BEDROOMS		
Total black homeowners	6,662	100.0
None	3	0.0
One	81	1.2
Two	935	14.0
Three	3,691	55.4
Four or more	1,952	29.3
NUMBER OF BATHROOMS		
Total black homeowners	6,662	100.0
None	34	0.5
One	1,645	24.7
One-and-one-half	1,241	18.6
Two or more	3,742	56.2
ROOMS USED FOR BUSINESS		
Total black homeowners	6,662	100.0
With room(s) used for business	2,002	30.1

* Single-family detached and mobile/manufactured homes only.
Note: Blacks are those who identify themselves as being of the race alone. "–" means not applicable.
Source: Bureau of the Census, American Housing Survey for the United States: 2011, Internet site http://www.census.gov/ housing/ahs/index.html; calculations by New Strategist

Table 4.46 Characteristics of Housing Units Occupied by Black Renters, 2011

(number and percent distribution of housing units occupied by black renters, 2011; numbers in thousands)

	number	percent distribution
Total black renters	**8,033**	**100.0%**
UNITS IN STRUCTURE		
Total black renters	**8,033**	**100.0**
One, detached	1,868	23.3
One, attached	688	8.6
Two to four	1,653	20.6
Five to nine	1,240	15.4
10 to 19	1,073	13.4
20 to 49	634	7.9
50 or more	756	9.4
Mobile home or trailer	120	1.5
Median square footage of unit*	1,300	–
NUMBER OF BEDROOMS		
Total black renters	**8,033**	**100.0**
None	94	1.2
One	1,996	24.8
Two	3,329	41.4
Three	2,033	25.3
Four or more	581	7.2
NUMBER OF BATHROOMS		
Total black renters	**8,033**	**100.0**
None	49	0.6
One	5,145	64.0
One-and-one-half	914	11.4
Two or more	1,925	24.0
ROOMS USED FOR BUSINESS		
Total black renters	**8,033**	**100.0**
With room(s) used for business	1,771	22.0

* Single-family detached and mobile/manufactured homes only.
Note: Blacks are those who identify themselves as being of the race alone. "–" means not applicable.
Source: Bureau of the Census, American Housing Survey for the United States: 2011, Internet site http://www.census.gov/housing/ahs/index.html; calculations by New Strategist

Table 4.47 Geographic Mobility of Blacks by Age, 2011–12

(total number of blacks aged 1 or older, and number and percent who moved between March 2011 and March 2012, by age and type of move; numbers in thousands)

	total	same house (nonmovers)	total movers	same county	different county, same state	different state total	different state same region	different state different region	movers from abroad
Total blacks	**42,051**	**35,399**	**6,652**	**4,687**	**1,136**	**690**	**368**	**322**	**140**
Aged 1 to 4	3,071	2,330	741	560	110	57	22	35	13
Aged 5 to 9	3,545	2,835	710	487	146	70	36	34	7
Aged 10 to 14	3,511	2,903	608	433	97	61	32	29	18
Aged 15 to 17	2,245	1,880	365	243	75	41	22	19	6
Aged 18 to 19	1,379	1,173	206	141	28	27	9	18	10
Aged 20 to 24	3,588	2,848	740	547	115	71	31	40	8
Aged 25 to 29	2,944	2,217	727	510	135	58	28	30	24
Aged 30 to 34	2,831	2,260	571	402	90	63	37	26	15
Aged 35 to 39	2,590	2,170	420	283	63	57	26	31	16
Aged 40 to 44	2,735	2,308	427	290	63	64	43	21	11
Aged 45 to 49	2,827	2,509	318	215	63	29	24	5	11
Aged 50 to 54	2,810	2,497	313	211	63	39	17	22	0
Aged 55 to 59	2,406	2,195	211	135	50	23	17	6	2
Aged 60 to 61	813	755	58	42	10	6	4	2	0
Aged 62 to 64	1,040	957	83	69	4	10	10	0	0
Aged 65 or older	3,717	3,563	154	119	22	14	10	4	0

PERCENT DISTRIBUTION BY MOBILITY STATUS

Total blacks	**100.0%**	**84.2%**	**15.8%**	**11.1%**	**2.7%**	**1.6%**	**0.9**	**0.8%**	**0.3%**
Aged 1 to 4	100.0	75.9	24.1	18.2	3.6	1.9	0.7	1.1	0.4
Aged 5 to 9	100.0	80.0	20.0	13.7	4.1	2.0	1.0	1.0	0.2
Aged 10 to 14	100.0	82.7	17.3	12.3	2.8	1.7	0.9	0.8	0.5
Aged 15 to 17	100.0	83.7	16.3	10.8	3.3	1.8	1.0	0.8	0.3
Aged 18 to 19	100.0	85.1	14.9	10.2	2.0	2.0	0.7	1.3	0.7
Aged 20 to 24	100.0	79.4	20.6	15.2	3.2	2.0	0.9	1.1	0.2
Aged 25 to 29	100.0	75.3	24.7	17.3	4.6	2.0	1.0	1.0	0.8
Aged 30 to 34	100.0	79.8	20.2	14.2	3.2	2.2	1.3	0.9	0.5
Aged 35 to 39	100.0	83.8	16.2	10.9	2.4	2.2	1.0	1.2	0.6
Aged 40 to 44	100.0	84.4	15.6	10.6	2.3	2.3	1.6	0.8	0.4
Aged 45 to 49	100.0	88.8	11.2	7.6	2.2	1.0	0.8	0.2	0.4
Aged 50 to 54	100.0	88.9	11.1	7.5	2.2	1.4	0.6	0.8	0.0
Aged 55 to 59	100.0	91.2	8.8	5.6	2.1	1.0	0.7	0.2	0.1
Aged 60 to 61	100.0	92.9	7.1	5.2	1.2	0.7	0.5	0.2	0.0
Aged 62 to 64	100.0	92.0	8.0	6.6	0.4	1.0	1.0	0.0	0.0
Aged 65 or older	100.0	95.9	4.1	3.2	0.6	0.4	0.3	0.1	0.0

Note: Blacks are those who identify themselves as being of the race alone and those who identify themselves as being of the race in combination with other races.
Source: Bureau of the Census, Geographic Mobility: 2011 to 2012, Internet site http://www.census.gov/hhes/migration/data/cps/cps2012.html; calculations by New Strategist

Table 4.48 Reasons for Moving among Black Movers, 2011–12

(number and percent distribution of black movers by main reason for move, 2011–12; numbers in thousands)

	number	percent distribution
Total black movers	**6,653**	**100.0%**
FAMILY REASONS	**1,874**	**28.2%**
Change in marital status	343	5.2
To establish own household	757	11.4
Other family reason	774	11.6
EMPLOYMENT REASONS	**899**	**13.5**
New job or job transfer	344	5.2
To look for work or lost job	92	1.4
To be closer to work, easier commute	341	5.1
Retired	24	0.4
Other job-related reason	98	1.5
HOUSING REASONS	**3,817**	**57.4**
Wanted own home, not rent	201	3.0
Wanted new or better home/apartment	1,331	20.0
Wanted better neighborhood, less crime	304	4.6
Wanted cheaper housing	739	11.1
Foreclosure, eviction	186	2.8
Other housing reason	1,056	15.9
OTHER REASONS	**61**	**0.9**
To attend or leave college	13	0.2
Change of climate	5	0.1
Health reasons	2	0.0
Natural disaster	8	0.1
Other reason	33	0.5

Note: Blacks are those who identify themselves as being of the race alone and those who identify themselves as being of the race in combination with other races.
Source: Bureau of the Census, Geographic Mobility: 2011 to 2012, Internet site http://www.census.gov/hhes/migration/data/cps/cps2012.html; calculations by New Strategist

Black Incomes Have Declined because of the Great Recession

The median income of black households fell by a substantial 16 percent between 2000 and 2011. Despite the decline, the $32,366 median of black households in 2011 was still 4 percent higher than in 1990, after adjusting for inflation.

The median income of black households was 65 percent as high as that of the average household in 2011, up from 62 percent in 1990. Black household income is below average because married couples—typically the most-affluent household type—head only 28 percent of black households. Female-headed families account for another 28 percent of black households. Black couples had a median income of $65,124 in 2011, while female-headed families had a much lower median of $26,332.

The median income of black households has fallen steeply since 2000 because of unemployment. Among black men who work full-time, median earnings have declined only 0.6 percent since 2000, after adjusting for inflation. Among black women who work full-time, median earnings grew 1.9 percent during those years. The earnings of blacks rise steadily with education. Black men with at least a bachelor's degree who work full-time earned a median of $55,734 in 2011.

The percentage of black married couples and female-headed families in poverty fell between 1990 and 2011, despite the Great Recession. Among married couples, the poverty rate declined from 12.6 to 9.4 percent. Among female-headed families, the rate fell from 48.1 to 39.3 percent. Black male-headed families, however, saw their poverty rate increase during those years, as it went from 20.6 to 24.2 percent.

■ Black household income will remain below average as long as female-headed families account for such a large share of black households.

Black household income fell more than average between 2000 and 2011

(percent change in median household income for total and black households, 2000 to 2011; in 2011 dollars)

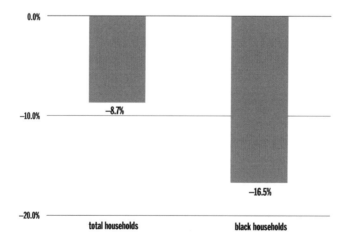

- 0.0%
- –10.0% — –8.7%
- –16.5%
- –20.0%
- total households
- black households

Table 4.49 Median Income of Total and Black Households, 1990 to 2011

(median income of total and black households, and index of black to total, 1990 to 2011; percent change in median for selected years; in 2011dollars)

	total households	black households	index, black to total
2011	$50,054	$32,366	65
2010	50,830	33,170	65
2009	52,195	34,341	66
2008	52,546	35,877	68
2007	54,489	36,979	68
2006	53,768	35,843	67
2005	53,371	35,661	67
2004	52,788	36,001	68
2003	52,973	36,306	69
2002	53,019	36,477	69
2001	53,646	37,438	70
2000	54,841	38,747	71
1999	54,932	37,673	69
1998	53,582	34,933	65
1997	51,704	35,000	68
1996	50,661	33,518	66
1995	49,935	32,815	66
1994	48,418	31,555	65
1993	47,884	29,939	63
1992	48,117	29,457	61
1991	48,516	30,287	62
1990	49,950	31,155	62
Percent change			
2007 to 2011	−8.1%	−12.5%	−
2000 to 2011	−8.7	−16.5	−
1990 to 2011	0.2	3.9	−

Note: Beginning in 2002, blacks are those who identify themselves as being of the race alone and being of the race in combination with other races. The index is calculated by dividing the black median by the total median and multiplying by 100. "–" means not applicable.
Source: Bureau of the Census, Current Population Surveys, Annual Social and Economic Supplement, Internet site http://www .census.gov/hhes/www/income/data/historical/household/index.html; calculations by New Strategist

Table 4.50 Black Household Income by Age of Householder, 2011

(number and percent distribution of black households by household income and age of householder, 2011; households in thousands as of 2012)

	total	15 to 24	25 to 34	35 to 44	45 to 54	55 to 64	65 or older total	65 to 74	75 or older
Black households	**16,165**	**1,119**	**3,029**	**3,175**	**3,332**	**2,910**	**2,599**	**1,567**	**1,033**
Under $5,000	1,135	158	285	188	252	158	94	58	36
$5,000 to $9,999	1,436	131	265	192	257	300	291	126	165
$10,000 to $14,999	1,538	129	222	173	236	305	473	261	213
$15,000 to $19,999	1,228	123	241	198	193	204	270	149	121
$20,000 to $24,999	1,185	116	207	220	204	217	221	117	104
$25,000 to $29,999	980	83	205	169	181	160	181	118	63
$30,000 to $34,999	984	61	202	187	196	178	159	96	63
$35,000 to $39,999	850	57	219	180	139	132	123	96	27
$40,000 to $44,999	750	61	139	164	153	107	124	78	46
$45,000 to $49,999	585	30	83	163	140	89	80	47	33
$50,000 to $54,999	659	32	116	148	167	120	76	57	20
$55,000 to $59,999	533	15	118	140	105	97	58	47	11
$60,000 to $64,999	485	19	109	127	105	77	49	38	10
$65,000 to $69,999	429	18	69	100	110	80	51	31	20
$70,000 to $74,999	373	5	71	101	89	69	39	30	9
$75,000 to $79,999	331	13	59	91	80	50	38	21	17
$80,000 to $84,999	297	7	45	75	60	72	38	25	13
$85,000 to $89,999	213	6	17	46	53	63	29	15	14
$90,000 to $94,999	268	9	61	63	58	60	18	13	5
$95,000 to $99,999	191	8	34	55	30	45	19	16	3
$100,000 to $124,999	714	21	115	154	211	138	77	55	22
$125,000 to $149,999	401	8	65	106	117	61	46	36	10
$150,000 to $174,999	237	4	32	66	78	39	16	13	3
$175,000 to $199,999	104	0	7	18	43	26	10	8	2
$200,000 or more	259	3	44	52	78	62	20	16	4
Median income	$32,366	$20,720	$31,684	$41,802	$40,193	$32,543	$23,616	$28,047	$19,226

PERCENT DISTRIBUTION

	total	15 to 24	25 to 34	35 to 44	45 to 54	55 to 64	65 or older total	65 to 74	75 or older
Black households	**100.0%**	**100.0%**	**100.0%**	**100.0%**	**100.0%**	**100.0%**	**100.0%**	**100.0%**	**100.0%**
Under $25,000	40.3	58.7	40.3	30.6	34.3	40.7	51.9	45.4	61.9
$25,000 to $49,999	25.7	26.1	28.0	27.2	24.3	22.9	25.7	27.8	22.5
$50,000 to $74,999	15.3	8.0	15.9	19.4	17.3	15.2	10.5	13.0	6.8
$75,000 to $99,999	8.0	3.8	7.1	10.4	8.4	10.0	5.5	5.7	5.0
$100,000 or more	10.6	3.2	8.7	12.5	15.8	11.2	6.5	8.2	4.0

Note: Blacks are those who identify themselves as being of the race alone and those who identify themselves as being of the race in combination with other races.
Source: Bureau of the Census, 2012 Current Population Survey, Internet site http://www.census.gov/hhes/www/income/data/incpovhlth/2011/dtables.html; calculations by New Strategist

Table 4.51 Black Household Income by Household Type, 2011

(number and percent distribution of black households by household income and household type, 2011; households in thousands as of 2012)

| | total | family households | | | nonfamily households | | | |
| | | married couples | female hh, no spouse present | male hh, no spouse present | female householder | | male householder | |
					total	living alone	total	living alone
Black households	**16,165**	**4,546**	**4,477**	**1,002**	**3,374**	**3,039**	**2,767**	**2,367**
Under $5,000	1,135	79	441	47	320	301	247	227
$5,000 to $9,999	1,436	88	410	43	541	530	354	335
$10,000 to $14,999	1,538	96	438	71	562	534	371	355
$15,000 to $19,999	1,228	142	431	71	341	316	244	218
$20,000 to $24,999	1,185	211	399	63	255	243	258	227
$25,000 to $29,999	980	181	351	63	204	171	182	159
$30,000 to $34,999	984	217	298	61	241	231	166	132
$35,000 to $39,999	850	236	266	74	140	130	134	110
$40,000 to $44,999	750	187	239	68	128	100	127	103
$45,000 to $49,999	585	170	191	29	87	75	109	90
$50,000 to $54,999	659	228	157	45	113	108	116	101
$55,000 to $59,999	533	237	135	38	65	45	56	41
$60,000 to $64,999	485	195	120	49	66	51	56	44
$65,000 to $69,999	429	195	84	39	58	36	53	34
$70,000 to $74,999	373	211	62	24	38	27	38	21
$75,000 to $79,999	331	175	54	28	35	27	38	28
$80,000 to $84,999	297	163	45	23	38	31	29	23
$85,000 to $89,999	213	122	42	26	17	8	7	5
$90,000 to $94,999	268	171	37	22	20	9	19	10
$95,000 to $99,999	191	102	45	17	11	5	16	5
$100,000 to $124,999	714	427	125	58	48	31	56	45
$125,000 to $149,999	401	285	48	14	14	11	39	17
$150,000 to $174,999	236	165	35	9	15	11	12	5
$175,000 to $199,999	104	82	5	8	2	1	8	3
$200,000 or more	259	182	17	12	16	8	32	27
Median income	$32,366	$65,124	$26,332	$40,501	$18,594	$17,075	$22,708	$20,858

PERCENT DISTRIBUTION

Black households	**100.0%**	**100.0%**	**100.0%**	**100.0%**	**100.0%**	**100.0%**	**100.0%**	**100.0%**
Under $25,000	40.4	13.6	47.4	29.4	59.8	63.3	53.2	57.5
$25,000 to $49,999	25.7	21.8	30.0	29.5	23.7	23.3	26.0	25.1
$50,000 to $74,999	15.3	23.5	12.5	19.4	10.1	8.8	11.5	10.2
$75,000 to $99,999	8.0	16.1	5.0	11.6	3.6	2.6	4.0	3.0
$100,000 or more	10.6	25.1	5.2	10.1	2.8	2.0	5.3	4.1

Note: Blacks are those who identify themselves as being of the race alone and those who identify themselves as being of the race in combination with other races. "hh" stands for householder.
Source: Bureau of the Census, 2012 Current Population Survey, Internet site http://www.census.gov/hhes/www/income/data/ incpovhlth/2011/dtables.html; calculations by New Strategist

Table 4.52 Income of Black Men by Age, 2011

(number and percent distribution of black men aged 15 or older by income and age, 2011; median income of men with income and of men working full-time, year-round; percent working full-time, year-round; men in thousands as of 2012)

	total	under 25	25 to 34	35 to 44	45 to 54	55 to 64	65 or older
TOTAL BLACK MEN	**14,499**	**3,506**	**2,642**	**2,404**	**2,582**	**1,872**	**1,493**
Without income	**2,937**	**1,789**	**395**	**251**	**305**	**124**	**74**
With income	**11,562**	**1,717**	**2,247**	**2,154**	**2,277**	**1,748**	**1,419**
Under $5,000	1,063	544	181	96	118	86	39
$5,000 to $9,999	1,469	406	257	171	231	249	155
$10,000 to $14,999	1,397	279	212	173	216	199	318
$15,000 to $19,999	1,007	170	175	166	164	140	192
$20,000 to $24,999	1,058	88	242	175	224	162	167
$25,000 to $29,999	806	67	198	183	145	126	85
$30,000 to $34,999	751	40	161	198	147	121	86
$35,000 to $39,999	647	53	149	145	102	115	83
$40,000 to $44,999	589	35	122	171	131	79	51
$45,000 to $49,999	436	4	104	105	118	64	41
$50,000 to $54,999	446	12	82	114	123	84	30
$55,000 to $59,999	211	5	58	44	47	22	36
$60,000 to $64,999	279	5	74	63	66	51	20
$65,000 to $69,999	207	0	37	55	64	34	16
$70,000 to $74,999	195	7	40	51	45	39	13
$75,000 to $79,999	130	2	28	34	44	22	1
$80,000 to $84,999	169	0	29	39	51	26	25
$85,000 to $89,999	70	0	7	21	27	12	4
$90,000 to $94,999	103	0	15	31	28	17	12
$95,000 to $99,999	34	0	4	5	12	9	4
$100,000 or more	493	0	72	115	174	89	42
MEDIAN INCOME							
Men with income	$23,584	$8,688	$26,062	$31,939	$30,932	$26,169	$20,153
Working full-time	40,136	21,350	36,734	41,169	45,439	41,969	49,873
Percent full-time	38.3%	11.6%	51.3%	59.5%	53.4%	43.4%	11.7%
PERCENT DISTRIBUTION							
TOTAL BLACK MEN	**100.0%**	**100.0%**	**100.0%**	**100.0%**	**100.0%**	**100.0%**	**100.0%**
Without income	**20.3**	**51.0**	**15.0**	**10.4**	**11.8**	**6.6**	**4.9**
With income	**79.7**	**49.0**	**85.0**	**89.6**	**88.2**	**93.4**	**95.1**
Under $15,000	27.1	35.0	24.6	18.3	21.9	28.5	34.2
$15,000 to $24,999	14.2	7.4	15.8	14.2	15.0	16.2	24.0
$25,000 to $34,999	10.7	3.1	13.6	15.8	11.3	13.2	11.5
$35,000 to $49,999	11.5	2.6	14.2	17.5	13.6	13.8	11.7
$50,000 to $74,999	9.2	0.8	11.0	13.6	13.4	12.3	7.7
$75,000 or more	6.9	0.1	5.9	10.2	13.0	9.3	5.8

Note: Blacks are those who identify themselves as being of the race alone and those who identify themselves as being of the race in combination with other races.
Source: Bureau of the Census, 2012 Current Population Survey Annual Social and Economic Supplement, Internet site http:// www.census.gov/hhes/www/cpstables/032012/perinc/toc.htm; calculations by New Strategist

Table 4.53 Income of Black Women by Age, 2011

(number and percent distribution of black women aged 15 or older by income and age, 2011; median income of women with income and of women working full-time, year-round; percent working full-time, year-round; women in thousands as of 2012)

	total	under 25	25 to 34	35 to 44	45 to 54	55 to 64	65 or older
TOTAL BLACK WOMEN	17,426	3,707	3,133	2,921	3,055	2,387	2,225
Without income	3,015	1,667	363	265	360	235	125
With income	14,411	2,040	2,770	2,656	2,694	2,152	2,099
Under $5,000	1,567	662	293	187	214	139	71
$5,000 to $9,999	2,155	455	345	229	344	278	504
$10,000 to $14,999	2,002	277	319	240	263	325	578
$15,000 to $19,999	1,598	232	331	272	276	232	256
$20,000 to $24,999	1,285	160	276	263	231	193	161
$25,000 to $29,999	990	72	243	191	223	140	122
$30,000 to $34,999	971	79	237	214	204	141	96
$35,000 to $39,999	803	42	216	196	156	128	65
$40,000 to $44,999	564	15	118	147	131	106	47
$45,000 to $49,999	419	7	77	132	99	68	37
$50,000 to $54,999	479	9	84	121	135	85	45
$55,000 to $59,999	279	16	51	90	61	42	20
$60,000 to $64,999	259	0	35	100	65	50	8
$65,000 to $69,999	156	4	30	51	38	23	10
$70,000 to $74,999	148	0	12	52	45	21	18
$75,000 to $79,999	131	2	16	34	35	27	16
$80,000 to $84,999	124	0	12	31	38	34	10
$85,000 to $89,999	52	0	13	9	13	13	4
$90,000 to $94,999	62	3	10	13	15	19	2
$95,000 to $99,999	48	0	6	13	13	13	2
$100,000 or more	318	4	46	72	94	75	27
MEDIAN INCOME							
Women with income	$19,561	$8,782	$21,222	$28,336	$25,296	$22,328	$13,925
Working full-time	35,090	20,782	31,744	37,576	36,604	38,810	43,796
Percent full-time	35.8%	13.2%	45.1%	57.8%	50.7%	38.0%	8.6%
PERCENT DISTRIBUTION							
TOTAL BLACK WOMEN	100.0%	100.0%	100.0%	100.0%	100.0%	100.0%	100.0%
Without income	17.3	45.0	11.6	9.1	11.8	9.8	5.6
With income	82.7	55.0	88.4	90.9	88.2	90.2	94.4
Under $15,000	32.8	37.6	30.5	22.4	26.9	31.1	51.9
$15,000 to $24,999	16.5	10.6	19.4	18.3	16.6	17.8	18.8
$25,000 to $34,999	11.3	4.1	15.3	13.9	14.0	11.8	9.8
$35,000 to $49,999	10.3	1.7	13.1	16.3	12.6	12.7	6.7
$50,000 to $74,999	7.6	0.8	6.8	14.1	11.3	9.3	4.5
$75,000 or more	4.2	0.3	3.3	5.9	6.8	7.6	2.7

Note: Blacks are those who identify themselves as being of the race alone and those who identify themselves as being of the race in combination with other races.
Source: Bureau of the Census, 2012 Current Population Survey Annual Social and Economic Supplement, Internet site http:// www.census.gov/hhes/www/cpstables/032012/perinc/toc.htm; calculations by New Strategist

Table 4.54 Median Earnings of Blacks Working Full-Time by Sex, 1990 to 2011

(median earnings of blacks working full-time, year-round by sex; index of black to total population median earnings, and black women's earnings as a percent of black men's earnings, 1990 to 2011; percent change in earnings for selected years; in 2011 dollars)

	black men		black women		women's earnings as a percent of men's earnings
	earnings	index	earnings	index	
2011	$39,094	81	$33,380	90	85.4%
2010	38,085	77	33,302	88	87.4
2009	39,318	80	33,446	88	85.1
2008	38,914	80	32,914	88	84.6
2007	39,170	80	33,701	89	86.0
2006	38,943	83	33,913	94	87.1
2005	37,991	80	34,194	93	90.0
2004	37,243	77	33,079	89	88.8
2003	39,445	79	33,004	88	83.7
2002	39,315	80	33,645	89	85.6
2001	39,828	82	33,786	91	84.8
2000	39,313	81	32,767	91	83.3
1999	40,142	82	32,701	92	81.5
1998	37,274	77	31,208	88	83.7
1997	36,931	78	30,787	88	83.4
1996	37,689	82	30,651	91	81.3
1995	35,797	78	30,282	92	84.6
1994	35,629	77	29,879	90	83.9
1993	35,282	76	30,372	91	86.1
1992	35,177	74	31,042	92	88.2
1991	35,550	75	30,147	91	84.8
1990	35,222	76	30,094	91	85.4

	percent change		percent change		percentage point change
2007 to 2011	−0.2%	–	−1.0%	–	−0.7
2000 to 2011	−0.6	–	1.9	–	2.0
1990 to 2011	11.0	–	10.9	–	−0.1

Note: Beginning in 2002, blacks are those who identify themselves as being of the race alone and being of the race in combination with other races. The black/total indexes are calculated by dividing the median earnings of black men and women by the median earnings of total men and women and multiplying by 100. "–" means not applicable.
Source: Bureau of the Census, Current Population Survey, Historical Tables, Internet site http://www.census.gov/hhes/www/income/data/historical/people/; calculations by New Strategist

Table 4.55 Median Earnings of Blacks Working Full-Time by Education and Sex, 2011

(median earnings of blacks aged 25 or older working full-time, year-round, by educational attainment and sex, and black women's earnings as a percent of black men's earnings, 2011)

	men	women	women's earnings as a percent of men's earnings
Total Asians	**$56,370**	**$41,733**	**74.0%**
Less than 9th grade	27,110	–	–
9th to 12th grade, no diploma	25,684	20,848	81.2
High school graduate	31,596	26,785	84.8
Some college, no degree	40,669	31,429	77.3
Associate's degree	41,052	35,442	86.3
Bachelor's degree or more	55,734	47,097	84.5
Bachelor's degree	50,405	44,171	87.6
Master's degree	70,455	55,371	78.6
Professional degree	–	72,449	–
Doctoral degree	–	–	–

Note: Blacks are those who identify themselves as being of the race alone and those who identify themselves as being of the race in combination with other races. "–" means data are not available.
Source: Bureau of the Census, 2012 Current Population Survey Annual Social and Economic Supplement, Internet site http://www.census.gov/hhes/www/cpstables/032012/perinc/toc.htm; calculations by New Strategist

Table 4.56 Poverty Status of Black Married Couples, 1990 to 2011

(total number of black married couples, and number and percent below poverty level by presence of children under age 18 at home, 1990 to 2011; percent change in numbers and percentage point change in rates for selected years; families in thousands as of March the following year)

		in poverty	
	total	number	percent
Total black married couples			
2011	4,547	426	9.4%
2010	4,473	407	9.1
2009	4,429	383	8.6
2008	4,530	365	8.0
2007	4,461	313	7.0
2006	4,490	356	7.9
2005	4,252	348	8.2
2004	4,264	386	9.1
2003	4,259	331	7.8
2002	4,268	340	8.0
2001	4,234	328	7.8
2000	4,214	266	6.3
1999	4,150	295	7.1
1998	3,979	290	7.3
1997	3,921	312	8.0
1996	3,851	352	9.1
1995	3,713	314	8.5
1994	3,842	336	8.7
1993	3,715	458	12.3
1992	3,777	490	13.0
1991	3,631	399	11.0
1990	3,569	448	12.6

	percent change		percentage point change
2007 to 2011	1.9%	36.1%	2.4
2000 to 2011	7.9	60.2	3.1
1990 to 2011	27.4	-4.9	-3.2

| | total | in poverty | |
		number	percent
Black married couples with children			
2011	2,224	272	12.2%
2010	2,205	279	12.7
2009	2,264	259	11.4
2008	2,298	225	9.8
2007	2,282	194	8.5
2006	2,433	221	9.1
2005	2,310	213	9.2
2004	2,292	213	9.3
2003	2,323	210	9.1
2002	2,340	199	8.5
2001	2,342	205	8.7
2000	2,343	157	6.7
1999	2,301	199	8.7
1998	2,198	189	8.6
1997	2,275	205	9.0
1996	2,174	239	11.0
1995	2,119	209	9.9
1994	2,147	245	11.4
1993	2,147	298	13.9
1992	2,229	343	15.4
1991	2,129	263	12.4
1990	2,104	301	14.3

	percent change		percentage point change
2007 to 2011	-2.5%	40.2%	3.7
2000 to 2011	-5.1	73.2	5.5
1990 to 2011	5.7	-9.6	-2.1

Note: Beginning in 2002, blacks are those who identify themselves as being of the race alone and those who identify themselves as being of the race in combination with other races.
Source: Bureau of the Census, Current Population Surveys, Historical Poverty Tables, Internet site http://www.census.gov/hhes/www/poverty/data/historical/families.html; calculations by New Strategist

Table 4.57 Poverty Status of Black Female-Headed Families, 1990 to 2011

(total number of black female-headed families, and number and percent below poverty level by presence of children under age 18 at home, 1990 to 2011; percent change in numbers and percentage point change in rates for selected years; families in thousands as of March the following year)

		in poverty	
	total	number	percent
Total black female-headed families			
2011	4,481	1,762	39.3%
2010	4,531	1,738	38.4
2009	4,264	1,569	36.8
2008	4,254	1,580	37.1
2007	4,218	1,570	37.2
2006	4,132	1,506	36.4
2005	4,215	1,524	36.2
2004	4,090	1,538	37.6
2003	4,068	1,496	36.8
2002	4,072	1,454	35.7
2001	3,838	1,351	35.2
2000	3,785	1,300	34.3
1999	3,797	1,487	39.2
1998	3,813	1,557	40.8
1997	3,926	1,563	39.8
1996	3,947	1,724	43.7
1995	3,769	1,701	45.1
1994	3,716	1,715	46.2
1993	3,828	1,908	49.9
1992	3,738	1,878	50.2
1991	3,582	1,834	51.2
1990	3,430	1,648	48.1

	percent change		percentage point change
2007 to 2011	6.2%	12.2%	2.1
2000 to 2011	18.4	35.5	5.0
1990 to 2011	30.6	6.9	-8.8

	total	in poverty	
		number	percent
Black female-headed families with children			
2011	3,213	1,532	47.7%
2010	3,188	1,501	47.1
2009	3,079	1,365	44.3
2008	3,187	1,416	44.4
2007	3,167	1,385	43.7
2006	3,112	1,347	43.3
2005	3,178	1,335	42.0
2004	3,092	1,339	43.3
2003	3,144	1,341	42.7
2002	3,120	1,288	41.3
2001	2,994	1,220	40.8
2000	2,873	1,177	41.0
1999	2,869	1,320	46.0
1998	2,940	1,397	47.5
1997	3,060	1,436	46.9
1996	3,120	1,593	51.0
1995	2,884	1,533	53.2
1994	2,951	1,591	53.9
1993	3,084	1,780	57.7
1992	2,971	1,706	57.4
1991	2,771	1,676	60.5
1990	2,698	1,513	56.1

	percent change		percentage point change
2007 to 2011	1.5%	10.6%	4.0
2000 to 2011	11.8	30.2	6.7
1990 to 2011	19.1	1.3	-8.4

Note: Beginning in 2002, blacks are those who identify themselves as being of the race alone and those who identify themselves as being of the race in combination with other races.
Source: Bureau of the Census, Current Population Surveys, Historical Poverty Tables, Internet site http://www.census.gov/hhes/ www/poverty/data/historical/families.html; calculations by New Strategist

Table 4.58 Poverty Status of Black Male-Headed Families, 1990 to 2011

(total number of black male-headed families, and number and percent below poverty level by presence of children under age 18 at home, 1990 to 2011; percent change in numbers and percentage point change in rates for selected years; families in thousands as of March the following year)

	total	in poverty number	in poverty percent
Total black male-headed families			
2011	1,002	242	24.2%
2010	979	257	26.3
2009	968	241	24.9
2008	840	167	19.8
2007	827	208	25.1
2006	882	180	20.4
2005	833	178	21.3
2004	760	158	20.7
2003	804	194	24.1
2002	793	165	20.8
2001	775	150	19.4
2000	732	120	16.3
1999	706	105	14.8
1998	660	134	20.3
1997	562	111	19.7
1996	657	130	19.8
1995	573	112	19.5
1994	535	161	30.1
1993	450	133	29.6
1992	467	116	24.8
1991	503	110	21.9
1990	472	97	20.6

	percent change		percentage point change
2007 to 2011	21.2%	16.3%	−0.9
2000 to 2011	36.9	101.7	7.9
1990 to 2011	112.3	149.5	3.6

Black male-headed families with children	total	in poverty	
		number	percent
2011	514	148	28.8%
2010	495	198	40.0
2009	535	163	30.5
2008	451	115	25.5
2007	434	128	29.5
2006	452	117	25.8
2005	442	131	29.6
2004	405	102	25.3
2003	476	146	30.7
2002	420	110	26.3
2001	404	99	24.6
2000	352	76	21.7
1999	386	84	21.7
1998	353	88	24.8
1997	312	81	25.8
1996	401	109	27.2
1995	337	79	23.4
1994	341	118	34.6
1993	294	93	31.6
1992	248	83	33.5
1991	243	77	31.7
1990	267	73	27.3

	percent change		percentage point change
2007 to 2011	18.4%	15.6%	–0.7
2000 to 2011	46.0	94.7	7.1
1990 to 2011	92.5	102.7	1.5

Note: Beginning in 2002, blacks are those who identify themselves as being of the race alone and those who identify themselves as being of the race in combination with other races.
Source: Bureau of the Census, Current Population Surveys, Historical Poverty Tables, Internet site http://www.census.gov/hhes/ www/poverty/data/historical/families.html; calculations by New Strategist

Table 4.59 Poverty Status of Blacks by Sex and Age, 2011

(total number of blacks, and number and percent below poverty level by sex and age, 2011; people in thousands as of 2012)

	total	in poverty number	in poverty percent
Total blacks	**42,648**	**11,730**	**27.5%**
Under age 18	12,968	4,849	37.4
Aged 18 to 24	4,967	1,536	30.9
Aged 25 to 34	5,775	1,522	26.4
Aged 35 to 44	5,325	1,037	19.5
Aged 45 to 54	5,637	1,242	22.0
Aged 55 to 59	2,406	576	23.9
Aged 60 to 64	1,853	327	17.7
Aged 65 or older	3,718	640	17.2
Black females	**22,659**	**6,650**	**29.4%**
Under age 18	6,331	2,413	38.1
Aged 18 to 24	2,607	893	34.2
Aged 25 to 34	3,133	993	31.7
Aged 35 to 44	2,921	660	22.6
Aged 45 to 54	3,055	732	24.0
Aged 55 to 59	1,305	316	24.2
Aged 60 to 64	1,082	182	16.8
Aged 65 or older	2,225	462	20.8
Black males	**19,989**	**5,079**	**25.4%**
Under age 18	6,637	2,436	36.7
Aged 18 to 24	2,360	643	27.3
Aged 25 to 34	2,642	530	20.0
Aged 35 to 44	2,404	377	15.7
Aged 45 to 54	2,582	510	19.8
Aged 55 to 59	1,101	260	23.6
Aged 60 to 64	771	146	18.9
Aged 65 or older	1,493	178	11.9

Note: Blacks are those who identify themselves as being of the race alone and those who identify themselves as being of the race in combination with other races.
Source: Bureau of the Census, 2012 Current Population Survey, Internet site http://www.census.gov/hhes/www/cpstables/032012/pov/toc.htm; calculations by New Strategist

Thirty Percent of Black Workers Are Managers or Professionals

The 30 percent of black workers who are employed as managers or professionals account for 9 percent of Americans who work in those occupations. Twenty-five percent of employed blacks work in sales and office jobs, and 25 percent are in service occupations. Blacks account for 11 percent of all workers, but for 23 percent of social workers, 23 percent of licensed practical nurses, 27 percent of security guards, and 38 percent of barbers.

Overall, 64 percent of black men and 60 percent of black women were in the labor force in 2012. Among black couples, 55 percent have both husband and wife in the labor force. Nevertheless, only 28 percent of black households have two or more earners because married couples head a relatively small share of black households.

Between 2010 and 2020, the number of black workers will grow 10 percent. The black share of the labor force will rise slightly from 11.6 to 12.0 percent during those years.

■ Until the Great Recession, black incomes had been rising because of the growing share of blacks in managerial and professional occupations.

Nearly 60 percent of black women are in the labor force

(percent of blacks aged 16 or older in the labor force, by sex, 2012)

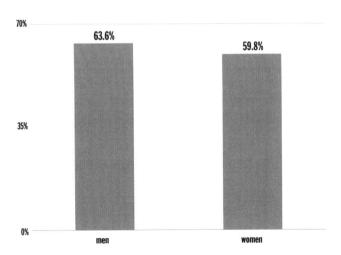

Table 4.60 Labor Force Participation Rate of Blacks by Age and Sex, 2012

(percent of blacks aged 16 or older in the civilian labor force, by age and sex, 2012)

	total	men	women
Total blacks	**61.5%**	**63.6%**	**59.8%**
Aged 16 to 19	26.9	25.6	28.2
Aged 20 to 24	66.5	66.4	66.5
Aged 25 to 29	79.1	81.8	76.8
Aged 30 to 34	79.8	83.3	77.1
Aged 35 to 39	81.9	85.5	79.1
Aged 40 to 44	79.5	81.6	77.7
Aged 45 to 49	76.9	79.3	74.8
Aged 50 to 54	72.1	72.5	71.9
Aged 55 to 59	61.7	63.3	60.4
Aged 60 to 64	47.2	49.1	45.7
Aged 65 or older	16.4	19.4	14.4
Aged 65 to 69	27.0	28.2	26.2
Aged 70 to 74	16.9	18.4	15.9
Aged 75 or older	6.6	10.8	4.2

Note: The civilian labor force equals the number of employed plus the number of unemployed.
Source: Bureau of Labor Statistics, Labor Force Statistics from the Current Population Survey, Internet site http://www.bls.gov/cps/tables.htm#empstat

Table 4.61 Employment Status of Blacks by Sex and Age, 2012

(number and percent of blacks aged 16 or older in the civilian labor force by sex, age, and employment status, 2012; numbers in thousands)

	civilian noninstitutional population	civilian labor force				
					unemployed	
		total	percent of population	employed	number	percent of labor force
Total blacks	**29,907**	**18,400**	**61.5%**	**15,856**	**2,544**	**13.8%**
Aged 16 to 19	2,643	711	26.9	438	272	38.3
Aged 20 to 24	3,326	2,210	66.5	1,700	510	23.1
Aged 25 to 34	5,455	4,333	79.4	3,693	640	14.8
Aged 35 to 44	5,107	4,120	80.7	3,662	457	11.1
Aged 45 to 54	5,446	4,057	74.5	3,660	397	9.8
Aged 55 to 64	4,281	2,369	55.3	2,161	209	8.8
Aged 65 or older	3,650	599	16.4	540	59	9.8
Black men	**13,508**	**8,594**	**63.6**	**7,302**	**1,292**	**15.0**
Aged 16 to 19	1,319	338	25.6	198	140	41.3
Aged 20 to 24	1,586	1,054	66.4	784	269	25.6
Aged 25 to 34	2,461	2,030	82.5	1,723	308	15.2
Aged 35 to 44	2,286	1,908	83.5	1,667	241	12.6
Aged 45 to 54	2,484	1,884	75.9	1,693	191	10.2
Aged 55 to 64	1,923	1,099	57.1	988	110	10.1
Aged 65 or older	1,449	281	19.4	249	32	11.5
Black women	**16,400**	**9,805**	**59.8**	**8,553**	**1,252**	**12.8**
Aged 16 to 19	1,324	373	28.2	240	133	35.6
Aged 20 to 24	1,740	1,157	66.5	916	241	20.8
Aged 25 to 34	2,994	2,303	76.9	1,970	333	14.4
Aged 35 to 44	2,821	2,212	78.4	1,995	216	9.8
Aged 45 to 54	2,963	2,173	73.3	1,968	205	9.4
Aged 55 to 64	2,358	1,271	53.9	1,173	98	7.7
Aged 65 or older	2,201	317	14.4	291	26	8.2

Note: The civilian labor force equals the number of the employed plus the number of the unemployed. The civilian population equals the number in the labor force plus the number not in the labor force.
Source: Bureau of Labor Statistics, Labor Force Statistics from the Current Population Survey, Internet site http://www.bls.gov/cps/tables.htm#empstat

Table 4.62 Black Workers by Occupation, 2012

(total number of employed persons aged 16 or older in the civilian labor force, number and percent distribution of employed blacks, and black share of total, by occupation, 2012; numbers in thousands)

	total	black number	black percent distribution	black share of total
TOTAL EMPLOYED	**142,469**	**15,856**	**100.0%**	**11.1%**
Management, professional and related occupations	**54,043**	**4,678**	**29.5**	**8.7**
Management, business, and financial operations	22,678	1,766	11.1	7.8
Management occupations	16,042	1,114	7.0	6.9
Business and financial operations occupations	6,636	651	4.1	9.8
Professional and related occupations	31,365	2,912	18.4	9.3
Computer and mathematical occupations	3,816	284	1.8	7.4
Architecture and engineering occupations	2,846	159	1.0	5.6
Life, physical, and social science occupations	1,316	85	0.5	6.5
Community and social services occupations	2,265	425	2.7	18.8
Legal occupations	1,786	127	0.8	7.1
Education, training, and library occupations	8,543	814	5.1	9.5
Arts, design, entertainment, sports, and media occupations	2,814	170	1.1	6.0
Health care practitioner and technical occupations	7,977	847	5.3	10.6
Service occupations	**25,459**	**4,039**	**25.5**	**15.9**
Health care support occupations	3,496	925	5.8	26.5
Protective service occupations	3,096	532	3.4	17.2
Food preparation and serving related occupations	8,018	968	6.1	12.1
Building and grounds cleaning and maintenance occupations	5,591	839	5.3	15.0
Personal care and service occupations	5,258	774	4.9	14.7
Sales and office occupations	**33,152**	**3,907**	**24.6**	**11.8**
Sales and related occupations	15,457	1,627	10.3	10.5
Office and administrative support occupations	17,695	2,280	14.4	12.9
Natural resources, construction, and maintenance occupations	**12,821**	**892**	**5.6**	**7.0**
Farming, fishing, and forestry occupations	994	53	0.3	5.3
Construction and extraction occupations	7,005	434	2.7	6.2
Installation, maintenance, and repair occupations	4,821	405	2.6	8.4
Production, transportation, and material moving occupations	**16,994**	**2,341**	**14.8**	**13.8**
Production occupations	8,455	985	6.2	11.6
Transportation and material moving occupations	8,540	1,356	8.6	15.9

Source: Bureau of Labor Statistics, Labor Force Statistics from the Current Population Survey, Internet site http://www.bls.gov/cps/tables.htm#empstat

Table 4.63 Black Workers by Detailed Occupation, 2012

(total number of employed workers agd 16 or older and percent black, by detailed occupation, 2012; numbers in thousands)

	total employed	black, share of total
TOTAL EMPLOYED AGED 16 OR OLDER	**142,469**	**11.1%**
Management, professional, and related occupations	**54,043**	**8.7**
Management, business, and financial operations occupations	22,678	7.8
Management occupations	16,042	6.9
Chief executives	1,513	3.7
General and operations managers	1,064	6.2
Legislators	11	–
Advertising and promotions managers	77	6.7
Marketing and sales managers	967	4.2
Public relations and fundraising managers	58	5.8
Administrative services managers	144	6.4
Computer and information systems managers	605	5.6
Financial managers	1,228	8.6
Compensation and benefits managers	15	–
Human resources managers	224	11.3
Training and development managers	36	–
Industrial production managers	261	3.4
Purchasing managers	218	8.4
Transportation, storage, and distribution managers	287	11.1
Farmers, ranchers, and other agricultural managers	944	0.8
Construction managers	983	3.7
Education administrators	811	13.8
Architectural and engineering managers	120	2.8
Food service managers	1,085	8.8
Funeral service managers	13	–
Gaming managers	26	–
Lodging managers	154	8.0
Medical and health services managers	585	10.9
Natural sciences managers	18	–
Postmasters and mail superintendents	39	–
Property, real estate, and community association managers	644	8.5
Social and community service managers	315	14.6
Emergency management directors	6	–
Managers, all other	3,594	7.3
Business and financial operations occupations	6,636	9.8
Agents and business managers of artists, performers, and athletes	47	–
Buyers and purchasing agents, farm products	13	–
Wholesale and retail buyers, except farm products	198	7.1

	total employed	black, share of total
Purchasing agents, except wholesale, retail, and farm products	261	6.1%
Claims adjusters, appraisers, examiners, and investigators	323	17.5
Compliance officers	199	9.1
Cost estimators	114	1.5
Human resources workers	603	15.4
Compensation, benefits, and job analysis specialists	71	6.9
Training and development specialists	126	15.9
Logisticians	94	12.3
Management analysts	773	6.8
Meeting, convention, and event planners	127	8.1
Fundraisers	86	5.1
Market research analysts and marketing specialists	219	5.4
Business operations specialists, all other	251	14.2
Accountants and auditors	1,765	9.7
Appraisers and assessors of real estate	93	9.8
Budget analysts	55	11.5
Credit analysts	30	–
Financial analysts	89	3.7
Personal financial advisors	378	4.8
Insurance underwriters	103	10.7
Financial examiners	14	–
Credit counselors and loan officers	333	13.2
Tax examiners and collectors, and revenue agents	82	13.9
Tax preparers	107	10.4
Financial specialists, all other	82	10.9
Professional and related occupations	31,365	9.3
Computer and mathematical occupations	3,816	7.4
Computer and information research scientists	29	–
Computer systems analysts	499	8.8
Information security analysts	52	11.8
Computer programmers	480	5.9
Software developers, applications and systems software	1,084	4.0
Web developers	190	4.1
Computer support specialists	476	12.0
Database administrators	101	4.1
Network and computer systems administrators	226	10.0
Computer network architects	127	10.0
Computer occupations, all other	341	11.4
Actuaries	26	–
Mathematicians	4	–
Operations research analysts	130	8.3
Statisticians	47	–
Miscellaneous mathematical science occupations	3	–
Other healthcare practitioners and technical occupations	75	8.8

	total employed	black, share of total
Architecture and engineering occupations	2,846	5.6%
Architects, except naval	195	1.3
Surveyors, cartographers, and photogrammetrists	51	4.3
Aerospace engineers	119	1.8
Agricultural engineers	4	–
Biomedical engineers	10	–
Chemical engineers	71	5.9
Civil engineers	358	5.4
Computer hardware engineers	91	8.5
Electrical and electronics engineers	335	3.5
Environmental engineers	43	–
Industrial engineers, including health and safety	197	6.2
Marine engineers and naval architects	8	–
Materials engineers	40	–
Mechanical engineers	288	6.3
Mining and geological engineers, including mining safety engineers	9	–
Nuclear engineers	11	–
Petroleum engineers	38	–
Engineers, all other	359	3.9
Drafters	149	3.0
Engineering technicians, except drafters	395	10.8
Surveying and mapping technicians	77	5.3
Life, physical, and social science occupations	1,316	6.5
Agricultural and food scientists	42	–
Biological scientists	101	3.7
Conservation scientists and foresters	25	–
Medical scientists	136	5.3
Astronomers and physicists	25	–
Atmospheric and space scientists	15	–
Chemists and materials scientists	105	4.0
Environmental scientists and geoscientists	105	7.0
Physical scientists, all other	154	2.7
Economists	26	–
Survey researchers	2	–
Psychologists	178	6.0
Sociologists	7	–
Urban and regional planners	28	–
Miscellaneous social scientists and related workers	57	10.8
Agricultural and food science technicians	32	–
Biological technicians	19	–
Chemical technicians	70	15.4
Geological and petroleum technicians	21	–
Nuclear technicians	3	–

	total employed	black, share of total
Social science research assistants	3	–
Miscellaneous life, physical, and social science technicians	160	12.8%
Community and social service occupations	2,265	18.8
Counselors	661	19.4
Social workers	734	23.0
Probation officers and correctional treatment specialists	88	20.7
Social and human service assistants	151	24.4
Miscellaneous community and social service specialists, including health educators and community health workers	94	16.9
Clergy	408	11.2
Directors, religious activities and education	61	7.4
Religious workers, all other	69	10.0
Legal occupations	1,786	7.1
Lawyers	1,061	4.4
Judicial law clerks	17	–
Judges, magistrates, and other judicial workers	67	12.8
Paralegals and legal assistants	418	10.7
Miscellaneous legal support workers	223	11.9
Education, training, and library occupations	8,543	9.5
Postsecondary teachers	1,350	7.9
Preschool and kindergarten teachers	678	11.8
Elementary and middle school teachers	2,838	9.8
Secondary school teachers	1,127	6.0
Special education teachers	366	6.9
Other teachers and instructors	860	10.7
Archivists, curators, and museum technicians	46	–
Librarians	181	7.9
Library technicians	45	–
Teacher assistants	898	14.5
Other education, training, and library workers	153	11.7
Arts, design, entertainment, sports, and media occupations	2,814	6.0
Artists and related workers	212	4.0
Designers	756	3.9
Actors	37	–
Producers and directors	121	8.2
Athletes, coaches, umpires, and related workers	267	6.4
Dancers and choreographers	21	–
Musicians, singers, and related workers	203	10.9
Entertainers and performers, sports and related workers, all other	41	–
Announcers	50	12.0
News analysts, reporters and correspondents	82	9.2
Public relations specialists	155	7.3
Editors	159	4.8

	total employed	black, share of total
Technical writers	58	2.7%
Writers and authors	208	5.4
Miscellaneous media and communication workers	98	5.6
Broadcast and sound engineering technicians and radio operators	108	4.1
Photographers	178	6.2
Television, video, and motion picture camera operators and editors	57	4.4
Media and communication equipment workers, all other	2	–
Health care practitioners and technical occupations	7,977	10.6
Chiropractors	58	0.0
Dentists	167	1.7
Dietitians and nutritionists	116	13.7
Optometrists	33	–
Pharmacists	286	6.8
Physicians and surgeons	911	7.2
Physician assistants	108	8.2
Podiatrists	9	–
Audiologists	14	–
Occupational therapists	118	2.5
Physical therapists	211	4.4
Radiation therapists	14	–
Recreational therapists	13	–
Respiratory therapists	111	12.1
Speech-language pathologists	146	3.1
Exercise physiologists	2	–
Therapists, all other	148	10.3
Veterinarians	85	1.9
Registered nurses	2,875	11.5
Nurse anesthetists	27	–
Nurse midwives	3	–
Nurse practitioners	103	4.5
Health diagnosing and treating practitioners, all other	23	–
Clinical laboratory technologists and technicians	319	13.5
Dental hygienists	163	3.3
Diagnostic related technologists and technicians	308	9.0
Emergency medical technicians and paramedics	172	5.0
Health practitioner support technologists and technicians	544	15.8
Licensed practical and licensed vocational nurses	531	23.3
Medical records and health information technicians	90	17.1
Opticians, dispensing	54	8.2
Miscellaneous health technologists and technicians	140	18.7
Other health care practitioners and technical occupations	75	8.8

	total employed	black, share of total
Service occupations	**25,459**	**15.9%**
Health care support occupations	3,496	26.5
Nursing, psychiatric, and home health aides	2,119	34.5
Occupational therapy assistants and aides	18	–
Physical therapist assistants and aides	66	14.7
Massage therapists	158	5.4
Dental assistants	274	9.6
Medical assistants	429	15.0
Medical transcriptionists	55	7.0
Pharmacy aides	45	–
Veterinary assistants and laboratory animal caretakers	47	–
Phlebotomists	119	26.5
Miscellaneous health care support occupations, including medical equipment preparers	166	21.9
Protective service occupations	3,096	17.2
First-line supervisors of correctional officers	46	–
First-line supervisors of police and detectives	112	9.2
First-line supervisors of fire fighting and prevention workers	64	10.7
First-line supervisors of protective service workers, all other	93	17.4
Firefighters	295	7.7
Fire inspectors	18	–
Bailiffs, correctional officers, and jailers	371	22.7
Detectives and criminal investigators	160	9.8
Fish and game wardens	7	–
Parking enforcement workers	4	–
Police and sheriff's patrol officers	657	12.8
Transit and railroad police	3	–
Animal control workers	11	–
Private detectives and investigators	103	8.0
Security guards and gaming surveillance officers	903	26.6
Crossing guards	61	19.7
Transportation security screeners	25	–
Lifeguards and other recreational, and all other protective service workers	162	7.8
Food preparation and serving related occupations	8,018	12.1
Chefs and head cooks	403	11.9
First-line supervisors of food preparation and serving workers	552	13.9
Cooks	1,970	16.6
Food preparation workers	868	12.1
Bartenders	412	5.2
Combined food preparation and serving workers, including fast food	343	14.1
Counter attendants, cafeteria, food concession, and coffee shop	233	10.9

	total employed	black, share of total
Waiters and waitresses	2,124	7.9%
Food servers, nonrestaurant	217	22.2
Dining room and cafeteria attendants and bartender helpers	359	10.0
Dishwashers	271	12.9
Hosts and hostesses, restaurant, lounge, and coffee shop	260	10.2
Food preparation and serving related workers, all other	6	–
Building and grounds cleaning and maintenance occupations	5,591	15.0
First-line supervisors of housekeeping and janitorial workers	277	16.9
First-line supervisors of landscaping, lawn service, and groundskeeping workers	281	6.6
Janitors and building cleaners	2,205	18.4
Maids and housekeeping cleaners	1,457	17.2
Pest control workers	73	7.7
Grounds maintenance workers	1,298	8.7
Personal care and service occupations	5,258	14.7
First-line supervisors of gaming workers	146	5.2
First-line supervisors of personal service workers	246	10.7
Animal trainers	44	–
Nonfarm animal caretakers	179	4.3
Gaming services workers	106	9.4
Motion picture projectionists	2	–
Ushers, lobby attendants, and ticket takers	43	–
Miscellaneous entertainment attendants and related workers	180	14.0
Embalmers and funeral attendants	16	–
Morticians, undertakers, and funeral directors	38	–
Barbers	109	38.2
Hairdressers, hairstylists, and cosmetologists	785	13.2
Miscellaneous personal appearance workers	300	5.3
Baggage porters, bellhops, and concierges	68	20.8
Tour and travel guides	51	3.6
Child care workers	1,314	15.3
Personal care aides	1,071	21.8
Recreation and fitness workers	406	10.0
Residential advisors	58	29.1
Personal care and service workers, all other	95	5.5
Sales and office occupations	**33,152**	**11.8**
Sales and related occupations	15,457	10.5
First-line supervisors of retail sales workers	3,237	8.6
First-line supervisors of nonretail sales workers	1,151	7.2
Cashiers	3,275	17.2
Counter and rental clerks	139	8.9
Parts salespersons	106	8.3
Retail salespersons	3,341	12.5
Advertising sales agents	230	9.9

	total employed	black, share of total
Insurance sales agents	540	8.1%
Securities, commodities, and financial services sales agents	280	3.4
Travel agents	73	2.5
Sales representatives, services, all other	457	7.9
Sales representatives, wholesale and manufacturing	1,277	3.7
Models, demonstrators, and product promoters	65	19.4
Real estate brokers and sales agents	761	4.0
Sales engineers	27	–
Telemarketers	97	23.0
Door-to-door sales workers, news and street vendors, and related workers	198	10.2
Sales and related workers, all other	204	7.7
Office and administrative support occupations	17,695	12.9
First-line supervisors of office and administrative support workers	1,416	11.3
Switchboard operators, including answering service	35	–
Telephone operators	42	–
Communications equipment operators, all other	9	–
Bill and account collectors	206	15.3
Billing and posting clerks	475	11.8
Bookkeeping, accounting, and auditing clerks	1,268	7.6
Gaming cage workers	8	–
Payroll and timekeeping clerks	155	9.5
Procurement clerks	27	–
Tellers	380	11.6
Financial clerks, all other	52	17.1
Brokerage clerks	5	–
Correspondence clerks	6	–
Court, municipal, and license clerks	85	23.0
Credit authorizers, checkers, and clerks	43	–
Customer service representatives	1,956	16.2
Eligibility interviewers, government programs	92	19.8
File clerks	292	14.1
Hotel, motel, and resort desk clerks	110	18.4
Interviewers, except eligibility and loan	135	20.0
Library assistants, clerical	97	7.0
Loan interviewers and clerks	144	10.9
New accounts clerks	26	–
Order clerks	104	5.8
Human resources assistants, except payroll and timekeeping	132	18.3
Receptionists and information clerks	1,237	12.1
Reservation and transportation ticket agents and travel clerks	117	21.8
Information and record clerks, all other	104	17.0
Cargo and freight agents	25	–
Couriers and messengers	213	13.0

	total employed	black, share of total
Dispatchers	277	13.5%
Meter readers, utilities	29	–
Postal service clerks	148	21.3
Postal service mail carriers	318	16.5
Postal service mail sorters, processors, and processing machine operators	66	28.6
Production, planning, and expediting clerks	272	11.0
Shipping, receiving, and traffic clerks	527	15.6
Stock clerks and order fillers	1,453	16.7
Weighers, measurers, checkers, and samplers, recordkeeping	74	19.9
Secretaries and administrative assistants	2,904	8.6
Computer operators	102	12.2
Data entry keyers	337	14.0
Word processors and typists	119	12.4
Desktop publishers	3	–
Insurance claims and policy processing clerks	230	12.7
Mail clerks and mail machine operators, except postal service	81	18.1
Office clerks, general	1,103	12.4
Office machine operators, except computer	46	–
Proofreaders and copy markers	10	–
Statistical assistants	32	–
Office and administrative support workers, all other	570	14.1
Natural resources, construction, and maintenance occupations	**12,821**	**7.0**
Farming, fishing, and forestry occupations	994	5.3
First-line supervisors of farming, fishing, and forestry workers	50	7.8
Agricultural inspectors	16	–
Animal breeders	6	–
Graders and sorters, agricultural products	118	16.6
Miscellaneous agricultural workers	711	3.2
Fishers and related fishing workers	33	–
Hunters and trappers	2	–
Forest and conservation workers	9	–
Logging workers	49	–
Construction and extraction occupations	7,005	6.2
First-line supervisors of construction trades and extraction workers	634	4.5
Boilermakers	23	–
Brickmasons, blockmasons, and stonemasons	122	5.8
Carpenters	1,223	4.2
Carpet, floor, and tile installers and finishers	150	8.8
Cement masons, concrete finishers, and terrazzo workers	68	5.8
Construction laborers	1,387	8.4
Paving, surfacing, and tamping equipment operators	23	–
Pile-driver operators	4	–
Operating engineers and other construction equipment operators	348	6.0

	total employed	black, share of total
Drywall installers, ceiling tile installers, and tapers	129	2.7%
Electricians	692	6.0
Glaziers	46	–
Insulation workers	44	–
Painters, construction and maintenance	485	5.5
Paperhangers	7	–
Pipelayers, plumbers, pipefitters, and steamfitters	534	6.6
Plasterers and stucco masons	18	–
Reinforcing iron and rebar workers	8	–
Roofers	196	7.0
Sheet metal workers	123	3.2
Structural iron and steel workers	65	6.5
Solar photovoltaic installers	7	–
Helpers, construction trades	53	12.1
Construction and building inspectors	118	5.5
Elevator installers and repairers	29	–
Fence erectors	33	–
Hazardous materials removal workers	38	–
Highway maintenance workers	108	11.0
Rail-track laying and maintenance equipment operators	10	–
Septic tank servicers and sewer pipe cleaners	8	–
Miscellaneous construction and related workers	32	–
Derrick, rotary drill, and service unit operators, oil, gas, and mining	37	–
Earth drillers, except oil and gas	35	–
Explosives workers, ordnance handling experts, and blasters	8	–
Mining machine operators	65	3.8
Roof bolters, mining	3	–
Roustabouts, oil and gas	14	–
Helpers—extraction workers	5	–
Other extraction workers	75	5.6
Installation, maintenance, and repair occupations	4,821	8.4
First-line supervisors of mechanics, installers, and repairers	292	11.3
Computer, automated teller, and office machine repairers	296	10.8
Radio and telecommunications equipment installers and repairers	158	11.2
Avionics technicians	14	–
Electric motor, power tool, and related repairers	37	–
Electrical and electronics installers and repairers, transportation equipment	5	–
Electrical and electronics repairers, industrial and utility	12	–
Electronic equipment installers and repairers, motor vehicles	18	–
Electronic home entertainment equipment installers and repairers	50	11.6
Security and fire alarm systems installers	41	–
Aircraft mechanics and service technicians	153	7.5
Automotive body and related repairers	140	5.7

	total employed	black, share of total
Automotive glass installers and repairers	22	–
Automotive service technicians and mechanics	867	9.6%
Bus and truck mechanics and diesel engine specialists	316	8.6
Heavy vehicle and mobile equipment service technicians and mechanics	194	5.4
Small engine mechanics	56	4.9
Miscellaneous vehicle and mobile equipment mechanics, installers, and repairers	87	8.0
Control and valve installers and repairers	27	–
Heating, air conditioning, and refrigeration mechanics and installers	340	7.1
Home appliance repairers	47	–
Industrial and refractory machinery mechanics	454	4.5
Maintenance and repair workers, general	442	8.4
Maintenance workers, machinery	28	–
Millwrights	53	2.1
Electrical power-line installers and repairers	110	7.8
Telecommunications line installers and repairers	177	11.2
Precision instrument and equipment repairers	60	9.1
Wind turbine service technicians	3	–
Coin, vending, and amusement machine servicers and repairers	33	–
Commercial divers	3	–
Locksmiths and safe repairers	31	–
Manufactured building and mobile home installers	5	–
Riggers	13	–
Signal and track switch repairers	5	–
Helpers—installation, maintenance, and repair workers	30	–
Other installation, maintenance, and repair workers	205	5.9
Production, transportation, and material moving occupations	**16,994**	**13.8**
Production occupations	8,455	11.6
First-line supervisors of production and operating workers	808	9.4
Aircraft structure, surfaces, rigging, and systems assemblers	23	–
Electrical, electronics, and electromechanical assemblers	166	13.4
Engine and other machine assemblers	32	–
Structural metal fabricators and fitters	25	–
Miscellaneous assemblers and fabricators	919	15.8
Bakers	199	15.6
Butchers and other meat, poultry, and fish processing workers	311	13.5
Food and tobacco roasting, baking, and drying machine operators and tenders	11	–
Food batchmakers	84	12.2
Food cooking machine operators and tenders	14	–
Food processing workers, all other	117	15.9
Computer control programmers and operators	67	6.4
Extruding and drawing machine setters, operators, and tenders, metal and plastic	10	–
Forging machine setters, operators, and tenders, metal and plastic	10	–
Rolling machine setters, operators, and tenders, metal and plastic	8	–

	total employed	black, share of total
Cutting, punching, and press machine setters, operators, and tenders, metal and plastic	87	8.4%
Drilling and boring machine tool setters, operators, and tenders, metal and plastic	3	–
Grinding, lapping, polishing, and buffing machine tool setters, operators, and tenders, metal and plastic	54	13.7
Lathe and turning machine tool setters, operators, and tenders, metal and plastic	17	–
Milling and planing machine setters, operators, and tenders, metal and plastic	3	–
Machinists	397	4.5
Metal furnace operators, tenders, pourers, and casters	17	–
Model makers and patternmakers, metal and plastic	11	–
Molders and molding machine setters, operators, and tenders, metal and plastic	37	–
Multiple machine tool setters, operators, and tenders, metal and plastic	5	–
Tool and die makers	56	3.1
Welding, soldering, and brazing workers	593	8.7
Heat treating equipment setters, operators, and tenders, metal and plastic	4	–
Layout workers, metal and plastic	4	–
Plating and coating machine setters, operators, and tenders, metal and plastic	18	–
Tool grinders, filers, and sharpeners	3	–
Metal workers and plastic workers, all other	375	14.4
Prepress technicians and workers	33	–
Printing press operators	201	10.1
Print binding and finishing workers	22	–
Laundry and dry-cleaning workers	185	20.8
Pressers, textile, garment, and related materials	54	17.0
Sewing machine operators	166	5.6
Shoe and leather workers and repairers	11	–
Shoe machine operators and tenders	11	–
Tailors, dressmakers, and sewers	86	5.9
Textile bleaching and dyeing machine operators and tenders	5	–
Textile cutting machine setters, operators, and tenders	12	–
Textile knitting and weaving machine setters, operators, and tenders	7	–
Textile winding, twisting, and drawing out machine setters, operators, and tenders	14	–
Extruding and forming machine setters, operators, and tenders, synthetic and glass fibers	1	–
Fabric and apparel patternmakers	3	–
Upholsterers	34	–
Textile, apparel, and furnishings workers, all other	14	–
Cabinetmakers and bench carpenters	45	–
Furniture finishers	7	–
Model makers and patternmakers, wood	0	–
Sawing machine setters, operators, and tenders, wood	30	–
Woodworking machine setters, operators, and tenders, except sawing	21	–
Woodworkers, all other	21	–
Power plant operators, distributors, and dispatchers	44	–

	total employed	black, share of total
Stationary engineers and boiler operators	121	10.4%
Water and wastewater treatment plant and system operators	72	8.4
Miscellaneous plant and system operators	39	–
Chemical processing machine setters, operators, and tenders	68	4.5
Crushing, grinding, polishing, mixing, and blending workers	100	14.5
Cutting workers	67	14.1
Extruding, forming, pressing, and compacting machine setters, operators, and tenders	45	–
Furnace, kiln, oven, drier, and kettle operators and tenders	16	–
Inspectors, testers, sorters, samplers, and weighers	689	11.5
Jewelers and precious stone and metal workers	46	–
Medical, dental, and ophthalmic laboratory technicians	95	1.6
Packaging and filling machine operators and tenders	261	14.1
Painting workers	150	5.7
Photographic process workers and processing machine operators	55	13.3
Semiconductor processors	4	–
Adhesive bonding machine operators and tenders	9	–
Cleaning, washing, and metal pickling equipment operators and tenders	7	–
Cooling and freezing equipment operators and tenders	2	–
Etchers and engravers	6	–
Molders, shapers, and casters, except metal and plastic	41	–
Paper goods machine setters, operators, and tenders	35	–
Tire builders	19	–
Helpers—production workers	59	19.8
Production workers, all other	933	13.7
Transportation and material moving occupations	8,540	15.9
Supervisors of transportation and material moving workers	200	13.5
Aircraft pilots and flight engineers	129	2.7
Air traffic controllers and airfield operations specialists	44	–
Flight attendants	88	11.8
Ambulance drivers and attendants, except emergency medical technicians	20	–
Bus drivers	558	25.3
Driver/sales workers and truck drivers	3,201	14.0
Taxi drivers and chauffeurs	336	24.8
Motor vehicle operators, all other	63	14.4
Locomotive engineers and operators	41	–
Railroad brake, signal, and switch operators	10	–
Railroad conductors and yardmasters	52	16.2
Subway, streetcar, and other rail transportation workers	11	–
Sailors and marine oilers	16	–
Ship and boat captains and operators	37	–
Ship engineers	7	–
Bridge and lock tenders	7	–
Parking lot attendants	81	23.5

	total employed	black, share of total
Automotive and watercraft service attendants	94	12.9%
Transportation inspectors	36	–
Transportation attendants, except flight attendants	38	–
Other transportation workers	17	–
Conveyor operators and tenders	4	–
Crane and tower operators	62	12.3
Dredge, excavating, and loading machine operators	42	–
Hoist and winch operators	5	–
Industrial truck and tractor operators	537	18.4
Cleaners of vehicles and equipment	315	16.8
Laborers and freight, stock, and material movers, hand	1,849	15.9
Machine feeders and offbearers	27	–
Packers and packagers, hand	431	14.0
Pumping station operators	25	–
Refuse and recyclable material collectors	106	24.9
Mine shuttle car operators	1	–
Tank car, truck, and ship loaders	4	–
Material moving workers, all other	45	–

Note: "–" means sample is too small to make a reliable estimate.
Source: Bureau of Labor Statistics, Labor Force Statistics from the Current Population Survey, Internet site http://www.bls.gov/ cps/tables.htm#empstat; calculations by New Strategist

Table 4.64 Black Workers by Industry, 2012

(total number of employed people aged 16 or older in the civilian labor force; number and percent distribution of employed blacks, and black share of total, by industry, 2012; numbers in thousands)

	total	black number	black percent distribution	black share of total
Total employed	**142,469**	**15,856**	**100.0%**	**11.1%**
Agriculture, forestry, fishing, and hunting	2,186	61	0.4	2.8
Mining	957	45	0.3	4.7
Construction	8,964	498	3.1	5.6
Manufacturing	14,686	1,283	8.1	8.7
Durable goods	9,244	705	4.4	7.6
Nondurable goods	5,443	578	3.6	10.6
Wholesale/retail trade	19,876	2,098	13.2	10.6
Wholesale trade	3,694	261	1.6	7.1
Retail trade	16,182	1,837	11.6	11.4
Transportation and utilities	7,271	1,159	7.3	15.9
Information	2,971	329	2.1	11.1
Financial activities	9,590	923	5.8	9.6
Professional and business services	16,539	1,582	10.0	9.6
Educational and health services	32,350	4,628	29.2	14.3
Leisure and hospitality	13,193	1,488	9.4	11.3
Other services	7,168	706	4.5	9.8
Other services, except private households	6,430	643	4.1	10.0
Private households	738	62	0.4	8.4
Public administration	6,717	1,056	6.7	15.7

Source: Bureau of Labor Statistics, Labor Force Statistics from the Current Population Survey, Internet site http://www.bls.gov/cps/tables.htm#empstat

Table 4.65 Black Workers by Full-Time and Part-Time Status, 2012

(number and percent distribution of employed blacks aged 16 or older by employment status and sex, 2012; numbers in thousands)

	total	men	women
Total employed blacks	**15,274**	**7,055**	**8,219**
Worked full-time	11,597	5,581	6,016
Worked part-time	3,678	1,474	2,203
For economic reasons	1,154	525	629
PERCENT DISTRIBUTION			
Total employed blacks	**100.0%**	**100.0%**	**100.0%**
Worked full-time	75.9	79.1	73.2
Worked part-time	24.1	20.9	26.8
For economic reasons	7.6	7.4	7.7

Note: Part-time work is less than 35 hours per week. Part-time workers exclude those who usually work full-time but who worked less than 35 hours in the previous week because of vacation, holidays, child care problems, weather issues, and other temporary, noneconomic reasons. "Economic reasons" means a worker's hours have been reduced or workers cannot find full-time employment.
Source: Bureau of Labor Statistics, Labor Force Statistics from the Current Population Survey, Internet site http://www.bls.gov/cps/tables.htm#empstat

Table 4.66 Black Workers by Educational Attainment, 2012

(number of total people and blacks aged 25 or older in the civilian labor force, black labor force participation rate, distribution of blacks in labor force, and black share of total labor force, by educational attainment, 2012; numbers in thousands)

	total labor force	black labor force number	participation rate	percent distribution	share of total
Total aged 25 or older	**133,690**	**15,478**	**64.7%**	**100.0%**	**11.6%**
Not a high school graduate	11,328	1,277	36.5	8.3	11.3
High school graduate only	36,772	5,080	61.9	32.8	13.8
Some college	22,685	3,303	69.4	21.3	14.6
Associate's degree	14,675	1,763	75.2	11.4	12.0
Bachelor's degree or more	48,230	4,057	79.0	26.2	8.4

Source: Bureau of Labor Statistics, Labor Force Statistics from the Current Population Survey, Internet site http://www.bls.gov/cps/tables.htm#empstat

Table 4.67 Black Workers by Job Tenure, 2012

(percent distribution of total and black wage and salary workers aged 16 or older by tenure with current employer, and index of black to total, 2012)

	total	black	index, black to total
Total workers	**100.0%**	**100.0%**	**100**
One year or less	21.1	22.2	105
13 months to 23 months	6.3	5.6	89
Two years	4.9	5.2	106
Three to four years	16.6	18.5	111
Five to nine years	21.8	22.1	101
10 to 14 years	12.5	12.4	99
15 to 19 years	6.1	4.5	74
20 or more years	10.6	9.5	90

Note: The index is calculated by dividing the black figure by the total figure and multiplying by 100.
Source: Bureau of Labor Statistics, Employee Tenure, Internet site http://www.bls.gov/news.release/tenure.toc.htm; calculations by New Strategist

Table 4.68 Black Households by Number of Earners, 2012

(number of total households, number and percent distribution of black households and black share of total, by number of earners per household, 2012; number of households in thousands)

		black		
	total	number	percent distribution	share of total
Total households	**121,084**	**16,165**	**100.0%**	**13.4%**
No earners	28,569	4,362	27.0	15.3
One earner	45,578	7,287	45.1	16.0
Two or more earners	46,938	4,515	27.9	9.6
Two earners	37,943	3,697	22.9	9.7
Three earners	6,905	648	4.0	9.4
Four or more earners	2,089	170	1.1	8.2
Average number of earners per household	1.28	1.11	–	–

Note: Blacks are those who identify themselves as being of the race alone alone and those who identify themselves as being of the race in combination with other races. "–" means not applicable.
Source: Bureau of the Census, 2012 Current Population Survey, Annual Social and Economic Supplement, Internet site http://www.census.gov/hhes/www/cpstables/032012/hhinc/toc.htm; calculations by New Strategist

Table 4.69 Labor Force Status of Black Married Couples, 2012

(number and percent distribution of black married couples by age of householder and labor force status of husband and wife, 2012; numbers in thousands)

| | total | husband and/or wife in labor force | | | neither husband nor wife in labor force |
		husband and wife	husband only	wife only	
Total black couples	**4,708**	**2,589**	**891**	**474**	**755**
Under age 25	100	44	45	0	11
Aged 25 to 29	272	178	75	19	1
Aged 30 to 34	436	301	106	15	14
Aged 35 to 39	491	347	86	32	27
Aged 40 to 44	600	441	86	47	25
Aged 45 to 54	1,134	741	225	105	63
Aged 55 to 64	948	447	182	130	188
Aged 65 to 74	514	74	61	105	273
Aged 75 or older	212	15	26	20	152
Total black couples	**100.0%**	**55.0%**	**18.9%**	**10.1%**	**16.0%**
Under age 25	100.0	44.0	45.0	0.0	11.0
Aged 25 to 29	100.0	65.4	27.6	7.0	0.4
Aged 30 to 34	100.0	69.0	24.3	3.4	3.2
Aged 35 to 39	100.0	70.7	17.5	6.5	5.5
Aged 40 to 44	100.0	73.5	14.3	7.8	4.2
Aged 45 to 54	100.0	65.3	19.8	9.3	5.6
Aged 55 to 64	100.0	47.2	19.2	13.7	19.8
Aged 65 to 74	100.0	14.4	11.9	20.4	53.1
Aged 75 or older	100.0	7.1	12.3	9.4	71.7

Note: Blacks are those who identify themselves as being of the race alone and those who identify themselves as being of the race in combination with other races.
Source: Bureau of the Census, America's Families and Living Arrangements: 2012, Internet site http://www.census.gov/hhes/ families/data/cps2012.html; calculations by New Strategist

Table 4.70 Black Minimum Wage Workers by Sex, 2011

(number of total and black employed wage and salary workers, number of total and black wage and salary workers paid hourly rates at or below minimum wage, and black share of total, by sex, 2011; numbers in thousands)

	total paid hourly rates	percent distribution	workers paid at or below minimum wage		
			number	percent distribution	share of total
Total workers aged 16 or older	**73,926**	**100.0%**	**3,828**	**100.0%**	**5.2%**
Black workers aged 16 or older	9,523	12.9	578	15.1	6.1
Black men	4,252	5.8	222	5.8	5.2
Black women	5,271	7.1	356	9.3	6.8

Source: Bureau of Labor Statistics, Characteristics of Minimum Wage Workers: 2011, Internet site http://www.bls.gov/cps/minwage2011tbls.htm; calculations by New Strategist

Table 4.71 Union Representation of Black Workers by Sex, 2012

(number of employed black wage and salary workers aged 16 or older, number and percent represented by unions, median weekly earnings of those working full-time by union representation status, and index of union median to average median, by sex, 2012; number in thousands)

	total	men	women
Total employed blacks	**14,975**	**6,753**	**8,222**
Number represented by unions	2,220	1,078	1,142
Percent represented by unions	14.8%	16.0%	13.9%
Median weekly earnings of black full-time workers	**$621**	**$665**	**$599**
Represented by unions	986	1,022	951
Not represented by unions	907	1,062	747
Index, median weekly earnings of black workers represented by unions to average black worker	**125**	**122**	**125**

Note: Workers represented by unions are either members of a labor union or workers who report no union affiliation but whose jobs are covered by a union or an employee association contract. The index is calculated by dividing median weekly earnings of workers represented by unions by median weekly earnings of the average black worker and multiplying by 100.
Source: Bureau of Labor Statistics, Labor Force Statistics from the Current Population Survey, Internet site http://www.bls.gov/cps/tables.htm#empstat

Table 4.72 Commuting Patterns of Black Workers, 2011

(number of total and black workers aged 16 or older, percent distribution by means of transportation to work, and index of black to total, 2011; numbers in thousands)

	total	black	index
Total workers aged 16 or older, number	138,270	15,670	–
Total workers aged 16 or older, percent	100.0%	100.0%	–
Drove alone in car, truck, or van	76.4	71.5	94
Carpooled in car, truck, or van	9.7	9.9	102
Public transportation (excluding taxicab)	5.0	11.2	224
Walked	2.8	3.0	107
Other means	1.7	1.7	100
Worked at home	4.3	2.6	60
Average travel time to work (minutes)	25.5	27.7	109

Note: Blacks are those who identify themselves as being of the race alone and those who identify themselves as being of the race in combination with other races. The index is calculated by dividing black figure by total figure and multiplying by 100. "–" means not applicable.
Source: Census Bureau, 2011 American Community Survey, Internet site http://factfinder2.census.gov/faces/nav/jsf/pages/index .xhtml; calculations by New Strategist

Table 4.73 Black Labor Force Projections, 2010 and 2020

(number and percent of blacks aged 16 or older in the civilian labor force by sex, 2010 and 2020; percent change in number and percentage point change in rate, 2010–20; numbers in thousands)

NUMBER	2010	2020	percent change
Total blacks in labor force	17,862	19,676	10.2%
Black men	8,415	9,393	11.6
Black women	9,447	10,283	8.8

PARTICIPATION RATE	2010	2020	percentage point change
Total blacks in labor force	62.2%	60.3%	–1.9
Black men	65.0	63.1	–1.9
Black women	59.9	57.9	–2.0

Note: Blacks are those who identify themselves as being of the race alone.
Source: Bureau of Labor Statistics, Labor Force Projections to 2020: A More Slowly Growing Workforce, Monthly Labor Review, January 2012, Internet site http://www.bls.gov/opub/mlr/2012/01/home.htm

Table 4.74 Black Share of Labor Force, 2010 and 2020

(total people and blacks aged 16 or older in the civilian labor force, and black share of total, 2010 and 2020; numbers in thousands)

	2010			2020		
	total	black	black share of total	total	black	black share of total
Total labor force	**153,889**	**17,862**	**11.6%**	**164,360**	**19,676**	**12.0%**
Men	81,985	8,415	10.3	87,128	9,393	10.8
Women	71,904	9,447	13.1	77,232	10,283	13.3

Note: Blacks are those who identify themselves as being of the race alone.
Source: Bureau of Labor Statistics, Labor Force Projections to 2020: A More Slowly Growing Workforce, Monthly Labor Review, January 2012, Internet site http://www.bls.gov/opub/mlr/2012/01/home.htm

Black Married Couples Slightly Outnumber Female-Headed Families

The 16 million households headed by blacks accounted for 13 percent of the nation's 121 million total households in 2012. Black households are more diverse than those of other racial and ethnic groups. Married couples head 28 percent of black households, while female-headed families account for another 28 percent.

Thirty-two percent of black households include children under age 18, a slightly larger share than the 29 percent figure for all households. Forty-five percent of black married couples have children at home, as do 61 percent of black female-headed families. Only 29 percent of black children live with their biological, married parents versus the 58 percent majority of all children. Nearly half (49 percent) of black children live with their mother only.

Among black men aged 18 or older, the largest share (45 percent) has never married. This compares with 30 percent of all men aged 18 or older who have never married. Among black women, 43 percent have never married versus the 25 percent figure among all women.

■ Because so many black households are female-headed families, the poorest household type, the income of black households is well below average.

Black households are diverse

(percent distribution of black households by household type, 2012)

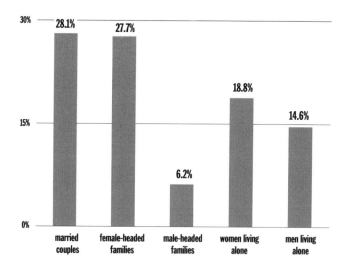

Table 4.75 Black Households by Age of Householder, 2012

(number of total households, number and percent distribution of black households, and black share of total, by age of householder, 2012, numbers in thousands)

	total	black		
		number	percent distribution	share of total
Total households	**121,084**	**16,165**	**100.0%**	**13.4%**
Under age 25	6,180	1,119	6.9	18.1
Aged 25 to 29	9,208	1,402	8.7	15.2
Aged 30 to 34	10,638	1,628	10.1	15.3
Aged 35 to 39	10,111	1,511	9.3	14.9
Aged 40 to 44	11,129	1,664	10.3	15.0
Aged 45 to 49	11,763	1,623	10.0	13.8
Aged 50 to 54	12,433	1,709	10.6	13.7
Aged 55 to 59	12,037	1,613	10.0	13.4
Aged 60 to 64	10,742	1,297	8.0	12.1
Aged 65 or older	26,843	2,599	16.1	9.7

Note: Blacks are those who identify themselves as being of the race alone and those who identify themselves as being of the race in combination with other races.
Source: Bureau of the Census, 2012 Current Population Survey, Internet site http://www.census.gov/hhes/www/income/data/ incpovhlth/2011/dtables.html; calculations by New Strategist

Table 4.76 Black Households by Household Type, 2012

(number of total households, number and percent distribution of black households, and black share of total, by household type, 2012; numbers in thousands)

	total	black number	black percent distribution	black share of total
TOTAL HOUSEHOLDS	**121,084**	**16,165**	**100.0%**	**13.4%**
Family households	**80,506**	**10,025**	**62.0**	**12.5**
Married couples	58,949	4,546	28.1	7.7
With children under age 18	25,114	2,333	14.4	9.3
Female householders, no spouse present	15,669	4,477	27.7	28.6
With children under age 18	10,380	3,208	19.8	30.9
Male householders, no spouse present	5,888	1,002	6.2	17.0
With children under age 18	2,982	514	3.2	17.2
Nonfamily households	**40,578**	**6,141**	**38.0**	**15.1**
Female householders	21,383	3,374	20.9	15.8
Living alone	18,354	3,039	18.8	16.6
Male householders	19,195	2,767	17.1	14.4
Living alone	14,835	2,367	14.6	16.0

Note: Blacks are those who identify themselves as being of the race alone and those who identify themselves as being of the race in combination with other races.
Source: Bureau of the Census, 2012 Current Population Survey, Internet site http://www.census.gov/hhes/www/income/data/incpovhlth/2011/dtables.html; calculations by New Strategist

Table 4.77 Black Households by Age of Householder and Household Type, 2012

(number and percent distribution of black households by age of householder and household type, 2012; numbers in thousands)

		family households			nonfamily households			
			female householder, no spouse present	male householder, no spouse present	female-headed		male-headed	
	total	married couples			total	living alone	total	living alone
Total black households	**16,165**	**4,546**	**4,477**	**1,002**	**3,374**	**3,039**	**2,767**	**2,367**
Under age 25	1,119	92	427	135	273	198	192	128
Aged 25 to 34	3,029	671	1,157	254	452	383	496	390
Aged 35 to 44	3,175	1,056	1,079	242	370	330	429	369
Aged 45 to 54	3,332	1,101	850	146	623	546	612	532
Aged 55 to 64	2,910	920	554	138	724	676	574	510
Aged 65 or older	2,599	705	410	89	932	906	464	437

PERCENT DISTRIBUTION BY HOUSEHOLD TYPE

Total black households	**100.0%**	**28.1%**	**27.7%**	**6.2%**	**20.9%**	**18.8%**	**17.1%**	**14.6%**
Under age 25	100.0	8.2	38.2	12.1	24.4	17.7	17.2	11.4
Aged 25 to 34	100.0	22.2	38.2	8.4	14.9	12.6	16.4	12.9
Aged 35 to 44	100.0	33.3	34.0	7.6	11.7	10.4	13.5	11.6
Aged 45 to 54	100.0	33.0	25.5	4.4	18.7	16.4	18.4	16.0
Aged 55 to 64	100.0	31.6	19.0	4.7	24.9	23.2	19.7	17.5
Aged 65 or older	100.0	27.1	15.8	3.4	35.9	34.9	17.9	16.8

PERCENT DISTRIBUTION BY AGE

Total black households	**100.0%**	**100.0%**	**100.0%**	**100.0%**	**100.0%**	**100.0%**	**100.0%**	**100.0%**
Under age 25	6.9	2.0	9.5	13.5	8.1	6.5	6.9	5.4
Aged 25 to 34	18.7	14.8	25.8	25.3	13.4	12.6	17.9	16.5
Aged 35 to 44	19.6	23.2	24.1	24.2	11.0	10.9	15.5	15.6
Aged 45 to 54	20.6	24.2	19.0	14.6	18.5	18.0	22.1	22.5
Aged 55 to 64	18.0	20.2	12.4	13.8	21.5	22.2	20.7	21.5
Aged 65 or older	16.1	15.5	9.2	8.9	27.6	29.8	16.8	18.5

Note: Blacks are those who identify themselves as being black alone and those who identify themselves as being black in combination with other races.
Source: Bureau of the Census, 2012 Current Population Survey, Internet site http://www.census.gov/hhes/www/income/data/incpovhlth/2011/dtables.html; calculations by New Strategist

Table 4.78 Black Households by Size, 2012

(number of total households, number and percent distribution of black households, and black share of total, by household size, 2012; number of households in thousands)

	total	black number	black percent distribution	black share of total
Total households	**121,084**	**16,165**	**100.0%**	**13.4%**
One person	33,188	5,406	33.4	16.3
Two people	40,983	4,388	27.1	10.7
Three people	19,241	2,771	17.1	14.4
Four people	16,049	1,942	12.0	12.1
Five people	7,271	976	6.0	13.4
Six people	2,734	413	2.6	15.1
Seven or more people	1,617	270	1.7	16.7
Average number of persons per household	2.55	2.55	–	–

Note: Blacks are those who identify themselves as being black alone and those who identify themselves as being black in combination with other races. "–" means not applicable.
Source: Bureau of the Census, Current Population Survey Annual Social and Economic Supplement, Internet site http://www .census.gov/hhes/www/income/dinctabs.html; calculations by New Strategist

Table 4.79 Black Households by Region, 2012

(number of total households, number and percent distribution of black households and black share of total, by region, 2012; numbers in thousands)

	total	black number	black percent distribution	black share of total
Total households	**121,084**	**16,165**	**100.0%**	**13.4%**
Northeast	21,774	2,749	17.0	12.6
Midwest	26,865	2,899	17.9	10.8
South	45,604	8,959	55.4	19.6
West	26,840	1,557	9.6	5.8

Note: Blacks are those who identify themselves as being black alone and those who identify themselves as being black in combination with other races.
Source: Bureau of the Census, Current Population Survey Annual Social and Economic Supplement, Internet site http://www .census.gov/hhes/www/income/dinctabs.html; calculations by New Strategist

Table 4.80 Black Households by Metropolitan Status, 2012

(number of total households, number and percent distribution of black households and black share of total, by metropolitan status, 2012; numbers in thousands)

	total	black		
		number	percent distribution	share of total
Total households	**121,084**	**16,165**	**100.0%**	**13.4%**
Inside metropolitan areas	101,526	14,541	90.0	14.3
Inside principal cities	40,616	8,320	51.5	20.5
Outside principal cities	60,910	6,221	38.5	10.2
Outside metropolitan areas	19,558	1,625	10.1	8.3

Note: Blacks are those who identify themselves as being black alone and those who identify themselves as being black in combination with other races.
Source: Bureau of the Census, Current Population Survey Annual Social and Economic Supplement, Internet site http://www .census.gov/hhes/www/income/dinctabs.html; calculations by New Strategist

Table 4.81 Blacks Living Alone by Sex and Age, 2012

(total number of blacks aged 15 or older, number and percent living alone, and percent distribution of blacks living alone, by sex and age, 2012; numbers in thousands)

	total	living alone number	living alone percent distribution	living alone share of total
Total blacks	**31,925**	**5,406**	**100.0%**	**16.9%**
Under age 25	7,212	326	6.0	4.5
Aged 25 to 34	5,775	773	14.3	13.4
Aged 35 to 44	5,325	699	12.9	13.1
Aged 45 to 54	5,637	1,078	19.9	19.1
Aged 55 to 64	4,258	1,186	21.9	27.9
Aged 65 to 74	2,266	749	13.9	33.1
Aged 75 or older	1,452	594	11.0	40.9
Black men	**14,499**	**2,367**	**100.0**	**16.3**
Under age 25	3,506	128	5.4	3.7
Aged 25 to 34	2,642	390	16.5	14.8
Aged 35 to 44	2,404	369	15.6	15.3
Aged 45 to 54	2,582	532	22.5	20.6
Aged 55 to 64	1,872	510	21.5	27.2
Aged 65 to 74	1,003	279	11.8	27.8
Aged 75 or older	490	158	6.7	32.3
Black women	**17,426**	**3,039**	**100.0**	**17.4**
Under age 25	3,707	198	6.5	5.3
Aged 25 to 34	3,133	383	12.6	12.2
Aged 35 to 44	2,921	330	10.9	11.3
Aged 45 to 54	3,055	546	18.0	17.9
Aged 55 to 64	2,387	676	22.2	28.3
Aged 65 to 74	1,263	470	15.5	37.2
Aged 75 or older	962	436	14.3	45.3

Note: Blacks include those who identify themselves as being black alone and those who identify themselves as being black in combination with other races.
Source: Bureau of the Census, Current Population Survey Annual Social and Economic Supplement, Internet site http://www .census.gov/hhes/www/income/dinctabs.html; calculations by New Strategist

Table 4.82 Black Households by Age of Householder, Type of Household, and Presence of Children, 2012

(number and percent distribution of black households by age of householder, type of household, and presence of own children under age 18, 2012; numbers in thousands)

	all households		married couples		female-headed families		male-headed families	
	total	with children	total	with children	total	with children	total	with children
Total black households	**16,165**	**5,163**	**4,546**	**2,024**	**4,477**	**2,725**	**1,002**	**414**
Under age 25	1,119	397	93	60	427	320	135	18
Aged 25 to 29	1,402	731	249	176	516	474	150	81
Aged 30 to 34	1,628	1,038	422	365	641	601	103	72
Aged 35 to 39	1,511	968	476	386	565	500	112	83
Aged 40 to 44	1,664	858	581	430	513	353	129	75
Aged 45 to 49	1,623	610	530	298	494	261	89	51
Aged 50 to 54	1,709	321	572	181	356	126	57	13
Aged 55 to 64	2,910	179	920	107	554	59	138	13
Aged 65 or older	2,599	60	705	21	410	32	89	7

PERCENT OF HOUSEHOLDS WITH CHILDREN BY TYPE

	all households		married couples		female-headed families		male-headed families	
Total black households	**100.0%**	**31.9%**	**100.0%**	**44.5%**	**100.0%**	**60.9%**	**100.0%**	**41.3%**
Under age 25	100.0	35.5	100.0	64.5	100.0	74.9	100.0	13.3
Aged 25 to 29	100.0	52.1	100.0	70.7	100.0	91.9	100.0	54.0
Aged 30 to 34	100.0	63.8	100.0	86.5	100.0	93.8	100.0	69.9
Aged 35 to 39	100.0	64.1	100.0	81.1	100.0	88.5	100.0	74.1
Aged 40 to 44	100.0	51.6	100.0	74.0	100.0	68.8	100.0	58.1
Aged 45 to 49	100.0	37.6	100.0	56.2	100.0	52.8	100.0	57.3
Aged 50 to 54	100.0	18.8	100.0	31.6	100.0	35.4	100.0	22.8
Aged 55 to 64	100.0	6.2	100.0	11.6	100.0	10.6	100.0	9.4
Aged 65 or older	100.0	2.3	100.0	3.0	100.0	7.8	100.0	7.9

Note: Blacks are those who identify themselves as being black alone and those who identify themselves as being black in combination with other races.
Source: Bureau of the Census, Current Population Survey Annual Social and Economic Supplement, America's Families and Living Arrangements: 2012, Internet site http://www.census.gov/hhes/families/data/cps2012.html; calculations by New Strategist

Table 4.83 Living Arrangements of Black Children, 2012

(number and percent distribution of black children under age 18 by living arrangement, 2012; numbers in thousands)

	number	percent distribution
BLACK CHILDREN	**13,012**	**100.0%**
Living with two parents	**5,200**	**40.0**
Married parents	4,537	34.9
Unmarried parents	663	5.1
Biological mother and father	4,364	33.5
Married parents	3,816	29.3
Biological mother and stepfather	518	4.0
Biological father and stepmother	160	1.2
Biological mother and adoptive father	22	0.2
Biological father and adoptive mother	3	0.0
Adoptive mother and father	101	0.8
Other	32	0.2
Living with one parent	**6,958**	**53.5**
Mother only	6,414	49.3
Father only	545	4.2
Living with no parents	**853**	**6.6**
Grandparents	494	3.8
Other	360	2.8
At least one biological parent	**11,907**	**91.5**
At least one stepparent	**750**	**5.8**
At least one adoptive parent	**205**	**1.6**

Note: Blacks are those who identify themselves as being of the race alone and those who identify themselves as being of the race in combination with other races.
Source: Bureau of the Census, Current Population Survey Annual Social and Economic Supplement, America's Families and Living Arrangements: 2012, Detailed Tables, Internet site http://www.census.gov/hhes/families/data/cps2012.html; calculations by New Strategist

Table 4.84 Marital Status of Black Men by Age, 2012

(number and percent distribution of black men aged 18 or older by age and current marital status, 2012; numbers in thousands)

	total	never married	married, spouse present	married, spouse absent	separated	divorced	widowed
Total black men	**13,340**	**5,973**	**4,824**	**235**	**598**	**1,400**	**310**
Aged 18 to 19	650	639	1	2	7	0	0
Aged 20 to 24	1,710	1,570	86	16	32	7	0
Aged 25 to 29	1,370	1,038	277	11	20	24	0
Aged 30 to 34	1,270	702	398	17	72	79	1
Aged 35 to 39	1,149	450	497	26	53	115	8
Aged 40 to 44	1,255	405	599	25	60	165	2
Aged 45 to 49	1,275	399	550	22	91	199	14
Aged 50 to 54	1,299	300	628	32	83	235	20
Aged 55 to 64	1,869	335	943	54	113	365	58
Aged 65 to 74	1,003	93	594	9	50	176	82
Aged 75 to 84	370	26	218	13	14	36	64
Aged 85 or older	120	15	34	7	4	0	60
Total black men	**100.0%**	**44.8%**	**36.2%**	**1.8%**	**4.5%**	**10.5%**	**2.3%**
Aged 18 to 19	100.0	98.3	0.2	0.3	1.1	0.0	0.0
Aged 20 to 24	100.0	91.8	5.0	0.9	1.9	0.4	0.0
Aged 25 to 29	100.0	75.8	20.2	0.8	1.5	1.8	0.0
Aged 30 to 34	100.0	55.3	31.3	1.3	5.7	6.2	0.1
Aged 35 to 39	100.0	39.2	43.3	2.3	4.6	10.0	0.7
Aged 40 to 44	100.0	32.3	47.7	2.0	4.8	13.1	0.2
Aged 45 to 49	100.0	31.3	43.1	1.7	7.1	15.6	1.1
Aged 50 to 54	100.0	23.1	48.3	2.5	6.4	18.1	1.5
Aged 55 to 64	100.0	17.9	50.5	2.9	6.0	19.5	3.1
Aged 65 to 74	100.0	9.3	59.2	0.9	5.0	17.5	8.2
Aged 75 to 84	100.0	7.0	58.9	3.5	3.8	9.7	17.3
Aged 85 or older	100.0	12.5	28.3	5.8	3.3	0.0	50.0

Note: Blacks are those who identify themselves as being black alone and those who identify themselves as being black in combination with other races.
Source: Bureau of the Census, Current Population Survey Annual Social and Economic Supplement, America's Families and Living Arrangements: 2012, Internet site http://www.census.gov/hhes/families/data/cps2012.html; calculations by New Strategist

Table 4.85 Marital Status of Black Women by Age, 2012

(number and percent distribution of black women aged 18 or older by age and current marital status, 2012; numbers in thousands)

	total	never married	married, spouse present	married, spouse absent	separated	divorced	widowed
Total black women	16,319	7,058	4,533	357	804	2,116	1,452
Aged 18 to 19	729	714	5	2	3	3	1
Aged 20 to 24	1,878	1,684	111	21	37	20	5
Aged 25 to 29	1,571	1,115	323	36	44	50	4
Aged 30 to 34	1,555	851	460	43	64	133	4
Aged 35 to 39	1,441	600	509	30	113	180	10
Aged 40 to 44	1,480	528	559	39	105	225	23
Aged 45 to 49	1,544	488	562	51	115	285	43
Aged 50 to 54	1,510	416	569	34	95	313	82
Aged 55 to 64	2,387	476	854	65	158	549	284
Aged 65 to 74	1,263	114	415	21	48	257	408
Aged 75 to 84	691	58	136	13	16	83	386
Aged 85 or older	271	14	28	2	4	19	204
Total black women	100.0%	43.3%	27.8%	2.2%	4.9%	13.0%	8.9%
Aged 18 to 19	100.0	97.9	0.7	0.3	0.4	0.4	0.1
Aged 20 to 24	100.0	89.7	5.9	1.1	2.0	1.1	0.3
Aged 25 to 29	100.0	71.0	20.6	2.3	2.8	3.2	0.3
Aged 30 to 34	100.0	54.7	29.6	2.8	4.1	8.6	0.3
Aged 35 to 39	100.0	41.6	35.3	2.1	7.8	12.5	0.7
Aged 40 to 44	100.0	35.7	37.8	2.6	7.1	15.2	1.6
Aged 45 to 49	100.0	31.6	36.4	3.3	7.4	18.5	2.8
Aged 50 to 54	100.0	27.5	37.7	2.3	6.3	20.7	5.4
Aged 55 to 64	100.0	19.9	35.8	2.7	6.6	23.0	11.9
Aged 65 to 74	100.0	9.0	32.9	1.7	3.8	20.3	32.3
Aged 75 to 84	100.0	8.4	19.7	1.9	2.3	12.0	55.9
Aged 85 or older	100.0	5.2	10.3	0.7	1.5	7.0	75.3

Note: Blacks are those who identify themselves as being black alone and those who identify themselves as being black in combination with other races.
Source: Bureau of the Census, Current Population Survey Annual Social and Economic Supplement, America's Families and Living Arrangements: 2012, Internet site http://www.census.gov/hhes/families/data/cps2012.html; calculations by New Strategist

Table 4.86 Marital History of Black Men by Age, 2009

(number of black men aged 15 or older and percent distribution by marital history and age, 2009; numbers in thousands)

	total	15–19	20–24	25–29	30–34	35–39	40–49	50–59	60–69	70+
TOTAL BLACK MEN, NUMBER	12,955	1,659	1,395	1,325	1,104	1,122	2,410	2,042	1,109	789
TOTAL BLACK MEN, PERCENT	100.0%	100.0%	100.0%	100.0%	100.0%	100.0%	100.0%	100.0%	100.0%	100.0%
Never married	46.9	98.4	91.7	73.1	54.5	43.1	24.2	17.5	9.4	8.1
Ever married	53.1	1.6	8.3	26.9	45.5	56.9	75.8	82.5	90.6	91.9
Married once	41.9	1.6	8.3	26.3	42.9	51.0	62.1	57.6	61.4	68.1
Still married	29.9	0.7	7.2	22.0	35.5	39.0	43.6	37.3	43.7	43.6
Married twice	9.2	0.0	0.0	0.5	2.6	5.7	12.6	20.5	20.1	19.5
Still married	6.8	0.0	0.0	0.3	2.6	4.5	9.2	15.4	15.5	11.8
Married three or more times	2.0	0.0	0.0	0.0	0.0	0.2	1.1	4.5	9.0	4.4
Still married	1.4	0.0	0.0	0.0	0.0	0.2	1.0	3.2	6.6	2.5
Ever divorced	17.7	0.4	0.2	3.1	6.6	14.7	26.5	39.2	34.6	22.9
Currently divorced	9.2	0.4	0.2	2.8	4.1	10.0	15.5	20.3	12.5	7.7
Ever widowed	3.7	0.5	0.0	0.5	0.0	0.6	2.2	3.2	10.7	28.2
Currently widowed	2.8	0.5	0.0	0.5	0.0	0.3	1.9	2.4	6.7	22.7

Note: Blacks are those who identify themselves as being of the race alone.
Source: Bureau of the Census, Number, Timing, and Duration of Marriages and Divorces: 2009, Detailed Tables, Internet site http://www.census.gov/hhes/socdemo/marriage/data/sipp/index.html

Table 4.87 Marital History of Black Women by Age, 2009

(number of black women aged 15 or older and percent distribution by marital history and age, 2009; numbers in thousands)

	total	15–19	20–24	25–29	30–34	35–39	40–49	50–59	60–69	70+
TOTAL BLACK WOMEN, NUMBER	**15,776**	**1,686**	**1,545**	**1,514**	**1,367**	**1,419**	**2,946**	**2,483**	**1,530**	**1,286**
TOTAL BLACK WOMEN, PERCENT	**100.0%**	**100.0%**	**100.0%**	**100.0%**	**100.0%**	**100.0%**	**100.0%**	**100.0%**	**100.0%**	**100.0%**
Never married	**45.2**	**98.3**	**88.6**	**70.5**	**53.6**	**39.2**	**30.7**	**21.5**	**14.5**	**7.0**
Ever married	**54.8**	**1.7**	**11.4**	**29.5**	**46.4**	**60.8**	**69.3**	**78.5**	**85.5**	**93.0**
Married once	44.6	1.5	11.1	29.0	42.4	52.5	59.2	58.8	62.8	71.0
Still married	24.8	1.3	9.0	23.1	30.2	33.7	37.0	30.4	30.8	14.6
Married twice	8.4	0.2	0.2	0.5	3.8	7.5	8.7	15.6	18.4	18.0
Still married	4.4	0.2	0.2	0.5	3.1	5.5	4.8	9.5	9.0	3.3
Married three or more times	1.7	0.0	0.0	0.0	0.2	0.8	1.4	4.1	4.3	3.9
Still married	0.8	0.0	0.0	0.0	0.0	0.4	0.9	1.7	2.4	0.8
Ever divorced	19.2	0.2	1.3	4.3	11.1	19.9	24.3	37.8	34.4	25.9
Currently divorced	12.3	0.0	1.1	3.8	7.9	13.8	17.3	24.7	18.5	12.0
Ever widowed	9.1	0.2	0.3	0.0	0.7	1.0	3.2	8.2	21.8	60.1
Currently widowed	8.3	0.2	0.3	0.0	0.3	0.6	2.6	6.5	19.9	58.2

Note: Blacks are those who identify themselves as being of the race alone.
Source: Bureau of the Census, Number, Timing, and Duration of Marriages and Divorces: 2009, Detailed Tables, Internet site http://www.census.gov/hhes/socdemo/marriage/data/sipp/index.html

Black Population Numbers 44 Million

The number of blacks in the United States grew 18 percent between 2000 and 2011, from 37 million to 44 million—a figure that includes blacks who identify themselves as being black alone and those who identify themselves as being black in combination with other races. Blacks account for 14 percent of the U.S. population, slightly less than the 17 percent share held by Hispanics.

More than half of blacks (54 percent) live in the South, where they account for 21 percent of the population. In Mississippi, 38 percent of the population is black, as is 33 percent of Louisiana's population, 32 percent of Georgia's, and 29 percent of South Carolina's. No single state is home to more than about 8 percent of the black population.

Among metropolitan areas, blacks account for the largest share of the population in Albany, Georgia (53 percent). Blacks account for more than 40 of the populations of 10 other metropolitan areas: Pine Bluff, AR; Jackson, MS; Sumter, SC; Memphis, TN–MS–AR; Rocky Mount, NC; Macon, GA; Montgomery, AL; Florence, SC; Columbus, GA–AL; and Hinesville–Fort Stewart, GA.

The American Time Use Survey reveals interesting facts about how blacks spend their time. Compared with the average person, blacks spend 32 percent more time in educational pursuits and 93 percent more time in religious activities.

■ Unlike Hispanics or Asians, most of whom live in only a few states, blacks are an important segment of the population throughout the country.

Blacks are a substantial share of the population in most regions

(black share of population by region, 2011)

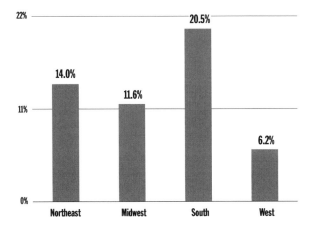

Table 4.88 Blacks by Racial Identification, 2000 and 2010

(total number of people, and number and percent distribution of blacks by racial identification, 2000 and 2010; percent change, 2000–10)

	2010		2000		percent change 2000–10
	number	percent distribution	number	percent distribution	
Total people	308,745,538	100.0%	281,421,906	100.0%	9.7%
Black alone or in combination with one or more other races	**42,020,743**	**13.6**	**37,104,248**	**13.2**	**13.3**
Black alone	38,929,319	12.6	34,658,190	12.3	12.3
Black in combination	3,091,424	1.0	2,446,058	0.9	26.4

Source: Bureau of the Census, An Overview: Race and Hispanic Origin and the 2010 Census, 2010 Census Briefs, Internet site http://www.census.gov/2010census/data/2010-census-briefs.php; calculations by New Strategist

Table 4.89 Blacks by Hispanic Origin, 2010

(number and percent distribution of blacks by Hispanic origin and racial identification, 2010)

	black alone or in combination		black alone	
	number	percent distribution	number	percent distribution
Total blacks	**42,020,743**	**100.0%**	**38,929,319**	**100.0%**
Not Hispanic	40,123,525	95.5	37,685,848	96.8
Hispanic	1,897,218	4.5	1,243,471	3.2

Source: Bureau of the Census, An Overview: Race and Hispanic Origin and the 2010 Census, 2010 Census Briefs, Internet site http://www.census.gov/2010census/data/2010-census-briefs.php; calculations by New Strategist

Table 4.90 Blacks by Age, 2000 to 2011

(number of blacks by age, 2000 to 2011; percent change, 2000–11)

	2011	2010	2000	percent change 2000–11
Total blacks	**43,884,130**	**42,020,743**	**37,104,248**	**18.3%**
Under age 5	3,700,516	3,537,623	3,238,758	14.3
Aged 5 to 9	3,507,394	3,389,399	3,563,220	–1.6
Aged 10 to 14	3,585,321	3,467,704	3,396,897	5.5
Aged 15 to 19	3,803,526	3,795,678	3,156,870	20.5
Aged 20 to 24	3,679,146	3,350,250	2,831,265	29.9
Aged 25 to 29	3,140,577	2,971,067	2,726,503	15.2
Aged 30 to 34	2,990,439	2,780,483	2,778,594	7.6
Aged 35 to 39	2,764,790	2,737,901	2,971,496	–7.0
Aged 40 to 44	2,863,594	2,772,659	2,826,656	1.3
Aged 45 to 49	2,960,897	2,922,195	2,374,543	24.7
Aged 50 to 54	2,877,343	2,774,537	1,880,832	53.0
Aged 55 to 59	2,404,382	2,267,305	1,355,395	77.4
Aged 60 to 64	1,904,295	1,731,892	1,099,969	73.1
Aged 65 to 69	1,255,252	1,191,992	908,984	38.1
Aged 70 to 74	919,772	872,582	752,674	22.2
Aged 75 to 79	668,111	630,948	565,015	18.2
Aged 80 to 84	448,633	434,553	355,482	26.2
Aged 85 or older	410,142	391,975	321,095	27.7
Aged 18 to 24	5,265,891	4,903,485	4,097,306	28.5
Aged 18 or older	30,874,118	29,383,574	25,014,544	23.4
Aged 65 or older	3,701,910	3,522,050	2,903,250	27.5

Note: Blacks are those who identify themselves as being of the race alone and those who identify themselves as being of the race in combination with other races.
Source: Bureau of the Census, 2000 Census, 2010 Census, and Population Estimates, Internet site http://www.census.gov/ popest/index.html; calculations by New Strategist

Table 4.91 Black Share of Total Population by Age, 2011

(total number of people, number and percent distribution of blacks, and black share of total, by age, 2011)

	total	black number	black percent distribution	black share of total
Total people	**311,591,917**	**43,884,130**	**100.0%**	**14.1%**
Under age 5	20,162,058	3,700,516	8.4	18.4
Aged 5 to 9	20,334,196	3,507,394	8.0	17.2
Aged 10 to 14	20,704,852	3,585,321	8.2	17.3
Aged 15 to 19	21,644,043	3,803,526	8.7	17.6
Aged 20 to 24	22,153,832	3,679,146	8.4	16.6
Aged 25 to 29	21,279,794	3,140,577	7.2	14.8
Aged 30 to 34	20,510,704	2,990,439	6.8	14.6
Aged 35 to 39	19,594,309	2,764,790	6.3	14.1
Aged 40 to 44	21,033,645	2,863,594	6.5	13.6
Aged 45 to 49	22,158,005	2,960,897	6.7	13.4
Aged 50 to 54	22,560,198	2,877,343	6.6	12.8
Aged 55 to 59	20,255,548	2,404,382	5.5	11.9
Aged 60 to 64	17,806,592	1,904,295	4.3	10.7
Aged 65 to 69	12,873,788	1,255,252	2.9	9.8
Aged 70 to 74	9,607,950	919,772	2.1	9.6
Aged 75 to 79	7,388,687	668,111	1.5	9.0
Aged 80 to 84	5,786,543	448,633	1.0	7.8
Aged 85 or older	5,737,173	410,142	0.9	7.1
Aged 18 to 24	31,064,709	5,265,891	12.0	17.0
Aged 18 or older	237,657,645	30,874,118	70.4	13.0
Aged 65 or older	41,394,141	3,701,910	8.4	8.9

Note: Blacks are those who identify themselves as being of the race alone and those who identify themselves as being of the race in combination with other races.
Source: Bureau of the Census, Population Estimates, Internet site http://www.census.gov/popest/index.html; calculations by New Strategist

Table 4.92 Blacks by Age and Sex, 2011

(number of blacks by age and sex, and sex ratio by age, 2011)

	total	females	males	sex ratio
Total blacks	**43,884,130**	**22,905,726**	**20,978,404**	**92**
Under age 5	3,700,516	1,821,157	1,879,359	103
Aged 5 to 9	3,507,394	1,729,534	1,777,860	103
Aged 10 to 14	3,585,321	1,765,037	1,820,284	103
Aged 15 to 19	3,803,526	1,870,540	1,932,986	103
Aged 20 to 24	3,679,146	1,852,555	1,826,591	99
Aged 25 to 29	3,140,577	1,624,587	1,515,990	93
Aged 30 to 34	2,990,439	1,572,699	1,417,740	90
Aged 35 to 39	2,764,790	1,466,001	1,298,789	89
Aged 40 to 44	2,863,594	1,515,447	1,348,147	89
Aged 45 to 49	2,960,897	1,567,117	1,393,780	89
Aged 50 to 54	2,877,343	1,530,986	1,346,357	88
Aged 55 to 59	2,404,382	1,300,298	1,104,084	85
Aged 60 to 64	1,904,295	1,049,195	855,100	82
Aged 65 to 69	1,255,252	709,341	545,911	77
Aged 70 to 74	919,772	536,378	383,394	71
Aged 75 to 79	668,111	408,006	260,105	64
Aged 80 to 84	448,633	292,236	156,397	54
Aged 85 or older	410,142	294,612	115,530	39
Aged 18 to 24	5,265,891	2,631,993	2,633,898	100
Aged 18 or older	30,874,118	16,498,896	14,375,222	87
Aged 65 or older	3,701,910	2,240,573	1,461,337	65

Note: Blacks are those who identify themselves as being of the race alone and those who identify themselves as being of the race in combination with other races. The sex ratio is the number of males divided by the number of females multiplied by 100.
Source: Bureau of the Census, Population Estimates, Internet site http://www.census.gov/popest/index.html; calculations by New Strategist

Table 4.93 Black Population Projections, 2012 to 2050

(number of blacks by age, and black share of total population, 2012 to 2050, percent and percentage point change, 2012–50; numbers in thousands)

NUMBER	2012	2020	2030	2040	2050	percent change 2012–50
Total blacks	**44,462**	**49,338**	**55,727**	**62,350**	**69,525**	**56.4%**
Under age 5	3,748	4,179	4,408	4,809	5,321	42.0
Aged 5 to 9	3,559	3,990	4,348	4,625	5,147	44.6
Aged 10 to 14	3,574	3,719	4,252	4,503	4,923	37.8
Aged 15 to 19	3,718	3,547	4,067	4,446	4,740	27.5
Aged 20 to 24	3,830	3,666	3,866	4,439	4,723	23.3
Aged 25 to 29	3,192	4,024	3,766	4,350	4,782	49.8
Aged 30 to 34	3,049	3,631	3,870	4,138	4,763	56.2
Aged 35 to 39	2,760	3,172	4,150	3,951	4,575	65.8
Aged 40 to 44	2,877	2,935	3,687	3,966	4,266	48.3
Aged 45 to 49	2,919	2,787	3,171	4,165	4,002	37.1
Aged 50 to 54	2,893	2,754	2,878	3,639	3,942	36.3
Aged 55 to 59	2,505	2,809	2,666	3,068	4,056	61.9
Aged 60 to 64	1,966	2,584	2,558	2,717	3,471	76.5
Aged 65 or older	3,871	5,541	8,039	9,534	10,814	179.3

SHARE OF TOTAL POPULATION	2012	2020	2030	2040	2050	percentage point change 2012–50
Total blacks	**14.2%**	**14.8%**	**15.5%**	**16.4%**	**17.4%**	**3.2**
Under age 5	18.5	19.2	19.8	20.9	22.1	3.6
Aged 5 to 9	17.4	18.7	19.4	20.2	21.5	4.1
Aged 10 to 14	17.3	18.0	19.0	19.7	20.8	3.5
Aged 15 to 19	17.4	17.0	18.5	19.2	20.0	2.6
Aged 20 to 24	17.0	16.9	17.6	18.6	19.3	2.3
Aged 25 to 29	14.9	17.2	16.6	18.0	18.8	3.8
Aged 30 to 34	14.6	15.9	16.6	17.3	18.4	3.8
Aged 35 to 39	14.2	14.5	17.0	16.5	17.9	3.8
Aged 40 to 44	13.7	14.4	15.8	16.5	17.3	3.6
Aged 45 to 49	13.5	13.9	14.5	16.9	16.5	3.0
Aged 50 to 54	12.8	13.5	14.3	15.7	16.5	3.7
Aged 55 to 59	12.1	12.9	13.7	14.3	16.8	4.8
Aged 60 to 64	11.0	12.3	13.1	14.1	15.5	4.5
Aged 65 or older	9.0	9.9	11.0	12.0	12.9	3.9

Note: Blacks are those who identify themselves as being of the race alone and those who identify themselves as being of the race in combination with other races.
Source: Bureau of the Census, Population Projections, Internet site http://www.census.gov/population/projections/; calculations by New Strategist

Table 4.94 Blacks by Region, 2000 to 2011

(number of blacks by region, 2000 to 2011; percent change, 2000–11)

	2011	2010	2000	percent change 2000–11
Total blacks	**43,884,130**	**42,020,743**	**36,419,434**	**20.5%**
Northeast	7,789,695	7,187,488	6,556,909	18.8
Midwest	7,767,061	7,594,486	6,838,669	13.6
South	23,841,902	23,105,082	19,528,231	22.1
West	4,485,472	4,133,687	3,495,625	28.3

Note: Blacks are those who identify themselves as being of the race alone and those who identify themselves as being of the race in combination with other races. Total blacks in 2000 do not match the 2000 total in some of the other tables because this figure has not been adjusted to eliminate the "some other race" category that was included in the census.
Source: Bureau of the Census, 2000 Census, 2010 Census, and Population Estimates, Internet site http://www.census.gov/popest/index.html; calculations by New Strategist

Table 4.95 Black Share of the Total Population by Region, 2011

(total number of people, number and percent distribution of blacks, and black share of total, by region, 2011)

		black		
	total	number	percent distribution	share of total
Total people	**311,587,816**	**43,884,130**	**100.0%**	**14.1%**
Northeast	55,597,646	7,789,695	17.8	14.0
Midwest	67,145,089	7,767,061	17.7	11.6
South	116,022,230	23,841,902	54.3	20.5
West	72,822,851	4,485,472	10.2	6.2

Note: Blacks are those who identify themselves as being of the race alone and those who identify themselves as being of the race in combination with other races.
Source: Bureau of the Census, Population Estimates, Internet site http://www.census.gov/popest/index.html; calculations by New Strategist

Table 4.96 Blacks by State, 2000 to 2011

(number of blacks by state, 2000 to 2011; percent change, 2000–11)

	2011	2010	2000	percent change 2000–11
Total blacks	**43,884,130**	**42,020,743**	**36,419,434**	**20.5%**
Alabama	1,303,027	1,281,118	1,168,998	11.5
Alaska	36,242	33,150	27,147	33.5
Arizona	351,551	318,665	185,599	89.4
Arkansas	477,900	468,710	427,152	11.9
California	2,893,884	2,683,914	2,513,041	15.2
Colorado	271,542	249,812	190,717	42.4
Connecticut	439,256	405,600	339,078	29.5
Delaware	212,543	205,923	157,152	35.2
District of Columbia	322,478	314,352	350,455	-8.0
Florida	3,335,564	3,200,663	2,471,730	34.9
Georgia	3,149,131	3,054,098	2,393,425	31.6
Hawaii	45,730	38,820	33,343	37.2
Idaho	19,002	15,940	8,127	133.8
Illinois	2,014,561	1,974,113	1,937,671	4.0
Indiana	675,140	654,415	538,015	25.5
Iowa	119,236	113,225	72,512	64.4
Kansas	211,959	202,149	170,610	24.2
Kentucky	389,415	376,213	311,878	24.9
Louisiana	1,516,689	1,486,885	1,468,317	3.3
Maine	23,033	21,764	9,553	141.1
Maryland	1,833,676	1,783,899	1,525,036	20.2
Massachusetts	581,032	508,413	398,479	45.8
Michigan	1,524,596	1,505,514	1,474,613	3.4
Minnesota	342,393	327,548	202,972	68.7
Mississippi	1,130,347	1,115,801	1,041,708	8.5
Missouri	759,917	747,474	655,377	16.0
Montana	9,660	7,917	4,441	117.5
Nebraska	103,849	98,959	75,833	36.9
Nevada	270,625	254,452	150,508	79.8
New Hampshire	24,331	21,736	12,218	99.1
New Jersey	1,383,879	1,300,363	1,211,750	14.2
New Mexico	66,471	57,040	42,412	56.7
New York	3,659,850	3,334,550	3,234,165	13.2
North Carolina	2,227,302	2,151,456	1,776,283	25.4
North Dakota	12,460	11,086	5,372	131.9
Ohio	1,569,826	1,541,771	1,372,501	14.4
Oklahoma	343,494	327,621	284,766	20.6
Oregon	108,329	98,479	72,647	49.1

	2011	2010	2000	percent change 2000–11
Pennsylvania	1,576,964	1,507,965	1,289,123	22.3%
Rhode Island	91,230	77,754	58,051	57.2
South Carolina	1,357,216	1,332,188	1,200,901	13.0
South Dakota	16,428	14,705	6,687	145.7
Tennessee	1,134,811	1,107,178	953,349	19.0
Texas	3,324,512	3,168,469	2,493,057	33.4
Utah	51,084	43,209	24,382	109.5
Vermont	10,120	9,343	4,492	125.3
Virginia	1,703,665	1,653,563	1,441,207	18.2
Washington	352,503	325,004	238,398	47.9
West Virginia	80,132	76,945	62,817	27.6
Wisconsin	416,696	403,527	326,506	27.6
Wyoming	8,849	7,285	4,863	82.0

Note: Blacks are those who identify themselves as being of the race alone and those who identify themselves as being of the race in combination with other races. Total blacks in 2000 do not match the 2000 total in some of the other tables because this figure has not been adjusted to eliminate the "some other race" category that was included in the census.
Source: Bureau of the Census, 2000 Census, 2010 Census, and Population Estimates, Internet site http://www.census.gov/popest/index.html; calculations by New Strategist

Table 4.97 Black Share of Total Population by State, 2011

(total number of people, number and percent distribution of blacks, and black share of total, by state, 2011)

	total	black number	percent distribution	share of total
Total people	**311,587,816**	**43,884,130**	**100.0%**	**14.1%**
Alabama	4,802,740	1,303,027	3.0	27.1
Alaska	722,718	36,242	0.1	5.0
Arizona	6,482,505	351,551	0.8	5.4
Arkansas	2,937,979	477,900	1.1	16.3
California	37,691,912	2,893,884	6.6	7.7
Colorado	5,116,796	271,542	0.6	5.3
Connecticut	3,580,709	439,256	1.0	12.3
Delaware	907,135	212,543	0.5	23.4
District of Columbia	617,996	322,478	0.7	52.2
Florida	19,057,542	3,335,564	7.6	17.5
Georgia	9,815,210	3,149,131	7.2	32.1
Hawaii	1,374,810	45,730	0.1	3.3
Idaho	1,584,985	19,002	0.0	1.2
Illinois	12,869,257	2,014,561	4.6	15.7
Indiana	6,516,922	675,140	1.5	10.4
Iowa	3,062,309	119,236	0.3	3.9
Kansas	2,871,238	211,959	0.5	7.4
Kentucky	4,369,356	389,415	0.9	8.9
Louisiana	4,574,836	1,516,689	3.5	33.2
Maine	1,328,188	23,033	0.1	1.7
Maryland	5,828,289	1,833,676	4.2	31.5
Massachusetts	6,587,536	581,032	1.3	8.8
Michigan	9,876,187	1,524,596	3.5	15.4
Minnesota	5,344,861	342,393	0.8	6.4
Mississippi	2,978,512	1,130,347	2.6	38.0
Missouri	6,010,688	759,917	1.7	12.6
Montana	998,199	9,660	0.0	1.0
Nebraska	1,842,641	103,849	0.2	5.6
Nevada	2,723,322	270,625	0.6	9.9
New Hampshire	1,318,194	24,331	0.1	1.8
New Jersey	8,821,155	1,383,879	3.2	15.7
New Mexico	2,082,224	66,471	0.2	3.2
New York	19,465,197	3,659,850	8.3	18.8
North Carolina	9,656,401	2,227,302	5.1	23.1
North Dakota	683,932	12,460	0.0	1.8
Ohio	11,544,951	1,569,826	3.6	13.6
Oklahoma	3,791,508	343,494	0.8	9.1

	total	black		
		number	percent distribution	share of total
Oregon	3,871,859	108,329	0.2%	2.8%
Pennsylvania	12,742,886	1,576,964	3.6	12.4
Rhode Island	1,051,302	91,230	0.2	8.7
South Carolina	4,679,230	1,357,216	3.1	29.0
South Dakota	824,082	16,428	0.0	2.0
Tennessee	6,403,353	1,134,811	2.6	17.7
Texas	25,674,681	3,324,512	7.6	12.9
Utah	2,817,222	51,084	0.1	1.8
Vermont	626,431	10,120	0.0	1.6
Virginia	8,096,604	1,703,665	3.9	21.0
Washington	6,830,038	352,503	0.8	5.2
West Virginia	1,855,364	80,132	0.2	4.3
Wisconsin	5,711,767	416,696	0.9	7.3
Wyoming	568,158	8,849	0.0	1.6

Note: Blacks are those who identify themselves as being of the race alone and those who identify themselves as being of the race in combination with other races.
Source: Bureau of the Census, Population Estimates, Internet site http://www.census.gov/popest/index.html; calculations by New Strategist

Table 4.98 Blacks by Metropolitan Area, 2010

(total number of people, number of blacks, and black share of total, for selected metropolitan areas, 2010)

	total population	black number	black share of total
Abilene, TX	165,252	13,969	8.5%
Akron, OH	703,200	93,126	13.2
Albany, GA	157,308	83,170	52.9
Albany–Schenectady–Troy, NY	870,716	78,991	9.1
Albuquerque, NM	887,077	31,886	3.6
Alexandria, LA	153,922	46,752	30.4
Allentown–Bethlehem–Easton, PA–NJ	821,173	50,408	6.1
Altoona, PA	127,089	3,034	2.4
Amarillo, TX	249,881	17,387	7.0
Ames, IA	89,542	2,770	3.1
Anchorage, AK	380,821	24,120	6.3
Anderson, IN	131,636	12,333	9.4
Anderson, SC	187,126	31,652	16.9
Ann Arbor, MI	344,791	49,305	14.3
Anniston–Oxford, AL	118,572	25,322	21.4
Appleton, WI	225,666	3,144	1.4
Asheville, NC	424,858	22,478	5.3
Athens–Clarke County, GA	192,541	39,097	20.3
Atlanta–Sandy Springs–Marietta, GA	5,268,860	1,772,569	33.6
Atlantic City–Hammonton, NJ	274,549	48,135	17.5
Auburn–Opelika, AL	140,247	32,884	23.4
Augusta–Richmond County, GA–SC	556,877	203,509	36.5
Austin–Round Rock–San Marcos, TX	1,716,289	142,344	8.3
Bakersfield–Delano, CA	839,631	56,494	6.7
Baltimore–Towson, MD	2,710,489	814,600	30.1
Bangor, ME	153,923	1,790	1.2
Barnstable Town, MA	215,888	6,012	2.8
Baton Rouge, LA	802,484	290,701	36.2
Battle Creek, MI	136,146	17,375	12.8
Bay City, MI	107,771	2,751	2.6
Beaumont–Port Arthur, TX	388,745	98,040	25.2
Bellingham, WA	201,140	3,512	1.7
Bend, OR	157,733	1,179	0.7
Billings, MT	158,050	1,925	1.2
Binghamton, NY	251,725	13,080	5.2
Birmingham–Hoover, AL	1,128,047	324,055	28.7
Bismarck, ND	108,779	996	0.9
Blacksburg–Christiansburg–Radford, VA	162,958	8,268	5.1

	total population	black	
		number	share of total
Bloomington, IN	192,714	6,084	3.2%
Bloomington–Normal, IL	169,572	14,531	8.6
Boise City–Nampa, ID	616,561	8,558	1.4
Boston–Cambridge–Quincy, MA–NH	4,552,402	379,885	8.3
Boulder, CO	294,567	4,007	1.4
Bowling Green, KY	125,953	11,729	9.3
Bremerton–Silverdale, WA	251,133	10,086	4.0
Bridgeport–Stamford–Norwalk, CT	916,829	108,575	11.8
Brownsville–Harlingen, TX	406,220	2,762	0.7
Brunswick, GA	112,370	27,313	24.3
Buffalo–Niagara Falls, NY	1,135,509	150,681	13.3
Burlington, NC	151,131	30,027	19.9
Burlington–South Burlington, VT	211,261	4,784	2.3
Canton–Massillon, OH	404,422	34,262	8.5
Cape Coral–Fort Myers, FL	618,754	56,014	9.1
Cape Girardeau–Jackson, MO–IL	96,275	9,158	9.5
Carson City, NV	55,274	1,297	2.3
Casper, WY	75,450	1,201	1.6
Cedar Rapids, IA	257,940	11,893	4.6
Champaign–Urbana, IL	231,891	27,801	12.0
Charleston, WV	304,284	17,548	5.8
Charleston–North Charleston–Summerville, SC	664,607	190,518	28.7
Charlotte–Gastonia–Rock Hill, NC–SC	1,758,038	441,500	25.1
Charlottesville, VA	201,559	27,462	13.6
Chattanooga, TN–GA	528,143	76,932	14.6
Cheyenne, WY	91,738	3,152	3.4
Chicago–Joliet–Naperville, IL–IN–WI	9,461,105	1,721,578	18.2
Chico, CA	220,000	5,386	2.4
Cincinnati–Middletown, OH–KY–IN	2,130,151	276,998	13.0
Clarksville, TN–KY	273,949	55,477	20.3
Cleveland, TN	115,788	5,037	4.4
Cleveland–Elyria–Mentor, OH	2,077,240	440,561	21.2
Coeur d'Alene, ID	138,494	950	0.7
College Station–Bryan, TX	228,660	28,562	12.5
Colorado Springs, CO	645,613	50,440	7.8
Columbia, MO	172,786	18,190	10.5
Columbia, SC	767,598	263,471	34.3
Columbus, GA–AL	294,865	123,480	41.9
Columbus, IN	76,794	1,937	2.5
Columbus, OH	1,836,536	300,094	16.3
Corpus Christi, TX	428,185	17,223	4.0

	total population	black	
		number	share of total
Corvallis, OR	85,579	1,267	1.5%
Crestview–Fort Walton Beach–Destin, FL	180,822	19,396	10.7
Cumberland, MD–WV	103,299	7,795	7.5
Dallas–Fort Worth–Arlington, TX	6,371,773	1,015,660	15.9
Dalton, GA	142,227	4,932	3.5
Danville, IL	81,625	11,626	14.2
Danville, VA	106,561	35,531	33.3
Davenport–Moline–Rock Island, IA–IL	379,690	31,450	8.3
Dayton, OH	841,502	136,745	16.3
Decatur, AL	153,829	19,135	12.4
Decatur, IL	110,768	19,971	18.0
Deltona–Daytona Beach–Ormond Beach, FL	494,593	56,417	11.4
Denver–Aurora–Broomfield, CO	2,543,482	171,107	6.7
Des Moines–West Des Moines, IA	569,633	32,728	5.7
Detroit–Warren–Livonia, MI	4,296,250	1,024,265	23.8
Dothan, AL	145,639	34,804	23.9
Dover, DE	162,310	42,508	26.2
Dubuque, IA	93,653	3,113	3.3
Duluth, MN–WI	279,771	5,749	2.1
Durham–Chapel Hill, NC	504,357	142,241	28.2
Eau Claire, WI	161,151	2,725	1.7
El Centro, CA	174,528	6,617	3.8
Elizabethtown, KY	119,736	14,778	12.3
Elkhart–Goshen, IN	197,559	13,745	7.0
Elmira, NY	88,830	7,391	8.3
El Paso, TX	800,647	29,546	3.7
Erie, PA	280,566	23,932	8.5
Eugene–Springfield, OR	351,715	6,203	1.8
Evansville, IN–KY	358,676	26,242	7.3
Fairbanks, AK	97,581	5,955	6.1
Fargo, ND–MN	208,777	5,567	2.7
Farmington, NM	130,044	1,344	1.0
Fayetteville, NC	366,383	142,452	38.9
Fayetteville–Springdale–Rogers, AR–MO	463,204	11,243	2.4
Flagstaff, AZ	134,421	2,385	1.8
Flint, MI	425,790	94,278	22.1
Florence, SC	205,566	86,531	42.1
Florence–Muscle Shoals, AL	147,137	19,034	12.9
Fond du Lac, WI	101,633	1,833	1.8
Fort Collins–Loveland, CO	299,630	4,117	1.4
Fort Smith, AR–OK	298,592	12,978	4.3
Fort Wayne, IN	416,257	48,052	11.5

	total population	black	
		number	share of total
Fresno, CA	930,450	57,795	6.2%
Gadsden, AL	104,430	16,468	15.8
Gainesville, FL	264,275	54,204	20.5
Gainesville, GA	179,684	14,397	8.0
Glens Falls, NY	128,923	3,098	2.4
Goldsboro, NC	122,623	39,932	32.6
Grand Forks, ND–MN	98,461	2,220	2.3
Grand Junction, CO	146,723	1,697	1.2
Grand Rapids–Wyoming, MI	774,160	72,814	9.4
Great Falls, MT	81,327	1,661	2.0
Greeley, CO	252,825	3,665	1.4
Green Bay, WI	306,241	7,761	2.5
Greensboro–High Point, NC	723,801	193,417	26.7
Greenville, NC	189,510	67,340	35.5
Greenville–Mauldin–Easley, SC	636,986	111,586	17.5
Gulfport–Biloxi, MS	248,820	50,589	20.3
Hagerstown–Martinsburg, MD–WV	269,140	25,694	9.5
Hanford–Corcoran, CA	152,982	12,701	8.3
Harrisburg–Carlisle, PA	549,475	64,242	11.7
Harrisonburg, VA	125,228	5,391	4.3
Hartford–West Hartford–East Hartford, CT	1,212,381	146,765	12.1
Hattiesburg, MS	142,842	41,354	29.0
Hickory–Lenoir–Morganton, NC	365,497	28,323	7.7
Hinesville–Fort Stewart, GA	77,917	32,558	41.8
Holland–Grand Haven, MI	263,801	5,635	2.1
Honolulu, HI	953,207	32,780	3.4
Hot Springs, AR	96,024	8,531	8.9
Houma–Bayou Cane–Thibodaux, LA	208,178	35,435	17.0
Houston–Sugar Land–Baytown, TX	5,946,800	1,071,344	18.0
Huntington–Ashland, WV–KY–OH	287,702	9,939	3.5
Huntsville, AL	417,593	94,913	22.7
Idaho Falls, ID	130,374	1,096	0.8
Indianapolis–Carmel, IN	1,756,241	283,549	16.1
Iowa City, IA	152,586	7,787	5.1
Ithaca, NY	101,564	5,411	5.3
Jackson, MI	160,248	15,199	9.5
Jackson, MS	539,057	259,879	48.2
Jackson, TN	115,425	38,204	33.1
Jacksonville, FL	1,345,596	308,264	22.9
Jacksonville, NC	177,772	31,426	17.7
Janesville, WI	160,331	9,856	6.1
Jefferson City, MO	149,807	12,378	8.3

	total population	black number	black share of total
Johnson City, TN	198,716	6,958	3.5%
Johnstown, PA	143,679	6,406	4.5
Jonesboro, AR	121,026	15,382	12.7
Joplin, MO	175,518	4,124	2.3
Kalamazoo–Portage, MI	326,589	36,064	11.0
Kankakee–Bradley, IL	113,449	18,489	16.3
Kansas City, MO–KS	2,035,334	279,618	13.7
Kennewick–Pasco–Richland, WA	253,340	5,497	2.2
Killeen–Temple–Fort Hood, TX	405,300	88,992	22.0
Kingsport–Bristol–Bristol, TN–VA	309,544	7,391	2.4
Kingston, NY	182,493	13,644	7.5
Knoxville, TN	698,030	50,448	7.2
Kokomo, IN	98,688	6,968	7.1
La Crosse, WI–MN	133,665	2,615	2.0
Lafayette, IN	201,789	8,610	4.3
Lafayette, LA	273,738	75,309	27.5
Lake Charles, LA	199,607	49,960	25.0
Lake Havasu City–Kingman, AZ	200,186	2,854	1.4
Lakeland–Winter Haven, FL	602,095	95,359	15.8
Lancaster, PA	519,445	24,600	4.7
Lansing–East Lansing, MI	464,036	49,570	10.7
Laredo, TX	250,304	1,442	0.6
Las Cruces, NM	209,233	4,847	2.3
Las Vegas–Paradise, NV	1,951,269	234,966	12.0
Lawrence, KS	110,826	6,004	5.4
Lawton, OK	124,098	25,251	20.3
Lebanon, PA	133,568	3,885	2.9
Lewiston, ID–WA	60,888	495	0.8
Lewiston–Auburn, ME	107,702	4,790	4.4
Lexington–Fayette, KY	472,099	56,802	12.0
Lima, OH	106,331	14,616	13.7
Lincoln, NE	302,157	13,941	4.6
Little Rock–North Little Rock–Conway, AR	699,757	160,875	23.0
Logan, UT–ID	125,442	1,073	0.9
Longview, TX	214,369	39,098	18.2
Longview, WA	102,410	1,260	1.2
Los Angeles–Long Beach–Santa Ana, CA	12,828,837	1,016,066	7.9
Louisville/Jefferson County, KY–IN	1,283,566	190,536	14.8
Lubbock, TX	284,890	23,077	8.1
Lynchburg, VA	252,634	46,902	18.6
Macon, GA	232,293	102,715	44.2
Madera–Chowchilla, CA	150,865	6,452	4.3

	total population	black number	black share of total
Madison, WI	568,593	32,365	5.7%
Manchester–Nashua, NH	400,721	11,151	2.8
Manhattan, KS	127,081	13,620	10.7
Mankato–North Mankato, MN	96,740	3,017	3.1
Mansfield, OH	124,475	13,120	10.5
McAllen–Edinburg–Mission, TX	774,769	5,663	0.7
Medford, OR	203,206	2,558	1.3
Memphis, TN–MS–AR	1,316,100	610,601	46.4
Merced, CA	255,793	12,189	4.8
Miami–Fort Lauderdale–Pompano Beach, FL	5,564,635	1,229,929	22.1
Michigan City–La Porte, IN	111,467	13,400	12.0
Midland, TX	136,872	9,991	7.3
Milwaukee–Waukesha–West Allis, WI	1,555,908	279,032	17.9
Minneapolis–St. Paul–Bloomington, MN–WI	3,279,833	285,989	8.7
Missoula, MT	109,299	970	0.9
Mobile, AL	412,992	145,793	35.3
Modesto, CA	514,453	19,606	3.8
Monroe, LA	176,441	63,436	36.0
Monroe, MI	152,021	4,372	2.9
Montgomery, AL	374,536	161,883	43.2
Morgantown, WV	129,709	4,765	3.7
Morristown, TN	136,608	4,628	3.4
Mount Vernon–Anacortes, WA	116,901	1,441	1.2
Muncie, IN	117,671	9,525	8.1
Muskegon–Norton Shores, MI	172,188	27,322	15.9
Myrtle Beach–North Myrtle Beach–Conway, SC	269,291	38,764	14.4
Napa, CA	136,484	3,488	2.6
Naples–Marco Island, FL	321,520	22,976	7.1
Nashville–Davidson–Murfreesboro–Franklin, TN	1,589,934	256,724	16.1
New Haven–Milford, CT	862,477	121,729	14.1
New Orleans–Metairie–Kenner, LA	1,167,764	406,890	34.8
New York–Northern New Jersey–Long Island, NY–NJ–PA	18,897,109	3,606,188	19.1
Niles–Benton Harbor, MI	156,813	25,882	16.5
North Port–Bradenton–Sarasota, FL	702,281	51,165	7.3
Norwich–New London, CT	274,055	21,103	7.7
Ocala, FL	331,298	43,757	13.2
Ocean City, NJ	97,265	5,542	5.7
Odessa, TX	137,130	6,847	5.0
Ogden–Clearfield, UT	547,184	10,282	1.9
Oklahoma City, OK	1,252,987	150,394	12.0
Olympia, WA	252,264	10,385	4.1

	total population	black	
		number	share of total
Omaha–Council Bluffs, NE–IA	865,350	78,192	9.0%
Orlando–Kissimmee–Sanford, FL	2,134,411	374,450	17.5
Oshkosh–Neenah, WI	166,994	3,934	2.4
Owensboro, KY	114,752	5,990	5.2
Oxnard–Thousand Oaks–Ventura, CA	823,318	20,931	2.5
Palm Bay–Melbourne–Titusville, FL	543,376	61,166	11.3
Palm Coast, FL	95,696	11,953	12.5
Panama City–Lynn Haven–Panama City Beach, FL	168,852	20,113	11.9
Parkersburg–Marietta–Vienna, WV–OH	162,056	2,808	1.7
Pascagoula, MS	162,246	33,086	20.4
Pensacola–Ferry Pass–Brent, FL	448,991	81,666	18.2
Peoria, IL	379,186	38,912	10.3
Philadelphia–Camden–Wilmington, PA–NJ–DE–MD	5,965,343	1,318,231	22.1
Phoenix–Mesa–Glendale, AZ	4,192,887	251,155	6.0
Pine Bluff, AR	100,258	48,557	48.4
Pittsburgh, PA	2,356,285	220,407	9.4
Pittsfield, MA	131,219	5,132	3.9
Pocatello, ID	90,656	1,085	1.2
Portland–South Portland–Biddeford, ME	514,098	10,915	2.1
Portland–Vancouver–Hillsboro, OR–WA	2,226,009	86,475	3.9
Port St. Lucie, FL	424,107	65,232	15.4
Poughkeepsie–Newburgh–Middletown, NY	670,301	77,655	11.6
Prescott, AZ	211,033	2,171	1.0
Providence–New Bedford–Fall River, RI–MA	1,600,852	102,784	6.4
Provo–Orem, UT	526,810	4,837	0.9
Pueblo, CO	159,063	4,325	2.7
Punta Gorda, FL	159,978	10,262	6.4
Racine, WI	195,408	24,471	12.5
Raleigh–Cary, NC	1,130,490	240,851	21.3
Rapid City, SD	126,382	2,436	1.9
Reading, PA	411,442	25,062	6.1
Redding, CA	177,223	2,784	1.6
Reno–Sparks, NV	425,417	13,372	3.1
Richmond, VA	1,258,251	391,055	31.1
Riverside–San Bernardino–Ontario, CA	4,224,851	374,838	8.9
Roanoke, VA	308,707	42,852	13.9
Rochester, MN	186,011	8,492	4.6
Rochester, NY	1,054,323	136,397	12.9
Rockford, IL	349,431	41,727	11.9
Rocky Mount, NC	152,392	69,427	45.6
Rome, GA	96,317	14,431	15.0

	total population	black number	black share of total
Sacramento–Arden–Arcade–Roseville, CA	2,149,127	195,136	9.1%
Saginaw–Saginaw Township North, MI	200,169	40,895	20.4
St. Cloud, MN	189,093	6,723	3.6
St. George, UT	138,115	1,368	1.0
St. Joseph, MO–KS	127,329	7,765	6.1
St. Louis, MO–IL	2,812,896	542,156	19.3
Salem, OR	390,738	6,423	1.6
Salinas, CA	415,057	16,554	4.0
Salisbury, MD	125,203	36,885	29.5
Salt Lake City, UT	1,124,197	23,707	2.1
San Angelo, TX	111,823	5,312	4.8
San Antonio–New Braunfels, TX	2,142,508	159,895	7.5
San Diego–Carlsbad–San Marcos, CA	3,095,313	194,788	6.3
Sandusky, OH	77,079	8,095	10.5
San Francisco–Oakland–Fremont, CA	4,335,391	420,311	9.7
San Jose–Sunnyvale–Santa Clara, CA	1,836,911	60,612	3.3
San Luis Obispo–Paso Robles, CA	269,637	7,089	2.6
Santa Barbara–Santa Maria–Goleta, CA	423,895	11,731	2.8
Santa Cruz–Watsonville, CA	262,382	4,757	1.8
Santa Fe, NM	144,170	1,892	1.3
Santa Rosa–Petaluma, CA	483,878	11,661	2.4
Savannah, GA	347,611	121,511	35.0
Scranton–Wilkes–Barre, PA	563,631	20,682	3.7
Seattle–Tacoma–Bellevue, WA	3,439,809	248,816	7.2
Sebastian–Vero Beach, FL	138,028	13,325	9.7
Sheboygan, WI	115,507	2,312	2.0
Sherman–Denison, TX	120,877	8,066	6.7
Shreveport–Bossier City, LA	398,604	158,435	39.7
Sioux City, IA–NE–SD	143,577	4,685	3.3
Sioux Falls, SD	228,261	8,650	3.8
South Bend–Mishawaka, IN–MI	319,224	41,894	13.1
Spartanburg, SC	284,307	61,037	21.5
Spokane, WA	471,221	13,414	2.8
Springfield, IL	210,170	26,280	12.5
Springfield, MA	692,942	55,142	8.0
Springfield, MO	436,712	12,471	2.9
Springfield, OH	138,333	14,415	10.4
State College, PA	153,990	5,491	3.6
Steubenville–Weirton, OH–WV	124,454	6,042	4.9
Stockton, CA	685,306	61,726	9.0
Sumter, SC	107,456	51,456	47.9
Syracuse, NY	662,577	62,278	9.4

	total population	black number	black share of total
Tallahassee, FL	367,413	122,996	33.5%
Tampa–St. Petersburg–Clearwater, FL	2,783,243	360,771	13.0
Terre Haute, IN	172,425	10,162	5.9
Texarkana, TX–Texarkana, AR	136,027	34,390	25.3
Toledo, OH	651,429	96,950	14.9
Topeka, KS	233,870	19,647	8.4
Trenton–Ewing, NJ	366,513	78,537	21.4
Tucson, AZ	980,263	44,332	4.5
Tulsa, OK	937,478	91,867	9.8
Tuscaloosa, AL	219,461	75,299	34.3
Tyler, TX	209,714	39,257	18.7
Utica–Rome, NY	299,397	18,524	6.2
Valdosta, GA	139,588	48,769	34.9
Vallejo–Fairfield, CA	413,344	71,375	17.3
Victoria, TX	115,384	7,163	6.2
Vineland–Millville–Bridgeton, NJ	156,898	34,752	22.1
Virginia Beach–Norfolk–Newport News, VA–NC	1,671,683	553,131	33.1
Visalia–Porterville, CA	442,179	9,720	2.2
Waco, TX	234,906	36,894	15.7
Warner Robins, GA	139,900	41,801	29.9
Washington–Arlington–Alexandria, DC–VA–MD–WV	5,582,170	1,520,870	27.2
Waterloo–Cedar Falls, IA	167,819	13,731	8.2
Wausau, WI	134,063	1,397	1.0
Wenatchee–East Wenatchee, WA	110,884	727	0.7
Wheeling, WV–OH	147,950	5,860	4.0
Wichita, KS	623,061	57,453	9.2
Wichita Falls, TX	151,306	15,350	10.1
Williamsport, PA	116,111	6,541	5.6
Wilmington, NC	362,315	54,597	15.1
Winchester, VA–WV	128,472	7,623	5.9
Winston–Salem, NC	477,717	101,926	21.3
Worcester, MA	798,552	40,856	5.1
Yakima, WA	243,231	3,666	1.5
York–Hanover, PA	434,972	29,371	6.8
Youngstown–Warren–Boardman, OH–PA	565,773	68,015	12.0
Yuba City, CA	166,892	6,272	3.8
Yuma, AZ	195,751	5,161	2.6

Note: Blacks are those who identify themselves as being of the race alone and those who identify themselves as being of the race in combination with other races.
Source: Bureau of the Census, 2010 Census, Internet site http://factfinder2.census.gov/faces/nav/jsf/pages/index.xhtml; calculations by New Strategist

Table 4.99 Time Use of Total Blacks, 2011

(average hours per day spent in primary activities by total people and blacks aged 15 or older, and index of black to total, by type of activity, 2011)

	total people	total blacks	index, black to total
Total, all activities	**24.00 hrs.**	**24.00 hrs.**	**100**
Personal care activities	9.47	9.83	104
Sleeping	8.71	8.94	103
Grooming	0.69	0.82	119
Household activities	1.78	1.36	76
Housework	0.58	0.48	83
Food preparation and cleanup	0.56	0.50	89
Lawn, garden, and houseplants	0.19	0.12	63
Animals and pets	0.09	0.03	33
Household management	0.18	0.11	61
Caring for and helping household members	0.43	0.31	72
Caring for and helping household children	0.34	0.24	71
Caring for and helping people in other households	0.15	0.15	100
Working and work-related activities	3.29	2.86	87
Educational activities	0.44	0.58	132
Consumer purchases	0.37	0.32	86
Eating and drinking	1.12	0.85	76
Socializing, relaxing, and leisure	4.65	5.29	114
Socializing and communicating	0.61	0.67	110
Watching television	2.75	3.38	123
Playing games (including computer games)	0.22	0.21	95
Computer use for leisure	0.22	0.25	114
Reading	0.30	0.13	43
Sports, exercise, and recreation	0.34	0.27	79
Religious and spiritual activities	0.15	0.29	193
Volunteering	0.15	0.16	107
Telephone calls	0.10	0.17	170
Traveling	1.21	1.19	98

Note: Hours per day do not add to 24.00 because not all activities are shown. Primary activities are those respondents identified as their main activity. Other activities done simultaneously are not included. The index is calculated by dividing time use of blacks by time use of the average person and multiplying by 100.
Source: Bureau of Labor Statistics, unpublished tables from the American Time Use Survey, Internet site http://www.bls.gov/tus/home.htm; calculations by New Strategist

Table 4.100 Time Use of Black Men, 2011

(average hours per day spent in primary activities by total and black men aged 15 or older, and index of black to total, by type of activity, 2011)

	total men	black men	index, black to total
Total, all activities	**24.00 hrs.**	**24.00 hrs.**	**100**
Personal care activities	9.23	9.40	102
Sleeping	8.62	8.71	101
Grooming	0.56	0.64	114
Household activities	1.36	1.06	78
Housework	0.27	0.23	85
Food preparation and cleanup	0.31	0.26	84
Lawn, garden, and houseplants	0.26	0.20	77
Animals and pets	0.08	0.03	38
Household management	0.15	0.11	73
Caring for and helping household members	0.27	0.18	67
Caring for and helping household children	0.21	0.12	57
Caring for and helping people in other households	0.15	0.11	73
Working and work-related activities	3.89	3.00	77
Educational activities	0.46	0.62	135
Consumer purchases	0.31	0.30	97
Eating and drinking	1.16	0.93	80
Socializing, relaxing, and leisure	4.88	5.86	120
Socializing and communicating	0.57	0.78	137
Watching television	2.99	3.71	124
Playing games (including computer games)	0.28	0.32	114
Computer use for leisure	0.26	0.35	135
Reading	0.24	0.11	46
Sports, exercise, and recreation	0.43	0.42	98
Religious and spiritual activities	0.12	0.22	183
Volunteering	0.13	0.13	100
Telephone calls	0.06	0.13	217
Traveling	1.25	1.26	101

Note: Hours per day do not add to 24.00 because not all activities are shown. Primary activities are those respondents identified as their main activity. Other activities done simultaneously are not included. The index is calculated by dividing time use of black men by time use of the average man and multiplying by 100.
Source: Bureau of Labor Statistics, unpublished tables from the American Time Use Survey, Internet site http://www.bls.gov/tus/home.htm; calculations by New Strategist

Table 4.101 Time Use of Black Women, 2011

(average hours per day spent in primary activities by total and black women aged 15 or older, and index of black to total, by type of activity, 2011)

	total women	black women	index, black to total
Total, all activities	**24.00 hrs.**	**24.00 hrs.**	**100**
Personal care activities	9.71	10.17	105
Sleeping	8.80	9.12	104
Grooming	0.82	0.96	117
Household activities	2.18	1.60	73
Housework	0.87	0.69	79
Food preparation and cleanup	0.79	0.70	89
Lawn, garden, and houseplants	0.13	0.05	38
Animals and pets	0.10	0.03	30
Household management	0.21	0.10	48
Caring for and helping household members	0.58	0.41	71
Caring for and helping household children	0.47	0.34	72
Caring for and helping people in other households	0.13	0.18	138
Working and work-related activities	2.73	2.74	100
Educational activities	0.42	0.55	131
Consumer purchases	0.43	0.34	79
Eating and drinking	1.09	0.78	72
Socializing, relaxing, and leisure	4.43	4.83	109
Socializing and communicating	0.66	0.58	88
Watching television	2.52	3.10	123
Playing games (including computer games)	0.16	0.12	75
Computer use for leisure	0.18	0.16	89
Reading	0.35	0.15	43
Sports, exercise, and recreation	0.25	0.14	56
Religious and spiritual activities	0.19	0.35	184
Volunteering	0.16	0.18	113
Telephone calls	0.13	0.20	154
Traveling	1.16	1.14	98

Note: Hours per day do not add to 24.00 because not all activities are shown. Primary activities are those respondents identified as their main activity. Other activities done simultaneously are not included. The index is calculated by dividing time use of black women by time use of the average woman and multiplying by 100.
Source: Bureau of Labor Statistics, unpublished tables from the American Time Use Survey, Internet site http://www.bls.gov/tus/home.htm; calculations by New Strategist

Table 4.102 Time Use of Blacks by Sex, 2011

(average hours per day spent in primary activities by black men and women aged 15 or older, and index of black women to men, by type of activity, 2011)

	black men	black women	index, women's time to men's
Total, all activities	**24.00 hrs.**	**24.00 hrs.**	**100**
Personal care activities	9.40	10.17	108
Sleeping	8.71	9.12	105
Grooming	0.64	0.96	150
Household activities	1.06	1.60	151
Housework	0.23	0.69	300
Food preparation and cleanup	0.26	0.70	269
Lawn, garden, and houseplants	0.20	0.05	25
Animals and pets	0.03	0.03	100
Household management	0.11	0.10	91
Caring for and helping household members	0.18	0.41	228
Caring for and helping household children	0.12	0.34	283
Caring for and helping people in other households	0.11	0.18	164
Working and work-related activities	3.00	2.74	91
Educational activities	0.62	0.55	89
Consumer purchases	0.30	0.34	113
Eating and drinking	0.93	0.78	84
Socializing, relaxing, and leisure	5.86	4.83	82
Socializing and communicating	0.78	0.58	74
Watching television	3.71	3.10	84
Playing games (including computer games)	0.32	0.12	38
Computer use for leisure	0.35	0.16	46
Reading	0.11	0.15	136
Sports, exercise, and recreation	0.42	0.14	33
Religious and spiritual activities	0.22	0.35	159
Volunteering	0.13	0.18	138
Telephone calls	0.13	0.20	154
Traveling	1.26	1.14	90

Note: Hours per day do not add to 24.00 because not all activities are shown. Primary activities are those respondents identified as their main activity. Other activities done simultaneously are not included. The index is calculated by dividing time use of black women by time use of black men and multiplying by 100.
Source: Bureau of Labor Statistics, unpublished tables from the American Time Use Survey, Internet site http://www.bls.gov/tus/ home.htm; calculations by New Strategist

Black Households Spend 74 Percent as Much as the Average Household

The nation's 15 million black households spent an average of $36,644 in 2011, according to the Bureau of Labor Statistics' Consumer Expenditure Survey. While the annual spending of black households (called consumer units by the Bureau of Labor Statistics) is less than the $49,705 spent by the average household, blacks spend more on some items.

One reason for the lower spending of blacks is that the most-affluent household type, married couples, is a minority of black households. Nevertheless blacks spend more than average on items such as pork, poultry, and fish. They are also big spenders on footwear, accounting for over 17 percent of consumer spending on shoes. Black households spend 7 percent more than average on soaps and laundry detergents and 41 percent more than average on rent.

■ Black spending is likely to approach or exceed the average on many more items in the years ahead.

Black households spend less than the average household

(average annual spending of total and black consumer units, 2011)

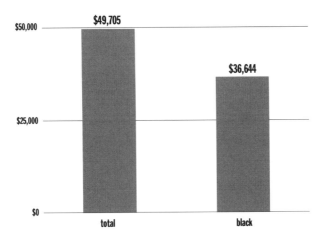

Table 4.103 Spending of Households Headed by Blacks, 2011

(average annual spending of total consumer units, and average annual, indexed, and market share of spending of consumer units headed by blacks, by product and service category, 2011)

	total consumer units	black consumer units average spending	black consumer units indexed spending	black consumer units market share
Number of consumer units (000s)	122,287	15,118	–	12.4%
Average number of persons per consumer unit	2.5	2.6	–	–
Average annual spending	**$49,705**	**$36,644**	**74**	**9.1%**
FOOD	**6,458**	**4,743**	**73**	**9.1**
Food at home	**3,838**	**2,989**	**78**	**9.6**
Cereals and bakery products	531	405	76	9.4
Cereals and cereal products	175	143	82	10.1
Bakery products	356	263	74	9.1
Meats, poultry, fish, and eggs	832	822	99	12.2
Beef	223	189	85	10.5
Pork	162	183	113	14.0
Other meats	123	86	70	8.6
Poultry	154	185	120	14.9
Fish and seafood	121	134	111	13.7
Eggs	50	46	92	11.4
Dairy products	407	246	60	7.5
Fresh milk and cream	150	98	65	8.1
Other dairy products	257	148	58	7.1
Fruits and vegetables	715	527	74	9.1
Fresh fruits	247	157	64	7.9
Fresh vegetables	224	145	65	8.0
Processed fruits	116	109	94	11.6
Processed vegetables	128	117	91	11.3
Other food at home	1,353	988	73	9.0
Sugar and other sweets	144	98	68	8.4
Fats and oils	110	94	85	10.6
Miscellaneous foods	690	502	73	9.0
Nonalcoholic beverages	361	280	78	9.6
Food prepared by consumer unit on trips	48	14	29	3.6
Food away from home	**2,620**	**1,754**	**67**	**8.3**
ALCOHOLIC BEVERAGES	**456**	**199**	**44**	**5.4**
HOUSING	**16,803**	**13,985**	**83**	**10.3**
Shelter	**9,825**	**8,111**	**83**	**10.2**
Owned dwellings	6,148	3,651	59	7.3
Mortgage interest and charges	3,184	2,151	68	8.4
Property taxes	1,845	930	50	6.2
Maintenance, repair, insurance, other expenses	1,120	570	51	6.3

	total consumer units	black consumer units		
		average spending	indexed spending	market share
Rented dwellings	$3,029	$4,268	141	17.4%
Other lodging	648	192	30	3.7
Utilities, fuels, and public services	**3,727**	**3,701**	**99**	**12.3**
Natural gas	420	429	102	12.6
Electricity	1,423	1,497	105	13.0
Fuel oil and other fuels	157	67	43	5.3
Telephone	1,226	1,242	101	12.5
Water and other public services	501	465	93	11.5
Household services	**1,122**	**810**	**72**	**8.9**
Personal services	398	307	77	9.5
Other household services	724	503	69	8.6
Housekeeping supplies	**615**	**426**	**69**	**8.6**
Laundry and cleaning supplies	145	155	107	13.2
Other household products	340	194	57	7.1
Postage and stationery	130	76	58	7.2
Household furnishings and equipment	**1,514**	**938**	**62**	**7.7**
Household textiles	109	52	48	5.9
Furniture	358	306	85	10.6
Floor coverings	20	10	50	6.2
Major appliances	194	152	78	9.7
Small appliances, misc. housewares	89	39	44	5.4
Miscellaneous household equipment	744	378	51	6.3
APPAREL AND RELATED SERVICES	**1,740**	**1,669**	**96**	**11.9**
Men and boys	**404**	**324**	**80**	**9.9**
Men, aged 16 or older	324	224	69	8.5
Boys, aged 2 to 15	80	99	124	15.3
Women and girls	**721**	**629**	**87**	**10.8**
Women, aged 16 or older	604	501	83	10.3
Girls, aged 2 to 15	117	128	109	13.5
Children under age 2	**68**	**77**	**113**	**14.0**
Footwear	**321**	**454**	**141**	**17.5**
Other apparel products and services	**226**	**185**	**82**	**10.1**
TRANSPORTATION	**8,293**	**5,944**	**72**	**8.9**
Vehicle purchases	**2,669**	**1,608**	**60**	**7.4**
Cars and trucks, new	1,265	634	50	6.2
Cars and trucks, used	1,339	959	72	8.9
Other vehicles	64	14	22	2.7
Gasoline and motor oil	**2,655**	**2,221**	**84**	**10.3**
Other vehicle expenses	**2,454**	**1,833**	**75**	**9.2**
Vehicle finance charges	233	194	83	10.3
Maintenance and repairs	805	587	73	9.0
Vehicle insurance	983	767	78	9.6
Vehicle rentals, leases, licenses, other charges	433	285	66	8.1
Public transportation	**516**	**283**	**55**	**6.8**

	total consumer units	black consumer units		
		average spending	indexed spending	market share
HEALTH CARE	**$3,313**	**$1,897**	**57**	**7.1%**
Health insurance	1,922	1,238	64	8.0
Medical services	768	300	39	4.8
Drugs	489	300	61	7.6
Medical supplies	134	59	44	5.4
ENTERTAINMENT	**2,572**	**1,432**	**56**	**6.9**
Fees and admissions	594	201	34	4.2
Audio and visual equipment and services	977	909	93	11.5
Pets, toys, and playground equipment	631	212	34	4.2
Other entertainment products and services	370	110	30	3.7
PERSONAL CARE PRODUCTS AND SERVICES	**634**	**533**	**84**	**10.4**
READING	**115**	**48**	**42**	**5.2**
EDUCATION	**1,051**	**479**	**46**	**5.6**
TOBACCO PRODUCTS AND SMOKING SUPPLIES	**351**	**260**	**74**	**9.2**
MISCELLANEOUS	**775**	**521**	**67**	**8.3**
CASH CONTRIBUTIONS	**1,721**	**1,341**	**78**	**9.6**
PERSONAL INSURANCE AND PENSIONS	**5,424**	**3,593**	**66**	**8.2**
Life and other personal insurance	317	250	79	9.7
Pensions and Social Security	5,106	3,344	65	8.1
PERSONAL TAXES	**2,012**	**500**	**25**	**3.1**
Federal income taxes	1,370	198	14	1.8
State and local income taxes	505	240	48	5.9
Other taxes	136	63	46	5.7
GIFTS FOR PEOPLE IN OTHER HOUSEHOLDS	**1,037**	**495**	**48**	**5.9**

Definitions: The index compares black to average consumer unit spending by dividing black spending by average spending in each category and multiplying by 100. An index of 125 means black spending is 25 percent above average, while an index of 75 means black spending is 25 percent below average. The market share is the percentage of total spending on a product or service category accounted for by consumer units headed by blacks.

Note: The Bureau of Labor Statistics uses consumer unit rather than household as the sampling unit in the Consumer Expenditure Survey. For the definition of consumer unit, see the glossary. Spending by category does not add to total spending because gift spending is also included in the preceding product and service categories and personal taxes are not included in the total. "–" means not applicable or sample is too small to make a reliable estimate.

Source: Bureau of Labor Statistics, 2011 Consumer Expenditure Survey, Internet site http://www.bls.gov/cex/; calculations by New Strategist

Black Households Have Little Wealth

The median net worth (assets minus debts) of black households was $6,314 in 2011, well below the $68,828 net worth of the average American household. Not only is the net worth of black households below average, but it fell by a steep 50 percent between 2005 and 2011, after adjusting for inflation. This decline exceeded the 36 percent loss for the average household during those years, according to the Census Bureau's Survey of Income and Program Participation.

Blacks are less likely than the average household to own most assets, the most important being a home. Only 44 percent of black households own a home compared with 65 percent of all households. Because housing equity accounts for a large share of Americans' net worth, the low homeownership rate of black households largely explains their below average net worth. Among black homeowners, median housing equity was $50,000 in 2011, substantially less than the $80,000 equity of the average homeowner.

Black households are less likely than average to be in debt (62 versus 69 percent). Among black households with debt, the median amount owed was just $35,000 compared with $70,000 owed by the average household. Blacks are more likely than average to have "other" debt, however, a category that includes student loans.

■ Eighty-four percent of blacks aged 65 or older receive income from Social Security, 29 percent from pensions, and 20 percent from earnings.

The median net worth of black households is less than one-tenth the overall median

(median net worth of total and black households, 2011)

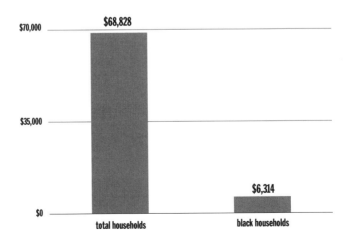

Table 4.104 Median Household Net Worth of Total and Black Households, 2005 and 2011

(median net worth of total and black households, 2005 and 2011; percent change, 2005–11; in 2011 dollars)

	2011	2005	percent change 2005–11
Total households	**$68,828**	**$107,344**	**–35.9%**
Black households	6,314	12,684	–50.2%

Note: Blacks are those who identify themselves as being black alone.
Source: Census Bureau, Wealth and Asset Ownership, Survey of Income and Program Participation, Internet site http://www
.census.gov/people/wealth/; calculations by New Strategist

Table 4.105 Distribution of Total and Black Households by Net Worth, 2011

(number of total and black households, median net worth of total and black households, and percent distribution of total and black households by net worth, 2011)

	total households	black households number	index
Number of households	**118,689,091**	**15,056,795**	–
Median net worth	**$68,828**	**$6,314**	**9**
DISTRIBUTION OF HOUSEHOLDS BY NET WORTH			
Total households	**100.0%**	**100.0%**	–
Zero or negative	18.1	33.5	185
$1 to $4,999	9.1	14.6	160
$5,000 to $9,999	4.8	7.0	146
$10,000 to $24,999	6.6	7.9	120
$25,000 to $49,999	6.9	6.6	96
$50,000 to $99,999	10.4	9.0	87
$100,000 to $249,999	17.9	12.6	70
$250,000 to $499,999	12.6	5.6	44
$500,000 or more	13.5	3.3	24

Note: Blacks are those who identify themselves as being black alone. The index is calculated by dividing the black figure by the total figure and multiplying by 100. "–" means not applicable.
Source: Census Bureau, Wealth and Asset Ownership, Survey of Income and Program Participation, Internet site http://www
.census.gov/people/wealth/; calculations by New Strategist

Table 4.106 Percent of Total and Black Households Owning Assets, 2011

(percent of total and black households owning selected assets, and index of black to total, 2011)

	total households	black households	
		percent	index
PERCENT WITH ASSET			
Interest earning asset at financial institution	69.8%	51.9%	74
Regular checking account	29.0	24.6	85
Stocks and mutal fund shares	19.6	6.4	33
Own business	13.8	7.4	54
Motor vehicles	84.7	70.5	83
Own home	65.3	43.8	67
Rental property	5.5	2.9	53
IRA or KEOGH account	28.9	11.2	39
401(k) and thrift savings	42.1	31.7	75

Note: Blacks are those who identify themselves as being black alone. The index is calculated by dividing the black figure by the total figure and multiplying by 100.
Source: Census Bureau, Wealth and Asset Ownership, Survey of Income and Program Participation, Internet site http://www .census.gov/people/wealth/; calculations by New Strategist

Table 4.107 Median Value or Equity of Assets Owned by Total and Black Households, 2011

(median value or equity of assets owned by total and black households, and index of black to total, 2011)

	total households	black households	
		median	index
MEDIAN VALUE OF ASSETS			
Interest earning asset at financial institution	$2,450	$500	20
Regular checking account	600	242	40
Stocks and mutal fund shares	20,000	4,750	24
Own business (equity)	8,000	2,000	25
Motor vehicles (equity)	6,824	3,916	57
Own home (equity)	80,000	50,000	63
Rental property (equity)	180,000	155,000	86
IRA or KEOGH account	34,000	15,000	44
401(k) and thrift savings	30,000	12,000	40

Note: Blacks are those who identify themselves as being black alone. The index is calculated by dividing the black figure by the total figure and multiplying by 100.
Source: Census Bureau, Wealth and Asset Ownership, Survey of Income and Program Participation, Internet site http://www .census.gov/people/wealth/; calculations by New Strategist

Table 4.108 Asset Ownership of Black Households, 2005 and 2011

(percent of black households owning financial assets, 2005 and 2011; percentage point change, 2005–11)

PERCENT OWNING ASSET	2011	2005	percentage point change
Interest earning asset at financial institution	51.9%	51.9%	0.0
Regular checking account	24.6	26.0	−1.4
Stocks and mutal fund shares	6.4	8.5	−2.1
Own business	7.4	8.5	−1.1
Motor vehicles	70.5	69.8	0.7
Own home	43.8	46.1	−2.3
Rental property	2.9	2.4	0.5
IRA or KEOGH account	11.2	11.9	−0.7
401(k) and thrift savings	31.7	30.2	1.5

Note: Blacks are those who identify themselves as being black alone.
Source: Census Bureau, Wealth and Asset Ownership, Survey of Income and Program Participation, Internet site http://www .census.gov/people/wealth/; calculations by New Strategist

Table 4.109 Median Value or Equity of Assets Owned by Black Households, 2005 and 2011

(median value or equity of assets owned by black households, 2005 and 2011; percent change, 2005–11; in 2011 dollars)

MEDIAN VALUE OF ASSETS	2011	2005	percent change
Interest earning asset at financial institution	$500	$1,037	−51.8%
Regular checking account	242	346	−30.0
Stocks and mutal fund shares	4,750	14,714	−67.7
Own business (equity)	2,000	5,759	−65.3
Motor vehicles (equity)	3,916	2,958	32.4
Own home (equity)	50,000	80,623	−38.0
Rental property (equity)	155,000	92,141	68.2
IRA or KEOGH account	15,000	17,276	−13.2
401(k) and thrift savings	12,000	14,973	−19.9

Note: Blacks are those who identify themselves as being black alone.
Source: Census Bureau, Wealth and Asset Ownership, Survey of Income and Program Participation, Internet site http://www .census.gov/people/wealth/; calculations by New Strategist

Table 4.110 Percent of Total and Black Households with Debt, 2011

(percent of total and black households with debt, and index of black to total, 2011)

	total households	black households percent	index
PERCENT WITH DEBT			
Total debt	**69.0%**	**62.0%**	**90**
Secured debt	55.3	44.1	80
Home debt	40.5	29.0	72
Business debt	4.1	2.0	49
Vehicle debt	30.4	25.3	83
Unsecured debt	46.2	44.3	96
Credit card debt	38.3	35.1	92
Loans	6.8	6.4	94
Other debt	18.6	21.2	114

Note: "Other debt" includes student loans. Blacks are those who identify themselves as being black alone. The index is calculated by dividing the black figure by the total figure and multiplying by 100.
Source: Census Bureau, Wealth and Asset Ownership, Survey of Income and Program Participation, Internet site http://www .census.gov/people/wealth/; calculations by New Strategist

Table 4.111 Median Debt of Total and Black Households, 2011

(median amount of debt for total and black households with debt, and index of black to total, 2011)

	total households	black households median	index
MEDIAN DEBT			
Total debt	**$70,000**	**$35,000**	**50**
Secured debt	91,000	60,000	66
Home debt	117,000	97,000	83
Business debt	25,000	18,000	72
Vehicle debt	10,000	9,000	90
Unsecured debt	7,000	6,800	97
Credit card debt	3,500	3,000	86
Loans	7,000	5,000	71
Other debt	10,000	10,000	100

Note: "Other debt" includes student loans. Blacks are those who identify themselves as being black alone. The index is calculated by dividing the black figure by the total figure and multiplying by 100.
Source: Census Bureau, Wealth and Asset Ownership, Survey of Income and Program Participation, Internet site http://www .census.gov/people/wealth/; calculations by New Strategist

Table 4.112 Total People and Blacks Aged 65 or Older Receiving Income by Source, 2011

(number of total people and blacks aged 65 or older receiving income, percent of blacks receiving income, and black share of total, 2011; ranked by number of total people receiving type of income; people in thousands as of 2012)

	total people receiving income	blacks receiving income		
		number	percent	black share of total
Total people aged 65 or older	**40,195**	**3,519**	**100.0%**	**8.8%**
Social Security	35,169	2,966	84.3	8.4
Interest	19,862	865	24.6	4.4
Retirement income	14,325	1,119	31.8	7.8
Pension income	12,460	1,011	28.7	8.1
Earnings	8,648	709	20.1	8.2
Dividends	7,584	176	5.0	2.3
Rents, royalties, estates, or trusts	3,103	129	3.7	4.2
Survivor benefits	1,859	116	3.3	6.2
Veteran's benefits	1,299	99	2.8	7.6
SSI (Supplemental Security Income)	1,297	263	7.5	20.3

Note: Blacks are those who identify themselves as being of the race alone and those who identify themselves as being of the race in combination with other races.
Source: Bureau of the Census, 2012 Current Population Survey Annual Social and Economic Supplement, Internet site http://www.census.gov/hhes/www/cpstables/032012/perinc/toc.htm; calculations by New Strategist

Table 4.113 Median Income of Total People and Blacks Aged 65 or Older by Source, 2011

(median income received by total people and blacks aged 65 or older and index of black to total, by type of income, 2011)

	median income for total people receiving income	median income for blacks receiving income	index, black to total
Total people aged 65 or older	**$19,939**	**$15,875**	**80**
Social Security	13,376	11,998	90
Interest	1,590	1,447	91
Retirement income	12,282	12,239	100
Pension income	12,458	12,528	101
Earnings	24,893	23,955	96
Dividends	2,023	1,631	81
Rents, royalties, estates, or trusts	3,855	3,724	97
Survivor benefits	7,913	5,224	66
Veteran's benefits	8,770	10,381	118
SSI (Supplemental Security Income)	5,322	3,946	74

Note: Blacks are those who identify themselves as being of the race alone and those who identify themselves as being of the race in combination with other races. The index is calculated by dividing the black figure by the total figure and multiplying by 100.
Source: Bureau of the Census, 2012 Current Population Survey Annual Social and Economic Supplement, Internet site http://www.census.gov/hhes/www/cpstables/032012/perinc/toc.htm; calculations by New Strategist

5

Hispanics

■ Hispanics are the largest minority in the United States, numbering 52 million in 2011 and accounting for 17 percent of the total population.

■ Only 65 percent of Hispanics aged 25 or older have a high school diploma.

■ Hispanics are more likely to be without health insurance than any other racial or ethnic group. In 2011, a substantial 30 percent did not have health insurance.

■ Forty-six percent of the nation's Hispanic households owned their home in 2012.

■ The $38,624 median income of Hispanic households in 2011 was 8 percent lower than in 2007, after adjusting for inflation. Behind the decline was job loss caused by the Great Recession.

■ Only 21 percent of Hispanic workers are in managerial or professional jobs, the figure ranging from a low of 17 percent among Mexican Americans to a high of 34 percent among Cuban Americans.

■ Forty-six percent of Hispanic households include children under age 18, a larger share than any other racial or ethnic group.

■ Twenty-eight percent of Hispanics live in California, where they account for 38 percent of the state's population.

■ Hispanic households spent an average of $42,086 in 2011. They spend 19 percent more than the average household on fresh fruit.

■ At just $7,683 in 2011, the median net worth of Hispanic households is far below the $68,828 median net worth of the average household.

Hispanics account for 17 percent of the U.S. population

(percent distribution of people by race and Hispanic origin, 2011)

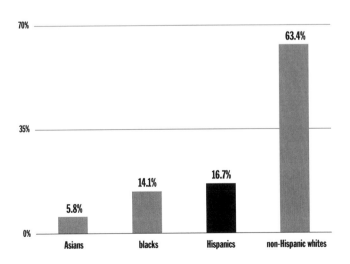

Hispanic Educational Attainment Lags Behind that of Asians, Blacks, and Non-Hispanic Whites

Hispanics are less educated than the average American because many are immigrants who came to the United States as adults with few years of schooling. Only 65 percent of Hispanics have a high school diploma versus 88 percent of the total population. Among Hispanics of Mexican origin, only 54 percent are high school graduates. Among those of Cuban descent, the figure is 75 percent.

Only 15 percent of Hispanics have a college degree, versus 31 percent of the total population. In 2011, nearly 3 million Hispanics were enrolled in college, accounting for 14 percent of the nation's college students. Many Hispanic college students (43 percent) attend two-year schools.

Hispanics earned 13 percent of associate's degrees awarded in 2010–11. They earned 9 percent of bachelor's degrees, 6 percent of master's degrees, and 5 percent of doctoral and first-professional degrees.

■ Although improving, the educational attainment of Hispanics will remain below average as long as poorly educated immigrants make up a large proportion of the Hispanic population.

Many Hispanics have not graduated from high school

(percent of Hispanics aged 25 or older by educational attainment, 2012)

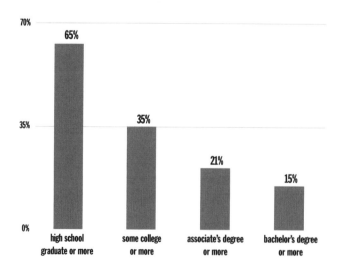

Table 5.1 Educational Attainment of Hispanics by Age, 2012

(number and percent distribution of Hispanics aged 25 or older by educational attainment and age, 2012; numbers in thousands)

	total	25 to 34	35 to 44	45 to 54	55 to 64	65 or older
Total Hispanics	**28,445**	**8,539**	**7,531**	**5,793**	**3,545**	**3,037**
Not a high school graduate	9,956	2,433	2,582	2,038	1,338	1,565
High school graduate only	8,538	2,793	2,270	1,686	1,037	751
Some college, no degree	3,887	1,385	1,011	777	467	247
Associate's degree	1,930	635	528	421	222	122
Bachelor's degree	2,935	998	807	603	312	215
Master's degree	903	216	269	193	135	87
Professional degree	169	53	32	47	16	21
Doctoral degree	126	27	30	28	16	25
High school graduate or more	18,488	6,107	4,947	3,755	2,205	1,468
Some college or more	9,950	3,314	2,677	2,069	1,168	717
Associate's degree or more	6,063	1,929	1,666	1,292	701	470
Bachelor's degree or more	4,133	1,294	1,138	871	479	348
PERCENT DISTRIBUTION						
Total Hispanics	**100.0%**	**100.0%**	**100.0%**	**100.0%**	**100.0%**	**100.0%**
Not a high school graduate	35.0	28.5	34.3	35.2	37.7	51.5
High school graduate only	30.0	32.7	30.1	29.1	29.3	24.7
Some college, no degree	13.7	16.2	13.4	13.4	13.2	8.1
Associate's degree	6.8	7.4	7.0	7.3	6.3	4.0
Bachelor's degree	10.3	11.7	10.7	10.4	8.8	7.1
Master's degree	3.2	2.5	3.6	3.3	3.8	2.9
Professional degree	0.6	0.6	0.4	0.8	0.5	0.7
Doctoral degree	0.4	0.3	0.4	0.5	0.5	0.8
High school graduate or more	65.0	71.5	65.7	64.8	62.2	48.3
Some college or more	35.0	38.8	35.5	35.7	32.9	23.6
Associate's degree or more	21.3	22.6	22.1	22.3	19.8	15.5
Bachelor's degree or more	14.5	15.2	15.1	15.0	13.5	11.5

Source: Bureau of the Census, Educational Attainment in the United States: 2012, Internet site http://www.census.gov/hhes/ socdemo/education/data/cps/2012/tables.html; calculations by New Strategist

Table 5.2 Educational Attainment of Hispanic Men by Age, 2012

(number and percent distribution of Hispanic men aged 25 or older by educational attainment and age, 2012; numbers in thousands)

	total	25 to 34	35 to 44	45 to 54	55 to 64	65 or older
Total Hispanic men	**14,165**	**4,456**	**3,823**	**2,898**	**1,687**	**1,299**
Not a high school graduate	5,102	1,371	1,356	1,113	611	651
High school graduate only	4,443	1,504	1,245	861	533	301
Some college, no degree	1,857	706	468	361	212	111
Associate's degree	884	308	251	169	104	51
Bachelor's degree	1,328	447	355	270	143	112
Master's degree	376	73	113	80	67	44
Professional degree	104	33	20	29	10	13
Doctoral degree	70	13	16	15	7	18
High school graduate or more	9,062	3,084	2,468	1,785	1,076	650
Some college or more	4,619	1,580	1,223	924	543	349
Associate's degree or more	2,762	874	755	563	331	238
Bachelor's degree or more	1,878	566	504	394	227	187

PERCENT DISTRIBUTION

	total	25 to 34	35 to 44	45 to 54	55 to 64	65 or older
Total Hispanic men	**100.0%**	**100.0%**	**100.0%**	**100.0%**	**100.0%**	**100.0%**
Not a high school graduate	36.0	30.8	35.5	38.4	36.2	50.1
High school graduate only	31.4	33.8	32.6	29.7	31.6	23.2
Some college, no degree	13.1	15.8	12.2	12.5	12.6	8.5
Associate's degree	6.2	6.9	6.6	5.8	6.2	3.9
Bachelor's degree	9.4	10.0	9.3	9.3	8.5	8.6
Master's degree	2.7	1.6	3.0	2.8	4.0	3.4
Professional degree	0.7	0.7	0.5	1.0	0.6	1.0
Doctoral degree	0.5	0.3	0.4	0.5	0.4	1.4
High school graduate or more	64.0	69.2	64.6	61.6	63.8	50.0
Some college or more	32.6	35.5	32.0	31.9	32.2	26.9
Associate's degree or more	19.5	19.6	19.7	19.4	19.6	18.3
Bachelor's degree or more	13.3	12.7	13.2	13.6	13.5	14.4

Source: Bureau of the Census, Educational Attainment in the United States: 2012, Internet site http://www.census.gov/hhes/socdemo/education/data/cps/2012/tables.html; calculations by New Strategist

Table 5.3 Educational Attainment of Hispanic Women by Age, 2012

(number and percent distribution of Hispanic women aged 25 or older by educational attainment and age, 2012; numbers in thousands)

	total	25 to 34	35 to 44	45 to 54	55 to 64	65 or older
Total Hispanic women	**14,281**	**4,083**	**3,708**	**2,895**	**1,858**	**1,737**
Not a high school graduate	4,854	1,062	1,227	927	729	916
High school graduate only	4,094	1,289	1,027	825	504	450
Some college, no degree	2,031	679	545	415	255	137
Associate's degree	1,047	328	277	253	117	73
Bachelor's degree	1,608	550	453	333	170	102
Master's degree	527	145	157	113	70	44
Professional degree	65	20	13	18	6	8
Doctoral degree	55	13	13	13	9	7
High school graduate or more	9,427	3,024	2,485	1,970	1,131	821
Some college or more	5,333	1,735	1,458	1,145	627	371
Associate's degree or more	3,302	1,056	913	730	372	234
Bachelor's degree or more	2,255	728	636	477	255	161

PERCENT DISTRIBUTION

	total	25 to 34	35 to 44	45 to 54	55 to 64	65 or older
Total Hispanic women	**100.0%**	**100.0%**	**100.0%**	**100.0%**	**100.0%**	**100.0%**
Not a high school graduate	34.0	26.0	33.1	32.0	39.2	52.7
High school graduate only	28.7	31.6	27.7	28.5	27.1	25.9
Some college, no degree	14.2	16.6	14.7	14.3	13.7	7.9
Associate's degree	7.3	8.0	7.5	8.7	6.3	4.2
Bachelor's degree	11.3	13.5	12.2	11.5	9.1	5.9
Master's degree	3.7	3.6	4.2	3.9	3.8	2.5
Professional degree	0.5	0.5	0.4	0.6	0.3	0.5
Doctoral degree	0.4	0.3	0.4	0.4	0.5	0.4
High school graduate or more	66.0	74.1	67.0	68.0	60.9	47.3
Some college or more	37.3	42.5	39.3	39.6	33.7	21.4
Associate's degree or more	23.1	25.9	24.6	25.2	20.0	13.5
Bachelor's degree or more	15.8	17.8	17.2	16.5	13.7	9.3

Source: Bureau of the Census, Educational Attainment in the United States: 2012, Internet site http://www.census.gov/hhes/ socdemo/education/data/cps/2012/tables.html; calculations by New Strategist

Table 5.4 Educational Attainment of Hispanics by Ethnicity, 2006–10

(number and percent distribution of Hispanics aged 25 or older by educational attainment and ethnicity, 2006–10; numbers in thousands)

	total	Mexican	Puerto Rican	Cuban	other Hispanic
Total Hispanics	**25,564**	**15,541**	**2,443**	**1,176**	**6,404**
Not a high school graduate	9,834	6,923	651	282	1,979
High school graduate only	6,862	4,127	730	325	1,680
Some college or associate's degree	5,538	3,070	675	274	1,519
Bachelor's degree	2,274	1,018	261	183	813
Graduate or professional degree	1,055	403	127	111	414
High school graduate or more	15,729	8,618	1,793	894	4,425
Some college or more	8,867	4,491	1,063	568	2,745
Bachelor's degree or more	3,329	1,421	388	294	1,226
PERCENT DISTRIBUTION					
Total Hispanics	**100.0 %**	**100.0%**	**100.0%**	**100.0%**	**100.0%**
Not a high school graduate	39.4	45.8	27.4	24.6	31.2
High school graduate only	28.2	27.9	31.2	28.1	27.8
Some college or associate's degree	19.8	17.7	25.9	22.2	22.2
Bachelor's degree	8.7	6.2	10.7	16.0	12.6
Graduate or professional degree	3.9	2.4	4.8	9.0	6.1
High school graduate or more	60.6	54.2	72.6	75.4	68.8
Some college or more	32.4	26.3	41.4	47.2	40.9
Bachelor's degree or more	12.5	8.6	15.5	25.0	18.7

Source: Bureau of the Census, 2006–10 American Community Survey, Internet site http://factfinder2.census.gov/faces/nav/jsf/pages/index.xhtml; calculations by New Strategist

Table 5.5 Educational Attainment of Hispanics by Region, 2006–10

(total number of Hispanics aged 25 or older and percent distribution by educational attainment and by region, 2006–10; numbers in thousands)

	total	Northeast	Midwest	South	West
Total Hispanics	**25,564**	**3,760**	**2,191**	**9,330**	**10,282**
Not a high school graduate	9,834	1,272	846	3,489	4,228
High school graduate only	6,862	1,119	626	2,467	2,651
Some college, no degree	4,151	573	334	1,469	1,774
Associate's degree	1,387	215	107	522	544
Bachelor's degree	2,274	384	186	946	759
Graduate degree	1,055	199	92	438	326
PERECENT DISTRIBUTION					
High school graduate or more	61.5%	66.2%	61.4%	62.6%	58.9%
Some college or more	34.7	36.4	32.8	36.2	33.1
Associate's degree or more	18.4	21.2	17.6	20.4	15.8
Bachelor's degree or more	13.0	15.5	12.7	14.8	10.6

Source: Bureau of the Census, 2006–10 American Community Survey, Internet site http://factfinder2.census.gov/faces/nav/jsf/pages/index.xhtml; calculations by New Strategist

Table 5.6 School Enrollment of Hispanics, 2011

(total number of people aged 3 or older enrolled in school, number of Hispanics enrolled, and Hispanic share of total, by age, October 2011; numbers in thousands)

	total	Hispanic number	Hispanic share of total
Total aged 3 or older	**79,043**	**16,131**	**20.4%**
Aged 3 to 4	4,597	956	20.8
Aged 5 to 6	8,009	2,050	25.6
Aged 7 to 9	12,319	3,005	24.4
Aged 10 to 13	15,941	3,506	22.0
Aged 14 to 15	7,825	1,604	20.5
Aged 16 to 17	7,906	1,591	20.1
Aged 18 to 19	6,017	1,136	18.9
Aged 20 to 21	4,618	775	16.8
Aged 22 to 24	3,961	598	15.1
Aged 25 to 29	3,139	429	13.7
Aged 30 to 34	1,571	183	11.6
Aged 35 to 44	1,688	186	11.0
Aged 45 to 54	1,012	73	7.2
Aged 55 or older	438	39	8.9

Source: Bureau of the Census, School Enrollment, CPS October 2011—Detailed Tables, Internet site http://www.census.gov/hhes/school/data/cps/2011/tables.html; calculations by New Strategist

Table 5.7 School Enrollment of Hispanics by Age and Sex, 2011

(number and percent of Hispanics aged 3 or older enrolled in school, by age and sex, October 2011; numbers in thousands)

	total		female		male	
	number	percent	number	percent	number	percent
Total Hispanics enrolled	**16,131**	**34.0%**	**7,860**	**34.1%**	**8,271**	**33.9%**
Aged 3 to 4	956	41.6	448	39.6	508	43.6
Aged 5 to 6	2,050	95.6	982	95.3	1,068	95.9
Aged 7 to 9	3,005	98.2	1,478	97.6	1,527	98.8
Aged 10 to 13	3,506	98.5	1,701	98.2	1,805	98.8
Aged 14 to 15	1,604	98.2	777	97.6	827	98.7
Aged 16 to 17	1,591	94.6	765	94.6	826	94.6
Aged 18 to 19	1,136	65.2	556	70.3	580	61.0
Aged 20 to 21	775	45.7	377	48.8	397	43.1
Aged 22 to 24	598	23.6	309	26.6	289	21.0
Aged 25 to 29	429	10.5	209	11.2	220	9.9
Aged 30 to 34	183	4.5	109	5.8	73	3.4
Aged 35 to 44	186	2.6	85	2.5	101	2.7
Aged 45 to 54	73	1.3	39	1.4	34	1.2
Aged 55 or older	39	0.6	24	0.7	15	0.5

Source: Bureau of the Census, School Enrollment, CPS October 2011—Detailed Tables, Internet site http://www.census.gov/hhes/school/data/cps/2011/tables.html; calculations by New Strategist

Table 5.8 Hispanic College Enrollment Rate, 2000 to 2011

(percentage of total people and Hispanics aged 16 to 24 who graduated from high school in the previous 12 months and were enrolled in college as of October, and index of Hispanic to total, 2000 to 2011; percentage point change in enrollment rate for selected years)

	total	Hispanic	index, Hispanic to total
2011	68.2%	66.6%	98
2010	68.1	59.7	88
2009	70.1	59.3	85
2008	68.6	63.9	93
2007	67.2	64.0	95
2006	66.0	57.9	88
2005	68.6	54.0	79
2004	66.7	61.8	93
2003	63.9	58.6	92
2002	65.2	53.6	82
2001	61.8	51.7	84
2000	63.3	52.9	84

PERCENTAGE POINT CHANGE

2000 to 2011	4.9	13.7	–

Note: The index is calculated by dividing the Hispanic figure by the total figure and multiplying by 100. "–" means not applicable.
Source: National Center for Education Statistics, Digest of Education Statistics 2012, Internet site ces.ed.gov/programs/digest/2012menu_tables.asp; calculations by New Strategist

Table 5.9 College Enrollment of Hispanics by Age, 2011

(total number of people aged 15 or older enrolled in college, number of Hispanics enrolled, and Hispanic share of total, by age, 2011; numbers in thousands)

		Hispanic	
	total	number	share of total
Total enrolled in college	**20,397**	**2,953**	**14.5%**
Under age 20	4,446	801	18.0
Aged 20 to 21	4,460	741	16.6
Aged 22 to 24	3,869	574	14.8
Aged 25 to 29	3,066	407	13.3
Aged 30 or older	4,559	431	9.5

Source: Bureau of the Census, School Enrollment, CPS October 2011—Detailed Tables, Internet site http://www.census.gov/ hhes/school/data/cps/2011/tables.html; calculations by New Strategist

Table 5.10 College Enrollment of Hispanics by Type of School and Sex, 2011

(number and percent distribution of Hispanics aged 15 or older enrolled in college by type of school and sex, and female share of total, 2011; numbers in thousands)

	total		men		women		
	number	percent distribution	number	percent distribution	number	percent distribution	share of total
Total Hispanics enrolled	**2,953**	**100.0%**	**1,438**	**100.0%**	**1,515**	**100.0%**	**51.3%**
Two-year undergraduate program	1,267	42.9	621	43.2	646	42.6	51.0
Four-year undergraduate program	1,393	47.2	649	45.1	745	49.2	53.5
Graduate school	292	9.9	168	11.7	124	8.2	42.5

Source: Bureau of the Census, School Enrollment, CPS October 2011—Detailed Tables, Internet site http://www.census.gov/ hhes/school/data/cps/2011/tables.html; calculations by New Strategist

Table 5.11 Associate's Degrees Earned by Hispanics by Field of Study, 2010–11

(total number of associate's degrees conferred and number and percent earned by Hispanics, by field of study, 2010–11)

	total	earned by Hispanics	
		number	share of total
Total associate's degrees	**942,327**	**125,616**	**13.3%**
Agriculture and natural resources	6,425	209	3.3
Architecture and related programs	569	161	28.3
Area, ethnic, and cultural studies	209	38	18.2
Biological and biomedical sciences	3,245	653	20.1
Business	139,986	16,601	11.9
Communication, journalism, and related programs	3,051	506	16.6
Communications technologies	4,209	414	9.8
Computer and information sciences	37,677	3,730	9.9
Construction trades	5,402	385	7.1
Education	20,459	2,952	14.4
Engineering	2,825	367	13.0
Engineering technologies	35,521	3,958	11.1
English language and literature/letters	2,019	476	23.6
Family and consumer sciences	8,532	1,602	18.8
Foreign languages and literatures	1,876	421	22.4
Health professions and related sciences	201,831	19,513	9.7
Homeland security, law enforcement, and firefighting	44,923	7,691	17.1
Legal professions and studies	11,620	1,534	13.2
Liberal arts and sciences, general studies, and humanities	306,670	47,746	15.6
Library science	160	20	12.5
Mathematics and statistics	1,644	385	23.4
Mechanic and repair technologies	19,969	2,493	12.5
Military technologies	856	110	12.9
Multi/interdisciplinary studies	23,729	4,038	17.0
Parks, recreation, leisure, and fitness	2,366	372	15.7
Philosophy and religion	283	53	18.7
Physical sciences	5,078	644	12.7
Precision production trades	3,254	216	6.6
Psychology	3,866	1,003	25.9
Public administration and social services	7,472	1,040	13.9
Social sciences and history	12,767	3,056	23.9
Theology and religious vocations	758	36	4.7
Transportation and material moving	1,697	253	14.9
Visual and performing arts	21,379	2,940	13.8

Source: National Center for Education Statistics, Digest of Education Statistics 2012, Internet site http://nces.ed.gov/programs/digest/2012menu_tables.asp; calculations by New Strategist

Table 5.12 Bachelor's Degrees Earned by Hispanics by Field of Study, 2010–11

(total number of bachelor's degrees conferred and number and percent earned by Hispanics, by field of study, 2010–11)

	total	earned by Hispanics number	earned by Hispanics share of total
Total bachelor's degrees	**1,715,913**	**154,063**	**9.0%**
Agriculture and natural resources	28,623	1,469	5.1
Architecture and related programs	9,832	1,228	12.5
Area, ethnic, and cultural studies	9,100	1,446	15.9
Biological and biomedical sciences	90,003	6,960	7.7
Business	365,093	32,394	8.9
Communication, journalism, and related programs	83,274	6,958	8.4
Communications technologies	4,858	494	10.2
Computer and information sciences	43,072	3,390	7.9
Construction trades	328	11	3.4
Education	103,992	6,585	6.3
Engineering	76,376	5,549	7.3
Engineering technologies	16,187	1,229	7.6
English language and literature/letters	52,744	4,507	8.5
Family and consumer sciences	22,444	1,837	8.2
Foreign languages, literatures, and linguistics	21,706	3,684	17.0
Health professions and related sciences	143,430	9,882	6.9
Homeland security, law enforcement, and firefighting	47,602	7,241	15.2
Legal professions and studies	4,429	547	12.4
Liberal arts and sciences, general studies, and humanities	46,727	4,911	10.5
Library science	96	3	3.1
Mathematics and statistics	17,182	1,158	6.7
Mechanic and repair technologies	226	18	8.0
Military technologies	64	2	3.1
Multi/interdisciplinary studies	42,228	5,254	12.4
Parks, recreation, leisure, and fitness	35,924	2,763	7.7
Philosophy and religion	12,836	970	7.6
Physical sciences	24,712	1,466	5.9
Precision production trades	43	4	9.3
Psychology	100,893	11,629	11.5
Public administration and social services	26,774	3,305	12.3
Social sciences and history	177,144	18,108	10.2
Theology and religious vocations	9,074	380	4.2
Transportation and material moving	4,941	379	7.7
Visual and performing arts	93,956	8,302	8.8

Source: National Center for Education Statistics, Digest of Education Statistics 2012, Internet site http://nces.ed.gov/programs/digest/2012menu_tables.asp; calculations by New Strategist

Table 5.13 Master's Degrees Earned by Hispanics by Field of Study, 2010–11

(total number of master's degrees conferred and number and percent earned by Hispanics, by field of study, 2010–11)

	total	earned by Hispanics number	earned by Hispanics share of total
Total master's degrees	**730,635**	**46,787**	**6.4%**
Agriculture and natural resources	5,773	222	3.8
Architecture and related programs	7,788	538	6.9
Area, ethnic, and cultural studies	1,914	200	10.4
Biological and biomedical sciences	11,327	600	5.3
Business	187,213	11,680	6.2
Communication, journalism, and related programs	8,303	577	6.9
Communications technologies	502	23	4.6
Computer and information sciences	19,446	688	3.5
Education	185,009	12,925	7.0
Engineering	38,719	1,547	4.0
Engineering technologies	4,515	220	4.9
English language and literature/letters	9,476	566	6.0
Family and consumer sciences	2,918	152	5.2
Foreign languages, literatures, and linguistics	3,727	592	15.9
Health professions and related sciences	75,579	4,547	6.0
Homeland security, law enforcement, and firefighting	7,433	640	8.6
Legal professions and studies	6,300	287	4.6
Liberal arts and sciences, general studies, and humanities	3,971	206	5.2
Library science	7,727	372	4.8
Mathematics and statistics	5,843	220	3.8
Multi/interdisciplinary studies	6,748	495	7.3
Parks, recreation, leisure, and fitness	6,553	334	5.1
Philosophy and religion	1,833	79	4.3
Physical sciences	6,386	268	4.2
Precision production trades	5	0	0.0
Psychology	25,051	2,255	9.0
Public administration and social services	38,634	3,696	9.6
Social sciences and history	21,084	1,362	6.5
Theology and religious vocations	13,191	507	3.8
Transportation and material moving	1,390	85	6.1
Visual and performing arts	16,277	904	5.6

Source: National Center for Education Statistics, Digest of Education Statistics 2012, Internet site http://nces.ed.gov/programs/digest/2012menu_tables.asp; calculations by New Strategist

Table 5.14 Doctoral and First-Professional Degrees Earned by Hispanics by Field of Study, 2010–11

(total number of doctoral and first-professional degrees conferred and number and percent earned by Hispanics, by field of study, 2010–11)

		earned by Hispanics	
	total	number	share of total
Total doctoral and first-professional degrees	**163,765**	**8,650**	**5.3%**
Agriculture and natural resources	1,246	48	3.9
Architecture and related programs	205	9	4.4
Area, ethnic, and cultural studies	278	16	5.8
Biological and biomedical sciences	7,693	342	4.4
Business	2,286	96	4.2
Communication, journalism, and related programs	577	14	2.4
Communications technologies	1	0	0.0
Computer and information sciences	1,588	21	1.3
Education	9,623	593	6.2
Engineering	8,369	200	2.4
Engineering technologies	56	1	1.8
English language and literature/letters	1,344	54	4.0
Family and consumer sciences	320	7	2.2
Foreign languages, literatures, and linguistics	1,158	84	7.3
Health professions and related sciences	60,153	2,875	4.8
Homeland security, law enforcement, and firefighting	131	4	3.1
Legal professions and studies	44,877	3,290	7.3
Liberal arts and sciences, general studies, and humanities	95	1	1.1
Library science	50	1	2.0
Mathematics and statistics	1,586	31	2.0
Multi/interdisciplinary studies	660	34	5.2
Parks, recreation, leisure, and fitness	257	5	1.9
Philosophy and religion	805	25	3.1
Physical sciences	5,295	144	2.7
Psychology	5,851	376	6.4
Public administration and social services	851	50	5.9
Social sciences and history	4,390	194	4.4
Theology and religious vocations	2,374	74	3.1
Visual and performing arts	1,646	61	3.7

Source: National Center for Education Statistics, Digest of Education Statistics 2012, Internet site http://nces.ed.gov/programs/digest/2012menu_tables.asp; calculations by New Strategist

Millions of Hispanics Lack Health Insurance

Fifty-six percent of Hispanics rate their health as "very good" or "excellent," less than the 60 percent share among the total population. One reason for the relatively poor health of Hispanics may be their limited access to health care because so many lack health insurance. Only 13 percent of Hispanics are cigarette smokers, while a larger 44 percent drink alcohol regularly. Two of three Hispanics are overweight, and more than 30 percent are obese.

More than 900,000 babies were born to Hispanic women in 2011, accounting for 23 percent of births that year. Mexican Americans account for 63 percent of Hispanic births. In California, nearly half of births are to Hispanics. The figure is 55 percent in New Mexico, 48 percent in Texas, and 39 percent in Arizona.

Hispanics are more likely to be without health insurance than any other racial or ethnic group. In 2011, a substantial 30 percent did not have health insurance, nearly double the 16 percent among the total population.

Despite the poorer health of Hispanics, their life expectancy is longer than any other racial or ethnic group. At birth, Hispanics have a life expectancy of 81.4 years versus 78.7 years for the average newborn. At age 65, Hispanics have a life expectancy of 20.8 years versus 19.2 years for the average 65-year-old.

■ The higher life expectancy of Hispanics is a medical mystery that has yet to be explained.

Thirty percent of Hispanics do not have health insurance

(percent distribution of Hispanics by health insurance coverage status, 2011)

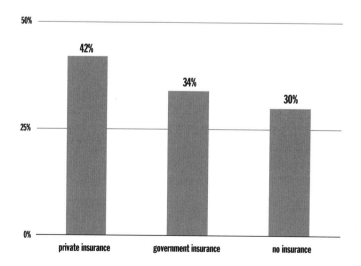

Table 5.15 Health Status of Total People and Hispanics, 2011

(number and percent distribution of total people and Hispanics aged 18 or older by self-reported health status, and index of Hispanic to total, 2011; numbers in thousands)

	total		Hispanic		index, Hispanic to total
	number	percent distribution	number	percent distribution	
Total people	**231,376**	**100.0%**	**32,762**	**100.0%**	–
Excellent/very good	139,424	60.3	18,218	55.6	92
Good	60,973	26.4	9,977	30.5	116
Fair/poor	30,856	13.3	4,567	13.9	105

Note: Numbers may not add to total because "unknown" is not shown. The index is calculated by dividing the Hispanic percentage by the total percentage and multiplying by 100. "–" means not applicable.
Source: National Center for Health Statistics, Summary Health Statistics for U.S. Adults: National Health Interview Survey, 2011, Vital and Health Statistics, Series 10, No. 256, 2012, Internet site http://www.cdc.gov/nchs/nhis.htm; calculations by New Strategist

Table 5.16 Weight of Hispanics by Age and Sex, 2007–10

(average weight in pounds of Hispanics aged 20 or older by age and sex, 2007–10)

	men	women
Total Hispanics	**186.1 lbs.**	**160.6 lbs.**
Aged 20 to 39	185.1	159.4
Aged 40 to 59	189.4	164.5
Aged 60 or older	180.8	155.8

Note: Data are based on measured weight of a sample of the civilian noninstitutionalized population.
Source: National Center for Health Statistics, Anthropometric Reference Data for Children and Adults: United States, 2007–2010, National Health Statistics Reports, Series 11, Number 252, 2012, Internet site http://www.cdc.gov/nchs/nhanes.htm

Table 5.17 Weight Status of Total People and Hispanics, 2011

(number and percent distribution of total people and Hispanics aged 18 or older by body mass index based on self-reported height and weight, and index of Hispanic to total, 2011; numbers in thousands)

	total number	total percent distribution	Hispanic number	Hispanic percent distribution	index, Hispanic to total
Total people	**231,376**	**100.0%**	**32,762**	**100.0%**	–
Underweight	3,549	1.5	288	0.9	57
Healthy weight	79,984	34.6	9,515	29.0	84
Overweight, total	141,072	61.0	21,931	66.9	110
Overweight, but not obese	77,586	33.5	11,862	36.2	108
Obese	63,486	27.4	10,069	30.7	112

Note: "Overweight" is defined as a body mass index of 25 or higher. "Obese" is defined as a body mass index of 30 or higher. Body mass index is calculated by dividing weight in kilograms by height in meters squared. Numbers may not add to total because "unknown" is not shown. The index is calculated by dividing the Hispanic percentage by the total percentage and multiplying by 100. "–" means not applicable.
Source: National Center for Health Statistics, Summary Health Statistics for U.S. Adults: National Health Interview Survey, 2011, Vital and Health Statistics, Series 10, No. 256, 2012, Internet site http://www.cdc.gov/nchs/nhis.htm; calculations by New Strategist

Table 5.18 Weight of Total and Hispanic High School Students by Sex, 2011

(percent of total and Hispanic 9th to 12th graders by weight status, by sex, 2011)

	total	Hispanic
MALES		
Measured as overweight*	31.2%	36.1%
Described themselves as overweight	23.9	27.4
Were trying to lose weight	31.6	39.6
FEMALES		
Measured as overweight*	25.2	26.6
Described themselves as overweight	34.8	36.3
Were trying to lose weight	61.2	66.4

* Students were classified as overweight if they were at or above the 85th percentile for body mass index, by age and sex, based on 2000 CDC growth charts.
Source: Centers for Disease Control and Prevention, Youth Risk Behavior Surveillance–United States, 2011, Mortality and Morbidity Weekly Report, Vol. 61, No. 4, June 8, 2012; Internet site http://www.cdc.gov/HealthyYouth/yrbs/index.htm

Table 5.19 Drinking Status of Total People and Hispanics, 2011

(number and percent distribution of total people and Hispanics aged 18 or older by drinking status, and index of Hispanic to total, 2011; numbers in thousands)

	total		Hispanic		index, Hispanic to total
	number	percent distribution	number	percent distribution	
Total people	**231,376**	**100.0%**	**32,762**	**100.0%**	–
Lifetime abstainer	45,367	19.6	9,504	29.0	148
Former drinker	33,663	14.5	4,250	13.0	89
Current drinker	148,970	64.4	18,494	56.4	88
Infrequent	31,158	13.5	4,173	12.7	95
Regular	117,812	50.9	14,321	43.7	86

Note: "Lifetime abstainers" have had fewer than 12 drinks in lifetime. "Former drinkers" have had 12 or more drinks in lifetime, none in past year. "Current infrequent drinkers" have had 12 or more drinks in lifetime and fewer than 12 drinks in past year. "Current regular drinkers" have had 12 or more drinks in lifetime and at least 12 drinks in past year. Numbers may not add to total because "unknown" is not shown. The index is calculated by dividing the Hispanic percentage by the total percentage and multiplying by 100. "–" means not applicable.
Source: National Center for Health Statistics, Summary Health Statistics for U.S. Adults: National Health Interview Survey, 2011, Vital and Health Statistics, Series 10, No. 256, 2012, Internet site http://www.cdc.gov/nchs/nhis.htm; calculations by New Strategist

Table 5.20 Smoking Status of Total People and Hispanics, 2011

(number and percent distribution of total people and Hispanics aged 18 or older by smoking status, and index of Hispanic to total, 2011; numbers in thousands)

	total		Hispanic		index, Hispanic to total
	number	percent distribution	number	percent distribution	
Total people	**231,376**	**100.0%**	**32,762**	**100.0%**	–
Never smoked	136,528	59.0	23,865	72.8	123
Former smoker	50,416	21.8	4,625	14.1	65
Current smoker	43,821	18.9	4,231	12.9	68

Note: "Never smoked" means fewer than 100 cigarettes in lifetime. "Former smokers" have smoked 100 or more cigarettes in lifetime but did not smoke at time of interview. "Current smokers" have smoked at least 100 cigarettes in lifetime and currently smoke. Numbers may not add to total because "unknown" is not shown. The index is calculated by dividing the Hispanic percentage by the total percentage and multiplying by 100. "–" means not applicable.
Source: National Center for Health Statistics, Summary Health Statistics for U.S. Adults: National Health Interview Survey, 2011, Vital and Health Statistics, Series 10, No. 256, 2012, Internet site http://www.cdc.gov/nchs/nhis.htm; calculations by New Strategist

Table 5.21 Births to Total and Hispanic Women by Age, 2011

(total number of births, number and percent distribution of births to Hispanics, and Hispanic share of total, by age, 2011)

	total	Hispanic number	Hispanic percent distribution	Hispanic share of total
Total births	3,953,593	912,290	100.0%	23.1%
Under age 15	3,974	1,570	0.2	39.5
Aged 15 to 19	329,797	109,218	12.0	33.1
Aged 20 to 24	925,213	242,411	26.6	26.2
Aged 25 to 29	1,127,592	246,635	27.0	21.9
Aged 30 to 34	986,661	191,047	20.9	19.4
Aged 35 to 39	463,815	97,538	10.7	21.0
Aged 40 to 44	108,891	22,635	2.5	20.8
Aged 45 to 54	7,651	1,236	0.1	16.2

Source: National Center for Health Statistics, Births: Preliminary Data for 2011, National Vital Statistics Report, Vol. 61, No. 5, 2012, Internet site http://www.cdc.gov/nchs/births.htm; calculations by New Strategist

Table 5.22 Births to Hispanics by Age and Ethnic Origin, 2010

(number and percent distribution of births to Hispanics by age and ethnic origin, 2010)

	total	Mexican	Puerto Rican	Cuban	Central and South American	other Hispanic
Total Hispanic births	**945,180**	**598,317**	**66,368**	**16,882**	**142,692**	**120,921**
Under age 20	123,609	82,507	10,170	1,047	10,224	19,661
Aged 20 to 24	254,723	163,348	20,864	3,873	30,819	35,819
Aged 25 to 29	254,982	161,693	16,776	4,689	40,433	31,391
Aged 30 to 34	191,334	117,607	11,720	4,055	36,491	21,461
Aged 35 to 39	97,554	59,597	5,477	2,632	19,767	10,081
Aged 40 to 44	21,783	12,950	1,278	550	4,647	2,358
Aged 45 or older	1,195	615	83	36	311	150

PERCENT DISTRIBUTION BY ETHNIC ORIGIN

	total	Mexican	Puerto Rican	Cuban	Central and South American	other Hispanic
Total Hispanic births	**100.0%**	**63.3%**	**7.0%**	**1.8%**	**15.1%**	**12.8%**
Under age 20	100.0	66.7	8.2	0.8	8.3	15.9
Aged 20 to 24	100.0	64.1	8.2	1.5	12.1	14.1
Aged 25 to 29	100.0	63.4	6.6	1.8	15.9	12.3
Aged 30 to 34	100.0	61.5	6.1	2.1	19.1	11.2
Aged 35 to 39	100.0	61.1	5.6	2.7	20.3	10.3
Aged 40 to 44	100.0	59.5	5.9	2.5	21.3	10.8
Aged 45 or older	100.0	51.5	6.9	3.0	26.0	12.6

PERCENT DISTRIBUTION BY AGE

	total	Mexican	Puerto Rican	Cuban	Central and South American	other Hispanic
Total Hispanic births	**100.0%**	**100.0%**	**100.0%**	**100.0%**	**100.0%**	**100.0%**
Under age 20	13.1	13.8	15.3	6.2	7.2	16.3
Aged 20 to 24	26.9	27.3	31.4	22.9	21.6	29.6
Aged 25 to 29	27.0	27.0	25.3	27.8	28.3	26.0
Aged 30 to 34	20.2	19.7	17.7	24.0	25.6	17.7
Aged 35 to 39	10.3	10.0	8.3	15.6	13.9	8.3
Aged 40 to 44	2.3	2.2	1.9	3.3	3.3	2.0
Aged 45 or older	0.1	0.1	0.1	0.2	0.2	0.1

Source: National Center for Health Statistics, Births: Final Data for 2010, National Vital Statistics Reports, Vol. 61, No. 1, 2012, Internet site http://www.cdc.gov/nchs/births.htm; calculations by New Strategist

Table 5.23 Births to Hispanic Women by Age and Marital Status, 2010

(total number of births to Hispanics, number of births to unmarried Hispanics, and unmarried share of total, by age, 2010)

		unmarried	
	total	number	share of total
Births to Hispanics	**945,180**	**504,411**	**53.4%**
Under age 15	1,811	1,792	99.0
Aged 15 to 19	121,798	105,130	86.3
Aged 20 to 24	254,723	165,963	65.2
Aged 25 to 29	254,982	119,900	47.0
Aged 30 to 34	191,334	70,963	37.1
Aged 35 to 39	97,554	32,823	33.6
Aged 40 or older	22,978	7,840	34.1

Source: National Center for Health Statistics, Births: Final Data for 2010, National Vital Statistics Reports, Vol. 61, No. 1, 2012, Internet site http://www.cdc.gov/nchs/births.htm; calculations by New Strategist

Table 5.24 Births to Total and Hispanic Women by Birth Order, 2011

(total number of births, number and percent distribution of births to Hispanics, and Hispanic share of total, by birth order, 2011)

		Hispanic		
	total	number	percent distribution	share of total
Total births	**3,953,593**	**912,290**	**100.0%**	**23.1%**
First child	1,577,344	313,032	34.3	19.8
Second child	1,239,136	272,840	29.9	22.0
Third child	648,124	180,818	19.8	27.9
Fourth or later child	458,777	140,921	15.4	30.7

Note: Numbers do not add to total because "not stated" is not shown.
Source: National Center for Health Statistics, Births: Preliminary Data for 2011, National Vital Statistics Report, Vol. 61, No. 5, 2012, Internet site http://www.cdc.gov/nchs/births.htm; calculations by New Strategist

Table 5.25 Births to Total and Hispanic Women by State, 2011

(total number of births, number and percent distribution of births to Hispanics, and Hispanic share of total, by state, 2011)

	total	Hispanic		
		number	percent distribution	share of total
Total births	**3,953,593**	**912,290**	**100.0%**	**23.1%**
Alabama	59,347	4,474	0.5	7.5
Alaska	11,455	757	0.1	6.6
Arizona	85,543	33,255	3.6	38.9
Arkansas	38,713	3,957	0.4	10.2
California	502,118	250,031	27.4	49.8
Colorado	65,055	18,077	2.0	27.8
Connecticut	37,280	8,388	0.9	22.5
Delaware	11,257	1,416	0.2	12.6
District of Columbia	9,314	1,373	0.2	14.7
Florida	213,344	58,735	6.4	27.5
Georgia	132,488	18,671	2.0	14.1
Hawaii	18,957	3,038	0.3	16.0
Idaho	22,305	3,475	0.4	15.6
Illinois	161,312	35,765	3.9	22.2
Indiana	83,702	7,180	0.8	8.6
Iowa	38,213	3,114	0.3	8.1
Kansas	39,642	6,294	0.7	15.9
Kentucky	55,377	2,781	0.3	5.0
Louisiana	61,889	3,607	0.4	5.8
Maine	12,704	207	0.0	1.6
Maryland	73,086	10,330	1.1	14.1
Massachusetts	73,225	6,764	0.7	9.2
Michigan	114,004	7,628	0.8	6.7
Minnesota	68,411	4,629	0.5	6.8
Mississippi	39,856	1,319	0.1	3.3
Missouri	76,117	4,114	0.5	5.4
Montana	12,069	449	0.0	3.7
Nebraska	25,720	3,646	0.4	14.2
Nevada	35,295	13,049	1.4	37.0
New Hampshire	12,852	524	0.1	4.1
New Jersey	105,886	28,010	3.1	26.5
New Mexico	27,289	15,061	1.7	55.2
New York	241,290	56,698	6.2	23.5
North Carolina	120,385	18,219	2.0	15.1
North Dakota	9,527	307	0.0	3.2
Ohio	137,916	6,337	0.7	4.6
Oklahoma	52,274	6,684	0.7	12.8

	total	Hispanic		
		number	percent distribution	share of total
Oregon	45,157	8,742	1.0%	19.4%
Pennsylvania	143,148	14,180	1.6	9.9
Rhode Island	10,960	2,417	0.3	22.1
South Carolina	57,368	4,747	0.5	8.3
South Dakota	11,849	505	0.1	4.3
Tennessee	79,588	7,022	0.8	8.8
Texas	377,449	182,510	20.0	48.4
Utah	51,223	7,686	0.8	15.0
Vermont	6,078	71	0.0	1.2
Virginia	102,648	12,473	1.4	12.2
Washington	86,976	15,976	1.8	18.4
West Virginia	20,720	207	0.0	1.0
Wisconsin	67,811	6,525	0.7	9.6
Wyoming	7,398	864	0.1	11.7

Source: National Center for Health Statistics, Births: Preliminary Data for 2011, National Vital Statistics Report, Vol. 61, No. 5, 2012, Internet site http://www.cdc.gov/nchs/births.htm; calculations by New Strategist

Table 5.26 Number of Births to Hispanic Women by State and Ethnicity, 2010

(number of births to Hispanics by state and ethnicity, 2010)

	total	Mexican	Puerto Rican	Cuban	Central and South American	other Hispanic
Total Hispanic births	**945,180**	**598,317**	**66,368**	**16,882**	**142,692**	**120,921**
Alabama	4,840	3,184	168	38	1,374	76
Alaska	661	333	67	13	99	149
Arizona	35,092	32,776	371	96	1,007	842
Arkansas	4,047	3,158	53	20	704	112
California	257,588	205,640	2,032	702	22,056	27,158
Colorado	19,458	13,356	364	94	1,034	4,610
Connecticut	8,235	1,000	4,375	88	2,664	108
Delaware	1,427	684	292	10	391	50
District of Columbia	1,359	155	36	10	1,015	143
Florida	59,605	13,246	11,046	11,362	21,093	2,858
Georgia	21,217	13,160	931	264	4,231	2,631
Hawaii	2,968	674	852	29	158	1,255
Idaho	3,639	3,001	42	9	149	438
Illinois	37,356	31,252	2,533	197	2,456	918
Indiana	7,569	6,042	350	36	614	527
Iowa	3,092	2,359	82	13	476	162
Kansas	6,429	4,741	144	41	645	858
Kentucky	2,858	1,868	185	144	485	176
Louisiana	3,586	1,682	170	92	1,450	192
Maine	210	24	28	8	41	109
Maryland	10,263	2,002	627	109	6,658	867
Massachusetts	10,618	479	4,494	63	5,418	164
Michigan	7,808	5,088	447	115	685	1,473
Minnesota	5,139	3,416	147	33	850	693
Mississippi	1,426	673	29	8	333	383
Missouri	4,334	2,911	186	59	700	478
Montana	433	244	14	4	38	133
Nebraska	3,943	2,904	50	43	648	298
Nevada	13,398	10,506	263	249	1,302	1,078
New Hampshire	529	93	123	14	108	191
New Jersey	28,003	6,192	6,512	731	12,070	2,498
New Mexico	15,478	5,935	84	46	309	9,104
New York	58,583	11,165	14,193	528	17,783	14,914
North Carolina	18,731	12,533	1,122	209	4,348	519
North Dakota	305	197	28	2	27	51
Ohio	6,323	3,105	1,363	77	990	788
Oklahoma	6,931	5,545	164	31	595	596
Oregon	9,257	8,092	113	56	541	455

	total	Mexican	Puerto Rican	Cuban	Central and South American	other Hispanic
Pennsylvania	13,736	2,830	6,914	190	1,562	2,240
Rhode Island	2,435	155	679	26	709	866
South Carolina	4,947	3,147	397	72	969	362
South Dakota	509	276	33	3	135	62
Tennessee	7,139	4,602	313	113	1,442	669
Texas	189,126	140,004	1,728	519	11,999	34,876
Utah	8,054	5,967	101	18	1,054	914
Vermont	77	23	16	3	16	19
Virginia	12,506	3,009	898	153	7,816	630
Washington	16,219	12,874	424	73	993	1,855
West Virginia	210	77	28	3	49	53
Wisconsin	6,545	5,275	740	57	361	112
Wyoming	939	663	17	9	42	208

Source: National Center for Health Statistics, Births: Final Data for 2010, National Vital Statistics Reports, Vol. 61, No. 1, 2012, Internet site http://www.cdc.gov/nchs/births.htm; calculations by New Strategist

Table 5.27 Percent Distribution of Births to Hispanic Women by State and Ethnicity, 2010

(percent distribution of births to Hispanics by state and ethnicity, 2010)

	total	Mexican	Puerto Rican	Cuban	Central and South American	other Hispanic
Total Hispanic births	100.0%	63.3%	7.0%	1.8%	15.1%	12.8%
Alabama	100.0	65.8	3.5	0.8	28.4	1.6
Alaska	100.0	50.4	10.1	2.0	15.0	22.5
Arizona	100.0	93.4	1.1	0.3	2.9	2.4
Arkansas	100.0	78.0	1.3	0.5	17.4	2.8
California	100.0	79.8	0.8	0.3	8.6	10.5
Colorado	100.0	68.6	1.9	0.5	5.3	23.7
Connecticut	100.0	12.1	53.1	1.1	32.3	1.3
Delaware	100.0	47.9	20.5	0.7	27.4	3.5
District of Columbia	100.0	11.4	2.6	0.7	74.7	10.5
Florida	100.0	22.2	18.5	19.1	35.4	4.8
Georgia	100.0	62.0	4.4	1.2	19.9	12.4
Hawaii	100.0	22.7	28.7	1.0	5.3	42.3
Idaho	100.0	82.5	1.2	0.2	4.1	12.0
Illinois	100.0	83.7	6.8	0.5	6.6	2.5
Indiana	100.0	79.8	4.6	0.5	8.1	7.0
Iowa	100.0	76.3	2.7	0.4	15.4	5.2
Kansas	100.0	73.7	2.2	0.6	10.0	13.3
Kentucky	100.0	65.4	6.5	5.0	17.0	6.2
Louisiana	100.0	46.9	4.7	2.6	40.4	5.4
Maine	100.0	11.4	13.3	3.8	19.5	51.9
Maryland	100.0	19.5	6.1	1.1	64.9	8.4
Massachusetts	100.0	4.5	42.3	0.6	51.0	1.5
Michigan	100.0	65.2	5.7	1.5	8.8	18.9
Minnesota	100.0	66.5	2.9	0.6	16.5	13.5
Mississippi	100.0	47.2	2.0	0.6	23.4	26.9
Missouri	100.0	67.2	4.3	1.4	16.2	11.0
Montana	100.0	56.4	3.2	0.9	8.8	30.7
Nebraska	100.0	73.6	1.3	1.1	16.4	7.6
Nevada	100.0	78.4	2.0	1.9	9.7	8.0
New Hampshire	100.0	17.6	23.3	2.6	20.4	36.1
New Jersey	100.0	22.1	23.3	2.6	43.1	8.9
New Mexico	100.0	38.3	0.5	0.3	2.0	58.8
New York	100.0	19.1	24.2	0.9	30.4	25.5
North Carolina	100.0	66.9	6.0	1.1	23.2	2.8
North Dakota	100.0	64.6	9.2	0.7	8.9	16.7
Ohio	100.0	49.1	21.6	1.2	15.7	12.5
Oklahoma	100.0	80.0	2.4	0.4	8.6	8.6
Oregon	100.0	87.4	1.2	0.6	5.8	4.9

	total	Mexican	Puerto Rican	Cuban	Central and South American	other Hispanic
Pennsylvania	100.0%	20.6%	50.3%	1.4%	11.4%	16.3%
Rhode Island	100.0	6.4	27.9	1.1	29.1	35.6
South Carolina	100.0	63.6	8.0	1.5	19.6	7.3
South Dakota	100.0	54.2	6.5	0.6	26.5	12.2
Tennessee	100.0	64.5	4.4	1.6	20.2	9.4
Texas	100.0	74.0	0.9	0.3	6.3	18.4
Utah	100.0	74.1	1.3	0.2	13.1	11.3
Vermont	100.0	29.9	20.8	3.9	20.8	24.7
Virginia	100.0	24.1	7.2	1.2	62.5	5.0
Washington	100.0	79.4	2.6	0.5	6.1	11.4
West Virginia	100.0	36.7	13.3	1.4	23.3	25.2
Wisconsin	100.0	80.6	11.3	0.9	5.5	1.7
Wyoming	100.0	70.6	1.8	1.0	4.5	22.2

Source: National Center for Health Statistics, Births: Final Data for 2010, National Vital Statistics Reports, Vol. 61, No. 1, 2012, Internet site http://www.cdc.gov/nchs/births.htm; calculations by New Strategist

Table 5.28 Health Insurance Coverage of Hispanics by Age, 2011

(number and percent distribution of Hispanics by age and health insurance coverage status, 2011; numbers in thousands)

		with health insurance coverage during year			not covered at any time during the year
	total	total	private	government	
Total Hispanics	**52,358**	**36,582**	**21,743**	**17,770**	**15,776**
Under age 18	17,679	15,016	6,729	9,444	2,663
Aged 18 to 24	6,234	3,667	2,498	1,430	2,567
Aged 25 to 34	8,539	4,537	3,469	1,276	4,002
Aged 35 to 44	7,531	4,458	3,566	1,104	3,073
Aged 45 to 54	5,794	3,673	2,916	949	2,120
Aged 55 to 64	3,545	2,427	1,658	934	1,118
Aged 65 or older	3,036	2,804	906	2,633	232

PERCENT DISTRIBUTION BY COVERAGE STATUS

Total Hispanics	**100.0%**	**69.9%**	**41.5%**	**33.9%**	**30.1%**
Under age 18	100.0	84.9	38.1	53.4	15.1
Aged 18 to 24	100.0	58.8	40.1	22.9	41.2
Aged 25 to 34	100.0	53.1	40.6	14.9	46.9
Aged 35 to 44	100.0	59.2	47.4	14.7	40.8
Aged 45 to 54	100.0	63.4	50.3	16.4	36.6
Aged 55 to 64	100.0	68.5	46.8	26.3	31.5
Aged 65 or older	100.0	92.4	29.8	86.7	7.6

Note: Numbers do not add to total because some people have more than one type of health insurance.
Source: Bureau of the Census, Health Insurance, Internet site http://www.census.gov/hhes/www/cpstables/032012/health/toc.htm; calculations by New Strategist

Table 5.29 Hispanics with Private Health Insurance Coverage by Age, 2011

(number and percent distribution of Hispanics by age and private health insurance coverage status, 2011; numbers in thousands)

| | | with private health insurance | | | |
| | | total | employment-based | | direct purchase |
	total	total	total	own	
Total Hispanics	**52,358**	**21,743**	**19,799**	**9,132**	**2,133**
Under age 18	17,679	6,729	6,245	50	579
Aged 18 to 24	6,234	2,498	2,048	631	206
Aged 25 to 34	8,539	3,469	3,225	2,347	336
Aged 35 to 44	7,531	3,566	3,355	2,453	272
Aged 45 to 54	5,794	2,916	2,746	2,058	268
Aged 55 to 64	3,545	1,658	1,524	1,137	169
Aged 65 or older	3,036	906	657	456	304
PERCENT DISTRIBUTION BY COVERAGE STATUS					
Total Hispanics	**100.0%**	**41.5%**	**37.8%**	**17.4%**	**4.1%**
Under age 18	100.0	38.1	35.3	0.3	3.3
Aged 18 to 24	100.0	40.1	32.9	10.1	3.3
Aged 25 to 34	100.0	40.6	37.8	27.5	3.9
Aged 35 to 44	100.0	47.4	44.5	32.6	3.6
Aged 45 to 54	100.0	50.3	47.4	35.5	4.6
Aged 55 to 64	100.0	46.8	43.0	32.1	4.8
Aged 65 or older	100.0	29.8	21.6	15.0	10.0

Note: Numbers do not add to total because some people have more than one type of health insurance.
Source: Bureau of the Census, Health Insurance, Internet site http://www.census.gov/hhes/www/cpstables/032012/health/toc .htm; calculations by New Strategist

Table 5.30 Hispanics with Government Health Insurance Coverage by Age, 2011

(number and percent distribution of Hispanics by age and government health insurance coverage status, 2011; numbers in thousands)

	total	with government health insurance			
		total	Medicaid	Medicare	military
Total Hispanics	**52,358**	**17,770**	**14,437**	**3,563**	**1,157**
Under age 18	17,679	9,444	9,086	115	370
Aged 18 to 24	6,234	1,430	1293	34	130
Aged 25 to 34	8,539	1,276	1068	84	179
Aged 35 to 44	7,531	1,104	949	115	121
Aged 45 to 54	5,794	949	760	217	93
Aged 55 to 64	3,545	934	575	393	149
Aged 65 or older	3,036	2,633	707	2,605	115

PERCENT DISTRIBUTION BY COVERAGE STATUS

Total Hispanics	**100.0%**	**33.9%**	**27.6%**	**6.8%**	**2.2%**
Under age 18	100.0	53.4	51.4	0.7	2.1
Aged 18 to 24	100.0	22.9	20.7	0.5	2.1
Aged 25 to 34	100.0	14.9	12.5	1.0	2.1
Aged 35 to 44	100.0	14.7	12.6	1.5	1.6
Aged 45 to 54	100.0	16.4	13.1	3.7	1.6
Aged 55 to 64	100.0	26.3	16.2	11.1	4.2
Aged 65 or older	100.0	86.7	23.3	85.8	3.8

Note: Numbers do not add to total because some people have more than one type of health insurance.
Source: Bureau of the Census, Health Insurance, Internet site http://www.census.gov/hhes/www/cpstables/032012/health/toc .htm; calculations by New Strategist

Table 5.31 Health Conditions among Total People and Hispanics Aged 18 or Older, 2011

(number of total people and Hispanics aged 18 or older with selected health conditions, percent of Hispanics with condition, and Hispanic share of total with condition, 2011; numbers in thousands)

	total	Hispanic number	Hispanic percent with condition	Hispanic share of total
TOTAL PEOPLE	231,376	32,762	100.0%	14.2%
Selected circulatory diseases				
Heart disease, all types	26,485	2,138	6.5	8.1
Coronary	15,300	1,352	4.1	8.8
Hypertension	58,959	5,623	17.2	9.5
Stroke	6,171	644	2.0	10.4
Selected respiratory conditions				
Emphysema	4,680	232	0.7	5.0
Asthma, ever	29,041	3,330	10.2	11.5
Asthma, still	18,869	1,959	6.0	10.4
Hay fever	16,869	1,708	5.2	10.1
Sinusitis	29,611	2,875	8.8	9.7
Chronic bronchitis	10,071	943	2.9	9.4
Selected types of cancer				
Any cancer	19,025	830	2.5	4.4
Breast cancer	3,221	163	0.5	5.1
Cervical cancer	1,188	82	0.3	6.9
Prostate cancer	2,280	111	0.3	4.9
Other selected diseases and conditions				
Diabetes	20,589	1,963	6.0	9.5
Ulcers	15,502	889	2.7	5.7
Kidney disease	4,381	409	1.2	9.3
Liver disease	3,016	261	0.8	8.7
Arthritis	53,782	2,295	7.0	4.3
Chronic joint symptoms	68,749	4,090	12.5	5.9
Migraines or severe headaches	37,904	5,397	16.5	14.2
Pain in neck	35,798	4,391	13.4	12.3
Pain in lower back	66,917	8,507	26.0	12.7
Pain in face or jaw	11,436	1,346	4.1	11.8
Selected sensory problems				
Hearing	37,122	3,006	9.2	8.1
Vision	21,232	2,672	8.2	12.6
Absence of all natural teeth	18,038	1,535	4.7	8.5

Note: The conditions shown are those that have ever been diagnosed by a doctor, except as noted. Hay fever, sinusitis, and chronic bronchitis have been diagnosed in the past 12 months. Kidney and liver disease have been diagnosed in the past 12 months and exclude kidney stones, bladder infections, and incontinence. Chronic joint symptoms are shown if respondent had pain, aching, or stiffness in or around a joint (excluding back and neck) and the condition began more than three months ago. Migraines, pain in neck, lower back, face, or jaw are shown only if pain lasted a whole day or more.
Source: National Center for Health Statistics, Summary Health Statistics for U.S. Adults: National Health Interview Survey, 2011, Vital and Health Statistics, Series 10, No. 256, 2012, Internet site http://www.cdc.gov/nchs/nhis.htm; calculations by New Strategist

Table 5.32 Health Conditions among Total and Hispanic Children, 2011

(number of total people and Hispanics under age 18 with selected health conditions, percent of Hispanics with condition, and Hispanic share of total, 2011; numbers in thousands)

		Hispanic		
	total	number	percent with condition	share of total
Total children	**74,518**	**17,517**	**100.0%**	**23.5%**
Ever told have asthma	10,463	2,452	14.0	23.4
Still have asthma	7,074	1,679	9.6	23.7
Hay fever in past 12 months	6,711	1,359	7.8	20.3
Respiratory allergies in past 12 months	8,269	1,104	6.3	13.4
Food allergies in past 12 months	4,126	707	4.0	17.1
Skin allergies in past 12 months	9,516	1,980	11.3	20.8
Prescription medication taken regularly for at least three months	10,019	1,635	9.3	16.3
Learning disability*	4,660	900	5.1	19.3
Attention deficit hyperactivity disorder*	5,240	802	4.6	15.3

* Diagnosed by a school representative or health professional; data exclude children under age 3.
Source: National Center for Health Statistics, Summary Health Statistics for U.S. Children: National Health Interview Survey, 2011, Vital and Health Statistics, Series 10, No. 254, 2012, Internet site http://www.cdc.gov/nchs/nhis.htm

Table 5.33 Health Care Office Visits by Total People and Hispanics, 2011

(number of total people and Hispanics aged 18 or older by visits to a health care provider in the past 12 months, percent distribution of Hispanics by number of visits, and Hispanic share of total, 2011; numbers in thousands)

		Hispanic		
	total	number	percent distribution	share of total
Total people	**231,376**	**32,762**	**100.0%**	**14.2%**
No visits	43,578	10,525	32.1	24.2
One visit	39,552	5,754	17.6	14.5
Two to three visits	59,226	7,082	21.6	12.0
Four to nine visits	55,721	6,064	18.5	10.9
10 or more visits	30,822	3,013	9.2	9.8

Note: Health care visits exclude overnight hospitalizations, visits to emergency rooms, home visits, dental visits, and telephone calls. Numbers may not add to total because "unknown" is not shown.
Source: National Center for Health Statistics, Summary Health Statistics for U.S. Adults: National Health Interview Survey, 2011, Vital and Health Statistics, Series 10, No. 256, 2012, Internet site http://www.cdc.gov/nchs/nhis.htm; calculations by New Strategist

Table 5.34 Difficulties in Physical Functioning among Total People and Hispanics, 2011

(number of total people and Hispanics aged 18 or older, number with difficulties in physical functioning, percentage of Hispanics with difficulty, and Hispanic share of total, by type of difficulty, 2011; numbers in thousands)

		Hispanic		
	total	number	percent	share of total
TOTAL PEOPLE	231,376	32,762	100.0%	14.2%
Total with any physical difficulty	37,368	3,785	15.3	10.1
Walk quarter of a mile	17,597	1,503	6.4	8.5
Climb 10 steps without resting	12,887	1,438	6.5	11.2
Stand for two hours	22,369	2,119	9.0	9.5
Sit for two hours	7,724	989	3.6	12.8
Stoop, bend, or kneel	21,677	2,163	9.1	10.0
Reach over head	6,550	714	3.1	10.9
Grasp or handle small objects	4,329	479	2.1	11.1
Lift or carry 10 pounds	10,677	1,383	6.2	13.0
Push or pull large objects	15,998	1,833	7.8	11.5

Note: Respondents were classified as having difficulties if they responded "very difficult" or "can't do at all."
Source: National Center for Health Statistics, Summary Health Statistics for U.S. Adults: National Health Interview Survey, 2011, Vital and Health Statistics, Series 10, No. 256, 2012, Internet site http://www.cdc.gov/nchs/nhis.htm; calculations by New Strategist

Table 5.35 AIDS Cases among Total People and Hispanics, through December 2009

(number of total AIDS cases diagnosed, number and percent distribution among Hispanics, and Hispanic share of total, by sex, through December 2009)

		Hispanic		
	total	number	percent distribution	share of total
Total diagnosed with AIDS	1,108,611	190,263	100.0%	17.2%
Males aged 13 or older	878,366	152,310	80.1	17.3
Females aged 13 or older	220,795	36,091	19.0	16.3
Children under age 13	9,448	1,862	1.0	19.7

Source: National Center for Health Statistics, Health United States 2011, Internet site http://www.cdc.gov/nchs/hus.htm; calculations by New Strategist

Table 5.36 Leading Causes of Death among Hispanics, 2009

(number and percent distribution of deaths to Hispanics accounted for by the 10 leading causes of death among Hispanics, 2009)

		number	percent distribution
Total Hispanic deaths		**141,576**	**100.0%**
1.	Malignant neoplasms (cancer) (2)	29,935	21.1
2.	Diseases of the heart (1)	29,611	20.9
3.	Accidents (unintentional injuries) (5)	10,654	7.5
4.	Cerebrovascular diseases (4)	7,065	5.0
5.	Diabetes mellitus (7)	6,311	4.5
6.	Chronic liver disease and cirrhosis	4,303	3.0
7.	Chronic lower respiratory disease (3)	4,026	2.8
8.	Influenza and pneumonia (8)	3,679	2.6
9.	Homicide	3,179	2.2
10.	Nephritis, nephrotic syndrome and nephrosis (9)	3,107	2.2
	All other causes	39,706	28.0

Note: Number in parentheses shows rank for all Americans if the cause of death is in top 10.
Source: National Center for Health Statistics, Deaths: Leading Causes for 2009, National Vital Statistics Report, Vol. 61, No. 7, 2012, Internet site http://www.cdc.gov/nchs/deaths.htm; calculations by New Strategist

Table 5.37 Life Expectancy of Total People and Hispanics by Sex, 2011

(average number of years of life remaining for total people and Hispanics at birth and age 65 by sex, and index of Hispanic life expectancy to total, 2011)

	total people	Hispanics	index, Hispanic to total
AT BIRTH			
Total	**78.7 yrs.**	**81.4 yrs.**	**103**
Female	81.1	83.7	103
Male	76.3	78.9	103
AT AGE 65			
Total	**19.2**	**20.8**	**108**
Female	20.4	21.9	107
Male	17.8	19.1	107

Note: The index is calculated by dividing Hispanic life expectancy by total life expectancy and multiplying by 100.
Source: National Center for Health Statistics, Deaths: Preliminary Data for 2011, National Vital Statistics Report, Vol. 61, No. 6, 2012, Internet site http://www.cdc.gov/nchs/deaths.htm; calculations by New Strategist

Hispanics Are Less Likely than the Average American to Own a Home

Forty-six percent of the nation's Hispanic households owned a home in 2012. This compares with a much higher homeownership rate of 65 percent for all households. Among Hispanic married couples, 60 percent own their home. By age, Hispanic homeownership surpasses 50 percent in the 45-or-older age groups. More than half of Hispanic households own their home in the Midwest and South. In the Northeast, only 29 percent of Hispanic households own their home.

The 80 percent majority of Hispanic homeowners live in a single-family detached house. The reported median value of the homes owned by Hispanics stood at $185,900, according to the 2006–10 American Community Survey, close to the $188,400 median for all homeowners.

Fifteen percent of Hispanics moved between 2011 and 2012, a higher mobility rate than the 12 percent for the population as a whole. The most common reason Hispanics moved was to find a new or better home or apartment.

■ Hispanic homeownership will continue to lag behind the national average because many Hispanics are immigrants with low incomes.

Hispanic homeownership is lowest in the Northeast

(percent of Hispanic households that own their home, by region, 2011)

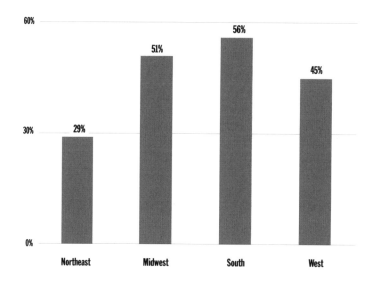

Table 5.38 Total and Hispanic Homeownership Rate, 2000 to 2012

(homeownership rate of total and Hispanic households and index of Hispanic to total, 2000 to 2012; percentage point change for selected years)

	total households	Hispanic households	index, Hispanic to total
2012	65.4%	46.1%	70
2011	66.1	46.9	71
2010	66.9	47.5	71
2009	67.4	48.4	72
2008	67.8	49.1	72
2007	68.1	49.7	73
2006	68.8	49.7	72
2005	68.9	49.5	72
2004	69.0	48.1	70
2003	68.3	46.7	68
2002	67.9	47.0	69
2001	67.8	47.3	70
2000	67.4	46.3	69

PERCENTAGE POINT CHANGE

2004 to 2012	–3.6	–2.0	–
2000 to 2012	–2.0	–0.2	–

Note: The index is calculated by dividing the Hispanic homeownership rate by the total rate and multiplying by 100. "–" means not applicable.
Source: Bureau of the Census, Housing Vacancies and Homeownership, Internet site http://www.census.gov/housing/hvs/; calculations by New Strategist

Table 5.39 Hispanic Homeownership Status by Age of Householder, 2011

(number and percent of Hispanic households by age of householder and homeownership status, 2011; numbers in thousands)

	total	owner		renter	
		number	percent	number	percent
Total Hispanic households	**13,841**	**6,530**	**47.2%**	**7,311**	**52.8%**
Under age 25	990	127	12.8	863	87.2
Aged 25 to 29	1,429	341	23.9	1,088	76.1
Aged 30 to 34	1,723	617	35.8	1,106	64.2
Aged 35 to 44	3,348	1,544	46.1	1,804	53.9
Aged 45 to 54	2,855	1,657	58.0	1,199	42.0
Aged 55 to 64	1,829	1,168	63.9	661	36.1
Aged 65 to 74	989	632	63.9	357	36.1
Aged 75 or older	679	445	65.5	234	34.5

Source: Bureau of the Census, American Housing Survey for the United States: 2011, Internet site http://www.census.gov/ housing/ahs/index.html; calculations by New Strategist

Table 5.40 Total and Hispanic Homeowners by Age of Householder, 2011

(number of total homeowners, number and percent distribution of Hispanic homeowners, and Hispanic share of total, by age of householder, 2011; numbers in thousands)

		Hispanic		
	total	number	percent distribution	share of total
Total homeowners	**76,091**	**6,530**	**100.0%**	**8.6%**
Under age 25	830	127	1.9	15.3
Aged 25 to 29	3,136	341	5.2	10.9
Aged 30 to 34	5,391	617	9.4	11.4
Aged 35 to 44	12,847	1,544	23.6	12.0
Aged 45 to 54	16,994	1,657	25.4	9.8
Aged 55 to 64	16,643	1,168	17.9	7.0
Aged 65 to 74	10,802	632	9.7	5.9
Aged 75 or older	9,448	445	6.8	4.7

Source: Bureau of the Census, American Housing Survey for the United States: 2011, Internet site http://www.census.gov/ housing/ahs/index.html; calculations by New Strategist

Table 5.41 Total and Hispanic Renters by Age of Householder, 2011

(number of total renters, number and percent distribution of Hispanic renters, and Hispanic share of total, by age of householder, 2011; numbers in thousands)

		Hispanic		
	total	number	percent distribution	share of total
Total renters	**38,816**	**7,311**	**100.0%**	**18.8%**
Under age 25	4,568	863	11.8	18.9
Aged 25 to 29	5,610	1,088	14.9	19.4
Aged 30 to 34	5,343	1,106	15.1	20.7
Aged 35 to 44	7,600	1,804	24.7	23.7
Aged 45 to 54	6,422	1,199	16.4	18.7
Aged 55 to 64	4,466	661	9.0	14.8
Aged 65 to 74	2,366	357	4.9	15.1
Aged 75 or older	2,442	234	3.2	9.6

Source: Bureau of the Census, American Housing Survey for the United States: 2011, Internet site http://www.census.gov/housing/ahs/index.html; calculations by New Strategist

Table 5.42 Hispanic Homeownership Status by Household Type, 2010

(number and percent of Hispanic households by household type and homeownership status, 2010; numbers in thousands)

	total	owner		renter	
		number	percent	number	percent
Total Hispanic households	**13,461**	**6,368**	**47.3%**	**7,093**	**52.7%**
Family households	10,558	5,418	51.3	5,140	48.7
Married couples	6,743	4,058	60.2	2,684	39.8
Female-headed family, no spouse present	2,589	906	35.0	1,683	65.0
Male-headed family, no spouse present	1,226	454	37.0	772	63.0
Nonfamily households	2,903	950	32.7	1,953	67.3
Female householder	1,309	474	36.2	835	63.8
Living alone	994	378	38.1	616	61.9
Male householder	1,595	477	29.9	1,118	70.1
Living alone	1,049	340	32.4	709	67.6

Source: Bureau of the Census, American Housing Survey for the United States: 2011, Internet site http://www.census.gov/housing/ahs/index.html; calculations by New Strategist

Table 5.43 Total and Hispanic Homeowners by Household Type, 2010

(number of total homeowners, number and percent distribution of Hispanic homeowners, and Hispanic share of total, by household type, 2010; numbers in thousands)

	total	Hispanic		
		number	percent distribution	share of total
Total homeowners	**75,986**	**6,368**	**100.0%**	**8.4%**
Family households	56,206	5,418	85.1	9.6
Married couples	45,801	4,058	63.7	8.9
Female-headed family, no spouse present	7,278	906	14.2	12.4
Male-headed family, no spouse present	3,127	454	7.1	14.5
Nonfamily households	19,780	950	14.9	4.8
Female householder	11,053	474	7.4	4.3
Living alone	9,625	378	5.9	3.9
Male householder	8,727	477	7.5	5.5
Living alone	6,828	340	5.3	5.0

Source: Bureau of the Census, 2010 Census, Internet site http://factfinder2.census.gov/faces/nav/jsf/pages/index.xhtml; calculations by New Strategist

Table 5.44 Total and Hispanic Renters by Household Type, 2010

(number of total renters, number and percent distribution of Hispanic renters, and Hispanic share of total, by household type, 2010; numbers in thousands)

	total	Hispanic number	Hispanic percent distribution	Hispanic share of total
Total homeowners	**75,986**	**6,368**	**100.0%**	**8.4%**
Family households	21,332	5,140	72.5	24.1
Married couples	10,710	2,684	37.8	25.1
Female-headed family, no spouse present	7,972	1,683	23.7	21.1
Male-headed family, no spouse present	2,651	772	10.9	29.1
Nonfamily households	19,398	1,953	27.5	10.1
Female householder	9,666	835	11.8	8.6
Living alone	7,673	616	8.7	8.0
Male householder	9,732	1,118	15.8	11.5
Living alone	7,078	709	10.0	10.0

Source: Bureau of the Census, 2010 Census, Internet site http://factfinder2.census.gov/faces/nav/jsf/pages/index.xhtml; calculations by New Strategist

Table 5.45 Hispanic Homeownership Status by Region, 2011

(number and percent of Hispanic households by homeownership status and region, 2011; numbers in thousands)

	total	owners number	owners percent	renters number	renters percent
Total Hispanic households	**13,841**	**6,530**	**47.2%**	**7,311**	**52.8%**
Northeast	2,119	604	28.5	1,515	71.5
Midwest	1,151	583	50.7	568	49.3
South	5,155	2,911	56.5	2,244	43.5
West	5,416	2,432	44.9	2,984	55.1

Source: Bureau of the Census, American Housing Survey for the United States: 2011, Internet site http://www.census.gov/housing/ahs/index.html; calculations by New Strategist

Table 5.46 Total and Hispanic Homeowners by Region, 2011

(number of total homeowners, number and percent distribution of Hispanic homeowners, and Hispanic share of total, by region, 2011; numbers in thousands)

| | | Hispanic | | |
	total	number	percent distribution	share of total
Total homeowners	**76,091**	**6,530**	**100.0%**	**8.6%**
Northeast	13,480	604	9.2	4.5
Midwest	18,032	583	8.9	3.2
South	29,119	2,911	44.6	10.0
West	15,460	2,432	37.2	15.7

Source: Bureau of the Census, American Housing Survey for the United States: 2011, Internet site http://www.census.gov/housing/ahs/index.html; calculations by New Strategist

Table 5.47 Total and Hispanic Renters by Region, 2011

(number of total renters, number and percent distribution of Hispanic renters, and Hispanic share of total, by region, 2011; numbers in thousands)

| | | Hispanic | | |
	total	number	percent distribution	share of total
Total renters	**38,816**	**7,311**	**100.0%**	**18.8%**
Northeast	7,585	1,515	20.7	20.0
Midwest	7,650	568	7.8	7.4
South	13,465	2,244	30.7	16.7
West	10,115	2,984	40.8	29.5

Source: Bureau of the Census, American Housing Survey for the United States: 2011, Internet site http://www.census.gov/housing/ahs/index.html; calculations by New Strategist

Table 5.48 Characteristics of Total and Hispanic Occupied Housing Units, 2006–10

(number of total and Hispanic occupied housing units, and percent distribution by selected characteristics, 2006–10; numbers in thousands)

	total number	total percent distribution	Hispanic number	Hispanic percent distribution
TOTAL OCCUPIED HOUSING UNITS	**114,236**	**100.0%**	**12,872**	**100.0%**
Year householder moved into unit				
Total households	**114,236**	**100.0**	**12,872**	**100.0**
2005 or later	39,766	34.8	5,860	45.5
2000 to 2004	26,517	23.2	3,350	26.0
1990 to 1999	23,883	20.9	2,236	17.4
1980 to 1989	10,804	9.5	740	5.8
1970 to 1979	7,147	6.3	432	3.4
Before 1970	6,120	5.4	253	2.0
Vehicles available				
Total households	**114,236**	**100.0**	**12,872**	**100.0**
None	10,113	8.9	1,632	12.7
One or more	104,123	91.1	11,240	87.3
House heating fuel				
Total households	**114,236**	**100.0**	**12,872**	**100.0**
Utility gas	57,018	49.9	6,313	49.0
Bottled gas	6,146	5.4	288	2.2
Electricity	39,066	34.2	5,183	40.3
Fuel oil or kerosene	8,073	7.1	603	4.7
Coal or coke	135	0.1	3	0.0
Wood	2,250	2.0	77	0.6
Solar energy	38	0.0	5	0.0
Other fuel	483	0.4	34	0.3
No heating fuel used	1,025	0.9	366	2.8
TOTAL OWNER-OCCUPIED HOMES	**76,090**	**100.0**	**6,273**	**100.0**
Housing units with a mortgage	51,697	67.9	4,816	76.8
Housing units without a mortgage	24,393	32.1	1,457	23.2
Median value of home	$188,400	–	$185,900	–
Median monthly owner costs with a mortgage	1,524	–	1,601	–
Median monthly owner costs without a mortgage	431	–	393	–
TOTAL RENTER-OCCUPIED HOMES	**38,146**	**100.0**	**6,598**	**100.0**
Occupied units paying rent	35,274	92.5	6,372	96.6
Median rent	$841	–	$877	–

Source: Bureau of the Census, 2006–10 American Community Survey, Internet site http://factfinder2.census.gov/faces/nav/jsf/pages/index.xhtml; calculations by New Strategist

Table 5.49 Characteristics of Housing Units Occupied by Hispanic Homeowners, 2011

(number and percent distribution of housing units occupied by Hispanic homeowners by selected housing characteristics, 2011; numbers in thousands)

	number	percent distribution
Total Hispanic homeowners	**6,530**	**100.0%**
UNITS IN STRUCTURE		
Total Hispanic homeowners	**6,530**	**100.0**
One, detached	5,234	80.2
One, attached	320	4.9
Two to four	177	2.7
Five to nine	59	0.9
10 to 19	46	0.7
20 to 49	39	0.6
50 or more	71	1.1
Mobile home or trailer	584	8.9
Median square footage of unit*	1,600	–
NUMBER OF BEDROOMS		
Total Hispanic homeowners	**6,530**	**100.0**
None	9	0.1
One	155	2.4
Two	1,137	17.4
Three	3,440	52.7
Four or more	1,791	27.4
NUMBER OF BATHROOMS		
Total Hispanic homeowners	**6,530**	**100.0**
None	25	0.4
One	1,628	24.9
One-and-one-half	806	12.3
Two or more	4,072	62.4
ROOMS USED FOR BUSINESS		
Total Hispanic homeowners	**6,530**	**100.0**
With room(s) used for business	1,530	23.4

* Single-family detached and mobile/manufactured homes only.
Note: "–" means not applicable.
Source: Bureau of the Census, American Housing Survey for the United States: 2011, Internet site http://www.census.gov/housing/ahs/index.html; calculations by New Strategist

Table 5.50 Characteristics of Housing Units Occupied by Hispanic Renters, 2011

(number and percent distribution of housing units occupied by Hispanic renters by selected housing characteristics, 2011; numbers in thousands)

	number	percent distribution
Total Hispanic renters	**7,311**	**100.0%**
UNITS IN STRUCTURE		
Total Hispanic renters	**7,311**	**100.0**
One, detached	1,887	25.8
One, attached	486	6.6
Two to four	1,482	20.3
Five to nine	1,019	13.9
10 to 19	862	11.8
20 to 49	734	10.0
50 or more	584	8.0
Mobile home or trailer	257	3.5
Median square footage of unit*	1,200	–
NUMBER OF BEDROOMS		
Total Hispanic renters	**7,311**	**100.0**
None	142	1.9
One	1,848	25.3
Two	3,055	41.8
Three	1,782	24.4
Four or more	485	6.6
NUMBER OF BATHROOMS		
Total Hispanic renters	**7,311**	**100.0**
None	57	0.8
One	4,762	65.1
One-and-one-half	563	7.7
Two or more	1,929	26.4
ROOMS USED FOR BUSINESS		
Total Hispanic renters	**7,311**	**100.0**
With room(s) used for business	1,344	18.4

* Single-family detached and mobile/manufactured homes only.
Note: "–" means not applicable.
Source: Bureau of the Census, American Housing Survey for the United States: 2011, Internet site http://www.census.gov/housing/ahs/index.html; calculations by New Strategist

Table 5.51 Geographic Mobility of Hispanics by Age, 2011–12

(total number of Hispanics aged 1 or older, and number and percent who moved between March 2011 and March 2012, by age and type of move; numbers in thousands)

	total	same house (nonmovers)	total movers	same county	different county, same state	different state total	different state same region	different state different region	movers from abroad
Total Hispanics	**51,352**	**43,587**	**7,765**	**5,524**	**1,093**	**826**	**434**	**392**	**321**
Aged 1 to 4	4,203	3,253	950	672	146	102	57	45	31
Aged 5 to 9	4,994	4,188	806	617	83	75	35	40	31
Aged 10 to 14	4,654	4,047	607	418	86	71	42	29	32
Aged 15 to 17	2,821	2,496	325	245	35	42	36	6	4
Aged 18 to 19	1,763	1,519	244	169	41	26	19	7	8
Aged 20 to 24	4,471	3,452	1,019	717	153	107	52	55	42
Aged 25 to 29	4,361	3,319	1,042	733	139	111	54	57	60
Aged 30 to 34	4,178	3,335	843	588	127	98	44	54	31
Aged 35 to 39	3,908	3,362	546	404	67	65	31	34	10
Aged 40 to 44	3,623	3,275	348	230	53	31	8	23	35
Aged 45 to 49	3,173	2,871	302	224	34	35	15	20	9
Aged 50 to 54	2,620	2,362	258	196	37	17	11	6	9
Aged 55 to 59	2,030	1,865	165	106	38	13	12	1	7
Aged 60 to 61	638	585	53	33	13	6	3	3	2
Aged 62 to 64	877	783	94	69	13	10	3	7	1
Aged 65 or older	3,037	2,874	163	104	29	19	13	6	11

PERCENT DISTRIBUTION BY MOBILITY STATUS

	total	same house (nonmovers)	total movers	same county	different county, same state	different state total	different state same region	different state different region	movers from abroad
Total Hispanics	**100.0%**	**84.9%**	**15.1%**	**10.8%**	**2.15%**	**1.6%**	**0.8%**	**0.8%**	**0.6%**
Aged 1 to 4	100.0	77.4	22.6	16.0	3.5	2.4	1.4	1.1	0.7
Aged 5 to 9	100.0	83.9	16.1	12.4	1.7	1.5	0.7	0.8	0.6
Aged 10 to 14	100.0	87.0	13.0	9.0	1.8	1.5	0.9	0.6	0.7
Aged 15 to 17	100.0	88.5	11.5	8.7	1.2	1.5	1.3	0.2	0.1
Aged 18 to 19	100.0	86.2	13.8	9.6	2.3	1.5	1.1	0.4	0.5
Aged 20 to 24	100.0	77.2	22.8	16.0	3.4	2.4	1.2	1.2	0.9
Aged 25 to 29	100.0	76.1	23.9	16.8	3.2	2.5	1.2	1.3	1.4
Aged 30 to 34	100.0	79.8	20.2	14.1	3.0	2.3	1.1	1.3	0.7
Aged 35 to 39	100.0	86.0	14.0	10.3	1.7	1.7	0.8	0.9	0.3
Aged 40 to 44	100.0	90.4	9.6	6.3	1.5	0.9	0.2	0.6	1.0
Aged 45 to 49	100.0	90.5	9.5	7.1	1.1	1.1	0.5	0.6	0.3
Aged 50 to 54	100.0	90.2	9.8	7.5	1.4	0.6	0.4	0.2	0.3
Aged 55 to 59	100.0	91.9	8.1	5.2	1.9	0.6	0.6	0.0	0.3
Aged 60 to 61	100.0	91.7	8.3	5.2	2.0	0.9	0.5	0.5	0.3
Aged 62 to 64	100.0	89.3	10.7	7.9	1.5	1.1	0.3	0.8	0.1
Aged 65 or older	100.0	94.6	5.4	3.4	1.0	0.6	0.4	0.2	0.4

Source: Bureau of the Census, Geographic Mobility: 2011 to 2012, Internet site http://www.census.gov/hhes/migration/data/cps/cps2012.html; calculations by New Strategist

Table 5.52 Reasons for Moving among Hispanic Movers, 2011–12

(number and percent distribution of Hispanic movers by main reason for move, 2011–12; numbers in thousands)

	number	percent distribution
Total Hispanic movers	**7,764**	**100.0%**
FAMILY REASONS	**2,296**	**29.6**
Change in marital status	398	5.1
To establish own household	947	12.2
Other family reason	951	12.2
EMPLOYMENT REASONS	**1,282**	**16.5**
New job or job transfer	568	7.3
To look for work or lost job	156	2.0
To be closer to work, easier commute	379	4.9
Retired	10	0.1
Other job-related reason	169	2.2
HOUSING REASONS	**4,131**	**53.2**
Wanted own home, not rent	356	4.6
Wanted new or better home/apartment	1,315	16.9
Wanted better neighborhood, less crime	265	3.4
Wanted cheaper housing	957	12.3
Foreclosure, eviction	244	3.1
Other housing reason	994	12.8
OTHER REASONS	**56**	**0.7**
To attend or leave college	9	0.1
Change of climate	0	0.0
Health reasons	3	0.0
Natural disaster	0	0.0
Other reason	44	0.6

Source: Bureau of the Census, Geographic Mobility: 2011 to 2012, Internet site http://www.census.gov/hhes/migration/data/cps/cps2012.html; calculations by New Strategist

The Incomes of Hispanics Are Well Below Average

The median income of Hispanic households fell 11 percent between 2000 and 2011, after adjusting for inflation. Despite the decline, the $38,624 median income of Hispanic households in 2011 was 4 percent higher than in 1990, after adjusting for inflation. The median income of Hispanic households is only 77 percent as high as that of the average household.

Between 2000 and 2011, the median earnings of Hispanic men who work full-time grew 2.5 percent, after adjusting for inflation. The median earnings of their female counterparts grew 7.6 percent during those years. Despite the increase, Hispanics with full-time jobs earn less than average because many are recent immigrants with little education.

Fully 15.9 percent of Hispanic married couples are poor—a higher poverty rate than is found among Asian, black, or non-Hispanic white couples. Poverty among Hispanic couples as well as female- and male-headed families has fallen since 1990.

■ The economic status of Hispanics will remain below that of the average American as long as immigrants account for a large share of the Hispanic population.

Hispanic incomes fell more than average between 2000 and 2011

(percent change in median income of total and Hispanic households, 2000 to 2011; in 2011 dollars)

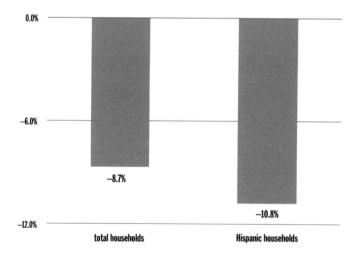

Table 5.53 Median Income of Total and Hispanic Households, 1990 to 2011

(median income of total and Hispanic households, and index of Hispanic to total, 1990 to 2011; percent change in median for selected years; in 2011 dollars)

	total households	Hispanic households	index, Hispanic to total
2011	$50,054	$38,624	77
2010	50,830	38,818	76
2009	52,195	39,887	76
2008	52,546	39,604	75
2007	54,489	41,956	77
2006	53,768	42,145	78
2005	53,371	41,437	78
2004	52,788	40,806	77
2003	52,973	40,351	76
2002	53,019	41,385	78
2001	53,646	42,640	79
2000	54,841	43,319	79
1999	54,932	41,501	76
1998	53,582	39,038	73
1997	51,704	37,205	72
1996	50,661	35,551	70
1995	49,935	33,499	67
1994	48,418	35,147	73
1993	47,884	35,078	73
1992	48,117	35,491	74
1991	48,516	36,542	75
1990	49,950	37,251	75

Percent change

2007 to 2011	–8.1%	–7.9%	–
2000 to 2011	–8.7	–10.8	–
1990 to 2011	0.2	3.7	–

Note: The index is calculated by dividing the Hispanic median by the total median and multiplying by 100. "–" means not applicable.
Source: Bureau of the Census, Current Population Surveys, Annual Social and Economic Supplement, Internet site http://www.census.gov/hhes/www/income/data/historical/household/index.html; calculations by New Strategist

Table 5.54 Hispanic Household Income by Age of Householder, 2011

(number and percent distribution of Hispanic households by household income and age of householder, 2011; households in thousands as of 2012)

	total	15 to 24	25 to 34	35 to 44	45 to 54	55 to 64	65 or older total	65 to 74	75 or older
Hispanic households	**14,939**	**1,288**	**3,554**	**3,618**	**2,943**	**1,935**	**1,600**	**977**	**623**
Under $5,000	688	120	173	137	96	95	65	42	24
$5,000 to $9,999	785	98	152	121	107	131	176	100	76
$10,000 to $14,999	992	56	195	184	157	147	253	108	145
$15,000 to $19,999	1,066	92	261	209	164	139	200	106	94
$20,000 to $24,999	1,126	103	265	280	190	146	142	91	50
$25,000 to $29,999	1,044	98	231	279	194	131	113	68	45
$30,000 to $34,999	1,047	110	279	253	211	91	103	66	37
$35,000 to $39,999	932	97	238	228	169	127	73	57	15
$40,000 to $44,999	850	84	207	222	164	110	62	33	30
$45,000 to $49,999	731	75	161	195	155	87	56	39	17
$50,000 to $54,999	684	59	186	165	151	72	52	37	15
$55,000 to $59,999	504	41	140	129	100	61	34	26	8
$60,000 to $64,999	578	54	140	152	117	80	35	30	5
$65,000 to $69,999	398	33	106	95	99	32	32	23	9
$70,000 to $74,999	379	29	97	106	73	57	17	10	7
$75,000 to $79,999	326	18	78	88	80	46	17	16	1
$80,000 to $84,999	291	16	75	92	70	30	9	6	3
$85,000 to $89,999	266	20	62	79	53	37	14	12	2
$90,000 to $94,999	256	3	62	72	64	35	20	15	4
$95,000 to $99,999	240	13	61	61	60	28	16	9	7
$100,000 to $124,999	725	42	190	188	180	100	27	24	5
$125,000 to $149,999	401	7	84	113	108	57	33	23	9
$150,000 to $174,999	259	10	54	82	72	27	16	10	5
$175,000 to $199,999	127	4	22	32	25	32	11	5	6
$200,000 or more	245	4	36	59	83	38	24	21	3
Median income	$38,624	$32,721	$39,552	$42,127	$40,193	$32,543	$23,627	$27,841	$18,618

PERCENT DISTRIBUTION

	total	15 to 24	25 to 34	35 to 44	45 to 54	55 to 64	65 or older total	65 to 74	75 or older
Hispanic households	100.0%	100.0%	100.0%	100.0%	100.0%	100.0%	100.0%	100.0%	100.0%
Under $25,000	31.2	36.4	29.4	25.7	24.3	34.0	52.3	45.8	62.4
$25,000 to $49,999	30.8	36.0	31.4	32.5	30.3	28.2	25.4	26.9	23.1
$50,000 to $74,999	17.0	16.8	18.8	17.9	18.3	15.6	10.6	12.9	7.1
$75,000 to $99,999	9.2	5.4	9.5	10.8	11.1	9.1	4.8	5.9	2.7
$100,000 or more	11.8	5.2	10.9	13.1	15.9	13.1	6.9	8.5	4.5

Source: Bureau of the Census, 2012 Current Population Survey, Internet site http://www.census.gov/hhes/www/income/data/incpovhlth/2011/dtables.html; calculations by New Strategist

Table 5.55 Hispanic Household Income by Household Type, 2011

(number and percent distribution of Hispanic households by household income and household type, 2011; households in thousands as of 2012)

| | | family households | | | nonfamily households | | | |
| | | married couples | female hh, no spouse present | male hh, no spouse present | female householder | | male householder | |
	total				total	living alone	total	living alone
Hispanic households	**14,939**	**7,222**	**3,086**	**1,277**	**1,535**	**1,251**	**1,818**	**1,264**
Under $5,000	4,261	712	1,087	150	1,262	1,154	1,051	924
$5,000 to $9,999	4,972	552	1,022	140	2,109	2,038	1,149	1,058
$10,000 to $14,999	7,127	985	1,208	263	2,993	2,874	1,677	1,556
$15,000 to $19,999	6,882	1,528	1,227	322	2,397	2,289	1,410	1,266
$20,000 to $24,999	7,095	2,157	1,258	390	1,753	1,599	1,537	1,308
$25,000 to $29,999	6,591	2,255	1,186	352	1,458	1,300	1,340	1,118
$30,000 to $34,999	6,667	2,500	1,096	408	1,356	1,223	1,308	1,087
$35,000 to $39,999	6,136	2,617	985	354	1,156	1,021	1,025	831
$40,000 to $44,999	5,795	2,538	943	309	988	812	1,017	797
$45,000 to $49,999	4,945	2,369	717	273	787	613	799	608
$50,000 to $54,999	5,170	2,536	676	291	799	633	869	674
$55,000 to $59,999	4,250	2,264	553	295	504	371	635	436
$60,000 to $64,999	4,432	2,376	502	286	581	453	687	517
$65,000 to $69,999	3,836	2,211	422	222	482	367	498	303
$70,000 to $74,999	3,606	2,170	350	209	404	268	473	301
$75,000 to $79,999	3,452	2,310	289	176	322	219	355	229
$80,000 to $84,999	3,036	1,990	241	155	239	163	411	249
$85,000 to $89,999	2,566	1,737	222	146	179	116	281	176
$90,000 to $94,999	2,594	1,826	193	106	183	115	285	157
$95,000 to $99,999	2,251	1,565	178	137	183	93	187	98
$100,000 to $124,999	9,129	6,773	590	385	531	291	849	479
$125,000 to $149,999	5,311	4,176	249	217	247	114	421	186
$150,000 to $174,999	3,829	2,955	189	133	205	110	347	205
$175,000 to $199,999	2,046	1,646	106	49	72	32	173	57
$200,000 or more	5,106	4,200	178	121	193	86	413	214
Median income	$38,624	$49,888	$28,206	$43,342	$20,955	$17,598	$30,238	$24,360

PERCENT DISTRIBUTION

Hispanic households	100.0%	100.0%	100.0%	100.0%	100.0%	100.0%	100.0%	100.0%
Under $25,000	31.2	19.4	44.5	22.5	54.6	61.4	41.5	51.2
$25,000 to $49,999	30.8	30.7	32.8	34.6	25.7	25.1	29.7	29.4
$50,000 to $74,999	17.0	19.7	14.2	18.9	10.7	8.4	15.2	13.0
$75,000 to $99,999	9.2	12.3	4.2	12.4	4.7	2.9	7.0	3.5
$100,000 or more	11.8	17.9	4.2	11.6	4.4	2.3	6.6	3.0

Note: "hh" stands for householder.
Source: Bureau of the Census, 2012 Current Population Survey, Internet site http://www.census.gov/hhes/www/income/data/incpovhlth/2011/dtables.html; calculations by New Strategist

Table 5.56 Income of Hispanic Men by Age, 2011

(number and percent distribution of Hispanic men aged 15 or older by income and age, 2011; median income of men with income and of men working full-time, year-round; percent working full-time, year-round; men in thousands as of 2012)

	total	under 25	25 to 34	35 to 44	45 to 54	55 to 64	65 or older
TOTAL HISPANIC MEN	**18,867**	**4,703**	**4,456**	**3,823**	**2,899**	**1,687**	**1,299**
Without income	**3,202**	**2,149**	**365**	**269**	**167**	**130**	**123**
With income	**15,665**	**2,554**	**4,091**	**3,554**	**2,732**	**1,558**	**1,176**
Under $5,000	1,144	594	221	121	94	74	40
$5,000 to $9,999	1,501	484	294	182	174	163	204
$10,000 to $14,999	1,925	425	443	341	259	182	275
$15,000 to $19,999	1,822	316	502	382	315	144	162
$20,000 to $24,999	1,749	258	521	401	296	158	114
$25,000 to $29,999	1,332	170	370	331	242	131	88
$30,000 to $34,999	1,210	99	376	323	227	123	62
$35,000 to $39,999	946	81	275	292	203	67	28
$40,000 to $44,999	834	46	270	216	160	111	31
$45,000 to $49,999	544	27	157	131	133	66	30
$50,000 to $54,999	560	6	151	171	149	59	24
$55,000 to $59,999	280	9	88	78	57	32	16
$60,000 to $64,999	370	12	95	112	68	58	24
$65,000 to $69,999	174	4	49	54	47	13	8
$70,000 to $74,999	203	2	56	77	34	23	10
$75,000 to $79,999	162	4	46	40	47	23	3
$80,000 to $84,999	148	5	31	57	21	20	14
$85,000 to $89,999	74	0	17	24	17	16	0
$90,000 to $94,999	87	1	23	21	21	14	6
$95,000 to $99,999	50	0	12	15	14	8	2
$100,000 or more	551	12	93	184	152	73	37
MEDIAN INCOME							
Men with income	$23,731	$11,829	$25,663	$30,171	$29,414	$26,494	$17,049
Working full-time	32,088	21,889	31,381	35,674	36,332	37,280	40,571
Percent full-time	48.2%	19.5%	61.8%	67.0%	64.4%	49.0%	12.9%
PERCENT DISTRIBUTION							
TOTAL HISPANIC MEN	**100.0%**	**100.0%**	**100.0%**	**100.0%**	**100.0%**	**100.0%**	**100.0%**
Without income	**17.0**	**45.7**	**8.2**	**7.0**	**5.8**	**7.7**	**9.5**
With income	**83.0**	**54.3**	**91.8**	**93.0**	**94.2**	**92.3**	**90.5**
Under $15,000	24.2	32.0	21.5	16.8	18.2	24.8	39.9
$15,000 to $24,999	18.9	12.2	23.0	20.5	21.1	17.9	21.3
$25,000 to $34,999	13.5	5.7	16.7	17.1	16.2	15.0	11.5
$35,000 to $49,999	12.3	3.3	15.8	16.7	17.1	14.4	6.8
$50,000 to $74,999	8.4	0.7	9.9	12.9	12.3	11.0	6.3
$75,000 or more	5.7	0.5	5.0	8.9	9.4	9.1	4.8

Source: Bureau of the Census, 2012 Current Population Survey Annual Social and Economic Supplement, Internet site http://www.census.gov/hhes/www/cpstables/032012/perinc/toc.htm; calculations by New Strategist

Table 5.57 Income of Hispanic Women by Age, 2011

(number and percent distribution of Hispanic women aged 15 or older by income and age, 2011; median income of women with income and of women working full-time, year-round; percent working full-time, year-round; women in thousands as of 2012)

	total	under 25	25 to 34	35 to 44	45 to 54	55 to 64	65 or older
TOTAL HISPANIC WOMEN	**18,633**	**4,352**	**4,083**	**3,708**	**2,895**	**1,858**	**1,737**
Without income	**5,355**	**2,157**	**1,133**	**846**	**575**	**420**	**224**
With income	**13,278**	**2,195**	**2,950**	**2,862**	**2,320**	**1,438**	**1,513**
Under $5,000	1,779	643	383	282	198	157	116
$5,000 to $9,999	2,188	476	379	296	250	268	520
$10,000 to $14,999	1,906	334	382	351	255	200	383
$15,000 to $19,999	1,650	271	344	362	339	161	173
$20,000 to $24,999	1,319	182	338	304	264	147	85
$25,000 to $29,999	888	76	236	250	190	86	50
$30,000 to $34,999	821	85	231	233	167	66	40
$35,000 to $39,999	629	59	163	187	121	64	34
$40,000 to $44,999	463	29	138	114	111	57	15
$45,000 to $49,999	309	7	90	88	75	33	17
$50,000 to $54,999	314	9	78	78	81	51	16
$55,000 to $59,999	149	3	35	45	38	15	13
$60,000 to $64,999	207	14	46	61	54	23	10
$65,000 to $69,999	101	0	22	32	22	19	7
$70,000 to $74,999	124	0	19	39	32	26	8
$75,000 to $79,999	83	0	19	24	27	7	7
$80,000 to $84,999	65	4	11	20	16	11	2
$85,000 to $89,999	45	0	4	21	10	10	0
$90,000 to $94,999	29	0	5	13	6	3	2
$95,000 to $99,999	23	0	4	6	6	5	3
$100,000 or more	187	3	23	57	59	31	14
MEDIAN INCOME							
Women with income	$16,829	$9,714	$19,690	$21,706	$21,741	$17,603	$11,308
Working full-time	30,102	21,725	30,187	31,308	31,121	30,739	31,968
Percent full-time	31.6%	13.3%	36.9%	45.2%	48.0%	33.0%	6.9%
PERCENT DISTRIBUTION							
TOTAL HISPANIC WOMEN	**100.0%**	**100.0%**	**100.0%**	**100.0%**	**100.0%**	**100.0%**	**100.0%**
Without income	**28.7**	**49.6**	**27.8**	**22.8**	**19.9**	**22.6**	**12.9**
With income	**71.3**	**50.4**	**72.2**	**77.2**	**80.1**	**77.4**	**87.1**
Under $15,000	31.5	33.4	28.0	25.1	24.3	33.6	58.6
$15,000 to $24,999	15.9	10.4	16.7	18.0	20.8	16.5	14.9
$25,000 to $34,999	9.2	3.7	11.4	13.0	12.3	8.2	5.2
$35,000 to $49,999	7.5	2.2	9.6	10.5	10.6	8.3	3.8
$50,000 to $74,999	4.8	0.6	4.9	6.9	7.8	7.1	3.1
$75,000 or more	2.3	0.2	1.6	3.8	4.3	3.6	1.6

Source: Bureau of the Census, 2012 Current Population Survey Annual Social and Economic Supplement, Internet site http:// www.census.gov/hhes/www/cpstables/032012/perinc/toc.htm; calculations by New Strategist

Table 5.58 Median Earnings of Hispanics Working Full-Time by Sex, 1990 to 2011

(median earnings of Hispanics working full-time, year-round by sex; index of Hispanic to total population median earnings, and Hispanic women's earnings as a percent of Hispanic men's earnings, 1990 to 2011; percent change in earnings for selected years; in 2011 dollars)

	Hispanic men		Hispanic women		women's earnings as a percent of
	earnings	index	earnings	index	men's earnings
2011	$31,843	66	$29,020	78	91.1%
2010	32,574	66	29,071	76	89.2
2009	32,918	67	28,501	75	86.6
2008	32,338	67	28,043	75	86.7
2007	32,757	67	28,867	76	88.1
2006	32,418	69	28,108	77	86.7
2005	30,840	65	27,896	76	90.5
2004	31,739	65	27,952	75	88.1
2003	31,896	64	27,347	73	85.7
2002	32,469	66	27,392	73	84.4
2001	31,865	66	27,304	74	85.7
2000	31,055	64	26,982	75	86.9
1999	30,260	62	26,166	74	86.5
1998	30,708	63	26,486	74	86.3
1997	30,201	64	26,509	76	87.8
1996	30,055	66	26,642	79	88.6
1995	29,863	65	25,173	76	84.3
1994	30,485	66	26,365	79	86.5
1993	30,883	66	25,685	77	83.2
1992	30,691	65	26,836	80	87.4
1991	31,840	67	26,160	79	82.2
1990	31,922	69	26,144	79	81.9
	percent change		percent change		percentage point change
2007 to 2011	−2.8%	–	0.5%	–	3.0
2000 to 2011	2.5	–	7.6	–	4.3
1990 to 2011	−0.2	–	11.0	–	9.2

Note: The Hispanic/total indexes are calculated by dividing the median earnings of Hispanic men and women by the median earnings of total men and women and multiplying by 100. "−" means not applicable.
Source: Bureau of the Census, Current Population Survey, Historical Tables, Internet site http://www.census.gov/hhes/www/income/data/historical/people/; calculations by New Strategist

Table 5.59 Median Earnings of Hispanics Working Full-Time by Education and Sex, 2011

(median earnings of Hispanics aged 25 or older working full-time, year-round, by educational attainment and sex, and Hispanic women's earnings as a percent of Hispanic men's earnings, 2011)

	men	women	Hispanic women's earnings as a percent of men's earnings
Total Hispanics	**$32,462**	**$29,492**	**90.9%**
Less than 9th grade	23,108	17,367	75.2
9th to 12th grade, no diploma	25,948	19,891	76.7
High school graduate	31,626	26,269	83.1
Some college, no degree	40,353	32,219	79.8
Associate's degree	42,286	32,365	76.5
Bachelor's degree or more	58,652	46,710	79.6
Bachelor's degree	52,261	41,684	79.8
Master's degree	65,771	56,128	85.3
Professional degree	–	–	–
Doctoral degree	–	–	–

Note: "–" means data are not available.
Source: Bureau of the Census, 2012 Current Population Survey Annual Social and Economic Supplement, Internet site http://www.census.gov/hhes/www/cpstables/032012/perinc/toc.htm; calculations by New Strategist

Table 5.60 Poverty Status of Hispanic Married Couples, 1990 to 2011

(total number of Hispanic married couples, and number and percent below poverty level by presence of children under age 18 at home, 1990 to 2011; percent change in numbers and percentage point change in rates for selected years; families in thousands as of March the following year)

		in poverty	
	total	number	percent
Total Hispanic married couples			
2011	7,222	1,145	15.9%
2010	7,065	1,221	17.3
2009	6,593	1,054	16.0
2008	6,911	1,078	15.6
2007	6,891	926	13.4
2006	6,764	903	13.3
2005	6,642	917	13.8
2004	6,353	934	14.7
2003	6,228	976	15.7
2002	6,189	927	15.0
2001	5,778	799	13.8
2000	5,426	772	14.2
1999	5,273	758	14.4
1998	4,945	775	15.7
1997	4,804	836	17.4
1996	4,520	815	18.0
1995	4,247	803	18.9
1994	4,236	827	19.5
1993	4,038	770	19.1
1992	3,940	743	18.8
1991	3,532	674	19.1
1990	3,454	605	17.5

	percent change		percentage point change
2007 to 2011	4.8%	23.7%	2.5
2000 to 2011	33.1	48.3	1.7
1990 to 2011	109.1	89.3	−1.6

	total	in poverty	
		number	percent
Hispanic married couples with children			
2011	4,656	916	19.7%
2010	4,684	1,022	21.8
2009	4,397	876	19.9
2008	4,617	874	18.9
2007	4,663	766	16.4
2006	4,607	718	15.6
2005	4,555	771	16.9
2004	4,365	778	17.8
2003	4,288	789	18.4
2002	4,242	752	17.7
2001	3,976	646	16.2
2000	3,857	649	16.8
1999	3,762	640	17.0
1998	3,398	656	19.3
1997	3,293	692	21.0
1996	3,124	687	22.0
1995	2,902	657	22.6
1994	2,923	698	23.9
1993	2,747	652	23.7
1992	2,692	615	22.9
1991	2,445	575	23.5
1990	2,405	501	20.8

	percent change		percentage point change
2007 to 2011	−0.2%	19.6%	3.3
2000 to 2011	20.7	41.1	2.9
1990 to 2011	93.6	82.8	−1.1

Source: Bureau of the Census, Current Population Surveys, Historical Poverty Tables, Internet site http://www.census.gov/hhes/ www/poverty/data/historical/families.html; calculations by New Strategist

Table 5.61 Poverty Status of Hispanic Female-Headed Families, 1990 to 2011

(total number of Hispanic female-headed families, and number and percent below poverty level by presence of children under age 18 at home, 1990 to 2011; percent change in numbers and percentage point change in rates for selected years; families in thousands as of March the following year)

| | total | in poverty | |
		number	percent
Total Hispanic **female-headed families**			
2011	3,090	1,272	41.2%
2010	2,978	1,270	42.6
2009	2,748	1,066	38.8
2008	2,571	1,007	39.2
2007	2,523	968	38.4
2006	2,446	881	36.0
2005	2,254	876	38.9
2004	2,241	872	38.9
2003	2,138	792	37.0
2002	2,033	717	35.3
2001	1,922	711	37.0
2000	1,826	664	36.4
1999	1,827	717	39.3
1998	1,728	756	43.7
1997	1,612	767	47.6
1996	1,617	823	50.9
1995	1,604	792	49.4
1994	1,485	773	52.1
1993	1,498	772	51.6
1992	1,348	664	49.3
1991	1,261	627	49.7
1990	1,186	573	48.3

	percent change		percentage point change
2007 to 2011	22.5%	31.4%	2.8
2000 to 2011	69.2	91.6	4.8
1990 to 2011	160.5	122.0	−7.1

	total	in poverty	
		number	percent
Hispanic female-headed families with children			
2011	2,361	1,159	49.1%
2010	2,296	1,159	50.5
2009	2,055	945	46.0
2008	1,957	912	46.6
2007	1,890	881	46.6
2006	1,908	811	42.5
2005	1,719	777	45.2
2004	1,753	806	46.0
2003	1,657	713	43.0
2002	1,587	657	41.4
2001	1,493	645	43.2
2000	1,391	597	42.9
1999	1,416	662	46.8
1998	1,355	707	52.2
1997	1,292	701	54.2
1996	1,274	760	59.7
1995	1,283	735	57.3
1994	1,182	700	59.2
1993	1,167	706	60.5
1992	1,037	598	57.7
1991	972	584	60.1
1990	921	536	58.2

	percent change		percentage point change
2007 to 2011	24.9%	31.6%	2.5
2000 to 2011	69.7	94.1	6.2
1990 to 2011	156.4	116.2	−9.1

Source: Bureau of the Census, Current Population Surveys, Historical Poverty Tables, Internet site http://www.census.gov/hhes/ www/poverty/data/historical/families.html; calculations by New Strategist

Table 5.62 Poverty Status of Hispanic Male-Headed Families, 1990 to 2011

(total number of Hispanic male-headed families, and number and percent below poverty level by presence of children under age 18 at home, 1990 to 2011; percent change in numbers and percentage point change in rates for selected years; families in thousands as of March the following year)

	total	in poverty	
		number	percent
Total Hispanic male-headed families			
2011	1,277	234	18.4%
2010	1,241	248	20.0
2009	1,081	249	23.0
2008	1,021	154	15.1
2007	983	151	15.3
2006	945	139	14.7
2005	972	155	15.9
2004	927	147	15.9
2003	908	157	17.3
2002	872	148	17.0
2001	817	139	17.0
2000	765	104	13.6
1999	688	117	17.0
1998	600	117	19.6
1997	545	119	21.7
1996	494	110	22.3
1995	436	100	22.9
1994	481	124	25.8
1993	410	83	20.2
1992	445	122	27.4
1991	383	71	18.5
1990	341	66	19.4

	percent change		percentage point change
2007 to 2011	29.9%	55.0%	3.1
2000 to 2011	66.9	125.0	4.8
1990 to 2011	274.5	254.5	−1.0

	total	in poverty	
		number	percent
Hispanic male-headed families with children			
2011	725	189	26.1%
2010	690	192	27.8
2009	606	183	30.2
2008	544	119	22.0
2007	507	112	22.0
2006	467	106	22.8
2005	496	102	20.6
2004	499	102	20.4
2003	508	127	24.9
2002	500	118	23.6
2001	468	115	24.5
2000	421	77	18.4
1999	377	98	26.1
1998	325	91	28.0
1997	324	99	30.5
1996	291	102	35.1
1995	237	78	32.9
1994	272	99	36.4
1993	239	66	27.6
1992	233	89	38.2
1991	204	60	29.4
1990	171	48	28.1

	percent change		percentage point change
2007 to 2011	43.0%	68.8%	4.1
2000 to 2011	72.2	145.5	7.7
1990 to 2011	324.0	293.8	−2.0

Source: Bureau of the Census, Current Population Surveys, Historical Poverty Tables, Internet site http://www.census.gov/hhes/www/poverty/data/historical/families.html; calculations by New Strategist

Table 5.63 Poverty Status of Hispanics by Sex and Age, 2011

(total number of Hispanics, and number and percent below poverty level by sex and age, 2011; people in thousands as of 2012)

	total	in poverty number	in poverty percent
Total Hispanics	**52,279**	**13,244**	**25.3%**
Under age 18	17,600	6,008	34.1
Aged 18 to 24	6,234	1,507	24.2
Aged 25 to 34	8,539	1,960	23.0
Aged 35 to 44	7,531	1,580	21.0
Aged 45 to 54	5,794	941	16.2
Aged 55 to 59	2,030	358	17.6
Aged 60 to 64	1,515	320	21.1
Aged 65 or older	3,036	569	18.7
Hispanic females	**25,876**	**7,166**	**27.7%**
Under age 18	8,630	3,036	35.2
Aged 18 to 24	2,965	824	27.8
Aged 25 to 34	4,083	1,203	29.5
Aged 35 to 44	3,708	873	23.6
Aged 45 to 54	2,895	494	17.0
Aged 55 to 59	1,049	197	18.8
Aged 60 to 64	809	197	24.4
Aged 65 or older	1,737	342	19.7
Hispanic males	**26,403**	**6,078**	**23.0%**
Under age 18	8,970	2,972	33.1
Aged 18 to 24	3,269	683	20.9
Aged 25 to 34	4,456	758	17.0
Aged 35 to 44	3,823	707	18.5
Aged 45 to 54	2,899	447	15.4
Aged 55 to 59	981	161	16.4
Aged 60 to 64	706	123	17.4
Aged 65 or older	1,299	227	17.5

Source: Bureau of the Census, 2012 Current Population Survey, Internet site http://www.census.gov/hhes/www/cpstables/032012/pov/toc.htm; calculations by New Strategist

Labor Force Participation Rate of Hispanic Men Is above Average

The labor force participation rate of Hispanic men, at 76 percent, is well above the 70 percent rate for all men. Hispanic women are only slightly less likely than the average women to be in the labor force—56.6 percent of Hispanics versus 57.7 percent of all women aged 16 or older. Among Hispanic women, those of Cuban origin are most likely to work, with a labor force participation rate of 61 percent.

Only 21 percent of Hispanic workers are in managerial or professional jobs, accounting for 8 percent of Americans employed in those occupations. The occupational distribution of Hispanics varies by ethnicity, however. More than one-third of Cuban Americans are employed in managerial or professional occupations. In contrast, the figure is just 17 percent among Mexican Americans. Hispanics account for 15 percent of all workers, but they are more than 40 percent of maids and housekeepers, grounds maintenance workers, and butchers, more than half of cement masons, and 62 percent of drywall installers.

Between 2010 and 2020, the number of Hispanic workers will grow 34 percent. Hispanics will account for nearly one in five workers by 2020.

■ Because a large share of Hispanics are poorly educated immigrants, they are less likely than the average worker to be employed in managerial or professional occupations.

More than three of four Hispanic men are in the labor force

(percent of Hispanics aged 16 or older in the labor force, by sex, 2012)

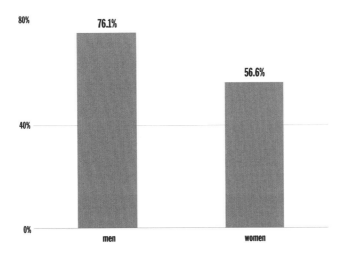

Table 5.64 Labor Force Participation Rate of Hispanics by Age and Sex, 2012

(percent of Hispanics aged 16 or older in the civilian labor force, by age and sex, 2012)

	total	men	women
Total Hispanics	**66.4%**	**76.1%**	**56.6%**
Aged 16 to 19	30.9	33.0	28.8
Aged 20 to 24	71.2	78.5	63.3
Aged 25 to 29	78.9	90.2	66.5
Aged 30 to 34	79.4	93.0	64.8
Aged 35 to 39	79.9	91.8	67.6
Aged 40 to 44	80.5	90.2	70.5
Aged 45 to 49	80.2	89.4	70.9
Aged 50 to 54	76.1	84.8	67.6
Aged 55 to 59	68.0	78.3	58.6
Aged 60 to 64	50.4	59.6	42.0
Aged 65 or older	16.5	21.1	13.2
Aged 65 to 69	27.0	30.3	24.3
Aged 70 to 74	16.4	22.0	12.5
Aged 75 or older	7.6	11.8	4.6

Note: The civilian labor force equals the number of employed plus the number of unemployed.
Source: Bureau of Labor Statistics, Labor Force Statistics from the Current Population Survey, Internet site http://www.bls.gov/cps/tables.htm#empstat

Table 5.65 Employment Status of Hispanics by Sex and Age, 2012

(number and percent of Hispanics aged 16 or older in the civilian labor force by sex, age, and employment status, 2012; numbers in thousands)

	civilian noninstitutional population	civilian labor force			unemployed	
		total	percent of population	employed	number	percent of labor force
Total Hispanics	**36,759**	**24,391**	**66.4%**	**21,878**	**2,514**	**10.3%**
Aged 16 to 19	3,656	1,131	30.9	808	324	28.6
Aged 20 to 24	4,502	3,205	71.2	2,761	444	13.8
Aged 25 to 34	8,512	6,736	79.1	6,119	618	9.2
Aged 35 to 44	7,551	6,053	80.2	5,552	502	8.3
Aged 45 to 54	5,831	4,569	78.4	4,188	381	8.3
Aged 55 to 64	3,613	2,185	60.5	1,983	201	9.2
Aged 65 or older	3,094	512	16.5	467	44	8.7
Hispanic men	**18,434**	**14,026**	**76.1**	**12,643**	**1,383**	**9.9**
Aged 16 to 19	1,879	620	33.0	431	189	30.5
Aged 20 to 24	2,341	1,837	78.5	1,584	254	13.8
Aged 25 to 34	4,424	4,053	91.6	3,714	339	8.4
Aged 35 to 44	3,822	3,480	91.1	3,229	251	7.2
Aged 45 to 54	2,911	2,542	87.3	2,334	208	8.2
Aged 55 to 64	1,729	1,215	70.3	1,097	119	9.8
Aged 65 or older	1,329	280	21.1	256	24	8.6
Hispanic women	**18,324**	**10,365**	**56.6**	**9,235**	**1,130**	**10.9**
Aged 16 to 19	1,776	512	28.8	377	135	26.4
Aged 20 to 24	2,161	1,368	63.3	1,178	190	13.9
Aged 25 to 34	4,088	2,683	65.6	2,405	278	10.4
Aged 35 to 44	3,729	2,574	69.0	2,323	251	9.7
Aged 45 to 54	2,920	2,027	69.4	1,854	173	8.5
Aged 55 to 64	1,884	969	51.4	887	83	8.5
Aged 65 or older	1,765	232	13.2	212	20	8.8

Note: The civilian labor force equals the number of the employed plus the number of the unemployed. The civilian population equals the number in the labor force plus the number not in the labor force.
Source: Bureau of Labor Statistics, Labor Force Statistics from the Current Population Survey, Internet site http://www.bls.gov/cps/tables.htm#empstat

Table 5.66 Employment Status of Hispanics by Sex and Ethnicity, 2012

(employment status of the civilian noninstitutionalized Hispanic population aged 16 or older, by sex and ethnicity, 2012; numbers in thousands)

	civilian noninstitutional population	civilian labor force				
					unemployed	
		total	percent of population	employed	number	percent of labor force
Total Hispanics	**36,759**	**24,391**	**66.4%**	**21,878**	**2,514**	**10.3%**
Mexican	22,716	15,128	66.6	13,552	1,577	10.4
Puerto Rican	3,462	2,090	60.4	1,830	260	12.4
Cuban	1,702	1,102	64.7	994	108	9.8
Hispanic men	**18,434**	**14,026**	**76.1**	**12,643**	**1,383**	**9.9**
Mexican	11,639	9,024	77.5	8,137	887	9.8
Puerto Rican	1,631	1,065	65.3	926	140	13.1
Cuban	842	579	68.9	525	55	9.4
Hispanic women	**18,324**	**10,365**	**56.6**	**9,235**	**1,130**	**10.9**
Mexican	11,078	6,105	55.1	5,414	690	11.3
Puerto Rican	1,831	1,025	55.9	904	120	11.7
Cuban	861	522	60.7	469	53	10.1

Note: The civilian labor force equals the number of the employed plus the number of the unemployed. The civilian population equals the number in the labor force plus the number not in the labor force.
Source: Bureau of Labor Statistics, Labor Force Statistics from the Current Population Survey, Internet site http://www.bls.gov/cps/tables.htm#empstat

Table 5.67 Hispanic Workers by Occupation, 2012

(total number of employed persons aged 16 or older in the civilian labor force, number and percent distribution of employed Hispanics, and Hispanic share of total, by occupation, 2012; numbers in thousands)

		Hispanic		
	total	number	percent distribution	share of total
TOTAL EMPLOYED	**142,469**	**21,878**	**100.0%**	**15.4%**
Management, professional and related occupations	**54,043**	**4,516**	**20.6**	**8.4**
Management, business, and financial operations	22,678	1,940	8.9	8.6
Management occupations	16,042	1,410	6.4	8.8
Business and financial operations occupations	6,636	530	2.4	8.0
Professional and related occupations	31,365	2,576	11.8	8.2
Computer and mathematical occupations	3,816	234	1.1	6.1
Architecture and engineering occupations	2,846	212	1.0	7.4
Life, physical, and social science occupations	1,316	88	0.4	6.7
Community and social services occupations	2,265	251	1.1	11.1
Legal occupations	1,786	133	0.6	7.4
Education, training, and library occupations	8,543	829	3.8	9.7
Arts, design, entertainment, sports, and media occupations	2,814	250	1.1	8.9
Health care practitioner and technical occupations	7,977	579	2.6	7.3
Service occupations	**25,459**	**5,754**	**26.3**	**22.6**
Health care support occupations	3,496	536	2.4	15.3
Protective service occupations	3,096	425	1.9	13.7
Food preparation and serving related occupations	8,018	1,911	8.7	23.8
Building and grounds cleaning and maintenance occupations	5,591	2,020	9.2	36.1
Personal care and service occupations	5,258	862	3.9	16.4
Sales and office occupations	**33,152**	**4,650**	**21.3**	**14.0**
Sales and related occupations	15,457	2,091	9.6	13.5
Office and administrative support occupations	17,695	2,559	11.7	14.5
Natural resources, construction, and maintenance occupations	**12,821**	**3,268**	**14.9**	**25.5**
Farming, fishing, and forestry occupations	994	440	2.0	44.3
Construction and extraction occupations	7,005	2,027	9.3	28.9
Installation, maintenance, and repair occupations	4,821	801	3.7	16.6
Production, transportation, and material moving occupations	**16,994**	**3,690**	**16.9**	**21.7**
Production occupations	8,455	1,838	8.4	21.7
Transportation and material moving occupations	8,540	1,852	8.5	21.7

Source: Bureau of Labor Statistics, Labor Force Statistics from the Current Population Survey, Internet site http://www.bls.gov/cps/tables.htm#empstat

Table 5.68 Hispanic Workers by Occupation and Ethnicity, 2012

(number of employed Hispanics aged 16 or older in the civilian labor force, by occupation and ethnicity, 2012; numbers in thousands)

	total	Mexican	Puerto Rican	Cuban
TOTAL EMPLOYED HISPANICS	**21,878**	**13,552**	**1,830**	**994**
Management, professional and related occupations	**4,516**	**2,361**	**538**	**338**
Management, business, and financial operations	1,940	1,037	202	154
Management occupations	1,410	747	141	122
Business and financial operations occupations	530	290	61	32
Professional and related occupations	2,576	1,324	336	185
Computer and mathematical occupations	234	106	34	12
Architecture and engineering occupations	212	116	16	16
Life, physical, and social science occupations	88	45	9	3
Community and social services occupations	251	135	47	6
Legal occupations	133	59	20	17
Education, training, and library occupations	829	446	97	72
Arts, design, entertainment, sports, and media occupations	250	123	23	11
Health care practitioner and technical occupations	579	295	89	48
Service occupations	**5,754**	**3,583**	**412**	**186**
Health care support occupations	536	293	68	32
Protective service occupations	425	241	69	26
Food preparation and serving related occupations	1,911	1,315	104	37
Building and grounds cleaning and maintenance occupations	2,020	1,244	95	63
Personal care and service occupations	862	489	75	28
Sales and office occupations	**4,650**	**2,763**	**515**	**237**
Sales and related occupations	2,091	1,260	202	108
Office and administrative support occupations	2,559	1,503	312	129
Natural resources, construction, and maintenance occupations	**3,268**	**2,352**	**126**	**96**
Farming, fishing, and forestry occupations	440	388	4	3
Construction and extraction occupations	2,027	1,455	60	53
Installation, maintenance, and repair occupations	801	509	62	39
Production, transportation, and material moving occupations	**3,690**	**2,493**	**239**	**136**
Production occupations	1,838	1,305	97	59
Transportation and material moving occupations	1,852	1,187	142	77

Note: Numbers do not add to total because not all ethnicities are shown.
Source: Bureau of Labor Statistics, Labor Force Statistics from the Current Population Survey, Internet site http://www.bls.gov/cps/tables.htm#empstat

Table 5.69 Percent Distribution of Hispanic Workers by Occupation and Ethnicity, 2012

(percent distribution of employed Hispanics aged 16 or older in the civilian labor force, by occupation and ethnicity, 2012; numbers in thousands)

	total	Mexican	Puerto Rican	Cuban
TOTAL EMPLOYED HISPANICS	**100.0%**	**100.0%**	**100.0%**	**100.0%**
Management, professional and related occupations	**20.6**	**17.4**	**29.4**	**34.0**
Management, business, and financial operations	8.9	7.7	11.0	15.5
Management occupations	6.4	5.5	7.7	12.3
Business and financial operations occupations	2.4	2.1	3.3	3.2
Professional and related occupations	11.8	9.8	18.4	18.6
Computer and mathematical occupations	1.1	0.8	1.9	1.2
Architecture and engineering occupations	1.0	0.9	0.9	1.6
Life, physical, and social science occupations	0.4	0.3	0.5	0.3
Community and social services occupations	1.1	1.0	2.6	0.6
Legal occupations	0.6	0.4	1.1	1.7
Education, training, and library occupations	3.8	3.3	5.3	7.2
Arts, design, entertainment, sports, and media occupations	1.1	0.9	1.3	1.1
Health care practitioner and technical occupations	2.6	2.2	4.9	4.8
Service occupations	**26.3**	**26.4**	**22.5**	**18.7**
Health care support occupations	2.4	2.2	3.7	3.2
Protective service occupations	1.9	1.8	3.8	2.6
Food preparation and serving related occupations	8.7	9.7	5.7	3.7
Building and grounds cleaning and maintenance occupations	9.2	9.2	5.2	6.3
Personal care and service occupations	3.9	3.6	4.1	2.8
Sales and office occupations	**21.3**	**20.4**	**28.1**	**23.8**
Sales and related occupations	9.6	9.3	11.0	10.9
Office and administrative support occupations	11.7	11.1	17.0	13.0
Natural resources, construction, and maintenance occupations	**14.9**	**17.4**	**6.9**	**9.7**
Farming, fishing, and forestry occupations	2.0	2.9	0.2	0.3
Construction and extraction occupations	9.3	10.7	3.3	5.3
Installation, maintenance, and repair occupations	3.7	3.8	3.4	3.9
Production, transportation, and material moving occupations	**16.9**	**18.4**	**13.1**	**13.7**
Production occupations	8.4	9.6	5.3	5.9
Transportation and material moving occupations	8.5	8.8	7.8	7.7

Source: Bureau of Labor Statistics, Labor Force Statistics from the Current Population Survey, Internet site http://www.bls.gov/cps/tables.htm#empstat

Table 5.70 Hispanic Workers by Detailed Occupation, 2012

(total number of employed workers agd 16 or older and percent Hispanic, by detailed occupation, 2012; numbers in thousands)

	total employed	Hispanic, share of total
TOTAL EMPLOYED AGED 16 OR OLDER	**142,469**	**15.4%**
Management, professional, and related occupations	**54,043**	**8.4**
Management, business, and financial operations occupations	22,678	8.6
Management occupations	16,042	8.8
Chief executives	1,513	4.7
General and operations managers	1,064	9.3
Legislators	11	–
Advertising and promotions managers	77	10.0
Marketing and sales managers	967	6.1
Public relations and fundraising managers	58	8.0
Administrative services managers	144	9.5
Computer and information systems managers	605	5.8
Financial managers	1,228	10.3
Compensation and benefits managers	15	–
Human resources managers	224	9.5
Training and development managers	36	–
Industrial production managers	261	11.4
Purchasing managers	218	10.4
Transportation, storage, and distribution managers	287	11.3
Farmers, ranchers, and other agricultural managers	944	4.0
Construction managers	983	9.4
Education administrators	811	7.9
Architectural and engineering managers	120	2.9
Food service managers	1,085	16.5
Funeral service managers	13	–
Gaming managers	26	–
Lodging managers	154	11.5
Medical and health services managers	585	8.1
Natural sciences managers	18	–
Postmasters and mail superintendents	39	–
Property, real estate, and community association managers	644	11.4
Social and community service managers	315	8.5
Emergency management directors	6	–
Managers, all other	3,594	9.3
Business and financial operations occupations	6,636	8.0
Agents and business managers of artists, performers, and athletes	47	–
Buyers and purchasing agents, farm products	13	–
Wholesale and retail buyers, except farm products	198	10.9

	total employed	Hispanic, share of total
Purchasing agents, except wholesale, retail, and farm products	261	9.8%
Claims adjusters, appraisers, examiners, and investigators	323	10.3
Compliance officers	199	8.2
Cost estimators	114	6.8
Human resources workers	603	11.8
Compensation, benefits, and job analysis specialists	71	11.8
Training and development specialists	126	10.8
Logisticians	94	11.9
Management analysts	773	4.4
Meeting, convention, and event planners	127	10.3
Fundraisers	86	3.4
Market research analysts and marketing specialists	219	4.7
Business operations specialists, all other	251	9.2
Accountants and auditors	1,765	6.8
Appraisers and assessors of real estate	93	1.0
Budget analysts	55	8.2
Credit analysts	30	–
Financial analysts	89	6.3
Personal financial advisors	378	4.5
Insurance underwriters	103	10.2
Financial examiners	14	–
Credit counselors and loan officers	333	9.3
Tax examiners and collectors, and revenue agents	82	13.9
Tax preparers	107	15.9
Financial specialists, all other	82	11.5
Professional and related occupations	31,365	8.2
Computer and mathematical occupations	3,816	6.1
Computer and information research scientists	29	–
Computer systems analysts	499	4.5
Information security analysts	52	4.0
Computer programmers	480	5.3
Software developers, applications and systems software	1,084	5.2
Web developers	190	5.6
Computer support specialists	476	9.7
Database administrators	101	9.8
Network and computer systems administrators	226	10.7
Computer network architects	127	4.6
Computer occupations, all other	341	5.9
Actuaries	26	–
Mathematicians	4	–
Operations research analysts	130	6.5
Statisticians	47	–
Miscellaneous mathematical science occupations	3	–

	total employed	Hispanic, share of total
Architecture and engineering occupations	2,846	7.4%
Architects, except naval	195	8.2
Surveyors, cartographers, and photogrammetrists	51	8.1
Aerospace engineers	119	4.6
Agricultural engineers	4	–
Biomedical engineers	10	–
Chemical engineers	71	6.7
Civil engineers	358	3.7
Computer hardware engineers	91	6.5
Electrical and electronics engineers	335	6.7
Environmental engineers	43	–
Industrial engineers, including health and safety	197	10.5
Marine engineers and naval architects	8	–
Materials engineers	40	–
Mechanical engineers	288	4.9
Mining and geological engineers, including mining safety engineers	9	–
Nuclear engineers	11	–
Petroleum engineers	38	–
Engineers, all other	359	5.9
Drafters	149	9.9
Engineering technicians, except drafters	395	12.3
Surveying and mapping technicians	77	13.5
Life, physical, and social science occupations	1,316	6.7
Agricultural and food scientists	42	–
Biological scientists	101	7.2
Conservation scientists and foresters	25	–
Medical scientists	136	5.8
Astronomers and physicists	25	–
Atmospheric and space scientists	15	–
Chemists and materials scientists	105	9.4
Environmental scientists and geoscientists	105	1.7
Physical scientists, all other	154	3.8
Economists	26	–
Survey researchers	2	–
Psychologists	178	6.3
Sociologists	7	–
Urban and regional planners	28	–
Miscellaneous social scientists and related workers	57	7.0
Agricultural and food science technicians	32	–
Biological technicians	19	–
Chemical technicians	70	7.4
Geological and petroleum technicians	21	–
Nuclear technicians	3	–

	total employed	Hispanic, share of total
Social science research assistants	3	–
Miscellaneous life, physical, and social science technicians	160	10.4%
Community and social service occupations	2,265	11.1
Counselors	661	10.7
Social workers	734	12.6
Probation officers and correctional treatment specialists	88	15.0
Social and human service assistants	151	15.5
Miscellaneous community and social service specialists, including health educators and community health workers	94	18.4
Clergy	408	6.1
Directors, religious activities and education	61	5.9
Religious workers, all other	69	8.9
Legal occupations	1,786	7.4
Lawyers	1,061	4.0
Judicial law clerks	17	–
Judges, magistrates, and other judicial workers	67	4.5
Paralegals and legal assistants	418	17.0
Miscellaneous legal support workers	223	7.0
Education, training, and library occupations	8,543	9.7
Postsecondary teachers	1,350	6.2
Preschool and kindergarten teachers	678	12.0
Elementary and middle school teachers	2,838	10.3
Secondary school teachers	1,127	7.6
Special education teachers	366	9.4
Other teachers and instructors	860	9.5
Archivists, curators, and museum technicians	46	–
Librarians	181	2.8
Library technicians	45	–
Teacher assistants	898	15.7
Other education, training, and library workers	153	11.8
Arts, design, entertainment, sports, and media occupations	2,814	8.9
Artists and related workers	212	6.6
Designers	756	8.9
Actors	37	–
Producers and directors	121	4.9
Athletes, coaches, umpires, and related workers	267	9.0
Dancers and choreographers	21	–
Musicians, singers, and related workers	203	6.7
Entertainers and performers, sports and related workers, all other	41	–
Announcers	50	15.3
News analysts, reporters and correspondents	82	5.9
Public relations specialists	155	8.0
Editors	159	6.5

	total employed	Hispanic, share of total
Technical writers	58	3.7%
Writers and authors	208	2.9
Miscellaneous media and communication workers	98	35.0
Broadcast and sound engineering technicians and radio operators	108	12.6
Photographers	178	10.7
Television, video, and motion picture camera operators and editors	57	10.7
Media and communication equipment workers, all other	2	–
Health care practitioners and technical occupations	7,977	7.3
Chiropractors	58	4.0
Dentists	167	2.5
Dietitians and nutritionists	116	7.2
Optometrists	33	–
Pharmacists	286	5.1
Physicians and surgeons	911	5.2
Physician assistants	108	8.8
Podiatrists	9	–
Audiologists	14	–
Occupational therapists	118	5.8
Physical therapists	211	9.4
Radiation therapists	14	–
Recreational therapists	13	–
Respiratory therapists	111	10.6
Speech-language pathologists	146	8.3
Exercise physiologists	2	–
Therapists, all other	148	8.7
Veterinarians	85	6.1
Registered nurses	2,875	6.2
Nurse anesthetists	27	–
Nurse midwives	3	–
Nurse practitioners	103	2.9
Health diagnosing and treating practitioners, all other	23	–
Clinical laboratory technologists and technicians	319	10.7
Dental hygienists	163	8.1
Diagnostic related technologists and technicians	308	7.8
Emergency medical technicians and paramedics	172	8.1
Health practitioner support technologists and technicians	544	12.2
Licensed practical and licensed vocational nurses	531	9.4
Medical records and health information technicians	90	15.6
Opticians, dispensing	54	4.1
Miscellaneous health technologists and technicians	140	10.0
Other health care practitioners and technical occupations	75	5.6

	total employed	Hispanic, share of total
Service occupations	**25,459**	**22.6%**
Health care support occupations	3,496	15.3
Nursing, psychiatric, and home health aides	2,119	14.2
Occupational therapy assistants and aides	18	–
Physical therapist assistants and aides	66	5.6
Massage therapists	158	12.0
Dental assistants	274	21.2
Medical assistants	429	22.9
Medical transcriptionists	55	4.0
Pharmacy aides	45	–
Veterinary assistants and laboratory animal caretakers	47	–
Phlebotomists	119	15.7
Miscellaneous health care support occupations, including medical equipment preparers	166	9.9
Protective service occupations	3,096	13.7
First-line supervisors of correctional officers	46	–
First-line supervisors of police and detectives	112	10.6
First-line supervisors of fire fighting and prevention workers	64	6.6
First-line supervisors of protective service workers, all other	93	12.5
Firefighters	295	9.9
Fire inspectors	18	–
Bailiffs, correctional officers, and jailers	371	18.3
Detectives and criminal investigators	160	10.4
Fish and game wardens	7	–
Parking enforcement workers	4	–
Police and sheriff's patrol officers	657	13.8
Transit and railroad police	3	–
Animal control workers	11	–
Private detectives and investigators	103	11.1
Security guards and gaming surveillance officers	903	15.8
Crossing guards	61	16.1
Transportation security screeners	25	–
Lifeguards and other recreational, and all other protective service workers	162	9.2
Food preparation and serving related occupations	8,018	23.8
Chefs and head cooks	403	18.6
First-line supervisors of food preparation and serving workers	552	17.2
Cooks	1,970	31.7
Food preparation workers	868	27.5
Bartenders	412	13.2
Combined food preparation and serving workers, including fast food	343	18.0
Counter attendants, cafeteria, food concession, and coffee shop	233	16.6

	total employed	Hispanic, share of total
Waiters and waitresses	2,124	19.6%
Food servers, nonrestaurant	217	20.1
Dining room and cafeteria attendants and bartender helpers	359	31.7
Dishwashers	271	40.5
Hosts and hostesses, restaurant, lounge, and coffee shop	260	14.8
Food preparation and serving related workers, all other	6	–
Building and grounds cleaning and maintenance occupations	5,591	36.1
First-line supervisors of housekeeping and janitorial workers	277	21.7
First-line supervisors of landscaping, lawn service, and groundskeeping workers	281	19.8
Janitors and building cleaners	2,205	30.9
Maids and housekeeping cleaners	1,457	43.3
Pest control workers	73	20.4
Grounds maintenance workers	1,298	44.4
Personal care and service occupations	5,258	16.4
First-line supervisors of gaming workers	146	10.1
First-line supervisors of personal service workers	246	9.3
Animal trainers	44	–
Nonfarm animal caretakers	179	12.2
Gaming services workers	106	13.5
Motion picture projectionists	2	–
Ushers, lobby attendants, and ticket takers	43	–
Miscellaneous entertainment attendants and related workers	180	17.6
Embalmers and funeral attendants	16	–
Morticians, undertakers, and funeral directors	38	–
Barbers	109	24.1
Hairdressers, hairstylists, and cosmetologists	785	15.0
Miscellaneous personal appearance workers	300	9.5
Baggage porters, bellhops, and concierges	68	18.0
Tour and travel guides	51	15.1
Child care workers	1,314	20.3
Personal care aides	1,071	21.2
Recreation and fitness workers	406	9.7
Residential advisors	58	5.4
Personal care and service workers, all other	95	17.5
Sales and office occupations	**33,152**	**14.0**
Sales and related occupations	15,457	13.5
First-line supervisors of retail sales workers	3,237	11.3
First-line supervisors of nonretail sales workers	1,151	10.4
Cashiers	3,275	19.9
Counter and rental clerks	139	19.6
Parts salespersons	106	12.3
Retail salespersons	3,341	15.3
Advertising sales agents	230	7.6

	total employed	Hispanic, share of total
Insurance sales agents	540	10.3%
Securities, commodities, and financial services sales agents	280	8.9
Travel agents	73	4.8
Sales representatives, services, all other	457	10.1
Sales representatives, wholesale and manufacturing	1,277	9.4
Models, demonstrators, and product promoters	65	10.6
Real estate brokers and sales agents	761	8.7
Sales engineers	27	–
Telemarketers	97	14.7
Door-to-door sales workers, news and street vendors, and related workers	198	13.5
Sales and related workers, all other	204	10.3
Office and administrative support occupations	17,695	14.5
First-line supervisors of office and administrative support workers	1,416	11.9
Switchboard operators, including answering service	35	–
Telephone operators	42	–
Communications equipment operators, all other	9	–
Bill and account collectors	206	17.6
Billing and posting clerks	475	16.2
Bookkeeping, accounting, and auditing clerks	1,268	9.0
Gaming cage workers	8	–
Payroll and timekeeping clerks	155	15.1
Procurement clerks	27	–
Tellers	380	18.6
Financial clerks, all other	52	16.6
Brokerage clerks	5	–
Correspondence clerks	6	–
Court, municipal, and license clerks	85	13.4
Credit authorizers, checkers, and clerks	43	–
Customer service representatives	1,956	18.0
Eligibility interviewers, government programs	92	23.1
File clerks	292	16.4
Hotel, motel, and resort desk clerks	110	18.6
Interviewers, except eligibility and loan	135	12.1
Library assistants, clerical	97	5.8
Loan interviewers and clerks	144	10.4
New accounts clerks	26	–
Order clerks	104	21.3
Human resources assistants, except payroll and timekeeping	132	7.9
Receptionists and information clerks	1,237	17.9
Reservation and transportation ticket agents and travel clerks	117	21.5
Information and record clerks, all other	104	13.4
Cargo and freight agents	25	–
Couriers and messengers	213	16.9

	total employed	Hispanic, share of total
Dispatchers	277	16.7%
Meter readers, utilities	29	–
Postal service clerks	148	12.0
Postal service mail carriers	318	8.8
Postal service mail sorters, processors, and processing machine operators	66	9.8
Production, planning, and expediting clerks	272	12.5
Shipping, receiving, and traffic clerks	527	23.7
Stock clerks and order fillers	1,453	18.1
Weighers, measurers, checkers, and samplers, recordkeeping	74	21.9
Secretaries and administrative assistants	2,904	10.3
Computer operators	102	10.7
Data entry keyers	337	13.8
Word processors and typists	119	12.9
Desktop publishers	3	–
Insurance claims and policy processing clerks	230	13.7
Mail clerks and mail machine operators, except postal service	81	10.1
Office clerks, general	1,103	16.9
Office machine operators, except computer	46	–
Proofreaders and copy markers	10	–
Statistical assistants	32	–
Office and administrative support workers, all other	570	11.0
Natural resources, construction, and maintenance occupations	**12,821**	**25.5**
Farming, fishing, and forestry occupations	994	44.2
First-line supervisors of farming, fishing, and forestry workers	50	23.9
Agricultural inspectors	16	–
Animal breeders	6	–
Graders and sorters, agricultural products	118	58.0
Miscellaneous agricultural workers	711	48.9
Fishers and related fishing workers	33	–
Hunters and trappers	2	–
Forest and conservation workers	9	–
Logging workers	49	–
Construction and extraction occupations	7,005	28.9
First-line supervisors of construction trades and extraction workers	634	14.0
Boilermakers	23	–
Brickmasons, blockmasons, and stonemasons	122	43.2
Carpenters	1,223	29.0
Carpet, floor, and tile installers and finishers	150	37.8
Cement masons, concrete finishers, and terrazzo workers	68	53.3
Construction laborers	1,387	41.2
Paving, surfacing, and tamping equipment operators	23	–
Pile-driver operators	4	–
Operating engineers and other construction equipment operators	348	17.1

	total employed	Hispanic, share of total
Drywall installers, ceiling tile installers, and tapers	129	62.0%
Electricians	692	14.8
Glaziers	46	–
Insulation workers	44	–
Painters, construction and maintenance	485	42.6
Paperhangers	7	–
Pipelayers, plumbers, pipefitters, and steamfitters	534	20.9
Plasterers and stucco masons	18	–
Reinforcing iron and rebar workers	8	–
Roofers	196	45.1
Sheet metal workers	123	12.1
Structural iron and steel workers	65	15.8
Solar photovoltaic installers	7	–
Helpers, construction trades	53	38.4
Construction and building inspectors	118	7.7
Elevator installers and repairers	29	–
Fence erectors	33	–
Hazardous materials removal workers	38	–
Highway maintenance workers	108	12.4
Rail-track laying and maintenance equipment operators	10	–
Septic tank servicers and sewer pipe cleaners	8	–
Miscellaneous construction and related workers	32	–
Derrick, rotary drill, and service unit operators, oil, gas, and mining	37	–
Earth drillers, except oil and gas	35	–
Explosives workers, ordnance handling experts, and blasters	8	–
Mining machine operators	65	17.2
Roof bolters, mining	3	–
Roustabouts, oil and gas	14	–
Helpers—extraction workers	5	–
Other extraction workers	75	26.2
Installation, maintenance, and repair occupations	4,821	16.6
First-line supervisors of mechanics, installers, and repairers	292	10.4
Computer, automated teller, and office machine repairers	296	9.9
Radio and telecommunications equipment installers and repairers	158	13.8
Avionics technicians	14	–
Electric motor, power tool, and related repairers	37	–
Electrical and electronics installers and repairers, transportation equipment	5	–
Electrical and electronics repairers, industrial and utility	12	–
Electronic equipment installers and repairers, motor vehicles	18	–
Electronic home entertainment equipment installers and repairers	50	13.2
Security and fire alarm systems installers	41	–
Aircraft mechanics and service technicians	153	14.3
Automotive body and related repairers	140	25.3

	total employed	Hispanic, share of total
Automotive glass installers and repairers	22	–
Automotive service technicians and mechanics	867	21.3%
Bus and truck mechanics and diesel engine specialists	316	13.4
Heavy vehicle and mobile equipment service technicians and mechanics	194	17.3
Small engine mechanics	56	12.2
Miscellaneous vehicle and mobile equipment mechanics, installers, and repairers	87	31.4
Control and valve installers and repairers	27	–
Heating, air conditioning, and refrigeration mechanics and installers	340	16.2
Home appliance repairers	47	–
Industrial and refractory machinery mechanics	454	13.3
Maintenance and repair workers, general	442	19.4
Maintenance workers, machinery	28	–
Millwrights	53	6.7
Electrical power-line installers and repairers	110	7.9
Telecommunications line installers and repairers	177	15.7
Precision instrument and equipment repairers	60	13.3
Wind turbine service technicians	3	–
Coin, vending, and amusement machine servicers and repairers	33	–
Commercial divers	3	–
Locksmiths and safe repairers	31	–
Manufactured building and mobile home installers	5	–
Riggers	13	–
Signal and track switch repairers	5	–
Helpers—installation, maintenance, and repair workers	30	–
Other installation, maintenance, and repair workers	205	21.2
Production, transportation, and material moving occupations	**16,994**	**21.7**
Production occupations	8,455	21.7
First-line supervisors of production and operating workers	808	13.9
Aircraft structure, surfaces, rigging, and systems assemblers	23	–
Electrical, electronics, and electromechanical assemblers	166	24.0
Engine and other machine assemblers	32	–
Structural metal fabricators and fitters	25	–
Miscellaneous assemblers and fabricators	919	19.3
Bakers	199	28.4
Butchers and other meat, poultry, and fish processing workers	311	41.6
Food and tobacco roasting, baking, and drying machine operators and tenders	11	–
Food batchmakers	84	33.5
Food cooking machine operators and tenders	14	–
Food processing workers, all other	117	34.6
Computer control programmers and operators	67	17.1
Extruding and drawing machine setters, operators, and tenders, metal and plastic	10	–
Forging machine setters, operators, and tenders, metal and plastic	10	–
Rolling machine setters, operators, and tenders, metal and plastic	8	–

	total employed	Hispanic, share of total
Cutting, punching, and press machine setters, operators, and tenders, metal and plastic	87	22.9%
Drilling and boring machine tool setters, operators, and tenders, metal and plastic	3	–
Grinding, lapping, polishing, and buffing machine tool setters, operators, and tenders, metal and plastic	54	21.8
Lathe and turning machine tool setters, operators, and tenders, metal and plastic	17	–
Milling and planing machine setters, operators, and tenders, metal and plastic	3	–
Machinists	397	11.7
Metal furnace operators, tenders, pourers, and casters	17	–
Model makers and patternmakers, metal and plastic	11	–
Molders and molding machine setters, operators, and tenders, metal and plastic	37	–
Multiple machine tool setters, operators, and tenders, metal and plastic	5	–
Tool and die makers	56	4.3
Welding, soldering, and brazing workers	593	23.0
Heat treating equipment setters, operators, and tenders, metal and plastic	4	–
Layout workers, metal and plastic	4	–
Plating and coating machine setters, operators, and tenders, metal and plastic	18	–
Tool grinders, filers, and sharpeners	3	–
Metal workers and plastic workers, all other	375	26.0
Prepress technicians and workers	33	–
Printing press operators	201	15.6
Print binding and finishing workers	22	–
Laundry and dry-cleaning workers	185	37.1
Pressers, textile, garment, and related materials	54	47.9
Sewing machine operators	166	43.8
Shoe and leather workers and repairers	11	–
Shoe machine operators and tenders	11	–
Tailors, dressmakers, and sewers	86	24.9
Textile bleaching and dyeing machine operators and tenders	5	–
Textile cutting machine setters, operators, and tenders	12	–
Textile knitting and weaving machine setters, operators, and tenders	7	–
Textile winding, twisting, and drawing out machine setters, operators, and tenders	14	–
Extruding and forming machine setters, operators, and tenders, synthetic and glass fibers	1	–
Fabric and apparel patternmakers	3	–
Upholsterers	34	–
Textile, apparel, and furnishings workers, all other	14	–
Cabinetmakers and bench carpenters	45	–
Furniture finishers	7	–
Model makers and patternmakers, wood	0	–
Sawing machine setters, operators, and tenders, wood	30	–
Woodworking machine setters, operators, and tenders, except sawing	21	–
Woodworkers, all other	21	–
Power plant operators, distributors, and dispatchers	44	–

	total employed	Hispanic, share of total
Stationary engineers and boiler operators	121	13.8%
Water and wastewater treatment plant and system operators	72	19.6
Miscellaneous plant and system operators	39	–
Chemical processing machine setters, operators, and tenders	68	10.7
Crushing, grinding, polishing, mixing, and blending workers	100	18.4
Cutting workers	67	15.8
Extruding, forming, pressing, and compacting machine setters, operators, and tenders	45	–
Furnace, kiln, oven, drier, and kettle operators and tenders	16	–
Inspectors, testers, sorters, samplers, and weighers	689	13.6
Jewelers and precious stone and metal workers	46	–
Medical, dental, and ophthalmic laboratory technicians	95	15.9
Packaging and filling machine operators and tenders	261	38.0
Painting workers	150	34.9
Photographic process workers and processing machine operators	55	18.7
Semiconductor processors	4	–
Adhesive bonding machine operators and tenders	9	–
Cleaning, washing, and metal pickling equipment operators and tenders	7	–
Cooling and freezing equipment operators and tenders	2	–
Etchers and engravers	6	–
Molders, shapers, and casters, except metal and plastic	41	–
Paper goods machine setters, operators, and tenders	35	–
Tire builders	19	–
Helpers—production workers	59	30.6
Production workers, all other	933	21.5
Transportation and material moving occupations	8,540	21.7
Supervisors of transportation and material moving workers	200	18.4
Aircraft pilots and flight engineers	129	5.0
Air traffic controllers and airfield operations specialists	44	–
Flight attendants	88	10.5
Ambulance drivers and attendants, except emergency medical technicians	20	–
Bus drivers	558	12.9
Driver/sales workers and truck drivers	3,201	19.3
Taxi drivers and chauffeurs	336	16.0
Motor vehicle operators, all other	63	10.5
Locomotive engineers and operators	41	–
Railroad brake, signal, and switch operators	10	–
Railroad conductors and yardmasters	52	12.5
Subway, streetcar, and other rail transportation workers	11	–
Sailors and marine oilers	16	–
Ship and boat captains and operators	37	–
Ship engineers	7	–
Bridge and lock tenders	7	–
Parking lot attendants	81	35.5

	total employed	Hispanic, share of total
Automotive and watercraft service attendants	94	12.5%
Transportation inspectors	36	–
Transportation attendants, except flight attendants	38	–
Other transportation workers	17	–
Conveyor operators and tenders	4	–
Crane and tower operators	62	12.2
Dredge, excavating, and loading machine operators	42	–
Hoist and winch operators	5	–
Industrial truck and tractor operators	537	31.3
Cleaners of vehicles and equipment	315	35.9
Laborers and freight, stock, and material movers, hand	1,849	23.0
Machine feeders and offbearers	27	–
Packers and packagers, hand	431	42.0
Pumping station operators	25	–
Refuse and recyclable material collectors	106	29.4
Mine shuttle car operators	1	–
Tank car, truck, and ship loaders	4	–
Material moving workers, all other	45	–

Note: "–" means sample is too small to make a reliable estimate.
Source: Bureau of Labor Statistics, Labor Force Statistics from the Current Population Survey, Internet site http://www.bls.gov/cps/tables.htm#empstat; calculations by New Strategist

Table 5.71 Hispanic Workers by Industry, 2012

(total number of employed people aged 16 or older in the civilian labor force; number and percent distribution of employed Hispanics, and Hispanic share of total, by industry, 2012; numbers in thousands)

	total	Hispanic number	Hispanic percent distribution	Hispanic share of total
Total employed	**142,469**	**21,878**	**100.0%**	**15.4%**
Agriculture, forestry, fishing, and hunting	2,168	491	2.2	22.6
Mining	819	167	0.8	20.4
Construction	10,974	2,188	10.0	19.9
Manufacturing	15,904	2,246	10.3	14.1
Wholesale/retail trade	20,585	3,075	14.1	14.9
Transportation and utilities	7,727	1,179	5.4	15.3
Information	3,481	303	1.4	8.7
Financial activities	10,228	1,119	5.1	10.9
Professional and business services	15,540	2,510	11.5	16.2
Educational and health services	31,402	3,675	16.8	11.7
Leisure and hospitality	12,767	2,891	13.2	22.6
Other services	7,005	1,287	5.9	18.4
Public administration	6,763	747	3.4	11.0

Source: Bureau of Labor Statistics, Labor Force Statistics from the Current Population Survey, Internet site http://www.bls.gov/cps/tables.htm#empstat

Table 5.72 Hispanic Workers by Full-Time and Part-Time Status, 2012

(number and percent distribution of employed Hispanics aged 16 or older by employment status and sex, 2012; numbers in thousands)

	total	men	women
Total employed Hispanics	**20,798**	**11,981**	**8,818**
Worked full-time	15,497	9,531	5,966
Worked part-time	5,301	2,449	2,852
For economic reasons	1,965	1,095	870
PERCENT DISTRIBUTION			
Total employed Hispanics	**100.0%**	**100.0%**	**100.0%**
Worked full-time	74.5	79.6	67.7
Worked part-time	25.5	20.4	32.3
For economic reasons	9.4	9.1	9.9

Note: Part-time work is less than 35 hours per week. Part-time workers exclude those who usually work full-time but who worked less than 35 hours in the previous week because of vacation, holidays, child care problems, weather issues, and other temporary, noneconomic reasons. "Economic reasons" means a worker's hours have been reduced or workers cannot find full-time employment.
Source: Bureau of Labor Statistics, Labor Force Statistics from the Current Population Survey, Internet site http://www.bls.gov/cps/tables.htm#empstat

Table 5.73 Hispanic Workers by Educational Attainment, 2012

(number of total people and Hispanics aged 25 or older in the civilian labor force, Hispanic labor force participation rate, distribution of Hispanics in labor force, and Hispanic share of total labor force, by educational attainment, 2012; numbers in thousands)

	total labor force	Hispanic labor force			
		number	participation rate	percent distribution	share of total
Total aged 25 or older	**133,690**	**20,055**	**70.1%**	**100.0%**	**15.0%**
Not a high school graduate	11,328	5,920	60.5	29.5	52.3
High school graduate only	36,772	6,168	71.4	30.8	16.8
Some college	22,685	2,973	75.6	14.8	13.1
Associate's degree	14,675	1,611	78.7	8.0	11.0
Bachelor's degree or more	48,230	3,384	80.4	16.9	7.0

Source: Bureau of Labor Statistics, Labor Force Statistics from the Current Population Survey, Internet site http://www.bls.gov/cps/tables.htm#empstat

Table 5.74 Hispanic Workers by Job Tenure, 2012

(percent distribution of total and Hispanic wage and salary workers aged 16 or older by tenure with current employer, and index of Hispanic to total, 2012)

	total	Hispanic	index, Hispanic to total
Total workers	**100.0%**	**100.0%**	**100**
One year or less	21.1	23.6	112
13 months to 23 months	6.3	5.9	94
Two years	4.9	6.6	135
Three to four years	16.6	20.1	121
Five to nine years	21.8	23.7	109
10 to 14 years	12.5	10.9	87
15 to 19 years	6.1	4.2	69
20 or more years	10.6	5.1	48

Note: The index is calculated by dividing the Hispanic figure by the total figure and multiplying by 100.
Source: Bureau of Labor Statistics, Employee Tenure, Internet site http://www.bls.gov/news.release/tenure.toc.htm; calculations by New Strategist

Table 5.75 Hispanic Households by Number of Earners, 2012

(number of total households, number and percent distribution of Hispanic households and Hispanic share of total, by number of earners per household, 2012; number of households in thousands)

	total	Hispanic number	Hispanic percent distribution	share of total
Total households	**121,084**	**14,939**	**100.0%**	**12.3%**
No earners	28,569	2,309	15.5	8.1
One earner	45,578	5,973	40.0	13.1
Two or more earners	46,938	6,657	44.6	14.2
Two earners	37,943	4,892	32.7	12.9
Three earners	6,905	1,260	8.4	18.2
Four or more earners	2,089	505	3.4	24.2
Average number of earners per household	1.28	1.53	–	–

Note: "–" means not applicable.
Source: Bureau of the Census, 2012 Current Population Survey, Annual Social and Economic Supplement, Internet site http://www.census.gov/hhes/www/cpstables/032012/hhinc/toc.htm; calculations by New Strategist

Table 5.76 Labor Force Status of Hispanic Married Couples, 2012

(number and percent distribution of Hispanic married couples by age of householder and labor force status of husband and wife, 2012; numbers in thousands)

	total	husband and/or wife in labor force			neither husband nor wife in labor force
		husband and wife	husband only	wife only	
Total Hispanic couples	**7,889**	**3,924**	**2,555**	**512**	**899**
Under age 25	307	135	150	12	10
Aged 25 to 29	705	356	320	24	6
Aged 30 to 34	1,093	609	424	39	21
Aged 35 to 39	1,080	609	421	29	20
Aged 40 to 44	1,106	677	342	49	38
Aged 45 to 54	1,811	1,062	533	125	91
Aged 55 to 64	1,057	404	295	152	205
Aged 65 to 74	490	63	57	64	305
Aged 75 or older	239	8	14	15	202
Total Hispanic couples	**100.0%**	**49.7%**	**32.4%**	**6.5%**	**11.4%**
Under age 25	100.0	44.0	48.9	3.9	3.3
Aged 25 to 29	100.0	50.5	45.4	3.4	0.9
Aged 30 to 34	100.0	55.7	38.8	3.6	1.9
Aged 35 to 39	100.0	56.4	39.0	2.7	1.9
Aged 40 to 44	100.0	61.2	30.9	4.4	3.4
Aged 45 to 54	100.0	58.6	29.4	6.9	5.0
Aged 55 to 64	100.0	38.2	27.9	14.4	19.4
Aged 65 to 74	100.0	12.9	11.6	13.1	62.2
Aged 75 or older	100.0	3.3	5.9	6.3	84.5

Source: Bureau of the Census, America's Families and Living Arrangements: 2012, Internet site http://www.census.gov/hhes/ families/data/cps2012.html; calculations by New Strategist

Table 5.77 Hispanic Minimum Wage Workers by Sex, 2011

(number of total and Hispanic employed wage and salary workers, number of total and Hispanic wage and salary workers paid hourly rates at or below minimum wage, and Hispanic share of total, by sex, 2011; numbers in thousands)

	total paid hourly rates	percent distribution	workers paid at or below minimum wage		
			number	percent distribution	share of total
Total workers aged 16 or older	**73,926**	**100.0%**	**3,828**	**100.0%**	**5.2%**
Hispanic workers aged 16 or older	13,264	17.9	720	18.8	5.4
Hispanic men	7,703	10.4	326	8.5	4.2
Hispanic women	5,561	7.5	394	10.3	7.1

Source: Bureau of Labor Statistics, Characteristics of Minimum Wage Workers: 2011, Internet site http://www.bls.gov/cps/minwage2011tbls.htm; calculations by New Strategist

Table 5.78 Union Representation of Hispanic Workers by Sex, 2012

(number of employed Hispanic wage and salary workers aged 16 or older, number and percent represented by unions, median weekly earnings of those working full-time by union representation status, and index of union median to average median, by sex, 2012; number in thousands)

	total	men	women
Total employed Hispanics	**20,144**	**11,415**	**8,730**
Number represented by unions	2,197	1,266	931
Percent represented by unions	10.9%	11.1%	10.7%
Median weekly earnings of Hispanic full-time workers	**$568**	**$592**	**$521**
Represented by unions	823	868	750
Not represented by unions	530	563	503
Index, median weekly earnings of Hispanic workers represented by unions to average Hispanic worker	**145**	**147**	**144**

Note: Workers represented by unions are either members of a labor union or workers who report no union affiliation but whose jobs are covered by a union or an employee association contract. The index is calculated by dividing median weekly earnings of workers represented by unions by median weekly earnings of the average Hispanic worker and multiplying by 100.
Source: Bureau of Labor Statistics, Labor Force Statistics from the Current Population Survey, Internet site http://www.bls.gov/cps/tables.htm#empstat

Table 5.79 Commuting Patterns of Hispanic Workers, 2011

(number of total and Hispanic workers aged 16 or older, percent distribution by means of transportation to work, and index of Hispanic to total, 2011; numbers in thousands)

	total	Hispanic	index
Total workers aged 16 or older, number	**138,270**	**20,943**	–
Total workers aged 16 or older, percent	**100.0%**	**100.0%**	–
Drove alone in car, truck, or van	76.4	68.2	89
Carpooled in car, truck, or van	9.7	15.3	158
Public transportation (excluding taxicab)	5.0	8.0	160
Walked	2.8	3.3	118
Other means	1.7	2.5	147
Worked at home	4.3	2.8	65
Average travel time to work (minutes)	25.5	26.4	104

Note: The index is calculated by dividing Hispanic figure by total figure and multiplying by 100. "–" means not applicable.
Source: Census Bureau, 2011 American Community Survey, Internet site http://factfinder2.census.gov/faces/nav/jsf/pages/index
.xhtml; calculations by New Strategist

Table 5.80 Hispanic Labor Force Projections, 2010 and 2020

(number and percent of Hispanics aged 16 or older in the civilian labor force by sex, 2010 and 2020; percent change in number and percentage point change in rate, 2010–20; numbers in thousands)

NUMBER	2010	2020	percent change
Total Hispanics in labor force	**22,748**	**30,493**	**34.0%**
Hispanic men	13,511	17,859	32.2
Hispanic women	9,238	12,634	36.8

PARTICIPATION RATE	2010	2020	percentage point change
Total Hispanics in labor force	**67.5%**	**66.2%**	**–1.3**
Hispanic men	77.8	75.9	–1.9
Hispanic women	56.5	56.1	–0.4

Source: Bureau of Labor Statistics, Labor Force Projections to 2020: A More Slowly Growing Workforce, Monthly Labor Review, January 2012, Internet site http://www.bls.gov/opub/mlr/2012/01/home.htm

Table 5.81 Hispanic Share of Labor Force, 2010 and 2020

(total people and Hispanics aged 16 or older in the civilian labor force, and Hispanic share of total, 2010 and 2020; numbers in thousands)

	2010			2020		
	total	Hispanic	Hispanic share of total	total	Hispanic	Hispanic share of total
Total labor force	**153,889**	**22,748**	**14.8%**	**164,360**	**30,493**	**18.6%**
Men	81,985	13,511	16.5	87,128	17,859	20.5
Women	71,904	9,238	12.8	77,232	12,634	16.4

Source: Bureau of Labor Statistics, Labor Force Projections to 2020: A More Slowly Growing Workforce, Monthly Labor Review, January 2012, Internet site http://www.bls.gov/opub/mlr/2012/01/home.htm

Most Hispanic Couples Have Children under Age 18 at Home

Among the nation's 121 million households in 2012, Hispanics headed 15 million, or 12 percent of the total. Hispanic householders are younger than average. Consequently, Hispanics account for a relatively large share of households headed by young adults. From 18 to 21 percent of householders under age 40 are Hispanic compared with only 6 percent of householders aged 65 or older.

Married couples account for fewer than half of Hispanic households (48 percent), and a substantial 21 percent are female-headed families. Hispanic households are less likely than the average household to be headed by a person living alone. Only 17 percent of Hispanic households are men or women who live by themselves versus 27 percent of households nationally.

Nearly half (46 percent) of Hispanic households include children under age 18—a much greater share than the 29 percent of households nationally that include children. Among Hispanic married couples, 60 percent have children at home. Fifty-four percent of Hispanic children live with their biological, married parents.

Because Hispanics are more likely than the average household to include children, Hispanic households are larger than average. The average Hispanic household is home to 3.36 people versus 2.55 people in households nationally.

■ Children are more common in Hispanic households because many Hispanics are immigrants from countries where traditional family life is the norm.

Married couples account for fewer than half of Hispanic households

(percent distribution of Hispanic households by household type, 2012)

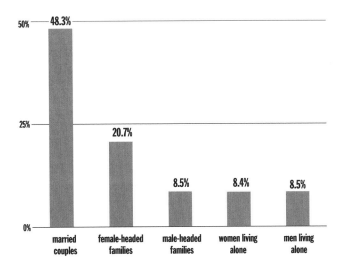

Table 5.82 Hispanic Households by Age of Householder, 2012

(number of total households, number and percent distribution of Hispanic households, and Hispanic share of total, by age of householder, 2012, numbers in thousands)

		Hispanic		
	total	number	percent distribution	share of total
Total households	**121,084**	**14,939**	**100.0%**	**12.3%**
Under age 25	6,180	1,288	8.6	20.8
Aged 25 to 29	9,208	1,621	10.9	17.6
Aged 30 to 34	10,638	1,933	12.9	18.2
Aged 35 to 39	10,111	1,842	12.3	18.2
Aged 40 to 44	11,129	1,777	11.9	16.0
Aged 45 to 49	11,763	1,598	10.7	13.6
Aged 50 to 54	12,433	1,345	9.0	10.8
Aged 55 to 59	12,037	1,085	7.3	9.0
Aged 60 to 64	10,742	850	5.7	7.9
Aged 65 or older	26,843	1,600	10.7	6.0

Source: Bureau of the Census, 2012 Current Population Survey, Internet site http://www.census.gov/hhes/www/income/data/incpovhlth/2011/dtables.html; calculations by New Strategist

Table 5.83 Hispanic Households by Household Type, 2012

(number of total households, number and percent distribution of Hispanic households, and Hispanic share of total, by type, 2012; numbers in thousands)

	total	Hispanic number	Hispanic percent distribution	Hispanic share of total
TOTAL HOUSEHOLDS	**121,084**	**14,939**	**100.0%**	**12.3%**
Family households	**80,506**	**11,585**	**77.6**	**14.4**
Married couples	58,949	7,222	48.3	12.3
With children under age 18	25,114	4,672	31.3	18.6
Female householders, no spouse present	15,669	3,086	20.7	19.7
With children under age 18	10,380	2,358	15.8	22.7
Male householders, no spouse present	5,888	1,277	8.5	21.7
With children under age 18	2,982	725	4.9	24.3
Nonfamily households	**40,578**	**3,353**	**22.4**	**8.3**
Female householders	21,383	1,535	10.3	7.2
Living alone	18,354	1,251	8.4	6.8
Male householders	19,195	1,818	12.2	9.5
Living alone	14,835	1,264	8.5	8.5

Source: Bureau of the Census, 2012 Current Population Survey Annual Social and Economic Supplement, Internet site http:// www.census.gov/hhes/www/cpstables/032012/hhinc/toc.htm; calculations by New Strategist

Table 5.84 Hispanic Households by Age of Householder and Household Type, 2012

(number and percent distribution of Hispanic households by age of householder and type of household, 2012; numbers in thousands)

| | | family households | | | nonfamily households | | | |
| | | | | | female-headed | | male-headed | |
	total	married couples	female householder, no spouse present	male householder, no spouse present	total	living alone	total	living alone
Total Hispanic households	**14,939**	**7,222**	**3,086**	**1,277**	**1,535**	**1,251**	**1,818**	**1,264**
Under age 25	1,288	240	422	259	172	77	194	78
Aged 25 to 34	3,554	1,668	806	410	207	142	463	269
Aged 35 to 44	3,618	2,031	811	265	133	110	378	273
Aged 45 to 54	2,943	1,653	540	206	234	190	310	245
Aged 55 to 64	1,935	959	296	98	327	292	255	212
Aged 65 or older	1,600	670	211	39	463	441	217	188

PERCENT DISTRIBUTION BY HOUSEHOLD TYPE

Total Hispanic households	**100.0%**	**48.3%**	**20.7%**	**8.5%**	**10.3%**	**8.4%**	**12.2%**	**8.5%**
Under age 25	100.0	6.4	16.7	19.9	28.3	11.5	28.7	16.0
Aged 25 to 34	100.0	51.3	7.9	9.1	12.3	8.3	19.4	12.1
Aged 35 to 44	100.0	71.5	10.1	3.8	6.8	5.7	7.8	6.3
Aged 45 to 54	100.0	71.4	10.5	3.8	6.7	6.4	7.6	6.1
Aged 55 to 64	100.0	68.0	10.2	4.7	8.4	7.3	8.8	6.8
Aged 65 or older	100.0	58.4	9.0	1.0	24.4	23.7	7.4	7.1

PERCENT DISTRIBUTION BY AGE

Total Hispanic households	**100.0%**	**100.0%**	**100.0%**	**100.0%**	**100.0%**	**100.0%**	**100.0%**	**100.0%**
Under age 25	8.6	3.3	13.7	20.3	11.2	6.2	10.7	6.2
Aged 25 to 34	23.8	23.1	26.1	32.1	13.5	11.4	25.5	21.3
Aged 35 to 44	24.2	28.1	26.3	20.8	8.7	8.8	20.8	21.6
Aged 45 to 54	19.7	22.9	17.5	16.1	15.2	15.2	17.1	19.4
Aged 55 to 64	13.0	13.3	9.6	7.7	21.3	23.3	14.0	16.8
Aged 65 or older	10.7	9.3	6.8	3.1	30.2	35.3	11.9	14.9

Source: Bureau of the Census, 2012 Current Population Survey, Internet site http://www.census.gov/hhes/www/income/data/incpovhlth/2011/dtables.html; calculations by New Strategist

Table 5.85 Hispanic Households by Size, 2012

(number of total households, number and percent distribution of Hispanic households, and Hispanic share of total, by household size, 2012; number of households in thousands)

		Hispanic		
	total	number	percent distribution	share of total
Total households	**121,084**	**14,939**	**100.0%**	**12.3%**
One person	33,188	2,516	16.8	7.6
Two people	40,983	3,396	22.7	8.3
Three people	19,241	2,926	19.6	15.2
Four people	16,049	2,912	19.5	18.1
Five people	7,271	1,798	12.0	24.7
Six people	2,734	776	5.2	28.4
Seven or more people	1,617	615	4.1	38.1
Average number of persons per household	2.55	3.36	–	–

Note: "–" means not applicable.
Source: Bureau of the Census, Current Population Survey Annual Social and Economic Supplement, Internet site http://www .census.gov/hhes/www/income/dinctabs.html; calculations by New Strategist

Table 5.86 Hispanic Households by Region, 2012

(number of total households, number and percent distribution of Hispanic households and Hispanic share of total, by region, 2012; numbers in thousands)

		Hispanic		
	total	number	percent distribution	share of total
Total households	121,084	14,939	100.0%	12.3%
Northeast	21,774	2,264	15.2	10.4
Midwest	26,865	1,215	8.1	4.5
South	45,604	5,529	37.0	12.1
West	26,840	5,930	39.7	22.1

Source: Bureau of the Census, Current Population Survey Annual Social and Economic Supplement, Internet site http://www .census.gov/hhes/www/income/dinctabs.html; calculations by New Strategist

Table 5.87 Hispanic Households by Metropolitan Status, 2012

(number of total households, number and percent distribution of Hispanic households and Hispanic share of total, by metropolitan status, 2012; numbers in thousands)

		Hispanic		
	total	number	percent distribution	share of total
Total households	121,084	14,939	100.0%	12.3%
Inside metropolitan areas	101,526	13,851	92.7	13.6
Inside principal cities	40,616	7,340	49.1	18.1
Outside principal cities	60,910	6,512	43.6	10.7
Outside metropolitan areas	19,558	1,087	7.3	5.6

Source: Bureau of the Census, Current Population Survey Annual Social and Economic Supplement, Internet site http://www .census.gov/hhes/www/income/dinctabs.html; calculations by New Strategist

Table 5.88 Hispanics Living Alone by Sex and Age, 2012

(total number of Hispanics aged 15 or older, number and percent living alone, and percent distribution of Hispanics living alone, by sex and age, 2012; numbers in thousands)

	total	living alone		
		number	percent distribution	share of total
Total Hispanics	**37,500**	**2,515**	**100.0%**	**6.7%**
Under age 25	9,055	155	6.2	1.7
Aged 25 to 34	8,539	411	16.3	4.8
Aged 35 to 44	7,531	383	15.2	5.1
Aged 45 to 54	5,794	435	17.3	7.5
Aged 55 to 64	3,545	504	20.0	14.2
Aged 65 to 74	1,844	337	13.4	18.3
Aged 75 or older	1,193	292	11.6	24.5
Hispanic men	**18,867**	**1,264**	**100.0**	**6.7**
Under age 25	4,703	78	6.2	1.7
Aged 25 to 34	4,456	269	21.3	6.0
Aged 35 to 44	3,823	273	21.6	7.1
Aged 45 to 54	2,899	245	19.4	8.5
Aged 55 to 64	1,687	212	16.8	12.6
Aged 65 to 74	819	117	9.3	14.3
Aged 75 or older	481	71	5.6	14.8
Hispanic women	**18,633**	**1,251**	**100.0**	**6.7**
Under age 25	4,352	77	6.2	1.8
Aged 25 to 34	4,083	142	11.4	3.5
Aged 35 to 44	3,708	110	8.8	3.0
Aged 45 to 54	2,895	190	15.2	6.6
Aged 55 to 64	1,858	292	23.3	15.7
Aged 65 to 74	1,025	220	17.6	21.5
Aged 75 or older	712	221	17.7	31.0

Source: Bureau of the Census, Current Population Survey Annual Social and Economic Supplement, Internet site http://www .census.gov/hhes/www/income/dinctabs.html; calculations by New Strategist

Table 5.89 Hispanic Households by Age of Householder, Type of Household, and Presence of Children, 2012

(number and percent distribution of Hispanic households by age of householder, type of household, and presence of own children under age 18, 2012; numbers in thousands)

	all households		married couples		female-headed families		male-headed families	
	total	with children	total	with children	total	with children	total	with children
Total Hispanic households	**14,939**	**6,912**	**7,222**	**4,367**	**3,086**	**2,040**	**1,277**	**505**
Under age 25	1,288	469	241	166	423	261	259	42
Aged 25 to 29	1,621	936	641	493	412	361	210	82
Aged 30 to 34	1,933	1,386	1,027	902	394	368	200	116
Aged 35 to 39	1,842	1,407	1,010	893	464	425	129	89
Aged 40 to 44	1,777	1,181	1,021	849	347	267	137	66
Aged 45 to 49	1,598	858	875	587	316	216	120	56
Aged 50 to 54	1,345	438	778	308	224	99	85	30
Aged 55 to 64	1,935	190	959	133	296	39	98	18
Aged 65 or older	1,600	46	670	36	211	4	39	4

PERCENT OF HOUSEHOLDS WITH CHILDREN BY TYPE

	all households		married couples		female-headed families		male-headed families	
Total Hispanic households	**100.0%**	**46.3%**	**100.0%**	**60.5%**	**100.0%**	**66.1%**	**100.0%**	**39.5%**
Under age 25	100.0	36.4	100.0	68.9	100.0	61.7	100.0	16.2
Aged 25 to 29	100.0	57.7	100.0	76.9	100.0	87.6	100.0	39.0
Aged 30 to 34	100.0	71.7	100.0	87.8	100.0	93.4	100.0	58.0
Aged 35 to 39	100.0	76.4	100.0	88.4	100.0	91.6	100.0	69.0
Aged 40 to 44	100.0	66.5	100.0	83.2	100.0	76.9	100.0	48.2
Aged 45 to 49	100.0	53.7	100.0	67.1	100.0	68.4	100.0	46.7
Aged 50 to 54	100.0	32.6	100.0	39.6	100.0	44.2	100.0	35.3
Aged 55 to 64	100.0	9.8	100.0	13.9	100.0	13.2	100.0	18.4
Aged 65 or older	100.0	2.9	100.0	5.4	100.0	1.9	100.0	10.3

Source: Bureau of the Census, Current Population Survey Annual Social and Economic Supplement, America's Families and Living Arrangements: 2012, Internet site http://www.census.gov/hhes/families/data/cps2012.html; calculations by New Strategist

Table 5.90 Living Arrangements of Hispanic Children, 2012

(number and percent distribution of Hispanic children under age 18 by living arrangement, 2012; numbers in thousands)

	number	percent distribution
HISPANIC CHILDREN	**17,570**	**100.0%**
Living with two parents	**11,542**	**65.7**
Married parents	10,364	59.0
Unmarried parents	1,178	6.7
Biological mother and father	10,589	60.3
Married parents	9,528	54.2
Biological mother and stepfather	680	3.9
Biological father and stepmother	125	0.7
Biological mother and adoptive father	29	0.2
Biological father and adoptive mother	1	0.0
Adoptive mother and father	86	0.5
Other	31	0.2
Living with one parent	**5,465**	**31.1**
Mother only	4,926	28.0
Father only	539	3.1
Living with no parents	**563**	**3.2**
Grandparents	265	1.5
Other	298	1.7
At least one biological parent	**16,822**	**95.7**
At least one stepparent	**864**	**4.9**
At least one adoptive parent	**160**	**0.9**

Source: Bureau of the Census, Current Population Survey Annual Social and Economic Supplement, America's Families and Living Arrangements: 2012, Detailed Tables, Internet site http://www.census.gov/hhes/families/data/cps2012.html; calculations by New Strategist

Table 5.91 Marital Status of Hispanic Men by Age, 2012

(number and percent distribution of Hispanic men aged 18 or older by age and current marital status, 2012; numbers in thousands)

	total	never married	married, spouse present	married, spouse absent	separated	divorced	widowed
Total Hispanic men	**17,425**	**6,958**	**7,870**	**660**	**536**	**1,147**	**253**
Aged 18 to 19	939	903	16	3	15	2	0
Aged 20 to 24	2,326	2,030	225	23	37	10	1
Aged 25 to 29	2,317	1,487	645	80	49	53	2
Aged 30 to 34	2,139	906	1,005	74	65	88	2
Aged 35 to 39	1,978	527	1,139	92	64	148	8
Aged 40 to 44	1,844	412	1,083	91	84	165	9
Aged 45 to 49	1,606	277	977	94	70	175	12
Aged 50 to 54	1,290	162	833	76	61	149	10
Aged 55 to 64	1,686	143	1,116	76	61	240	50
Aged 65 to 74	819	81	531	29	14	97	66
Aged 75 to 84	369	20	251	15	14	17	52
Aged 85 or older	112	9	48	7	2	4	41
Total Hispanic men	**100.0%**	**39.9%**	**45.2%**	**3.8%**	**3.1%**	**6.6%**	**1.5%**
Aged 18 to 19	100.0	96.2	1.7	0.3	1.6	0.2	0.0
Aged 20 to 24	100.0	87.3	9.7	1.0	1.6	0.4	0.0
Aged 25 to 29	100.0	64.2	27.8	3.5	2.1	2.3	0.1
Aged 30 to 34	100.0	42.4	47.0	3.5	3.0	4.1	0.1
Aged 35 to 39	100.0	26.6	57.6	4.7	3.2	7.5	0.4
Aged 40 to 44	100.0	22.3	58.7	4.9	4.6	8.9	0.5
Aged 45 to 49	100.0	17.2	60.8	5.9	4.4	10.9	0.7
Aged 50 to 54	100.0	12.6	64.6	5.9	4.7	11.6	0.8
Aged 55 to 64	100.0	8.5	66.2	4.5	3.6	14.2	3.0
Aged 65 to 74	100.0	9.9	64.8	3.5	1.7	11.8	8.1
Aged 75 to 84	100.0	5.4	68.0	4.1	3.8	4.6	14.1
Aged 85 or older	100.0	8.0	42.9	6.3	1.8	3.6	36.6

Source: Bureau of the Census, Current Population Survey Annual Social and Economic Supplement, America's Families and Living Arrangements: 2012, Internet site http://www.census.gov/hhes/families/data/cps2012.html; calculations by New Strategist

Table 5.92 Marital Status of Hispanic Women by Age, 2012

(number and percent distribution of Hispanic women aged 18 or older by age and current marital status, 2012; numbers in thousands)

	total	never married	married, spouse present	married, spouse absent	separated	divorced	widowed
Total Hispanic women	**17,240**	**5,246**	**8,104**	**390**	**820**	**1,708**	**972**
Aged 18 to 19	824	793	16	8	4	3	0
Aged 20 to 24	2,141	1,651	359	43	57	27	3
Aged 25 to 29	2,045	941	875	41	88	95	5
Aged 30 to 34	2,033	526	1,217	46	109	127	8
Aged 35 to 39	1,930	383	1,144	41	128	225	9
Aged 40 to 44	1,778	271	1,102	47	113	226	19
Aged 45 to 49	1,567	230	946	30	78	242	42
Aged 50 to 54	1,328	132	812	42	81	201	60
Aged 55 to 64	1,858	207	966	51	113	319	202
Aged 65 to 74	1,025	75	483	29	41	163	233
Aged 75 to 84	513	26	157	8	6	63	253
Aged 85 or older	199	11	28	3	1	17	139
Total Hispanic women	**100.0%**	**30.4%**	**47.0%**	**2.3%**	**4.8%**	**9.9%**	**5.6%**
Aged 18 to 19	100.0	96.2	1.9	1.0	0.5	0.4	0.0
Aged 20 to 24	100.0	77.1	16.8	2.0	2.7	1.3	0.1
Aged 25 to 29	100.0	46.0	42.8	2.0	4.3	4.6	0.2
Aged 30 to 34	100.0	25.9	59.9	2.3	5.4	6.2	0.4
Aged 35 to 39	100.0	19.8	59.3	2.1	6.6	11.7	0.5
Aged 40 to 44	100.0	15.2	62.0	2.6	6.4	12.7	1.1
Aged 45 to 49	100.0	14.7	60.4	1.9	5.0	15.4	2.7
Aged 50 to 54	100.0	9.9	61.1	3.2	6.1	15.1	4.5
Aged 55 to 64	100.0	11.1	52.0	2.7	6.1	17.2	10.9
Aged 65 to 74	100.0	7.3	47.1	2.8	4.0	15.9	22.7
Aged 75 to 84	100.0	5.1	30.6	1.6	1.2	12.3	49.3
Aged 85 or older	100.0	5.5	14.1	1.5	0.5	8.5	69.8

Source: Bureau of the Census, Current Population Survey Annual Social and Economic Supplement, America's Families and Living Arrangements: 2012, Internet site http://www.census.gov/hhes/families/data/cps2012.html; calculations by New Strategist

Table 5.93 Marital History of Hispanic Men by Age, 2009

(number of Hispanic men aged 15 or older and percent distribution by marital history and age, 2009; numbers in thousands)

	total	15–19	20–24	25–29	30–34	35–39	40–49	50–59	60–69	70+
TOTAL HISPANIC MEN, NUMBER	17,120	2,071	1,779	2,298	2,065	2,095	3,059	2,125	992	636
TOTAL HISPANIC MEN, PERCENT	100.0%	100.0%	100.0%	100.0%	100.0%	100.0%	100.0%	100.0%	100.0%	100.0%
Never married	39.7	96.9	79.5	56.8	34.2	24.9	17.5	11.1	4.7	4.5
Ever married	60.3	3.1	20.5	43.2	65.8	75.1	82.5	88.9	95.3	95.5
Married once	52.6	3.1	20.5	42.2	62.7	68.0	70.9	73.2	70.2	71.9
Still married	44.1	2.6	18.9	37.4	55.3	57.2	59.5	59.2	57.9	47.3
Married twice	6.5	0.0	0.0	0.9	3.2	6.8	9.2	13.3	20.4	19.7
Still married	4.8	0.0	0.0	0.6	2.7	5.7	7.0	9.9	14.3	11.4
Married three or more times	1.2	0.0	0.0	0.2	0.0	0.3	2.4	2.5	4.6	3.9
Still married	0.8	0.0	0.0	0.2	0.0	0.3	1.4	1.4	3.1	3.0
Ever divorced	12.9	0.1	0.9	4.9	7.9	13.5	19.3	25.0	34.1	25.6
Currently divorced	7.0	0.1	0.9	4.2	4.9	7.3	10.3	13.9	14.7	12.6
Ever widowed	1.7	0.4	0.1	0.0	0.2	0.2	1.7	1.7	2.9	25.6
Currently widowed	1.2	0.4	0.1	0.0	0.2	0.0	1.0	0.8	2.2	18.5

Source: Bureau of the Census, Number, Timing, and Duration of Marriages and Divorces: 2009, Detailed Tables, Internet site http://www.census.gov/hhes/socdemo/marriage/data/sipp/index.html

Table 5.94 Marital History of Hispanic Women by Age, 2009

(number of Hispanic women aged 15 or older and percent distribution by marital history and age, 2009; numbers in thousands)

	total	15–19	20–24	25–29	30–34	35–39	40–49	50–59	60–69	70+
TOTAL HISPANIC WOMEN, NUMBER	**16,207**	**1,917**	**1,719**	**1,930**	**1,690**	**1,805**	**3,038**	**2,049**	**1,216**	**843**
TOTAL HISPANIC WOMEN, PERCENT	**100.0%**	**100.0%**	**100.0%**	**100.0%**	**100.0%**	**100.0%**	**100.0%**	**100.0%**	**100.0%**	**100.0%**
Never married	**32.3**	**94.4**	**66.8**	**36.8**	**27.2**	**15.1**	**14.1**	**11.0**	**7.6**	**9.9**
Ever married	**67.7**	**5.6**	**33.2**	**63.2**	**72.8**	**84.9**	**85.9**	**89.0**	**92.4**	**90.1**
Married once	59.9	5.6	32.8	61.8	66.1	76.3	74.4	74.7	74.8	76.2
Still married	44.9	4.4	29.0	52.5	57.0	61.5	57.6	51.9	49.1	24.0
Married twice	6.8	0.0	0.4	1.4	6.3	7.9	10.9	11.0	14.1	11.0
Still married	4.6	0.0	0.4	1.3	5.7	6.1	8.4	6.3	9.3	1.9
Married three or more times	1.1	0.0	0.0	0.0	0.5	0.6	0.7	3.3	3.4	3.0
Still married	0.6	0.0	0.0	0.0	0.5	0.4	0.4	2.8	1.2	0.0
Ever divorced	14.0	0.1	1.2	6.6	11.9	15.3	20.3	26.9	23.1	21.8
Currently divorced	8.5	0.1	0.8	5.4	5.5	8.7	12.1	17.4	13.3	14.0
Ever widowed	5.9	0.6	0.3	0.6	0.6	2.0	3.5	6.4	18.8	49.3
Currently widowed	5.3	0.6	0.3	0.5	0.6	1.2	2.4	6.1	15.7	48.3

Source: Bureau of the Census, Number, Timing, and Duration of Marriages and Divorces: 2009, Detailed Tables, Internet site http://www.census.gov/hhes/socdemo/marriage/data/sipp/index.html

Hispanics Are the Largest Minority Group in the United States

The Hispanic population grew 47 percent between 2000 and 2011, expanding from 35 million to 52 million. Hispanics account for 17 percent of the total U.S. population. The number of Hispanics is growing rapidly because of immigration. Thirty-eight percent of immigrants to the United States in 2011 were from Mexico, Latin America, the Caribbean, or Spain.

Hispanic is an ethnic identity, not a race. There are white, black, American Indian, and Asian Hispanics. According to the 2010 census, 53 percent of Hispanics identify their race as white and another 37 percent identify themselves as "some other race" (most of whom are white).

Among Hispanics, Mexicans are the largest ethnic group (63 percent). Thirteen percent of U.S. residents speak Spanish at home, with the proportion peaking at nearly 30 percent in California, New Mexico, and Texas.

Hispanics are most likely to live in the West (41 percent) and South (36 percent). Twenty-eight percent of Hispanics live in California, where they account for 38 percent of the state's population. Los Angeles is home to nearly 6 million Hispanics, more than any other metropolitan area. Hispanics account for 44 percent of the Los Angeles population.

The American Time Use Survey reveals interesting facts about how Hispanics spend their time. Compared with the average person, Hispanics spend 35 percent more time caring for household children and 50 percent more time in educational activities because many are young adults.

■ Since 2000, the number of Hispanics has more than doubled in 12 states.

Hispanics account for more than one-quarter of the population in the West

(Hispanic share of population by region, 2011)

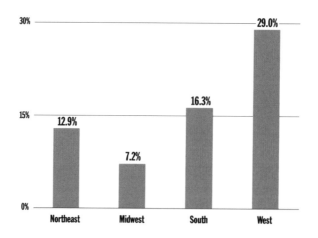

Table 5.95 Hispanics by Race, 2010

(total number of people, and number and percent distribution of Hispanics by racial identification, 2000 and 2010; percent change, 2000–10)

	number	percent distribution
Total people	**308,745,538**	**100.0%**
Hispanics	50,477,594	16.3
Total Hispanics	**50,477,594**	**100.0**
One race	47,435,002	94.0
American Indian	685,150	1.4
Asian	209,128	0.4
Black	1,243,471	2.5
Native Hawaiian	58,437	0.1
White	26,735,713	53.0
Some other race	18,503,103	36.7
Two or more races	3,042,592	6.0

Note: Most Hispanics who identified themselves as "some other race" are white. American Indians include Alaska Natives. Native Hawaiians include other Pacific Islanders.
Source: Bureau of the Census, An Overview: Race and Hispanic Origin and the 2010 Census, 2010 Census Briefs, Internet site http://www.census.gov/2010census/data/2010-census-briefs.php; calculations by New Strategist

Table 5.96 Hispanics by Ethnic Origin, 2000 and 2010

(number and percent distribution of Hispanics by ethnic origin, 2000 and 2010; percent change in number, 2000–10)

	2010		2000		percent change 2000–10
	number	percent distribution	number	percent distribution	
Total Hispanics	**50,477,594**	**100.0%**	**35,305,818**	**100.0%**	**43.0%**
Mexican	31,798,258	63.0	20,640,711	58.5	54.1
Puerto Rican	4,623,716	9.2	3,406,178	9.6	35.7
Cuban	1,785,547	3.5	1,241,685	3.5	43.8
Other Hispanic origin	12,270,073	24.3	10,017,244	28.4	22.5
Dominican (Dominican Republic)	1,414,703	2.8	764,945	2.2	84.9
Central American	3,998,280	7.9	1,686,937	4.8	137.0
Costa Rican	126,418	0.3	68,588	0.2	84.3
Guatemalan	1,044,209	2.1	372,487	1.1	180.3
Honduran	633,401	1.3	217,569	0.6	191.1
Nicaraguan	348,202	0.7	177,684	0.5	96.0
Panamanian	165,456	0.3	91,723	0.3	80.4
Salvadoran	1,648,968	3.3	655,165	1.9	151.7
Other Central American	31,626	0.1	103,721	0.3	−69.5
South American	2,769,434	5.5	1,353,562	3.8	104.6
Argentinean	224,952	0.4	100,864	0.3	123.0
Bolivian	99,210	0.2	42,068	0.1	135.8
Chilean	126,810	0.3	68,849	0.2	84.2
Colombian	908,734	1.8	470,684	1.3	93.1
Ecuadorian	564,631	1.1	260,559	0.7	116.7
Paraguayan	20,023	0.0	8,769	0.0	128.3
Peruvian	531,358	1.1	233,926	0.7	127.1
Uruguayan	56,884	0.1	18,804	0.1	202.5
Venezuelan	215,023	0.4	91,507	0.3	135.0
Other South American	21,809	0.0	57,532	0.2	−62.1
Spaniard	635,253	1.3	100,135	0.3	534.4
Other Hispanic	3,452,403	6.8	6,111,665	17.3	−43.5

Source: Bureau of the Census, The Hispanic Population: 2010, 2010 Census Brief, Internet site http://www.census .gov/2010census/data/2010-census-briefs.php

Table 5.97 Hispanics by Age, 2000 to 2011

(number of Hispanics by age, 2000 to 2011; percent change, 2000–11)

	2011	2010	2000	percent change 2000–11
Total Hispanics	**52,045,277**	**50,477,594**	**35,305,818**	**47.4%**
Under age 5	5,192,122	5,114,488	3,717,974	39.6
Aged 5 to 9	4,910,449	4,790,771	3,623,680	35.5
Aged 10 to 14	4,627,827	4,525,242	3,163,412	46.3
Aged 15 to 19	4,581,506	4,532,155	3,171,646	44.5
Aged 20 to 24	4,477,698	4,322,275	3,409,427	31.3
Aged 25 to 29	4,368,028	4,310,471	3,385,334	29.0
Aged 30 to 34	4,237,092	4,124,483	3,124,901	35.6
Aged 35 to 39	3,932,814	3,856,340	2,825,158	39.2
Aged 40 to 44	3,574,975	3,442,400	2,304,152	55.2
Aged 45 to 49	3,137,366	3,022,074	1,775,168	76.7
Aged 50 to 54	2,578,717	2,441,454	1,360,935	89.5
Aged 55 to 59	1,975,066	1,841,432	960,033	105.7
Aged 60 to 64	1,482,636	1,372,385	750,407	97.6
Aged 65 to 69	1,019,022	948,576	599,353	70.0
Aged 70 to 74	736,472	700,142	477,266	54.3
Aged 75 to 79	535,048	510,808	326,726	63.8
Aged 80 to 84	374,753	351,488	179,538	108.7
Aged 85 or older	303,686	270,610	150,708	101.5
Aged 18 to 24	6,339,530	6,154,040	4,743,880	33.6
Aged 18 or older	34,595,205	33,346,703	22,963,559	50.7
Aged 65 or older	2,968,981	2,781,624	1,733,591	71.3

Source: Bureau of the Census, 2000 Census, 2010 Census, and Population Estimates, Internet site http://www.census.gov/ popest/index.html; calculations by New Strategist

Table 5.98 Hispanic Share of Total Population by Age, 2011

(total number of people, number and percent distribution of Hispanics, and Hispanic share of total, by age, 2011)

	total	Hispanic number	Hispanic percent distribution	Hispanic share of total
Total people	311,591,917	52,045,277	100.0%	16.7%
Under age 5	20,162,058	5,192,122	10.0	25.8
Aged 5 to 9	20,334,196	4,910,449	9.4	24.1
Aged 10 to 14	20,704,852	4,627,827	8.9	22.4
Aged 15 to 19	21,644,043	4,581,506	8.8	21.2
Aged 20 to 24	22,153,832	4,477,698	8.6	20.2
Aged 25 to 29	21,279,794	4,368,028	8.4	20.5
Aged 30 to 34	20,510,704	4,237,092	8.1	20.7
Aged 35 to 39	19,594,309	3,932,814	7.6	20.1
Aged 40 to 44	21,033,645	3,574,975	6.9	17.0
Aged 45 to 49	22,158,005	3,137,366	6.0	14.2
Aged 50 to 54	22,560,198	2,578,717	5.0	11.4
Aged 55 to 59	20,255,548	1,975,066	3.8	9.8
Aged 60 to 64	17,806,592	1,482,636	2.8	8.3
Aged 65 to 69	12,873,788	1,019,022	2.0	7.9
Aged 70 to 74	9,607,950	736,472	1.4	7.7
Aged 75 to 79	7,388,687	535,048	1.0	7.2
Aged 80 to 84	5,786,543	374,753	0.7	6.5
Aged 85 or older	5,737,173	303,686	0.6	5.3
Aged 18 to 24	31,064,709	6,339,530	12.2	20.4
Aged 18 or older	237,657,645	34,595,205	66.5	14.6
Aged 65 or older	41,394,141	2,968,981	5.7	7.2

Source: Bureau of the Census, Population Estimates, Internet site http://www.census.gov/popest/index.html; calculations by New Strategist

Table 5.99 Hispanics by Age and Sex, 2011

(number of Hispanics by age and sex, and sex ratio by age, 2011)

	total	females	males	sex ratio
Total Hispanics	**52,045,277**	**25,602,066**	**26,443,211**	**103**
Under age 5	5,192,122	2,541,220	2,650,902	104
Aged 5 to 9	4,910,449	2,406,221	2,504,228	104
Aged 10 to 14	4,627,827	2,264,121	2,363,706	104
Aged 15 to 19	4,581,506	2,212,656	2,368,850	107
Aged 20 to 24	4,477,698	2,101,640	2,376,058	113
Aged 25 to 29	4,368,028	2,046,563	2,321,465	113
Aged 30 to 34	4,237,092	2,023,293	2,213,799	109
Aged 35 to 39	3,932,814	1,916,474	2,016,340	105
Aged 40 to 44	3,574,975	1,745,750	1,829,225	105
Aged 45 to 49	3,137,366	1,546,188	1,591,178	103
Aged 50 to 54	2,578,717	1,295,583	1,283,134	99
Aged 55 to 59	1,975,066	1,017,783	957,283	94
Aged 60 to 64	1,482,636	782,227	700,409	90
Aged 65 to 69	1,019,022	555,639	463,383	83
Aged 70 to 74	736,472	413,747	322,725	78
Aged 75 to 79	535,048	310,739	224,309	72
Aged 80 to 84	374,753	225,393	149,360	66
Aged 85 or older	303,686	196,829	106,857	54
Aged 18 to 24	6,339,530	2,993,233	3,346,297	112
Aged 18 or older	34,595,205	17,069,441	17,525,764	103
Aged 65 or older	2,968,981	1,702,347	1,266,634	74

Note: The sex ratio is the number of males divided by the number of females multiplied by 100.
Source: Bureau of the Census, Population Estimates, Internet site http://www.census.gov/popest/index.html; calculations by New Strategist

Table 5.100 Hispanic Population Projections, 2012 to 2050

(number of Hispanics by age, and Hispanic share of total population, 2012 to 2050, percent and percentage point change, 2012–50; numbers in thousands)

NUMBER	2012	2020	2030	2040	2050	percent change 2012–50
Total Hispanics	**53,274**	**63,784**	**78,655**	**94,876**	**111,732**	**109.7%**
Under age 5	5,267	6,035	6,924	7,970	8,930	69.5
Aged 5 to 9	5,026	5,715	6,597	7,591	8,628	71.7
Aged 10 to 14	4,689	5,329	6,289	7,211	8,264	76.2
Aged 15 to 19	4,579	5,069	6,063	6,987	7,988	74.4
Aged 20 to 24	4,616	5,079	6,065	7,117	8,061	74.6
Aged 25 to 29	4,401	5,239	6,027	7,173	8,130	84.7
Aged 30 to 34	4,326	4,878	5,837	6,958	8,031	85.6
Aged 35 to 39	4,001	4,633	5,701	6,579	7,731	93.2
Aged 40 to 44	3,680	4,295	5,100	6,112	7,241	96.8
Aged 45 to 49	3,215	3,910	4,687	5,788	6,675	107.6
Aged 50 to 54	2,688	3,434	4,249	5,057	6,083	126.3
Aged 55 to 59	2,093	2,968	3,805	4,566	5,673	171.0
Aged 60 to 64	1,548	2,370	3,288	4,072	4,876	214.9
Aged 65 or older	3,142	4,831	8,023	11,695	15,421	390.8

SHARE OF TOTAL POPULATION	2012	2020	2030	2040	2050	percentage point change 2012–50
Total Hispanics	**17.0%**	**19.1%**	**21.9%**	**25.0%**	**27.9%**	**11.0**
Under age 5	26.0	27.7	31.1	34.6	37.0	11.0
Aged 5 to 9	24.6	26.8	29.4	33.2	36.0	11.4
Aged 10 to 14	22.7	25.8	28.1	31.5	34.9	12.2
Aged 15 to 19	21.5	24.4	27.6	30.1	33.8	12.3
Aged 20 to 24	20.5	23.5	27.6	29.8	33.0	12.5
Aged 25 to 29	20.6	22.4	26.5	29.7	31.9	11.3
Aged 30 to 34	20.7	21.3	25.0	29.1	30.9	10.2
Aged 35 to 39	20.5	21.2	23.3	27.4	30.3	9.8
Aged 40 to 44	17.5	21.1	21.8	25.5	29.4	11.9
Aged 45 to 49	14.8	19.5	21.4	23.5	27.5	12.7
Aged 50 to 54	11.9	16.8	21.2	21.8	25.5	13.6
Aged 55 to 59	10.1	13.6	19.6	21.3	23.5	13.5
Aged 60 to 64	8.7	11.3	16.9	21.2	21.8	13.1
Aged 65 or older	7.3	8.6	11.0	14.7	18.4	11.1

Source: Bureau of the Census, Population Projections, Internet site http://www.census.gov/population/projections/; calculations by New Strategist

Table 5.101 Hispanics by Region, 2000 to 2011

(number of Hispanics by region, 2000 to 2011; percent change, 2000–11)

	2011	2010	2000	percent change 2000–11
Total Hispanics	52,045,277	50,477,594	35,305,818	47.4%
Northeast	7,192,169	6,991,969	5,254,087	36.9
Midwest	4,809,029	4,661,678	3,124,532	53.9
South	18,893,534	18,227,508	11,586,696	63.1
West	21,150,545	20,596,439	15,340,503	37.9

Source: Bureau of the Census, 2000 Census, 2010 Census, and Population Estimates, Internet site http://www.census.gov/popest/index.html; calculations by New Strategist

Table 5.102 Hispanic Share of the Total Population by Region, 2011

(total number of people, number and percent distribution of Hispanics, and Hispanic share of total, by region, 2011)

	total	Hispanic number	percent distribution	share of total
Total people	311,587,816	52,045,277	100.0%	16.7%
Northeast	55,597,646	7,192,169	13.8	12.9
Midwest	67,145,089	4,809,029	9.2	7.2
South	116,022,230	18,893,534	36.3	16.3
West	72,822,851	21,150,545	40.6	29.0

Source: Bureau of the Census, Population Estimates, Internet site http://www.census.gov/popest/index.html; calculations by New Strategist

Table 5.103 Hispanics by State, 2000 to 2011

(number of Hispanics by state, 2000 to 2011; percent change, 2000–11)

	2011	2010	2000	percent change 2000–11
Total Hispanics	**52,045,277**	**50,477,594**	**35,305,818**	**47.4%**
Alabama	193,868	185,602	75,830	155.7
Alaska	42,113	39,249	25,852	62.9
Arizona	1,949,294	1,895,149	1,295,617	50.5
Arkansas	195,075	186,050	86,866	124.6
California	14,359,500	14,013,719	10,966,556	30.9
Colorado	1,070,566	1,038,687	735,601	45.5
Connecticut	494,290	479,087	320,323	54.3
Delaware	76,153	73,221	37,277	104.3
District of Columbia	58,744	54,749	44,953	30.7
Florida	4,355,525	4,223,806	2,682,715	62.4
Georgia	892,010	853,689	435,227	105.0
Hawaii	126,418	120,842	87,699	44.1
Idaho	182,080	175,901	101,690	79.1
Illinois	2,079,697	2,027,578	1,530,262	35.9
Indiana	403,796	389,707	214,536	88.2
Iowa	158,014	151,544	82,473	91.6
Kansas	309,914	300,042	188,252	64.6
Kentucky	138,563	132,836	59,939	131.2
Louisiana	202,233	192,560	107,738	87.7
Maine	17,958	16,935	9,360	91.9
Maryland	490,716	470,632	227,916	115.3
Massachusetts	650,621	627,654	428,729	51.8
Michigan	447,917	436,358	323,877	38.3
Minnesota	259,297	250,258	143,382	80.8
Mississippi	85,631	81,481	39,569	116.4
Missouri	221,155	212,470	118,592	86.5
Montana	30,502	28,565	18,081	68.7
Nebraska	174,516	167,405	94,425	84.8
Nevada	737,221	716,501	393,970	87.1
New Hampshire	38,560	36,704	20,489	88.2
New Jersey	1,600,690	1,555,144	1,117,191	43.3
New Mexico	973,050	953,403	765,386	27.1
New York	3,495,138	3,416,922	2,867,583	21.9
North Carolina	832,405	800,120	378,963	119.7
North Dakota	15,318	13,467	7,786	96.7
Ohio	367,116	354,674	217,123	69.1
Oklahoma	347,620	332,007	179,304	93.9
Oregon	466,069	450,062	275,314	69.3

	2011	2010	2000	percent change 2000–11
Pennsylvania	750,431	719,660	394,088	90.4%
Rhode Island	134,714	130,655	90,820	48.3
South Carolina	245,660	235,682	95,076	158.4
South Dakota	24,020	22,119	10,903	120.3
Tennessee	303,119	290,059	123,838	144.8
Texas	9,791,582	9,460,921	6,669,666	46.8
Utah	372,912	358,340	201,559	85.0
Vermont	9,767	9,208	5,504	77.5
Virginia	660,730	631,825	329,540	100.5
Washington	789,060	755,790	441,509	78.7
West Virginia	23,900	22,268	12,279	94.6
Wisconsin	348,269	336,056	192,921	80.5
Wyoming	51,760	50,231	31,669	63.4

Source: Bureau of the Census, 2000 Census, 2010 Census, and Population Estimates, Internet site http://www.census.gov/popest/index.html; calculations by New Strategist

Table 5.104 Hispanic Share of Total Population by State, 2011

(total number of people, number and percent distribution of Hispanics, and Hispanic share of total, by state, 2011)

	total	Hispanic number	percent distribution	share of total
Total people	**311,587,816**	**52,045,277**	**100.0%**	**16.7%**
Alabama	4,802,740	193,868	0.4	4.0
Alaska	722,718	42,113	0.1	5.8
Arizona	6,482,505	1,949,294	3.7	30.1
Arkansas	2,937,979	195,075	0.4	6.6
California	37,691,912	14,359,500	27.6	38.1
Colorado	5,116,796	1,070,566	2.1	20.9
Connecticut	3,580,709	494,290	0.9	13.8
Delaware	907,135	76,153	0.1	8.4
District of Columbia	617,996	58,744	0.1	9.5
Florida	19,057,542	4,355,525	8.4	22.9
Georgia	9,815,210	892,010	1.7	9.1
Hawaii	1,374,810	126,418	0.2	9.2
Idaho	1,584,985	182,080	0.3	11.5
Illinois	12,869,257	2,079,697	4.0	16.2
Indiana	6,516,922	403,796	0.8	6.2
Iowa	3,062,309	158,014	0.3	5.2
Kansas	2,871,238	309,914	0.6	10.8
Kentucky	4,369,356	138,563	0.3	3.2
Louisiana	4,574,836	202,233	0.4	4.4
Maine	1,328,188	17,958	0.0	1.4
Maryland	5,828,289	490,716	0.9	8.4
Massachusetts	6,587,536	650,621	1.3	9.9
Michigan	9,876,187	447,917	0.9	4.5
Minnesota	5,344,861	259,297	0.5	4.9
Mississippi	2,978,512	85,631	0.2	2.9
Missouri	6,010,688	221,155	0.4	3.7
Montana	998,199	30,502	0.1	3.1
Nebraska	1,842,641	174,516	0.3	9.5
Nevada	2,723,322	737,221	1.4	27.1
New Hampshire	1,318,194	38,560	0.1	2.9
New Jersey	8,821,155	1,600,690	3.1	18.1
New Mexico	2,082,224	973,050	1.9	46.7
New York	19,465,197	3,495,138	6.7	18.0
North Carolina	9,656,401	832,405	1.6	8.6
North Dakota	683,932	15,318	0.0	2.2
Ohio	11,544,951	367,116	0.7	3.2
Oklahoma	3,791,508	347,620	0.7	9.2

	total	Hispanic		
		number	percent distribution	share of total
Oregon	3,871,859	466,069	0.9%	12.0%
Pennsylvania	12,742,886	750,431	1.4	5.9
Rhode Island	1,051,302	134,714	0.3	12.8
South Carolina	4,679,230	245,660	0.5	5.3
South Dakota	824,082	24,020	0.0	2.9
Tennessee	6,403,353	303,119	0.6	4.7
Texas	25,674,681	9,791,582	18.8	38.1
Utah	2,817,222	372,912	0.7	13.2
Vermont	626,431	9,767	0.0	1.6
Virginia	8,096,604	660,730	1.3	8.2
Washington	6,830,038	789,060	1.5	11.6
West Virginia	1,855,364	23,900	0.0	1.3
Wisconsin	5,711,767	348,269	0.7	6.1
Wyoming	568,158	51,760	0.1	9.1

Source: Bureau of the Census, Population Estimates, Internet site http://www.census.gov/popest/index.html; calculations by New Strategist

Table 5.105 Number of Hispanics by State and Ethnicity, 2010

(number of Hispanics by state and ethnicity, 2010)

	total	Mexican	Puerto Rican	Cuban	Dominican	Central American	South American	other Hispanic
Total Hispanics	50,477,594	31,798,258	4,623,716	1,785,547	1,414,703	3,998,280	2,769,434	4,087,656
Alabama	185,602	122,911	12,225	4,064	852	22,800	5,938	16,812
Alaska	39,249	21,642	4,502	927	1,909	2,509	2,345	5,415
Arizona	1,895,149	1,657,668	34,787	10,692	3,103	36,642	21,895	130,362
Arkansas	186,050	138,194	4,789	1,493	384	23,216	3,028	14,946
California	14,013,719	11,423,146	189,945	88,607	11,455	1,132,520	293,880	874,166
Colorado	1,038,687	757,181	22,995	6,253	1,744	29,386	19,117	202,011
Connecticut	479,087	50,658	252,972	9,490	26,093	35,023	71,355	33,496
Delaware	73,221	30,283	22,533	1,443	2,035	8,112	3,849	4,966
District of Columbia	54,749	8,507	3,129	1,789	2,508	23,354	7,639	7,823
Florida	4,223,806	629,718	847,550	1,213,438	172,451	432,665	674,542	253,442
Georgia	853,689	519,502	71,987	25,048	14,941	106,987	57,707	57,517
Hawaii	120,842	35,415	44,116	1,544	600	2,962	3,549	32,656
Idaho	175,901	148,923	2,910	825	185	3,494	3,707	15,857
Illinois	2,027,578	1,602,403	182,989	22,541	5,691	70,000	67,862	76,092
Indiana	389,707	295,373	30,304	4,042	2,340	22,093	10,032	25,523
Iowa	151,544	117,090	4,885	1,226	429	13,289	3,754	10,871
Kansas	300,042	247,297	9,247	2,723	764	15,293	5,845	18,873
Kentucky	132,836	82,110	11,454	9,323	1,065	11,479	5,405	12,000
Louisiana	192,560	78,643	11,603	10,330	3,238	51,722	8,871	28,153
Maine	16,935	5,134	4,377	783	610	1,708	1,515	2,808
Maryland	470,632	88,004	42,572	10,366	14,873	195,692	61,400	57,725
Massachusetts	627,654	38,379	266,125	11,306	103,292	96,958	54,398	57,196
Michigan	436,358	317,903	37,267	9,922	5,012	17,785	13,243	35,226
Minnesota	250,258	176,007	10,807	3,661	1,294	19,908	18,075	20,506
Mississippi	81,481	52,459	5,888	2,063	733	8,343	2,833	9,162
Missouri	212,470	147,254	12,236	4,979	1,503	17,763	8,731	20,004
Montana	28,565	20,048	1,491	421	95	735	997	4,778
Nebraska	167,405	128,060	3,242	2,152	358	17,242	2,824	13,527
Nevada	716,501	540,978	20,664	21,459	2,446	55,937	19,056	55,961
New Hampshire	36,704	7,822	11,729	1,349	4,460	2,731	4,266	4,347
New Jersey	1,555,144	217,715	434,092	83,362	197,922	176,611	325,179	120,263
New Mexico	953,403	590,890	7,964	4,298	492	6,621	4,841	338,297
New York	3,416,922	457,288	1,070,558	70,803	674,787	353,589	513,417	276,480
North Carolina	800,120	486,960	71,800	18,079	15,225	105,066	46,307	56,683
North Dakota	13,467	9,223	987	260	90	452	539	1,916
Ohio	354,674	172,029	94,965	7,523	6,453	22,756	17,571	33,377
Oklahoma	332,007	267,016	12,223	2,755	727	15,641	7,134	26,511
Oregon	450,062	369,817	8,845	4,923	574	18,190	9,648	38,065
Pennsylvania	719,660	129,568	366,082	17,930	62,348	35,453	48,126	60,153
Rhode Island	130,655	9,090	34,979	1,640	35,008	23,817	14,013	12,108
South Carolina	235,682	138,358	26,493	5,955	3,018	26,290	17,856	17,712

	total	Mexican	Puerto Rican	Cuban	Dominican	Central American	South American	other Hispanic
South Dakota	22,119	13,839	1,483	265	79	2,891	617	2,945
Tennessee	290,059	186,615	21,060	7,773	2,113	36,856	11,039	24,603
Texas	9,460,921	7,951,193	130,576	46,541	13,353	420,683	133,808	764,767
Utah	358,340	258,905	7,182	1,963	1,252	20,442	26,028	42,568
Vermont	9,208	2,534	2,261	510	282	671	1,204	1,746
Virginia	631,825	155,067	73,958	15,229	10,504	206,568	101,480	69,019
Washington	755,790	601,768	25,838	6,744	1,819	33,661	20,742	65,218
West Virginia	22,268	9,704	3,701	764	363	2,081	1,700	3,955
Wisconsin	336,056	244,248	46,323	3,696	1,786	10,616	9,675	19,712
Wyoming	50,231	37,719	1,026	275	45	977	852	9,337

Note: "Other Hispanic" includes Spaniard.
Source: Bureau of the Census, 2010 Census, Internet site http://factfinder2.census.gov/faces/nav/jsf/pages/index.xhtml;
calculations by New Strategist

Table 5.106 Distribution of Hispanics by State and Ethnicity, 2010

(percent distribution of Hispanics by state and ethnicity, 2010)

	total	Mexican	Puerto Rican	Cuban	Dominican	Central American	South American	other Hispanic
Total Hispanics	**100.0%**	**63.0%**	**9.2%**	**3.5%**	**2.8%**	**7.9%**	**5.5%**	**8.1%**
Alabama	100.0	66.2	6.6	2.2	0.5	12.3	3.2	9.1
Alaska	100.0	55.1	11.5	2.4	4.9	6.4	6.0	13.8
Arizona	100.0	87.5	1.8	0.6	0.2	1.9	1.2	6.9
Arkansas	100.0	74.3	2.6	0.8	0.2	12.5	1.6	8.0
California	100.0	81.5	1.4	0.6	0.1	8.1	2.1	6.2
Colorado	100.0	72.9	2.2	0.6	0.2	2.8	1.8	19.4
Connecticut	100.0	10.6	52.8	2.0	5.4	7.3	14.9	7.0
Delaware	100.0	41.4	30.8	2.0	2.8	11.1	5.3	6.8
District of Columbia	100.0	15.5	5.7	3.3	4.6	42.7	14.0	14.3
Florida	100.0	14.9	20.1	28.7	4.1	10.2	16.0	6.0
Georgia	100.0	60.9	8.4	2.9	1.8	12.5	6.8	6.7
Hawaii	100.0	29.3	36.5	1.3	0.5	2.5	2.9	27.0
Idaho	100.0	84.7	1.7	0.5	0.1	2.0	2.1	9.0
Illinois	100.0	79.0	9.0	1.1	0.3	3.5	3.3	3.8
Indiana	100.0	75.8	7.8	1.0	0.6	5.7	2.6	6.5
Iowa	100.0	77.3	3.2	0.8	0.3	8.8	2.5	7.2
Kansas	100.0	82.4	3.1	0.9	0.3	5.1	1.9	6.3
Kentucky	100.0	61.8	8.6	7.0	0.8	8.6	4.1	9.0
Louisiana	100.0	40.8	6.0	5.4	1.7	26.9	4.6	14.6
Maine	100.0	30.3	25.8	4.6	3.6	10.1	8.9	16.6
Maryland	100.0	18.7	9.0	2.2	3.2	41.6	13.0	12.3
Massachusetts	100.0	6.1	42.4	1.8	16.5	15.4	8.7	9.1
Michigan	100.0	72.9	8.5	2.3	1.1	4.1	3.0	8.1
Minnesota	100.0	70.3	4.3	1.5	0.5	8.0	7.2	8.2
Mississippi	100.0	64.4	7.2	2.5	0.9	10.2	3.5	11.2
Missouri	100.0	69.3	5.8	2.3	0.7	8.4	4.1	9.4
Montana	100.0	70.2	5.2	1.5	0.3	2.6	3.5	16.7
Nebraska	100.0	76.5	1.9	1.3	0.2	10.3	1.7	8.1
Nevada	100.0	75.5	2.9	3.0	0.3	7.8	2.7	7.8
New Hampshire	100.0	21.3	32.0	3.7	12.2	7.4	11.6	11.8
New Jersey	100.0	14.0	27.9	5.4	12.7	11.4	20.9	7.7
New Mexico	100.0	62.0	0.8	0.5	0.1	0.7	0.5	35.5
New York	100.0	13.4	31.3	2.1	19.7	10.3	15.0	8.1
North Carolina	100.0	60.9	9.0	2.3	1.9	13.1	5.8	7.1
North Dakota	100.0	68.5	7.3	1.9	0.7	3.4	4.0	14.2
Ohio	100.0	48.5	26.8	2.1	1.8	6.4	5.0	9.4
Oklahoma	100.0	80.4	3.7	0.8	0.2	4.7	2.1	8.0
Oregon	100.0	82.2	2.0	1.1	0.1	4.0	2.1	8.5
Pennsylvania	100.0	18.0	50.9	2.5	8.7	4.9	6.7	8.4
Rhode Island	100.0	7.0	26.8	1.3	26.8	18.2	10.7	9.3
South Carolina	100.0	58.7	11.2	2.5	1.3	11.2	7.6	7.5

	total	Mexican	Puerto Rican	Cuban	Dominican	Central American	South American	other Hispanic
South Dakota	100.0%	62.6%	6.7%	1.2%	0.4%	13.1%	2.8%	13.3%
Tennessee	100.0	64.3	7.3	2.7	0.7	12.7	3.8	8.5
Texas	100.0	84.0	1.4	0.5	0.1	4.4	1.4	8.1
Utah	100.0	72.3	2.0	0.5	0.3	5.7	7.3	11.9
Vermont	100.0	27.5	24.6	5.5	3.1	7.3	13.1	19.0
Virginia	100.0	24.5	11.7	2.4	1.7	32.7	16.1	10.9
Washington	100.0	79.6	3.4	0.9	0.2	4.5	2.7	8.6
West Virginia	100.0	43.6	16.6	3.4	1.6	9.3	7.6	17.8
Wisconsin	100.0	72.7	13.8	1.1	0.5	3.2	2.9	5.9
Wyoming	100.0	75.1	2.0	0.5	0.1	1.9	1.7	18.6

Note: "Other Hispanic" includes Spaniard.
Source: Bureau of the Census, 2010 Census, Internet site http://factfinder2.census.gov/faces/nav/jsf/pages/index.xhtml;
calculations by New Strategist

Table 5.107 Hispanics by Metropolitan Area, 2010

(total number of people, number of Hispanics, and Hispanic share of total, for selected metropolitan areas, 2010)

	total population	Hispanic number	Hispanic share of total
Abilene, TX	165,252	35,108	21.2%
Akron, OH	703,200	10,733	1.5
Albany, GA	157,308	3,270	2.1
Albany–Schenectady–Troy, NY	870,716	36,027	4.1
Albuquerque, NM	887,077	414,222	46.7
Alexandria, LA	153,922	4,349	2.8
Allentown–Bethlehem–Easton, PA–NJ	821,173	106,598	13.0
Altoona, PA	127,089	1,230	1.0
Amarillo, TX	249,881	63,116	25.3
Ames, IA	89,542	2,695	3.0
Anchorage, AK	380,821	25,362	6.7
Anderson, IN	131,636	4,189	3.2
Anderson, SC	187,126	5,447	2.9
Ann Arbor, MI	344,791	13,860	4.0
Anniston–Oxford, AL	118,572	3,893	3.3
Appleton, WI	225,666	8,049	3.6
Asheville, NC	424,858	27,100	6.4
Athens–Clarke County, GA	192,541	15,313	8.0
Atlanta–Sandy Springs–Marietta, GA	5,268,860	547,400	10.4
Atlantic City–Hammonton, NJ	274,549	46,241	16.8
Auburn–Opelika, AL	140,247	4,571	3.3
Augusta–Richmond County, GA–SC	556,877	24,712	4.4
Austin–Round Rock–San Marcos, TX	1,716,289	538,313	31.4
Bakersfield–Delano, CA	839,631	413,033	49.2
Baltimore–Towson, MD	2,710,489	123,754	4.6
Bangor, ME	153,923	1,620	1.1
Barnstable Town, MA	215,888	4,687	2.2
Baton Rouge, LA	802,484	27,357	3.4
Battle Creek, MI	136,146	6,177	4.5
Bay City, MI	107,771	5,093	4.7
Beaumont–Port Arthur, TX	388,745	50,049	12.9
Bellingham, WA	201,140	15,756	7.8
Bend, OR	157,733	11,718	7.4
Billings, MT	158,050	7,143	4.5
Binghamton, NY	251,725	7,472	3.0
Birmingham–Hoover, AL	1,128,047	48,530	4.3
Bismarck, ND	108,779	1,386	1.3
Blacksburg–Christiansburg–Radford, VA	162,958	3,562	2.2

	total population	Hispanic	
		number	share of total
Bloomington, IN	192,714	4,549	2.4%
Bloomington–Normal, IL	169,572	7,434	4.4
Boise City–Nampa, ID	616,561	77,538	12.6
Boston–Cambridge–Quincy, MA–NH	4,552,402	410,516	9.0
Boulder, CO	294,567	39,276	13.3
Bowling Green, KY	125,953	5,274	4.2
Bremerton–Silverdale, WA	251,133	15,686	6.2
Bridgeport–Stamford–Norwalk, CT	916,829	155,025	16.9
Brownsville–Harlingen, TX	406,220	357,747	88.1
Brunswick, GA	112,370	5,696	5.1
Buffalo–Niagara Falls, NY	1,135,509	46,425	4.1
Burlington, NC	151,131	16,639	11.0
Burlington–South Burlington, VT	211,261	3,507	1.7
Canton–Massillon, OH	404,422	6,203	1.5
Cape Coral–Fort Myers, FL	618,754	113,308	18.3
Cape Girardeau–Jackson, MO–IL	96,275	1,729	1.8
Carson City, NV	55,274	11,777	21.3
Casper, WY	75,450	5,231	6.9
Cedar Rapids, IA	257,940	6,079	2.4
Champaign–Urbana, IL	231,891	11,068	4.8
Charleston, WV	304,284	2,522	0.8
Charleston–North Charleston–Summerville, SC	664,607	35,707	5.4
Charlotte–Gastonia–Rock Hill, NC–SC	1,758,038	172,766	9.8
Charlottesville, VA	201,559	9,640	4.8
Chattanooga, TN–GA	528,143	18,690	3.5
Cheyenne, WY	91,738	11,978	13.1
Chicago–Joliet–Naperville, IL–IN–WI	9,461,105	1,957,080	20.7
Chico, CA	220,000	31,116	14.1
Cincinnati–Middletown, OH–KY–IN	2,130,151	55,120	2.6
Clarksville, TN–KY	273,949	18,718	6.8
Cleveland, TN	115,788	4,897	4.2
Cleveland–Elyria–Mentor, OH	2,077,240	98,133	4.7
Coeur d'Alene, ID	138,494	5,268	3.8
College Station–Bryan, TX	228,660	51,561	22.5
Colorado Springs, CO	645,613	94,959	14.7
Columbia, MO	172,786	5,017	2.9
Columbia, SC	767,598	39,153	5.1
Columbus, GA–AL	294,865	16,896	5.7
Columbus, IN	76,794	4,762	6.2
Columbus, OH	1,836,536	66,460	3.6
Corpus Christi, TX	428,185	247,231	57.7
Corvallis, OR	85,579	5,467	6.4

	total population	Hispanic	
		number	share of total
Crestview–Fort Walton Beach–Destin, FL	180,822	12,296	6.8%
Cumberland, MD–WV	103,299	1,287	1.2
Dallas–Fort Worth–Arlington, TX	6,371,773	1,752,166	27.5
Dalton, GA	142,227	37,625	26.5
Danville, IL	81,625	3,441	4.2
Danville, VA	106,561	2,577	2.4
Davenport–Moline–Rock Island, IA–IL	379,690	29,024	7.6
Dayton, OH	841,502	17,211	2.0
Decatur, AL	153,829	9,730	6.3
Decatur, IL	110,768	2,072	1.9
Deltona–Daytona Beach–Ormond Beach, FL	494,593	55,217	11.2
Denver–Aurora–Broomfield, CO	2,543,482	571,131	22.5
Des Moines–West Des Moines, IA	569,633	38,004	6.7
Detroit–Warren–Livonia, MI	4,296,250	168,065	3.9
Dothan, AL	145,639	4,304	3.0
Dover, DE	162,310	9,346	5.8
Dubuque, IA	93,653	1,807	1.9
Duluth, MN–WI	279,771	3,387	1.2
Durham–Chapel Hill, NC	504,357	56,915	11.3
Eau Claire, WI	161,151	2,604	1.6
El Centro, CA	174,528	140,271	80.4
Elizabethtown, KY	119,736	5,718	4.8
Elkhart–Goshen, IN	197,559	27,886	14.1
Elmira, NY	88,830	2,240	2.5
El Paso, TX	800,647	658,134	82.2
Erie, PA	280,566	9,518	3.4
Eugene–Springfield, OR	351,715	26,167	7.4
Evansville, IN–KY	358,676	6,946	1.9
Fairbanks, AK	97,581	5,651	5.8
Fargo, ND–MN	208,777	5,071	2.4
Farmington, NM	130,044	24,776	19.1
Fayetteville, NC	366,383	36,013	9.8
Fayetteville–Springdale–Rogers, AR–MO	463,204	69,087	14.9
Flagstaff, AZ	134,421	18,166	13.5
Flint, MI	425,790	12,983	3.0
Florence, SC	205,566	4,170	2.0
Florence–Muscle Shoals, AL	147,137	3,175	2.2
Fond du Lac, WI	101,633	4,368	4.3
Fort Collins–Loveland, CO	299,630	31,628	10.6
Fort Smith, AR–OK	298,592	24,468	8.2
Fort Wayne, IN	416,257	24,172	5.8
Fresno, CA	930,450	468,070	50.3

	total population	Hispanic	
		number	share of total
Gadsden, AL	104,430	3,447	3.3%
Gainesville, FL	264,275	21,597	8.2
Gainesville, GA	179,684	46,906	26.1
Glens Falls, NY	128,923	2,624	2.0
Goldsboro, NC	122,623	12,162	9.9
Grand Forks, ND–MN	98,461	3,671	3.7
Grand Junction, CO	146,723	19,552	13.3
Grand Rapids–Wyoming, MI	774,160	65,227	8.4
Great Falls, MT	81,327	2,711	3.3
Greeley, CO	252,825	71,680	28.4
Green Bay, WI	306,241	18,967	6.2
Greensboro–High Point, NC	723,801	54,683	7.6
Greenville, NC	189,510	12,256	6.5
Greenville–Mauldin–Easley, SC	636,986	42,967	6.7
Gulfport–Biloxi, MS	248,820	11,622	4.7
Hagerstown–Martinsburg, MD–WV	269,140	9,248	3.4
Hanford–Corcoran, CA	152,982	77,866	50.9
Harrisburg–Carlisle, PA	549,475	25,831	4.7
Harrisonburg, VA	125,228	11,741	9.4
Hartford–West Hartford–East Hartford, CT	1,212,381	151,219	12.5
Hattiesburg, MS	142,842	3,961	2.8
Hickory–Lenoir–Morganton, NC	365,497	23,063	6.3
Hinesville–Fort Stewart, GA	77,917	7,937	10.2
Holland–Grand Haven, MI	263,801	22,761	8.6
Honolulu, HI	953,207	77,433	8.1
Hot Springs, AR	96,024	4,622	4.8
Houma–Bayou Cane–Thibodaux, LA	208,178	8,068	3.9
Houston–Sugar Land–Baytown, TX	5,946,800	2,099,412	35.3
Huntington–Ashland, WV–KY–OH	287,702	2,707	0.9
Huntsville, AL	417,593	19,995	4.8
Idaho Falls, ID	130,374	14,553	11.2
Indianapolis–Carmel, IN	1,756,241	108,259	6.2
Iowa City, IA	152,586	7,338	4.8
Ithaca, NY	101,564	4,264	4.2
Jackson, MI	160,248	4,837	3.0
Jackson, MS	539,057	11,391	2.1
Jackson, TN	115,425	3,649	3.2
Jacksonville, FL	1,345,596	92,879	6.9
Jacksonville, NC	177,772	17,896	10.1
Janesville, WI	160,331	12,124	7.6
Jefferson City, MO	149,807	3,172	2.1
Johnson City, TN	198,716	5,217	2.6

	total population	Hispanic number	Hispanic share of total
Johnstown, PA	143,679	2,006	1.4%
Jonesboro, AR	121,026	4,820	4.0
Joplin, MO	175,518	10,564	6.0
Kalamazoo–Portage, MI	326,589	17,717	5.4
Kankakee–Bradley, IL	113,449	10,167	9.0
Kansas City, MO–KS	2,035,334	166,683	8.2
Kennewick–Pasco–Richland, WA	253,340	72,700	28.7
Killeen–Temple–Fort Hood, TX	405,300	82,426	20.3
Kingsport–Bristol–Bristol, TN–VA	309,544	4,169	1.3
Kingston, NY	182,493	15,909	8.7
Knoxville, TN	698,030	23,865	3.4
Kokomo, IN	98,688	2,549	2.6
La Crosse, WI–MN	133,665	1,873	1.4
Lafayette, IN	201,789	14,089	7.0
Lafayette, LA	273,738	9,668	3.5
Lake Charles, LA	199,607	5,099	2.6
Lake Havasu City–Kingman, AZ	200,186	29,569	14.8
Lakeland–Winter Haven, FL	602,095	106,532	17.7
Lancaster, PA	519,445	44,930	8.6
Lansing–East Lansing, MI	464,036	28,574	6.2
Laredo, TX	250,304	239,653	95.7
Las Cruces, NM	209,233	137,514	65.7
Las Vegas–Paradise, NV	1,951,269	568,644	29.1
Lawrence, KS	110,826	5,651	5.1
Lawton, OK	124,098	13,896	11.2
Lebanon, PA	133,568	12,410	9.3
Lewiston, ID–WA	60,888	1,752	2.9
Lewiston–Auburn, ME	107,702	1,669	1.5
Lexington–Fayette, KY	472,099	27,760	5.9
Lima, OH	106,331	2,513	2.4
Lincoln, NE	302,157	16,957	5.6
Little Rock–North Little Rock–Conway, AR	699,757	33,575	4.8
Logan, UT–ID	125,442	12,054	9.6
Longview, TX	214,369	30,240	14.1
Longview, WA	102,410	7,975	7.8
Los Angeles–Long Beach–Santa Ana, CA	12,828,837	5,700,862	44.4
Louisville/Jefferson County, KY–IN	1,283,566	50,388	3.9
Lubbock, TX	284,890	92,095	32.3
Lynchburg, VA	252,634	5,234	2.1
Macon, GA	232,293	5,664	2.4
Madera–Chowchilla, CA	150,865	80,992	53.7
Madison, WI	568,593	30,705	5.4

	total population	Hispanic number	share of total
Manchester–Nashua, NH	400,721	21,241	5.3%
Manhattan, KS	127,081	9,819	7.7
Mankato–North Mankato, MN	96,740	2,812	2.9
Mansfield, OH	124,475	1,732	1.4
McAllen–Edinburg–Mission, TX	774,769	702,206	90.6
Medford, OR	203,206	21,745	10.7
Memphis, TN–MS–AR	1,316,100	65,395	5.0
Merced, CA	255,793	140,485	54.9
Miami–Fort Lauderdale–Pompano Beach, FL	5,564,635	2,312,929	41.6
Michigan City–La Porte, IN	111,467	6,093	5.5
Midland, TX	136,872	51,600	37.7
Milwaukee–Waukesha–West Allis, WI	1,555,908	147,503	9.5
Minneapolis–St. Paul–Bloomington, MN–WI	3,279,833	176,283	5.4
Missoula, MT	109,299	2,861	2.6
Mobile, AL	412,992	9,936	2.4
Modesto, CA	514,453	215,658	41.9
Monroe, LA	176,441	3,703	2.1
Monroe, MI	152,021	4,667	3.1
Montgomery, AL	374,536	11,840	3.2
Morgantown, WV	129,709	1,921	1.5
Morristown, TN	136,608	8,860	6.5
Mount Vernon–Anacortes, WA	116,901	19,709	16.9
Muncie, IN	117,671	2,088	1.8
Muskegon–Norton Shores, MI	172,188	8,261	4.8
Myrtle Beach–North Myrtle Beach–Conway, SC	269,291	16,683	6.2
Napa, CA	136,484	44,010	32.2
Naples–Marco Island, FL	321,520	83,177	25.9
Nashville–Davidson–Murfreesboro–Franklin, TN	1,589,934	105,367	6.6
New Haven–Milford, CT	862,477	129,743	15.0
New Orleans–Metairie–Kenner, LA	1,167,764	91,922	7.9
New York–Northern New Jersey–Long Island, NY–NJ–PA	18,897,109	4,327,560	22.9
Niles–Benton Harbor, MI	156,813	7,054	4.5
North Port–Bradenton–Sarasota, FL	702,281	77,988	11.1
Norwich–New London, CT	274,055	23,214	8.5
Ocala, FL	331,298	36,137	10.9
Ocean City, NJ	97,265	6,054	6.2
Odessa, TX	137,130	72,331	52.7
Ogden–Clearfield, UT	547,184	64,690	11.8
Oklahoma City, OK	1,252,987	142,042	11.3
Olympia, WA	252,264	17,787	7.1
Omaha–Council Bluffs, NE–IA	865,350	77,508	9.0

	total population	Hispanic number	share of total
Orlando–Kissimmee–Sanford, FL	2,134,411	538,856	25.2%
Oshkosh–Neenah, WI	166,994	5,784	3.5
Owensboro, KY	114,752	2,725	2.4
Oxnard–Thousand Oaks–Ventura, CA	823,318	331,567	40.3
Palm Bay–Melbourne–Titusville, FL	543,376	43,943	8.1
Palm Coast, FL	95,696	8,251	8.6
Panama City–Lynn Haven–Panama City Beach, FL	168,852	8,107	4.8
Parkersburg–Marietta–Vienna, WV–OH	162,056	1,292	0.8
Pascagoula, MS	162,246	6,831	4.2
Pensacola–Ferry Pass–Brent, FL	448,991	20,568	4.6
Peoria, IL	379,186	10,516	2.8
Philadelphia–Camden–Wilmington, PA–NJ–DE–MD	5,965,343	468,168	7.8
Phoenix–Mesa–Glendale, AZ	4,192,887	1,235,718	29.5
Pine Bluff, AR	100,258	1,816	1.8
Pittsburgh, PA	2,356,285	29,969	1.3
Pittsfield, MA	131,219	4,530	3.5
Pocatello, ID	90,656	7,915	8.7
Portland–South Portland–Biddeford, ME	514,098	7,976	1.6
Portland–Vancouver–Hillsboro, OR–WA	2,226,009	241,844	10.9
Port St. Lucie, FL	424,107	63,876	15.1
Poughkeepsie–Newburgh–Middletown, NY	670,301	98,452	14.7
Prescott, AZ	211,033	28,728	13.6
Providence–New Bedford–Fall River, RI–MA	1,600,852	163,675	10.2
Provo–Orem, UT	526,810	56,172	10.7
Pueblo, CO	159,063	65,811	41.4
Punta Gorda, FL	159,978	9,213	5.8
Racine, WI	195,408	22,546	11.5
Raleigh–Cary, NC	1,130,490	114,512	10.1
Rapid City, SD	126,382	4,817	3.8
Reading, PA	411,442	67,355	16.4
Redding, CA	177,223	14,878	8.4
Reno–Sparks, NV	425,417	93,952	22.1
Richmond, VA	1,258,251	63,289	5.0
Riverside–San Bernardino–Ontario, CA	4,224,851	1,996,402	47.3
Roanoke, VA	308,707	9,713	3.1
Rochester, MN	186,011	7,588	4.1
Rochester, NY	1,054,323	64,719	6.1
Rockford, IL	349,431	43,144	12.3
Rocky Mount, NC	152,392	8,119	5.3
Rome, GA	96,317	8,987	9.3
Sacramento–Arden–Arcade–Roseville, CA	2,149,127	433,734	20.2
Saginaw–Saginaw Township North, MI	200,169	15,573	7.8

	total population	Hispanic	
		number	share of total
St. Cloud, MN	189,093	4,822	2.6%
St. George, UT	138,115	13,486	9.8
St. Joseph, MO–KS	127,329	5,348	4.2
St. Louis, MO–IL	2,812,896	72,019	2.6
Salem, OR	390,738	85,682	21.9
Salinas, CA	415,057	230,003	55.4
Salisbury, MD	125,203	5,341	4.3
Salt Lake City, UT	1,124,197	186,866	16.6
San Angelo, TX	111,823	39,722	35.5
San Antonio–New Braunfels, TX	2,142,508	1,158,148	54.1
San Diego–Carlsbad–San Marcos, CA	3,095,313	991,348	32.0
Sandusky, OH	77,079	2,604	3.4
San Francisco–Oakland–Fremont, CA	4,335,391	938,794	21.7
San Jose–Sunnyvale–Santa Clara, CA	1,836,911	510,396	27.8
San Luis Obispo–Paso Robles, CA	269,637	55,973	20.8
Santa Barbara–Santa Maria–Goleta, CA	423,895	181,687	42.9
Santa Cruz–Watsonville, CA	262,382	84,092	32.0
Santa Fe, NM	144,170	73,015	50.6
Santa Rosa–Petaluma, CA	483,878	120,430	24.9
Savannah, GA	347,611	17,207	5.0
Scranton–Wilkes–Barre, PA	563,631	32,610	5.8
Seattle–Tacoma–Bellevue, WA	3,439,809	309,476	9.0
Sebastian–Vero Beach, FL	138,028	15,465	11.2
Sheboygan, WI	115,507	6,329	5.5
Sherman–Denison, TX	120,877	13,688	11.3
Shreveport–Bossier City, LA	398,604	13,816	3.5
Sioux City, IA–NE–SD	143,577	22,339	15.6
Sioux Falls, SD	228,261	7,746	3.4
South Bend–Mishawaka, IN–MI	319,224	20,965	6.6
Spartanburg, SC	284,307	16,658	5.9
Spokane, WA	471,221	21,260	4.5
Springfield, IL	210,170	3,601	1.7
Springfield, MA	692,942	106,481	15.4
Springfield, MO	436,712	11,592	2.7
Springfield, OH	138,333	3,805	2.8
State College, PA	153,990	3,690	2.4
Steubenville–Weirton, OH–WV	124,454	1,250	1.0
Stockton, CA	685,306	266,341	38.9
Sumter, SC	107,456	3,532	3.3
Syracuse, NY	662,577	22,697	3.4
Tallahassee, FL	367,413	21,342	5.8
Tampa–St. Petersburg–Clearwater, FL	2,783,243	452,208	16.2

	total population	Hispanic	
		number	share of total
Terre Haute, IN	172,425	3,200	1.9%
Texarkana, TX–Texarkana, AR	136,027	7,100	5.2
Toledo, OH	651,429	37,733	5.8
Topeka, KS	233,870	20,615	8.8
Trenton–Ewing, NJ	366,513	55,318	15.1
Tucson, AZ	980,263	338,802	34.6
Tulsa, OK	937,478	78,446	8.4
Tuscaloosa, AL	219,461	6,158	2.8
Tyler, TX	209,714	36,088	17.2
Utica–Rome, NY	299,397	11,859	4.0
Valdosta, GA	139,588	7,735	5.5
Vallejo–Fairfield, CA	413,344	99,356	24.0
Victoria, TX	115,384	50,497	43.8
Vineland–Millville–Bridgeton, NJ	156,898	42,457	27.1
Virginia Beach–Norfolk–Newport News, VA–NC	1,671,683	89,567	5.4
Visalia–Porterville, CA	442,179	268,065	60.6
Waco, TX	234,906	55,471	23.6
Warner Robins, GA	139,900	8,515	6.1
Washington–Arlington–Alexandria, DC–VA–MD–WV	5,582,170	770,795	13.8
Waterloo–Cedar Falls, IA	167,819	5,268	3.1
Wausau, WI	134,063	2,992	2.2
Wenatchee–East Wenatchee, WA	110,884	29,726	26.8
Wheeling, WV–OH	147,950	1,056	0.7
Wichita, KS	623,061	72,082	11.6
Wichita Falls, TX	151,306	23,001	15.2
Williamsport, PA	116,111	1,559	1.3
Wilmington, NC	362,315	19,459	5.4
Winchester, VA–WV	128,472	9,451	7.4
Winston–Salem, NC	477,717	49,274	10.3
Worcester, MA	798,552	75,422	9.4
Yakima, WA	243,231	109,470	45.0
York–Hanover, PA	434,972	24,397	5.6
Youngstown–Warren–Boardman, OH–PA	565,773	15,185	2.7
Yuba City, CA	166,892	45,302	27.1
Yuma, AZ	195,751	116,912	59.7

Source: Bureau of the Census, 2010 Census, Internet site http://factfinder2.census.gov/faces/nav/jsf/pages/index.xhtml; calculations by New Strategist

Table 5.108 Immigrants from Latin America and Spain, 2011

(total number of immigrants admitted for legal permanent residence, and number and percent distribution of immigrants from Latin America and Spain, by country of birth, 2011)

	number	percent distribution
Total immigrants	**1,062,040**	**100.0%**
Immigrants from Latin America and Spain	408,621	38.5
Immigrants from Latin America and Spain	**408,621**	**100.0**
Mexico	143,446	35.1
Caribbean	133,679	32.7
Cuba	36,452	8.9
Dominican Republic	46,109	11.3
Haiti	22,111	5.4
Jamaica	19,662	4.8
Other Caribbean	9,345	2.3
Central America	43,707	10.7
Belize	905	0.2
Costa Rica	2,135	0.5
El Salvador	18,667	4.6
Guatemala	11,092	2.7
Honduras	6,133	1.5
Nicaragua	3,401	0.8
Panama	1,374	0.3
South America	85,899	21.0
Argentina	4,473	1.1
Bolivia	2,173	0.5
Brazil	11,763	2.9
Chile	1,853	0.5
Colombia	22,635	5.5
Ecuador	11,103	2.7
Guyana	6,599	1.6
Paraguay	500	0.1
Peru	196	0.0
Suriname	14,064	3.4
Uruguay	1,553	0.4
Venezuela	9,183	2.2
Spain	1,890	0.5

Note: Immigrants are those granted legal permanent residence in the United States. They either arrive in the United States with immigrant visas issued abroad or adjust their status in the United States from temporary to permanent residence.
Source: Department of Homeland Security, 2011 Yearbook of Immigration Statistics, Internet site http://www.dhs.gov/yearbook-immigration-statistics

Table 5.109 People Who Speak Spanish at Home, by State, 2009–11

(total number of people aged 5 or older and number and percent who speak Spanish at home, by state, 2009–11)

	total people aged 5 or older	speak Spanish at home	
		number	percent
United States	**288,553,996**	**36,932,973**	**12.8%**
Alabama	4,477,927	151,801	3.4
Alaska	658,127	23,264	3.5
Arizona	5,956,673	1,218,399	20.5
Arkansas	2,721,294	143,695	5.3
California	34,793,018	10,030,509	28.8
Colorado	4,702,519	561,264	11.9
Connecticut	3,372,311	361,008	10.7
Delaware	843,743	57,288	6.8
District of Columbia	571,129	38,897	6.8
Florida	17,774,767	3,569,483	20.1
Georgia	9,033,746	696,112	7.7
Hawaii	1,273,878	25,887	2.0
Idaho	1,449,701	112,653	7.8
Illinois	12,003,172	1,571,392	13.1
Indiana	6,057,433	272,367	4.5
Iowa	2,848,477	112,205	3.9
Kansas	2,651,027	192,452	7.3
Kentucky	4,063,448	101,453	2.5
Louisiana	4,223,687	150,074	3.6
Maine	1,260,061	11,445	0.9
Maryland	5,416,438	364,524	6.7
Massachusetts	6,187,386	482,811	7.8
Michigan	9,292,971	265,718	2.9
Minnesota	4,959,424	192,651	3.9
Mississippi	2,759,514	65,472	2.4
Missouri	5,602,736	149,841	2.7
Montana	930,061	14,100	1.5
Nebraska	1,697,746	115,547	6.8
Nevada	2,516,454	506,745	20.1
New Hampshire	1,247,618	26,631	2.1
New Jersey	8,253,094	1,254,965	15.2
New Mexico	1,917,278	553,719	28.9
New York	18,233,396	2,675,028	14.7
North Carolina	8,926,372	644,380	7.2
North Dakota	630,522	7,213	1.1
Ohio	10,821,383	240,060	2.2
Oklahoma	3,493,183	216,049	6.2

	total people aged 5 or older	speak Spanish at home	
		number	percent
Oregon	3,603,503	319,851	8.9%
Pennsylvania	11,982,323	511,731	4.3
Rhode Island	995,269	107,044	10.8
South Carolina	4,333,308	193,373	4.5
South Dakota	757,925	15,919	2.1
Tennessee	5,949,415	229,635	3.9
Texas	23,304,988	6,867,338	29.5
Utah	2,509,875	241,535	9.6
Vermont	594,196	6,311	1.1
Virginia	7,508,820	502,160	6.7
Washington	6,307,524	505,620	8.0
West Virginia	1,749,410	17,188	1.0
Wisconsin	5,335,726	238,166	4.5
Wyoming	515,858	23,514	4.6

Note: Data for Wyoming are an ACS 5-year estimate, 2007–2011.
Source: Bureau of the Census, 2009–11 American Community Survey 3-Year Estimates, Internet site Internet site http://factfinder2.census.gov/faces/nav/jsf/pages/index.xhtml; calculations by New Strategist

Table 5.110 Time Use of Total Hispanics, 2011

(average hours per day spent in primary activities by total people and Hispanics aged 15 or older, and index of Hispanic to total, by type of activity, 2011)

	total people	total Hispanics	index, Hispanic to total
Total, all activities	**24.00 hrs.**	**24.00 hrs.**	**100**
Personal care activities	9.47	9.89	104
Sleeping	8.71	9.11	105
Grooming	0.69	0.73	106
Household activities	1.78	1.82	102
Housework	0.58	0.72	124
Food preparation and cleanup	0.56	0.68	121
Lawn, garden, and houseplants	0.19	0.12	63
Animals and pets	0.09	0.06	67
Household management	0.18	0.09	50
Caring for and helping household members	0.43	0.56	130
Caring for and helping household children	0.34	0.46	135
Caring for and helping people in other households	0.15	0.09	60
Working and work-related activities	3.29	3.10	94
Educational activities	0.44	0.66	150
Consumer purchases	0.37	0.39	105
Eating and drinking	1.12	1.09	97
Socializing, relaxing, and leisure	4.65	4.25	91
Socializing and communicating	0.61	0.62	102
Watching television	2.75	2.65	96
Playing games (including computer games)	0.22	0.14	64
Computer use for leisure	0.22	0.17	77
Reading	0.30	0.12	40
Sports, exercise, and recreation	0.34	0.35	103
Religious and spiritual activities	0.15	0.17	113
Volunteering	0.15	0.06	40
Telephone calls	0.10	0.07	70
Traveling	1.21	1.19	98

Note: Hours per day do not add to 24.00 because not all activities are shown. Primary activities are those respondents identified as their main activity. Other activities done simultaneously are not included. The index is calculated by dividing time use of Hispanics by time use of the average person and multiplying by 100.
Source: Bureau of Labor Statistics, unpublished tables from the American Time Use Survey, Internet site http://www.bls.gov/tus/home.htm; calculations by New Strategist

Table 5.111 Time Use of Hispanic Men, 2011

(average hours per day spent in primary activities by total and Hispanic men aged 15 or older, and index of Hispanic to total, by type of activity, 2011)

	total men	Hispanic men	index, Hispanic to total
Total, all activities	**24.00 hrs.**	**24.00 hrs.**	**100**
Personal care activities	9.23	9.70	105
Sleeping	8.62	9.04	105
Grooming	0.56	0.64	114
Household activities	1.36	1.15	85
Housework	0.27	0.30	111
Food preparation and cleanup	0.31	0.29	94
Lawn, garden, and houseplants	0.26	0.18	69
Animals and pets	0.08	0.06	75
Household management	0.15	0.09	60
Caring for and helping household members	0.27	0.30	111
Caring for and helping household children	0.21	0.24	114
Caring for and helping people in other households	0.15	0.10	67
Working and work-related activities	3.89	3.71	95
Educational activities	0.46	0.74	161
Consumer purchases	0.31	0.35	113
Eating and drinking	1.16	1.11	96
Socializing, relaxing, and leisure	4.88	4.55	93
Socializing and communicating	0.57	0.59	104
Watching television	2.99	2.92	98
Playing games (including computer games)	0.28	0.23	82
Computer use for leisure	0.26	0.21	81
Reading	0.24	0.08	33
Sports, exercise, and recreation	0.43	0.05	12
Religious and spiritual activities	0.12	0.15	125
Volunteering	0.13	0.05	38
Telephone calls	0.06	0.06	100
Traveling	1.25	1.23	98

Note: Hours per day do not add to 24.00 because not all activities are shown. Primary activities are those respondents identified as their main activity. Other activities done simultaneously are not included. The index is calculated by dividing time use of Hispanic men by time use of the average man and multiplying by 100.
Source: Bureau of Labor Statistics, unpublished tables from the American Time Use Survey, Internet site http://www.bls.gov/tus/home.htm; calculations by New Strategist

Table 5.112 Time Use of Hispanic Women, 2011

(average hours per day spent in primary activities by total and Hispanic women aged 15 or older, and index of Hispanic to total, by type of activity, 2011)

	total women	Hispanic women	index, Hispanic to total
Total, all activities	**24.00 hrs.**	**24.00 hrs.**	**100**
Personal care activities	9.71	10.09	104
Sleeping	8.80	9.18	104
Grooming	0.82	0.82	100
Household activities	2.18	2.53	116
Housework	0.87	1.16	133
Food preparation and cleanup	0.79	1.09	138
Lawn, garden, and houseplants	0.13	0.07	54
Animals and pets	0.10	0.05	50
Household management	0.21	0.10	48
Caring for and helping household members	0.58	0.83	143
Caring for and helping household children	0.47	0.69	147
Caring for and helping people in other households	0.13	0.08	62
Working and work-related activities	2.73	2.45	90
Educational activities	0.42	0.57	136
Consumer purchases	0.43	0.43	100
Eating and drinking	1.09	1.07	98
Socializing, relaxing, and leisure	4.43	3.93	89
Socializing and communicating	0.66	0.66	100
Watching television	2.52	2.35	93
Playing games (including computer games)	0.16	0.05	31
Computer use for leisure	0.18	0.12	67
Reading	0.35	0.16	46
Sports, exercise, and recreation	0.25	0.19	76
Religious and spiritual activities	0.19	0.19	100
Volunteering	0.16	0.07	44
Telephone calls	0.13	0.08	62
Traveling	1.16	1.15	99

Note: Hours per day do not add to 24.00 because not all activities are shown. Primary activities are those respondents identified as their main activity. Other activities done simultaneously are not included. The index is calculated by dividing time use of Hispanic women by time use of the average woman and multiplying by 100.
Source: Bureau of Labor Statistics, unpublished tables from the American Time Use Survey, Internet site http://www.bls.gov/tus/home.htm; calculations by New Strategist

Table 5.113 Time Use of Hispanics by Sex, 2011

(average hours per day spent in primary activities by Hispanic men and women aged 15 or older, and index of Hispanic women to men, by type of activity, 2011)

	Hispanic men 24.00 hrs.	Hispanic women 24.00 hrs.	index, women's time to men's 100
Total, all activities	**24.00 hrs.**	**24.00 hrs.**	**100**
Personal care activities	9.70	10.09	104
Sleeping	9.04	9.18	102
Grooming	0.64	0.82	128
Household activities	1.15	2.53	220
Housework	0.30	1.16	387
Food preparation and cleanup	0.29	1.09	376
Lawn, garden, and houseplants	0.18	0.07	39
Animals and pets	0.06	0.05	83
Household management	0.09	0.10	111
Caring for and helping household members	0.30	0.83	277
Caring for and helping household children	0.24	0.69	288
Caring for and helping people in other households	0.10	0.08	80
Working and work-related activities	3.71	2.45	66
Educational activities	0.74	0.57	77
Consumer purchases	0.35	0.43	123
Eating and drinking	1.11	1.07	96
Socializing, relaxing, and leisure	4.55	3.93	86
Socializing and communicating	0.59	0.66	112
Watching television	2.92	2.35	80
Playing games (including computer games)	0.23	0.05	22
Computer use for leisure	0.21	0.12	57
Reading	0.08	0.16	200
Sports, exercise, and recreation	0.05	0.19	380
Religious and spiritual activities	0.15	0.19	127
Volunteering	0.05	0.07	140
Telephone calls	0.06	0.08	133
Traveling	1.23	1.15	93

Note: Hours per day do not add to 24.00 because not all activities are shown. Primary activities are those respondents identified as their main activity. Other activities done simultaneously are not included. The index is calculated by dividing time use of Hispanic women by time use of Hispanic men and multiplying by 100.
Source: Bureau of Labor Statistics, unpublished tables from the American Time Use Survey, Internet site http://www.bls.gov/tus/home.htm; calculations by New Strategist

Hispanic Households Spend Less than the Average Household

The nation's 15 million Hispanic households spent an average of $42,086 in 2011, according to the Bureau of Labor Statistics' Consumer Expenditure Survey. While the annual spending of Hispanic households (called consumer units by the Bureau of Labor Statistics) is less than the $49,705 spent by the average household, Hispanics spend more on many items.

Hispanic households spend less than average because their incomes are relatively low. Hispanic incomes are low because many Hispanics have little education or earning power. Despite their larger household size—3.4 people versus 2.5 people in the average household—Hispanics spend only an average amount on food at home (groceries). But they spend 32 percent more than average on eggs, 27 percent more than average on poultry, and 19 percent more than average on fresh fruit. They are also big buyers of infants' clothes, spending 34 percent more than the average household on this item and accounting for 17 percent the market. Hispanic households spend 34 percent more than average on laundry and cleaning supplies.

■ Hispanic spending will remain below average as long as poorly educated immigrants account for a large share of the Hispanic population.

Hispanic households spend 15 percent less than the average household

(average annual spending of total and Hispanic consumer units, 2011)

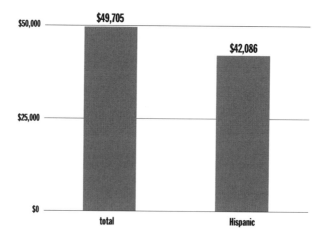

Table 5.114 Spending of Households Headed by Hispanics, 2011

(average annual spending of total consumer units, and average annual, indexed, and market share of spending of consumer units headed by Hispanics, by product and service category, 2011)

	total consumer units	Hispanic consumer units		
		average spending	indexed spending	market share
Number of consumer units (000s)	122,287	15,222	–	12.4%
Average number of persons per consumer unit	2.5	3.4	–	–
Average annual spending	**$49,705**	**$42,086**	**85**	**10.5%**
FOOD	**6,458**	**6,373**	**99**	**12.3**
Food at home	**3,838**	**3,849**	**100**	**12.5**
Cereals and bakery products	531	493	93	11.6
Cereals and cereal products	175	181	103	12.9
Bakery products	356	312	88	10.9
Meats, poultry, fish, and eggs	832	968	116	14.5
Beef	223	268	120	15.0
Pork	162	191	118	14.7
Other meats	123	110	89	11.1
Poultry	154	196	127	15.8
Fish and seafood	121	138	114	14.2
Eggs	50	66	132	16.4
Dairy products	407	388	95	11.9
Fresh milk and cream	150	163	109	13.5
Other dairy products	257	226	88	10.9
Fruits and vegetables	715	778	109	13.5
Fresh fruits	247	293	119	14.8
Fresh vegetables	224	241	108	13.4
Processed fruits	116	120	103	12.9
Processed vegetables	128	124	97	12.1
Other food at home	1,353	1,221	90	11.2
Sugar and other sweets	144	117	81	10.1
Fats and oils	110	122	111	13.8
Miscellaneous foods	690	580	84	10.5
Nonalcoholic beverages	361	370	102	12.8
Food prepared by consumer unit on trips	48	32	67	8.3
Food away from home	**2,620**	**2,524**	**96**	**12.0**
ALCOHOLIC BEVERAGES	**456**	**281**	**62**	**7.7**
HOUSING	**16,803**	**15,648**	**93**	**11.6**
Shelter	**9,825**	**9,766**	**99**	**12.4**
Owned dwellings	6,148	4,713	77	9.5
Mortgage interest and charges	3,184	2,814	88	11.0
Property taxes	1,845	1,202	65	8.1
Maintenance, repair, insurance, other expenses	1,120	697	62	7.7

	total consumer units	Hispanic consumer units		
		average spending	indexed spending	market share
Rented dwellings	$3,029	$4,806	159	19.8%
Other lodging	648	248	38	4.8
Utilities, fuels, and public services	**3,727**	**3,462**	**93**	**11.6**
Natural gas	420	350	83	10.4
Electricity	1,423	1,283	90	11.2
Fuel oil and other fuels	157	42	27	3.3
Telephone	1,226	1,288	105	13.1
Water and other public services	501	499	100	12.4
Household services	**1,122**	**755**	**67**	**8.4**
Personal services	398	319	80	10.0
Other household services	724	436	60	7.5
Housekeeping supplies	**615**	**536**	**87**	**10.8**
Laundry and cleaning supplies	145	195	134	16.7
Other household products	340	255	75	9.3
Postage and stationery	130	86	66	8.2
Household furnishings and equipment	**1,514**	**1,129**	**75**	**9.3**
Household textiles	109	73	67	8.3
Furniture	358	310	87	10.8
Floor coverings	20	7	35	4.4
Major appliances	194	128	66	8.2
Small appliances, misc. housewares	89	61	69	8.5
Miscellaneous household equipment	744	550	74	9.2
APPAREL AND RELATED SERVICES	**1,740**	**1,989**	**114**	**14.2**
Men and boys	**404**	**518**	**128**	**16.0**
Men, aged 16 or older	324	402	124	15.4
Boys, aged 2 to 15	80	116	145	18.0
Women and girls	**721**	**672**	**93**	**11.6**
Women, aged 16 or older	604	532	88	11.0
Girls, aged 2 to 15	117	140	120	14.9
Children under age 2	**68**	**91**	**134**	**16.7**
Footwear	**321**	**452**	**141**	**17.5**
Other apparel products and services	**226**	**256**	**113**	**14.1**
TRANSPORTATION	**8,293**	**7,520**	**91**	**11.3**
Vehicle purchases	**2,669**	**2,208**	**83**	**10.3**
Cars and trucks, new	1,265	691	55	6.8
Cars and trucks, used	1,339	1,511	113	14.0
Other vehicles	64	6	9	1.2
Gasoline and motor oil	**2,655**	**2,721**	**102**	**12.8**
Other vehicle expenses	**2,454**	**2,174**	**89**	**11.0**
Vehicle finance charges	233	215	92	11.5
Maintenance and repairs	805	638	79	9.9
Vehicle insurance	983	934	95	11.8
Vehicle rentals, leases, licenses, other charges	433	386	89	11.1
Public transportation	**516**	**417**	**81**	**10.1**

	total consumer units	Hispanic consumer units		
		average spending	indexed spending	market share
HEALTH CARE	**$3,313**	**$1,774**	**54**	**6.7%**
Health insurance	1,922	1,008	52	6.5
Medical services	768	453	59	7.3
Drugs	489	237	48	6.0
Medical supplies	134	75	56	7.0
ENTERTAINMENT	**2,572**	**1,738**	**68**	**8.4**
Fees and admissions	594	339	57	7.1
Audio and visual equipment and services	977	839	86	10.7
Pets, toys, and playground equipment	631	392	62	7.7
Other entertainment products and services	370	167	45	5.6
PERSONAL CARE PRODUCTS AND SERVICES	**634**	**611**	**96**	**12.0**
READING	**115**	**46**	**40**	**5.0**
EDUCATION	**1,051**	**624**	**59**	**7.4**
TOBACCO PRODUCTS AND SMOKING SUPPLIES	**351**	**164**	**47**	**5.8**
MISCELLANEOUS	**775**	**476**	**61**	**7.6**
CASH CONTRIBUTIONS	**1,721**	**812**	**47**	**5.9**
PERSONAL INSURANCE AND PENSIONS	**5,424**	**4,030**	**74**	**9.2**
Life and other personal insurance	317	115	36	4.5
Pensions and Social Security	5,106	3,915	77	9.5
PERSONAL TAXES	**2,012**	**465**	**23**	**2.9**
Federal income taxes	1,370	236	17	2.1
State and local income taxes	505	186	37	4.6
Other taxes	136	43	32	3.9
GIFTS FOR PEOPLE IN OTHER HOUSEHOLDS	**1,037**	**585**	**56**	**7.0**

Definitions: The index compares Hispanic to average consumer unit spending by dividing Hispanic spending by average spending in each category and multiplying by 100. An index of 125 means Hispanic spending is 25 percent above average, while an index of 75 means Hispanic spending is 25 percent below average. The market share is the percentage of total spending on a product or service category accounted for by consumer units headed by Hispanics.
Note: The Bureau of Labor Statistics uses consumer unit rather than household as the sampling unit in the Consumer Expenditure Survey. For the definition of consumer unit, see the glossary. Spending by category does not add to total spending because gift spending is also included in the preceding product and service categories and personal taxes are not included in the total. "–" means not applicable or sample is too small to make a reliable estimate.
Source: Bureau of Labor Statistics, 2011 Consumer Expenditure Survey, Internet site http://www.bls.gov/cex/; calculations by New Strategist

Hispanic Households Have Little Wealth

The median net worth (assets minus debts) of Hispanic households was $7,683 in 2011, well below the $68,828 net worth of the average American household. Not only is the net worth of Hispanic households below average, but it fell by a steep 61 percent between 2005 and 2011, after adjusting for inflation—the largest decline among racial and ethnic groups. This decline far exceeded the 36 percent loss for the average household during those years, according to the Census Bureau's Survey of Income and Program Participation.

Hispanics are less likely than the average household to own most assets, the most important being a home. Only 47 percent of Hispanic households own a home compared with 65 percent of all households. Because housing equity accounts for a large share of Americans' net worth, the low homeownership rate of Hispanic households largely explains their below average net worth. Among Hispanic homeowners, median housing equity was $47,000 in 2011, substantially less than the $80,000 median equity of the average homeowner.

Hispanic households are less likely than average to be in debt (63 versus 69 percent). Among Hispanic households with debt, the median amount owed was just $41,000 compared with $70,000 owed by the average household.

■ Eighty-two percent of Hispanics aged 65 or older receive income from Social Security, 20 percent from earnings, and 16 percent from pensions.

The net worth of Hispanic households is far below average

(median net worth of total and Hispanic households, 2011)

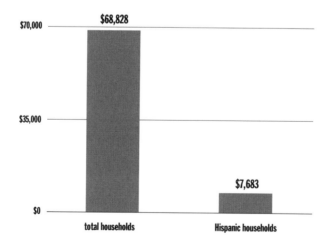

Table 5.115 Median Household Net Worth of Total and Hispanic Households, 2005 and 2011

(median net worth of total and Hispanic households, 2005 and 2011; percent change, 2005–11; in 2011 dollars)

	2011	2005	percent change 2005–11
Total households	**$68,828**	**$107,344**	**–35.9%**
Hispanic households	7,683	19,670	–60.9

Source: Census Bureau, Wealth and Asset Ownership, Survey of Income and Program Participation, Internet site http://www
.census.gov/people/wealth/; calculations by New Strategist

Table 5.116 Distribution of Total and Hispanic Households by Net Worth, 2011

(number of total and Hispanic households, median net worth of total and Hispanic households, and percent distribution of total and Hispanic households by net worth, 2011)

	total households	Hispanic households	
		number	index
Number of households	**118,689,091**	**14,099,126**	–
Median net worth	**$68,828**	**$7,683**	**11**
DISTRIBUTION OF HOUSEHOLDS BY NET WORTH			
Total households	**100.0%**	**100.0%**	–
Zero or negative	18.1	28.5	158
$1 to $4,999	9.1	16.5	181
$5,000 to $9,999	4.8	7.4	154
$10,000 to $24,999	6.6	8.4	127
$25,000 to $49,999	6.9	8.0	116
$50,000 to $99,999	10.4	9.9	95
$100,000 to $249,999	17.9	11.2	63
$250,000 to $499,999	12.6	6.1	48
$500,000 or more	13.5	3.9	29

Note: The index is calculated by dividing the Hispanic figure by the total figure and multiplying by 100. "–" means not applicable.
Source: Census Bureau, Wealth and Asset Ownership, Survey of Income and Program Participation, Internet site http://www
.census.gov/people/wealth/; calculations by New Strategist

Table 5.117 Percent of Total and Hispanic Households Owning Assets, 2011

(percent of total and Hispanic households owning selected assets, and index of Hispanic to total, 2011)

	total households	Hispanic households	
PERCENT WITH ASSET		percent	index
Interest earning asset at financial institution	69.8%	53.6%	77
Regular checking account	29.0	30.2	104
Stocks and mutal fund shares	19.6	4.3	22
Own business	13.8	11.5	84
Motor vehicles	84.7	77.3	91
Own home	65.3	47.2	72
Rental property	5.5	2.6	47
IRA or KEOGH account	28.9	9.9	34
401(k) and thrift savings	42.1	25.8	61

Note: The index is calculated by dividing the Hispanic figure by the total figure and multiplying by 100.
Source: Census Bureau, Wealth and Asset Ownership, Survey of Income and Program Participation, Internet site http://www .census.gov/people/wealth/; calculations by New Strategist

Table 5.118 Median Value or Equity of Assets Owned by Total and Hispanic Households, 2011

(median value or equity of assets owned by total and Hispanic households, and index of Hispanic to total, 2011)

	total households	Hispanic households	
MEDIAN VALUE OF ASSETS		median	index
Interest earning asset at financial institution	$2,450	$700	29
Regular checking account	600	300	50
Stocks and mutal fund shares	20,000	8,000	40
Own business (equity)	8,000	2,000	25
Motor vehicles (equity)	6,824	5,267	77
Own home (equity)	80,000	47,000	59
Rental property (equity)	180,000	150,000	83
IRA or KEOGH account	34,000	17,000	50
401(k) and thrift savings	30,000	15,000	50

Note: The index is calculated by dividing the Hispanic figure by the total figure and multiplying by 100.
Source: Census Bureau, Wealth and Asset Ownership, Survey of Income and Program Participation, Internet site http://www .census.gov/people/wealth/; calculations by New Strategist

Table 5.119 Asset Ownership of Hispanic Households, 2005 and 2011

(percent of Hispanic households owning financial assets, 2005 and 2011; percentage point change, 2005–11)

	2011	2005	percentage point change
PERCENT OWNING ASSET			
Interest earning asset at financial institution	53.6%	51.0%	2.6
Regular checking account	30.2	31.4	–1.2
Stocks and mutal fund shares	4.3	8.2	–3.9
Own business	11.5	11.7	–0.2
Motor vehicles	77.3	79.6	–2.3
Own home	47.2	50.9	–3.7
Rental property	2.6	2.2	0.4
IRA or KEOGH account	9.9	11.8	–1.9
401(k) and thrift savings	25.8	26.5	–0.7

Source: Census Bureau, Wealth and Asset Ownership, Survey of Income and Program Participation, Internet site http://www .census.gov/people/wealth/; calculations by New Strategist

Table 5.120 Median Value or Equity of Assets Owned by Hispanic Households, 2005 and 2011

(median value or equity of assets owned by Hispanic households, 2005 and 2011; percent change, 2005–11; in 2011 dollars)

	2011	2005	percent change
MEDIAN VALUE OF ASSETS			
Interest earning asset at financial institution	$700	$1,382	–49.4%
Regular checking account	300	576	–47.9
Stocks and mutal fund shares	8,000	22,114	–63.8
Own business (equity)	2,000	5,759	–65.3
Motor vehicles (equity)	5,267	3,862	36.4
Own home (equity)	47,000	103,659	–54.7
Rental property (equity)	150,000	172,765	–13.2
IRA or KEOGH account	17,000	14,973	13.5
401(k) and thrift savings	15,000	12,669	18.4

Source: Census Bureau, Wealth and Asset Ownership, Survey of Income and Program Participation, Internet site http://www .census.gov/people/wealth/; calculations by New Strategist

Table 5.121 Percent of Total and Hispanic Households with Debt, 2011

(percent of total and Hispanic households with debt, and index of Hispanic to total, 2011)

PERCENT WITH DEBT	total households	Hispanic households	
		percent	index
Total debt	**69.0%**	**63.3%**	**92**
Secured debt	55.3	48.6	88
Home debt	40.5	31.7	78
Business debt	4.1	2.4	59
Vehicle debt	30.4	29.2	96
Unsecured debt	46.2	41.5	90
Credit card debt	38.3	34.3	90
Loans	6.8	5.8	85
Other debt	18.6	14.8	80

Note: "Other debt" includes student loans. The index is calculated by dividing the Hispanic figure by the total figure and multiplying by 100.
Source: Census Bureau, Wealth and Asset Ownership, Survey of Income and Program Participation, Internet site http://www .census.gov/people/wealth/; calculations by New Strategist

Table 5.122 Median Debt of Total and Hispanic Households, 2011

(median amount of debt for total and Hispanic households with debt, and index of Hispanic to total, 2011)

MEDIAN DEBT	total households	Hispanic households	
		median	index
Total debt	**$70,000**	**$41,000**	**59**
Secured debt	91,000	77,000	85
Home debt	117,000	120,000	103
Business debt	25,000	12,000	48
Vehicle debt	10,000	10,000	100
Unsecured debt	7,000	5,000	71
Credit card debt	3,500	3,100	89
Loans	7,000	5,000	71
Other debt	10,000	8,000	80

Note: "Other debt" includes student loans. The index is calculated by dividing the Hispanic figure by the total figure and multiplying by 100.
Source: Census Bureau, Wealth and Asset Ownership, Survey of Income and Program Participation, Internet site http://www .census.gov/people/wealth/; calculations by New Strategist

Table 5.123 Total People and Hispanics Aged 65 or Older Receiving Income by Source, 2011

(number of total people and Hispanics aged 65 or older receiving income, percent of Hispanics receiving income, and Hispanic share of total, 2011; ranked by number of total people receiving type of income; people in thousands as of 2012)

	total people receiving income	Hispanics receiving income		
		number	percent	Hispanic share of total
Total people aged 65 or older	**40,195**	**2,690**	**100.0%**	**6.7%**
Social Security	35,169	2,202	81.9	6.3
Interest	19,862	612	22.8	3.1
Retirement income	14,325	519	19.3	3.6
Pension income	12,460	441	16.4	3.5
Earnings	8,648	538	20.0	6.2
Dividends	7,584	127	4.7	1.7
Rents, royalties, estates, or trusts	3,103	104	3.9	3.4
Survivor benefits	1,859	54	2.0	2.9
Veteran's benefits	1,299	45	1.7	3.5
SSI (Supplemental Security Income)	1,297	255	9.5	19.7

Source: Bureau of the Census, 2012 Current Population Survey Annual Social and Economic Supplement, Internet site http://www.census.gov/hhes/www/cpstables/032012/perinc/toc.htm; calculations by New Strategist

Table 5.124 Median Income of Total People and Hispanics Aged 65 or Older by Source, 2011

(median income received by total people and Hispanics aged 65 or older and index of Hispanics to total, by type of income, 2011)

	median income for total people receiving income	median income for Hispanic receiving income	index, Hispanic to total
Total people aged 65 or older	**$19,939**	**$13,105**	**66**
Social Security	13,376	10,653	80
Interest	1,590	1,508	95
Retirement income	12,282	11,481	93
Pension income	12,458	11,920	96
Earnings	24,893	21,974	88
Dividends	2,023	1,884	93
Rents, royalties, estates, or trusts	3,855	3,835	99
Survivor benefits	7,913	–	–
Veteran's benefits	8,770	–	–
SSI (Supplemental Security Income)	5,322	4,429	83

Note: The index is calculated by dividing the Hispanic figure by the total figure and multiplying by 100. "–" means sample is too small to make a reliable estimate.
Source: Bureau of the Census, 2012 Current Population Survey Annual Social and Economic Supplement, Internet site http://www.census.gov/hhes/www/cpstables/032012/perinc/toc.htm; calculations by New Strategist

Non-Hispanic Whites

■ The non-Hispanic white population accounted for 63 percent of the total U.S. population in 2011, down from 69 percent in 2000.

■ Thirty-four percent of non-Hispanic whites aged 25 or older have a bachelor's degree, far below the 50 percent of Asians who are college graduates.

■ Only 54 percent of the nation's births are to non-Hispanic whites.

■ Nearly 74 percent of the nation's non-Hispanic white households own their home, a higher share than any other racial or ethnic group.

■ The $55,412 median income of non-Hispanic white households in 2011 was 7 percent less than in 2007. Behind the decline was job loss caused by the Great Recession.

■ Between 2010 and 2020, the number of non-Hispanic white workers will shrink by nearly 2 percent, and the non-Hispanic white share of the labor force will fall from 68 to 62 percent.

■ Only 25 percent of non-Hispanic white households include children under age 18, the smallest share among racial and ethnic groups.

■ The non-Hispanic white share of the population ranges from a low of 52 percent in the West to a high of 78 percent in the Midwest.

■ The nation's non-Hispanic white and other households spent an average of $53,056 in 2011, or 7 percent more than the average household.

■ The median net worth of non-Hispanic white households was $110,500 in 2011, far above the $68,828 median net worth of the average household.

Non-Hispanic whites account for 63 percent of the U.S. population

(percent distribution of people by race and Hispanic origin, 2011)

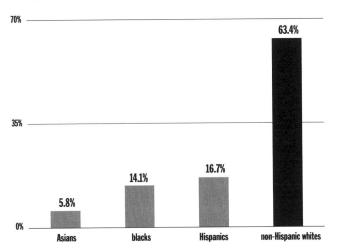

Non-Hispanic Whites Are Less Educated than Asians

The educational attainment of non-Hispanic whites is slightly above average. Thirty-four percent of non-Hispanic whites have a college degree versus 31 percent of the total population. Asians are more likely to have a college degree (50 percent). Ninety-two percent of non-Hispanic whites are high school graduates—the largest proportion among all racial and ethnic groups.

Because non-Hispanic whites account for the majority of Americans, they also earn most college degrees. Non-Hispanic whites earned 64 percent of associate's degree in 2010–11. They were awarded 69 percent of bachelor's degrees, 63 percent of master's degrees, and 65 percent of doctoral and first-professional degrees.

■ The share of college degrees earned by non-Hispanic whites is shrinking as minorities make up a growing proportion of college students.

More than one-third of non-Hispanic whites aged 25 or older have a bachelor's degree

(percent of non-Hispanic whites aged 25 or older by educational attainment, 2012)

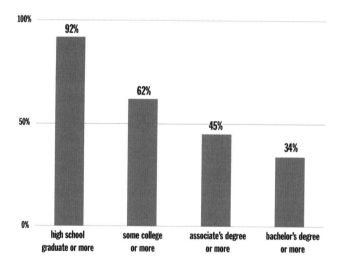

Table 6.1 Educational Attainment of Non-Hispanic Whites by Age, 2012

(number and percent distribution of non-Hispanic whites aged 25 or older by educational attainment and age, 2012; numbers in thousands)

	total	25 to 34	35 to 44	45 to 54	55 to 64	65 or older
Total non-Hispanic whites	**139,001**	**23,933**	**24,200**	**29,896**	**28,068**	**32,905**
Not a high school graduate	10,449	1,223	1,110	1,821	1,608	4,687
High school graduate only	42,457	5,920	6,169	9,504	8,631	12,233
Some college, no degree	23,727	4,433	4,215	5,000	4,927	5,152
Associate's degree	14,436	2,632	2,960	3,363	3,216	2,268
Bachelor's degree	30,552	7,082	6,335	6,602	5,718	4,815
Master's degree	12,538	1,945	2,575	2,634	2,884	2,499
Professional degree	2,398	418	428	538	508	507
Doctoral degree	2,443	281	406	434	578	743
High school graduate or more	128,551	22,711	23,088	28,075	26,462	28,217
Some college or more	86,094	16,791	16,919	18,571	17,831	15,984
Associate's degree or more	62,367	12,358	12,704	13,571	12,904	10,832
Bachelor's degree or more	47,931	9,726	9,744	10,208	9,688	8,564

PERCENT DISTRIBUTION

	total	25 to 34	35 to 44	45 to 54	55 to 64	65 or older
Total non-Hispanic whites	**100.0%**	**100.0%**	**100.0%**	**100.0%**	**100.0%**	**100.0%**
Not a high school graduate	7.5	5.1	4.6	6.1	5.7	14.2
High school graduate only	30.5	24.7	25.5	31.8	30.8	37.2
Some college, no degree	17.1	18.5	17.4	16.7	17.6	15.7
Associate's degree	10.4	11.0	12.2	11.2	11.5	6.9
Bachelor's degree	22.0	29.6	26.2	22.1	20.4	14.6
Master's degree	9.0	8.1	10.6	8.8	10.3	7.6
Professional degree	1.7	1.7	1.8	1.8	1.8	1.5
Doctoral degree	1.8	1.2	1.7	1.5	2.1	2.3
High school graduate or more	92.5	94.9	95.4	93.9	94.3	85.8
Some college or more	61.9	70.2	69.9	62.1	63.5	48.6
Associate's degree or more	44.9	51.6	52.5	45.4	46.0	32.9
Bachelor's degree or more	34.5	40.6	40.3	34.1	34.5	26.0

Note: Non-Hispanic whites are those who identify themselves as white alone and not Hispanic.
Source: Bureau of the Census, Educational Attainment in the United States: 2012, Internet site http://www.census.gov/hhes/ socdemo/education/data/cps/2012/tables.html; calculations by New Strategist

Table 6.2 Educational Attainment of Non-Hispanic White Men by Age, 2012

(number and percent distribution of non-Hispanic white men aged 25 or older by educational attainment and age, 2012; numbers in thousands)

	total	25 to 34	35 to 44	45 to 54	55 to 64	65 or older
Total non-Hispanic white men	**67,204**	**11,993**	**12,094**	**14,741**	**13,643**	**14,731**
Not a high school graduate	5,219	703	647	1,018	831	2,022
High school graduate only	20,568	3,527	3,433	4,844	4,134	4,629
Some college, no degree	11,216	2,173	2,126	2,306	2,326	2,286
Associate's degree	6,318	1,205	1,276	1,538	1,326	973
Bachelor's degree	14,983	3,355	2,971	3,211	2,931	2,514
Master's degree	5,747	695	1,163	1,201	1,355	1,332
Professional degree	1,558	217	239	354	356	392
Doctoral degree	1,594	121	238	268	384	582
High school graduate or more	61,984	11,293	11,446	13,722	12,812	12,708
Some college or more	41,416	7,766	8,013	8,878	8,678	8,079
Associate's degree or more	30,200	5,593	5,887	6,572	6,352	5,793
Bachelor's degree or more	23,882	4,388	4,611	5,034	5,026	4,820

PERCENT DISTRIBUTION

	total	25 to 34	35 to 44	45 to 54	55 to 64	65 or older
Total non-Hispanic white men	**100.0%**	**100.0%**	**100.0%**	**100.0%**	**100.0%**	**100.0%**
Not a high school graduate	7.8	5.9	5.3	6.9	6.1	13.7
High school graduate only	30.6	29.4	28.4	32.9	30.3	31.4
Some college, no degree	16.7	18.1	17.6	15.6	17.0	15.5
Associate's degree	9.4	10.0	10.6	10.4	9.7	6.6
Bachelor's degree	22.3	28.0	24.6	21.8	21.5	17.1
Master's degree	8.6	5.8	9.6	8.1	9.9	9.0
Professional degree	2.3	1.8	2.0	2.4	2.6	2.7
Doctoral degree	2.4	1.0	2.0	1.8	2.8	4.0
High school graduate or more	92.2	94.2	94.6	93.1	93.9	86.3
Some college or more	61.6	64.8	66.3	60.2	63.6	54.8
Associate's degree or more	44.9	46.6	48.7	44.6	46.6	39.3
Bachelor's degree or more	35.5	36.6	38.1	34.1	36.8	32.7

Note: Non-Hispanic whites are those who identify themselves as white alone and not Hispanic.
Source: Bureau of the Census, Educational Attainment in the United States: 2012, Internet site http://www.census.gov/hhes/socdemo/education/data/cps/2012/tables.html; calculations by New Strategist

Table 6.3 Educational Attainment of Non-Hispanic White Women by Age, 2012

(number and percent distribution of non-Hispanic white women aged 25 or older by educational attainment and age, 2012; numbers in thousands)

	total	25 to 34	35 to 44	45 to 54	55 to 64	65 or older
Total non-Hispanic white women	**71,797**	**11,939**	**12,105**	**15,155**	**14,425**	**18,173**
Not a high school graduate	5,230	522	465	803	776	2,665
High school graduate only	21,889	2,394	2,736	4,659	4,498	7,604
Some college, no degree	12,510	2,260	2,089	2,695	2,601	2,866
Associate's degree	8,118	1,427	1,683	1,824	1,889	1,292
Bachelor's degree	15,569	3,726	3,364	3,391	2,787	2,301
Master's degree	6,791	1,250	1,412	1,433	1,530	1,166
Professional degree	840	200	189	184	151	116
Doctoral degree	849	160	168	166	194	162
High school graduate or more	9,427	3,024	2,485	1,970	1,131	821
Some college or more	5,333	1,735	1,458	1,145	627	371
Associate's degree or more	3,302	1,056	913	730	372	234
Bachelor's degree or more	2,255	728	636	477	255	161

PERCENT DISTRIBUTION

	total	25 to 34	35 to 44	45 to 54	55 to 64	65 or older
Total non-Hispanic white women	**100.0%**	**100.0%**	**100.0%**	**100.0%**	**100.0%**	**100.0%**
Not a high school graduate	7.3	4.4	3.8	5.3	5.4	14.7
High school graduate only	30.5	20.1	22.6	30.7	31.2	41.8
Some college, no degree	17.4	18.9	17.3	17.8	18.0	15.8
Associate's degree	11.3	12.0	13.9	12.0	13.1	7.1
Bachelor's degree	21.7	31.2	27.8	22.4	19.3	12.7
Master's degree	9.5	10.5	11.7	9.5	10.6	6.4
Professional degree	1.2	1.7	1.6	1.2	1.0	0.6
Doctoral degree	1.2	1.3	1.4	1.1	1.3	0.9
High school graduate or more	92.7	95.6	96.2	94.7	94.6	85.3
Some college or more	62.2	75.6	73.6	64.0	63.4	43.5
Associate's degree or more	44.8	56.6	56.3	46.2	45.4	27.7
Bachelor's degree or more	33.5	44.7	42.4	34.1	32.3	20.6

Note: Non-Hispanic whites are those who identify themselves as white alone and not Hispanic.
Source: Bureau of the Census, Educational Attainment in the United States: 2012, Internet site http://www.census.gov/hhes/ socdemo/education/data/cps/2012/tables.html; calculations by New Strategist

Table 6.4 Educational Attainment of Non-Hispanic Whites by Region, 2006–10

(total number of non-Hispanic whites aged 25 or older and percent distribution by educational attainment and region, 2006–10; numbers in thousands)

	total	Northeast	Midwest	South	West
Total non-Hispanic whites	**138,362**	**27,152**	**35,893**	**48,246**	**27,071**
Not a high school graduate	13,863	2,569	3,513	5,914	1,867
High school graduate only	41,118	8,586	11,763	14,437	6,332
Some college, no degree	29,596	4,462	7,756	10,361	7,017
Associate's degree	11,009	2,172	2,947	3,505	2,385
Bachelor's degree	26,865	5,510	6,446	8,944	5,965
Graduate degree	15,911	3,853	3,468	5,085	3,504
PERECENT DISTRIBUTION					
High school graduate or more	90.0%	90.5%	90.2%	87.7%	93.1%
Some college or more	60.3	58.9	57.4	57.8	69.7
Associate's degree or more	38.9	42.5	35.8	36.3	43.8
Bachelor's degree or more	30.9	34.5	27.6	29.1	35.0

Note: Non-Hispanic whites are those who identify themselves as white alone and not Hispanic.
Source: Bureau of the Census, 2006–10 American Community Survey, Internet site http://factfinder2.census.gov/faces/nav/jsf/pages/index.xhtml; calculations by New Strategist

Table 6.5 School Enrollment of Non-Hispanic Whites, 2011

(total number of people aged 3 or older enrolled in school, number of non-Hispanic whites enrolled, and non-Hispanic white share of total, by age, October 2011; numbers in thousands)

| | | non-Hispanic white | |
	total	number	share of total
Total aged 3 or older	**79,043**	**44,951**	**56.9%**
Aged 3 to 4	4,597	2,484	54.0
Aged 5 to 6	8,009	4,219	52.7
Aged 7 to 9	12,319	6,565	53.3
Aged 10 to 13	15,941	8,890	55.8
Aged 14 to 15	7,825	4,509	57.6
Aged 16 to 17	7,906	4,535	57.4
Aged 18 to 19	6,017	3,525	58.6
Aged 20 to 21	4,618	2,953	63.9
Aged 22 to 24	3,961	2,465	62.2
Aged 25 to 29	3,139	1,927	61.4
Aged 30 to 34	1,571	939	59.8
Aged 35 to 44	1,688	963	57.0
Aged 45 to 54	1,012	701	69.3
Aged 55 or older	438	275	62.8

Note: Non-Hispanic whites are those who identify themselves as white alone and not Hispanic.
Source: Bureau of the Census, School Enrollment, CPS October 2011—Detailed Tables, Internet site http://www.census.gov/hhes/school/data/cps/2011/tables.html; calculations by New Strategist

Table 6.6 School Enrollment of Non-Hispanic Whites by Age and Sex, 2011

(number and percent of non-Hispanic whites aged 3 or older enrolled in school, by age and sex, October 2011; numbers in thousands)

	total		female		male	
	number	percent	number	percent	number	percent
Total non-Hispanic whites enrolled	**44,951**	**23.6%**	**22,616**	**23.3%**	**22,336**	**23.9%**
Aged 3 to 4	2,484	56.2	1,216	56.1	1,269	56.4
Aged 5 to 6	4,219	95.8	2,070	96.1	2,149	95.5
Aged 7 to 9	6,565	98.2	3,208	98.1	3,357	98.3
Aged 10 to 13	8,890	98.5	4,315	98.5	4,575	98.5
Aged 14 to 15	4,509	98.9	2,189	99.3	2,319	98.4
Aged 16 to 17	4,535	95.9	2,211	95.9	2,325	95.8
Aged 18 to 19	3,525	72.1	1,798	74.3	1,727	69.9
Aged 20 to 21	2,953	56.2	1,557	59.5	1,396	53.0
Aged 22 to 24	2,465	32.9	1,220	32.7	1,246	33.1
Aged 25 to 29	1,927	15.2	1,091	17.3	835	13.2
Aged 30 to 34	939	7.8	522	8.5	417	7.0
Aged 35 to 44	963	4.0	584	4.8	379	3.1
Aged 45 to 54	701	2.3	451	2.9	250	1.7
Aged 55 or older	275	0.5	182	0.6	93	0.3

Note: Non-Hispanic whites are those who identify themselves as white alone and not Hispanic.
Source: Bureau of the Census, School Enrollment, CPS October 2011—Detailed Tables, Internet site http://www.census.gov/ hhes/school/data/cps/2011/tables.html; calculations by New Strategist

Table 6.7 Non-Hispanic White College Enrollment Rate, 2000 to 2011

(percentage of total people and non-Hispanic whites aged 16 to 24 who graduated from high school in the previous 12 months and were enrolled in college as of October, and index of non-Hispanic white to total, 2000 to 2011; percentage point change in enrollment rate for selected years)

	total	non-Hispanic white	index, non-Hispanic white to total
2011	68.2%	68.3%	100
2010	68.1	70.5	104
2009	70.1	71.3	102
2008	68.6	71.7	105
2007	67.2	69.5	103
2006	66.0	68.5	104
2005	68.6	73.2	107
2004	66.7	68.8	103
2003	63.9	66.2	104
2002	65.2	69.1	106
2001	61.8	64.3	104
2000	63.3	65.7	104

PERCENTAGE POINT CHANGE

2000 to 2011	4.9	2.6	–

Note: Non-Hispanic whites are those who identify themselves as white alone and not Hispanic. The index is calculated by dividing the non-Hispanic white figure by the total figure and multiplying by 100. "–" means not applicable.
Source: National Center for Education Statistics, Digest of Education Statistics 2012, Internet site ces.ed.gov/programs/digest/2012menu_tables.asp; calculations by New Strategist

Table 6.8 College Enrollment of Non-Hispanic Whites by Age, 2011

(total number of people aged 15 or older enrolled in college, number of non-Hispanic whites enrolled, and non-Hispanic white share of total, by age, 2011; numbers in thousands)

| | | non-Hispanic white | |
	total	number	share of total
Total enrolled in college	**20,397**	**12,703**	**62.3%**
Under age 20	4,446	2,693	60.6
Aged 20 to 21	4,460	2,868	64.3
Aged 22 to 24	3,869	2,425	62.7
Aged 25 to 29	3,066	1,893	61.7
Aged 30 or older	4,559	2,823	61.9

Note: Non-Hispanic whites are those who identify themselves as being white alone and not Hispanic.
Source: Bureau of the Census, School Enrollment, CPS October 2011—Detailed Tables, Internet site http://www.census.gov/hhes/school/data/cps/2011/tables.html; calculations by New Strategist

Table 6.9 College Enrollment of Non-Hispanic Whites by Type of School and Sex, 2011

(number and percent distribution of non-Hispanic whites aged 15 or older enrolled in college by type of school and sex, and female share of total, 2011; numbers in thousands)

| | total | | men | | women | | |
	number	percent distribution	number	percent distribution	number	percent distribution	share of total
Total non-Hispanic whites enrolled	**12,703**	**100.0%**	**5,731**	**100.0%**	**6,972**	**100.0%**	**54.9%**
Two-year undergraduate program	3,062	24.1	1,320	23.0	1,741	25.0	56.9
Four-year undergraduate program	7,130	56.1	3,347	58.4	3,783	54.3	53.1
Graduate school	2,511	19.8	1,064	18.6	1,447	20.8	57.6

Note: Non-Hispanic whites are those who identify themselves as white alone and not Hispanic.
Source: Bureau of the Census, School Enrollment, CPS October 2011—Detailed Tables, Internet site http://www.census.gov/hhes/school/data/cps/2011/tables.html; calculations by New Strategist

Table 6.10 Associate's Degrees Earned by Non-Hispanic Whites by Field of Study, 2010–11

(total number of associate's degrees conferred and number and percent earned by non-Hispanic whites, by field of study, 2010–11)

		earned by non-Hispanic whites	
	total	number	share of total
Total associate's degrees	**942,327**	**604,110**	**64.1%**
Agriculture and natural resources	6,425	5,942	92.5
Architecture and related programs	569	310	54.5
Area, ethnic, and cultural studies	209	45	21.5
Biological and biomedical sciences	3,245	1,656	51.0
Business	139,986	84,192	60.1
Communication, journalism, and related programs	3,051	1,955	64.1
Communications technologies	4,209	2,956	70.2
Computer and information sciences	37,677	25,050	66.5
Construction trades	5,402	4,282	79.3
Education	20,459	13,278	64.9
Engineering	2,825	1,794	63.5
Engineering technologies	35,521	25,100	70.7
English language and literature/letters	2,019	1,080	53.5
Family and consumer sciences	8,532	4,430	51.9
Foreign languages and literatures	1,876	1,193	63.6
Health professions and related sciences	201,831	139,071	68.9
Homeland security, law enforcement, and firefighting	44,923	27,248	60.7
Legal professions and studies	11,620	7,440	64.0
Liberal arts and sciences, general studies, and humanities	306,670	192,864	62.9
Library science	160	128	80.0
Mathematics and statistics	1,644	778	47.3
Mechanic and repair technologies	19,969	14,078	70.5
Military technologies	856	582	68.0
Multi/interdisciplinary studies	23,729	13,787	58.1
Parks, recreation, leisure, and fitness	2,366	1,457	61.6
Philosophy and religion	283	152	53.7
Physical sciences	5,078	2,866	56.4
Precision production trades	3,254	2,741	84.2
Psychology	3,866	2,125	55.0
Public administration and social services	7,472	3,889	52.0
Social sciences and history	12,767	6,316	49.5
Theology and religious vocations	758	520	68.6
Transportation and material moving	1,697	1,137	67.0
Visual and performing arts	21,379	13,668	63.9

Source: National Center for Education Statistics, Digest of Education Statistics 2012, Internet site http://nces.ed.gov/programs/digest/2012menu_tables.asp; calculations by New Strategist

Table 6.11 Bachelor's Degrees Earned by Non-Hispanic Whites by Field of Study, 2010–11

(total number of bachelor's degrees conferred and number and percent earned by non-Hispanic whites, by field of study, 2010–11)

	total	earned by non-Hispanic whites	
		number	share of total
Total bachelor's degrees	**1,715,913**	**1,182,405**	**68.9%**
Agriculture and natural resources	28,623	24,278	84.8
Architecture and related programs	9,832	6,619	67.3
Area, ethnic, and cultural studies	9,100	4,534	49.8
Biological and biomedical sciences	90,003	56,460	62.7
Business	365,093	238,786	65.4
Communication, journalism, and related programs	83,274	60,577	72.7
Communications technologies	4,858	3,360	69.2
Computer and information sciences	43,072	28,031	65.1
Construction trades	328	295	89.9
Education	103,992	85,234	82.0
Engineering	76,376	51,718	67.7
Engineering technologies	16,187	11,989	74.1
English language and literature/letters	52,744	40,147	76.1
Family and consumer sciences	22,444	16,065	71.6
Foreign languages, literatures, and linguistics	21,706	14,821	68.3
Health professions and related sciences	143,430	102,055	71.2
Homeland security, law enforcement, and firefighting	47,602	28,088	59.0
Legal professions and studies	4,429	2,769	62.5
Liberal arts and sciences, general studies, and humanities	46,727	31,056	66.5
Library science	96	85	88.5
Mathematics and statistics	17,182	11,836	68.9
Mechanic and repair technologies	226	158	69.9
Military technologies	64	43	67.2
Multi/interdisciplinary studies	42,228	28,286	67.0
Parks, recreation, leisure, and fitness	35,924	26,998	75.2
Philosophy and religion	12,836	9,752	76.0
Physical sciences	24,712	17,842	72.2
Precision production trades	43	29	67.4
Psychology	100,893	66,122	65.5
Public administration and social services	26,774	15,336	57.3
Social sciences and history	177,144	118,979	67.2
Theology and religious vocations	9,074	7,555	83.3
Transportation and material moving	4,941	3,812	77.2
Visual and performing arts	93,956	68,690	73.1

Source: National Center for Education Statistics, Digest of Education Statistics 2012, Internet site http://nces.ed.gov/programs/digest/2012menu_tables.asp; calculations by New Strategist

Table 6.12 Master's Degrees Earned by Non-Hispanic Whites by Field of Study, 2010–11

(total number of master's degrees conferred and number and percent earned by non-Hispanic whites, by field of study, 2010–11)

		earned by non-Hispanic whites	
	total	number	share of total
Total master's degrees	**730,635**	**462,903**	**63.4%**
Agriculture and natural resources	5,773	4,166	72.2
Architecture and related programs	7,788	5,017	64.4
Area, ethnic, and cultural studies	1,914	1,071	56.0
Biological and biomedical sciences	11,327	6,461	57.0
Business	187,213	105,520	56.4
Communication, journalism, and related programs	8,303	5,136	61.9
Communications technologies	502	214	42.6
Computer and information sciences	19,446	6,501	33.4
Education	185,009	139,909	75.6
Engineering	38,719	14,807	38.2
Engineering technologies	4,515	2,190	48.5
English language and literature/letters	9,476	7,529	79.5
Family and consumer sciences	2,918	2,056	70.5
Foreign languages, literatures, and linguistics	3,727	2,114	56.7
Health professions and related sciences	75,579	52,288	69.2
Homeland security, law enforcement, and firefighting	7,433	4,664	62.7
Legal professions and studies	6,300	2,185	34.7
Liberal arts and sciences, general studies, and humanities	3,971	2,859	72.0
Library science	7,727	6,474	83.8
Mathematics and statistics	5,843	2,636	45.1
Multi/interdisciplinary studies	6,748	4,576	67.8
Parks, recreation, leisure, and fitness	6,553	4,882	74.5
Philosophy and religion	1,833	1,400	76.4
Physical sciences	6,386	3,707	58.0
Precision production trades	5	4	80.0
Psychology	25,051	17,066	68.1
Public administration and social services	38,634	22,912	59.3
Social sciences and history	21,084	13,469	63.9
Theology and religious vocations	13,191	9,088	68.9
Transportation and material moving	1,390	1,105	79.5
Visual and performing arts	16,277	10,897	66.9

Source: National Center for Education Statistics, Digest of Education Statistics 2012, Internet site http://nces.ed.gov/programs/digest/2012menu_tables.asp; calculations by New Strategist

Table 6.13 Doctoral and First-Professional Degrees Earned by Non-Hispanic Whites by Field of Study, 2010–11

(total number of doctoral and first-professional degrees conferred and number and percent earned by non-Hispanic whites, by field of study, 2010–11)

		earned by non-Hispanic whites	
	total	number	share of total
Total doctoral and first-professional degrees	**163,765**	**105,932**	**64.7%**
Agriculture and natural resources	1,246	610	49.0
Architecture and related programs	205	68	33.2
Area, ethnic, and cultural studies	278	141	50.7
Biological and biomedical sciences	7,693	4,214	54.8
Business	2,286	1,089	47.6
Communication, journalism, and related programs	577	358	62.0
Communications technologies	1	0	0.0
Computer and information sciences	1,588	581	36.6
Education	9,623	6,172	64.1
Engineering	8,369	2,599	31.1
Engineering technologies	56	32	57.1
English language and literature/letters	1,344	1,044	77.7
Family and consumer sciences	320	189	59.1
Foreign languages, literatures, and linguistics	1,158	625	54.0
Health professions and related sciences	60,153	41,177	68.5
Homeland security, law enforcement, and firefighting	131	89	67.9
Legal professions and studies	44,877	32,762	73.0
Liberal arts and sciences, general studies, and humanities	95	73	76.8
Library science	50	26	52.0
Mathematics and statistics	1,586	685	43.2
Multi/interdisciplinary studies	660	372	56.4
Parks, recreation, leisure, and fitness	257	163	63.4
Philosophy and religion	805	550	68.3
Physical sciences	5,295	2,579	48.7
Psychology	5,851	4,303	73.5
Public administration and social services	851	458	53.8
Social sciences and history	4,390	2,509	57.2
Theology and religious vocations	2,374	1,417	59.7
Visual and performing arts	1,646	1,047	63.6

Source: National Center for Education Statistics, Digest of Education Statistics 2012, Internet site http://nces.ed.gov/programs/digest/2012menu_tables.asp; calculations by New Strategist

Most Non-Hispanic Whites Say Their Health Is Very Good or Excellent

Sixty-three percent of non-Hispanic whites report being in "very good" or "excellent" health. Only 12 percent say their health is "fair" or "poor." Non-Hispanic whites rate their health highly although 60 percent are overweight. Twenty-one percent of non-Hispanic whites smoke cigarettes, and the majority drinks alcohol regularly.

Fifty-four percent of the nation's births in 2011 were to non-Hispanic white women. In 11 states (Arizona, California, Florida, Georgia, Hawaii, Maryland, Nevada, New Jersey, New Mexico, New York, and Texas) and the District of Columbia, non-Hispanic whites account for a minority of births. In California, the most-populous state, only 29 percent of births are to non-Hispanic whites.

Among all racial and ethnic groups, non-Hispanic whites are least likely to be without health insurance. Only 11 percent were uninsured in 2011. More than 60 percent of non-Hispanic whites are covered by employment-based private health insurance. Among Hispanics, in contrast, only 38 percent are covered by health insurance through an employer.

Because the non-Hispanic white population is older than the Asian, black, and Hispanic populations, non-Hispanic whites account for a disproportionate 72 percent of adults with difficulties in physical functioning. Fifteen percent of non-Hispanic whites aged 18 or older have physical difficulties.

Among non-Hispanic whites, heart disease and cancer are the two leading causes of death, accounting for half the total. Alzheimer's disease is the sixth-leading cause of death among non-Hispanic whites.

■ As the non-Hispanic white population ages, the percentage of Americans with disabilities will rise.

Non-Hispanic whites are most likely to be covered by employment-based health insurance

(percent of people covered by employment-based private health insurance, by race and Hispanic origin, 2011)

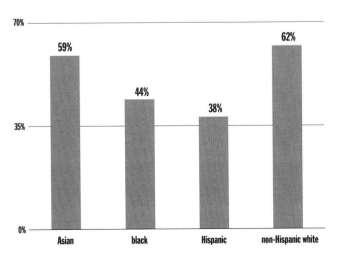

Table 6.14 Health Status of Total People and Non-Hispanic Whites, 2011

(number and percent distribution of total people and non-Hispanic whites aged 18 or older by self-reported health status, and index of non-Hispanic white to total, 2011; numbers in thousands)

	total		non-Hispanic white		index, non-Hispanic white to total
	number	percent distribution	number	percent distribution	
Total people	**231,376**	**100.0%**	**156,482**	**100.0%**	–
Excellent/very good	139,424	60.3	98,718	63.1	105
Good	60,973	26.4	38,402	24.5	93
Fair/poor	30,856	13.3	19,251	12.3	92

Note: Non-Hispanic whites are those who identify themselves as being white alone and not Hispanic. Numbers may not add to total because "unknown" is not shown. The index is calculated by dividing the non-Hispanic white percentage by the total percentage and multiplying by 100. "–" means not applicable.
Source: National Center for Health Statistics, Summary Health Statistics for U.S. Adults: National Health Interview Survey, 2011, Vital and Health Statistics, Series 10, No. 256, 2012, Internet site http://www.cdc.gov/nchs/nhis.htm; calculations by New Strategist

Table 6.15 Weight of Non-Hispanic Whites by Age and Sex, 2007–10

(average weight in pounds of non-Hispanic whites aged 20 or older by age and sex, 2007–10)

	men	women
Total non-Hispanic whites	**199.2 lbs.**	**165.4 lbs.**
Aged 20 to 39	194.7	164.7
Aged 40 to 59	204.9	167.7
Aged 60 or older	196.3	163.0

Note: Data are based on measured weight of a sample of the civilian noninstitutionalized population.
Source: National Center for Health Statistics, Anthropometric Reference Data for Children and Adults: United States, 2007–2010, National Health Statistics Reports, Series 11, Number 252, 2012, Internet site http://www.cdc.gov/nchs/nhanes.htm

Table 6.16 Weight Status of Total People and Non-Hispanic Whites, 2011

(number and percent distribution of total people and non-Hispanic whites aged 18 or older by body mass index based on self-reported height and weight, and index of non-Hispanic white to total, 2011; numbers in thousands)

	total		non-Hispanic white		index, non-Hispanic white to total
	number	percent distribution	number	percent distribution	
Total people	**231,376**	**100.0%**	**156,482**	**100.0%**	–
Underweight	3,549	1.5	2,456	1.6	102
Healthy weight	79,984	34.6	56,201	35.9	104
Overweight, total	141,072	61.0	93,284	59.6	98
Overweight, but not obese	77,586	33.5	52,535	33.6	100
Obese	63,486	27.4	40,749	26.0	95

Note: "Overweight" is defined as a body mass index of 25 or higher. "Obese" is defined as a body mass index of 30 or higher. Body mass index is calculated by dividing weight in kilograms by height in meters squared. Non-Hispanic whites are those who identify themselves as being white alone and not Hispanic. Numbers may not add to total because "unknown" is not shown. The index is calculated by dividing the non-Hispanic white percentage by the total percentage and multiplying by 100. "–" means not applicable.
Source: National Center for Health Statistics, Summary Health Statistics for U.S. Adults: National Health Interview Survey, 2011, Vital and Health Statistics, Series 10, No. 256, 2012, Internet site http://www.cdc.gov/nchs/nhis.htm; calculations by New Strategist

Table 6.17 Weight of Total and Non-Hispanic White High School Students by Sex, 2011

(percent of total and non-Hispanic white 9th to 12th graders by weight status, by sex, 2011)

	total	non-Hispanic white
MALES		
Measured as overweight*	31.2%	29.7%
Described themselves as overweight	23.9	23.7
Were trying to lose weight	31.6	29.2
FEMALES		
Measured as overweight*	25.2	21.5
Described themselves as overweight	34.8	33.7
Were trying to lose weight	61.2	61.4

* Students were classified as overweight if they were at or above the 85th percentile for body mass index, by age and sex, based on 2000 CDC growth charts.
Source: Centers for Disease Control and Prevention, Youth Risk Behavior Surveillance–United States, 2011, Mortality and Morbidity Weekly Report, Vol. 61, No. 4, June 8, 2012; Internet site http://www.cdc.gov/HealthyYouth/yrbs/index.htm

Table 6.18 Drinking Status of Total People and Non-Hispanic Whites, 2011

(number and percent distribution of total people and non-Hispanic whites aged 18 or older by drinking status, and index of non-Hispanic white to total, 2011; numbers in thousands)

	total		non-Hispanic white		index, non-Hispanic white to total
	number	percent distribution	number	percent distribution	
Total people	**231,376**	**100.0%**	**156,482**	**100.0%**	–
Lifetime abstainer	45,367	19.6	22,871	14.6	75
Former drinker	33,663	14.5	23,264	14.9	102
Current drinker	148,970	64.4	108,167	69.1	107
Infrequent	31,158	13.5	21,235	13.6	101
Regular	117,812	50.9	86,932	55.6	109

Note: "Lifetime abstainers" have had fewer than 12 drinks in lifetime. "Former drinkers" have had 12 or more drinks in lifetime, none in past year. "Current infrequent drinkers" have had 12 or more drinks in lifetime and fewer than 12 drinks in past year. "Current regular drinkers" have had 12 or more drinks in lifetime and at least 12 drinks in past year. Non-Hispanic whites are those who identify themselves as being white alone and not Hispanic. The index is calculated by dividing the non-Hispanic white figure by the total figure and multiplying by 100. "–" means not applicable.
Source: National Center for Health Statistics, Summary Health Statistics for U.S. Adults: National Health Interview Survey, 2011, Vital and Health Statistics, Series 10, No. 256, 2012, Internet site http://www.cdc.gov/nchs/nhis.htm; calculations by New Strategist

Table 6.19 Smoking Status of Total People and Non-Hispanic Whites, 2011

(number and percent distribution of total people and non-Hispanic whites aged 18 or older by smoking status, and index of non-Hispanic white to total, 2011; numbers in thousands)

	total		non-Hispanic white		index, non-Hispanic white to total
	number	percent distribution	number	percent distribution	
Total people	**231,376**	**100.0%**	**156,482**	**100.0%**	–
Never smoked	136,528	59.0	84,365	53.9	91
Former smoker	50,416	21.8	39,578	25.3	116
Current smoker	43,821	18.9	32,108	20.5	108

Note: "Never smoked" means fewer than 100 cigarettes in lifetime. "Former smokers" have smoked 100 or more cigarettes in lifetime but did not smoke at time of interview. "Current smokers" have smoked at least 100 cigarettes in lifetime and currently smoke. Non-Hispanic whites are those who identify themselves as being white alone and not Hispanic. The index is calculated by dividing the non-Hispanic white figure by the total figure and multiplying by 100. "–" means not applicable.
Source: National Center for Health Statistics, Summary Health Statistics for U.S. Adults: National Health Interview Survey, 2011, Vital and Health Statistics, Series 10, No. 256, 2012, Internet site http://www.cdc.gov/nchs/nhis.htm; calculations by New Strategist

Table 6.20 Births to Total and Non-Hispanic White Women by Age, 2011

(total number of births, number and percent distribution of births to non-Hispanic whites, and non-Hispanic white share of total, by age, 2011)

| | | non-Hispanic white | | |
	total	number	percent distribution	share of total
Total births	**3,953,593**	**2,150,926**	**100.0%**	**54.4%**
Under age 15	3,974	875	0.0	22.0
Aged 15 to 19	329,797	129,693	6.0	39.3
Aged 20 to 24	925,213	453,006	21.1	49.0
Aged 25 to 29	1,127,592	648,883	30.2	57.5
Aged 30 to 34	986,661	592,239	27.5	60.0
Aged 35 to 39	463,815	261,098	12.1	56.3
Aged 40 to 44	108,891	60,807	2.8	55.8
Aged 45 to 54	7,651	4,325	0.2	56.5

Source: National Center for Health Statistics, Births: Preliminary Data for 2011, National Vital Statistics Report, Vol. 61, No. 5, 2012, Internet site http://www.cdc.gov/nchs/births.htm; calculations by New Strategist

Table 6.21 Births to Non-Hispanic White Women by Age and Marital Status, 2010

(total number of births to non-Hispanic whites, number of births to unmarried non-Hispanic whites, and unmarried share of total, by age, 2010)

	total	unmarried number	share of total
Births to non-Hispanic whites	**2,162,406**	**627,541**	**29.0%**
Under age 15	968	959	99.1
Aged 15 to 19	144,102	120,831	83.9
Aged 20 to 24	464,849	246,000	52.9
Aged 25 to 29	648,610	147,405	22.7
Aged 30 to 34	574,627	70,862	12.3
Aged 35 to 39	264,126	31,728	12.0
Aged 40 or older	65,124	9,756	15.0

Source: National Center for Health Statistics, Births: Final Data for 2010, National Vital Statistics Reports, Vol. 61, No. 1, 2012, Internet site http://www.cdc.gov/nchs/births.htm; calculations by New Strategist

Table 06.22 Births to Total and Non-Hispanic White Women by Birth Order, 2011

(total number of births, number and percent distribution of births to non-Hispanic whites, and non-Hispanic white share of total, by birth order, 2011)

	total	non-Hispanic white number	percent distribution	share of total
Total births	**3,953,593**	**2,150,926**	**100.0%**	**54.4%**
First child	1,577,344	905,847	42.1	57.4
Second child	1,239,136	699,455	32.5	56.4
Third child	648,124	329,989	15.3	50.9
Fourth or later child	458,777	203,075	9.4	44.3

Note: Numbers do not add to total because "not stated" is not shown.
Source: National Center for Health Statistics, Births: Preliminary Data for 2011, National Vital Statistics Report, Vol. 61, No. 5, 2012, Internet site http://www.cdc.gov/nchs/births.htm; calculations by New Strategist

Table 6.23 Births to Total and Non-Hispanic White Women by State, 2011

(total number of births, number and percent distribution of births to non-Hispanic whites, and non-Hispanic white share of total, by state, 2011)

	total	non-Hispanic white number	non-Hispanic white percent distribution	non-Hispanic white share of total
Total births	**3,953,593**	**2,150,926**	**100.0%**	**54.4%**
Alabama	59,347	35,687	1.7	60.1
Alaska	11,455	6,081	0.3	53.1
Arizona	85,543	38,987	1.8	45.6
Arkansas	38,713	26,407	1.2	68.2
California	502,118	144,583	6.7	28.8
Colorado	65,055	40,439	1.9	62.2
Connecticut	37,280	21,541	1.0	57.8
Delaware	11,257	6,221	0.3	55.3
District of Columbia	9,314	2,637	0.1	28.3
Florida	213,344	97,250	4.5	45.6
Georgia	132,488	60,672	2.8	45.8
Hawaii	18,957	4,861	0.2	25.6
Idaho	22,305	17,869	0.8	80.1
Illinois	161,312	87,952	4.1	54.5
Indiana	83,702	64,490	3.0	77.0
Iowa	38,213	31,927	1.5	83.6
Kansas	39,642	28,814	1.3	72.7
Kentucky	55,377	46,200	2.1	83.4
Louisiana	61,889	33,114	1.5	53.5
Maine	12,704	11,746	0.5	92.5
Maryland	73,086	33,261	1.5	45.5
Massachusetts	73,225	50,918	2.4	69.5
Michigan	114,004	79,604	3.7	69.8
Minnesota	68,411	50,296	2.3	73.5
Mississippi	39,856	20,499	1.0	51.4
Missouri	76,117	57,811	2.7	76.0
Montana	12,069	9,934	0.5	82.3
Nebraska	25,720	19,301	0.9	75.0
Nevada	35,295	15,259	0.7	43.2
New Hampshire	12,852	11,403	0.5	88.7
New Jersey	105,886	49,664	2.3	46.9
New Mexico	27,289	7,719	0.4	28.3
New York	241,290	117,198	5.4	48.6
North Carolina	120,385	67,685	3.1	56.2
North Dakota	9,527	7,759	0.4	81.4
Ohio	137,916	104,505	4.9	75.8
Oklahoma	52,274	33,361	1.6	63.8

	total	non-Hispanic white		
		number	percent distribution	share of total
Oregon	45,157	31,768	1.5%	70.4%
Pennsylvania	143,148	100,767	4.7	70.4
Rhode Island	10,960	6,758	0.3	61.7
South Carolina	57,368	32,960	1.5	57.5
South Dakota	11,849	8,862	0.4	74.8
Tennessee	79,588	54,131	2.5	68.0
Texas	377,449	133,890	6.2	35.5
Utah	51,223	40,860	1.9	79.8
Vermont	6,078	5,728	0.3	94.2
Virginia	102,648	60,369	2.8	58.8
Washington	86,976	55,084	2.6	63.3
West Virginia	20,720	19,521	0.9	94.2
Wisconsin	67,811	50,500	2.3	74.5
Wyoming	7,398	6,071	0.3	82.1

Source: National Center for Health Statistics, Births: Preliminary Data for 2011, National Vital Statistics Report, Vol. 61, No. 5, 2012, Internet site http://www.cdc.gov/nchs/births.htm; calculations by New Strategist

Table 6.24 Health Insurance Coverage of Non-Hispanic Whites by Age, 2011

(number and percent distribution of non-Hispanic whites by age and health insurance coverage status, 2011; numbers in thousands)

	total	with health insurance coverage during year			not covered at any time during the year
		total	private	government	
Total non-Hispanic whites	**195,148**	**173,466**	**141,783**	**60,184**	**21,681**
Under age 18	39,143	36,499	28,544	11,035	2,644
Aged 18 to 24	17,004	13,874	12,004	2,723	3,130
Aged 25 to 34	23,933	19,038	16,661	3,290	4,895
Aged 35 to 44	24,199	20,594	18,712	2,900	3,605
Aged 45 to 54	29,896	25,934	23,280	3,909	3,962
Aged 55 to 64	28,069	24,903	21,716	5,281	3,166
Aged 65 or older	32,904	32,624	20,865	31,046	280

PERCENT DISTRIBUTION BY COVERAGE STATUS

Total non-Hispanic whites	**100.0%**	**88.9%**	**72.7%**	**30.8%**	**11.1%**
Under age 18	100.0	93.2	72.9	28.2	6.8
Aged 18 to 24	100.0	81.6	70.6	16.0	18.4
Aged 25 to 34	100.0	79.5	69.6	13.7	20.5
Aged 35 to 44	100.0	85.1	77.3	12.0	14.9
Aged 45 to 54	100.0	86.7	77.9	13.1	13.3
Aged 55 to 64	100.0	88.7	77.4	18.8	11.3
Aged 65 or older	100.0	99.1	63.4	94.4	0.9

Note: Non-Hispanic whites are those who identify themselves as being white alone and not Hispanic. Numbers do not add to total because some people have more than one type of health insurance.
Source: Bureau of the Census, Health Insurance, Internet site http://www.census.gov/hhes/www/cpstables/032012/health/toc .htm; calculations by New Strategist

Table 6.25 Non-Hispanic Whites with Private Health Insurance Coverage by Age, 2011

(number and percent distribution of non-Hispanic whites by age and private health insurance coverage status, 2011; numbers in thousands)

| | total | with private health insurance | | | |
| | | total | employment-based | | direct purchase |
			total	own	
Total non-Hispanic whites	**195,148**	**141,783**	**120,268**	**63,791**	**24,092**
Under age 18	39,143	28,544	26,232	97	2,888
Aged 18 to 24	17,004	12,004	9,155	2,157	1,301
Aged 25 to 34	23,933	16,661	15,151	11,291	1,711
Aged 35 to 44	24,199	18,712	17,402	12,210	1,877
Aged 45 to 54	29,896	23,280	21,305	15,101	2,877
Aged 55 to 64	28,069	21,716	19,184	13,954	3,287
Aged 65 or older	32,904	20,865	11,840	8,980	10,151

PERCENT DISTRIBUTION BY COVERAGE STATUS

Total non-Hispanic whites	**100.0%**	**72.7%**	**61.6%**	**32.7%**	**12.3%**
Under age 18	100.0	72.9	67.0	0.2	7.4
Aged 18 to 24	100.0	70.6	53.8	12.7	7.7
Aged 25 to 34	100.0	69.6	63.3	47.2	7.1
Aged 35 to 44	100.0	77.3	71.9	50.5	7.8
Aged 45 to 54	100.0	77.9	71.3	50.5	9.6
Aged 55 to 64	100.0	77.4	68.3	49.7	11.7
Aged 65 or older	100.0	63.4	36.0	27.3	30.9

Note: Non-Hispanic whites are those who identify themselves as being white alone and not Hispanic. Numbers do not add to total because some people have more than one type of health insurance.
Source: Bureau of the Census, Health Insurance, Internet site http://www.census.gov/hhes/www/cpstables/032012/health/toc .htm; calculations by New Strategist

Table 6.26 Non-Hispanic Whites with Government Health Insurance Coverage by Age, 2011

(number and percent distribution of non-Hispanic whites by age and government health insurance coverage status, 2011; numbers in thousands)

	total	with government health insurance			
		total	Medicaid	Medicare	military
Total non-Hispanic whites	**195,148**	**60,184**	**21,799**	**36,271**	**9,949**
Under age 18	39,143	11,035	9,543	301	1,577
Aged 18 to 24	17,004	2,723	2,084	128	610
Aged 25 to 34	23,933	3,290	2,173	384	967
Aged 35 to 44	24,199	2,900	1,749	624	813
Aged 45 to 54	29,896	3,909	2,157	1,378	1006
Aged 55 to 64	28,069	5,281	1,989	2,553	1,714
Aged 65 or older	32,904	31,046	2,104	30,903	3,262

PERCENT DISTRIBUTION BY COVERAGE STATUS

Total non-Hispanic whites	**100.0%**	**30.8%**	**11.2%**	**18.6%**	**5.1%**
Under age 18	100.0	28.2	24.4	0.8	4.0
Aged 18 to 24	100.0	16.0	12.3	0.8	3.6
Aged 25 to 34	100.0	13.7	9.1	1.6	4.0
Aged 35 to 44	100.0	12.0	7.2	2.6	3.4
Aged 45 to 54	100.0	13.1	7.2	4.6	3.4
Aged 55 to 64	100.0	18.8	7.1	9.1	6.1
Aged 65 or older	100.0	94.4	6.4	93.9	9.9

Note: Non-Hispanic whites are those who identify themselves as being white alone and not Hispanic. Numbers do not add to total because some people have more than one type of health insurance.
Source: Bureau of the Census, Health Insurance, Internet site http://www.census.gov/hhes/www/cpstables/032012/health/toc .htm; calculations by New Strategist

Table 6.27 Health Conditions among Total People and Non-Hispanic Whites Aged 18 or Older, 2011

(number of total people and non-Hispanic whites aged 18 or older with selected health conditions, percent of non-Hispanic whites with condition, and non-Hispanic white share of total with condition, 2011; numbers in thousands)

	total	non-Hispanic white number	non-Hispanic white percent with condition	non-Hispanic white share of total
TOTAL PEOPLE	231,376	156,482	100.0%	67.6%
Selected circulatory diseases				
Heart disease, all types	26,485	20,323	13.0	76.7
Coronary	15,300	11,548	7.4	75.5
Hypertension	58,959	41,606	26.6	70.6
Stroke	6,171	3,963	2.5	64.2
Selected respiratory conditions				
Emphysema	4,680	3,749	2.4	80.1
Asthma, ever	29,041	19,852	12.7	68.4
Asthma, still	18,869	13,050	8.3	69.2
Hay fever	16,869	12,659	8.1	75.0
Sinusitis	29,611	22,110	14.1	74.7
Chronic bronchitis	10,071	7,402	4.7	73.5
Selected types of cancer				
Any cancer	19,025	16,370	10.5	86.0
Breast cancer	3,221	2,658	1.7	82.5
Cervical cancer	1,188	1,008	0.6	84.8
Prostate cancer	2,280	1,811	1.2	79.4
Other selected diseases and conditions				
Diabetes	20,589	13,023	8.3	63.3
Ulcers	15,502	11,362	7.3	73.3
Kidney disease	4,381	2,846	1.8	65.0
Liver disease	3,016	1,913	1.2	63.4
Arthritis	53,782	41,448	26.5	77.1
Chronic joint symptoms	68,749	51,279	32.8	74.6
Migraines or severe headaches	37,904	25,606	16.4	67.6
Pain in neck	35,798	25,922	16.6	72.4
Pain in lower back	66,917	47,221	30.2	70.6
Pain in face or jaw	11,436	8,285	5.3	72.4
Selected sensory problems				
Hearing	37,122	29,920	19.1	80.6
Vision	21,232	14,461	9.2	68.1
Absence of all natural teeth	18,038	13,067	8.4	72.4

Note: The conditions shown are those that have ever been diagnosed by a doctor, except as noted. Hay fever, sinusitis, and chronic bronchitis have been diagnosed in the past 12 months. Kidney and liver disease have been diagnosed in the past 12 months and exclude kidney stones, bladder infections, and incontinence. Chronic joint symptoms are shown if respondent had pain, aching, or stiffness in or around a joint (excluding back and neck) and the condition began more than three months ago. Migraines, pain in neck, lower back, face, or jaw are shown only if pain lasted a whole day or more. Non-Hispanic whites are those who identify themselves as being white alone and not Hispanic.
Source: National Center for Health Statistics, Summary Health Statistics for U.S. Adults: National Health Interview Survey, 2011, Vital and Health Statistics, Series 10, No. 256, 2012, Internet site http://www.cdc.gov/nchs/nhis.htm; calculations by New Strategist

Table 6.28 Health Conditions among Total and Non-Hispanic White Children, 2011

(number of total people and non-Hispanic whites under age 18 with selected health conditions, percent of non-Hispanic whites with condition, and non-Hispanic white share of total, 2011; numbers in thousands)

| | | non-Hispanic white | | |
	total	number	percent with condition	share of total
Total children	**74,518**	**40,459**	**100.0%**	**54.3%**
Ever told have asthma	10,463	4,993	12.3	47.7
Still have asthma	7,074	3,157	7.8	44.6
Hay fever in past 12 months	6,711	3,998	9.9	59.6
Respiratory allergies in past 12 months	8,269	4,781	11.8	57.8
Food allergies in past 12 months	4,126	2,361	5.8	57.2
Skin allergies in past 12 months	9,516	4,920	12.2	51.7
Prescription medication taken regularly for at least three months	10,019	6,087	15.0	60.8
Learning disability*	4,660	2,743	6.8	58.9
Attention deficit hyperactivity disorder*	5,240	3,435	8.5	65.6

* Diagnosed by a school representative or health professional; data exclude children under age 3.
Note: Non-Hispanic whites are those who identify themselves as being white alone and not Hispanic.
Source: National Center for Health Statistics, Summary Health Statistics for U.S. Children: National Health Interview Survey, 2011, Vital and Health Statistics, Series 10, No. 254, 2012, Internet site http://www.cdc.gov/nchs/nhis.htm

Table 6.29 Health Care Office Visits by Total People and Non-Hispanic Whites, 2011

(number of total people and non-Hispanic whites aged 18 or older by visits to a health care provider in the past 12 months, percent distribution of non-Hispanic whites by number of visits, and non-Hispanic white share of total, 2011; numbers in thousands)

| | | non-Hispanic white | | |
	total	number	percent distribution	share of total
Total people	**231,376**	**156,482**	**100.0%**	**67.6%**
No visits	43,578	24,085	15.4	55.3
One visit	39,552	26,334	16.8	66.6
Two to three visits	59,226	41,175	26.3	69.5
Four to nine visits	55,721	40,349	25.8	72.4
10 or more visits	30,822	22,914	14.6	74.3

Note: Health care visits exclude overnight hospitalizations, visits to emergency rooms, home visits, dental visits, and telephone calls. Non-Hispanic whites are those who identify themselves as being white alone and not Hispanic. Numbers may not add to total because "unknown" is not shown.
Source: National Center for Health Statistics, Summary Health Statistics for U.S. Adults: National Health Interview Survey, 2011, Vital and Health Statistics, Series 10, No. 256, 2012, Internet site http://www.cdc.gov/nchs/nhis.htm; calculations by New Strategist

Table 6.30 Difficulties in Physical Functioning among Total People and Non-Hispanic Whites, 2011

(number of total people and non-Hispanic whites aged 18 or older, number with difficulties in physical functioning, percentage of non-Hispanic whites with difficulty, and non-Hispanic white share of total, by type of difficulty, 2011; numbers in thousands)

| | | non-Hispanic white | | |
	total	number	percent	share of total
TOTAL PEOPLE	**231,376**	**156,482**	**100.0%**	**67.6%**
Total with any physical difficulty	**37,368**	**26,775**	**15.3**	**71.7**
Walk quarter of a mile	17,597	12,726	7.2	72.3
Climb 10 steps without resting	12,887	8,887	5.0	69.0
Stand for two hours	22,369	16,168	9.2	72.3
Sit for two hours	7,724	5,233	3.0	67.7
Stoop, bend, or kneel	21,677	15,800	8.9	72.9
Reach over head	6,550	4,618	2.6	70.5
Grasp or handle small objects	4,329	3,073	1.7	71.0
Lift or carry 10 pounds	10,677	6,879	3.9	64.4
Push or pull large objects	15,998	10,970	6.2	68.6

Note: Respondents were classified as having difficulties if they responded "very difficult" or "can't do at all." Non-Hispanic whites are those who identify themselves as being white alone and not Hispanic.
Source: National Center for Health Statistics, Summary Health Statistics for U.S. Adults: National Health Interview Survey, 2011, Vital and Health Statistics, Series 10, No. 256, 2012, Internet site http://www.cdc.gov/nchs/nhis.htm; calculations by New Strategist

---

Table 6.31 AIDS Cases among Total People and Non-Hispanic Whites, through December 2009

(number of total AIDS cases diagnosed, number and percent distribution among non-Hispanic whites, and non-Hispanic white share of total, by sex, through December 2009)

| | | non-Hispanic white | | |
	total	number	percent distribution	share of total
Total diagnosed with AIDS	**982,498**	**426,102**	**100.0%**	**43.4%**
Males aged 13 or older	783,786	381,898	89.6	48.7
Females aged 13 or older	189,566	42,602	10.0	22.5
Children under age 13	9,144	1,602	0.4	17.5

Source: National Center for Health Statistics, Health United States 2011, Internet site http://www.cdc.gov/nchs/hus.htm; calculations by New Strategist

Table 6.32 Leading Causes of Death Among Non-Hispanic Whites, 2009

(number and percent distribution of deaths to non-Hispanic whites accounted for by the 10 leading causes of death among non-Hispanic whites, 2009)

		number	percent distribution
Total non-Hispanic white deaths		**1,944,606**	**100.0%**
1.	Diseases of the heart (1)	485,779	25.0
2.	Malignant neoplasms (cancer) (2)	457,189	23.5
3.	Cerebrovascular diseases (4)	122,605	6.3
4.	Chronic lower respiratory disease (3)	101,703	5.2
5.	Accidents (unintentional injuries) (5)	91,416	4.7
6.	Alzheimer's disease (6)	69,695	3.6
7.	Diabetes mellitus (7)	47,851	2.5
8.	Influenza and pneumonia (8)	42,752	2.2
9.	Nephritis, nephrotic syndrome, and nephrosis (9)	35,670	1.8
10.	Suicide (10)	30,813	1.6
All other causes		459,133	23.6

Note: Number in parentheses shows rank for all Americans if the cause of death is in top 10.
Source: National Center for Health Statistics, Deaths: Leading Causes for 2009, National Vital Statistics Report, Vol. 61, No. 7, 2012, Internet site http://www.cdc.gov/nchs/deaths.htm; calculations by New Strategist

Table 6.33 Life Expectancy of Total People and Non-Hispanic Whites by Sex, 2011

(average number of years of life remaining for total people and non-Hispanic whites at birth and age 65 by sex, and index of non-Hispanic white life expectancy to total, 2011)

	total people	non-Hispanic white	index, non-Hispanic white to total
AT BIRTH			
Total	**78.7 yrs.**	**78.8 yrs.**	**100**
Female	81.1	81.1	100
Male	76.3	76.4	100
AT AGE 65			
Total	**19.2**	**19.2**	**100**
Female	20.4	20.3	100
Male	17.8	17.8	100

Note: The index is calculated by dividing non-Hispanic white life expectancy by total life expectancy and multiplying by 100.
Source: National Center for Health Statistics, Deaths: Preliminary Data for 2011, National Vital Statistics Report, Vol. 61, No. 6, 2012, Internet site http://www.cdc.gov/nchs/deaths.htm; calculations by New Strategist

Nearly Three of Four Non-Hispanic White Households Own Their Home

Seventy-three percent of the nation's non-Hispanic white households own a home, a greater share than the 65 percent among all households. Homeownership surpasses 80 percent among non-Hispanic white married couples and among householders aged 55 or older. Homeownership among non-Hispanic whites does not vary much by region, ranging from a low of 69 percent in the West to a high of 76 percent in the Midwest and South.

The reported median value of the homes owned by non-Hispanic whites stood at $190,000, according to the 2006–10 American Community Survey, close to the $188,400 median of all homeowners. About two-thirds of non-Hispanic white homeowners have a mortgage, and among those who do median monthly housing costs are $1,500.

Only 10 percent of non-Hispanic whites moved between 2011 and 2012, a lower mobility rate than for Asians, blacks, or Hispanics. Among non-Hispanic whites who moved, the most common reason was the desire for a new or better home or apartment.

■ The homeownership rate of non-Hispanic whites fell 2.5 percentage points between 2004 and 2012 as the housing market collapsed during the Great Recession.

Non-Hispanic white homeownership is lowest in the West

(percent of non-Hispanic white households that own their home, by region, 2011)

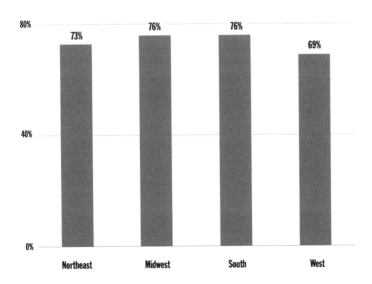

Table 6.34 Total and Non-Hispanic White Homeownership Rate, 2000 to 2012

(homeownership rate of total and non-Hispanic white households and index of non-Hispanic white to total, 2000 to 2012; percentage point change for selected years)

	total households	non-Hispanic white households	index, non-Hispanic white to total
2012	65.4%	73.5%	112
2011	66.1	73.8	112
2010	66.9	74.4	111
2009	67.4	74.8	111
2008	67.8	75.0	111
2007	68.1	75.2	110
2006	68.8	75.8	110
2005	68.9	75.8	110
2004	69.0	76.0	110
2003	68.3	75.4	110
2002	67.9	74.7	110
2001	67.8	74.3	110
2000	67.4	73.8	109

PERCENTAGE POINT CHANGE

2004 to 2012	–3.6	–2.5	–
2000 to 2012	–2.0	–0.3	–

Note: Non-Hispanic whites are those who identify themselves as white alone and not Hispanic. The index is calculated by dividing the non-Hispanic white homeownership rate by the total rate and multiplying by 100. "–" means not applicable.
Source: Bureau of the Census, Housing Vacancies and Homeownership, Internet site http://www.census.gov/housing/hvs/; calculations by New Strategist

Table 6.35 Non-Hispanic White and Other Homeownership Status by Age of Householder, 2011

(number and percent of non-Hispanic white and other households by age of householder and homeownership status, 2011; numbers in thousands)

	total	owner number	owner percent	renter number	renter percent
Total non-Hispanic white and other households	**86,371**	**62,899**	**72.8%**	**23,472**	**27.2%**
Under age 25	3,593	657	18.3	2,936	81.7
Aged 25 to 29	6,075	2,605	42.9	3,470	57.1
Aged 30 to 34	7,485	4,376	58.5	3,109	41.5
Aged 35 to 44	14,143	10,072	71.2	4,071	28.8
Aged 45 to 54	17,363	13,657	78.7	3,706	21.3
Aged 55 to 64	16,750	13,986	83.5	2,764	16.5
Aged 65 to 74	10,745	9,255	86.1	1,490	13.9
Aged 75 or older	10,216	8,290	81.1	1,926	18.9

Note: Non-Hispanic whites are those who identify themselves as white alone and not Hispanic. Others are Asians, American Indians, and people who identify themselves as being of two or more races.
Source: Bureau of the Census, American Housing Survey for the United States: 2011, Internet site http://www.census.gov/housing/ahs/index.html; calculations by New Strategist

Table 6.36 Total and Non-Hispanic White and Other Homeowners by Age of Householder, 2011

(number of total homeowners, number and percent distribution of non-Hispanic white and other homeowners, and non-Hispanic white and other share of total, by age of householder, 2011; numbers in thousands)

	total	non-Hispanic white and other number	non-Hispanic white and other percent distribution	non-Hispanic white and other share of total
Total homeowners	**76,091**	**62,899**	**100.0%**	**82.7%**
Under age 25	830	657	1.0	79.2
Aged 25 to 29	3,136	2,605	4.1	83.1
Aged 30 to 34	5,391	4,376	7.0	81.2
Aged 35 to 44	12,847	10,072	16.0	78.4
Aged 45 to 54	16,994	13,657	21.7	80.4
Aged 55 to 64	16,643	13,986	22.2	84.0
Aged 65 to 74	10,802	9,255	14.7	85.7
Aged 75 or older	9,448	8,290	13.2	87.7

Note: Non-Hispanic whites are those who identify themselves as white alone and not Hispanic. Others are Asians, American Indians, and people who identify themselves as being of two or more races.
Source: Bureau of the Census, American Housing Survey for the United States: 2011, Internet site http://www.census.gov/housing/ahs/index.html; calculations by New Strategist

Table 6.37 Total and Non-Hispanic White and Other Renters by Age of Householder, 2011

(number of total renters, number and percent distribution of non-Hispanic white and other renters, and non-Hispanic white and other share of total, by age of householder, 2011; numbers in thousands)

| | | non-Hispanic white and other | | |
	total	number	percent distribution	share of total
Total renters	**38,816**	**23,472**	**100.0%**	**60.5%**
Under age 25	4,568	2,936	12.5	64.3
Aged 25 to 29	5,610	3,470	14.8	61.9
Aged 30 to 34	5,343	3,109	13.2	58.2
Aged 35 to 44	7,600	4,071	17.3	53.6
Aged 45 to 54	6,422	3,706	15.8	57.7
Aged 55 to 64	4,466	2,764	11.8	61.9
Aged 65 to 74	2,366	1,490	6.3	63.0
Aged 75 or older	2,442	1,926	8.2	78.9

Note: Non-Hispanic whites are those who identify themselves as white alone and not Hispanic. Others are Asians, American Indians, and people who identify themselves as being of two or more races.
Source: Bureau of the Census, American Housing Survey for the United States: 2011, Internet site http://www.census.gov/housing/ahs/index.html; calculations by New Strategist

Table 6.38 Non-Hispanic White Homeownership Status by Household Type, 2010

(number and percent of non-Hispanic white households by household type and homeownership status, 2010; numbers in thousands)

| | | owner | | renter | |
	total	number	percent	number	percent
Total non-Hispanic white households	**82,333**	**59,484**	**72.2%**	**22,849**	**27.8%**
Family households	52,977	43,058	81.3	9,919	18.7
Married couples	42,088	36,460	86.6	5,627	13.4
Female-headed family, no spouse present	7,597	4,501	59.2	3,096	40.8
Male-headed family, no spouse present	3,293	2,097	63.7	1,195	36.3
Nonfamily households	29,356	16,425	56.0	12,930	44.0
Female householder	15,736	9,200	58.5	6,536	41.5
Living alone	13,210	8,038	60.8	5,172	39.2
Male householder	13,619	7,225	53.0	6,394	47.0
Living alone	10,313	5,651	54.8	4,663	45.2

Note: Non-Hispanic whites are those who identify themselves as white alone and not Hispanic.
Source: Bureau of the Census, 2010 Census, Internet site http://factfinder2.census.gov/faces/nav/jsf/pages/index.xhtml; calculations by New Strategist

Table 6.39 Total and Non-Hispanic White Homeowners by Household Type, 2010

(number of total homeowners, number and percent distribution of non-Hispanic white homeowners, and non-Hispanic white share of total, by household type, 2010; numbers in thousands)

| | total | non-Hispanic white | | |
		number	percent distribution	share of total
Total homeowners	**75,986**	**59,484**	**100.0%**	**78.3%**
Family households	56,206	43,058	72.4	76.6
Married couples	45,801	36,460	61.3	79.6
Female-headed family, no spouse present	7,278	4,501	7.6	61.8
Male-headed family, no spouse present	3,127	2,097	3.5	67.1
Nonfamily households	19,780	16,425	27.6	83.0
Female householder	11,053	9,200	15.5	83.2
Living alone	9,625	8,038	13.5	83.5
Male householder	8,727	7,225	12.1	82.8
Living alone	6,828	5,651	9.5	82.8

Note: Non-Hispanic whites are those who identify themselves as white alone and not Hispanic.
Source: Bureau of the Census, 2010 Census, Internet site http://factfinder2.census.gov/faces/nav/jsf/pages/index.xhtml; calculations by New Strategist

Table 6.40 Total and Non-Hispanic White Renters by Household Type, 2010

(number of total renters, number and percent distribution of non-Hispanic white renters, and non-Hispanic white share of total, by household type, 2010; numbers in thousands)

	total	non-Hispanic white		
		number	percent distribution	share of total
Total renters	**40,730**	**22,849**	**100.0%**	**56.1%**
Family households	21,332	9,919	43.4	46.5
Married couples	10,710	5,627	24.6	52.5
Female-headed family, no spouse present	7,972	3,096	13.6	38.8
Male-headed family, no spouse present	2,651	1,195	5.2	45.1
Nonfamily households	19,398	12,930	56.6	66.7
Female householder	9,666	6,536	28.6	67.6
Living alone	7,673	5,172	22.6	67.4
Male householder	9,732	6,394	28.0	65.7
Living alone	7,078	4,663	20.4	65.9

Note: Non-Hispanic whites are those who identify themselves as white alone and not Hispanic.
Source: Bureau of the Census, 2010 Census, Internet site http://factfinder2.census.gov/faces/nav/jsf/pages/index.xhtml; calculations by New Strategist

Table 6.41 Non-Hispanic White Homeownership Status by Region, 2011

(number and percent of non-Hispanic white households by homeownership status and region, 2011; numbers in thousands)

		owners		renters	
	total	number	share of total	number	share of total
Total non-Hispanic white households	**80,190**	**59,274**	**73.9%**	**20,916**	**26.1%**
Northeast	15,435	11,291	73.2	4,144	26.8
Midwest	20,962	15,844	75.6	5,118	24.4
South	27,884	21,198	76.0	6,686	24.0
West	15,910	10,942	68.8	4,968	31.2

Note: Non-Hispanic whites are those who identify themselves as white alone and not Hispanic.
Source: Bureau of the Census, American Housing Survey for the United States: 2011, Internet site http://www.census.gov/housing/ahs/index.html; calculations by New Strategist

Table 6.42 Total and Non-Hispanic White Homeowners by Region, 2011

(number of total homeowners, number and percent distribution of non-Hispanic white homeowners, and non-Hispanic white share of total, by region, 2011; numbers in thousands)

		non-Hispanic white		
	total	number	percent distribution	share of total
Total homeowners	**76,091**	**59,274**	**100.0%**	**77.9%**
Northeast	13,480	11,291	19.0	83.8
Midwest	18,032	15,844	26.7	87.9
South	29,119	21,198	35.8	72.8
West	15,460	10,942	18.5	70.8

Note: Non-Hispanic whites are those who identify themselves as white alone and not Hispanic.
Source: Bureau of the Census, American Housing Survey for the United States: 2011, Internet site http://www.census.gov/housing/ahs/index.html; calculations by New Strategist

Table 6.43 Total and Non-Hispanic White Renters by Region, 2011

(number of total renters, number and percent distribution of non-Hispanic white renters, and non-Hispanic white share of total, by region, 2011; numbers in thousands)

| | total | non-Hispanic white | | |
		number	percent distribution	share of total
Total renters	**38,816**	**20,916**	**100.0%**	**53.9%**
Northeast	7,585	4,144	19.8	54.6
Midwest	7,650	5,118	24.5	66.9
South	13,465	6,686	32.0	49.7
West	10,115	4,968	23.8	49.1

Note: Non-Hispanic whites are those who identify themselves as white alone and not Hispanic.
Source: Bureau of the Census, American Housing Survey for the United States: 2011, Internet site http://www.census.gov/housing/ahs/index.html; calculations by New Strategist

Table 6.44 Characteristics of Total and Non-Hispanic White Occupied Housing Units, 2006–10

(number of total and non-Hispanic white occupied housing units, and percent distribution by selected characteristics, 2006–10; numbers in thousands)

	total		non-Hispanic white	
	number	percent distribution	number	percent distribution
TOTAL OCCUPIED HOUSING UNITS	**114,236**	**100.0%**	**81,236**	**100.0%**
Year householder moved into unit				
Total households	**114,236**	**100.0**	**81,236**	**100.0**
2005 or later	39,766	34.8	25,273	31.1
2000 to 2004	26,517	23.2	18,500	22.8
1990 to 1999	23,883	20.9	18,059	22.2
1980 to 1989	10,804	9.5	8,581	10.6
1970 to 1979	7,147	6.3	5,678	7.0
Before 1970	6,120	5.4	5,144	6.3
Vehicles available				
Total households	**114,236**	**100.0**	**81,236**	**100.0**
None	10,113	8.9	5,087	6.3
One or more	104,123	91.1	76,148	93.7
House heating fuel				
Total households	**114,236**	**100.0**	**81,236**	**100.0**
Utility gas	57,018	49.9	40,412	49.7
Bottled gas	6,146	5.4	5,208	6.4
Electricity	39,066	34.2	26,137	32.2
Fuel oil or kerosene	8,073	7.1	6,533	8.0
Coal or coke	135	0.1	126	0.2
Wood	2,250	2.0	2,019	2.5
Solar energy	38	0.0	25	0.0
Other fuel	483	0.4	389	0.5
No heating fuel used	1,025	0.9	385	0.5
TOTAL OWNER-OCCUPIED HOMES	**76,090**	**100.0**	**59,782**	**100.0**
Housing units with a mortgage	51,697	67.9	39,383	65.9
Housing units without a mortgage	24,393	32.1	20,399	34.1
Median value of home	$188,400	–	$190,000	–
Median monthly owner costs with a mortgage	1,524	–	1,500	–
Median monthly owner costs without a mortgage	431	–	435	–
TOTAL RENTER-OCCUPIED HOMES	**38,146**	**100.0**	**21,454**	**100.0**
Occupied units paying rent	35,274	92.5	19,926	92.9
Median rent	$841	–	$833	–

Note: Non-Hispanic whites are those who identify themselves as white alone and not Hispanic. "–" means not applicable.
Source: Bureau of the Census, 2006–10 American Community Survey, Internet site http://factfinder2.census.gov/faces/nav/jsf/pages/index.xhtml; calculations by New Strategist

Table 6.45 Geographic Mobility of Non-Hispanic Whites by Age, 2011–12

(total number of non-Hispanic whites aged 1 or older, and number and percent who moved between March 2011 and March 2012, by age and type of move; numbers in thousands)

	total	same house (nonmovers)	total movers	same county	different county, same state	different state total	same region	different region	movers from abroad
Total non-Hispanic whites	193,189	173,443	19,746	12,107	4,172	3,103	1,339	1,764	364
Aged 1 to 4	8,056	6,753	1,303	823	260	203	83	120	18
Aged 5 to 9	10,659	9,410	1,249	832	243	164	70	94	9
Aged 10 to 14	11,260	10,171	1,089	712	208	158	69	89	11
Aged 15 to 17	7,209	6,638	571	377	110	78	28	50	7
Aged 18 to 19	4,634	4,024	610	378	163	59	21	38	11
Aged 20 to 24	12,370	9,160	3,210	1,996	643	505	219	286	66
Aged 25 to 29	12,110	9,188	2,922	1,726	573	540	276	264	83
Aged 30 to 34	11,823	9,848	1,975	1,219	412	292	130	162	52
Aged 35 to 39	11,182	9,795	1,387	892	278	201	77	124	16
Aged 40 to 44	13,018	11,896	1,122	665	271	159	54	105	27
Aged 45 to 49	14,247	13,227	1,020	631	217	159	68	91	13
Aged 50 to 54	15,649	14,718	931	523	215	186	74	112	8
Aged 55 to 59	14,876	14,116	760	461	171	104	47	57	24
Aged 60 to 61	5,478	5,231	247	143	58	41	13	28	5
Aged 62 to 64	7,714	7,386	328	175	82	70	23	47	0
Aged 65 or older	32,905	31,883	1,022	553	269	183	86	97	15

PERCENT DISTRIBUTION BY MOBILITY STATUS

	total	same house (nonmovers)	total movers	same county	different county, same state	different state total	same region	different region	movers from abroad
Total non-Hispanic whites	100.0%	89.8%	10.2%	6.3%	2.2%	1.6%	0.7%	0.9%	0.2%
Aged 1 to 4	100.0	83.8	16.2	10.2	3.2	2.5	1.0	1.5	0.2
Aged 5 to 9	100.0	88.3	11.7	7.8	2.3	1.5	0.7	0.9	0.1
Aged 10 to 14	100.0	90.3	9.7	6.3	1.8	1.4	0.6	0.8	0.1
Aged 15 to 17	100.0	92.1	7.9	5.2	1.5	1.1	0.4	0.7	0.1
Aged 18 to 19	100.0	86.8	13.2	8.2	3.5	1.3	0.5	0.8	0.2
Aged 20 to 24	100.0	74.1	25.9	16.1	5.2	4.1	1.8	2.3	0.5
Aged 25 to 29	100.0	75.9	24.1	14.3	4.7	4.5	2.3	2.2	0.7
Aged 30 to 34	100.0	83.3	16.7	10.3	3.5	2.5	1.1	1.4	0.4
Aged 35 to 39	100.0	87.6	12.4	8.0	2.5	1.8	0.7	1.1	0.1
Aged 40 to 44	100.0	91.4	8.6	5.1	2.1	1.2	0.4	0.8	0.2
Aged 45 to 49	100.0	92.8	7.2	4.4	1.5	1.1	0.5	0.6	0.1
Aged 50 to 54	100.0	94.1	5.9	3.3	1.4	1.2	0.5	0.7	0.1
Aged 55 to 59	100.0	94.9	5.1	3.1	1.1	0.7	0.3	0.4	0.2
Aged 60 to 61	100.0	95.5	4.5	2.6	1.1	0.7	0.2	0.5	0.1
Aged 62 to 64	100.0	95.7	4.3	2.3	1.1	0.9	0.3	0.6	0.0
Aged 65 or older	100.0	96.9	3.1	1.7	0.8	0.6	0.3	0.3	0.0

Note: Non-Hispanic whites are those who identify themselves as white alone and not Hispanic.
Source: Bureau of the Census, Geographic Mobility: 2011 to 2012, Internet site http://www.census.gov/hhes/migration/data/cps/cps2012.html; calculations by New Strategist

Table 6.46 Reasons for Moving among Non-Hispanic White Movers, 2011–12

(number and percent distribution of non-Hispanic white movers by main reason for move, 2011–12; numbers in thousands)

	number	percent distribution
Total non-Hispanic white movers	**19,746**	**100.0%**
FAMILY REASONS	**5,916**	**30.0**
Change in marital status	95	4.2
To establish own household	151	6.7
Other family reason	248	10.9
EMPLOYMENT REASONS	**4,197**	**21.3**
New job or job transfer	2,183	11.1
To look for work or lost job	356	1.8
To be closer to work, easier commute	1,121	5.7
Retired	125	0.6
Other job-related reason	412	2.1
HOUSING REASONS	**9,170**	**46.4**
Wanted own home, not rent	1,034	5.2
Wanted new or better home/apartment	2,864	14.5
Wanted better neighborhood, less crime	602	3.0
Wanted cheaper housing	1,426	7.2
Foreclosure, eviction	357	1.8
Other housing reason	2,887	14.6
OTHER REASONS	**462**	**2.3**
To attend or leave college	123	0.6
Change of climate	11	0.1
Health reasons	81	0.4
Natural disaster	26	0.1
Other reason	221	1.1

Note: Non-Hispanic whites are those who identify themselves as white alone and not Hispanic.
Source: Bureau of the Census, Geographic Mobility: 2011 to 2012, Internet site http://www.census.gov/hhes/migration/data/cps/cps2012.html; calculations by New Strategist

Non-Hispanic Whites Have Above-Average Incomes

The $55,412 median income of non-Hispanic white households in 2011 was 11 percent greater than the all-household average. Between 2000 and 2011, the median income of non-Hispanic white households fell 7.0 percent, less than the 8.7 percent loss for all households during those years.

The median earnings of non-Hispanic white men who work full-time fell 2.9 percent between 2000 and 2011, after adjusting for inflation, while their female counterparts experienced a 3.5 percent increase. Even during the 2007 to 2011 time period, when many workers lost ground, non-Hispanic white women with full-time jobs saw their earnings grow.

Non-Hispanic whites are less likely to be poor than Asians, blacks, or Hispanics. The poverty rate of non-Hispanic white couples stood at 4.1 percent in 2011. Among non-Hispanic white female-headed families, the poverty rate was a higher 23.4 percent.

■ The median income of non-Hispanic white households did not decline as much as the incomes of Asian, black, and Hispanic households because non-Hispanic whites are older, on average, and were less affected by the unemployment of the Great Recession.

Non-Hispanic white household income fell less than average between 2000 and 2011

(percent change in total and non-Hispanic white median household income, 2000 to 2011; in 2011 dollars)

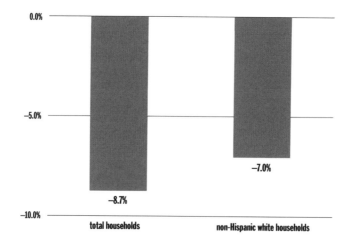

Table 6.47 Median Income of Total and Non-Hispanic White Households, 1990 to 2011

(median income of total and non-Hispanic white households, and index of non-Hispanic white to total, 1990 to 2011; percent change in median for selected years; in 2011 dollars)

	total households	non-Hispanic white households	index, non-Hispanic white to total
2011	$50,054	$55,412	111
2010	50,830	56,178	111
2009	52,195	57,106	109
2008	52,546	58,006	110
2007	54,489	59,573	109
2006	53,768	58,478	109
2005	53,371	58,507	110
2004	52,788	58,237	110
2003	52,973	58,426	110
2002	53,019	58,634	111
2001	53,646	58,825	110
2000	54,841	59,586	109
1999	54,932	59,604	109
1998	53,582	58,480	109
1997	51,704	56,695	110
1996	50,661	55,365	109
1995	49,935	54,480	109
1994	48,418	52,713	109
1993	47,884	52,377	109
1992	48,117	52,286	109
1991	48,516	52,054	107
1990	49,950	53,290	107
Percent change			
2007 to 2011	−8.1%	−7.0%	–
2000 to 2011	−8.7	−7.0	–
1990 to 2011	0.2	4.0	–

Note: Beginning in 2002, non-Hispanic whites are those who identify themselves as white alone and not Hispanic. The index is calculated by dividing the non-Hispanic white median by the total median and multiplying by 100. "–" means not applicable.
Source: Bureau of the Census, Current Population Surveys, Annual Social and Economic Supplement, Internet site http://www .census.gov/hhes/www/income/data/historical/household/index.html; calculations by New Strategist

Table 6.48 Non-Hispanic White Household Income by Age of Householder, 2011

(number and percent distribution of non-Hispanic white households by household income and age of householder, 2011; households in thousands as of 2012)

	total	15 to 24	25 to 34	35 to 44	45 to 54	55 to 64	65 or older total	65 to 74	75 or older
Non-Hispanic white households	**83,573**	**3,367**	**11,958**	**13,065**	**16,589**	**16,886**	**21,708**	**11,409**	**10,299**
Under $5,000	2,168	266	325	253	457	512	355	129	226
$5,000 to $9,999	2,589	210	290	243	423	540	883	358	525
$10,000 to $14,999	4,324	271	362	338	539	715	2,099	731	1,369
$15,000 to $19,999	4,306	218	426	352	457	661	2,192	789	1,403
$20,000 to $24,999	4,491	318	560	429	554	678	1,951	801	1,150
$25,000 to $29,999	4,281	226	544	451	533	670	1,857	876	982
$30,000 to $34,999	4,339	283	658	532	574	760	1,532	713	818
$35,000 to $39,999	4,065	201	623	486	610	801	1,343	731	612
$40,000 to $44,999	3,959	233	627	536	671	814	1,078	598	480
$45,000 to $49,999	3,395	157	565	504	627	662	879	485	395
$50,000 to $54,999	3,576	114	649	558	633	717	904	568	336
$55,000 to $59,999	3,024	135	559	479	605	551	694	459	236
$60,000 to $64,999	3,140	128	592	551	656	605	608	401	207
$65,000 to $69,999	2,787	114	457	488	507	616	604	391	213
$70,000 to $74,999	2,643	97	433	516	607	545	445	276	169
$75,000 to $79,999	2,603	42	478	479	531	571	501	355	146
$80,000 to $84,999	2,223	44	396	441	514	457	370	233	137
$85,000 to $89,999	1,935	32	345	394	439	419	306	223	83
$90,000 to $94,999	1,942	29	285	367	514	446	301	216	84
$95,000 to $99,999	1,682	33	275	327	427	329	290	209	81
$100,000 to $124,999	7,016	82	1,078	1,580	1,771	1,500	1,005	744	263
$125,000 to $149,999	4,121	45	593	861	1,135	1,001	486	350	136
$150,000 to $174,999	3,110	33	328	670	927	762	387	291	95
$175,000 to $199,999	1,670	30	169	356	521	421	171	122	50
$200,000 or more	4,187	25	339	872	1,356	1,133	463	362	101
Median income	$55,412	$32,312	$57,501	$72,371	$73,159	$62,497	$34,944	$44,839	$27,306

PERCENT DISTRIBUTION

	total	15 to 24	25 to 34	35 to 44	45 to 54	55 to 64	65 or older total	65 to 74	75 or older
Non-Hispanic white households	100.0%	100.0%	100.0%	100.0%	100.0%	100.0%	100.0%	100.0%	100.0%
Under $25,000	21.4	38.1	16.4	12.4	14.6	18.4	34.5	24.6	45.4
$25,000 to $49,999	24.0	32.7	25.2	19.2	18.2	22.0	30.8	29.8	31.9
$50,000 to $74,999	18.2	17.5	22.5	19.8	18.1	18.0	15.0	18.4	11.3
$75,000 to $99,999	12.4	5.3	14.9	15.4	14.6	13.2	8.1	10.8	5.2
$100,000 or more	24.1	6.4	21.0	33.2	34.4	28.5	11.6	16.4	6.3

Note: Non-Hispanic whites are those who identify themselves as white alone and not Hispanic.
Source: Bureau of the Census, 2012 Current Population Survey, Internet site http://www.census.gov/hhes/www/income/data/incpovhlth/2011/dtables.html; calculations by New Strategist

Table 6.49 Non-Hispanic White Household Income by Household Type, 2011

(number and percent distribution of non-Hispanic white households by household income and household type, 2011; households in thousands as of 2012)

| | total | family households | | | nonfamily households | | | |
| | | married couples | female hh, no spouse present | male hh, no spouse present | female householder | | male householder | |
					total	living alone	total	living alone
Non-Hispanic white households	83,573	43,376	7,539	3,231	15,635	13,395	13,792	10,629
Under $5,000	2,168	435	349	63	715	671	606	542
$5,000 to $9,999	2,589	301	351	37	1,274	1,226	627	571
$10,000 to $14,999	4,324	552	463	137	2,119	2,043	1,054	976
$15,000 to $19,999	4,306	884	486	147	1,855	1,792	934	849
$20,000 to $24,999	4,491	1,312	553	201	1,367	1,243	1,058	908
$25,000 to $29,999	4,281	1,497	544	157	1,105	1,001	978	823
$30,000 to $34,999	4,339	1,700	497	236	935	847	971	834
$35,000 to $39,999	4,065	1,751	491	167	882	774	773	638
$40,000 to $44,999	3,959	1,811	478	165	765	636	739	593
$45,000 to $49,999	3,395	1,648	363	160	639	493	585	459
$50,000 to $54,999	3,576	1,784	384	163	603	470	642	492
$55,000 to $59,999	3,024	1,628	298	189	392	294	517	364
$60,000 to $64,999	3,140	1,736	285	159	433	343	527	391
$65,000 to $69,999	2,787	1,633	235	142	378	303	398	251
$70,000 to $74,999	2,643	1,605	213	131	313	209	382	252
$75,000 to $79,999	2,603	1,810	193	89	246	163	265	175
$80,000 to $84,999	2,223	1,504	151	94	155	111	318	192
$85,000 to $89,999	1,935	1,328	146	73	152	101	237	161
$90,000 to $94,999	1,942	1,400	115	61	139	91	226	124
$95,000 to $99,999	1,682	1,196	101	83	149	73	152	83
$100,000 to $124,999	7,016	5,345	357	223	411	220	680	385
$125,000 to $149,999	4,121	3,284	152	145	207	96	333	152
$150,000 to $174,999	3,110	2,413	127	94	176	93	301	187
$175,000 to $199,999	1,668	1,350	81	28	68	30	142	49
$200,000 or more	4,187	3,470	123	87	158	72	349	180
Median income	$55,412	$78,546	$40,317	$54,243	$26,791	$23,778	$39,027	$33,199

PERCENT DISTRIBUTION

	total	married couples	female hh, no spouse present	male hh, no spouse present	female householder total	living alone	male householder total	living alone
Non-Hispanic white households	100.0%	100.0%	100.0%	100.0%	100.0%	100.0%	100.0%	100.0%
Under $25,000	21.4	8.0	29.2	18.1	46.9	52.1	31.0	36.2
$25,000 to $49,999	24.0	19.4	31.5	27.4	27.7	28.0	29.3	31.5
$50,000 to $74,999	18.2	19.3	18.8	24.3	13.5	12.1	17.9	16.5
$75,000 to $99,999	12.4	16.7	9.4	12.4	5.4	4.0	8.7	6.9
$100,000 or more	24.1	36.6	11.1	17.9	6.5	3.8	13.1	9.0

Note: Non-Hispanic whites are those who identify themselves as white alone and not Hispanic. "hh" stands for householder. Source: Bureau of the Census, 2012 Current Population Survey, Internet site http://www.census.gov/hhes/www/income/data/ incpovhlth/2011/dtables.html; calculations by New Strategist

Table 6.50 Income of Non-Hispanic White Men by Age, 2011

(number and percent distribution of non-Hispanic white men aged 15 or older by income and age, 2011; median income of men with income and of men working full-time, year-round; percent working full-time, year-round; men in thousands as of 2012)

	total	under 25	25 to 34	35 to 44	45 to 54	55 to 64	65 or older
TOTAL NON-HISPANIC WHITE MEN	**79,468**	**12,264**	**11,994**	**12,094**	**14,742**	**13,644**	**14,731**
Without income	**6,566**	**4,187**	**683**	**465**	**598**	**444**	**189**
With income	**72,902**	**8,077**	**11,310**	**11,629**	**14,144**	**13,200**	**14,542**
Under $5,000	4,410	2,444	499	323	375	530	240
$5,000 to $9,999	3,913	1,418	537	359	490	551	558
$10,000 to $14,999	5,229	1,009	604	478	723	817	1,598
$15,000 to $19,999	5,306	814	701	477	592	721	2,001
$20,000 to $24,999	5,251	756	858	619	685	746	1,586
$25,000 to $29,999	4,612	454	882	551	647	698	1,380
$30,000 to $34,999	4,697	389	1,005	682	710	779	1,132
$35,000 to $39,999	4,147	241	822	682	853	714	834
$40,000 to $44,999	4,021	174	851	717	810	741	728
$45,000 to $49,999	3,360	91	669	685	753	570	592
$50,000 to $54,999	3,636	75	730	695	787	727	623
$55,000 to $59,999	2,417	37	438	508	535	504	396
$60,000 to $64,999	2,780	65	482	609	686	572	365
$65,000 to $69,999	1,855	14	335	409	393	448	255
$70,000 to $74,999	1,900	9	290	412	491	433	265
$75,000 to $79,999	1,631	6	238	374	414	373	226
$80,000 to $84,999	1,636	20	221	358	484	362	192
$85,000 to $89,999	1,034	3	142	242	268	231	149
$90,000 to $94,999	1,075	8	158	237	303	220	149
$95,000 to $99,999	737	6	98	143	189	187	114
$100,000 or more	9,254	42	750	2,070	2,955	2,278	1,160
MEDIAN INCOME							
Men with income	$38,148	$10,606	$37,513	$51,106	$51,903	$47,179	$29,658
Working full-time	55,763	25,673	45,931	60,083	62,402	64,856	68,104
Percent full-time	50.1%	18.2%	67.7%	75.1%	71.8%	56.4%	14.1%
PERCENT DISTRIBUTION TOTAL NON-HISPANIC WHITE MEN	**100.0%**	**100.0%**	**100.0%**	**100.0%**	**100.0%**	**100.0%**	**100.0%**
Without income	**8.3**	**34.1**	**5.7**	**3.8**	**4.1**	**3.3**	**1.3**
With income	**91.7**	**65.9**	**94.3**	**96.2**	**95.9**	**96.7**	**98.7**
Under $15,000	17.1	39.7	13.7	9.6	10.8	13.9	16.3
$15,000 to $24,999	13.3	12.8	13.0	9.1	8.7	10.8	24.3
$25,000 to $34,999	11.7	6.9	15.7	10.2	9.2	10.8	17.1
$35,000 to $49,999	14.5	4.1	19.5	17.2	16.4	14.8	14.6
$50,000 to $74,999	15.8	1.6	19.0	21.8	19.6	19.7	12.9
$75,000 or more	19.3	0.7	13.4	28.3	31.3	26.8	13.5

Note: Non-Hispanic whites are those who identify themselves as white alone and not Hispanic.
Source: Bureau of the Census, 2012 Current Population Survey Annual Social and Economic Supplement, Internet site http://www.census.gov/hhes/www/cpstables/032012/perinc/toc.htm; calculations by New Strategist

Table 6.51 Income of Non-Hispanic White Women by Age, 2011

(number and percent distribution of non-Hispanic white women aged 15 or older by income and age, 2011; median income of women with income and of women working full-time, year-round; percent working full-time, year-round; women in thousands as of 2012)

	total	under 25	25 to 34	35 to 44	45 to 54	55 to 64	65 or older
TOTAL NON-HISPANIC WHITE WOMEN	**83,747**	**11,950**	**11,939**	**12,105**	**15,154**	**14,425**	**18,173**
Without income	**9,541**	**4,058**	**1,325**	**1,219**	**1,382**	**1,114**	**444**
With income	**74,206**	**7,891**	**10,614**	**10,887**	**13,773**	**13,311**	**17,730**
Under $5,000	8,196	2,553	1,152	1,174	1,305	1,256	756
$5,000 to $9,999	9,048	1,623	842	735	1,109	1,293	3,446
$10,000 to $14,999	9,448	1,194	880	893	1,133	1,382	3,965
$15,000 to $19,999	7,129	770	843	753	1,044	1,073	2,646
$20,000 to $24,999	6,083	629	887	817	1,019	1,057	1,675
$25,000 to $29,999	5,042	360	831	762	1,009	879	1,202
$30,000 to $34,999	4,716	242	1,036	777	923	882	856
$35,000 to $39,999	4,084	195	780	760	879	851	620
$40,000 to $44,999	3,479	114	693	667	785	694	526
$45,000 to $49,999	2,637	52	542	503	656	497	389
$50,000 to $54,999	2,669	47	472	524	659	615	353
$55,000 to $59,999	1,610	24	301	350	442	305	187
$60,000 to $64,999	1,742	24	284	355	451	437	190
$65,000 to $69,999	1,307	15	198	312	310	320	152
$70,000 to $74,999	1,078	18	185	238	293	232	112
$75,000 to $79,999	860	6	126	183	252	176	118
$80,000 to $84,999	758	6	116	167	216	185	68
$85,000 to $89,999	491	2	57	94	145	145	48
$90,000 to $94,999	539	6	47	102	155	177	52
$95,000 to $99,999	350	10	38	67	99	80	56
$100,000 or more	2,941	2	305	653	892	776	312
MEDIAN INCOME							
Women with income	$22,226	$9,225	$28,790	$31,459	$31,095	$27,782	$16,194
Working full-time	41,373	23,153	38,421	44,499	44,470	44,098	46,009
Percent full-time	34.4%	13.5%	50.1%	50.5%	52.4%	41.4%	6.6%
PERCENT DISTRIBUTION							
TOTAL NON-HISPANIC WHITE WOMEN	**100.0%**	**100.0%**	**100.0%**	**100.0%**	**100.0%**	**100.0%**	**100.0%**
Without income	**11.4**	**34.0**	**11.1**	**10.1**	**9.1**	**7.7**	**2.4**
With income	**88.6**	**66.0**	**88.9**	**89.9**	**90.9**	**92.3**	**97.6**
Under $15,000	31.9	44.9	24.1	23.2	23.4	27.3	44.9
$15,000 to $24,999	15.8	11.7	14.5	13.0	13.6	14.8	23.8
$25,000 to $34,999	11.7	5.0	15.6	12.7	12.7	12.2	11.3
$35,000 to $49,999	12.2	3.0	16.9	15.9	15.3	14.2	8.4
$50,000 to $74,999	10.0	1.1	12.1	14.7	14.2	13.2	5.5
$75,000 or more	7.1	0.3	5.8	10.5	11.6	10.7	3.6

Note: Non-Hispanic whites are those who identify themselves as white alone and not Hispanic.
Source: Bureau of the Census, 2012 Current Population Survey Annual Social and Economic Supplement, Internet site http://www.census.gov/hhes/www/cpstables/032012/perinc/toc.htm; calculations by New Strategist

Table 6.52 Median Earnings of Non-Hispanic Whites Working Full-Time by Sex, 1990 to 2011

(median earnings of non-Hispanic whites working full-time, year-round by sex; index of non-Hispanic white to total population median earnings, and non-Hispanic white women's earnings as a percent of non-Hispanic white men's earnings, 1990 to 2011; percent change in earnings for selected years; in 2011 dollars)

	non-Hispanic white men		non-Hispanic white women		women's earnings as a percent of men's earnings
	earnings	index	earnings	index	
2011	$52,318	109	$40,335	109	77.1%
2010	53,599	108	41,558	109	77.5
2009	53,902	109	40,405	106	75.0
2008	53,529	111	39,056	105	73.0
2007	54,594	112	39,858	105	73.0
2006	54,013	115	39,861	110	73.8
2005	53,499	112	39,302	107	73.5
2004	54,226	112	38,729	104	71.4
2003	54,732	110	39,201	104	71.6
2002	53,106	108	39,258	104	73.9
2001	52,951	109	39,129	105	73.9
2000	53,872	111	38,969	109	72.3
1999	54,595	111	37,030	104	67.8
1998	51,998	107	37,039	104	71.2
1997	51,134	109	36,209	104	70.8
1996	50,590	110	35,528	105	70.2
1995	50,413	109	34,674	105	68.8
1994	48,981	106	34,810	104	71.1
1993	49,002	105	34,307	103	70.0
1992	49,821	105	34,387	102	69.0
1991	49,999	106	33,970	103	67.9
1990	50,267	109	33,959	103	67.6

	percent change		percent change		percentage point change
2007 to 2011	−4.2%	–	1.2%	–	4.1
2000 to 2011	−2.9	–	3.5	–	4.8
1990 to 2011	4.1	–	18.8	–	9.5

Note: Beginning in 2002, non-Hispanic whites are those who identify themselves as white alone and not Hispanic. The non-Hispanic white/total indexes are calculated by dividing the median earnings of non-Hispanic white men and women by the median earnings of total men and women and multiplying by 100. "–" means not applicable.
Source: Bureau of the Census, Current Population Survey, Historical Tables, Internet site http://www.census.gov/hhes/www/income/data/historical/people/; calculations by New Strategist

Table 6.53 Median Earnings of Non-Hispanic Whites Working Full-Time by Education and Sex, 2011

(median earnings of non-Hispanic whites aged 25 or older working full-time, year-round, by educational attainment and sex, and non-Hispanic white women's earnings as a percent of non-Hispanic white men's earnings, 2011)

	men	women	women's earnings as a percent of men's earnings
Total non-Hispanic whites	**$53,380**	**$41,058**	**76.9%**
Less than 9th grade	30,740	17,857	58.1
9th to 12th grade, no diploma	32,130	22,495	70.0
High school graduate	42,194	30,840	73.1
Some college, no degree	49,581	34,468	69.5
Associate's degree	51,430	40,485	78.7
Bachelor's degree or more	75,329	52,465	69.6
Bachelor's degree	66,810	48,762	73.0
Master's degree	81,386	59,630	73.3
Professional degree	120,176	76,832	63.9
Doctoral degree	101,606	80,065	78.8

Note: Non-Hispanic whites are those who identify themselves as white alone and not Hispanic.
Source: Bureau of the Census, 2012 Current Population Survey Annual Social and Economic Supplement, Internet site http://www.census.gov/hhes/www/cpstables/032012/perinc/toc.htm; calculations by New Strategist

Table 6.54 Poverty Status of Non-Hispanic White Married Couples, 1990 to 2011

(total number of non-Hispanic white married couples, and number and percent below poverty level by presence of children under age 18 at home, 1990 to 2011; percent change in numbers and percentage point change in rates for selected years; families in thousands as of March the following year)

Total non-Hispanic white married couples	total	in poverty	
		number	percent
2011	43,382	1,787	4.1%
2010	43,508	1,802	4.1
2009	43,966	1,697	3.9
2008	44,281	1,545	3.5
2007	43,758	1,388	3.2
2006	44,343	1,436	3.2
2005	44,123	1,450	3.3
2004	44,206	1,710	3.9
2003	44,200	1,575	3.6
2002	44,109	1,628	3.7
2001	44,124	1,477	3.3
2000	44,278	1,435	3.2
1999	44,443	1,474	3.3
1998	43,669	1,639	3.8
1997	43,427	1,501	3.5
1996	43,276	1,628	3.8
1995	43,771	1,664	3.8
1994	44,178	1,915	4.3
1993	43,745	2,042	4.7
1992	43,661	1,978	4.5
1991	43,724	1,918	4.4
1990	43,682	1,799	4.1

	percent change		percentage point change
2007 to 2011	−0.9%	28.7%	0.9
2000 to 2011	−2.0	24.5	0.9
1990 to 2011	−0.7	−0.7	0.0

		in poverty	
	total	number	percent
Non-Hispanic white married couples with children			
2011	16,241	846	5.2%
2010	16,903	872	5.2
2009	17,582	854	4.9
2008	17,750	738	4.2
2007	17,730	678	3.8
2006	18,494	683	3.7
2005	18,580	661	3.6
2004	18,698	800	4.3
2003	18,628	746	4.0
2002	18,879	781	4.1
2001	19,076	696	3.6
2000	19,356	709	3.7
1999	19,209	743	3.9
1998	19,327	859	4.5
1997	19,588	842	4.3
1996	19,729	884	4.5
1995	19,866	948	4.8
1994	20,276	1,101	5.4
1993	20,166	1,263	6.3
1992	19,905	1,177	5.9
1991	19,845	1,152	5.8
1990	19,957	1,085	5.4

	percent change		percentage point change
2007 to 2011	−8.4%	24.8%	1.4
2000 to 2011	−16.1	19.3	1.5
1990 to 2011	−18.6	−22.0	−0.2

Note: Beginning in 2002, non-Hispanic whites are those who identify themselves as white alone and not Hispanic.
Source: Bureau of the Census, Current Population Surveys, Historical Poverty Tables, Internet site http://www.census.gov/hhes/ www/poverty/data/historical/families.html; calculations by New Strategist

Table 6.55 Poverty Status of Non-Hispanic White Female-Headed Families, 1990 to 2011

(total number of non-Hispanic white female-headed families, and number and percent below poverty level by presence of children under age 18 at home, 1990 to 2011; percent change in numbers and percentage point change in rates for selected years; families in thousands as of March the following year)

		in poverty	
	total	number	percent
Total non-Hispanic white female-headed families			
2011	7,541	1,766	23.4%
2010	7,220	1,743	24.1
2009	7,294	1,701	23.3
2008	7,100	1,473	20.7
2007	7,178	1,489	20.7
2006	7,390	1,628	22.0
2005	7,138	1,537	21.5
2004	7,164	1,491	20.8
2003	7,121	1,455	20.4
2002	7,072	1,374	19.4
2001	6,886	1,305	19.0
2000	6,891	1,226	17.8
1999	6,770	1,248	18.4
1998	6,909	1,428	20.7
1997	6,826	1,598	23.4
1996	6,875	1,538	22.4
1995	6,792	1,463	21.5
1994	6,764	1,678	24.8
1993	6,798	1,699	25.0
1992	6,629	1,637	24.7
1991	6,553	1,610	24.6
1990	6,408	1,480	23.1

	percent change		percentage point change
2007 to 2011	5.1%	18.6%	2.7
2000 to 2011	9.4	44.0	5.6
1990 to 2011	17.7	19.3	0.3

Non-Hispanic white female-headed families with children	total	in poverty	
		number	percent
2011	4,539	1,496	33.0%
2010	4,436	1,447	32.6
2009	4,449	1,412	31.7
2008	4,368	1,246	28.5
2007	4,398	1,283	29.2
2006	4,650	1,405	30.2
2005	4,487	1,308	29.2
2004	4,562	1,287	28.2
2003	4,518	1,269	28.1
2002	4,470	1,170	26.2
2001	4,414	1,135	25.7
2000	4,305	1,058	24.6
1999	4,233	1,069	25.3
1998	4,427	1,275	28.8
1997	4,320	1,420	32.9
1996	4,357	1,351	31.0
1995	4,361	1,294	29.7
1994	4,386	1,471	33.5
1993	4,330	1,506	34.8
1992	4,150	1,474	35.5
1991	4,067	1,429	35.1
1990	3,929	1,317	33.5

	percent change		percentage point change
2007 to 2011	3.2%	16.6%	3.8
2000 to 2011	5.4	41.4	8.4
1990 to 2011	15.5	13.6	−0.5

Note: Beginning in 2002, non-Hispanic whites are those who identify themselves as white alone and not Hispanic.
Source: Bureau of the Census, Current Population Surveys, Historical Poverty Tables, Internet site http://www.census.gov/hhes/ www/poverty/data/historical/families.html; calculations by New Strategist

Table 6.56 Poverty Status of Non-Hispanic White Male-Headed Families, 1990 to 2011

(total number of non-Hispanic white male-headed families, and number and percent below poverty level by presence of children under age 18 at home, 1990 to 2011; percent change in numbers and percentage point change in rates for selected years; families in thousands as of March the following year)

	total	in poverty	
		number	percent
Total non-Hispanic white male-headed families			
2011	3,231	403	12.5%
2010	3,058	336	11.0
2009	3,200	399	12.5
2008	3,069	365	11.9
2007	2,991	308	10.3
2006	2,924	309	10.6
2005	3,003	298	9.9
2004	2,892	304	10.5
2003	2,710	241	8.9
2002	2,679	207	7.7
2001	2,618	270	10.3
2000	2,559	236	9.2
1999	2,481	231	9.3
1998	2,530	197	7.8
1997	2,622	258	9.8
1996	2,475	267	10.8
1995	2,298	257	11.2
1994	2,087	241	11.5
1993	1,927	248	12.9
1992	2,011	225	11.2
1991	2,011	190	9.4
1990	1,948	163	8.4

	percent change		percentage point change
2007 to 2011	8.0%	30.8%	2.2
2000 to 2011	26.3	70.8	3.3
1990 to 2011	65.9	147.2	4.1

		in poverty	
	total	number	percent
Non-Hispanic white male-headed families with children			
2011	1,597	276	17.3%
2010	1,475	253	17.2
2009	1,550	286	18.5
2008	1,538	217	14.1
2007	1,633	215	13.2
2006	1,521	208	13.6
2005	1,534	201	13.1
2004	1,506	207	13.8
2003	1,358	170	12.5
2002	1,315	137	10.4
2001	1,371	184	13.4
2000	1,404	173	12.3
1999	1,347	161	12.0
1998	1,355	148	10.9
1997	1,466	215	14.7
1996	1,295	190	14.7
1995	1,270	202	15.9
1994	1,072	161	15.0
1993	981	177	18.0
1992	1,034	166	16.1
1991	997	141	14.1
1990	878	119	13.6

	percent change		percentage point change
2007 to 2011	−2.2%	28.4%	4.1
2000 to 2011	13.7	59.5	5.0
1990 to 2011	81.9	131.9	3.7

Note: Beginning in 2002, non-Hispanic whites are those who identify themselves as white alone and not Hispanic.
Source: Bureau of the Census, Current Population Surveys, Historical Poverty Tables, Internet site http://www.census.gov/hhes/www/poverty/data/historical/families.html; calculations by New Strategist

Table 6.57 Poverty Status of Non-Hispanic Whites by Sex and Age, 2011

(total number of non-Hispanic whites, and number and percent below poverty level by sex and age, 2011; people in thousands as of 2012)

		in poverty	
	total	number	percent
Total Non-Hispanic whites	**194,960**	**19,171**	**9.8%**
Under age 18	38,955	4,850	12.5
Aged 18 to 24	17,004	2,747	16.2
Aged 25 to 34	23,933	2,738	11.4
Aged 35 to 44	24,199	1,991	8.2
Aged 45 to 54	29,896	2,346	7.8
Aged 55 to 59	14,876	1,159	7.8
Aged 60 to 64	13,192	1,131	8.6
Aged 65 or older	32,904	2,210	6.7
Non-Hispanic white females	**99,213**	**10,806**	**10.9%**
Under age 18	18,947	2,334	12.3
Aged 18 to 24	8,469	1,556	18.4
Aged 25 to 34	11,939	1,642	13.8
Aged 35 to 44	12,105	1,150	9.5
Aged 45 to 54	15,154	1,311	8.7
Aged 55 to 59	7,590	662	8.7
Aged 60 to 64	6,835	599	8.8
Aged 65 or older	18,173	1,552	8.5
Non-Hispanic white males	**95,748**	**8,366**	**8.7%**
Under age 18	20,009	2,516	12.6
Aged 18 to 24	8,535	1,192	14.0
Aged 25 to 34	11,994	1,095	9.1
Aged 35 to 44	12,094	841	7.0
Aged 45 to 54	14,742	1,035	7.0
Aged 55 to 59	7,286	497	6.8
Aged 60 to 64	6,357	532	8.4
Aged 65 or older	14,731	658	4.5

Note: Non-Hispanic whites are those who identify themselves as white alone and not Hispanic.
Source: Bureau of the Census, 2012 Current Population Survey, Internet site http://www.census.gov/hhes/www/cpstables/032012/pov/toc.htm; calculations by New Strategist

Three of Four Managerial and Professional Workers Are Non-Hispanic White

Seventy-one percent of white men and 57 percent of white women were in the labor force in 2012. Because whites comprise the great majority of the population, their labor force participation rate closely matches that of the total population. (The Bureau of Labor Statistics' employment figures for whites include most Hispanics, since Hispanics may be of any race and most are white.)

By detailed occupation, the non-Hispanic white share of employment varies greatly. More than 90 percent of farmers, chiropractors, and veterinarians are non-Hispanic white. At the other end of the scale, only 23 percent of graders and sorters of agricultural products are non-Hispanic white.

Thirty-nine percent of non-Hispanic white households have two or more earners. Among non-Hispanic white couples, the 52 percent majority are dual earners. Non-Hispanic white workers are 16 percent more likely than the average worker to work at home.

Between 2010 and 2020, the number of non-Hispanic white workers will decline by 1.5 percent. The decline will be much larger among men (–2.3 percent) than women (–0.7 percent). In the year 2020, non-Hispanic white workers will account for just 63 percent of the labor force.

■ Non-Hispanic white men will account for only 33 percent of the labor force in 2020, down from 36 percent in 2010.

More than 70 percent of white men are in the labor force

(percent of whites aged 16 or older in the labor force, by sex, 2012)

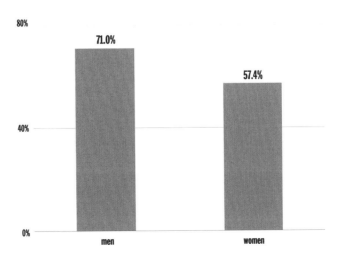

Table 6.58 Labor Force Participation Rate of Whites by Age and Sex, 2012

(percent of whites aged 16 or older in the civilian labor force, by age and sex, 2012)

	total	men	women
Total whites	**64.0%**	**71.0%**	**57.4%**
Aged 16 to 19	36.9	36.7	37.1
Aged 20 to 24	73.1	77.2	69.0
Aged 25 to 29	82.4	89.9	74.9
Aged 30 to 34	82.8	91.8	73.7
Aged 35 to 39	82.6	92.3	73.1
Aged 40 to 44	83.6	91.4	75.9
Aged 45 to 49	82.7	89.4	76.1
Aged 50 to 54	79.9	85.6	74.3
Aged 55 to 59	74.1	79.9	68.5
Aged 60 to 64	56.4	61.9	51.3
Aged 65 or older	18.7	24.0	14.4
Aged 65 to 69	32.9	38.2	28.0
Aged 70 to 74	19.7	24.6	15.4
Aged 75 or older	7.7	11.5	5.1

Note: Whites include Hispanics because Hispanics may be of any race and most are white. The civilian labor force equals the number of employed plus the number of unemployed.
Source: Bureau of Labor Statistics, Labor Force Statistics from the Current Population Survey, Internet site http://www.bls.gov/ cps/tables.htm#empstat

Table 6.59 Employment Status of Whites by Sex and Age, 2012

(number and percent of whites aged 16 or older in the civilian labor force by sex, age, and employment status, 2012; numbers in thousands)

	civilian noninstitutional population	civilian labor force			unemployed	
		total	percent of population	employed	number	percent of labor force
Total whites	**193,204**	**123,684**	**64.0%**	**114,769**	**8,915**	**7.2%**
Aged 16 to 19	12,658	4,669	36.9	3,665	1,004	21.5
Aged 20 to 24	16,289	11,914	73.1	10,561	1,353	11.4
Aged 25 to 34	31,242	25,806	82.6	23,925	1,881	7.3
Aged 35 to 44	30,597	25,445	83.2	23,931	1,514	5.9
Aged 45 to 54	34,935	28,384	81.2	26,769	1,614	5.7
Aged 55 to 64	31,511	20,752	65.9	19,608	1,144	5.5
Aged 65 or older	35,973	6,714	18.7	6,309	405	6.0
White men	**94,266**	**66,921**	**71.0**	**61,990**	**4,931**	**7.4**
Aged 16 to 19	6,486	2,382	36.7	1,797	584	24.5
Aged 20 to 24	8,211	6,339	77.2	5,547	792	12.5
Aged 25 to 34	15,691	14,256	90.9	13,212	1,044	7.3
Aged 35 to 44	15,263	14,018	91.8	13,224	794	5.7
Aged 45 to 54	17,287	15,121	87.5	14,264	856	5.7
Aged 55 to 64	15,333	10,970	71.6	10,334	637	5.8
Aged 65 or older	15,995	3,835	24.0	3,611	224	5.8
White women	**98,938**	**56,763**	**57.4**	**52,779**	**3,985**	**7.0**
Aged 16 to 19	6,172	2,288	37.1	1,868	420	18.4
Aged 20 to 24	8,078	5,575	69.0	5,014	561	10.1
Aged 25 to 34	15,550	11,550	74.3	10,713	837	7.2
Aged 35 to 44	15,334	11,428	74.5	10,708	720	6.3
Aged 45 to 54	17,648	13,263	75.2	12,505	758	5.7
Aged 55 to 64	16,179	9,782	60.5	9,274	508	5.2
Aged 65 or older	19,978	2,879	14.4	2,698	181	6.3

Note: Whites include Hispanics because Hispanics may be of any race and most are white. The civilian labor force equals the number of the employed plus the number of the unemployed. The civilian population equals the number in the labor force plus the number not in the labor force.
Source: Bureau of Labor Statistics, Labor Force Statistics from the Current Population Survey, Internet site http://www.bls.gov/ cps/tables.htm#empstat

Table 6.60 White Workers by Occupation, 2012

(total number of employed persons aged 16 or older in the civilian labor force, number and percent distribution of employed whites, and white share of total, by occupation, 2012; numbers in thousands)

	total	white number	white percent distribution	white share of total
TOTAL EMPLOYED	**142,469**	**114,769**	**100.0%**	**80.6%**
Management, professional and related occupations	**54,043**	**44,375**	**38.7**	**82.1**
Management, business, and financial operations	22,678	1,940	8.9	8.6
Management occupations	16,042	1,410	6.4	8.8
Business and financial operations occupations	6,636	530	2.4	8.0
Professional and related occupations	31,365	2,576	11.8	8.2
Computer and mathematical occupations	3,816	2,773	2.4	72.7
Architecture and engineering occupations	2,846	2,339	2.0	82.2
Life, physical, and social science occupations	1,316	1,077	0.9	81.8
Community and social services occupations	2,265	1,711	1.5	75.5
Legal occupations	1,786	1,552	1.4	86.9
Education, training, and library occupations	8,543	7,161	6.2	83.8
Arts, design, entertainment, sports, and media occupations	2,814	2,395	2.1	85.1
Health care practitioner and technical occupations	7,977	6,273	5.5	78.6
Service occupations	**33,152**	**26,733**	**23.3**	**80.6**
Health care support occupations	3,496	2,294	2.0	65.6
Protective service occupations	3,096	2,350	2.0	75.9
Food preparation and serving related occupations	8,018	6,209	5.4	77.4
Building and grounds cleaning and maintenance occupations	5,591	4,365	3.8	78.1
Personal care and service occupations	5,258	3,783	3.3	71.9
Sales and office occupations	**33,152**	**4,650**	**21.3**	**14.0**
Sales and related occupations	15,457	12,563	10.9	81.3
Office and administrative support occupations	17,695	14,169	12.3	80.1
Natural resources, construction, and maintenance occupations	**12,821**	**11,272**	**9.8**	**87.9**
Farming, fishing, and forestry occupations	994	889	0.8	89.4
Construction and extraction occupations	7,005	6,253	5.4	89.3
Installation, maintenance, and repair occupations	4,821	4,130	3.6	85.7
Production, transportation, and material moving occupations	**16,994**	**13,389**	**11.7**	**78.8**
Production occupations	8,455	6,702	5.8	79.3
Transportation and material moving occupations	8,540	6,686	5.8	78.3

Note: Whites includes Hispanics because Hispanics may be of any race and most are white.
Source: Bureau of Labor Statistics, Labor Force Statistics from the Current Population Survey, Internet site http://www.bls.gov/cps/tables.htm#empstat

Table 6.61 Non-Hispanic White Workers by Detailed Occupation, 2012

(total number of employed workers aged 16 or older and percent non-Hispanic white, by detailed occupation, 2012; numbers in thousands)

	total employed	non-Hispanic white, share of total
TOTAL EMPLOYED AGED 16 OR OLDER	**142,469**	**68.1%**
Management, professional, and related occupations	**54,043**	**76.0**
Management, business, and financial operations occupations	22,678	77.8
Management occupations	16,042	5.1
Management occupations	16,042	79.2
Chief executives	1,513	87.4
General and operations managers	1,064	79.8
Legislators	11	–
Advertising and promotions managers	77	79.0
Marketing and sales managers	967	83.7
Public relations and fundraising managers	58	82.8
Administrative services managers	144	79.7
Computer and information systems managers	605	74.1
Financial managers	1,228	75.4
Compensation and benefits managers	15	–
Human resources managers	224	76.8
Training and development managers	36	–
Industrial production managers	261	80.1
Purchasing managers	218	76.6
Transportation, storage, and distribution managers	287	74.3
Farmers, ranchers, and other agricultural managers	944	94.0
Construction managers	983	84.7
Education administrators	811	76.1
Architectural and engineering managers	120	86.6
Food service managers	1,085	65.2
Funeral service managers	13	–
Gaming managers	26	–
Lodging managers	154	66.6
Medical and health services managers	585	75.9
Natural sciences managers	18	–
Postmasters and mail superintendents	39	–
Property, real estate, and community association managers	644	76.7
Social and community service managers	315	73.2
Emergency management directors	6	–
Managers, all other	3,594	78.4
Business and financial operations occupations	6,636	74.8
Agents and business managers of artists, performers, and athletes	47	–
Buyers and purchasing agents, farm products	13	–

	total employed	non-Hispanic white, share of total
Wholesale and retail buyers, except farm products	198	74.3%
Purchasing agents, except wholesale, retail, and farm products	261	79.7
Claims adjusters, appraisers, examiners, and investigators	323	69.1
Compliance officers	199	79.4
Cost estimators	114	89.7
Human resources workers	603	68.4
Compensation, benefits, and job analysis specialists	71	77.1
Training and development specialists	126	72.5
Logisticians	94	73.6
Management analysts	773	80.0
Meeting, convention, and event planners	127	77.4
Fundraisers	86	86.9
Market research analysts and marketing specialists	219	80.8
Business operations specialists, all other	251	71.0
Accountants and auditors	1,765	71.5
Appraisers and assessors of real estate	93	86.5
Budget analysts	55	71.6
Credit analysts	30	–
Financial analysts	89	81.0
Personal financial advisors	378	84.5
Insurance underwriters	103	78.4
Financial examiners	14	–
Credit counselors and loan officers	333	71.5
Tax examiners and collectors, and revenue agents	82	60.7
Tax preparers	107	66.6
Financial specialists, all other	82	69.2
Professional and related occupations	31,365	74.7
Computer and mathematical occupations	3,816	69.0
Computer and information research scientists	29	–
Computer systems analysts	499	70.9
Information security analysts	52	70.0
Computer programmers	480	71.5
Software developers, applications and systems software	1,084	61.4
Web developers	190	82.3
Computer support specialists	476	70.6
Database administrators	101	76.1
Network and computer systems administrators	226	68.3
Computer network architects	127	70.8
Computer occupations, all other	341	71.0
Actuaries	26	–
Mathematicians	4	–
Operations research analysts	130	75.9
Statisticians	47	–
Miscellaneous mathematical science occupations	3	–

	total employed	non-Hispanic white, share of total
Architecture and engineering occupations	2,846	76.2%
Architects, except naval	195	84.3
Surveyors, cartographers, and photogrammetrists	51	82.2
Aerospace engineers	119	80.2
Agricultural engineers	4	–
Biomedical engineers	10	–
Chemical engineers	71	78.1
Civil engineers	358	81.9
Computer hardware engineers	91	64.2
Electrical and electronics engineers	335	73.2
Environmental engineers	43	–
Industrial engineers, including health and safety	197	73.7
Marine engineers and naval architects	8	–
Materials engineers	40	–
Mechanical engineers	288	76.5
Mining and geological engineers, including mining safety engineers	9	–
Nuclear engineers	11	–
Petroleum engineers	38	–
Engineers, all other	359	74.8
Drafters	149	79.4
Engineering technicians, except drafters	395	71.9
Surveying and mapping technicians	77	78.7
Life, physical, and social science occupations	1,316	76.9
Agricultural and food scientists	42	–
Biological scientists	101	77.4
Conservation scientists and foresters	25	–
Medical scientists	136	66.5
Astronomers and physicists	25	–
Atmospheric and space scientists	15	–
Chemists and materials scientists	105	77.4
Environmental scientists and geoscientists	105	90.0
Physical scientists, all other	154	73.1
Economists	26	–
Survey researchers	2	–
Psychologists	178	83.8
Sociologists	7	–
Urban and regional planners	28	–
Miscellaneous social scientists and related workers	57	76.7
Agricultural and food science technicians	32	–
Biological technicians	19	–
Chemical technicians	70	72.4
Geological and petroleum technicians	21	–
Nuclear technicians	3	–

	total employed	non-Hispanic white, share of total
Social science research assistants	3	–
Miscellaneous life, physical, and social science technicians	160	62.4%
Community and social service occupations	2,265	66.9
Counselors	661	67.0
Social workers	734	61.3
Probation officers and correctional treatment specialists	88	63.0
Social and human service assistants	151	56.3
Miscellaneous community and social service specialists, including health educators and community health workers	94	62.3
Clergy	408	78.5
Directors, religious activities and education	61	84.6
Religious workers, all other	69	78.3
Legal occupations	1,786	81.6
Lawyers	1,061	87.3
Judicial law clerks	17	–
Judges, magistrates, and other judicial workers	67	82.0
Paralegals and legal assistants	418	67.7
Miscellaneous legal support workers	223	79.7
Education, training, and library occupations	8,543	76.5
Postsecondary teachers	1,350	74.6
Preschool and kindergarten teachers	678	72.0
Elementary and middle school teachers	2,838	77.8
Secondary school teachers	1,127	83.3
Special education teachers	366	82.6
Other teachers and instructors	860	73.9
Archivists, curators, and museum technicians	46	–
Librarians	181	86.8
Library technicians	45	–
Teacher assistants	898	67.1
Other education, training, and library workers	153	74.0
Arts, design, entertainment, sports, and media occupations	2,814	79.9
Artists and related workers	212	80.1
Designers	756	81.3
Actors	37	–
Producers and directors	121	83.6
Athletes, coaches, umpires, and related workers	267	83.2
Dancers and choreographers	21	–
Musicians, singers, and related workers	203	79.6
Entertainers and performers, sports and related workers, all other	41	–
Announcers	50	64.4
News analysts, reporters and correspondents	82	78.8
Public relations specialists	155	78.9
Editors	159	85.5

	total employed	non-Hispanic white, share of total
Technical writers	58	86.9%
Writers and authors	208	87.5
Miscellaneous media and communication workers	98	44.4
Broadcast and sound engineering technicians and radio operators	108	81.7
Photographers	178	78.8
Television, video, and motion picture camera operators and editors	57	79.3
Media and communication equipment workers, all other	2	–
Health care practitioners and technical occupations	7,977	73.7
Chiropractors	58	92.5
Dentists	167	85.2
Dietitians and nutritionists	116	74.0
Optometrists	33	–
Pharmacists	286	69.6
Physicians and surgeons	911	69.5
Physician assistants	108	74.0
Podiatrists	9	–
Audiologists	14	–
Occupational therapists	118	87.7
Physical therapists	211	77.1
Radiation therapists	14	–
Recreational therapists	13	–
Respiratory therapists	111	71.7
Speech-language pathologists	146	86.9
Exercise physiologists	2	–
Therapists, all other	148	78.1
Veterinarians	85	90.7
Registered nurses	2,875	75.0
Nurse anesthetists	27	–
Nurse midwives	3	–
Nurse practitioners	103	88.0
Health diagnosing and treating practitioners, all other	23	–
Clinical laboratory technologists and technicians	319	61.8
Dental hygienists	163	83.0
Diagnostic related technologists and technicians	308	79.1
Emergency medical technicians and paramedics	172	85.3
Health practitioner support technologists and technicians	544	66.1
Licensed practical and licensed vocational nurses	531	62.2
Medical records and health information technicians	90	63.0
Opticians, dispensing	54	83.9
Miscellaneous health technologists and technicians	140	60.3
Other health care practitioners and technical occupations	75	82.5

	total employed	non-Hispanic white, share of total
Service occupations	**25,459**	**55.9%**
Health care support occupations	3,496	53.7
Nursing, psychiatric, and home health aides	2,119	46.7
Occupational therapy assistants and aides	18	–
Physical therapist assistants and aides	66	76.1
Massage therapists	158	74.9
Dental assistants	274	65.6
Medical assistants	429	58.3
Medical transcriptionists	55	88.7
Pharmacy aides	45	–
Veterinary assistants and laboratory animal caretakers	47	–
Phlebotomists	119	53.0
Miscellaneous health care support occupations, including medical equipment preparers	166	64.2
Protective service occupations	3,096	66.4
First-line supervisors of correctional officers	46	–
First-line supervisors of police and detectives	112	75.8
First-line supervisors of fire fighting and prevention workers	64	82.7
First-line supervisors of protective service workers, all other	93	69.7
Firefighters	295	81.3
Fire inspectors	18	–
Bailiffs, correctional officers, and jailers	371	57.9
Detectives and criminal investigators	160	76.3
Fish and game wardens	7	–
Parking enforcement workers	4	–
Police and sheriff's patrol officers	657	70.3
Transit and railroad police	3	–
Animal control workers	11	–
Private detectives and investigators	103	78.7
Security guards and gaming surveillance officers	903	53.5
Crossing guards	61	62.4
Transportation security screeners	25	–
Lifeguards and other recreational, and all other protective service workers	162	81.8
Food preparation and serving related occupations	8,018	57.9
Chefs and head cooks	403	55.3
First-line supervisors of food preparation and serving workers	552	64.9
Cooks	1,970	45.7
Food preparation workers	868	54.7
Bartenders	412	78.1
Combined food preparation and serving workers, including fast food	343	64.8
Counter attendants, cafeteria, food concession, and coffee shop	233	67.7

	total employed	non-Hispanic white, share of total
Waiters and waitresses	2,124	65.4%
Food servers, nonrestaurant	217	51.3
Dining room and cafeteria attendants and bartender helpers	359	52.8
Dishwashers	271	41.1
Hosts and hostesses, restaurant, lounge, and coffee shop	260	69.6
Food preparation and serving related workers, all other	6	–
Building and grounds cleaning and maintenance occupations	5,591	45.6
First-line supervisors of housekeeping and janitorial workers	277	58.1
First-line supervisors of landscaping, lawn service, and groundskeeping workers	281	72.5
Janitors and building cleaners	2,205	47.1
Maids and housekeeping cleaners	1,457	34.7
Pest control workers	73	71.8
Grounds maintenance workers	1,298	45.2
Personal care and service occupations	5,258	59.4
First-line supervisors of gaming workers	146	75.5
First-line supervisors of personal service workers	246	60.2
Animal trainers	44	–
Nonfarm animal caretakers	179	81.7
Gaming services workers	106	52.8
Motion picture projectionists	2	–
Ushers, lobby attendants, and ticket takers	43	–
Miscellaneous entertainment attendants and related workers	180	63.3
Embalmers and funeral attendants	16	–
Morticians, undertakers, and funeral directors	38	–
Barbers	109	35.2
Hairdressers, hairstylists, and cosmetologists	785	65.3
Miscellaneous personal appearance workers	300	25.6
Baggage porters, bellhops, and concierges	68	48.1
Tour and travel guides	51	74.2
Child care workers	1,314	61.1
Personal care aides	1,071	49.1
Recreation and fitness workers	406	75.8
Residential advisors	58	64.1
Personal care and service workers, all other	95	73.7
Sales and office occupations	**33,152**	**69.5**
Sales and related occupations	15,457	70.7
First-line supervisors of retail sales workers	3,237	74.2
First-line supervisors of nonretail sales workers	1,151	77.4
Cashiers	3,275	55.6
Counter and rental clerks	139	66.3
Parts salespersons	106	75.3
Retail salespersons	3,341	67.8
Advertising sales agents	230	80.2

	total employed	non-Hispanic white, share of total
Insurance sales agents	540	79.8%
Securities, commodities, and financial services sales agents	280	79.4
Travel agents	73	83.4
Sales representatives, services, all other	457	78.3
Sales representatives, wholesale and manufacturing	1,277	83.2
Models, demonstrators, and product promoters	65	66.0
Real estate brokers and sales agents	761	82.6
Sales engineers	27	–
Telemarketers	97	61.2
Door-to-door sales workers, news and street vendors, and related workers	198	72.5
Sales and related workers, all other	204	77.3
Office and administrative support occupations	17,695	68.4
First-line supervisors of office and administrative support workers	1,416	73.3
Switchboard operators, including answering service	35	–
Telephone operators	42	–
Communications equipment operators, all other	9	–
Bill and account collectors	206	63.5
Billing and posting clerks	475	68.0
Bookkeeping, accounting, and auditing clerks	1,268	78.4
Gaming cage workers	8	–
Payroll and timekeeping clerks	155	70.8
Procurement clerks	27	–
Tellers	380	64.1
Financial clerks, all other	52	62.2
Brokerage clerks	5	–
Correspondence clerks	6	–
Court, municipal, and license clerks	85	62.4
Credit authorizers, checkers, and clerks	43	–
Customer service representatives	1,956	61.6
Eligibility interviewers, government programs	92	55.0
File clerks	292	64.9
Hotel, motel, and resort desk clerks	110	56.7
Interviewers, except eligibility and loan	135	61.9
Library assistants, clerical	97	84.0
Loan interviewers and clerks	144	74.7
New accounts clerks	26	–
Order clerks	104	68.8
Human resources assistants, except payroll and timekeeping	132	71.9
Receptionists and information clerks	1,237	65.7
Reservation and transportation ticket agents and travel clerks	117	45.8
Information and record clerks, all other	104	67.1
Cargo and freight agents	25	–
Couriers and messengers	213	67.7

	total employed	non-Hispanic white, share of total
Dispatchers	277	67.5%
Meter readers, utilities	29	–
Postal service clerks	148	57.2
Postal service mail carriers	318	68.0
Postal service mail sorters, processors, and processing machine operators	66	48.9
Production, planning, and expediting clerks	272	73.3
Shipping, receiving, and traffic clerks	527	57.1
Stock clerks and order fillers	1,453	60.7
Weighers, measurers, checkers, and samplers, recordkeeping	74	55.4
Secretaries and administrative assistants	2,904	77.9
Computer operators	102	70.6
Data entry keyers	337	67.1
Word processors and typists	119	71.9
Desktop publishers	3	–
Insurance claims and policy processing clerks	230	70.0
Mail clerks and mail machine operators, except postal service	81	61.2
Office clerks, general	1,103	65.7
Office machine operators, except computer	46	–
Proofreaders and copy markers	10	–
Statistical assistants	32	–
Office and administrative support workers, all other	570	71.0
Natural resources, construction, and maintenance occupations	**12,821**	**65.4**
Farming, fishing, and forestry occupations	994	48.7
First-line supervisors of farming, fishing, and forestry workers	50	64.1
Agricultural inspectors	16	–
Animal breeders	6	–
Graders and sorters, agricultural products	118	23.3
Miscellaneous agricultural workers	711	46.4
Fishers and related fishing workers	33	–
Hunters and trappers	2	–
Forest and conservation workers	9	–
Logging workers	49	–
Construction and extraction occupations	7,005	63.3
First-line supervisors of construction trades and extraction workers	634	80.2
Boilermakers	23	–
Brickmasons, blockmasons, and stonemasons	122	50.7
Carpenters	1,223	64.9
Carpet, floor, and tile installers and finishers	150	53.0
Cement masons, concrete finishers, and terrazzo workers	68	37.8
Construction laborers	1,387	48.4
Paving, surfacing, and tamping equipment operators	23	–
Pile-driver operators	4	–
Operating engineers and other construction equipment operators	348	76.7

	total employed	non-Hispanic white, share of total
Drywall installers, ceiling tile installers, and tapers	129	35.3%
Electricians	692	76.9
Glaziers	46	–
Insulation workers	44	–
Painters, construction and maintenance	485	49.9
Paperhangers	7	–
Pipelayers, plumbers, pipefitters, and steamfitters	534	71.0
Plasterers and stucco masons	18	–
Reinforcing iron and rebar workers	8	–
Roofers	196	47.4
Sheet metal workers	123	83.0
Structural iron and steel workers	65	77.7
Solar photovoltaic installers	7	–
Helpers, construction trades	53	48.2
Construction and building inspectors	118	84.7
Elevator installers and repairers	29	–
Fence erectors	33	–
Hazardous materials removal workers	38	–
Highway maintenance workers	108	76.5
Rail-track laying and maintenance equipment operators	10	–
Septic tank servicers and sewer pipe cleaners	8	–
Miscellaneous construction and related workers	32	–
Derrick, rotary drill, and service unit operators, oil, gas, and mining	37	–
Earth drillers, except oil and gas	35	–
Explosives workers, ordnance handling experts, and blasters	8	–
Mining machine operators	65	79.0
Roof bolters, mining	3	–
Roustabouts, oil and gas	14	–
Helpers—extraction workers	5	–
Other extraction workers	75	67.2
Installation, maintenance, and repair occupations	4,821	72.0
First-line supervisors of mechanics, installers, and repairers	292	77.3
Computer, automated teller, and office machine repairers	296	72.1
Radio and telecommunications equipment installers and repairers	158	71.8
Avionics technicians	14	–
Electric motor, power tool, and related repairers	37	–
Electrical and electronics installers and repairers, transportation equipment	5	–
Electrical and electronics repairers, industrial and utility	12	–
Electronic equipment installers and repairers, motor vehicles	18	–
Electronic home entertainment equipment installers and repairers	50	70.9
Security and fire alarm systems installers	41	–
Aircraft mechanics and service technicians	153	72.8
Automotive body and related repairers	140	66.7

	total employed	non-Hispanic white, share of total
Automotive service technicians and mechanics	867	64.4%
Bus and truck mechanics and diesel engine specialists	316	76.7
Heavy vehicle and mobile equipment service technicians and mechanics	194	75.3
Small engine mechanics	56	82.7
Miscellaneous vehicle and mobile equipment mechanics, installers, and repairers	87	60.6
Control and valve installers and repairers	27	–
Heating, air conditioning, and refrigeration mechanics and installers	340	73.5
Home appliance repairers	47	–
Industrial and refractory machinery mechanics	454	79.3
Maintenance and repair workers, general	442	69.0
Maintenance workers, machinery	28	–
Millwrights	53	89.8
Electrical power-line installers and repairers	110	84.0
Telecommunications line installers and repairers	177	71.2
Precision instrument and equipment repairers	60	76.5
Wind turbine service technicians	3	–
Coin, vending, and amusement machine servicers and repairers	33	–
Commercial divers	3	–
Locksmiths and safe repairers	31	–
Manufactured building and mobile home installers	5	–
Riggers	13	–
Signal and track switch repairers	5	–
Helpers—installation, maintenance, and repair workers	30	–
Other installation, maintenance, and repair workers	205	71.5
Production, transportation, and material moving occupations	**16,994**	**60.3**
Production occupations	8,455	60.9
First-line supervisors of production and operating workers	808	70.9
Aircraft structure, surfaces, rigging, and systems assemblers	23	–
Electrical, electronics, and electromechanical assemblers	166	46.3
Engine and other machine assemblers	32	–
Structural metal fabricators and fitters	25	–
Miscellaneous assemblers and fabricators	919	58.0
Bakers	199	50.9
Butchers and other meat, poultry, and fish processing workers	311	37.0
Food and tobacco roasting, baking, and drying machine operators and tenders	11	–
Food batchmakers	84	48.6
Food cooking machine operators and tenders	14	–
Food processing workers, all other	117	43.6
Computer control programmers and operators	67	73.2
Extruding and drawing machine setters, operators, and tenders, metal and plastic	10	–
Forging machine setters, operators, and tenders, metal and plastic	10	–
Rolling machine setters, operators, and tenders, metal and plastic	8	–

	total employed	non-Hispanic white, share of total
Cutting, punching, and press machine setters, operators, and tenders, metal and plastic	87	65.4%
Drilling and boring machine tool setters, operators, and tenders, metal and plastic	3	–
Grinding, lapping, polishing, and buffing machine tool setters, operators, and tenders, metal and plastic	54	63.8
Lathe and turning machine tool setters, operators, and tenders, metal and plastic	17	–
Milling and planing machine setters, operators, and tenders, metal and plastic	3	–
Machinists	397	78.9
Metal furnace operators, tenders, pourers, and casters	17	–
Model makers and patternmakers, metal and plastic	11	–
Molders and molding machine setters, operators, and tenders, metal and plastic	37	–
Multiple machine tool setters, operators, and tenders, metal and plastic	5	–
Tool and die makers	56	87.0
Welding, soldering, and brazing workers	593	65.7
Heat treating equipment setters, operators, and tenders, metal and plastic	4	–
Layout workers, metal and plastic	4	–
Plating and coating machine setters, operators, and tenders, metal and plastic	18	–
Tool grinders, filers, and sharpeners	3	–
Metal workers and plastic workers, all other	375	53.0
Prepress technicians and workers	33	–
Printing press operators	201	70.9
Print binding and finishing workers	22	–
Laundry and dry-cleaning workers	185	31.8
Pressers, textile, garment, and related materials	54	31.6
Sewing machine operators	166	39.2
Shoe and leather workers and repairers	11	–
Shoe machine operators and tenders	11	–
Tailors, dressmakers, and sewers	86	49.7
Textile bleaching and dyeing machine operators and tenders	5	–
Textile cutting machine setters, operators, and tenders	12	–
Textile knitting and weaving machine setters, operators, and tenders	7	–
Textile winding, twisting, and drawing out machine setters, operators, and tenders	14	–
Extruding and forming machine setters, operators, and tenders, synthetic and glass fibers	1	–
Fabric and apparel patternmakers	3	–
Upholsterers	34	–
Textile, apparel, and furnishings workers, all other	14	–
Cabinetmakers and bench carpenters	45	–
Furniture finishers	7	–
Model makers and patternmakers, wood	0	–
Sawing machine setters, operators, and tenders, wood	30	–
Woodworking machine setters, operators, and tenders, except sawing	21	–
Woodworkers, all other	21	–
Power plant operators, distributors, and dispatchers	44	–

	total employed	non-Hispanic white, share of total
Stationary engineers and boiler operators	121	71.5%
Water and wastewater treatment plant and system operators	72	70.3
Miscellaneous plant and system operators	39	–
Chemical processing machine setters, operators, and tenders	68	84.0
Crushing, grinding, polishing, mixing, and blending workers	100	60.3
Cutting workers	67	66.6
Extruding, forming, pressing, and compacting machine setters, operators, and tenders	45	–
Furnace, kiln, oven, drier, and kettle operators and tenders	16	–
Inspectors, testers, sorters, samplers, and weighers	689	68.2
Jewelers and precious stone and metal workers	46	–
Medical, dental, and ophthalmic laboratory technicians	95	73.6
Packaging and filling machine operators and tenders	261	39.1
Painting workers	150	55.1
Photographic process workers and processing machine operators	55	63.1
Semiconductor processors	4	–
Adhesive bonding machine operators and tenders	9	–
Cleaning, washing, and metal pickling equipment operators and tenders	7	–
Cooling and freezing equipment operators and tenders	2	–
Etchers and engravers	6	–
Molders, shapers, and casters, except metal and plastic	41	–
Paper goods machine setters, operators, and tenders	35	–
Tire builders	19	–
Helpers—production workers	59	46.7
Production workers, all other	933	60.8
Transportation and material moving occupations	8,540	59.7
Supervisors of transportation and material moving workers	200	63.7
Aircraft pilots and flight engineers	129	89.8
Air traffic controllers and airfield operations specialists	44	–
Flight attendants	88	71.8
Ambulance drivers and attendants, except emergency medical technicians	20	–
Bus drivers	558	59.5
Driver/sales workers and truck drivers	3,201	65.1
Taxi drivers and chauffeurs	336	45.4
Motor vehicle operators, all other	63	73.7
Locomotive engineers and operators	41	–
Railroad brake, signal, and switch operators	10	–
Railroad conductors and yardmasters	52	70.6
Subway, streetcar, and other rail transportation workers	11	–
Sailors and marine oilers	16	–
Ship and boat captains and operators	37	–
Ship engineers	7	–
Bridge and lock tenders	7	–
Parking lot attendants	81	35.7

	total employed	non-Hispanic white, share of total
Automotive and watercraft service attendants	94	69.4%
Transportation inspectors	36	–
Transportation attendants, except flight attendants	38	–
Other transportation workers	17	–
Conveyor operators and tenders	4	–
Crane and tower operators	62	74.6
Dredge, excavating, and loading machine operators	42	–
Hoist and winch operators	5	–
Industrial truck and tractor operators	537	48.7
Cleaners of vehicles and equipment	315	44.6
Laborers and freight, stock, and material movers, hand	1,849	58.6
Machine feeders and offbearers	27	–
Packers and packagers, hand	431	40.5
Pumping station operators	25	–
Refuse and recyclable material collectors	106	44.3
Mine shuttle car operators	1	–
Tank car, truck, and ship loaders	4	–
Material moving workers, all other	45	–

Note: The non-Hispanic white share of the employed by occupation is calculated by subtracting the Asian, black, and Hispanic shares from the total. "–" means sample is too small to make a reliable estimate.
Source: Bureau of Labor Statistics, Labor Force Statistics from the Current Population Survey, Internet site http://www.bls.gov/cps/tables.htm#empstat; calculations by New Strategist

Table 6.62 White Workers by Industry, 2012

(total number of employed people aged 16 or older in the civilian labor force; number and percent distribution of employed whites, and white share of total, by industry, 2012; numbers in thousands)

		white		
	total	number	percent distribution	share of total
Total employed	**142,469**	**114,769**	**100.0%**	**80.6%**
Agriculture, forestry, fishing, and hunting	2,186	2,033	1.8	93.0
Mining	957	865	0.8	90.4
Construction	8,964	8,050	7.0	89.8
Manufacturing	14,686	12,121	10.6	82.5
Durable goods	9,244	7,688	6.7	83.2
Nondurable goods	5,443	4,433	3.9	81.4
Wholesale/retail trade	19,876	16,180	14.1	81.4
Wholesale trade	3,694	3,175	2.8	86.0
Retail trade	16,182	13,006	11.3	80.4
Transportation and utilities	7,271	5,611	4.9	77.2
Information	2,971	2,373	2.1	79.9
Financial activities	9,590	7,900	6.9	82.4
Professional and business services	16,539	13,396	11.7	81.0
Educational and health services	32,350	25,135	21.9	77.7
Leisure and hospitality	13,193	10,266	8.9	77.8
Other services	7,168	5,706	5.0	79.6
Other services, except private households	6,430	5,088	4.4	79.1
Private households	738	618	0.5	83.7
Public administration	6,717	5,133	4.5	76.4

Note: Whites include Hispanics because Hispanics may be of any race and most are white.
Source: Bureau of Labor Statistics, Labor Force Statistics from the Current Population Survey, Internet site http://www.bls.gov/cps/tables.htm#empstat

Table 6.63 White Workers by Full-Time and Part-Time Status, 2012

(number and percent distribution of employed whites aged 16 or older by employment status and sex, 2012; numbers in thousands)

	total	men	women
Total employed whites	**108,587**	**58,669**	**49,918**
Worked full-time	81,073	47,609	33,464
Worked part-time	27,514	11,060	16,454
For economic reasons	6,189	3,141	3,048
PERCENT DISTRIBUTION			
Total employed whites	**100.0%**	**100.0%**	**100.0%**
Worked full-time	74.7	81.1	67.0
Worked part-time	25.3	18.9	33.0
For economic reasons	5.7	5.4	6.1

Note: Part-time work is less than 35 hours per week. Part-time workers exclude those who usually work full-time but who worked less than 35 hours in the previous week because of vacation, holidays, child care problems, weather issues, and other temporary, noneconomic reasons. "Economic reasons" means a worker's hours have been reduced or workers cannot find full-time employment. Whites include Hispanics because Hispanics may be of any race and most are white.
Source: Bureau of Labor Statistics, Labor Force Statistics from the Current Population Survey, Internet site http://www.bls.gov/cps/tables.htm#empstat

Table 6.64 White Workers by Educational Attainment, 2012

(number of total people and whites aged 25 or older in the civilian labor force, white labor force participation rate, distribution of whites in labor force, and white share of total labor force, by educational attainment, 2012; numbers in thousands)

	total labor force	white labor force			
		number	participation rate	percent distribution	share of total
Total aged 25 or older	**133,690**	**107,101**	**65.2%**	**100.0%**	**80.1%**
Not a high school graduate	11,328	9,147	47.2	8.5	80.7
High school graduate only	36,772	29,298	58.9	27.4	79.7
Some college	22,685	17,819	65.3	16.6	78.5
Associate's degree	14,675	11,909	73.1	11.1	81.2
Bachelor's degree or more	48,230	38,928	75.6	36.3	80.7

Note: Whites include Hispanics because Hispanics may be of any race and most are white.
Source: Bureau of Labor Statistics, Labor Force Statistics from the Current Population Survey, Internet site http://www.bls.gov/cps/tables.htm#empstat

Table 6.65 White Workers by Job Tenure, 2012

(percent distribution of total and white wage and salary workers aged 16 or older by tenure with current employer, and index of white to total, 2012)

	total	white	index, white to total
Total workers	**100.0%**	**100.0%**	**100**
One year or less	21.1	20.7	98
13 months to 23 months	6.3	6.4	102
Two years	4.9	4.8	98
Three to four years	16.6	16.1	97
Five to nine years	21.8	21.7	100
10 to 14 years	12.5	12.6	101
15 to 19 years	6.1	6.6	108
20 or more years	10.6	11.3	107

Note: The index is calculated by dividing the white figure by the total figure and multiplying by 100. Whites include Hispanics because Hispanics may be of any race and most are white.
Source: Bureau of Labor Statistics, Employee Tenure, Internet site http://www.bls.gov/news.release/tenure.toc.htm; calculations by New Strategist

Table 6.66 Non-Hispanic White Households by Number of Earners, 2012

(number of total households, number and percent distribution of non-Hispanic white households and non-Hispanic white share of total, by number of earners per household, 2012; number of households in thousands)

		non-Hispanic white		
	total	number	percent distribution	share of total
Total households	**121,084**	**83,573**	**100.0%**	**69.0%**
No earners	28,569	20,898	25.0	73.2
One earner	45,578	29,829	35.7	65.4
Two or more earners	46,938	32,846	39.3	70.0
Two earners	37,943	27,051	32.4	71.3
Three earners	6,905	4,544	5.4	65.8
Four or more earners	2,089	1,250	1.5	59.8
Average number of earners per household	1.28	1.25	–	–

Note: Non-Hispanic whites are those who identify themselves as white alone and not Hispanic. "–" means not applicable.
Source: Bureau of the Census, 2012 Current Population Survey, Annual Social and Economic Supplement, Internet site http://www.census.gov/hhes/www/cpstables/032012/hhinc/toc.htm; calculations by New Strategist

Table 6.67 Labor Force Status of Non-Hispanic White Married Couples, 2012

(number and percent distribution of non-Hispanic white married couples by age of householder and labor force status of husband and wife, 2012; numbers in thousands)

	total	husband and/or wife in labor force			neither husband nor wife in labor force
		husband and wife	husband only	wife only	
Total non-Hispanic white couples	**44,264**	**23,162**	**9,218**	**3,253**	**8,632**
Under age 25	769	440	268	37	26
Aged 25 to 29	2,358	1,579	618	93	68
Aged 30 to 34	3,495	2,448	874	118	57
Aged 35 to 39	3,591	2,532	898	108	52
Aged 40 to 44	4,426	3,162	1,010	138	115
Aged 45 to 54	9,878	6,891	2,060	539	388
Aged 55 to 64	9,656	4,954	2,071	1,225	1,406
Aged 65 to 74	6,344	1,000	1,107	824	3,414
Aged 75 or older	3,746	156	313	171	3,106
Total non-Hispanic white couples	**100.0%**	**52.3%**	**20.8%**	**7.3%**	**19.5%**
Under age 25	100.0	57.2	34.9	4.8	3.4
Aged 25 to 29	100.0	67.0	26.2	3.9	2.9
Aged 30 to 34	100.0	70.0	25.0	3.4	1.6
Aged 35 to 39	100.0	70.5	25.0	3.0	1.4
Aged 40 to 44	100.0	71.4	22.8	3.1	2.6
Aged 45 to 54	100.0	69.8	20.9	5.5	3.9
Aged 55 to 64	100.0	51.3	21.4	12.7	14.6
Aged 65 to 74	100.0	15.8	17.4	13.0	53.8
Aged 75 or older	100.0	4.2	8.4	4.6	82.9

Note: Non-Hispanic whites are those who identify themselves as white alone and not Hispanic.
Source: Bureau of the Census, America's Families and Living Arrangements: 2012, Internet site http://www.census.gov/hhes/families/data/cps2012.html; calculations by New Strategist

Table 6.68 White Minimum Wage Workers by Sex, 2011

(number of total and white employed wage and salary workers, number of total and white wage and salary workers paid hourly rates at or below minimum wage, and white share of total, by sex, 2011; numbers in thousands)

| | total paid hourly rates | percent distribution | workers paid at or below minimum wage | | |
			number	percent distribution	share of total
Total workers aged 16 or older	**73,926**	**100.0%**	**3,828**	**100.0%**	**5.2%**
White workers aged 16 or older	59,314	80.2	3,006	78.5	5.1
White men	29,743	40.2	1,108	28.9	3.7
White women	29,571	40.0	1,898	49.6	6.4

Note: Whites include Hispanics because Hispanics may be of any race and most are white.
Source: Bureau of Labor Statistics, Characteristics of Minimum Wage Workers: 2011, Internet site http://www.bls.gov/cps/minwage2011tbls.htm; calculations by New Strategist

Table 6.69 Union Representation of White Workers by Sex, 2012

(number of employed white wage and salary workers aged 16 or older, number and percent represented by unions, median weekly earnings of those working full-time by union representation status, and index of union median to average median, by sex, 2012; number in thousands)

	total	men	women
Total employed whites	**101,851**	**53,542**	**48,309**
Number represented by unions	12,517	6,933	5,584
Percent represented by unions	12.3%	12.9%	11.6%
Median weekly earnings of white full-time workers	**$792**	**$879**	**$710**
Represented by unions	960	1,017	890
Not represented by unions	762	845	681
Index, median weekly earnings of white workers represented by unions to average white worker	**121**	**116**	**125**

Note: Workers represented by unions are either members of a labor union or workers who report no union affiliation but whose jobs are covered by a union or an employee association contract. The index is calculated by dividing median weekly earnings of workers represented by unions by median weekly earnings of the average white worker and multiplying by 100. Whites include Hispanics because Hispanics may be of any race and most are white.
Source: Bureau of Labor Statistics, Labor Force Statistics from the Current Population Survey, Internet site http://www.bls.gov/cps/tables.htm#empstat

Table 6.70 Commuting Patterns of Non-Hispanic White Workers, 2011

(number of total and non-Hispanic white workers aged 16 or older, percent distribution by means of transportation to work, and index of non-Hispanic white to total, 2011; numbers in thousands)

	total	non-Hispanic white	index
Total workers aged 16 or older, number	**138,270**	**92,616**	–
Total workers aged 16 or older, percent	**100.0%**	**100.0%**	–
Drove alone in car, truck, or van	76.4	79.9	105
Carpooled in car, truck, or van	9.7	8.0	82
Public transportation (excluding taxicab)	5.0	3.0	60
Walked	2.8	2.6	93
Other means	1.7	1.6	94
Worked at home	4.3	5.0	116
Average travel time to work (minutes)	25.5	24.7	97

Note: Non-Hispanic whites are those who identify themselves as being white alone and not Hispanic. The index is calculated by dividing non-Hispanic white figure by total figure and multiplying by 100. "–" means not applicable.
Source: Census Bureau, 2011 American Community Survey, Internet site http://factfinder2.census.gov/faces/nav/jsf/pages/index .xhtml; calculations by New Strategist

Table 6.71 Non-Hispanic White Labor Force Projections, 2010 and 2020

(number and percent of non-Hispanic whites aged 16 or older in the civilian labor force by sex, 2010 and 2020; percent change in number and percentage point change in rate, 2010–20; numbers in thousands)

NUMBER	2010	2020	percent change
Total non-Hispanic whites in labor force	**103,947**	**102,371**	**–1.5%**
Non-Hispanic white men	55,116	53,867	–2.3
Non-Hispanic white women	48,831	48,504	–0.7

PARTICIPATION RATE	2010	2020	percentage point change
Total non-Hispanic whites in labor force	**64.6%**	**62.0%**	**–2.6**
Non-Hispanic white men	70.7	67.2	–3.5
Non-Hispanic white women	58.9	57.2	–1.7

Note: Non-Hispanic whites are those who identify themselves as white alone and not Hispanic.
Source: Bureau of Labor Statistics, Labor Force Projections to 2020: A More Slowly Growing Workforce, Monthly Labor Review, January 2012, Internet site http://www.bls.gov/opub/mlr/2012/01/home.htm

Table 6.72 Non-Hispanic White Share of Labor Force, 2010 and 2020

(total people and non-Hispanic whites aged 16 or older in the civilian labor force, and non-Hispanic white share of total, 2010 and 2020; numbers in thousands)

	2010			2020		
	total	non-Hispanic white	non-Hispanic white share of total	total	non-Hispanic white	non-Hispanic white share of total
Total labor force	**153,889**	**103,947**	**67.5%**	**164,360**	**102,371**	**62.3%**
Men	81,985	55,116	67.2	87,128	53,867	61.8
Women	71,904	48,831	67.9	77,232	48,504	62.8

Note: Non-Hispanic whites are those who identify themselves as white alone and not Hispanic.
Source: Bureau of Labor Statistics, Labor Force Projections to 2020: A More Slowly Growing Workforce, Monthly Labor Review, January 2012, Internet site http://www.bls.gov/opub/mlr/2012/01/home.htm

Married Couples Head Most Non-Hispanic White Households

Non-Hispanic whites account for 69 percent of the nation's 121 million households. The proportion ranges from a low of 54 percent among householders under age 25 to a high of 81 percent among householders aged 65 or older.

Married couples account for the 52 percent majority of non-Hispanic white households. Only 9 percent are female-headed families. People who live alone head a substantial 29 percent of non-Hispanic white households. Half of non-Hispanic white women who live by themselves are aged 65 or older.

Only 25 percent of non-Hispanic white households include children under age 18. Even among non-Hispanic white married couples, just 36 percent have children under age 18 at home. Sixty-seven percent of non-Hispanic white children live with their biological, married parents. Another 16 percent live with only their mother.

Fifty-nine percent of non-Hispanic white men aged 18 or older are currently married. The proportion is a slightly smaller 55 percent among non-Hispanic white women. Twenty-three percent of non-Hispanic white men have ever divorced, the proportion peaking at 37 percent among men in their fifties and sixties. The figures are even higher for non-Hispanic white women: 25 percent have ever divorced, and the proportion reaches 39 percent among women in their fifties.

■ Non-Hispanic white households are more likely than average to be headed by people who live alone because of the older age of the non-Hispanic white population.

Many non-Hispanic white households are people who live alone

(percent distribution of non-Hispanic white households by household type, 2012)

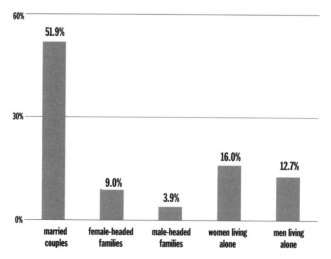

Table 6.73 Non-Hispanic White Households by Age of Householder, 2012

(number of total households, number and percent distribution of non-Hispanic white households, and non-Hispanic white share of total, by age of householder, 2012, numbers in thousands)

| | | non-Hispanic white | | |
	total	number	percent distribution	share of total
Total households	**121,084**	**83,573**	**100.0%**	**69.0%**
Under age 25	6,180	3,367	4.0	54.5
Aged 25 to 29	9,208	5,626	6.7	61.1
Aged 30 to 34	10,638	6,333	7.6	59.5
Aged 35 to 39	10,111	6,015	7.2	59.5
Aged 40 to 44	11,129	7,050	8.4	63.3
Aged 45 to 49	11,763	7,847	9.4	66.7
Aged 50 to 54	12,433	8,742	10.5	70.3
Aged 55 to 59	12,037	8,765	10.5	72.8
Aged 60 to 64	10,742	8,121	9.7	75.6
Aged 65 or older	26,843	21,708	26.0	80.9

Note: Non-Hispanic whites are those who identify themselves as being white alone and not Hispanic.
Source: Bureau of the Census, 2012 Current Population Survey, Internet site http://www.census.gov/hhes/www/income/data/incpovhlth/2011/dtables.html; calculations by New Strategist

Table 6.74 Non-Hispanic White Households by Household Type, 2012

(number of total households, number and percent distribution of non-Hispanic white households, and non-Hispanic white share of total, by type, 2012; numbers in thousands)

	total	non-Hispanic white number	non-Hispanic white percent distribution	non-Hispanic white share of total
TOTAL HOUSEHOLDS	**121,084**	**83,573**	**100.0%**	**69.0%**
Family households	**80,506**	**54,146**	**64.8**	**67.3**
Married couples	58,949	43,376	51.9	73.6
With children under age 18	25,114	16,258	19.5	64.7
Female householders, no spouse present	15,669	7,539	9.0	48.1
With children under age 18	10,380	4,549	5.4	43.8
Male householders, no spouse present	5,888	3,231	3.9	54.9
With children under age 18	2,982	1,599	1.9	53.6
Nonfamily households	**40,578**	**29,426**	**35.2**	**72.5**
Female householders	21,383	15,635	18.7	73.1
Living alone	18,354	13,395	16.0	73.0
Male householders	19,195	13,792	16.5	71.9
Living alone	14,835	10,629	12.7	71.7

Note: Non-Hispanic whites are those who identify themselves as being white alone and not Hispanic.
Source: Bureau of the Census, 2012 Current Population Survey Annual Social and Economic Supplement, Internet site http://www.census.gov/hhes/www/cpstables/032012/hhinc/toc.htm; calculations by New Strategist

Table 6.75 Non-Hispanic White Households by Age of Householder and Household Type, 2012

(number and percent distribution of non-Hispanic white households by age of householder and household type, 2012; numbers in thousands)

| | | family households | | | nonfamily households | | | |
| | | | | | female-headed | | male-headed | |
	total	married couples	female householder, no spouse present	male householder, no spouse present	total	living alone	total	living alone
Total non-Hispanic white households	83,573	43,376	7,539	3,231	15,635	13,395	13,792	10,629
Under age 25	3,367	673	547	343	889	411	914	384
Aged 25 to 34	11,958	5,690	1,335	666	1,701	1,106	2,567	1,515
Aged 35 to 44	13,065	7,863	1,692	586	1,039	796	1,885	1,404
Aged 45 to 54	16,589	9,631	1,629	698	2,007	1,657	2,624	2,175
Aged 55 to 64	16,886	9,524	1,064	506	2,995	2,647	2,797	2,400
Aged 65 or older	21,708	9,996	1,272	433	7,003	6,778	3,004	2,751

PERCENT DISTRIBUTION BY HOUSEHOLD TYPE

Total non-Hispanic white households	100.0%	51.9%	9.0%	3.9%	18.7%	16.0%	16.5%	12.7%
Under age 25	100.0	20.0	16.2	10.2	26.4	12.2	27.1	11.4
Aged 25 to 34	100.0	47.6	11.2	5.6	14.2	9.2	21.5	12.7
Aged 35 to 44	100.0	60.2	13.0	4.5	8.0	6.1	14.4	10.7
Aged 45 to 54	100.0	58.1	9.8	4.2	12.1	10.0	15.8	13.1
Aged 55 to 64	100.0	56.4	6.3	3.0	17.7	15.7	16.6	14.2
Aged 65 or older	100.0	46.0	5.9	2.0	32.3	31.2	13.8	12.7

PERCENT DISTRIBUTION BY AGE

Total non-Hispanic white households	100.0%	100.0%	100.0%	100.0%	100.0%	100.0%	100.0%	100.0%
Under age 25	4.0	1.6	7.3	10.6	5.7	3.1	6.6	3.6
Aged 25 to 34	14.3	13.1	17.7	20.6	10.9	8.3	18.6	14.3
Aged 35 to 44	15.6	18.1	22.4	18.1	6.6	5.9	13.7	13.2
Aged 45 to 54	19.8	22.2	21.6	21.6	12.8	12.4	19.0	20.5
Aged 55 to 64	20.2	22.0	14.1	15.7	19.2	19.8	20.3	22.6
Aged 65 or older	26.0	23.0	16.9	13.4	44.8	50.6	21.8	25.9

Note: Non-Hispanic whites are those who identify themselves as being white alone and not Hispanic.
Source: Bureau of the Census, 2012 Current Population Survey, Internet site http://www.census.gov/hhes/www/income/data/incpovhlth/2011/dtables.html; calculations by New Strategist

Table 6.76 Non-Hispanic White Households by Size, 2012

(number of total households, number and percent distribution of non-Hispanic white households, and non-Hispanic white share of total, by household size, 2012; number of households in thousands)

		non-Hispanic white		
	total	number	percent distribution	share of total
Total households	**121,084**	**83,573**	**100.0%**	**69.0%**
One person	33,188	24,024	28.7	72.4
Two people	40,983	31,274	37.4	76.3
Three people	19,241	12,335	14.8	64.1
Four people	16,049	9,970	11.9	62.1
Five people	7,271	4,016	4.8	55.2
Six people	2,734	1,367	1.6	50.0
Seven or more people	1,617	586	0.7	36.2
Average number of persons per household	2.55	2.38	–	–

Note: Non-Hispanic whites are those who identify themselves as being white alone and not Hispanic. "–" means not applicable.
Source: Bureau of the Census, Current Population Survey Annual Social and Economic Supplement, Internet site http://www .census.gov/hhes/www/income/dinctabs.html; calculations by New Strategist

Table 6.77 Non-Hispanic White Households by Region, 2012

(number of total households, number and percent distribution of non-Hispanic white households and non-Hispanic white share of total, by region, 2012; numbers in thousands)

| | total | non-Hispanic white | | |
		number	percent distribution	share of total
Total households	**121,084**	**83,573**	**100.0%**	**69.0%**
Northeast	21,774	15,849	19.0	72.8
Midwest	26,865	21,833	26.1	81.3
South	45,604	29,487	35.3	64.7
West	26,840	16,404	19.6	61.1

Note: Non-Hispanic whites are those who identify themselves as being white alone and not Hispanic.
Source: Bureau of the Census, Current Population Survey Annual Social and Economic Supplement, Internet site http://www.census.gov/hhes/www/income/dinctabs.html; calculations by New Strategist

Table 6.78 Non-Hispanic White Households by Metropolitan Status, 2012

(number of total households, number and percent distribution of non-Hispanic white households and non-Hispanic white share of total, by metropolitan status, 2012; numbers in thousands)

| | total | non-Hispanic white | | |
		number	percent distribution	share of total
Total households	**121,084**	**83,573**	**100.0%**	**69.0%**
Inside metropolitan areas	101,526	67,440	80.7	66.4
Inside principal cities	40,616	22,112	26.5	54.4
Outside principal cities	60,910	45,328	54.2	74.4
Outside metropolitan areas	19,558	16,133	19.3	82.5

Note: Non-Hispanic whites are those who identify themselves as being white alone and not Hispanic.
Source: Bureau of the Census, Current Population Survey Annual Social and Economic Supplement, Internet site http://www.census.gov/hhes/www/income/dinctabs.html; calculations by New Strategist

Table 6.79 Non-Hispanic Whites Living Alone by Sex and Age, 2012

(total number of non-Hispanic whites aged 15 or older, number and percent living alone, and percent distribution of non-Hispanic whites living alone, by sex and age, 2012; numbers in thousands)

	total	living alone number	percent distribution	share of total
Total non-Hispanic whites	**163,215**	**24,024**	**100.0%**	**14.7%**
Under age 25	24,213	795	3.3	3.3
Aged 25 to 34	23,933	2,621	10.9	11.0
Aged 35 to 44	24,199	2,200	9.2	9.1
Aged 45 to 54	29,896	3,832	16.0	12.8
Aged 55 to 64	28,069	5,047	21.0	18.0
Aged 65 to 74	18,155	3,960	16.5	21.8
Aged 75 or older	14,749	5,569	23.2	37.8
Non-Hispanic white men	**79,468**	**10,629**	**100.0**	**13.4**
Under age 25	12,264	384	3.6	3.1
Aged 25 to 34	11,994	1,515	14.3	12.6
Aged 35 to 44	12,094	1,404	13.2	11.6
Aged 45 to 54	14,742	2,175	20.5	14.8
Aged 55 to 64	13,644	2,400	22.6	17.6
Aged 65 to 74	8,637	1,389	13.1	16.1
Aged 75 or older	6,093	1,362	12.8	22.4
Non-Hispanic white women	**83,747**	**13,395**	**100.0**	**16.0**
Under age 25	11,950	411	3.1	3.4
Aged 25 to 34	11,939	1,106	8.3	9.3
Aged 35 to 44	12,105	796	5.9	6.6
Aged 45 to 54	15,154	1,657	12.4	10.9
Aged 55 to 64	14,425	2,647	19.8	18.3
Aged 65 to 74	9,518	2,571	19.2	27.0
Aged 75 or older	8,655	4,207	31.4	48.6

Note: Non-Hispanic whites are those who identify themselves as being white alone and not Hispanic.
Source: Bureau of the Census, Current Population Survey Annual Social and Economic Supplement, Internet site http://www.census.gov/hhes/www/income/dinctabs.html; calculations by New Strategist

Table 6.80 Non-Hispanic White Households by Age of Householder, Type of Household, and Presence of Children, 2012

(number and percent distribution of non-Hispanic white households by age of householder, type of household, and presence of own children under age 18, 2012; numbers in thousands)

	all households		married couples		female-headed families		male-headed families	
	total	with children	total	with children	total	with children	total	with children
Total non-Hispanic white households	**83,573**	**20,790**	**43,376**	**15,467**	**7,539**	**3,924**	**3,231**	**1,399**
Under age 25	3,367	826	674	341	547	387	343	96
Aged 25 to 29	5,626	2,049	2,271	1,301	637	555	357	193
Aged 30 to 34	6,333	3,402	3,418	2,549	698	648	308	205
Aged 35 to 39	6,015	3,912	3,530	2,959	811	724	287	228
Aged 40 to 44	7,050	4,197	4,333	3,286	880	681	299	230
Aged 45 to 49	7,847	3,357	4,552	2,637	850	503	364	217
Aged 50 to 54	8,742	1,926	5,079	1,517	780	295	333	114
Aged 55 to 64	16,886	958	9,524	760	1,064	110	506	89
Aged 65 or older	21,708	163	9,995	116	1,271	20	433	25

PERCENT OF HOUSEHOLDS WITH CHILDREN BY TYPE

Total non-Hispanic white households	**100.0%**	**24.9%**	**100.0%**	**35.7%**	**100.0%**	**52.0%**	**100.0%**	**43.3%**
Under age 25	100.0	24.5	100.0	50.6	100.0	70.7	100.0	28.0
Aged 25 to 29	100.0	36.4	100.0	57.3	100.0	87.1	100.0	54.1
Aged 30 to 34	100.0	53.7	100.0	74.6	100.0	92.8	100.0	66.6
Aged 35 to 39	100.0	65.0	100.0	83.8	100.0	89.3	100.0	79.4
Aged 40 to 44	100.0	59.5	100.0	75.8	100.0	77.4	100.0	76.9
Aged 45 to 49	100.0	42.8	100.0	57.9	100.0	59.2	100.0	59.6
Aged 50 to 54	100.0	22.0	100.0	29.9	100.0	37.8	100.0	34.2
Aged 55 to 64	100.0	5.7	100.0	8.0	100.0	10.3	100.0	17.6
Aged 65 or older	100.0	0.8	100.0	1.2	100.0	1.6	100.0	5.8

Note: Non-Hispanic whites are those who identify themselves as being white alone and not Hispanic.
Source: Bureau of the Census, Current Population Survey Annual Social and Economic Supplement, America's Families and Living Arrangements: 2012, Internet site http://www.census.gov/hhes/families/data/cps2012.html; calculations by New Strategist

Table 6.81 Living Arrangements of Non-Hispanic White Children, 2012

(number and percent distribution of non-Hispanic white children under age 18 by living arrangement, 2012; numbers in thousands)

	number	percent distribution
NON-HISPANIC WHITE CHILDREN	**39,062**	**100.0%**
Living with two parents	**29,881**	**76.5**
Married parents	28,806	73.7
Unmarried parents	1,075	2.8
Biological mother and father	26,888	68.8
Married parents	25,997	66.6
Biological mother and stepfather	1,742	4.5
Biological father and stepmother	587	1.5
Biological mother and adoptive father	118	0.3
Biological father and adoptive mother	28	0.1
Adoptive mother and father	364	0.9
Other	154	0.4
Living with one parent	**8,090**	**20.7**
Mother only	6,423	16.4
Father only	1,667	4.3
Living with no parents	**1,091**	**2.8**
Grandparents	627	1.6
Other	463	1.2
At least one biological parent	**37,339**	**95.6**
At least one stepparent	**2,519**	**6.4**
At least one adoptive parent	**600**	**1.5**

Note: Non-Hispanic whites are those who identify themselves as being white alone and not Hispanic.
Source: Bureau of the Census, Current Population Survey Annual Social and Economic Supplement, America's Families and Living Arrangements: 2012, Detailed Tables, Internet site http://www.census.gov/hhes/families/data/cps2012.html; calculations by New Strategist

Table 6.82 Marital Status of Non-Hispanic White Men by Age, 2012

(number and percent distribution of non-Hispanic white men aged 18 or older by age and current marital status, 2012; numbers in thousands)

	total	never married	married, spouse present	married, spouse absent	separated	divorced	widowed
Total non-Hispanic white men	**75,700**	**19,459**	**44,320**	**671**	**1,233**	**7,823**	**2,194**
Aged 18 to 19	2,331	2,263	26	12	19	8	4
Aged 20 to 24	6,203	5,510	530	44	61	51	8
Aged 25 to 29	6,037	3,580	2,063	49	116	221	9
Aged 30 to 34	5,952	2,073	3,307	67	92	407	5
Aged 35 to 39	5,595	1,220	3,659	25	117	554	21
Aged 40 to 44	6,493	1,149	4,252	86	152	837	16
Aged 45 to 49	7,039	1,104	4,585	44	218	1,038	50
Aged 50 to 54	7,690	856	5,334	68	140	1,200	92
Aged 55 to 64	13,628	1,142	9,696	111	215	2,149	314
Aged 65 to 74	8,637	365	6,621	76	77	985	514
Aged 75 to 84	4,574	143	3,408	61	23	319	619
Aged 85 or older	1,520	53	837	29	3	56	542
Total non-Hispanic white men	**100.0%**	**25.7%**	**58.5%**	**0.9%**	**1.6%**	**10.3%**	**2.9%**
Aged 18 to 19	100.0	97.1	1.1	0.5	0.8	0.3	0.2
Aged 20 to 24	100.0	88.8	8.5	0.7	1.0	0.8	0.1
Aged 25 to 29	100.0	59.3	34.2	0.8	1.9	3.7	0.1
Aged 30 to 34	100.0	34.8	55.6	1.1	1.5	6.8	0.1
Aged 35 to 39	100.0	21.8	65.4	0.4	2.1	9.9	0.4
Aged 40 to 44	100.0	17.7	65.5	1.3	2.3	12.9	0.2
Aged 45 to 49	100.0	15.7	65.1	0.6	3.1	14.7	0.7
Aged 50 to 54	100.0	11.1	69.4	0.9	1.8	15.6	1.2
Aged 55 to 64	100.0	8.4	71.1	0.8	1.6	15.8	2.3
Aged 65 to 74	100.0	4.2	76.7	0.9	0.9	11.4	6.0
Aged 75 to 84	100.0	3.1	74.5	1.3	0.5	7.0	13.5
Aged 85 or older	100.0	3.5	55.1	1.9	0.2	3.7	35.7

Note: Non-Hispanic whites are those who identify themselves as being white alone and not Hispanic
Source: Bureau of the Census, Current Population Survey Annual Social and Economic Supplement, America's Families and Living Arrangements: 2012, Internet site http://www.census.gov/hhes/families/data/cps2012.html; calculations by New Strategist

Table 6.83 Marital Status of Non-Hispanic White Women by Age, 2012

(number and percent distribution of non-Hispanic white women aged 18 or older by age and current marital status, 2012; numbers in thousands)

	total	never married	married, spouse present	married, spouse absent	separated	divorced	widowed
Total non-Hispanic white women	**80,232**	**15,977**	**43,920**	**780**	**1,426**	**9,889**	**8,241**
Aged 18 to 19	2,300	2,209	39	15	19	7	10
Aged 20 to 24	6,166	4,941	952	73	120	67	13
Aged 25 to 29	6,072	2,884	2,692	53	116	304	23
Aged 30 to 34	5,867	1,473	3,597	59	182	539	17
Aged 35 to 39	5,578	861	3,717	76	194	678	52
Aged 40 to 44	6,522	734	4,524	67	159	956	83
Aged 45 to 49	7,199	648	4,942	75	208	1,194	130
Aged 50 to 54	7,950	596	5,386	74	146	1,453	295
Aged 55 to 64	14,418	975	9,476	150	173	2,595	1,049
Aged 65 to 74	9,508	369	5,637	48	70	1,439	1,944
Aged 75 to 84	6,028	190	2,511	59	24	544	2,700
Aged 85 or older	2,624	96	447	31	12	112	1,925
Total non-Hispanic white women	**100.0%**	**19.9%**	**54.7%**	**1.0%**	**1.8%**	**12.3%**	**10.3%**
Aged 18 to 19	100.0	96.0	1.7	0.7	0.8	0.3	0.4
Aged 20 to 24	100.0	80.1	15.4	1.2	1.9	1.1	0.2
Aged 25 to 29	100.0	47.5	44.3	0.9	1.9	5.0	0.4
Aged 30 to 34	100.0	25.1	61.3	1.0	3.1	9.2	0.3
Aged 35 to 39	100.0	15.4	66.6	1.4	3.5	12.2	0.9
Aged 40 to 44	100.0	11.3	69.4	1.0	2.4	14.7	1.3
Aged 45 to 49	100.0	9.0	68.6	1.0	2.9	16.6	1.8
Aged 50 to 54	100.0	7.5	67.7	0.9	1.8	18.3	3.7
Aged 55 to 64	100.0	6.8	65.7	1.0	1.2	18.0	7.3
Aged 65 to 74	100.0	3.9	59.3	0.5	0.7	15.1	20.4
Aged 75 to 84	100.0	3.2	41.7	1.0	0.4	9.0	44.8
Aged 85 or older	100.0	3.7	17.0	1.2	0.5	4.3	73.4

Note: Non-Hispanic whites are those who identify themselves as being white alone and not Hispanic.
Source: Bureau of the Census, Current Population Survey Annual Social and Economic Supplement, America's Families and Living Arrangements: 2012, Internet site http://www.census.gov/hhes/families/data/cps2012.html; calculations by New Strategist

Table 6.84 Marital History of Non-Hispanic White Men by Age, 2009

(number of non-Hispanic white men aged 15 or older and percent distribution by marital history and age, 2009; numbers in thousands)

	total	15–19	20–24	25–29	30–34	35–39	40–49	50–59	60–69	70+
TOTAL NON-HISPANIC WHITE MEN, NUMBER	79,170	6,376	6,466	6,258	5,778	6,113	14,703	14,465	10,042	8,969
TOTAL NON-HISPANIC WHITE MEN, PERCENT	100.0%	100.0%	100.0%	100.0%	100.0%	100.0%	100.0%	100.0%	100.0%	100.0%
Never married	29.0	98.2	88.0	56.9	32.3	20.3	15.0	10.0	4.3	2.9
Ever married	71.0	1.8	12.0	43.1	67.7	79.7	85.0	90.0	95.7	97.1
Married once	53.7	1.6	12.0	41.0	61.3	68.2	64.6	62.1	63.8	72.2
Still married	43.9	1.1	10.7	36.1	53.4	57.6	51.1	50.2	53.8	54.9
Married twice	13.5	0.2	0.1	2.0	6.0	10.1	16.9	21.3	23.0	19.2
Still married	10.5	0.1	0.1	1.8	4.9	8.7	12.8	16.6	18.5	13.8
Married three or more times	3.8	0.0	0.0	0.1	0.4	1.3	3.5	6.6	8.9	5.7
Still married	2.9	0.0	0.0	0.0	0.3	1.1	2.7	5.0	6.9	4.1
Ever divorced	23.2	0.3	0.9	5.8	12.7	20.1	31.7	37.4	37.4	23.6
Currently divorced	9.7	0.2	0.9	3.9	7.4	10.2	15.4	15.3	12.0	6.8
Ever widowed	4.1	0.4	0.1	0.2	0.3	0.6	1.2	2.5	6.1	22.2
Currently widowed	2.9	0.3	0.1	0.2	0.1	0.4	0.8	1.6	3.6	16.9

Source: Bureau of the Census, Number, Timing, and Duration of Marriages and Divorces: 2009, Detailed Tables, Internet site http://www.census.gov/hhes/socdemo/marriage/data/sipp/index.html

Table 6.85 Marital History of Non-Hispanic White Women by Age, 2009

(number of non-Hispanic white women aged 15 or older and percent distribution by marital history and age, 2009; numbers in thousands)

	total	15–19	20–24	25–29	30–34	35–39	40–49	50–59	60–69	70+
TOTAL NON-HISPANIC WHITE WOMEN, NUMBER	84,053	6,238	6,316	6,322	5,867	6,267	14,794	14,998	10,836	12,415
TOTAL NON-HISPANIC WHITE WOMEN, PERCENT	100.0%	100.0%	100.0%	100.0%	100.0%	100.0%	100.0%	100.0%	100.0%	100.0%
Never married	**23.0**	**98.1**	**76.3**	**43.3**	**22.0**	**13.5**	**9.8**	**7.2**	**4.5**	**3.8**
Ever married	**77.0**	**1.9**	**23.7**	**56.7**	**78.0**	**86.5**	**90.2**	**92.8**	**95.5**	**96.2**
Married once	59.1	1.9	23.3	53.5	67.4	69.6	67.0	64.7	67.4	76.5
Still married	42.1	1.3	20.8	45.6	57.1	57.4	52.5	48.8	47.1	32.0
Married twice	14.0	0.0	0.3	3.3	9.7	14.5	18.3	21.4	21.1	15.2
Still married	9.3	0.0	0.2	2.8	8.3	11.5	13.0	15.2	14.3	5.6
Married three or more times	3.9	0.0	0.0	0.0	0.9	2.5	4.9	6.7	7.0	4.6
Still married	2.4	0.0	0.0	0.0	0.8	1.8	3.3	4.7	4.1	1.6
Ever divorced	25.0	0.2	2.0	8.6	18.4	26.2	34.8	39.4	36.4	20.9
Currently divorced	12.0	0.2	1.8	5.8	9.1	12.4	17.5	18.3	16.2	9.4
Ever widowed	11.1	0.2	0.0	0.1	0.4	1.3	2.3	6.0	15.8	50.4
Currently widowed	9.8	0.2	0.0	0.1	0.4	0.7	1.5	4.4	12.6	47.3

Source: Bureau of the Census, Number, Timing, and Duration of Marriages and Divorces: 2009, Detailed Tables, Internet site http://www.census.gov/hhes/socdemo/marriage/data/sipp/index.html

Non-Hispanic White Population Barely Grew between 2000 and 2011

Non-Hispanic whites accounted for 63 percent of the total population in 2011, down from 69 percent in 2000. The non-Hispanic white population grew only 1 percent during those years, well below the 10 percent gain for the population as a whole.

Non-Hispanic whites account for a much smaller share of children and young adults than of older Americans because Hispanics, blacks, and Asians are a growing proportion of the younger age groups. Just 50 percent of children under age 5 are non-Hispanic white versus 84 percent of people aged 85 or older.

The non-Hispanic white share of regional populations varies substantially. In the Midwest, 78 percent of the population is non-Hispanic white. In the West, only 52 percent of residents are non-Hispanic white. Variations by state are even greater. In Maine and Vermont, 94 percent of the population is non-Hispanic white. In California, Hawaii, New Mexico, and Texas, fewer than 50 percent of residents are non-Hispanic white. In Parkersburg–Marietta–Vienna, West Virginia, and Altoona, Pennsylvania, fully 96 percent of the population is non-Hispanic white. In contrast, non-Hispanic whites account for only 3 percent of the residents of Laredo, Texas.

■ In a growing number of states and metropolitan areas, non-Hispanic whites are no longer in the majority, changing America's social fabric.

The non-Hispanic white share of regional populations varies substantially

(non-Hispanic white share of population by region, 2011)

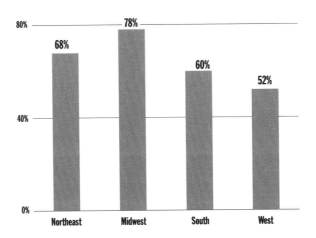

Table 6.86 Whites by Racial Identification, 2000 and 2010

(total number of people, and number and percent distribution of whites by racial identification, 2000 and 2010; percent change, 2000–10)

	2010 number	2010 percent distribution	2000 number	2000 percent distribution	percent change 2000–10
Total people	**308,745,538**	**100.0%**	**281,421,906**	**100.0%**	**9.7%**
White alone or in combination with one or more other races	**231,040,398**	**74.8**	**216,930,975**	**77.1**	**6.5**
White alone	223,553,265	72.4	211,460,626	75.1	5.7
White alone, not Hispanic	196,817,552	63.7	194,552,774	69.1	1.2
White in combination	7,487,133	2.4	5,470,349	1.9	36.9

Source: Bureau of the Census, An Overview: Race and Hispanic Origin and the 2010 Census, 2010 Census Briefs, Internet site http://www.census.gov/2010census/data/2010-census-briefs.php; calculations by New Strategist

Table 6.87 Whites by Hispanic Origin, 2010

(number and percent distribution of whites by Hispanic origin and racial identification, 2010)

	white alone or in combination number	white alone or in combination percent distribution	white alone number	white alone percent distribution
Total whites	**231,040,398**	**100.0%**	**223,553,265**	**100.0%**
Not Hispanic	201,856,108	87.4	196,817,552	88.0
Hispanic	29,184,290	12.6	26,735,713	12.0

Source: Bureau of the Census, An Overview: Race and Hispanic Origin and the 2010 Census, 2010 Census Briefs, Internet site http://www.census.gov/2010census/data/2010-census-briefs.php; calculations by New Strategist

Table 6.88 Non-Hispanic Whites by Age, 2000 to 2011

(number of non-Hispanic whites by age, 2000 to 2011; percent change, 2000–11)

	2011	2010	2000	percent change 2000–11
Total non-Hispanic whites	**197,510,927**	**196,817,552**	**195,575,485**	**1.0%**
Under age 5	10,140,660	10,254,079	11,287,342	–10.2
Aged 5 to 9	10,733,903	10,838,062	12,392,199	–13.4
Aged 10 to 14	11,338,734	11,403,383	12,961,174	–12.5
Aged 15 to 19	12,064,584	12,341,592	12,837,017	–6.0
Aged 20 to 24	12,639,890	12,426,842	11,682,056	8.2
Aged 25 to 29	12,321,092	12,226,930	12,076,702	2.0
Aged 30 to 34	11,843,984	11,495,910	13,450,700	–11.9
Aged 35 to 39	11,423,098	11,984,317	15,752,098	–27.5
Aged 40 to 44	13,189,150	13,218,304	16,212,924	–18.7
Aged 45 to 49	14,738,772	15,355,524	14,972,438	–1.6
Aged 50 to 54	15,865,922	15,785,646	13,529,816	17.3
Aged 55 to 59	14,780,602	14,454,799	10,581,448	39.7
Aged 60 to 64	13,504,933	12,822,733	8,510,782	58.7
Aged 65 to 69	9,975,049	9,682,945	7,674,574	30.0
Aged 70 to 74	7,494,164	7,257,878	7,348,333	2.0
Aged 75 to 79	5,865,434	5,861,366	6,324,955	–7.3
Aged 80 to 84	4,748,408	4,746,881	4,296,367	10.5
Aged 85 or older	4,842,548	4,660,361	3,684,560	31.4
Aged 18 to 24	17,609,336	17,547,396	16,828,781	4.6
Aged 18 or older	158,202,492	157,100,990	151,244,478	4.6
Aged 65 or older	32,925,603	32,209,431	29,328,789	12.3

Note: Non-Hispanic whites are those who identify themselves as being white alone and not Hispanic.
Source: Bureau of the Census, 2000 Census, 2010 Census, and Population Estimates, Internet site http://www.census.gov/popest/index.html; calculations by New Strategist

Table 6.89 Non-Hispanic White Share of Total Population by Age, 2011

(total number of people, number and percent distribution of non-Hispanic whites, and non-Hispanic white share of total, by age, 2011)

	total	non-Hispanic white number	percent distribution	share of total
Total people	**311,591,917**	**197,510,927**	**100.0%**	**63.4%**
Under age 5	20,162,058	10,140,660	5.1	50.3
Aged 5 to 9	20,334,196	10,733,903	5.4	52.8
Aged 10 to 14	20,704,852	11,338,734	5.7	54.8
Aged 15 to 19	21,644,043	12,064,584	6.1	55.7
Aged 20 to 24	22,153,832	12,639,890	6.4	57.1
Aged 25 to 29	21,279,794	12,321,092	6.2	57.9
Aged 30 to 34	20,510,704	11,843,984	6.0	57.7
Aged 35 to 39	19,594,309	11,423,098	5.8	58.3
Aged 40 to 44	21,033,645	13,189,150	6.7	62.7
Aged 45 to 49	22,158,005	14,738,772	7.5	66.5
Aged 50 to 54	22,560,198	15,865,922	8.0	70.3
Aged 55 to 59	20,255,548	14,780,602	7.5	73.0
Aged 60 to 64	17,806,592	13,504,933	6.8	75.8
Aged 65 to 69	12,873,788	9,975,049	5.1	77.5
Aged 70 to 74	9,607,950	7,494,164	3.8	78.0
Aged 75 to 79	7,388,687	5,865,434	3.0	79.4
Aged 80 to 84	5,786,543	4,748,408	2.4	82.1
Aged 85 or older	5,737,173	4,842,548	2.5	84.4
Aged 18 to 24	31,064,709	17,609,336	8.9	56.7
Aged 18 or older	237,657,645	158,202,492	80.1	66.6
Aged 65 or older	41,394,141	32,925,603	16.7	79.5

Note: Non-Hispanic whites are those who identify themselves as being white alone and not Hispanic.
Source: Bureau of the Census, Population Estimates, Internet site http://www.census.gov/popest/index.html; calculations by New Strategist

Table 6.90 Non-Hispanic Whites by Age and Sex, 2011

(number of non-Hispanic whites by age and sex, and sex ratio by age, 2011)

	total	females	males	sex ratio
Total non-Hispanic whites	**197,510,927**	**100,352,466**	**97,158,461**	**97**
Under age 5	10,140,660	4,946,558	5,194,102	105
Aged 5 to 9	10,733,903	5,226,352	5,507,551	105
Aged 10 to 14	11,338,734	5,518,231	5,820,503	105
Aged 15 to 19	12,064,584	5,858,219	6,206,365	106
Aged 20 to 24	12,639,890	6,218,246	6,421,644	103
Aged 25 to 29	12,321,092	6,097,468	6,223,624	102
Aged 30 to 34	11,843,984	5,869,618	5,974,366	102
Aged 35 to 39	11,423,098	5,677,282	5,745,816	101
Aged 40 to 44	13,189,150	6,570,351	6,618,799	101
Aged 45 to 49	14,738,772	7,398,096	7,340,676	99
Aged 50 to 54	15,865,922	8,009,651	7,856,271	98
Aged 55 to 59	14,780,602	7,529,593	7,251,009	96
Aged 60 to 64	13,504,933	6,934,893	6,570,040	95
Aged 65 to 69	9,975,049	5,199,329	4,775,720	92
Aged 70 to 74	7,494,164	4,005,807	3,488,357	87
Aged 75 to 79	5,865,434	3,255,733	2,609,701	80
Aged 80 to 84	4,748,408	2,799,751	1,948,657	70
Aged 85 or older	4,842,548	3,237,288	1,605,260	50
Aged 18 to 24	17,609,336	8,633,259	8,976,077	104
Aged 18 or older	158,202,492	81,218,119	76,984,373	95
Aged 65 or older	32,925,603	18,497,908	14,427,695	78

Note: Non-Hispanic whites are those who identify themselves as being white alone and not Hispanic. The sex ratio is the number of males divided by the number of females multiplied by 100.
Source: Bureau of the Census, Population Estimates, Internet site http://www.census.gov/popest/index.html; calculations by New Strategist

Table 6.91 Non-Hispanic White Population Projections, 2012 to 2050

(number of non-Hispanic whites by age, 2012 to 2050, percent change for selected years; numbers in thousands)

NUMBER	2012	2020	2030	2040	2050	percent change 2012–50
Total non-Hispanic whites	**197,762**	**199,313**	**198,817**	**193,887**	**186,334**	**–5.8%**
Under age 5	10,114	10,291	9,527	8,751	8,311	–17.8
Aged 5 to 9	10,676	10,314	10,060	9,144	8,597	–19.5
Aged 10 to 14	11,215	10,324	10,379	9,631	8,863	–21.0
Aged 15 to 19	11,840	10,902	10,396	10,155	9,245	–21.9
Aged 20 to 24	12,729	11,539	10,496	10,577	9,843	–22.7
Aged 25 to 29	12,315	12,486	11,153	10,694	10,472	–15.0
Aged 30 to 34	12,040	12,639	11,763	10,773	10,873	–9.7
Aged 35 to 39	11,248	12,344	12,613	11,334	10,896	–3.1
Aged 40 to 44	12,998	11,554	12,659	11,833	10,870	–16.4
Aged 45 to 49	14,219	11,745	12,249	12,562	11,324	–20.4
Aged 50 to 54	15,737	12,882	11,333	12,474	11,700	–25.7
Aged 55 to 59	15,038	14,661	11,356	11,920	12,279	–18.3
Aged 60 to 64	13,351	14,870	12,241	10,860	12,029	–9.9
Aged 65 or older	34,243	42,761	52,594	53,180	51,033	49.0

SHARE OF TOTAL POPULATION	2012	2020	2030	2040	2050	percentage point change 2012–50
Total non-Hispanic whites	**63.0%**	**59.7%**	**55.5%**	**51.0%**	**46.6%**	**–16.4**
Under age 5	49.9	47.2	42.8	38.0	34.5	–15.4
Aged 5 to 9	52.2	48.4	44.8	40.0	35.8	–16.3
Aged 10 to 14	54.3	50.1	46.4	42.1	37.4	–16.9
Aged 15 to 19	55.5	52.4	47.4	43.8	39.1	–16.4
Aged 20 to 24	56.4	53.3	47.8	44.3	40.2	–16.2
Aged 25 to 29	57.6	53.4	49.1	44.3	41.1	–16.5
Aged 30 to 34	57.6	55.2	50.4	45.0	41.9	–15.7
Aged 35 to 39	57.7	56.4	51.6	47.2	42.7	–15.0
Aged 40 to 44	61.8	56.7	54.1	49.3	44.1	–17.8
Aged 45 to 49	65.6	58.7	55.8	51.1	46.7	–18.9
Aged 50 to 54	69.7	62.9	56.4	53.8	49.0	–20.7
Aged 55 to 59	72.4	67.4	58.6	55.7	51.0	–21.4
Aged 60 to 64	75.0	70.8	62.9	56.4	53.8	–21.1
Aged 65 or older	79.3	76.4	72.3	66.7	60.9	–18.4

Note: Non-Hispanic whites are those who identify themselves as being white alone and not Hispanic.
Source: Bureau of the Census, Population Projections, Internet site http://www.census.gov/population/projections/; calculations by New Strategist

Table 6.92 Non-Hispanic Whites by Region, 2000 to 2011

(number of non-Hispanic whites by region, 2000 to 2011; percent change, 2000–11)

	2011	2010	2000	percent change 2000–11
Total non-Hispanic whites	**197,510,927**	**196,817,552**	**194,552,774**	**1.5%**
Northeast	38,014,596	38,008,094	39,327,262	–3.3
Midwest	52,120,571	52,096,633	52,386,131	–0.5
South	69,151,884	68,706,462	65,927,794	4.9
West	38,223,876	38,006,363	36,911,587	3.6

Note: Non-Hispanic whites are those who identify themselves as being white alone and not Hispanic. Total non-Hispanic whites in 2000 do not match the 2000 total in some of the other tables because this figure has not been adjusted to eliminate the "some other race" category that was included in the census.
Source: Bureau of the Census, 2000 Census, 2010 Census, and Population Estimates, Internet site http://www.census.gov/popest/index.html; calculations by New Strategist

Table 6.93 Non-Hispanic White Share of the Total Population by Region, 2011

(total number of people, number and percent distribution of non-Hispanic whites, and non-Hispanic white share of total, by region, 2011)

	total	non-Hispanic white		share of total
		number	percent distribution	
Total people	**311,587,816**	**197,510,927**	**100.0%**	**63.4%**
Northeast	55,597,646	38,014,596	19.2	68.4
Midwest	67,145,089	52,120,571	26.4	77.6
South	116,022,230	69,151,884	35.0	59.6
West	72,822,851	38,223,876	19.4	52.5

Note: Non-Hispanic whites are those who identify themselves as being white alone and not Hispanic.
Source: Bureau of the Census, Population Estimates, Internet site http://www.census.gov/popest/index.html; calculations by New Strategist

Table 6.94 Non-Hispanic Whites by State, 2000 to 2011

(number of non-Hispanic whites by state, 2000 to 2011; percent change, 2000–11)

	2011	2010	2000	percent change 2000–11
Total non-Hispanic whites	**197,510,927**	**196,817,552**	**194,552,774**	**1.5%**
Alabama	3,206,541	3,204,402	3,125,819	2.6
Alabama	4,802,740	4,779,736	4,447,100	8.0
Alaska	722,718	710,231	626,932	15.3
Arizona	6,482,505	6,392,017	5,130,632	26.3
Arkansas	2,937,979	2,915,918	2,673,400	9.9
California	37,691,912	37,253,956	33,871,648	11.3
Colorado	5,116,796	5,029,196	4,301,261	19.0
Connecticut	3,580,709	3,574,097	3,405,565	5.1
Delaware	907,135	897,934	783,600	15.8
District of Columbia	617,996	601,723	572,059	8.0
Florida	19,057,542	18,801,310	15,982,378	19.2
Georgia	9,815,210	9,687,653	8,186,453	19.9
Hawaii	1,374,810	1,360,301	1,211,537	13.5
Idaho	1,584,985	1,567,582	1,293,953	22.5
Illinois	12,869,257	12,830,632	12,419,293	3.6
Indiana	6,516,922	6,483,802	6,080,485	7.2
Iowa	3,062,309	3,046,355	2,926,324	4.6
Kansas	2,871,238	2,853,118	2,688,418	6.8
Kentucky	4,369,356	4,339,367	4,041,769	8.1
Louisiana	4,574,836	4,533,372	4,468,976	2.4
Maine	1,328,188	1,328,361	1,274,923	4.2
Maryland	5,828,289	5,773,552	5,296,486	10.0
Massachusetts	6,587,536	6,547,629	6,349,097	3.8
Michigan	9,876,187	9,883,640	9,938,444	–0.6
Minnesota	5,344,861	5,303,925	4,919,479	8.6
Mississippi	2,978,512	2,967,297	2,844,658	4.7
Missouri	6,010,688	5,988,927	5,595,211	7.4
Montana	998,199	989,415	902,195	10.6
Nebraska	1,842,641	1,826,341	1,711,263	7.7
Nevada	2,723,322	2,700,551	1,998,257	36.3
New Hampshire	1,318,194	1,316,470	1,235,786	6.7
New Jersey	8,821,155	8,791,894	8,414,350	4.8
New Mexico	2,082,224	2,059,179	1,819,046	14.5
New York	19,465,197	19,378,102	18,976,457	2.6
North Carolina	9,656,401	9,535,483	8,049,313	20.0
North Dakota	683,932	672,591	642,200	6.5
Ohio	11,544,951	11,536,504	11,353,140	1.7
Oklahoma	3,791,508	3,751,351	3,450,654	9.9

	2011	2010	2000	percent change 2000–11
Oregon	3,871,859	3,831,074	3,421,399	13.2%
Pennsylvania	12,742,886	12,702,379	12,281,054	3.8
South Carolina	4,679,230	4,625,364	4,012,012	16.6
South Dakota	824,082	814,180	754,844	9.2
Tennessee	6,403,353	6,346,105	5,689,283	12.6
Texas	25,674,681	25,145,561	20,851,820	23.1
Utah	2,817,222	2,763,885	2,233,169	26.2
Vermont	626,431	625,741	608,827	2.9
Virginia	8,096,604	8,001,024	7,078,515	14.4
Washington	6,830,038	6,724,540	5,894,121	15.9
West Virginia	1,855,364	1,852,994	1,808,344	2.6
Wisconsin	5,711,767	5,686,986	5,363,675	6.5
Wyoming	568,158	563,626	493,782	15.1

Note: Non-Hispanic whites are those who identify themselves as being white alone and not Hispanic. Total non-Hispanic whites in 2000 do not match the 2000 total in some of the other tables because this figure has not been adjusted to eliminate the "some other race" category that was included in the census.
Source: Bureau of the Census, 2000 Census, 2010 Census, and Population Estimates, Internet site http://www.census.gov/ popest/index.html; calculations by New Strategist

Table 6.95 Non-Hispanic White Share of Total Population by State, 2011

(total number of people, number and percent distribution of non-Hispanic whites, and non-Hispanic white share of total, by state, 2011)

| | | non-Hispanic white | | |
	total	number	percent distribution	share of total
Total people	**311,591,917**	**197,510,927**	**100.0%**	**63.4%**
Alabama	4,802,740	3,206,541	1.6	66.8
Alaska	722,718	460,501	0.2	63.7
Arizona	6,482,505	3,720,143	1.9	57.4
Arkansas	2,937,979	2,179,905	1.1	74.2
California	37,691,912	14,977,120	7.6	39.7
Colorado	5,116,796	3,567,583	1.8	69.7
Connecticut	3,580,709	2,540,031	1.3	70.9
Delaware	907,135	590,287	0.3	65.1
District of Columbia	617,996	218,278	0.1	35.3
Florida	19,057,542	10,962,466	5.6	57.5
Georgia	9,815,210	5,450,015	2.8	55.5
Hawaii	1,374,810	315,513	0.2	22.9
Idaho	1,584,985	1,325,244	0.7	83.6
Illinois	12,869,257	8,147,277	4.1	63.3
Indiana	6,516,922	5,299,190	2.7	81.3
Iowa	3,062,309	2,705,821	1.4	88.4
Kansas	2,871,238	2,234,288	1.1	77.8
Kentucky	4,369,356	3,763,369	1.9	86.1
Louisiana	4,574,836	2,748,876	1.4	60.1
Maine	1,328,188	1,252,674	0.6	94.3
Maryland	5,828,289	3,169,834	1.6	54.4
Massachusetts	6,587,536	5,032,600	2.5	76.4
Michigan	9,876,187	7,546,042	3.8	76.4
Minnesota	5,344,861	4,425,203	2.2	82.8
Mississippi	2,978,512	1,719,069	0.9	57.7
Missouri	6,010,688	4,858,955	2.5	80.8
Montana	998,199	873,186	0.4	87.5
Nebraska	1,842,641	1,506,941	0.8	81.8
Nevada	2,723,322	1,458,510	0.7	53.6
New Hampshire	1,318,194	1,214,726	0.6	92.2
New Jersey	8,821,155	5,194,384	2.6	58.9
New Mexico	2,082,224	836,611	0.4	40.2
New York	19,465,197	11,293,771	5.7	58.0
North Carolina	9,656,401	6,276,916	3.2	65.0
North Dakota	683,932	605,688	0.3	88.6
Ohio	11,544,951	9,351,839	4.7	81.0
Oklahoma	3,791,508	2,587,379	1.3	68.2

		non-Hispanic white		
	total	number	percent distribution	share of total
Oregon	3,871,859	3,024,723	1.5%	78.1%
Pennsylvania	12,742,886	10,092,308	5.1	79.2
Rhode Island	1,051,302	804,081	0.4	76.5
South Carolina	4,679,230	2,993,966	1.5	64.0
South Dakota	824,082	695,376	0.4	84.4
Tennessee	6,403,353	4,829,515	2.4	75.4
Texas	25,674,681	11,508,453	5.8	44.8
Utah	2,817,222	2,255,459	1.1	80.1
Vermont	626,431	590,021	0.3	94.2
Virginia	8,096,604	5,222,122	2.6	64.5
Washington	6,830,038	4,923,700	2.5	72.1
West Virginia	1,855,364	1,724,893	0.9	93.0
Wisconsin	5,711,767	4,743,951	2.4	83.1
Wyoming	568,158	485,583	0.2	85.5

Note: Non-Hispanic whites are those who identify themselves as being white alone and not Hispanic.
Source: Bureau of the Census, Population Estimates, Internet site http://www.census.gov/popest/index.html; calculations by New Strategist

Table 6.96 Non-Hispanic Whites by Metropolitan Area, 2010

(total number of people, number of non-Hispanic whites, and non-Hispanic white share of total, for selected metropolitan areas, 2010)

	total population	non-Hispanic white number	non-Hispanic white share of total
Abilene, TX	165,252	112,735	68.2%
Akron, OH	703,200	579,151	82.4
Albany, GA	157,308	68,820	43.7
Albany–Schenectady–Troy, NY	870,716	721,505	82.9
Albuquerque, NM	887,077	374,214	42.2
Alexandria, LA	153,922	98,984	64.3
Allentown–Bethlehem–Easton, PA–NJ	821,173	645,741	78.6
Altoona, PA	127,089	121,495	95.6
Amarillo, TX	249,881	160,881	64.4
Ames, IA	89,542	77,812	86.9
Anchorage, AK	380,821	256,490	67.4
Anderson, IN	131,636	113,577	86.3
Anderson, SC	187,126	147,362	78.8
Ann Arbor, MI	344,791	248,675	72.1
Anniston–Oxford, AL	118,572	87,285	73.6
Appleton, WI	225,666	203,691	90.3
Asheville, NC	424,858	366,448	86.3
Athens–Clarke County, GA	192,541	130,515	67.8
Atlanta–Sandy Springs–Marietta, GA	5,268,860	2,671,757	50.7
Atlantic City–Hammonton, NJ	274,549	160,871	58.6
Auburn–Opelika, AL	140,247	97,900	69.8
Augusta–Richmond County, GA–SC	556,877	314,669	56.5
Austin–Round Rock–San Marcos, TX	1,716,289	938,474	54.7
Bakersfield–Delano, CA	839,631	323,794	38.6
Baltimore–Towson, MD	2,710,489	1,626,199	60.0
Bangor, ME	153,923	145,700	94.7
Barnstable Town, MA	215,888	197,327	91.4
Baton Rouge, LA	802,484	465,308	58.0
Battle Creek, MI	136,146	108,664	79.8
Bay City, MI	107,771	98,241	91.2
Beaumont–Port Arthur, TX	388,745	228,486	58.8
Bellingham, WA	201,140	164,675	81.9
Bend, OR	157,733	139,470	88.4
Billings, MT	158,050	140,131	88.7
Binghamton, NY	251,725	222,179	88.3
Birmingham–Hoover, AL	1,128,047	733,656	65.0
Bismarck, ND	108,779	100,591	92.5
Blacksburg–Christiansburg–Radford, VA	162,958	143,718	88.2

	total population	non-Hispanic white	
		number	share of total
Bloomington, IN	192,714	172,163	89.3%
Bloomington–Normal, IL	169,572	138,835	81.9
Boise City–Nampa, ID	616,561	505,202	81.9
Boston–Cambridge–Quincy, MA–NH	4,552,402	3,408,585	74.9
Boulder, CO	294,567	233,741	79.4
Bowling Green, KY	125,953	104,540	83.0
Bremerton–Silverdale, WA	251,133	198,745	79.1
Bridgeport–Stamford–Norwalk, CT	916,829	606,716	66.2
Brownsville–Harlingen, TX	406,220	43,427	10.7
Brunswick, GA	112,370	77,516	69.0
Buffalo–Niagara Falls, NY	1,135,509	903,063	79.5
Burlington, NC	151,131	101,718	67.3
Burlington–South Burlington, VT	211,261	194,738	92.2
Canton–Massillon, OH	404,422	357,541	88.4
Cape Coral–Fort Myers, FL	618,754	439,048	71.0
Cape Girardeau–Jackson, MO–IL	96,275	83,552	86.8
Carson City, NV	55,274	39,083	70.7
Casper, WY	75,450	67,191	89.1
Cedar Rapids, IA	257,940	233,695	90.6
Champaign–Urbana, IL	231,891	172,266	74.3
Charleston, WV	304,284	279,242	91.8
Charleston–North Charleston–Summerville, SC	664,607	420,240	63.2
Charlotte–Gastonia–Rock Hill, NC–SC	1,758,038	1,076,021	61.2
Charlottesville, VA	201,559	154,343	76.6
Chattanooga, TN–GA	528,143	420,172	79.6
Cheyenne, WY	91,738	74,120	80.8
Chicago–Joliet–Naperville, IL–IN–WI	9,461,105	5,204,489	55.0
Chico, CA	220,000	165,416	75.2
Cincinnati–Middletown, OH–KY–IN	2,130,151	1,738,775	81.6
Clarksville, TN–KY	273,949	191,406	69.9
Cleveland, TN	115,788	103,851	89.7
Cleveland–Elyria–Mentor, OH	2,077,240	1,490,074	71.7
Coeur d'Alene, ID	138,494	127,454	92.0
College Station–Bryan, TX	228,660	136,769	59.8
Colorado Springs, CO	645,613	469,095	72.7
Columbia, MO	172,786	140,917	81.6
Columbia, SC	767,598	447,927	58.4
Columbus, GA–AL	294,865	147,518	50.0
Columbus, IN	76,794	66,817	87.0
Columbus, OH	1,836,536	1,394,399	75.9
Corpus Christi, TX	428,185	155,550	36.3
Corvallis, OR	85,579	71,552	83.6

	total population	non-Hispanic white	
		number	share of total
Crestview–Fort Walton Beach–Destin, FL	180,822	139,500	77.1%
Cumberland, MD–WV	103,299	92,937	90.0
Dallas–Fort Worth–Arlington, TX	6,371,773	3,201,677	50.2
Dalton, GA	142,227	97,484	68.5
Danville, IL	81,625	65,590	80.4
Danville, VA	106,561	67,357	63.2
Davenport–Moline–Rock Island, IA–IL	379,690	311,053	81.9
Dayton, OH	841,502	663,353	78.8
Decatur, AL	153,829	119,005	77.4
Decatur, IL	110,768	86,822	78.4
Deltona–Daytona Beach–Ormond Beach, FL	494,593	372,982	75.4
Denver–Aurora–Broomfield, CO	2,543,482	1,673,709	65.8
Des Moines–West Des Moines, IA	569,633	476,434	83.6
Detroit–Warren–Livonia, MI	4,296,250	2,916,144	67.9
Dothan, AL	145,639	104,154	71.5
Dover, DE	162,310	105,891	65.2
Dubuque, IA	93,653	86,981	92.9
Duluth, MN–WI	279,771	257,081	91.9
Durham–Chapel Hill, NC	504,357	278,907	55.3
Eau Claire, WI	161,151	149,946	93.0
El Centro, CA	174,528	23,927	13.7
Elizabethtown, KY	119,736	95,235	79.5
Elkhart–Goshen, IN	197,559	152,555	77.2
Elmira, NY	88,830	77,643	87.4
El Paso, TX	800,647	105,246	13.1
Erie, PA	280,566	242,787	86.5
Eugene–Springfield, OR	351,715	297,808	84.7
Evansville, IN–KY	358,676	318,979	88.9
Fairbanks, AK	97,581	72,259	74.1
Fargo, ND–MN	208,777	188,964	90.5
Farmington, NM	130,044	55,254	42.5
Fayetteville, NC	366,383	169,891	46.4
Fayetteville–Springdale–Rogers, AR–MO	463,204	353,302	76.3
Flagstaff, AZ	134,421	74,231	55.2
Flint, MI	425,790	309,683	72.7
Florence, SC	205,566	112,098	54.5
Florence–Muscle Shoals, AL	147,137	122,562	83.3
Fond du Lac, WI	101,633	93,398	91.9
Fort Collins–Loveland, CO	299,630	253,047	84.5
Fort Smith, AR–OK	298,592	226,828	76.0
Fort Wayne, IN	416,257	330,540	79.4
Fresno, CA	930,450	304,522	32.7

	total population	non-Hispanic white	
		number	share of total
Gadsden, AL	104,430	82,789	79.3%
Gainesville, FL	264,275	172,348	65.2
Gainesville, GA	179,684	114,300	63.6
Glens Falls, NY	128,923	121,581	94.3
Goldsboro, NC	122,623	68,216	55.6
Grand Forks, ND–MN	98,461	87,768	89.1
Grand Junction, CO	146,723	121,944	83.1
Grand Rapids–Wyoming, MI	774,160	615,337	79.5
Great Falls, MT	81,327	71,100	87.4
Greeley, CO	252,825	170,827	67.6
Green Bay, WI	306,241	263,593	86.1
Greensboro–High Point, NC	723,801	449,177	62.1
Greenville, NC	189,510	106,076	56.0
Greenville–Mauldin–Easley, SC	636,986	467,055	73.3
Gulfport–Biloxi, MS	248,820	177,475	71.3
Hagerstown–Martinsburg, MD–WV	269,140	229,076	85.1
Hanford–Corcoran, CA	152,982	53,879	35.2
Harrisburg–Carlisle, PA	549,475	442,343	80.5
Harrisonburg, VA	125,228	105,031	83.9
Hartford–West Hartford–East Hartford, CT	1,212,381	868,016	71.6
Hattiesburg, MS	142,842	95,576	66.9
Hickory–Lenoir–Morganton, NC	365,497	302,096	82.7
Hinesville–Fort Stewart, GA	77,917	35,576	45.7
Holland–Grand Haven, MI	263,801	226,156	85.7
Honolulu, HI	953,207	181,684	19.1
Hot Springs, AR	96,024	80,621	84.0
Houma–Bayou Cane–Thibodaux, LA	208,178	151,869	73.0
Houston–Sugar Land–Baytown, TX	5,946,800	2,360,472	39.7
Huntington–Ashland, WV–KY–OH	287,702	270,988	94.2
Huntsville, AL	417,593	286,557	68.6
Idaho Falls, ID	130,374	111,798	85.8
Indianapolis–Carmel, IN	1,756,241	1,310,092	74.6
Iowa City, IA	152,586	128,881	84.5
Ithaca, NY	101,564	81,490	80.2
Jackson, MI	160,248	137,588	85.9
Jackson, MS	539,057	260,512	48.3
Jackson, TN	115,425	71,897	62.3
Jacksonville, FL	1,345,596	885,040	65.8
Jacksonville, NC	177,772	122,558	68.9
Janesville, WI	160,331	135,526	84.5
Jefferson City, MO	149,807	131,411	87.7
Johnson City, TN	198,716	183,099	92.1

	total population	non-Hispanic white	
		number	share of total
Johnstown, PA	143,679	134,073	93.3%
Jonesboro, AR	121,026	98,641	81.5
Joplin, MO	175,518	151,986	86.6
Kalamazoo–Portage, MI	326,589	263,075	80.6
Kankakee–Bradley, IL	113,449	83,218	73.4
Kansas City, MO–KS	2,035,334	1,514,888	74.4
Kennewick–Pasco–Richland, WA	253,340	164,241	64.8
Killeen–Temple–Fort Hood, TX	405,300	218,901	54.0
Kingsport–Bristol–Bristol, TN–VA	309,544	293,968	95.0
Kingston, NY	182,493	149,099	81.7
Knoxville, TN	698,030	606,269	86.9
Kokomo, IN	98,688	87,446	88.6
La Crosse, WI–MN	133,665	122,899	91.9
Lafayette, IN	201,789	166,341	82.4
Lafayette, LA	273,738	182,803	66.8
Lake Charles, LA	199,607	140,168	70.2
Lake Havasu City–Kingman, AZ	200,186	159,378	79.6
Lakeland–Winter Haven, FL	602,095	388,769	64.6
Lancaster, PA	519,445	440,969	84.9
Lansing–East Lansing, MI	464,036	363,242	78.3
Laredo, TX	250,304	8,345	3.3
Las Cruces, NM	209,233	62,992	30.1
Las Vegas–Paradise, NV	1,951,269	935,955	48.0
Lawrence, KS	110,826	90,532	81.7
Lawton, OK	124,098	73,122	58.9
Lebanon, PA	133,568	116,010	86.9
Lewiston, ID–WA	60,888	54,861	90.1
Lewiston–Auburn, ME	107,702	98,931	91.9
Lexington–Fayette, KY	472,099	372,839	79.0
Lima, OH	106,331	87,708	82.5
Lincoln, NE	302,157	256,854	85.0
Little Rock–North Little Rock–Conway, AR	699,757	487,009	69.6
Logan, UT–ID	125,442	108,026	86.1
Longview, TX	214,369	141,499	66.0
Longview, WA	102,410	87,825	85.8
Los Angeles–Long Beach–Santa Ana, CA	12,828,837	4,056,820	31.6
Louisville/Jefferson County, KY–IN	1,283,566	1,012,081	78.8
Lubbock, TX	284,890	162,440	57.0
Lynchburg, VA	252,634	194,849	77.1
Macon, GA	232,293	119,766	51.6
Madera–Chowchilla, CA	150,865	57,380	38.0
Madison, WI	568,593	476,020	83.7

	total population	non-Hispanic white	
		number	share of total
Manchester–Nashua, NH	400,721	351,224	87.6%
Manhattan, KS	127,081	96,848	76.2
Mankato–North Mankato, MN	96,740	88,338	91.3
Mansfield, OH	124,475	107,726	86.5
McAllen–Edinburg–Mission, TX	774,769	60,553	7.8
Medford, OR	203,206	170,023	83.7
Memphis, TN–MS–AR	1,316,100	608,449	46.2
Merced, CA	255,793	81,599	31.9
Miami–Fort Lauderdale–Pompano Beach, FL	5,564,635	1,937,939	34.8
Michigan City–La Porte, IN	111,467	90,695	81.4
Midland, TX	136,872	72,822	53.2
Milwaukee–Waukesha–West Allis, WI	1,555,908	1,073,109	69.0
Minneapolis–St. Paul–Bloomington, MN–WI	3,279,833	2,578,117	78.6
Missoula, MT	109,299	99,489	91.0
Mobile, AL	412,992	243,904	59.1
Modesto, CA	514,453	240,423	46.7
Monroe, LA	176,441	106,971	60.6
Monroe, MI	152,021	140,609	92.5
Montgomery, AL	374,536	192,543	51.4
Morgantown, WV	129,709	118,855	91.6
Morristown, TN	136,608	121,337	88.8
Mount Vernon–Anacortes, WA	116,901	89,694	76.7
Muncie, IN	117,671	103,721	88.1
Muskegon–Norton Shores, MI	172,188	133,132	77.3
Myrtle Beach–North Myrtle Beach–Conway, SC	269,291	208,096	77.3
Napa, CA	136,484	76,967	56.4
Naples–Marco Island, FL	321,520	211,156	65.7
Nashville–Davidson–Murfreesboro–Franklin, TN	1,589,934	1,176,069	74.0
New Haven–Milford, CT	862,477	582,384	67.5
New Orleans–Metairie–Kenner, LA	1,167,764	628,878	53.9
New York–Northern New Jersey–Long Island, NY–NJ–PA	18,897,109	9,233,812	48.9
Niles–Benton Harbor, MI	156,813	119,389	76.1
North Port–Bradenton–Sarasota, FL	702,281	558,928	79.6
Norwich–New London, CT	274,055	214,605	78.3
Ocala, FL	331,298	245,136	74.0
Ocean City, NJ	97,265	84,522	86.9
Odessa, TX	137,130	56,306	41.1
Ogden–Clearfield, UT	547,184	452,785	82.7
Oklahoma City, OK	1,252,987	845,104	67.4
Olympia, WA	252,264	199,019	78.9
Omaha–Council Bluffs, NE–IA	865,350	681,172	78.7

	total population	non-Hispanic white	
		number	share of total
Orlando–Kissimmee–Sanford, FL	2,134,411	1,136,863	53.3%
Oshkosh–Neenah, WI	166,994	151,509	90.7
Owensboro, KY	114,752	104,565	91.1
Oxnard–Thousand Oaks–Ventura, CA	823,318	400,868	48.7
Palm Bay–Melbourne–Titusville, FL	543,376	421,466	77.6
Palm Coast, FL	95,696	72,860	76.1
Panama City–Lynn Haven–Panama City Beach, FL	168,852	133,790	79.2
Parkersburg–Marietta–Vienna, WV–OH	162,056	155,597	96.0
Pascagoula, MS	162,246	117,679	72.5
Pensacola–Ferry Pass–Brent, FL	448,991	325,627	72.5
Peoria, IL	379,186	319,493	84.3
Philadelphia–Camden–Wilmington, PA–NJ–DE–MD	5,965,343	3,875,845	65.0
Phoenix–Mesa–Glendale, AZ	4,192,887	2,460,541	58.7
Pine Bluff, AR	100,258	48,740	48.6
Pittsburgh, PA	2,356,285	2,051,163	87.1
Pittsfield, MA	131,219	118,926	90.6
Pocatello, ID	90,656	76,730	84.6
Portland–South Portland–Biddeford, ME	514,098	480,553	93.5
Portland–Vancouver–Hillsboro, OR–WA	2,226,009	1,698,126	76.3
Port St. Lucie, FL	424,107	287,564	67.8
Poughkeepsie–Newburgh–Middletown, NY	670,301	476,071	71.0
Prescott, AZ	211,033	172,968	82.0
Providence–New Bedford–Fall River, RI–MA	1,600,852	1,273,029	79.5
Provo–Orem, UT	526,810	444,339	84.3
Pueblo, CO	159,063	86,054	54.1
Punta Gorda, FL	159,978	137,628	86.0
Racine, WI	195,408	145,414	74.4
Raleigh–Cary, NC	1,130,490	716,883	63.4
Rapid City, SD	126,382	105,389	83.4
Reading, PA	411,442	316,406	76.9
Redding, CA	177,223	146,044	82.4
Reno–Sparks, NV	425,417	281,745	66.2
Richmond, VA	1,258,251	754,328	60.0
Riverside–San Bernardino–Ontario, CA	4,224,851	1,546,666	36.6
Roanoke, VA	308,707	248,968	80.6
Rochester, MN	186,011	159,840	85.9
Rochester, NY	1,054,323	824,425	78.2
Rockford, IL	349,431	254,953	73.0
Rocky Mount, NC	152,392	73,130	48.0
Rome, GA	96,317	70,959	73.7
Sacramento–Arden–Arcade–Roseville, CA	2,149,127	1,197,389	55.7
Saginaw–Saginaw Township North, MI	200,169	141,187	70.5

	total population	non-Hispanic white	
		number	share of total
St. Cloud, MN	189,093	172,353	91.1%
St. George, UT	138,115	118,282	85.6
St. Joseph, MO–KS	127,329	111,905	87.9
St. Louis, MO–IL	2,812,896	2,112,954	75.1
Salem, OR	390,738	277,460	71.0
Salinas, CA	415,057	136,435	32.9
Salisbury, MD	125,203	79,563	63.5
Salt Lake City, UT	1,124,197	842,071	74.9
San Angelo, TX	111,823	64,952	58.1
San Antonio–New Braunfels, TX	2,142,508	773,807	36.1
San Diego–Carlsbad–San Marcos, CA	3,095,313	1,500,047	48.5
Sandusky, OH	77,079	65,463	84.9
San Francisco–Oakland–Fremont, CA	4,335,391	1,840,372	42.4
San Jose–Sunnyvale–Santa Clara, CA	1,836,911	648,063	35.3
San Luis Obispo–Paso Robles, CA	269,637	191,696	71.1
Santa Barbara–Santa Maria–Goleta, CA	423,895	203,122	47.9
Santa Cruz–Watsonville, CA	262,382	156,397	59.6
Santa Fe, NM	144,170	63,291	43.9
Santa Rosa–Petaluma, CA	483,878	320,027	66.1
Savannah, GA	347,611	199,249	57.3
Scranton–Wilkes–Barre, PA	563,631	502,578	89.2
Seattle–Tacoma–Bellevue, WA	3,439,809	2,340,274	68.0
Sebastian–Vero Beach, FL	138,028	106,780	77.4
Sheboygan, WI	115,507	100,520	87.0
Sherman–Denison, TX	120,877	95,103	78.7
Shreveport–Bossier City, LA	398,604	218,052	54.7
Sioux City, IA–NE–SD	143,577	109,779	76.5
Sioux Falls, SD	228,261	202,388	88.7
South Bend–Mishawaka, IN–MI	319,224	247,405	77.5
Spartanburg, SC	284,307	199,184	70.1
Spokane, WA	471,221	408,629	86.7
Springfield, IL	210,170	175,307	83.4
Springfield, MA	692,942	516,073	74.5
Springfield, MO	436,712	399,431	91.5
Springfield, OH	138,333	117,976	85.3
State College, PA	153,990	135,427	87.9
Steubenville–Weirton, OH–WV	124,454	115,903	93.1
Stockton, CA	685,306	245,919	35.9
Sumter, SC	107,456	50,423	46.9
Syracuse, NY	662,577	555,047	83.8
Tallahassee, FL	367,413	211,958	57.7
Tampa–St. Petersburg–Clearwater, FL	2,783,243	1,879,437	67.5

	total population	non-Hispanic white	
		number	share of total
Terre Haute, IN	172,425	155,488	90.2%
Texarkana, TX–Texarkana, AR	136,027	92,034	67.7
Toledo, OH	651,429	503,966	77.4
Topeka, KS	233,870	186,502	79.7
Trenton–Ewing, NJ	366,513	199,909	54.5
Tucson, AZ	980,263	541,700	55.3
Tulsa, OK	937,478	635,628	67.8
Tuscaloosa, AL	219,461	134,386	61.2
Tyler, TX	209,714	130,246	62.1
Utica–Rome, NY	299,397	260,944	87.2
Valdosta, GA	139,588	80,113	57.4
Vallejo–Fairfield, CA	413,344	168,628	40.8
Victoria, TX	115,384	55,695	48.3
Vineland–Millville–Bridgeton, NJ	156,898	78,931	50.3
Virginia Beach–Norfolk–Newport News, VA–NC	1,671,683	955,896	57.2
Visalia–Porterville, CA	442,179	143,935	32.6
Waco, TX	234,906	138,295	58.9
Warner Robins, GA	139,900	84,703	60.5
Washington–Arlington–Alexandria, DC–VA–MD–WV	5,582,170	2,711,258	48.6
Waterloo–Cedar Falls, IA	167,819	145,617	86.8
Wausau, WI	134,063	121,007	90.3
Wenatchee–East Wenatchee, WA	110,884	77,272	69.7
Wheeling, WV–OH	147,950	139,308	94.2
Wichita, KS	623,061	459,730	73.8
Wichita Falls, TX	151,306	108,124	71.5
Williamsport, PA	116,111	106,710	91.9
Wilmington, NC	362,315	281,017	77.6
Winchester, VA–WV	128,472	108,821	84.7
Winston–Salem, NC	477,717	317,660	66.5
Worcester, MA	798,552	644,299	80.7
Yakima, WA	243,231	116,024	47.7
York–Hanover, PA	434,972	374,779	86.2
Youngstown–Warren–Boardman, OH–PA	565,773	476,794	84.3
Yuba City, CA	166,892	90,198	54.0
Yuma, AZ	195,751	69,022	35.3

Note: Non-Hispanic whites are those who identify themselves as being white alone and not Hispanic.
Source: Bureau of the Census, 2010 Census, Internet site http://factfinder2.census.gov/faces/nav/jsf/pages/index.xhtml;
calculations by New Strategist

Spending of Non-Hispanic Whites and "Others" Is above Average

The nation's 92 million non-Hispanic white and "other" households spent an average of $53,056 in 2011, according to the Bureau of Labor Statistics' Consumer Expenditure Survey. This is more than the average household spends but well below the spending of Asian households. "Others" include Alaska Natives, American Indians, Asians, Pacific Islanders, and those who identify themselves as being of two or more races.

Non-Hispanic white and other households spend 14 percent more than the average household on health care, 15 percent more on alcoholic beverages, and 22 percent more on other lodging (a category that includes hotel and motel expenses). The segment spends 16 percent less than average on rent and 12 percent less on shoes.

■ Because the non-Hispanic white population is older than the black and Hispanic populations, its spending on health care is above average.

Non-Hispanic white and other households spend 7 percent more than the average household

(average annual spending of total and non-Hispanic white and other consumer units, 2011)

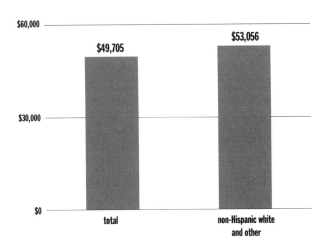

Table 6.97 Spending of Households Headed by Non-Hispanic Whites and Others, 2011

(average annual spending of total consumer units, and average annual, indexed, and market share of spending of consumer units headed by non-Hispanic whites and others, by product and service category, 2011)

	total consumer units	non-Hispanic white and other consumer units		
		average spending	indexed spending	market share
Number of consumer units (000s)	122,287	92,163	–	75.4%
Average number of persons per consumer unit	2.5	2.4	–	–
Average annual spending	**$49,705**	**$53,056**	**107**	**80.4%**
FOOD	**6,458**	**6,743**	**104**	**78.7**
Food at home	**3,838**	**3,970**	**103**	**78.0**
Cereals and bakery products	531	556	105	78.9
Cereals and cereal products	175	179	102	77.1
Bakery products	356	377	106	79.8
Meats, poultry, fish, and eggs	832	813	98	73.6
Beef	223	221	99	74.7
Pork	162	154	95	71.6
Other meats	123	130	106	79.7
Poultry	154	143	93	70.0
Fish and seafood	121	116	96	72.3
Eggs	50	48	96	72.4
Dairy products	407	435	107	80.6
Fresh milk and cream	150	156	104	78.4
Other dairy products	257	279	109	81.8
Fruits and vegetables	715	735	103	77.5
Fresh fruits	247	255	103	77.8
Fresh vegetables	224	234	104	78.7
Processed fruits	116	116	100	75.4
Processed vegetables	128	130	102	76.5
Other food at home	1,353	1,431	106	79.7
Sugar and other sweets	144	156	108	81.6
Fats and oils	110	110	100	75.4
Miscellaneous foods	690	737	107	80.5
Nonalcoholic beverages	361	373	103	77.9
Food prepared by consumer unit on trips	48	55	115	86.4
Food away from home	**2,620**	**2,773**	**106**	**79.8**
ALCOHOLIC BEVERAGES	**456**	**525**	**115**	**86.8**
HOUSING	**16,803**	**17,449**	**104**	**78.3**
Shelter	**9,825**	**10,122**	**103**	**77.6**
Owned dwellings	6,148	6,791	110	83.2
Mortgage interest and charges	3,184	3,412	107	80.8
Property taxes	1,845	2,100	114	85.8
Maintenance, repair, insurance, other expenses	1,120	1,278	114	86.0

	total consumer units	non-Hispanic white and other consumer units		
		average spending	indexed spending	market share
Rented dwellings	$3,029	$2,543	84	63.3%
Other lodging	648	788	122	91.6
Utilities, fuels, and public services	**3,727**	**3,773**	**101**	**76.3**
Natural gas	420	429	102	77.0
Electricity	1,423	1,433	101	75.9
Fuel oil and other fuels	157	190	121	91.2
Telephone	1,226	1,214	99	74.6
Water and other public services	501	506	101	76.1
Household services	**1,122**	**1,233**	**110**	**82.8**
Personal services	398	426	107	80.7
Other household services	724	807	111	84.0
Housekeeping supplies	**615**	**656**	**107**	**80.4**
Laundry and cleaning supplies	145	136	94	70.7
Other household products	340	375	110	83.1
Postage and stationery	130	145	112	84.1
Household furnishings and equipment	**1,514**	**1,666**	**110**	**82.9**
Household textiles	109	124	114	85.7
Furniture	358	374	104	78.7
Floor coverings	20	24	120	90.4
Major appliances	194	211	109	82.0
Small appliances, misc. housewares	89	102	115	86.4
Miscellaneous household equipment	744	831	112	84.2
APPAREL AND RELATED SERVICES	**1,740**	**1,714**	**99**	**74.2**
Men and boys	**404**	**399**	**99**	**74.4**
Men, aged 16 or older	324	328	101	76.3
Boys, aged 2 to 15	80	71	89	66.9
Women and girls	**721**	**743**	**103**	**77.7**
Women, aged 16 or older	604	631	104	78.7
Girls, aged 2 to 15	117	112	96	72.1
Children under age 2	**68**	**63**	**93**	**69.8**
Footwear	**321**	**281**	**88**	**66.0**
Other apparel products and services	**226**	**227**	**100**	**75.7**
TRANSPORTATION	**8,293**	**8,798**	**106**	**80.0**
Vehicle purchases	**2,669**	**2,919**	**109**	**82.4**
Cars and trucks, new	1,265	1,464	116	87.2
Cars and trucks, used	1,339	1,373	103	77.3
Other vehicles	64	82	128	96.6
Gasoline and motor oil	**2,655**	**2,714**	**102**	**77.0**
Other vehicle expenses	**2,454**	**2,596**	**106**	**79.7**
Vehicle finance charges	233	242	104	78.3
Maintenance and repairs	805	867	108	81.2
Vehicle insurance	983	1,023	104	78.4
Vehicle rentals, leases, licenses, other charges	433	464	107	80.8
Public transportation	**516**	**570**	**110**	**83.3**

	total consumer units	non-Hispanic white and other consumer units		
		average spending	indexed spending	market share
HEALTH CARE	**$3,313**	**$3,793**	**114**	**86.3%**
Health insurance	1,922	2,182	114	85.6
Medical services	768	896	117	87.9
Drugs	489	560	115	86.3
Medical supplies	134	155	116	87.2
ENTERTAINMENT	**2,572**	**2,888**	**112**	**84.6**
Fees and admissions	594	699	118	88.7
Audio and visual equipment and services	977	1,009	103	77.8
Pets, toys, and playground equipment	631	734	116	87.7
Other entertainment products and services	370	445	120	90.6
PERSONAL CARE PRODUCTS AND SERVICES	**634**	**654**	**103**	**77.7**
READING	**115**	**138**	**120**	**90.4**
EDUCATION	**1,051**	**1,212**	**115**	**86.9**
TOBACCO PRODUCTS AND SMOKING SUPPLIES	**351**	**396**	**113**	**85.0**
MISCELLANEOUS	**775**	**864**	**111**	**84.0**
CASH CONTRIBUTIONS	**1,721**	**1,930**	**112**	**84.5**
PERSONAL INSURANCE AND PENSIONS	**5,424**	**5,951**	**110**	**82.7**
Life and other personal insurance	317	361	114	85.8
Pensions and Social Security	5,106	5,590	109	82.5
PERSONAL TAXES	**2,012**	**2,511**	**125**	**94.1**
Federal income taxes	1,370	1,747	128	96.1
State and local income taxes	505	601	119	89.7
Other taxes	136	163	120	90.3
GIFTS FOR PEOPLE IN OTHER HOUSEHOLDS	**1,037**	**1,198**	**116**	**87.1**

Definitions: The index compares the spending of non-Hispanic white and other householders to average consumer unit spending by dividing non-Hispanic white and other spending by average spending in each category and multiplying by 100. An index of 125 means non-Hispanic white and other spending is 25 percent above average, while an index of 75 means non-Hispanic white and other spending is 25 percent below average. The market share is the percentage of total spending on a product or service category accounted for by consumer units headed by non-Hispanic whites and others. "Other" includes Alaska Natives, American Indians, Asians, Native Hawaiians, and other Pacific Islanders as well as those who report being of more than one race.
Note: The Bureau of Labor Statistics uses consumer unit rather than household as the sampling unit in the Consumer Expenditure Survey. For the definition of consumer unit, see the glossary. Spending by category does not add to total spending because gift spending is also included in the preceding product and service categories and personal taxes are not included in the total. "–" means not applicable.
Source: Bureau of Labor Statistics, 2011 Consumer Expenditure Survey, Internet site http://www.bls.gov/cex/; calculations by New Strategist

Non-Hispanic Whites Have the Most Household Wealth

The median net worth (assets minus debts) of non-Hispanic white households was $110,500 in 2011, far above the $68,828 net worth of the average American household. Not only is the net worth of non-Hispanic white households well above average, but it fell by only 26 percent between 2005 and 2011, after adjusting for inflation—the smallest decline among racial and ethnic groups. This decline was much less than the 36 percent loss for the average household during those years, according to the Census Bureau's Survey of Income and Program Participation.

Non-Hispanic whites are more likely than the average household to own most assets. Most important is homeownership, since housing equity accounts for a large share of net worth for the average American household. Nearly 73 percent of non-Hispanic white households are homeowners, much greater than the 65 percent homeownership rate among all households. Among non-Hispanic white homeowners, median housing equity was $85,000 in 2011, greater than the $80,000 average.

Non-Hispanic white households are slightly more likely than the average household to be in debt (71 versus 69 percent). Their home-secured debt (mortgages) is equal to the average, at $117,000.

■ Eighty-nine percent of non-Hispanic whites aged 65 or older receive income from Social Security, 33 percent from pensions, and 22 percent from earnings.

The net worth of non-Hispanic whites is far above average

(median net worth of total and non-Hispanic white households, 2011)

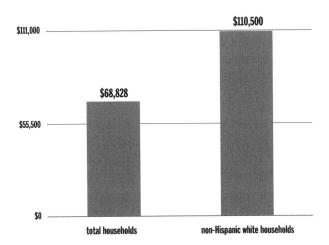

Table 6.98 Median Household Net Worth of Total and Non-Hispanic White Households, 2005 and 2011

(median net worth of total and non-Hispanic white households, 2005 and 2011; percent change, 2005–11; in 2011 dollars)

	2011	2005	percent change 2005–11
Total households	**$68,828**	**$107,344**	**−35.9%**
Non-Hispanic white households	110,500	150,132	−26.4

Note: Non-Hispanic whites are those who identify themselves as being white alone and not Hispanic.
Source: Census Bureau, Wealth and Asset Ownership, Survey of Income and Program Participation, Internet site http://www.census.gov/people/wealth/; calculations by New Strategist

Table 6.99 Distribution of Total and Hispanic Households by Net Worth, 2011

(number of total and Hispanic households, median net worth of total and Hispanic households, and percent distribution of total and Hispanic households by net worth, 2011)

	total households	non-Hispanic white households	
		number	index
Number of households	**118,689,091**	**83,245,166**	**–**
Median net worth	**$68,828**	**$110,500**	**161**

DISTRIBUTION OF HOUSEHOLDS BY NET WORTH

Total households	**100.0%**	**100.0%**	**–**
Zero or negative	18.1	13.7	76
$1 to $4,999	9.1	6.8	75
$5,000 to $9,999	4.8	3.9	81
$10,000 to $24,999	6.6	6.0	91
$25,000 to $49,999	6.9	6.7	97
$50,000 to $99,999	10.4	10.8	104
$100,000 to $249,999	17.9	20.1	112
$250,000 to $499,999	12.6	15.1	120
$500,000 or more	13.5	16.9	125

Note: Non-Hispanic whites are those who identify themselves as being white alone and not Hispanic. The index is calculated by dividing the non-Hispanic white figure by the total figure and multiplying by 100. "–" means not applicable.
Source: Census Bureau, Wealth and Asset Ownership, Survey of Income and Program Participation, Internet site http://www.census.gov/people/wealth/; calculations by New Strategist

Table 6.100 Percent of Total and Non-Hispanic White Households Owning Assets, 2011

(percent of total and non-Hispanic white households owning selected assets, and index of non-Hispanic white to total, 2011)

	total households	non-Hispanic white households	
		percent	index
PERCENT WITH ASSET			
Interest earning asset at financial institution	69.8%	75.4%	108
Regular checking account	29.0	29.1	100
Stocks and mutal fund shares	19.6	24.5	125
Own business	13.8	15.3	111
Motor vehicles	84.7	88.3	104
Own home	65.3	72.6	111
Rental property	5.5	6.4	116
IRA or KEOGH account	28.9	35.4	122
401(k) and thrift savings	42.1	46.4	110

Note: Non-Hispanic whites are those who identify themselves as being white alone and not Hispanic. The index is calculated by dividing the non-Hispanic white figure by the total figure and multiplying by 100.
Source: Census Bureau, Wealth and Asset Ownership, Survey of Income and Program Participation, Internet site http://www .census.gov/people/wealth/; calculations by New Strategist

Table 6.101 Median Value or Equity of Assets Owned by Total and Non-Hispanic White Households, 2011

(median value or equity of assets owned by total and non-Hispanic white households, and index of non-Hispanic white to total, 2011)

	total households	non-Hispanic white households	
		median	index
MEDIAN VALUE OF ASSETS			
Interest earning asset at financial institution	$2,450	$3,250	133
Regular checking account	600	800	133
Stocks and mutal fund shares	20,000	24,000	120
Own business (equity)	8,000	10,000	125
Motor vehicles (equity)	6,824	7,113	104
Own home (equity)	80,000	85,000	106
Rental property (equity)	180,000	180,000	100
IRA or KEOGH account	34,000	36,500	107
401(k) and thrift savings	30,000	35,000	117

Note: Non-Hispanic whites are those who identify themselves as being white alone and not Hispanic. The index is calculated by dividing the non-Hispanic white figure by the total figure and multiplying by 100.
Source: Census Bureau, Wealth and Asset Ownership, Survey of Income and Program Participation, Internet site http://www .census.gov/people/wealth/; calculations by New Strategist

Table 6.102 Asset Ownership of Non-Hispanic White Households, 2005 and 2011

(percent of non-Hispanic white households owning financial assets, 2005 and 2011; percentage point change, 2005–11)

PERCENT OWNING ASSET	2011	2005	percentage point change
Interest earning asset at financial institution	75.4%	76.6%	–1.2
Regular checking account	29.1	34.6	–5.5
Stocks and mutal fund shares	24.5	30.6	–6.1
Own business	15.3	16.6	–1.3
Motor vehicles	88.3	89.9	–1.6
Own home	72.6	74.0	–1.4
Rental property	6.4	5.7	0.7
IRA or KEOGH account	35.4	36.9	–1.5
401(k) and thrift savings	46.4	44.8	1.6

Note: Non-Hispanic whites are those who identify themselves as being white alone and not Hispanic.
Source: Census Bureau, Wealth and Asset Ownership, Survey of Income and Program Participation, Internet site http://www .census.gov/people/wealth/; calculations by New Strategist

Table 6.103 Median Value or Equity of Assets Owned by Non-Hispanic White Households, 2005 and 2011

(median value or equity of assets owned by non-Hispanic white households, 2005 and 2011; percent change, 2005–11; in 2011 dollars)

MEDIAN VALUE OF ASSETS	2011	2005	percent change
Interest earning asset at financial institution	$3,250	$4,835	–32.8%
Regular checking account	800	1,037	–22.8
Stocks and mutal fund shares	24,000	28,794	–16.6
Own business (equity)	10,000	11,518	–13.2
Motor vehicles (equity)	7,113	6,091	16.8
Own home (equity)	85,000	119,783	–29.0
Rental property (equity)	180,000	222,290	–19.0
IRA or KEOGH account	36,500	28,794	26.8
401(k) and thrift savings	35,000	34,553	1.3

Note: Non-Hispanic whites are those who identify themselves as being white alone and not Hispanic.
Source: Census Bureau, Wealth and Asset Ownership, Survey of Income and Program Participation, Internet site http://www .census.gov/people/wealth/; calculations by New Strategist

Table 6.104 Percent of Total and Non-Hispanic White Households with Debt, 2011

(percent of total and non-Hispanic white households with debt, and index of non-Hispanic white to total, 2011)

	total households	non-Hispanic white households	
		percent	index
PERCENT WITH DEBT			
Total debt	**69.0%**	**70.9%**	**103**
Secured debt	55.3	58.3	105
Home debt	40.5	44.0	109
Business debt	4.1	4.8	117
Vehicle debt	30.4	31.5	104
Unsecured debt	46.2	47.2	102
Credit card debt	38.3	39.4	103
Loans	6.8	7.1	104
Other debt	18.6	18.8	101

Note: "Other debt" includes student loans. Non-Hispanic whites are those who identify themselves as being white alone and not Hispanic. The index is calculated by dividing the non-Hispanic white figure by the total figure and multiplying by 100.
Source: Census Bureau, Wealth and Asset Ownership, Survey of Income and Program Participation, Internet site http://www .census.gov/people/wealth/; calculations by New Strategist

Table 6.105 Median Debt of Total and Non-Hispanic White Households, 2011

(median amount of debt for total and non-Hispanic white households with debt, and index of non-Hispanic white to total, 2011)

	total households	non-Hispanic white households	
		median	index
MEDIAN DEBT			
Total debt	**$70,000**	**$80,000**	**114**
Secured debt	91,000	97,500	107
Home debt	117,000	117,000	100
Business debt	25,000	25,000	100
Vehicle debt	10,000	10,000	100
Unsecured debt	7,000	7,470	107
Credit card debt	3,500	3,650	104
Loans	7,000	7,200	103
Other debt	10,000	10,800	108

Note: "Other debt" includes student loans. Non-Hispanic whites are those who identify themselves as being white alone and not Hispanic. The index is calculated by dividing the non-Hispanic white figure by the total figure and multiplying by 100.
Source: Census Bureau, Wealth and Asset Ownership, Survey of Income and Program Participation, Internet site http://www .census.gov/people/wealth/; calculations by New Strategist

Table 6.106 Total People and Non-Hispanic Whites Aged 65 or Older Receiving Income by Source, 2011

(number of total people and non-Hispanic whites aged 65 or older receiving income, percent of non-Hispanic whites receiving income, and non-Hispanic white share of total, 2011; ranked by number of total people receiving type of income; people in thousands as of 2012)

		non-Hispanic whites receiving income		
	total people receiving income	number	percent	non-Hispanic white share of total
Total people aged 65 or older	**40,195**	**32,271**	**100.0%**	**80.3%**
Social Security	35,169	28,726	89.0	81.7
Interest	19,862	17,678	54.8	89.0
Retirement income	14,325	12,250	38.0	85.5
Pension income	12,460	10,633	32.9	85.3
Earnings	8,648	6,996	21.7	80.9
Dividends	7,584	7,007	21.7	92.4
Rents, royalties, estates, or trusts	3,103	2,751	8.5	88.7
Survivor benefits	1,859	1,638	5.1	88.1
Veteran's benefits	1,299	1,111	3.4	85.5
SSI (Supplemental Security Income)	1,297	572	1.8	44.1

Note: Non-Hispanic whites are those who identify themselves as being white alone and not Hispanic.
Source: Bureau of the Census, 2012 Current Population Survey Annual Social and Economic Supplement, Internet site http://www.census.gov/hhes/www/cpstables/032012/perinc/toc.htm; calculations by New Strategist

Table 6.107 Median Income of Total People and Non-Hispanic Whites Aged 65 or Older by Source, 2011

(median income received by total people and non-Hispanic whites aged 65 or older and index of non-Hispanic white to total, by type of income, 2011)

	median income for total people receiving income	median income for non-Hispanic whites receiving income	index, non-Hispanic white to total
Total people aged 65 or older	**$19,939**	**$21,309**	**107**
Social Security	13,376	13,811	103
Interest	1,590	1,600	101
Retirement income	12,282	12,301	100
Pension income	12,458	12,457	100
Earnings	24,893	25,051	101
Dividends	2,023	2,039	101
Rents, royalties, estates, or trusts	3,855	3,816	99
Survivor benefits	7,913	8,148	103
Veteran's benefits	8,770	8,188	93
SSI (Supplemental Security Income)	5,322	5,861	110

Note: Non-Hispanic whites are those who identify themselves as being white alone and not Hispanic. The index is calculated by dividing the non-Hispanic white figure by the total figure and multiplying by 100.
Source: Bureau of the Census, 2012 Current Population Survey Annual Social and Economic Supplement, Internet site http://www.census.gov/hhes/www/cpstables/032012/perinc/toc.htm; calculations by New Strategist

Total Population

■ The U.S. population grew from 282 million in 2000 to 312 million in 2011. The non-Hispanic white share of the population fell from 69 to 63 percent during those years.

■ Thirty-one percent of Americans aged 25 or older had a bachelor's degree in 2012. The proportion ranges from a low of 15 percent among Hispanics to a high of 50 percent among Asians.

■ Nearly 4 million babies were born to American women in 2011, and only 54 percent were non-Hispanic white.

■ Seventy-four percent of the nation's homeowners are non-Hispanic white.

■ The $50,054 median income of U.S. households in 2011 was 8 percent lower than in 2007, after adjusting for inflation. Behind the decline was job loss due to the Great Recession.

■ The non-Hispanic white share of workers will fall from 68 to 62 percent between 2010 and 2020.

■ Among householders under age 45, more than one in three are Asian, black, Hispanic, or another minority.

■ Twenty-one percent of U.S. residents speak a language other than English at home. In California, the proportion is 44 percent.

■ Asian households spend the most—21 percent more than the average household. Black and Hispanic households spend less than average.

■ The median net worth of non-Hispanic white households stood at $110,500 in 2011, much greater than the median net worth of any other racial or ethnic group.

Minority share of U.S. population will grow rapidly

(percent of U.S. residents who are American Indian, Asian, black, or Hispanic, 2012 to 2050)

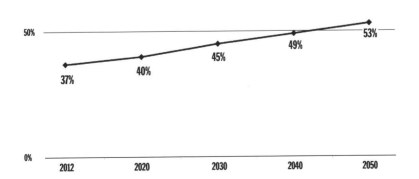

Educational Attainment of Americans Varies Greatly by Race and Hispanic Origin

Overall, 88 percent of Americans had a high school diploma in 2012. But the figure ranges from a low of 65 percent among Hispanics to a high of 92 percent among non-Hispanic whites. The proportion of all Americans with a high school diploma did not top 50 percent until the late 1960s, then rose rapidly as the well-educated baby-boom generation entered adulthood.

Thirty-one percent of Americans had a bachelor's degree in 2012. Again, the proportion varies greatly by race and Hispanic origin—ranging from a low of 15 percent among Hispanics to a high of 50 percent among Asians.

Seventy-nine million Americans aged 3 or older are enrolled in school. Blacks, Hispanics, Asians, and other minorities are an ever-growing share of students, including more than 40 percent of students under age 20.

■ The educational attainment of Americans will continue to rise as well-educated younger adults replace less-educated older people.

Most Americans aged 25 or older have at least some college experience

(percent of total people aged 25 or older by educational attainment, 2012)

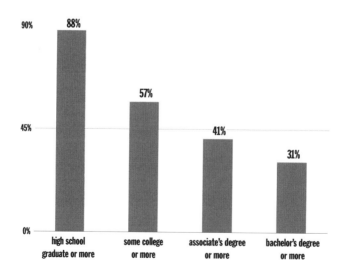

Table 7.1 Educational Attainment of Total People by Age, 2012

(number and percent distribution of people aged 25 or older by educational attainment and age, 2012; numbers in thousands)

	total	25 to 34	35 to 44	45 to 54	55 to 64	65 or older
Total people	**204,579**	**41,219**	**39,927**	**43,955**	**37,971**	**41,506**
Not a high school graduate	25,276	4,414	4,388	4,807	3,827	7,842
High school graduate only	62,113	10,974	10,681	13,927	11,773	14,759
Some college, no degree	34,163	7,676	6,686	7,217	6,495	6,088
Associate's degree	19,737	4,089	4,301	4,588	4,014	2,745
Bachelor's degree	40,561	10,144	8,886	8,726	7,099	5,704
Master's degree	16,459	2,906	3,756	3,408	3,477	2,911
Professional degree	3,093	609	596	684	599	606
Doctoral degree	3,178	405	633	599	687	853
High school graduate or more	179,304	36,803	35,539	39,149	34,144	33,666
Some college or more	117,191	25,829	24,858	25,222	22,371	18,907
Associate's degree or more	83,028	18,153	18,172	18,005	15,876	12,819
Bachelor's degree or more	63,291	14,064	13,871	13,417	11,862	10,074

PERCENT DISTRIBUTION

	total	25 to 34	35 to 44	45 to 54	55 to 64	65 or older
Total people	**100.0%**	**100.0%**	**100.0%**	**100.0%**	**100.0%**	**100.0%**
Not a high school graduate	12.4	10.7	11.0	10.9	10.1	18.9
High school graduate only	30.4	26.6	26.8	31.7	31.0	35.6
Some college, no degree	16.7	18.6	16.7	16.4	17.1	14.7
Associate's degree	9.6	9.9	10.8	10.4	10.6	6.6
Bachelor's degree	19.8	24.6	22.3	19.9	18.7	13.7
Master's degree	8.0	7.1	9.4	7.8	9.2	7.0
Professional degree	1.5	1.5	1.5	1.6	1.6	1.5
Doctoral degree	1.6	1.0	1.6	1.4	1.8	2.1
High school graduate or more	87.6	89.3	89.0	89.1	89.9	81.1
Some college or more	57.3	62.7	62.3	57.4	58.9	45.6
Associate's degree or more	40.6	44.0	45.5	41.0	41.8	30.9
Bachelor's degree or more	30.9	34.1	34.7	30.5	31.2	24.3

Source: Bureau of the Census, Educational Attainment in the United States: 2012, Internet site http://www.census.gov/hhes/ socdemo/education/data/cps/2012/tables.html; calculations by New Strategist

Table 7.2 Educational Attainment of Total Men by Age, 2012

(number and percent distribution of men aged 25 or older by educational attainment and age, 2012; numbers in thousands)

	total	25 to 34	35 to 44	45 to 54	55 to 64	65 or older
Total men	**98,119**	**20,464**	**19,676**	**21,490**	**18,157**	**18,333**
Not a high school graduate	12,504	2,447	2,342	2,572	1,845	3,299
High school graduate only	30,216	6,126	5,805	7,064	5,608	5,612
Some college, no degree	16,072	3,758	3,244	3,334	3,025	2,713
Associate's degree	8,560	1,862	1,827	2,036	1,669	1166
Bachelor's degree	19,415	4,703	4,095	4,141	3,543	2,933
Master's degree	7,397	1,076	1,676	1,546	1,610	1,490
Professional degree	1,938	315	323	435	400	465
Doctoral degree	2,016	176	366	364	457	653
High school graduate or more	85,614	18,016	17,336	18,920	16,312	15,032
Some college or more	55,398	11,890	11,531	11,856	10,704	9,420
Associate's degree or more	39,326	8,132	8,287	8,522	7,679	6,707
Bachelor's degree or more	30,766	6,270	6,460	6,486	6,010	5,541

PERCENT DISTRIBUTION

	total	25 to 34	35 to 44	45 to 54	55 to 64	65 or older
Total men	**100.0%**	**100.0%**	**100.0%**	**100.0%**	**100.0%**	**100.0%**
Not a high school graduate	12.7	12.0	11.9	12.0	10.2	18.0
High school graduate only	30.8	29.9	29.5	32.9	30.9	30.6
Some college, no degree	16.4	18.4	16.5	15.5	16.7	14.8
Associate's degree	8.7	9.1	9.3	9.5	9.2	6.4
Bachelor's degree	19.8	23.0	20.8	19.3	19.5	16.0
Master's degree	7.5	5.3	8.5	7.2	8.9	8.1
Professional degree	2.0	1.5	1.6	2.0	2.2	2.5
Doctoral degree	2.1	0.9	1.9	1.7	2.5	3.6
High school graduate or more	87.3	88.0	88.1	88.0	89.8	82.0
Some college or more	56.5	58.1	58.6	55.2	59.0	51.4
Associate's degree or more	40.1	39.7	42.1	39.7	42.3	36.6
Bachelor's degree or more	31.4	30.6	32.8	30.2	33.1	30.2

Source: Bureau of the Census, Educational Attainment in the United States: 2012, Internet site http://www.census.gov/hhes/socdemo/education/data/cps/2012/tables.html; calculations by New Strategist

Table 7.3 Educational Attainment of Total Women by Age, 2012

(number and percent distribution of women aged 25 or older by educational attainment and age, 2012; numbers in thousands)

	total	25 to 34	35 to 44	45 to 54	55 to 64	65 or older
Total women	**106,460**	**20,756**	**20,251**	**22,466**	**19,815**	**23,175**
Not a high school graduate	12,771	1,968	2,047	2,233	1,983	4,544
High school graduate only	31,898	4,848	4,877	6,863	6,165	9,147
Some college, no degree	18,091	3,918	3,444	3,884	3,470	3,376
Associate's degree	11,176	2,227	2,474	2,551	2,346	1,579
Bachelor's degree	21,146	5,442	4,791	4,586	3,556	2,771
Master's degree	9,062	1,830	2,080	1,863	1,867	1421
Professional degree	1,155	294	273	250	199	140
Doctoral degree	1162	229	266	235	231	200
High school graduate or more	93,690	18,788	18,205	20,232	17,834	18,634
Some college or more	61,792	13,940	13,328	13,369	11,669	9,487
Associate's degree or more	43,701	10,022	9,884	9,485	8,199	6,111
Bachelor's degree or more	32,525	7,795	7,410	6,934	5,853	4,532

PERCENT DISTRIBUTION

Total women	**100.0%**	**100.0%**	**100.0%**	**100.0%**	**100.0%**	**100.0%**
Not a high school graduate	12.0	9.5	10.1	9.9	10.0	19.6
High school graduate only	30.0	23.4	24.1	30.5	31.1	39.5
Some college, no degree	17.0	18.9	17.0	17.3	17.5	14.6
Associate's degree	10.5	10.7	12.2	11.4	11.8	6.8
Bachelor's degree	19.9	26.2	23.7	20.4	17.9	12.0
Master's degree	8.5	8.8	10.3	8.3	9.4	6.1
Professional degree	1.1	1.4	1.3	1.1	1.0	0.6
Doctoral degree	1.1	1.1	1.3	1.0	1.2	0.9
High school graduate or more	88.0	90.5	89.9	90.1	90.0	80.4
Some college or more	58.0	67.2	65.8	59.5	58.9	40.9
Associate's degree or more	41.0	48.3	48.8	42.2	41.4	26.4
Bachelor's degree or more	30.6	37.6	36.6	30.9	29.5	19.6

Source: Bureau of the Census, Educational Attainment in the United States: 2012, Internet site http://www.census.gov/hhes/socdemo/education/data/cps/2012/tables.html; calculations by New Strategist

Table 7.4 Educational Attainment by Race and Hispanic Origin, 2012

(number and percent distribution of people aged 25 or older by educational attainment, race, and Hispanic origin, 2012; numbers in thousands)

	total	Asian	black	Hispanic	non-Hispanic white
Total people	**204,579**	**11,400**	**24,713**	**28,445**	**139,001**
Not a high school graduate	25,276	1,251	3,684	9,956	10,449
High school graduate or more	179,304	10,146	21,028	18,488	128,551
Some college or more	117,191	7,792	12,669	9,950	86,094
Associate's degree or more	83,028	6,564	7,632	6,063	62,367
Bachelor's degree or more	63,291	5,747	5,282	4,133	47,931

PERCENT DISTRIBUTION BY EDUCATIONAL ATTAINMENT

Total people	**100.0 %**	**100.0%**	**100.0%**	**100.0%**	**100.0%**
Not a high school graduate	12.4	11.0	14.9	35.0	7.5
High school graduate or more	87.6	89.0	85.1	65.0	92.5
Some college or more	57.3	68.4	51.3	35.0	61.9
Associate's degree or more	40.6	57.6	30.9	21.3	44.9
Bachelor's degree or more	30.9	50.4	21.4	14.5	34.5

PERCENT DISTRIBUTION BY RACE AND HISPANIC ORIGIN

Total people	**100.0%**	**5.6%**	**12.1%**	**13.9%**	**67.9%**
Not a high school graduate	100.0	4.9	14.6	39.4	41.3
High school graduate or more	100.0	5.7	11.7	10.3	71.7
Some college or more	100.0	6.6	10.8	8.5	73.5
Associate's degree or more	100.0	7.9	9.2	7.3	75.1
Bachelor's degree or more	100.0	9.1	8.3	6.5	75.7

Note: Numbers by race and Hispanic origin do not sum to total because Asians and blacks are those who identify themselves as being of the race alone and those who identify themselves as being of the race in combination with other races, Hispanics may be of any race, and not all races are shown. Non-Hispanic whites are those who identify themselves as being white alone and not Hispanic.
Source: Bureau of the Census, Educational Attainment in the United States: 2012, Internet site http://www.census.gov/hhes/socdemo/education/data/cps/2012/tables.html; calculations by New Strategist

Table 7.5 Educational Attainment of the Total Population by Region, 2006–10

(total number of people aged 25 or older and percent distribution by educational attainment and region, 2006–10; numbers in thousands)

	total	Northeast	Midwest	South	West
Total people	**199,727**	**37,103**	**43,723**	**73,448**	**45,452**
Not a high school graduate	29,898	4,944	5,320	12,430	7,205
High school graduate only	57,903	11,423	13,983	21,774	10,723
Some college, no degree	41,176	6,059	9,403	15,203	10,510
Associate's degree	15,022	2,814	3,457	5,119	3,632
Bachelor's degree	35,148	7,041	7,435	12,078	8,594
Graduate degree	20,579	4,823	4,124	6,844	4,787
PERECENT DISTRIBUTION					
High school graduate or more	85.0%	86.7%	87.8%	83.1%	84.1%
Some college or more	56.0	55.9	55.9	53.4	60.6
Associate's degree or more	35.4	39.6	34.3	32.7	37.4
Bachelor's degree or more	27.9	32.0	26.4	25.8	29.4

Source: Bureau of the Census, 2006–10 American Community Survey, Internet site http://factfinder2.census.gov/faces/nav/jsf/ pages/index.xhtml; calculations by New Strategist

Table 7.6 School Enrollment of Total People by Age and Sex, 2011

(number and percent of people aged 3 or older enrolled in school, by age and sex, October 2011; numbers in thousands)

	total		female		male	
	number	percent	number	percent	number	percent
Total people enrolled	**79,043**	**26.6%**	**39,798**	**26.5%**	**39,245**	**27.2%**
Aged 3 to 4	4,597	54.5	2,239	52.1	2,358	52.8
Aged 5 to 6	8,009	94.7	3,866	95.2	4,143	95.1
Aged 7 to 9	12,319	98.1	6,066	97.9	6,253	98.1
Aged 10 to 13	15,941	98.6	7,780	98.4	8,161	98.6
Aged 14 to 15	7,825	98.7	3,836	98.9	3,990	98.4
Aged 16 to 17	7,906	94.3	3,882	96.0	4,025	95.4
Aged 18 to 19	6,017	66.8	3,029	73.5	2,987	68.8
Aged 20 to 21	4,618	48.4	2,406	56.4	2,213	49.2
Aged 22 to 24	3,961	27.3	2,031	32.0	1,931	30.3
Aged 25 to 29	3,139	12.4	1,761	16.8	1,378	12.9
Aged 30 to 34	1,571	7.2	919	8.9	653	6.4
Aged 35 to 44	1,688	3.8	1,032	5.2	656	3.4
Aged 45 to 54	1012	2.4	669	3.0	343	1.6
Aged 55 or older	438	0.4	283	0.7	155	0.4

Source: Bureau of the Census, School Enrollment, CPS October 2011—Detailed Tables, Internet site http://www.census.gov/hhes/school/data/cps/2011/tables.html; calculations by New Strategist

Table 7.7 School Enrollment by Age, Race, and Hispanic Origin, 2011

(total number of people aged 3 or older enrolled in school by age and percent distribution by race, and Hispanic origin, October 2011; numbers in thousands)

	total		Asian	black	Hispanic	non-Hispanic white
	number	percent				
Total people enrolled	**79,043**	**100.0%**	**5.8%**	**16.8%**	**20.4%**	**56.9%**
Aged 3 to 4	4,597	100.0	5.8	19.1	20.8	54.0
Aged 5 to 6	8,009	100.0	5.9	16.6	25.6	52.7
Aged 7 to 9	12,319	100.0	5.8	16.9	24.4	53.3
Aged 10 to 13	15,941	100.0	5.6	16.4	22.0	55.8
Aged 14 to 15	7,825	100.0	5.0	16.3	20.5	57.6
Aged 16 to 17	7,906	100.0	5.3	16.5	20.1	57.4
Aged 18 to 19	6,017	100.0	5.3	17.0	18.9	58.6
Aged 20 to 21	4,618	100.0	7.3	12.3	16.8	63.9
Aged 22 to 24	3,961	100.0	6.2	16.1	15.1	62.2
Aged 25 to 29	3,139	100.0	7.0	17.5	13.7	61.4
Aged 30 to 34	1,571	100.0	7.7	20.9	11.6	59.8
Aged 35 to 44	1,688	100.0	7.3	23.4	11.0	57.0
Aged 45 to 54	1012	100.0	2.3	20.4	7.2	69.3
Aged 55 or older	438	100.0	4.3	22.4	8.9	62.8

Note: Numbers by race and Hispanic origin do not sum to total because Asians and blacks are those who identify themselves as being of the race alone and those who identify themselves as being of the race in combination with other races, Hispanics may be of any race, and not all races are shown. Non-Hispanic whites are those who identify themselves as being white alone and not Hispanic.
Source: Bureau of the Census, School Enrollment, CPS October 2011—Detailed Tables, Internet site http://www.census.gov/ hhes/school/data/cps/2011/tables.html; calculations by New Strategist

Table 7.8 College Enrollment by Age, Race, and Hispanic Origin, 2011

(total number of people aged 15 or older enrolled in college by age and percent distribution by race, and Hispanic origin, October 2011; numbers in thousands)

| | total | | | | | non-Hispanic |
	number	percent	Asian	black	Hispanic	white
Total enrolled in college	**20,397**	**100.0%**	**5.9%**	**15.4%**	**14.5%**	**62.3%**
Under age 20	4,446	100.0	5.9	13.9	18.0	60.6
Aged 20 to 21	4,460	100.0	6.3	11.0	16.6	64.3
Aged 22 to 24	3,869	100.0	5.9	14.7	14.8	62.7
Aged 25 to 29	3,066	100.0	6.2	16.7	13.3	61.7
Aged 30 or older	4,559	100.0	5.4	20.9	9.5	61.9

Note: Percentages by race and Hispanic origin do not sum to total because Asians and blacks are those who identify themselves as being of the race alone, Hispanics may be of any race, and not all races are shown. Non-Hispanic whites are those who identify themselves as being white alone and not Hispanic.
Source: Bureau of the Census, School Enrollment, CPS October 2011—Detailed Tables, Internet site http://www.census.gov/ hhes/school/data/cps/2011/tables.html; calculations by New Strategist

Table 7.9 College Enrollment of Total People by Type of School and Enrollment Status, 2011

(number and percent distribution of total people aged 15 or older enrolled in college by type of school and percent distribution of enrollment by race and Hispanic origin, October 2011; numbers in thousands)

| | total | | percent distribution by race and Hispanic origin | | | | |
	number	percent distribution	total	Asian	black	Hispanic	non-Hispanic white
Total people enrolled	**20,397**	**100.0%**	**100.0%**	**5.9%**	**15.4%**	**14.5%**	**62.3%**
Two-year undergraduate program	5,705	28.0	100.0	3.8	17.9	22.2	53.7
Four-year undergraduate program	10,920	53.5	100.0	5.8	14.4	12.8	65.3
Graduate school	3,773	18.5	100.0	9.3	14.6	7.7	66.6
Total men enrolled	**9,132**	**100.0**	**100.0**	**6.2**	**13.3**	**15.7**	**62.8**
Two-year undergraduate program	2,453	26.9	100.0	3.8	14.5	25.3	53.8
Four-year undergraduate program	5,061	55.4	100.0	6.4	13.0	12.8	66.1
Graduate school	1,617	17.7	100.0	9.2	12.2	10.4	65.8
Total women enrolled	**11,266**	**100.0**	**100.0**	**5.7**	**17.2**	**13.4**	**61.9**
Two-year undergraduate program	3,252	28.9	100.0	3.8	20.5	19.9	53.5
Four-year undergraduate program	5,858	52.0	100.0	5.3	15.7	12.7	64.6
Graduate school	2,155	19.1	100.0	9.4	16.3	5.8	67.1

Note: Percentages by race and Hispanic origin do not sum to total because Asians and blacks are those who identify themselves as being of the race alone, Hispanics may be of any race, and not all races are shown. Non-Hispanic whites are those who identify themselves as being white alone and not Hispanic.
Source: Bureau of the Census, School Enrollment, CPS October 2011—Detailed Tables, Internet site http://www.census.gov/ hhes/school/data/cps/2011/tables.html; calculations by New Strategist

Table 7.10 Degrees Earned by Race and Hispanic Origin, 2010–11

(total number of degrees conferred and percent distribution by race and Hispanic origin, 2010–11)

	total	Asian	black	Hispanic	non-Hispanic white
Total degrees	**3,552,640**	**227,748**	**393,351**	**335,116**	**2,355,350**
Associate's degrees	942,327	45,876	128,703	125,616	604,110
Bachelor's degrees	1,715,913	121,066	173,017	154,063	1,182,405
Master's degrees	730,635	43,728	80,706	46,787	462,903
Doctoral and first-professional degrees	163,765	17,078	10,925	8,650	105,932

PERCENT DISTRIBUTION BY RACE AND HISPANIC ORIGIN

Associate's degrees	100.0%	4.9%	13.7%	13.3%	64.1%
Bachelor's degrees	100.0	7.1	10.1	9.0	68.9
Master's degrees	100.0	6.0	11.0	6.4	63.4
Doctoral and first-professional degrees	100.0	10.4	6.7	5.3	64.7

Note: Numbers do not add to total because Hispanics may be of any race, not all races are shown, and "nonresident aliens" are not shown.
Source: National Center for Education Statistics, Digest of Education Statistics 2012, Internet site http://nces.ed.gov/programs/digest/2012menu_tables.asp; calculations by New Strategist

As the Asian, Black, and Hispanic Populations Grow, a Smaller Share of Newborns Are Non-Hispanic White

About 4 million babies were born to American women in 2011, and only a slim majority—54 percent—was non-Hispanic white. Twenty-three percent of babies born in 2011 were Hispanic, 15 percent were black, 6 percent were Asian, and 1 percent were American Indian. As these children grow up, the United States will become an increasingly multicultural society.

Eighty-four percent of Americans had health insurance in 2011, leaving a substantial 16 percent without coverage. The majority of those without health insurance are Asian, black, or Hispanic. Non-Hispanic whites account for only 45 percent of the uninsured.

Sixteen percent of Americans aged 18 or older have difficulties in physical functioning, and 8 percent say they would find it "very difficult" or impossible to walk a quarter of a mile. Heart disease and cancer are the leading causes of death and accounted for 48 percent of all deaths in 2009.

■ Because of the aging of the population, the proportion of Americans with disabilities is certain to rise.

Minorities are the majority of those without health insurance

(percent distribution of people without health insurance by race and Hispanic origin, 2011)

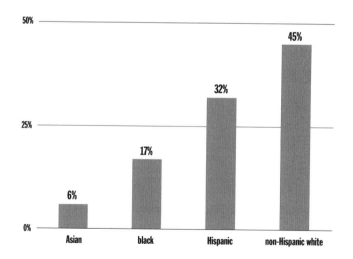

Table 7.11 Weight of Total People by Age and Sex, 2007–10

(average weight in pounds of people aged 20 or older by age and sex, 2007–10)

	men	women
Total people	**195.5 lbs.**	**166.2 lbs.**
Aged 20 to 29	183.9	161.9
Aged 30 to 39	199.5	169.1
Aged 40 to 49	200.6	168.0
Aged 50 to 59	201.3	170.0
Aged 60 to 69	199.4	170.5
Aged 70 to 79	190.6	164.9
Aged 80 or older	174.9	143.1

Note: Data are based on measured weight of a sample of the civilian noninstitutionalized population.
Source: National Center for Health Statistics, Anthropometric Reference Data for Children and Adults: United States, 2007–2010, National Health Statistics Reports, Series 11, Number 252, 2012, Internet site http://www.cdc.gov/nchs/nhanes.htm

Table 7.12 Births to Total Women by Age, 2011

(number and percent distribution of births to women by age, 2011)

	number	percent distribution
Total births	**3,953,593**	**100.0%**
Under age 15	3,974	0.1
Aged 15 to 19	329,797	8.3
Aged 20 to 24	925,213	23.4
Aged 25 to 29	1,127,592	28.5
Aged 30 to 34	986,661	25.0
Aged 35 to 39	463,815	11.7
Aged 40 to 44	108,891	2.8
Aged 45 to 54	7,651	0.2

Source: National Center for Health Statistics, Births: Preliminary Data for 2011, National Vital Statistics Report, Vol. 61, No. 5, 2012, Internet site http://www.cdc.gov/nchs/births.htm; calculations by New Strategist

Table 7.13 Births by Age, Race, and Hispanic Origin, 2011

(total number of births and percent distribution by age, race, and Hispanic origin of mother, 2011)

| | total | | American | | | | non-Hispanic |
	number	percent	Indian	Asian	black	Hispanic	white
Total births	**3,953,593**	**100.0%**	**1.2%**	**6.4%**	**14.7%**	**23.1%**	**54.4%**
Under age 15	3,974	100.0	2.4	1.7	34.7	39.5	22.0
Aged 15 to 19	329,797	100.0	2.1	1.7	23.8	33.1	39.3
Aged 20 to 24	925,213	100.0	1.7	3.0	20.2	26.2	49.0
Aged 25 to 29	1,127,592	100.0	1.1	6.2	13.1	21.9	57.5
Aged 30 to 34	986,661	100.0	0.8	9.0	10.6	19.4	60.0
Aged 35 to 39	463,815	100.0	0.7	10.7	10.8	21.0	56.3
Aged 40 to 44	108,891	100.0	0.7	10.1	11.9	20.8	55.8
Aged 45 to 54	7,651	100.0	0.4	10.6	13.2	16.2	56.5

Note: Births by race and Hispanic origin do not add to total because Hispanics may be of any race and "not stated" is not shown.
Source: National Center for Health Statistics, Births: Preliminary Data for 2011, National Vital Statistics Report, Vol. 61, No. 5, 2012, Internet site http://www.cdc.gov/nchs/births.htm; calculations by New Strategist

Table 7.14 Births to Unmarried Women by Age, 2010

(total number of births, number and percent to unmarried women and unmarried share of total, by age, 2010)

| | | unmarried | | |
	total	number	percent distribution	percent of total
Total births	**3,999,386**	**1,633,471**	**100.0%**	**40.8%**
Under age 15	4,497	4,465	0.3	99.3
Aged 15 to 19	367,678	323,862	19.8	88.1
Aged 20 to 24	951,688	600,833	36.8	63.1
Aged 25 to 29	1,133,713	384,865	23.6	33.9
Aged 30 to 34	962,170	203,479	12.5	21.1
Aged 35 to 39	464,870	91,089	5.6	19.6
Aged 40 to 54	114,770	24,878	1.5	21.7

Source: National Center for Health Statistics, Births: Final Data for 2010, National Vital Statistics Reports, Vol. 61, No. 1, 2012, Internet site http://www.cdc.gov/nchs/births.htm; calculations by New Strategist

Table 7.15 Births to Unmarried Women by Age, Race, and Hispanic Origin, 2010

(number and percent distribution of births to unmarried women by age, race, and Hispanic origin of mother, 2010)

	total number	American Indian	Asian	black	Hispanic	non-Hispanic white
Total births to unmarried women	**1,633,471**	**30,670**	**42,069**	**427,687**	**504,411**	**627,541**
Under age 15	4,465	100	47	1,571	1,792	959
Aged 15 to 19	323,862	6,744	5,069	86,250	105,130	120,831
Aged 20 to 24	600,833	11,686	12,498	164,547	165,963	246,000
Aged 25 to 29	384,865	6,867	11,886	98,495	119,900	147,405
Aged 30 to 34	203,479	3,528	7,291	50,558	70,963	70,862
Aged 35 to 39	91,089	1,402	3,987	20,831	32,823	31,728
Aged 40 or older	24,878	343	1,291	5,435	7,840	9,756
Total births to unmarried women	**100.0%**	**1.9%**	**2.6%**	**26.2%**	**30.9%**	**38.4%**
Under age 15	100.0	2.2	1.1	35.2	40.1	21.5
Aged 15 to 19	100.0	2.1	1.6	26.6	32.5	37.3
Aged 20 to 24	100.0	1.9	2.1	27.4	27.6	40.9
Aged 25 to 29	100.0	1.8	3.1	25.6	31.2	38.3
Aged 30 to 34	100.0	1.7	3.6	24.8	34.9	34.8
Aged 35 to 39	100.0	1.5	4.4	22.9	36.0	34.8
Aged 40 or older	100.0	1.4	5.2	21.8	31.5	39.2

Note: Births by race and Hispanic origin do not add to total because Hispanics may be of any race and "not stated" is not shown. American Indians include Alaska Natives. Asians include Pacific Islanders.
Source: National Center for Health Statistics, Births: Final Data for 2010, National Vital Statistics Reports, Vol. 61, No. 1, 2012, Internet site http://www.cdc.gov/nchs/births.htm; calculations by New Strategist

Table 7.16 Births to Total Women by Birth Order, 2011

(number and percent distribution of births to women by birth order, 2011)

	number	percent distribution
Total births	**3,953,593**	**100.0%**
First child	1,577,344	39.9
Second child	1,239,136	31.3
Third child	648,124	16.4
Fourth or later child	458,777	11.6

Note: Numbers do not add to total because "not stated" is not shown.
Source: National Center for Health Statistics, Births: Preliminary Data for 2011, National Vital Statistics Report, Vol. 61, No. 5, 2012, Internet site http://www.cdc.gov/nchs/births.htm; calculations by New Strategist

Table 7.17 Births by State, Race, and Hispanic Origin, 2011

(total number of births and percent distribution by race and Hispanic origin of mother, by state, 2011)

	total		American Indian	Asian	non-Hispanic black	Hispanic	non-Hispanic white
	number	percent					
Total births	**3,953,593**	**100.0%**	**1.2%**	**6.4%**	**14.7%**	**23.1%**	**54.4%**
Alabama	59,347	100.0	0.3	1.7	30.3	7.5	60.1
Alaska	11,455	100.0	24.8	9.1	3.8	6.6	53.1
Arizona	85,543	100.0	7.0	4.2	4.8	38.9	45.6
Arkansas	38,713	100.0	0.7	2.0	18.7	10.2	68.2
California	502,118	100.0	0.7	14.0	6.0	49.8	28.8
Colorado	65,055	100.0	1.0	3.9	4.7	27.8	62.2
Connecticut	37,280	100.0	0.7	6.1	12.8	22.5	57.8
Delaware	11,257	100.0	0.2	4.9	26.9	12.6	55.3
District of Columbia	9,314	100.0	0.2	6.0	51.7	14.7	28.3
Florida	213,344	100.0	0.2	3.4	23.0	27.5	45.6
Georgia	132,488	100.0	0.3	4.7	33.7	14.1	45.8
Hawaii	18,957	100.0	0.4	64.6	2.7	16.0	25.6
Idaho	22,305	100.0	1.9	2.0	0.9	15.6	80.1
Illinois	161,312	100.0	0.1	6.0	16.9	22.2	54.5
Indiana	83,702	100.0	0.2	2.4	11.7	8.6	77.0
Iowa	38,213	100.0	0.7	3.2	4.8	8.1	83.6
Kansas	39,642	100.0	1.0	3.4	7.4	15.9	72.7
Kentucky	55,377	100.0	0.2	2.2	9.4	5.0	83.4
Louisiana	61,889	100.0	0.6	2.2	38.1	5.8	53.5
Maine	12,704	100.0	0.9	1.7	3.1	1.6	92.5
Maryland	73,086	100.0	0.3	7.8	32.6	14.1	45.5
Massachusetts	73,225	100.0	0.4	8.5	10.8	9.2	69.5
Michigan	114,004	100.0	0.7	3.5	19.1	6.7	69.8
Minnesota	68,411	100.0	2.3	7.5	9.5	6.8	73.5
Mississippi	39,856	100.0	0.7	1.1	43.4	3.3	51.4
Missouri	76,117	100.0	0.5	2.6	15.0	5.4	76.0
Montana	12,069	100.0	12.3	1.2	0.6	3.7	82.3
Nebraska	25,720	100.0	2.0	2.8	6.6	14.2	75.0
Nevada	35,295	100.0	1.3	8.4	10.5	37.0	43.2
New Hampshire	12,852	100.0	0.2	4.0	1.8	4.1	88.7
New Jersey	105,886	100.0	0.2	11.2	15.2	26.5	46.9
New Mexico	27,289	100.0	13.2	1.9	1.7	55.2	28.3
New York	241,290	100.0	0.5	10.3	16.2	23.5	48.6
North Carolina	120,385	100.0	1.6	4.3	23.8	15.1	56.2
North Dakota	9,527	100.0	10.9	1.8	2.3	3.2	81.4
Ohio	137,916	100.0	0.2	2.5	16.6	4.6	75.8
Oklahoma	52,274	100.0	11.8	2.8	9.2	12.8	63.8
Oregon	45,157	100.0	1.9	6.0	2.6	19.4	70.4
Pennsylvania	143,148	100.0	0.3	4.4	14.7	9.9	70.4
Rhode Island	10,960	100.0	1.4	5.4	8.8	22.1	61.7
South Carolina	57,368	100.0	0.4	2.1	31.9	8.3	57.5

| | total | | American | | non-Hispanic | | non-Hispanic |
	number	percent	Indian	Asian	black	Hispanic	white
South Dakota	11,849	100.0%	17.7%	1.9%	2.2%	4.3%	74.8%
Tennessee	79,588	100.0	0.3	2.4	20.8	8.8	68.0
Texas	377,449	100.0	0.3	4.6	11.4	48.4	35.5
Utah	51,223	100.0	1.5	3.3	1.1	15.0	79.8
Vermont	6,078	100.0	0.3	2.6	1.5	1.2	94.2
Virginia	102,648	100.0	0.1	7.4	21.4	12.2	58.8
Washington	86,976	100.0	2.6	10.9	4.9	18.4	63.3
West Virginia	20,720	100.0	0.1	0.9	3.5	1.0	94.2
Wisconsin	67,811	100.0	1.4	4.6	9.7	9.6	74.5
Wyoming	7,398	100.0	3.6	1.4	0.9	11.7	82.1

Note: Numbers do not add to total because not all races are shown and Hispanics may be of any race. American Indians include Alaska Natives. Asians include Pacific Islanders.
Source: National Center for Health Statistics, Births: Preliminary Data for 2011, National Vital Statistics Report, Vol. 61, No. 5, 2012, Internet site http://www.cdc.gov/nchs/births.htm; calculations by New Strategist

Table 7.18 Health Insurance Coverage of the Total Population by Age, 2011

(number and percent distribution of total people by age and health insurance coverage status, 2011; numbers in thousands)

	total	with health insurance coverage during year			not covered at any time during the year
		total	private	government	
Total people	**308,827**	**260,214**	**197,323**	**99,497**	**48,613**
Under age 18	74,108	67,143	44,047	28,747	6,964
Aged 18 to 24	30,140	22,491	18,088	5,865	7,649
Aged 25 to 34	41,219	29,690	24,976	6,092	11,529
Aged 35 to 44	39,927	31,528	27,678	5,421	8,399
Aged 45 to 54	43,955	36,102	31,330	6,634	7,853
Aged 55 to 64	37,971	32,442	27,106	8,026	5,529
Aged 65 or older	41,507	40,817	24,098	38,712	690

PERCENT DISTRIBUTION BY COVERAGE STATUS

Total people	**100.0%**	**84.3%**	**63.9%**	**32.2%**	**15.7%**
Under age 18	100.0	90.6	59.4	38.8	9.4
Aged 18 to 24	100.0	74.6	60.0	19.5	25.4
Aged 25 to 34	100.0	72.0	60.6	14.8	28.0
Aged 35 to 44	100.0	79.0	69.3	13.6	21.0
Aged 45 to 54	100.0	82.1	71.3	15.1	17.9
Aged 55 to 64	100.0	85.4	71.4	21.1	14.6
Aged 65 or older	100.0	98.3	58.1	93.3	1.7

Note: Numbers do not add to total because some people have more than one type of health insurance.
Source: Bureau of the Census, Health Insurance, Internet site http://www.census.gov/hhes/www/cpstables/032012/health/toc .htm; calculations by New Strategist

Table 7.19 Total People with Private Health Insurance Coverage by Age, 2011

(number and percent distribution of total people by age and private health insurance coverage status, 2011; numbers in thousands)

| | | with private health insurance | | | |
| | | | employment-based | | |
	total	total	total	own	direct purchase
Total people	**308,827**	**197,323**	**170,102**	**88,237**	**30,244**
Under age 18	74,108	44,047	40,561	198	4,254
Aged 18 to 24	30,140	18,088	13,945	3,508	1,923
Aged 25 to 34	41,219	24,976	22,799	17,024	2,516
Aged 35 to 44	39,927	27,678	25,793	18,389	2,618
Aged 45 to 54	43,955	31,330	28,759	20,709	3,754
Aged 55 to 64	37,971	27,106	24,108	17,703	3,901
Aged 65 or older	41,507	24,098	14,137	10,705	11,276

PERCENT DISTRIBUTION BY COVERAGE STATUS

Total people	**100.0%**	**63.9%**	**55.1%**	**28.6%**	**9.8%**
Under age 18	100.0	59.4	54.7	0.3	5.7
Aged 18 to 24	100.0	60.0	46.3	11.6	6.4
Aged 25 to 34	100.0	60.6	55.3	41.3	6.1
Aged 35 to 44	100.0	69.3	64.6	46.1	6.6
Aged 45 to 54	100.0	71.3	65.4	47.1	8.5
Aged 55 to 64	100.0	71.4	63.5	46.6	10.3
Aged 65 or older	100.0	58.1	34.1	25.8	27.2

Note: Numbers by type of insurance do not add to total because some people have more than one type of health insurance coverage.
Source: Bureau of the Census, Health Insurance, Internet site http://www.census.gov/hhes/www/cpstables/032012/health/toc .htm; calculations by New Strategist

Table 7.20 Total People with Government Health Insurance Coverage by Age, 2011

(number and percent distribution of total people by age and government health insurance coverage status, 2011; numbers in thousands)

		with government health insurance			
	total	total	Medicaid	Medicare	military
Total people	**308,827**	**99,497**	**50,835**	**46,922**	**13,712**
Under age 18	74,108	28,747	26,345	611	2,586
Aged 18 to 24	30,140	5,865	4,832	255	980
Aged 25 to 34	41,219	6,092	4,495	624	1,372
Aged 35 to 44	39,927	5,421	3,771	998	1,177
Aged 45 to 54	43,955	6,634	4,014	2,101	1,518
Aged 55 to 64	37,971	8,026	3,494	3,836	2,263
Aged 65 or older	41,507	38,712	3,883	38,496	3,816

PERCENT DISTRIBUTION BY COVERAGE STATUS

Total people	**100.0%**	**32.2%**	**16.5%**	**15.2%**	**4.4%**
Under age 18	100.0	38.8	35.5	0.8	3.5
Aged 18 to 24	100.0	19.5	16.0	0.8	3.3
Aged 25 to 34	100.0	14.8	10.9	1.5	3.3
Aged 35 to 44	100.0	13.6	9.4	2.5	2.9
Aged 45 to 54	100.0	15.1	9.1	4.8	3.5
Aged 55 to 64	100.0	21.1	9.2	10.1	6.0
Aged 65 or older	100.0	93.3	9.4	92.7	9.2

Note: Numbers by type of insurance do not add to total because some people have more than one type of health insurance coverage.
Source: Bureau of the Census, Health Insurance, Internet site http://www.census.gov/hhes/www/cpstables/032012/health/toc .htm; calculations by New Strategist

Table 7.21 People without Health Insurance Coverage by Age, Race, and Hispanic Origin, 2011

(total number of people without health insurance coverage during the year and percent distribution by age, race, and Hispanic origin, 2011; numbers in thousands)

	total number	total percent	Asian	black	Hispanic	non-Hispanic white
Total people without health insurance	**48,613**	**100.0%**	**5.9%**	**16.8%**	**32.5%**	**44.6%**
Under age 18	6,964	100.0	5.4	18.6	38.2	38.0
Aged 18 to 24	7,649	100.0	5.9	19.7	33.6	40.9
Aged 25 to 34	11,529	100.0	6.2	17.1	34.7	42.5
Aged 35 to 44	8,399	100.0	5.8	14.5	36.6	42.9
Aged 45 to 54	7,853	100.0	5.2	16.5	27.0	50.5
Aged 55 to 64	5,529	100.0	6.9	14.4	20.2	57.3
Aged 65 or older	690	100.0	9.4	15.4	33.6	40.6

Note: Percentages do not sum to total because Asians and blacks are those who identify themselves as being of the race alone and those who identify themselves as being of the race in combination with other races, not all races are shown, and Hispanics may be of any race. Non-Hispanic whites are those who identify themselves as being white alone and not Hispanic.
Source: Bureau of the Census, Health Insurance, Internet site http://www.census.gov/hhes/www/cpstables/032012/health/toc .htm; calculations by New Strategist

Table 7.22 Health Conditions among Total People Aged 18 or Older, 2011

(number and percent of total people aged 18 or older with selected health conditions, 2011; numbers in thousands)

	number	percent with condition
TOTAL PEOPLE	**231,376**	**100.0%**
Selected circulatory diseases		
Heart disease, all types	26,485	11.4
Coronary	15,300	6.6
Hypertension	58,959	25.5
Stroke	6,171	2.7
Selected respiratory conditions		
Emphysema	4,680	2.0
Asthma, ever	29,041	12.6
Asthma, still	18,869	8.2
Hay fever	16,869	7.3
Sinusitis	29,611	12.8
Chronic bronchitis	10,071	4.4
Selected types of cancer		
Any cancer	19,025	8.2
Breast cancer	3,221	1.4
Cervical cancer	1,188	0.5
Prostate cancer	2,280	1.0
Other selected diseases and conditions		
Diabetes	20,589	8.9
Ulcers	15,502	6.7
Kidney disease	4,381	1.9
Liver disease	3,016	1.3
Arthritis	53,782	23.2
Chronic joint symptoms	68,749	29.7
Migraines or severe headaches	37,904	16.4
Pain in neck	35,798	15.5
Pain in lower back	66,917	28.9
Pain in face or jaw	11,436	4.9
Selected sensory problems		
Hearing	37,122	16.0
Vision	21,232	9.2
Absence of all natural teeth	18,038	7.8

Note: The conditions shown are those that have ever been diagnosed by a doctor, except as noted. Hay fever, sinusitis, and chronic bronchitis have been diagnosed in the past 12 months. Kidney and liver disease have been diagnosed in the past 12 months and exclude kidney stones, bladder infections, and incontinence. Chronic joint symptoms are shown if respondent had pain, aching, or stiffness in or around a joint (excluding back and neck) and the condition began more than three months ago. Migraines, pain in neck, lower back, face, or jaw are shown only if pain lasted a whole day or more.
Source: National Center for Health Statistics, Summary Health Statistics for U.S. Adults: National Health Interview Survey, 2011, Vital and Health Statistics, Series 10, No. 256, 2012, Internet site http://www.cdc.gov/nchs/nhis.htm; calculations by New Strategist

Table 7.23 Health Conditions among Total Children, 2011

(number and percent of total children under age 18 with selected health conditions, 2011; numbers in thousands)

	number	percent with condition
Total children	**74,518**	**100.0%**
Ever told have asthma	10,463	14.0
Still have asthma	7,074	9.5
Hay fever in past 12 months	6,711	9.0
Respiratory allergies in past 12 months	8,269	11.1
Food allergies in past 12 months	4,126	5.5
Skin allergies in past 12 months	9,516	12.8
Prescription medication taken regularly for at least three months	10,019	13.4
Learning disability*	4,660	6.3
Attention deficit hyperactivity disorder*	5,240	7.0

* Diagnosed by a school representative or health professional; data exclude children under age 3.
Source: National Center for Health Statistics, Summary Health Statistics for U.S. Children: National Health Interview Survey, 2011, Vital and Health Statistics, Series 10, No. 254, 2012, Internet site http://www.cdc.gov/nchs/nhis.htm

Table 7.24 Difficulties in Physical Functioning among Total People, 2011

(number and percent of people aged 18 or older with difficulties in physical functioning, by type of difficulty, 2011; numbers in thousands)

	number	percent
TOTAL PEOPLE	**231,376**	**100.0%**
Total with any physical difficulty	**37,368**	**16.2**
Walk quarter of a mile	17,597	7.6
Climb 10 steps without resting	12,887	5.6
Stand for two hours	22,369	9.7
Sit for two hours	7,724	3.3
Stoop, bend, or kneel	21,677	9.4
Reach over head	6,550	2.8
Grasp or handle small objects	4,329	1.9
Lift or carry 10 pounds	10,677	4.6
Push or pull large objects	15,998	6.9

Note: Respondents were classified as having difficulties if they responded "very difficult" or "can't do at all."
Source: National Center for Health Statistics, Summary Health Statistics for U.S. Adults: National Health Interview Survey, 2011, Vital and Health Statistics, Series 10, No. 256, 2012, Internet site http://www.cdc.gov/nchs/nhis.htm; calculations by New Strategist

Table 7.25 Health Care Office Visits by Total People, 2011

(number and percent distribution of the population aged 18 or older by number of office visits to a health care provider in past 12 months, 2011; numbers in thousands)

	total	percent distribution
Total people	**231,376**	**100.0%**
No visits	43,578	18.8
One visit	39,552	17.1
Two to three visits	59,226	25.6
Four to nine visits	55,721	24.1
10 or more visits	30,822	13.3

Note: Health care visits exclude overnight hospitalizations, visits to emergency rooms, home visits, dental visits, and telephone calls.
Source: National Center for Health Statistics, Summary Health Statistics for U.S. Adults: National Health Interview Survey, 2011, Vital and Health Statistics, Series 10, No. 256, 2012, Internet site http://www.cdc.gov/nchs/nhis.htm; calculations by New Strategist

Table 7.26 Deaths from the 10 Leading Causes, 2009

(total number of deaths caused by the 10 leading causes of death, 2009; ranked by total number of deaths)

	number	percent distribution
Total deaths	**2,437,163**	**100.0%**
1. Diseases of the heart	599,413	24.6
2. Malignant neoplasms (cancer)	567,628	23.3
3. Chronic lower respiratory diseases	137,353	5.6
4. Cerebrovascular diseases	128,842	5.3
5. Accidents	118,021	4.8
6. Alzheimer's disease	79,003	3.2
7. Diabetes mellitus	68,705	2.8
8. Influenza and pneumonia	53,692	2.2
9. Nephritis, nephrotic syndrome and nephrosis	48,935	2.0
10. Suicide	36,909	1.5
All other causes	598,662	24.6

Source: National Center for Health Statistics, Deaths: Leading Causes for 2009, National Vital Statistics Report, Vol. 61, No. 7, 2012, Internet site http://www.cdc.gov/nchs/deaths.htm; calculations by New Strategist

Homeownership Is Highest for Non-Hispanic Whites

Among the nation's homeowners in 2011, nearly 78 percent were non-Hispanic white. Because non-Hispanic whites are the largest population segment and have the highest homeownership rate, they account for the great majority of homeowners. The pattern is different among renters. Only 54 percent of the nation's renters are non-Hispanic white, while 21 percent are black and 19 percent are Hispanic.

Twelve percent of Americans moved between March 2011 and March 2012. Non-Hispanic whites account for only 54 percent of movers. Blacks and Hispanics account for 18 and 21 percent of movers, respectively, and Asians for 6 percent. Among people who moved in the past year, non-Hispanic whites account for 69 percent of those who moved because of retirement and 80 percent of those who moved for health reasons. Non-Hispanic whites were just 44 percent of those who moved because they wanted cheaper housing.

■ The economic downturn has reduced homeownership rates in every racial and ethnic group.

Non-Hispanic whites are the great majority of homeowners, but only about half of renters

(percent distribution of homeowners and renters by race and Hispanic origin of householder, 2011)

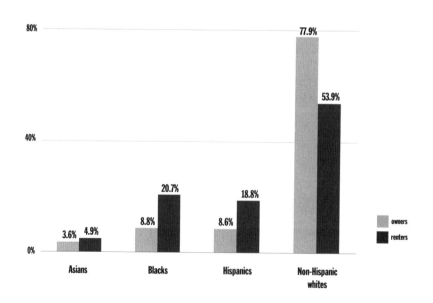

Table 7.27 Homeowners by Race and Hispanic Origin, 2011

(number of total households, and number, percent, and percent distribution of households by homeownership status, by race and Hispanic origin of householder, 2011; numbers in thousands)

| | total | homeowners | | | renters | | |
		number	percent of total	percent distribution	number	percent of total	percent distribution
Total households	114,907	76,091	66.2%	100.0%	38,816	33.8%	100.0%
RACE							
Asian alone	4,620	2,714	58.7	3.6	1,907	41.3	4.9
Black alone	14,694	6,662	45.3	8.8	8,033	54.7	20.7
White alone	92,820	65,357	70.4	85.9	27,463	29.6	70.8
Two or more races	1,480	793	53.6	1.0	688	46.5	1.8
HISPANIC ORIGIN							
Hispanic	13,841	6,530	47.2	8.6	7,311	52.8	18.8
Non-Hispanic white	80,190	59,274	73.9	77.9	20,916	26.1	53.9

Note: Hispanics may be of any race. Non-Hispanic whites are those who identify themselves as being white alone and not Hispanic.
Source: Bureau of the Census, American Housing Survey for the United States: 2011, Internet site http://www.census.gov/ housing/ahs/index.html; calculations by New Strategist

Table 7.28 **Homeownership Status by Age of Householder, 2011**

(number and percent of total households by age of householder and homeownership status, 2011; numbers in thousands)

	total	owner		renter	
		number	percent	number	percent
Total households	**114,907**	**76,091**	**66.2%**	**38,816**	**33.8%**
Under age 25	5,398	830	15.4	4,568	84.6
Aged 25 to 29	8,745	3,136	35.9	5,610	64.2
Aged 30 to 34	10,735	5,391	50.2	5,343	49.8
Aged 35 to 44	20,447	12,847	62.8	7,600	37.2
Aged 45 to 54	23,416	16,994	72.6	6,422	27.4
Aged 55 to 64	21,108	16,643	78.8	4,466	21.2
Aged 65 to 74	13,168	10,802	82.0	2,366	18.0
Aged 75 or older	11,890	9,448	79.5	2,442	20.5

Source: Bureau of the Census, American Housing Survey for the United States: 2011, Internet site http://www.census.gov/housing/ahs/index.html; calculations by New Strategist

Table 7.29 **Total Homeowners by Age of Householder, 2011**

(number and percent distribution of total homeowners, by age of householder, 2011; numbers in thousands)

	number	percent distribution
Total homeowners	**76,091**	**100.0%**
Under age 25	830	1.1
Aged 25 to 29	3,136	4.1
Aged 30 to 34	5,391	7.1
Aged 35 to 44	12,847	16.9
Aged 45 to 54	16,994	22.3
Aged 55 to 64	16,643	21.9
Aged 65 to 74	10,802	14.2
Aged 75 or older	9,448	12.4

Source: Bureau of the Census, American Housing Survey for the United States: 2011, Internet site http://www.census.gov/housing/ahs/index.html; calculations by New Strategist

Table 7.30 Total Renters by Age of Householder, 2011

(number and percent distribution of total renters, by age of householder, 2011; numbers in thousands)

	number	percent distribution
Total renters	**38,816**	**100.0%**
Under age 25	4,568	11.8
Aged 25 to 29	5,610	14.5
Aged 30 to 34	5,343	13.8
Aged 35 to 44	7,600	19.6
Aged 45 to 54	6,422	16.5
Aged 55 to 64	4,466	11.5
Aged 65 to 74	2,366	6.1
Aged 75 or older	2,442	6.3

Source: Bureau of the Census, American Housing Survey for the United States: 2011, Internet site http://www.census.gov/housing/ahs/index.html; calculations by New Strategist

Table 7.31 Homeownership Status by Household Type, 2010

(number and percent of total households by household type and homeownership status, 2010; numbers in thousands)

	total	owner		renter	
		number	percent	number	percent
Total households	**116,716**	**75,986**	**65.1%**	**40,730**	**34.9%**
Family households	**77,538**	**56,206**	**72.5**	**21,332**	**27.5**
Married couples	56,510	45,801	81.0	10,710	19.0
Female-headed family, no spouse present	15,250	7,278	47.7	7,972	52.3
Male-headed family, no spouse present	5,778	3,127	54.1	2,651	45.9
Nonfamily households	**39,178**	**19,780**	**50.5**	**19,398**	**49.5**
Female householder	20,719	11,053	53.3	9,666	46.7
Living alone	17,299	9,625	55.6	7,673	44.4
Male householder	18,459	8,727	47.3	9,732	52.7
Living alone	13,906	6,828	49.1	7,078	50.9

Source: Bureau of the Census, 2010 Census, Internet site http://factfinder2.census.gov/faces/nav/jsf/pages/index.xhtml; calculations by New Strategist

Table 7.32 Total Homeowners by Household Type, 2010

(number and percent distribution of total homeowners, by household type, 2010; numbers in thousands)

	total	percent distribution
Total homeowners	**75,986**	**100.0%**
Family households	**56,206**	**74.0**
Married couples	45,801	60.3
Female-headed family, no spouse present	7,278	9.6
Male-headed family, no spouse present	3,127	4.1
Nonfamily households	**19,780**	**26.0**
Female householder	11,053	14.5
Living alone	9,625	12.7
Male householder	8,727	11.5
Living alone	6,828	9.0

Source: Bureau of the Census, 2010 Census, Internet site http://factfinder2.census.gov/faces/nav/jsf/pages/index.xhtml; calculations by New Strategist

Table 7.33 Total Renters by Household Type, 2010

(number and percent distribution of total renters, by household type, 2010; numbers in thousands)

	total	percent distribution
Total renters	**40,730**	**100.0%**
Family households	**21,332**	**52.4**
Married couples	10,710	26.3
Female-headed family, no spouse present	7,972	19.6
Male-headed family, no spouse present	2,651	6.5
Nonfamily households	**19,398**	**47.6**
Female householder	9,666	23.7
Living alone	7,673	18.8
Male householder	9,732	23.9
Living alone	7,078	17.4

Source: Bureau of the Census, 2010 Census, Internet site http://factfinder2.census.gov/faces/nav/jsf/pages/index.xhtml; calculations by New Strategist

Table 7.34 Homeownership Status by Region, 2011

(number and percent of total households by region and homeownership status, 2011; numbers in thousands)

	total	owners		renters	
		number	percent	number	percent
Total households	**114,907**	**76,091**	**66.2%**	**38,816**	**33.8%**
Northeast	21,066	13,480	64.0	7,585	36.0
Midwest	25,682	18,032	70.2	7,650	29.8
South	42,584	29,119	68.4	13,465	31.6
West	25,575	15,460	60.4	10,115	39.6

Source: Bureau of the Census, American Housing Survey for the United States: 2011, Internet site http://www.census.gov/housing/ahs/index.html; calculations by New Strategist

Table 7.35 Homeowners by Region, 2011

(number and percent distribution of total homeowners by region, 2011; numbers in thousands)

	number	percent distribution
Total homeowners	**76,091**	**100.0%**
Northeast	13,480	17.7
Midwest	18,032	23.7
South	29,119	38.3
West	15,460	20.3

Source: Bureau of the Census, American Housing Survey for the United States: 2011, Internet site http://www.census.gov/housing/ahs/index.html; calculations by New Strategist

Table 7.36 Renters by Region, 2011

(number and percent distribution of total renters by region, 2011; numbers in thousands)

	number	percent distribution
Total renters	**38,816**	**100.0%**
Northeast	7,585	19.5
Midwest	7,650	19.7
South	13,465	34.7
West	10,115	26.1

Source: Bureau of the Census, American Housing Survey for the United States: 2011, Internet site http://www.census.gov/ housing/ahs/index.html; calculations by New Strategist

Table 7.37 **Characteristics of Occupied Housing Units by Homeownership Status, 2011**

(number and percent distribution of total occupied housing units by selected housing characteristics and homeownership status, 2011; numbers in thousands)

	total	owner-occupied		renter-occupied	
		number	percent distribution	number	percent distribution
UNITS IN STRUCTURE					
Total households	**114,907**	**76,091**	**100.0%**	**38,816**	**100.0%**
One, detached	73,761	62,662	82.4	11,099	28.6
One, attached	6,744	4,090	5.4	2,654	6.8
Two to four	8,956	1,419	1.9	7,537	19.4
Five to nine	5,410	583	0.8	4,827	12.4
10 to 19	5,032	518	0.7	4,514	11.6
20 to 49	3,665	408	0.5	3,257	8.4
50 or more	4,150	734	1.0	3,415	8.8
Mobile home or trailer	7,190	5,678	7.5	1,512	3.9
Median square footage of unit*	1,800	1,800	–	1,301	–
NUMBER OF BEDROOMS					
Total households	**114,907**	**76,091**	**100.0**	**38,816**	**100.0**
None	912	72	0.1	840	2.2
One	12,067	1,731	2.3	10,336	26.6
Two	28,656	13,197	17.3	15,459	39.8
Three	48,565	39,306	51.7	9,259	23.9
Four or more	24,707	21,785	28.6	2,921	7.5
NUMBER OF BATHROOMS					
Total households	**114,907**	**76,091**	**100.0**	**38,816**	**100.0**
None	494	190	0.2	304	0.8
One	39,268	15,118	19.9	24,150	62.2
One-and-one-half	15,066	11,232	14.8	3,834	9.9
Two or more	60,079	49,551	65.1	10,528	27.1
ROOM USED FOR BUSINESS					
Total households	**114,907**	**76,091**	**100.0**	**38,816**	**100.0**
With room(s) used for business	32,425	24,068	31.6	8,355	21.5

* *Single-family detached and mobile/manufactured homes only.*
Note: "–" means not applicable.
Source: Bureau of the Census, American Housing Survey for the United States: 2011, Internet site http://www.census.gov/housing/ahs/index.html; calculations by New Strategist

Table 7.38 Geographic Mobility of Total People by Age, 2011–12

(total number of people aged 1 or older, number and percent who moved between March 2011 and March 2012, and percent distribution of movers by type of move, by age; numbers in thousands)

	total	same house (nonmovers)	total movers	same county	different county, same state	different state total	different state same region	different state different region	movers from abroad
Total, aged 1 or older	**304,924**	**268,436**	**36,488**	**23,493**	**6,782**	**5,059**	**2,319**	**2,740**	**1,154**
Aged 1 to 4	16,207	13,117	3,090	2,086	521	400	178	222	83
Aged 5 to 9	20,416	17,532	2,884	1,993	496	332	142	190	62
Aged 10 to 14	20,605	18,221	2,384	1,612	403	308	144	164	60
Aged 15 to 17	12,977	11,666	1,311	880	225	172	90	82	34
Aged 18 to 19	8,262	7,109	1,153	744	249	117	48	69	43
Aged 20 to 24	21,878	16,491	5,387	3,486	957	732	334	398	213
Aged 25 to 29	20,893	15,756	5,137	3,204	912	795	410	385	226
Aged 30 to 34	20,326	16,663	3,663	2,341	674	522	236	286	126
Aged 35 to 39	19,140	16,606	2,534	1,657	434	377	141	236	66
Aged 40 to 44	20,787	18,770	2,017	1,237	420	270	113	157	90
Aged 45 to 49	21,583	19,807	1,776	1,139	341	249	113	136	47
Aged 50 to 54	22,372	20,746	1,626	1,004	345	249	105	144	27
Aged 55 to 59	20,470	19,275	1,195	729	276	153	87	66	38
Aged 60 to 61	7,344	6,970	374	223	84	56	23	33	10
Aged 62 to 64	10,157	9,625	532	334	102	92	37	55	3
Aged 65 or older	41,506	40,080	1,426	823	344	234	118	116	25

PERCENT DISTRIBUTION BY MOBILITY STATUS

	total	same house (nonmovers)	total movers	same county	different county, same state	different state total	different state same region	different state different region	movers from abroad
Total, aged 1 or older	**100.0%**	**88.0%**	**12.0%**	**7.7%**	**2.2%**	**1.7%**	**0.8%**	**0.9%**	**0.4%**
Aged 1 to 4	100.0	80.9	19.1	12.9	3.2	2.5	1.1	1.4	0.5
Aged 5 to 9	100.0	85.9	14.1	9.8	2.4	1.6	0.7	0.9	0.3
Aged 10 to 14	100.0	88.4	11.6	7.8	2.0	1.5	0.7	0.8	0.3
Aged 15 to 17	100.0	89.9	10.1	6.8	1.7	1.3	0.7	0.6	0.3
Aged 18 to 19	100.0	86.0	14.0	9.0	3.0	1.4	0.6	0.8	0.5
Aged 20 to 24	100.0	75.4	24.6	15.9	4.4	3.3	1.5	1.8	1.0
Aged 25 to 29	100.0	75.4	24.6	15.3	4.4	3.8	2.0	1.8	1.1
Aged 30 to 34	100.0	82.0	18.0	11.5	3.3	2.6	1.2	1.4	0.6
Aged 35 to 39	100.0	86.8	13.2	8.7	2.3	2.0	0.7	1.2	0.3
Aged 40 to 44	100.0	90.3	9.7	6.0	2.0	1.3	0.5	0.8	0.4
Aged 45 to 49	100.0	91.8	8.2	5.3	1.6	1.2	0.5	0.6	0.2
Aged 50 to 54	100.0	92.7	7.3	4.5	1.5	1.1	0.5	0.6	0.1
Aged 55 to 59	100.0	94.2	5.8	3.6	1.3	0.7	0.4	0.3	0.2
Aged 60 to 61	100.0	94.9	5.1	3.0	1.1	0.8	0.3	0.4	0.1
Aged 62 to 64	100.0	94.8	5.2	3.3	1.0	0.9	0.4	0.5	0.0
Aged 65 or older	100.0	96.6	3.4	2.0	0.8	0.6	0.3	0.3	0.1

Source: Bureau of the Census, Geographic Mobility: 2011 to 2012, Internet site http://www.census.gov/hhes/migration/data/cps/cps2012.html; calculations by New Strategist

Table 7.39 Movers by Age, Race, and Hispanic Origin, 2011–12

(total number of people aged 1 or older who moved between March 2011 and March 2012 and percent distribution by age, race, and Hispanic origin; numbers in thousands)

	total		Asian	black	Hispanic	non-Hispanic white
	number	percent				
Total movers	**36,488**	**100.0%**	**6.2%**	**18.2%**	**21.3%**	**54.1%**
Aged 1 to 4	3,090	100.0	5.7	24.0	30.7	42.2
Aged 5 to 9	2,884	100.0	4.7	24.6	27.9	43.3
Aged 10 to 14	2,384	100.0	4.3	25.5	25.5	45.7
Aged 15 to 17	1,311	100.0	4.4	27.8	24.8	43.6
Aged 18 to 19	1,153	100.0	5.4	17.9	21.2	52.9
Aged 20 to 24	5,387	100.0	7.0	13.7	18.9	59.6
Aged 25 to 29	5,137	100.0	8.2	14.2	20.3	56.9
Aged 30 to 34	3,663	100.0	7.1	15.6	23.0	53.9
Aged 35 to 39	2,534	100.0	7.6	16.6	21.5	54.7
Aged 40 to 44	2,017	100.0	5.3	21.2	17.3	55.6
Aged 45 to 49	1,776	100.0	7.0	17.9	17.0	57.4
Aged 50 to 54	1,626	100.0	4.9	19.2	15.9	57.3
Aged 55 to 59	1,195	100.0	4.9	17.7	13.8	63.6
Aged 60 to 61	374	100.0	2.7	15.5	14.2	66.0
Aged 62 to 64	532	100.0	4.5	15.6	17.7	61.7
Aged 65 or older	1,426	100.0	5.8	10.8	11.4	71.7

Note: Numbers by race and Hispanic origin do not sum to total because Asians and blacks are those who identify themselves as being of the race alone, Hispanics may be of any race, and not all races are shown. Non-Hispanic whites are those who identify themselves as being white alone and not Hispanic.
Source: Bureau of the Census, Geographic Mobility: 2011 to 2012, Internet site http://www.census.gov/hhes/migration/data/cps/cps2012.html; calculations by New Strategist

Table 7.40 Reasons for Moving by Race and Hispanic Origin, 2011–12

(total number of movers by main reason for move and percent distribution by race and Hispanic origin, 2011–12; numbers in thousands)

	total		Asian	black	Hispanic	non-Hispanic white
	number	percent				
Total movers	**36,488**	**100.0%**	**6.2%**	**18.2%**	**21.3%**	**54.1%**
FAMILY REASONS	**10,693**	**100.0%**	**4.6%**	**17.5%**	**21.5%**	**55.3%**
Change in marital status	2,300	100.0	4.1	14.9	17.3	63.0
To establish own household	3,906	100.0	3.9	19.4	24.2	52.0
Other family reason	4,487	100.0	5.5	17.2	21.2	54.3
EMPLOYMENT REASONS	**7,058**	**100.0%**	**9.4%**	**12.7%**	**18.2%**	**59.5%**
New job or job transfer	3,470	100.0	10.8	9.9	16.4	62.9
To look for work or lost job	659	100.0	7.6	14.0	23.7	54.0
To be closer to work, easier commute	1,997	100.0	7.8	17.1	19.0	56.1
Retired	182	100.0	12.1	13.2	5.5	68.7
Other job-related reason	750	100.0	8.4	13.1	22.5	54.9
HOUSING REASONS	**18,041**	**100.0%**	**5.6%**	**21.2%**	**22.9%**	**50.8%**
Wanted own home, not rent	1,711	100.0	7.7	11.7	20.8	60.4
Wanted new or better home/apartment	5,810	100.0	5.0	22.9	22.6	49.3
Wanted better neighborhood, less crime	1,229	100.0	4.7	24.7	21.6	49.0
Wanted cheaper housing	3,260	100.0	4.4	22.7	29.4	43.7
Foreclosure, eviction	792	100.0	3.3	23.5	30.8	45.1
Other housing reason	5,239	100.0	7.0	20.2	19.0	55.1
OTHER REASONS	**698**	**100.0%**	**13.5%**	**8.7%**	**8.0%**	**66.2%**
To attend or leave college	198	100.0	24.7	6.6	4.5	62.1
Change of climate	16	100.0	0.0	31.3	0.0	68.8
Health reasons	101	100.0	13.9	2.0	3.0	80.2
Natural disaster	55	100.0	3.6	14.5	0.0	47.3
Other reason	328	100.0	8.8	10.1	13.4	67.4

Note: Numbers by race and Hispanic origin do not sum to total because Asians and blacks are those who identify themselves as being of the race alone and those who identify themselves as being of the race in combination with other races, Hispanics may be of any race, and not all races are shown. Non-Hispanic whites are those who identify themselves as being white alone and not Hispanic.
Source: Bureau of the Census, Geographic Mobility: 2011 to 2012, Internet site http://www.census.gov/hhes/migration/data/cps/cps2012.html; calculations by New Strategist

Asians, Blacks, Hispanics, and Non-Hispanic Whites Lost Ground between 2000 and 2011

The median income of American households fell 8.7 percent between 2000 and 2011, to $50,054 after adjusting for inflation. Non-Hispanic white households lost the least, their median income falling 7.0 percent compared with 11 percent losses for Asians and Hispanics and a 16.5 percent loss for blacks.

By age, median household income peaks among Asian householders aged 35 to 54, at more than $80,000. It is lowest (below $19,000) among the oldest Hispanic householders. By household type, median income is highest for Asian married couples, with a median of $81,842 and lowest for black women who live alone, at just $17,075.

Non-Hispanic whites account for the 49 percent plurality of poor married couples and 42 percent of poor male-headed families. They account for 36 percent of poor female-headed families, and blacks account for another 36 percent. Among the nation's 46 million poor people, non-Hispanic whites are a 41 percent minority. Blacks account for 25 percent, and Hispanics account for a larger 29 percent of the poor.

■ Hispanic household incomes lag behind those of Asians and non-Hispanic whites because of their low educational attainment. Black household incomes lag because married couples head relatively few black households.

Asian incomes are the highest

(median household income by race and Hispanic origin, 2011)

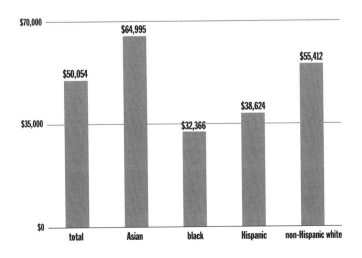

Table 7.41 Median Income of Households by Race and Hispanic Origin, 1990 to 2011

(median income of households by race and Hispanic origin, percent change in median for selected years, and index of median by race/Hispanic origin to total, 1990 to 2011; in 2011 dollars)

	total	Asian	black	Hispanic	non-Hispanic white
Median					
2011	$50,054	$64,995	$32,366	$38,624	$55,412
2010	50,830	65,531	33,170	38,818	56,178
2009	52,195	68,234	34,341	39,887	57,106
2008	52,546	68,491	35,877	39,604	58,006
2007	54,489	71,458	36,979	41,956	59,573
2006	53,768	71,281	35,843	42,145	58,478
2005	53,371	70,332	35,661	41,437	58,507
2004	52,788	68,404	36,001	40,806	58,237
2003	52,973	67,579	36,306	40,351	58,426
2002	53,019	65,366	36,477	41,385	58,634
2001	53,646	68,137	37,438	42,640	58,825
2000	54,841	72,821	38,747	43,319	59,586
1999	54,932	68,787	37,673	41,501	59,604
1998	53,582	64,265	34,933	39,038	58,480
1997	51,704	63,222	35,000	37,205	56,695
1996	50,661	61,772	33,518	35,551	55,365
1995	49,935	59,516	32,815	33,499	54,480
1994	48,418	60,751	31,555	35,147	52,713
1993	47,884	58,775	29,939	35,078	52,377
1992	48,117	59,371	29,457	35,491	52,286
1991	48,516	58,699	30,287	36,542	52,054
1990	49,950	64,142	31,155	37,251	53,290
Percent change					
2007 to 2011	−8.1%	−9.0%	−12.5%	−7.9%	−7.0%
2000 to 2011	−8.7	−10.7	−16.5	−10.8	−7.0
1990 to 2011	0.2	1.3	3.9	3.7	4.0

Index	total	Asian	black	Hispanic	non-Hispanic white
2011	100	130	65	77	111
2010	100	129	65	76	111
2009	100	131	66	76	109
2008	100	130	68	75	110
2007	100	131	68	77	109
2006	100	133	67	78	109
2005	100	132	67	78	110
2004	100	130	68	77	110
2003	100	128	69	76	110
2002	100	123	69	78	111
2001	100	127	70	79	110
2000	100	133	71	79	109
1999	100	125	69	76	109
1998	100	120	65	73	109
1997	100	122	68	72	110
1996	100	122	66	70	109
1995	100	119	66	67	109
1994	100	125	65	73	109
1993	100	123	63	73	109
1992	100	123	61	74	109
1991	100	121	62	75	107
1990	100	128	62	75	107

Note: Beginning in 2002, Asians and blacks are those who identify themselves as being of the race alone and those who identify themselves as being of the race in combination with other races. Hispanics may be of any race. Beginning in 2002, data for non-Hispanic whites are for those who identify themselves as being white alone and not Hispanic. The index is calculated by dividing the median income of each race/Hispanic origin group by the national median and multiplying by 100.
Source: Bureau of the Census, Current Population Surveys, Annual Social and Economic Supplement, Internet site http://www .census.gov/hhes/www/income/data/historical/household/index.html; calculations by New Strategist

Table 7.42 Total Household Income by Age of Householder, 2011

(number and percent distribution of households by household income and age of householder, 2011; households in thousands as of 2012)

	total	15 to 24	25 to 34	35 to 44	45 to 54	55 to 64	65 or older total	65 to 74	75 or older
Total households	**121,084**	**6,180**	**19,846**	**21,241**	**24,195**	**22,779**	**26,843**	**14,517**	**12,326**
Under $5,000	4,261	624	829	611	839	809	550	246	305
$5,000 to $9,999	4,972	460	744	580	808	992	1,388	604	785
$10,000 to $14,999	7,127	481	817	712	987	1,209	2,921	1,144	1,777
$15,000 to $19,999	6,882	469	985	795	853	1,047	2,734	1,082	1,652
$20,000 to $24,999	7,095	569	1,094	969	995	1,082	2,386	1,046	1,340
$25,000 to $29,999	6,591	429	1,020	937	968	1,016	2,222	1,093	1,129
$30,000 to $34,999	6,667	490	1,218	1,028	1,027	1,061	1,845	905	940
$35,000 to $39,999	6,136	385	1,146	930	974	1,111	1,590	915	675
$40,000 to $44,999	5,795	386	1,028	975	1,032	1,066	1,308	734	575
$45,000 to $49,999	4,945	271	845	927	990	868	1,043	590	453
$50,000 to $54,999	5,170	220	1,004	923	999	960	1,064	685	379
$55,000 to $59,999	4,250	203	853	784	847	749	814	551	263
$60,000 to $64,999	4,432	222	899	890	903	802	716	489	227
$65,000 to $69,999	3,836	177	675	724	761	775	723	472	251
$70,000 to $74,999	3,606	136	644	779	816	697	534	338	196
$75,000 to $79,999	3,452	78	662	693	745	700	574	404	171
$80,000 to $84,999	3,036	74	587	660	683	598	434	281	153
$85,000 to $89,999	2,566	59	469	553	578	538	369	261	108
$90,000 to $94,999	2,594	42	435	533	674	565	345	249	96
$95,000 to $99,999	2,251	58	383	492	557	422	339	241	98
$100,000 to $124,999	9,130	160	1,526	2,110	2,320	1,847	1,169	867	301
$125,000 to $149,999	5,311	64	819	1,169	1,465	1,195	599	432	167
$150,000 to $174,999	3,830	49	455	878	1,135	881	434	324	110
$175,000 to $199,999	2,045	35	230	449	626	497	208	143	64
$200,000 or more	5,106	40	482	1,139	1,616	1,294	535	421	113
Median income	$50,054	$30,460	$50,774	$61,916	$63,861	$55,937	$33,118	$41,598	$26,277

PERCENT DISTRIBUTION

	total	15 to 24	25 to 34	35 to 44	45 to 54	55 to 64	65 or older total	65 to 74	75 or older
Total households	**100.0%**	**100.0%**	**100.0%**	**100.0%**	**100.0%**	**100.0%**	**100.0%**	**100.0%**	**100.0%**
Under $25,000	25.1	42.1	22.5	17.3	18.5	22.6	37.2	28.4	47.5
$25,000 to $49,999	24.9	31.7	26.5	22.6	20.6	22.5	29.8	29.2	30.6
$50,000 to $74,999	17.6	15.5	20.5	19.3	17.9	17.5	14.3	17.5	10.7
$75,000 to $99,999	11.5	5.0	12.8	13.8	13.4	12.4	7.7	9.9	5.1
$100,000 or more	21.0	5.6	17.7	27.0	29.6	25.1	11.0	15.1	6.1

Source: Bureau of the Census, 2012 Current Population Survey, Internet site http://www.census.gov/hhes/www/income/data/incpovhlth/2011/dtables.html; calculations by New Strategist

Table 7.43 Median Household Income by Age, Race, and Hispanic Origin of Householder, 2011

(median income of households by age, race, and Hispanic origin of householder, and index of race/Hisapnic origin median to national median by age, 2011)

	total	Asian	black	Hispanic	non-Hispanic white
Total households	**$50,054**	**$64,995**	**$32,366**	**$38,624**	**$55,412**
Under age 25	30,460	25,855	20,720	32,721	32,312
Aged 25 to 34	50,774	67,721	31,684	39,552	57,501
Aged 35 to 44	61,916	80,265	41,802	42,127	72,371
Aged 45 to 54	63,861	80,138	40,193	40,193	73,159
Aged 55 to 64	55,937	68,636	32,543	32,543	62,497
Aged 65 or older	33,118	38,938	23,616	23,627	34,944
Aged 65 to 74	41,598	48,340	28,047	27,841	44,839
Aged 75 or older	26,277	28,969	19,226	18,618	27,306
Index					
Total households	**100**	**130**	**65**	**77**	**111**
Under age 25	61	52	41	65	65
Aged 25 to 34	101	135	63	79	115
Aged 35 to 44	124	160	84	84	145
Aged 45 to 54	128	160	80	80	146
Aged 55 to 64	112	137	65	65	125
Aged 65 or older	66	78	47	47	70
Aged 65 to 74	83	97	56	56	90
Aged 75 or older	52	58	38	37	55

Note: Asians and blacks are those who identify themselves as being of the race alone and those who identify themselves as being of the race in combination with other races. Non-Hispanic whites are those who identify themselves as being white alone and not Hispanic. Hispanics may be of any race. The index is calculated by dividing the median income of each race/Hispanic origin group by the national median and multiplying by 100.
Source: Bureau of the Census, 2012 Current Population Survey, Internet site http://www.census.gov/hhes/www/income/data/incpovhlth/2011/dtables.html; calculations by New Strategist

Table 7.44 Total Household Income by Household Type, 2011

(number and percent distribution of households by household income and household type, 2011; households in thousands as of 2012)

| | | family households | | | nonfamily households | | | |
| | | | | | female householder | | male householder | |
	total	married couples	female hh, no spouse present	male hh, no spouse present	total	living alone	total	living alone
Total households	**121,084**	**58,949**	**15,669**	**5,888**	**21,383**	**18,354**	**19,195**	**14,835**
Under $5,000	4,261	712	1,087	150	1,262	1,154	1,051	924
$5,000 to $9,999	4,972	552	1,022	140	2,109	2,038	1,149	1,058
$10,000 to $14,999	7,127	985	1,208	263	2,993	2,874	1,677	1,556
$15,000 to $19,999	6,882	1,528	1,227	322	2,397	2,289	1,410	1,266
$20,000 to $24,999	7,095	2,157	1,258	390	1,753	1,599	1,537	1,308
$25,000 to $29,999	6,591	2,255	1,186	352	1,458	1,300	1,340	1,118
$30,000 to $34,999	6,667	2,500	1,096	408	1,356	1,223	1,308	1,087
$35,000 to $39,999	6,136	2,617	985	354	1,156	1,021	1,025	831
$40,000 to $44,999	5,795	2,538	943	309	988	812	1,017	797
$45,000 to $49,999	4,945	2,369	717	273	787	613	799	608
$50,000 to $54,999	5,170	2,536	676	291	799	633	869	674
$55,000 to $59,999	4,250	2,264	553	295	504	371	635	436
$60,000 to $64,999	4,432	2,376	502	286	581	453	687	517
$65,000 to $69,999	3,836	2,211	422	222	482	367	498	303
$70,000 to $74,999	3,606	2,170	350	209	404	268	473	301
$75,000 to $79,999	3,452	2,310	289	176	322	219	355	229
$80,000 to $84,999	3,036	1,990	241	155	239	163	411	249
$85,000 to $89,999	2,566	1,737	222	146	179	116	281	176
$90,000 to $94,999	2,594	1,826	193	106	183	115	285	157
$95,000 to $99,999	2,251	1,565	178	137	183	93	187	98
$100,000 to $124,999	9,129	6,773	590	385	531	291	849	479
$125,000 to $149,999	5,311	4,176	249	217	247	114	421	186
$150,000 to $174,999	3,829	2,955	189	133	205	110	347	205
$175,000 to $199,999	2,046	1,646	106	49	72	32	173	57
$200,000 or more	5,106	4,200	178	121	193	86	413	214
Median income	$50,054	$74,130	$33,637	$49,567	$25,492	$22,262	$35,482	$30,623

PERCENT DISTRIBUTION

Total households	**100.0%**	**100.0%**	**100.0%**	**100.0%**	**100.0%**	**100.0%**	**100.0%**	**100.0%**
Under $25,000	25.1	10.1	37.0	21.5	49.2	54.2	35.5	41.2
$25,000 to $49,999	24.9	20.8	31.4	28.8	26.9	27.1	28.6	29.9
$50,000 to $74,999	17.6	19.6	16.0	22.1	13.0	11.4	16.5	15.0
$75,000 to $99,999	11.5	16.0	7.2	12.2	5.2	3.8	7.9	6.1
$100,000 or more	21.0	33.5	8.4	15.4	5.8	3.4	11.5	7.7

Note: "hh" stands for householder.
Source: Bureau of the Census, 2012 Current Population Survey, Internet site http://www.census.gov/hhes/www/income/data/incpovhlth/2011/dtables.html; calculations by New Strategist

Table 7.45 Median Household Income by Household Type and Race and Hispanic Origin of Householder, 2011

(median income of households by type of household, race, and Hispanic origin of householder, and index of race/Hispanic origin median to national median by household type, 2011)

	total	Asian	black	Hispanic	non-Hispanic white
Total households	**$50,054**	**$64,995**	**$32,366**	**$38,624**	**$55,412**
Married couples	74,130	81,842	65,124	49,888	78,546
Female householder, no spouse present	33,637	47,171	26,332	28,206	40,317
Male householder, no spouse present	49,567	59,645	40,501	43,342	54,243
Female-headed nonfamily household	25,492	32,571	18,594	20,955	26,791
Women living alone	22,262	30,584	17,075	17,598	23,778
Male-headed nonfamily household	35,482	37,496	22,708	30,238	39,027
Men living alone	30,623	31,093	20,858	24,360	33,199
Index					
Total households	**100**	**130**	**65**	**77**	**111**
Married couples	148	164	130	100	157
Female householder, no spouse present	67	94	53	56	81
Male householder, no spouse present	99	119	81	87	108
Female-headed nonfamily household	51	65	37	42	54
Women living alone	44	61	34	35	48
Male-headed nonfamily household	71	75	45	60	78
Men living alone	61	62	42	49	66

Note: Asians and blacks are those who identify themselves as being of the race alone and those who identify themselves as being of the race in combination with other races. Non-Hispanic whites are those who identify themselves as being white alone and not Hispanic. Hispanics may be of any race. The index is calculated by dividing the median income of each race/Hispanic origin group by the national median and multiplying by 100.
Source: Bureau of the Census, 2012 Current Population Survey, Internet site http://www.census.gov/hhes/www/income/data/incpovhlth/2011/dtables.html; calculations by New Strategist

Table 7.46 Income of Total Men by Age, 2011

(number and percent distribution of men aged 15 or older by income and age, 2011; median income of men with income and of men working full-time, year-round; percent working full-time, year-round; men in thousands as of 2012)

	total	under 25	25 to 34	35 to 44	45 to 54	55 to 64	65 or older
TOTAL MEN	**119,946**	**21,826**	**20,464**	**19,677**	**21,490**	**18,157**	**18,332**
Without income	**13,718**	**8,740**	**1,581**	**1,065**	**1,169**	**749**	**414**
With income	**106,228**	**13,086**	**18,883**	**18,612**	**20,320**	**17,408**	**17,918**
Under $5,000	7,090	3,798	952	589	646	744	362
$5,000 to $9,999	7,441	2,490	1,182	754	951	1,034	1,030
$10,000 to $14,999	9,020	1,801	1,331	1,045	1,272	1,274	2,296
$15,000 to $19,999	8,537	1,350	1,483	1,065	1,129	1,084	2,427
$20,000 to $24,999	8,522	1,181	1,708	1,273	1,284	1,132	1,945
$25,000 to $29,999	7,054	726	1,522	1,102	1,094	1,001	1,610
$30,000 to $34,999	7,019	560	1,625	1,264	1,149	1,083	1,337
$35,000 to $39,999	6,010	380	1,350	1,169	1,204	935	972
$40,000 to $44,999	5,672	256	1,292	1,151	1,164	973	835
$45,000 to $49,999	4,567	131	978	983	1,053	730	692
$50,000 to $54,999	4,903	106	1,039	1,041	1,120	901	697
$55,000 to $59,999	3,066	51	601	682	673	590	468
$60,000 to $64,999	3,646	90	702	858	858	708	429
$65,000 to $69,999	2,339	18	456	536	535	509	285
$70,000 to $74,999	2,472	20	421	604	601	526	299
$75,000 to $79,999	2,058	12	346	483	544	431	242
$80,000 to $84,999	2,125	27	309	524	602	428	235
$85,000 to $89,999	1,271	3	193	308	337	271	157
$90,000 to $94,999	1,375	11	219	320	377	274	175
$95,000 to $99,999	917	10	129	193	241	218	126
$100,000 or more	11,123	66	1,044	2,666	3,486	2,562	1,300

MEDIAN INCOME

Men with income	$32,986	$10,518	$32,581	$43,967	$45,950	$41,550	$27,707
Working full-time	50,316	24,423	41,433	51,926	56,675	60,388	64,655
Percent full-time	48.4%	17.1%	63.7%	71.7%	68.5%	54.4%	14.0%

PERCENT DISTRIBUTION

TOTAL MEN	**100.0%**	**100.0%**	**100.0%**	**100.0%**	**100.0%**	**100.0%**	**100.0%**
Without income	**11.4**	**40.0**	**7.7**	**5.4**	**5.4**	**4.1**	**2.3**
With income	**88.6**	**60.0**	**92.3**	**94.6**	**94.6**	**95.9**	**97.7**
Under $15,000	19.6	37.1	16.9	12.1	13.4	16.8	20.1
$15,000 to $24,999	14.2	11.6	15.6	11.9	11.2	12.2	23.8
$25,000 to $34,999	11.7	5.9	15.4	12.0	10.4	11.5	16.1
$35,000 to $49,999	13.5	3.5	17.7	16.8	15.9	14.5	13.6
$50,000 to $74,999	13.7	1.3	15.7	18.9	17.6	17.8	11.9
$75,000 or more	15.7	0.6	10.9	22.8	26.0	23.0	12.2

Source: Bureau of the Census, 2012 Current Population Survey Annual Social and Economic Supplement, Internet site http:// www.census.gov/hhes/www/cpstables/032012/perinc/toc.htm; calculations by New Strategist

Table 7.47 Income of Total Women by Age, 2011

(number and percent distribution of women aged 15 or older by income and age, 2011; median income of women with income and of women working full-time, year-round; percent working full-time, year-round; women in thousands as of 2012)

	total	under 25	25 to 34	35 to 44	45 to 54	55 to 64	65 or older
TOTAL WOMEN	127,751	21,291	20,755	20,251	22,465	19,814	23,174
Without income	19,419	8,363	3,120	2,578	2,512	1,948	898
With income	108,332	12,927	17,635	17,672	19,954	17,867	22,276
Under $5,000	12,472	4,152	1,971	1,830	1,847	1,656	1,016
$5,000 to $9,999	14,270	2,740	1,698	1,335	1,802	1,950	4,744
$10,000 to $14,999	14,043	1,909	1,662	1,595	1,748	2,006	5,123
$15,000 to $19,999	10,865	1,318	1,605	1,482	1,755	1,540	3,164
$20,000 to $24,999	9,218	1,018	1,596	1,485	1,630	1,502	1,988
$25,000 to $29,999	7,341	537	1,422	1,283	1,498	1,173	1,429
$30,000 to $34,999	6,908	429	1,632	1,302	1,378	1,144	1,022
$35,000 to $39,999	5,785	313	1,223	1,197	1,219	1,079	753
$40,000 to $44,999	4,809	181	1,042	996	1,088	897	605
$45,000 to $49,999	3,537	74	754	744	889	623	452
$50,000 to $54,999	3,677	69	695	771	918	795	430
$55,000 to $59,999	2,144	50	416	503	558	383	233
$60,000 to $64,999	2,365	43	406	554	601	545	217
$65,000 to $69,999	1,647	19	270	420	382	386	170
$70,000 to $74,999	1,430	18	244	347	383	292	146
$75,000 to $79,999	1,186	8	182	278	347	225	146
$80,000 to $84,999	1,053	11	161	255	289	247	89
$85,000 to $89,999	636	2	82	144	180	171	55
$90,000 to $94,999	690	10	77	145	188	212	59
$95,000 to $99,999	451	10	48	98	129	101	65
$100,000 or more	3,807	16	449	907	1,125	938	372
MEDIAN INCOME							
Women with income	$21,102	$9,107	$25,723	$29,095	$28,460	$25,923	$15,362
Working full-time	38,685	22,360	36,199	40,868	41,274	41,888	44,893
Percent full-time	34.2%	13.1%	46.2%	50.4%	51.5%	40.2%	6.8%
PERCENT DISTRIBUTION							
TOTAL WOMEN	100.0%	100.0%	100.0%	100.0%	100.0%	100.0%	100.0%
Without income	15.2	39.3	15.0	12.7	11.2	9.8	3.9
With income	84.8	60.7	85.0	87.3	88.8	90.2	96.1
Under $15,000	31.9	41.3	25.7	23.5	24.0	28.3	47.0
$15,000 to $24,999	15.7	11.0	15.4	14.7	15.1	15.4	22.2
$25,000 to $34,999	11.2	4.5	14.7	12.8	12.8	11.7	10.6
$35,000 to $49,999	11.1	2.7	14.5	14.5	14.2	13.1	7.8
$50,000 to $74,999	8.8	0.9	9.8	12.8	12.6	12.1	5.2
$75,000 or more	6.1	0.3	4.8	9.0	10.1	9.6	3.4

Source: Bureau of the Census, 2012 Current Population Survey Annual Social and Economic Supplement, Internet site http://www.census.gov/hhes/www/cpstables/032012/perinc/toc.htm; calculations by New Strategist

Table 7.48 Median Earnings of People Working Full-Time by Sex, 1990 to 2011

(median earnings of total people aged 15 or older working full-time, year-round by sex, and women's earnings as a percent of men's income, 1990 to 2011; percent change in earnings for selected years; in 2011 dollars)

	men	women	women's earnings as a percent of men's earnings
2011	$48,202	$37,118	77.0%
2010	49,464	38,052	76.9
2009	49,416	38,040	77.0
2008	48,435	37,339	77.1
2007	48,935	38,076	77.8
2006	47,142	36,271	76.9
2005	47,680	36,703	77.0
2004	48,576	37,197	76.6
2003	49,732	37,572	75.5
2002	49,294	37,759	76.6
2001	48,624	37,114	76.3
2000	48,653	35,867	73.7
1999	49,121	35,522	72.3
1998	48,704	35,637	73.2
1997	47,050	34,892	74.2
1996	45,882	33,844	73.8
1995	46,154	32,967	71.4
1994	46,302	33,323	72.0
1993	46,605	33,332	71.5
1992	47,428	33,572	70.8
1991	47,381	33,099	69.9
1990	46,172	33,067	71.6

	percent change		percentage point change
2007 to 2011	−1.5%	−2.5%	−0.8
2000 to 2011	−0.9	3.5	3.3
1990 to 2011	4.4	12.3	5.4

Source: Bureau of the Census, Current Population Survey, Historical Tables, Internet site http://www.census.gov/hhes/www/income/data/historical/people/; calculations by New Strategist

Table 7.49 Median Earnings of Total People Working Full-Time by Education and Sex, 2011

(median earnings of total people aged 25 or older working full-time, year-round, by educational attainment and sex, and women's earnings as a percent of men's earnings, 2011)

	men	women	women's earnings as a percent of men's earnings
Total people	**$50,361**	**$38,294**	**76.0%**
Less than 9th grade	24,453	18,239	74.6
9th to 12th grade, no diploma	29,435	20,883	70.9
High school graduate	40,055	29,857	74.5
Some college, no degree	46,434	33,401	71.9
Associate's degree	50,282	37,773	75.1
Bachelor's degree or more	71,778	51,942	72.4
Bachelor's degree	63,737	47,435	74.4
Master's degree	80,958	59,099	73.0
Professional degree	115,298	76,737	66.6
Doctoral degree	101,222	77,392	76.5

Source: Bureau of the Census, 2012 Current Population Survey Annual Social and Economic Supplement, Internet site http://www.census.gov/hhes/www/cpstables/032012/perinc/toc.htm; calculations by New Strategist

Table 7.50 Poverty Status of Married Couples, 1990 to 2011

(total number of married couples, and number and percent below poverty level by presence of children under age 18 at home, 1990 to 2011; percent change in numbers and percentage point change in rates for selected years; families in thousands as of March the following year)

	total	in poverty	
		number	percent
Total married couples			
2011	58,963	3,652	6.2%
2010	58,667	3,681	6.3
2009	58,428	3,409	5.8
2008	59,137	3,261	5.5
2007	58,395	2,849	4.9
2006	58,964	2,910	4.9
2005	58,189	2,944	5.1
2004	57,983	3,216	5.5
2003	57,725	3,115	5.4
2002	57,327	3,052	5.3
2001	56,755	2,760	4.9
2000	56,598	2,637	4.7
1999	56,290	2,748	4.9
1998	54,778	2,879	5.3
1997	54,321	2,821	5.2
1996	53,604	3,010	5.6
1995	53,570	2,982	5.6
1994	53,865	3,272	6.1
1993	53,181	3,481	6.5
1992	53,090	3,385	6.4
1991	52,457	3,158	6.0
1990	52,147	2,981	5.7

	percent change		percentage point change
2007 to 2011	1.0%	28.2%	1.3
2000 to 2011	4.2	38.5	1.5
1990 to 2011	13.1	22.5	0.5

	total	in poverty	
		number	percent
Married couples with children			
2011	25,081	2,216	8.8%
2010	25,687	2,309	9.0
2009	26,119	2,161	8.3
2008	26,490	1,989	7.5
2007	26,450	1,765	6.7
2006	27,317	1,746	6.4
2005	27,147	1,777	6.5
2004	27,137	1,903	7.0
2003	26,959	1,885	7.0
2002	27,052	1,831	6.8
2001	26,931	1,643	6.1
2000	27,121	1,615	6.0
1999	26,694	1,711	6.4
1998	26,226	1,822	6.9
1997	26,430	1,863	7.1
1996	26,184	1,964	7.5
1995	26,034	1,961	7.5
1994	26,367	2,197	8.3
1993	26,121	2,363	9.0
1992	25,907	2,237	8.6
1991	25,357	2,106	8.3
1990	25,410	1,990	7.8

	percent change		percentage point change
2007 to 2011	−5.2%	25.6%	2.1
2000 to 2011	−7.5	37.2	2.8
1990 to 2011	−1.3	11.4	1.0

Source: Bureau of the Census, Current Population Surveys, Historical Poverty Tables, Internet site http://www.census.gov/hhes/ www/poverty/data/historical/families.html; calculations by New Strategist

Table 7.51 Poverty Status of Female-Headed Families, 1990 to 2011

(total number of female-headed families, and number and percent below poverty level by presence of children under age 18 at home, 1990 to 2011; percent change in numbers and percentage point change in rates for selected years; families in thousands as of March the following year)

		in poverty	
	total	number	percent
Total female-headed families			
2011	15,678	4,894	31.2%
2010	15,243	4,827	31.7
2009	14,857	4,441	29.9
2008	14,482	4,163	28.7
2007	14,411	4,078	28.3
2006	14,424	4,087	28.3
2005	14,095	4,044	28.7
2004	13,981	3,962	28.3
2003	13,791	3,856	28.0
2002	13,626	3,613	26.5
2001	13,146	3,470	26.4
2000	12,903	3,278	25.4
1999	12,818	3,559	27.8
1998	12,796	3,831	29.9
1997	12,652	3,995	31.6
1996	12,790	4,167	32.6
1995	12,514	4,057	32.4
1994	12,220	4,232	34.6
1993	12,411	4,424	35.6
1992	12,061	4,275	35.4
1991	11,693	4,161	35.6
1990	11,268	3,768	33.4

	percent change		percentage point change
2007 to 2011	8.8%	20.0%	2.9
2000 to 2011	21.5	49.3	5.8
1990 to 2011	39.1	29.9	−2.2

		in poverty	
	total	number	percent
Female-headed families with children			
2011	10,379	4,243	40.9%
2010	10,178	4,163	40.9
2009	9,872	3,800	38.5
2008	9,796	3,645	37.2
2007	9,718	3,593	37.0
2006	9,894	3,615	36.5
2005	9,638	3,493	36.2
2004	9,676	3,477	35.9
2003	9,614	3,416	35.5
2002	9,414	3,171	33.7
2001	9,171	3,083	33.6
2000	8,813	2,906	33.0
1999	8,793	3,139	35.7
1998	8,934	3,456	38.7
1997	8,822	3,614	41.0
1996	8,957	3,755	41.9
1995	8,751	3,634	41.5
1994	8,665	3,816	44.0
1993	8,758	4,034	46.1
1992	8,375	3,867	46.2
1991	7,991	3,767	47.1
1990	7,707	3,426	44.5

	percent change		percentage point change
2007 to 2011	6.8%	18.1%	3.9
2000 to 2011	17.8	46.0	7.9
1990 to 2011	34.7	23.8	−3.6

Source: Bureau of the Census, Current Population Surveys, Historical Poverty Tables, Internet site http://www.census.gov/hhes/ www/poverty/data/historical/families.html; calculations by New Strategist

Table 7.52 Poverty Status of Male-Headed Families, 1990 to 2011

(total number of male-headed families, and number and percent below poverty level by presence of children under age 18 at home, 1990 to 2011; percent change in numbers and percentage point change in rates for selected years; families in thousands as of March the following year)

	total	in poverty	
		number	percent
Total male-headed families			
2011	5,888	950	16.1%
2010	5,649	892	15.8
2009	5,582	942	16.9
2008	5,255	723	13.8
2007	5,103	696	13.6
2006	5,067	671	13.2
2005	5,134	669	13.0
2004	4,901	657	13.4
2003	4,717	636	13.5
2002	4,663	564	12.1
2001	4,440	583	13.1
2000	4,277	485	11.3
1999	4,099	485	11.8
1998	3,977	476	12.0
1997	3,911	507	13.0
1996	3,847	531	13.8
1995	3,513	493	14.0
1994	3,228	549	17.0
1993	2,914	488	16.8
1992	3,065	484	15.8
1991	3,025	392	13.0
1990	2,907	349	12.0

	percent change		percentage point change
2007 to 2011	15.4%	36.5%	2.5
2000 to 2011	37.7	95.9	4.8
1990 to 2011	102.5	172.2	4.1

	total	in poverty	
		number	percent
Male-headed families with children			
2011	2,976	652	21.9%
2010	2,789	673	24.1
2009	2,829	670	23.7
2008	2,676	471	17.6
2007	2,700	471	17.5
2006	2,569	461	17.9
2005	2,609	459	17.6
2004	2,562	439	17.1
2003	2,456	470	19.1
2002	2,380	395	16.6
2001	2,325	412	17.7
2000	2,256	345	15.3
1999	2,200	360	16.3
1998	2,107	350	16.6
1997	2,175	407	18.7
1996	2,063	412	20.0
1995	1,934	381	19.7
1994	1,750	395	22.6
1993	1,577	354	22.5
1992	1,569	353	22.5
1991	1,513	297	19.6
1990	1,386	260	18.8

	percent change		percentage point change
2007 to 2011	10.2%	38.4%	4.4
2000 to 2011	31.9	89.0	6.6
1990 to 2011	114.7	150.8	3.1

Source: Bureau of the Census, Current Population Surveys, Historical Poverty Tables, Internet site http://www.census.gov/hhes/www/poverty/data/historical/families.html; calculations by New Strategist

Table 7.53 Families in Poverty by Family Type, Race, and Hispanic Origin, 2011

(number and percent of families in poverty, and percent distribution of families in poverty, by type of family and race and Hispanic origin of householder, 2011; families in thousands as of 2012)

	total	Asian	black	Hispanic	non-Hispanic white
NUMBER IN POVERTY					
Total families in poverty	**9,497**	**434**	**2,431**	**2,651**	**3,955**
Married couples	3,652	265	426	1,145	1,787
Female householders, no spouse present	4,894	122	1,762	1,272	1,766
Male householders, no spouse present	950	47	242	234	403
PERCENT IN POVERTY					
Total families	**11.8%**	**10.0%**	**24.2%**	**22.9%**	**7.3%**
Married couples	6.2	7.7	9.4	15.9	4.1
Female householders, no spouse present	31.2	21.4	39.3	41.2	23.4
Male householders, no spouse present	16.1	14.0	24.2	18.4	12.5
PERCENT DISTRIBUTION OF FAMILIES IN POVERTY BY RACE AND HISPANIC ORIGIN					
Total families in poverty	**100.0%**	**4.6%**	**25.6%**	**27.9%**	**41.6%**
Married couples	100.0	7.3	11.7	31.4	48.9
Female householders, no spouse present	100.0	2.5	36.0	26.0	36.1
Male householders, no spouse present	100.0	4.9	25.5	24.6	42.4
PERCENT DISTRIBUTION OF FAMILIES IN POVERTY BY FAMILY TYPE					
Total families in poverty	**100.0%**	**100.0%**	**100.0%**	**100.0%**	**100.0%**
Married couples	38.5	61.1	17.5	43.2	45.2
Female householders, no spouse present	51.5	28.1	72.5	48.0	44.7
Male householders, no spouse present	10.0	10.8	10.0	8.8	10.2

Note: Numbers do not add to total because Asians and blacks are those who identify themselves as being of the race alone and those who identify themselves as being of the race in combination with other races. Non-Hispanic whites are those who identify themselves as being white alone and not Hispanic. Hispanics may be of any race.
Source: Bureau of the Census, 2012 Current Population Survey, Internet site http://www.census.gov/hhes/www/ cpstables/032012/pov/toc.htm; calculations by New Strategist

Table 7.54 Families with Children in Poverty by Family Type, Race, and Hispanic Origin, 2011

(number and percent of families with children under age 18 in poverty, and percent distribution of families with children in poverty, by type of family and race and Hispanic origin of householder, 2011; families in thousands as of 2012)

	total	Asian	black	Hispanic	non-Hispanic white
NUMBER IN POVERTY					
Total families with children in poverty	**7,111**	**287**	**1,951**	**2,265**	**2,618**
Married couples	2,216	168	272	916	846
Female householders, no spouse present	4,243	92	1,532	1,159	1,496
Male householders, no spouse present	652	27	148	189	276
PERCENT IN POVERTY					
Total families with children	**18.5%**	**12.6%**	**32.8%**	**29.3%**	**11.7%**
Married couples	8.8	9.1	12.2	19.7	5.2
Female householders, no spouse present	40.9	30.1	47.7	49.1	33.0
Male householders, no spouse present	21.9	22.6	28.8	26.1	17.3
PERCENT DISTRIBUTION OF FAMILIES IN POVERTY BY RACE AND HISPANIC ORIGIN					
Total families with children in poverty	**100.0%**	**4.0%**	**27.4%**	**31.9%**	**36.8%**
Married couples	100.0	7.6	12.3	41.3	38.2
Female householders, no spouse present	100.0	2.2	36.1	27.3	35.3
Male householders, no spouse present	100.0	4.1	22.7	29.0	42.3
PERCENT DISTRIBUTION OF FAMILIES IN POVERTY BY FAMILY TYPE					
Total families with children in poverty	**100.0%**	**100.0%**	**100.0%**	**100.0%**	**100.0%**
Married couples	31.2	58.5	13.9	40.4	32.3
Female householders, no spouse present	59.7	32.1	78.5	51.2	57.1
Male householders, no spouse present	9.2	9.4	7.6	8.3	10.5

Note: Numbers do not add to total because Asians and blacks are those who identify themselves as being of the race alone and those who identify themselves as being of the race in combination with other races. Non-Hispanic whites are those who identify themselves as being white alone and not Hispanic. Hispanics may be of any race.
Source: Bureau of the Census, 2012 Current Population Survey, Internet site http://www.census.gov/hhes/www/ cpstables/032012/pov/toc.htm; calculations by New Strategist

Table 7.55 Poverty Status by Sex and Age, 2011

(total number of people, and number and percent below poverty level by sex and age, 2011; people in thousands as of 2012)

	total	in poverty number	in poverty percent
Total people	**308,456**	**46,247**	**15.0%**
Under age 18	73,737	16,134	21.9
Aged 18 to 24	30,140	6,209	20.6
Aged 25 to 34	41,219	6,537	15.9
Aged 35 to 44	39,927	4,873	12.2
Aged 45 to 54	43,955	4,795	10.9
Aged 55 to 59	20,470	2,181	10.7
Aged 60 to 64	17,501	1,898	10.8
Aged 65 or older	41,507	3,620	8.7
Total females	**157,466**	**25,746**	**16.3%**
Under age 18	36,026	8,002	22.2
Aged 18 to 24	14,980	3,487	23.3
Aged 25 to 34	20,755	4,021	19.4
Aged 35 to 44	20,251	2,827	14.0
Aged 45 to 54	22,465	2,656	11.8
Aged 55 to 59	10,592	1,221	11.5
Aged 60 to 64	9,223	1,045	11.3
Aged 65 or older	23,174	2,486	10.7
Total males	**150,990**	**20,501**	**13.6%**
Under age 18	37,711	8,132	21.6
Aged 18 to 24	15,160	2,722	18.0
Aged 25 to 34	20,464	2,516	12.3
Aged 35 to 44	19,677	2,046	10.4
Aged 45 to 54	21,490	2,138	10.0
Aged 55 to 59	9,879	960	9.7
Aged 60 to 64	8,278	854	10.3
Aged 65 or older	18,332	1,134	6.2

Source: Bureau of the Census, Current Population Surveys, Historical Poverty Tables, Internet site http://www.census.gov/hhes/www/poverty/data/historical/families.html; calculations by New Strategist

Table 7.56 People in Poverty by Age, Race, and Hispanic Origin, 2011

(number and percent of people in poverty and percent distribution of poor, by age, race, and Hispanic origin, 2011; people in thousands as of 2012)

	total	Asian	black	Hispanic	non-Hispanic white
NUMBER OF POOR					
Total people in poverty	**46,247**	**2,189**	**11,730**	**13,244**	**19,171**
Under age 18	16,134	607	4,849	6,008	4,850
Aged 18 to 24	6,209	420	1,536	1,507	2,747
Aged 25 to 34	6,537	347	1,522	1,960	2,738
Aged 35 to 44	4,873	265	1037	1,580	1,991
Aged 45 to 54	4,795	217	1242	941	2,346
Aged 55 to 59	2,181	65	576	358	1,159
Aged 60 to 64	1,898	83	327	320	1131
Aged 65 or older	3,620	185	640	569	2,210
PERCENT IN POVERTY					
Total people	**15.0%**	**12.3%**	**27.5%**	**25.3%**	**9.8%**
Under age 18	21.9	13.3	37.4	34.1	12.5
Aged 18 to 24	20.6	22.8	30.9	24.2	16.2
Aged 25 to 34	15.9	11.8	26.4	23.0	11.4
Aged 35 to 44	12.2	9.5	19.5	21.0	8.2
Aged 45 to 54	10.9	9.3	22.0	16.2	7.8
Aged 55 to 59	10.7	6.8	23.9	17.6	7.8
Aged 60 to 64	10.8	10.5	17.7	21.1	8.6
Aged 65 or older	8.7	11.7	17.2	18.7	6.7
PERCENT DISTRIBUTION OF POOR BY RACE AND HISPANIC ORIGIN					
Total people in poverty	**100.0%**	**4.7%**	**25.4%**	**28.6%**	**41.5%**
Under age 18	100.0	3.8	30.1	37.2	30.1
Aged 18 to 24	100.0	6.8	24.7	24.3	44.2
Aged 25 to 34	100.0	5.3	23.3	30.0	41.9
Aged 35 to 44	100.0	5.4	21.3	32.4	40.9
Aged 45 to 54	100.0	4.5	25.9	19.6	48.9
Aged 55 to 59	100.0	3.0	26.4	16.4	53.1
Aged 60 to 64	100.0	4.4	17.2	16.9	59.6
Aged 65 or older	100.0	5.1	17.7	15.7	61.0

Note: Numbers do not add to total because Asians and blacks are those who identify themselves as being of the race alone and those who identify themselves as being of the race in combination with other races. Non-Hispanic whites are those who identify themselves as being white alone and not Hispanic. Hispanics may be of any race.
Source: Bureau of the Census, 2012 Current Population Survey, Internet site http://www.census.gov/hhes/www/ cpstables/032012/pov/toc.htm; calculations by New Strategist

Thirty-Eight Percent of American Workers Are Managers or Professionals

Sixty-four percent of Americans aged 16 or older are in the labor force, including 70 percent of men and 58 percent of women. Among the nation's 155 million workers in 2012, 47 percent were women.

The largest share of workers—38 percent—is employed in managerial or professional occupations. Another 23 percent hold sales or office jobs. Eighteen percent of Americans are employed as service workers in jobs such as food preparation, personal care, and building maintenance.

Among all married couples, 52 percent are dual earners with both husband and wife in the labor force. Just 23 percent have only the husband in the labor force. Thirty-nine percent of households have two or more earners, while 24 percent have no earners—most of them retired.

Between 2010 and 2020, the labor force will expand by 7 percent. The non-Hispanic white share of workers will decline during the decade from 68 to 62 percent. In 2020, Hispanics will account for 19 percent of workers, blacks for 12 percent, Asians for 6 percent, and other racial groups for 3 percent.

■ The labor force as a whole is becoming more diverse, but some occupations are far more diverse than others.

Most men and women work

(percent of people aged 16 or older in the civilian labor force, by sex, 2012)

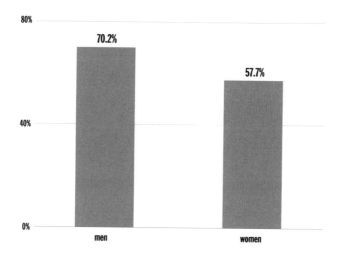

Table 7.57 Labor Force Participation Rate of Total People by Age and Sex, 2012

(percent of persons aged 16 or older in the civilian labor force, by age and sex, 2012)

	total	men	women
Total people	**63.7%**	**70.2%**	**57.7%**
Aged 16 to 19	34.3	34.0	34.6
Aged 20 to 24	70.9	74.5	67.4
Aged 25 to 29	81.3	88.4	74.4
Aged 30 to 34	82.0	90.7	73.7
Aged 35 to 39	82.3	91.3	73.7
Aged 40 to 44	82.8	90.1	75.8
Aged 45 to 49	81.7	88.1	75.6
Aged 50 to 54	78.8	84.1	73.7
Aged 55 to 59	72.5	78.0	67.3
Aged 60 to 64	55.2	60.5	50.4
Aged 65 or older	18.5	23.6	14.4
Aged 65 to 69	32.1	37.1	27.6
Aged 70 to 74	19.5	24.2	15.4
Aged 75 or older	7.6	11.3	5.0

Note: The civilian labor force equals the number of employed plus the number of unemployed.
Source: Bureau of Labor Statistics, Labor Force Statistics from the Current Population Survey, Internet site http://www.bls.gov/cps/tables.htm#empstat

Table 7.58 Employment Status of Total People by Sex and Age, 2012

(number and percent of people aged 16 or older in the civilian labor force by sex, age, and employment status, 2012; numbers in thousands)

	civilian noninstitutional population	civilian labor force total	percent of population	employed	unemployed number	percent of labor force
Total people	**243,284**	**154,975**	**63.7%**	**142,469**	**12,506**	**8.1%**
Aged 16 to 19	16,984	5,823	34.3	4,426	1,397	24.0
Aged 20 to 24	21,799	15,462	70.9	13,408	2,054	13.3
Aged 25 to 34	40,975	33,465	81.7	30,701	2,764	8.3
Aged 35 to 44	39,642	32,734	82.6	30,576	2,158	6.6
Aged 45 to 54	43,697	35,054	80.2	32,874	2,181	6.2
Aged 55 to 64	38,318	24,710	64.5	23,239	1,470	5.9
Aged 65 or older	41,869	7,727	18.5	7,245	482	6.2
Total men	**117,343**	**82,327**	**70.2**	**75,555**	**6,771**	**8.2**
Aged 16 to 19	8,657	2,940	34.0	2,152	787	26.8
Aged 20 to 24	10,889	8,110	74.5	6,948	1,163	14.3
Aged 25 to 34	20,205	18,083	89.5	16,607	1,476	8.2
Aged 35 to 44	19,416	17,607	90.7	16,483	1,124	6.4
Aged 45 to 54	21,339	18,363	86.1	17,221	1,142	6.2
Aged 55 to 64	18,416	12,879	69.9	12,068	811	6.3
Aged 65 or older	18,422	4,345	23.6	4,077	268	6.2
Total women	**125,941**	**72,648**	**57.7**	**66,914**	**5,734**	**7.9**
Aged 16 to 19	8,327	2,883	34.6	2,274	609	21.1
Aged 20 to 24	10,910	7,352	67.4	6,460	891	12.1
Aged 25 to 34	20,770	15,382	74.1	14,094	1,288	8.4
Aged 35 to 44	20,226	15,127	74.8	14,093	1,034	6.8
Aged 45 to 54	22,358	16,692	74.7	15,653	1,039	6.2
Aged 55 to 64	19,902	11,830	59.4	11,171	659	5.6
Aged 65 or older	23,447	3,383	14.4	3,168	214	6.3

Note: The civilian labor force equals the number of the employed plus the number of the unemployed. The civilian population equals the number in the labor force plus the number not in the labor force.
Source: Bureau of Labor Statistics, Labor Force Statistics from the Current Population Survey, Internet site http://www.bls.gov/cps/tables.htm#empstat

Table 7.59 Total Workers by Occupation, 2012

(number and percent distribution of employed persons aged 16 or older in the civilian labor force, by occupation, 2012; numbers in thousands)

	total	percent distribution
TOTAL EMPLOYED	**142,469**	**100.0%**
Management, professional and related occupations	**54,043**	**37.9**
Management, business, and financial operations	22,678	15.9
Management occupations	16,042	11.3
Business and financial operations occupations	6,636	4.7
Professional and related occupations	31,365	22.0
Computer and mathematical occupations	3,816	2.7
Architecture and engineering occupations	2,846	2.0
Life, physical, and social science occupations	1,316	0.9
Community and social services occupations	2,265	1.6
Legal occupations	1,786	1.3
Education, training, and library occupations	8,543	6.0
Arts, design, entertainment, sports, and media occupations	2,814	2.0
Health care practitioner and technical occupations	7,977	5.6
Service occupations	**25,459**	**17.9**
Health care support occupations	3,496	2.5
Protective service occupations	3,096	2.2
Food preparation and serving related occupations	8,018	5.6
Building and grounds cleaning and maintenance occupations	5,591	3.9
Personal care and service occupations	5,258	3.7
Sales and office occupations	**33,152**	**23.3**
Sales and related occupations	15,457	10.8
Office and administrative support occupations	17,695	12.4
Natural resources, construction, and maintenance occupations	**12,821**	**9.0**
Farming, fishing, and forestry occupations	994	0.7
Construction and extraction occupations	7,005	4.9
Installation, maintenance, and repair occupations	4,821	3.4
Production, transportation, and material moving occupations	**16,994**	**11.9**
Production occupations	8,455	5.9
Transportation and material moving occupations	8,540	6.0

Source: Bureau of Labor Statistics, Labor Force Statistics from the Current Population Survey, Internet site http://www.bls.gov/cps/tables.htm#empstat

Table 7.60 Total Workers by Industry, 2012

(number and percent distribution of employed people aged 16 or older in the civilian labor force, by industry, 2012; numbers in thousands)

	number	percent distribution
Total employed	**142,469**	**100.0%**
Agriculture, forestry, fishing, and hunting	2,186	1.5
Mining	957	0.7
Construction	8,964	6.3
Manufacturing	14,686	10.3
Durable goods	9,244	6.5
Nondurable goods	5,443	3.8
Wholesale/retail trade	19,876	14.0
Wholesale trade	3,694	2.6
Retail trade	16,182	11.4
Transportation and utilities	7,271	5.1
Information	2,971	2.1
Financial activities	9,590	6.7
Professional and business services	16,539	11.6
Educational and health services	32,350	22.7
Leisure and hospitality	13,193	9.3
Other services	7,168	5.0
Other services, except private households	6,430	4.5
Private households	738	0.5
Public administration	6,717	4.7

Source: Bureau of Labor Statistics, Labor Force Statistics from the Current Population Survey, Internet site http://www.bls.gov/cps/tables.htm#empstat

Table 7.61 Total Workers by Full-Time and Part-Time Status, 2012

(number and percent distribution of employed people aged 16 or older by employment status and sex, 2012; numbers in thousands)

	total	men	women
Total employed	**135,235**	**71,765**	**63,470**
Worked full-time	101,383	58,149	43,233
Worked part-time	33,852	13,616	20,236
For economic reasons	8,003	3,981	4,022
PERCENT DISTRIBUTION			
Total employed	**100.0%**	**100.0%**	**100.0%**
Worked full-time	75.0	81.0	68.1
Worked part-time	25.0	19.0	31.9
For economic reasons	5.9	5.5	6.3

Note: Part-time work is less than 35 hours per week. Part-time workers exclude those who usually work full-time but who worked less than 35 hours in the previous week because of vacation, holidays, child care problems, weather issues, and other temporary, noneconomic reasons. "Economic reasons" means a worker's hours have been reduced or workers cannot find full-time employment.
Source: Bureau of Labor Statistics, Labor Force Statistics from the Current Population Survey, Internet site http://www.bls.gov/cps/tables.htm#empstat

Table 7.62 Total Workers by Educational Attainment, 2012

(number, participation rate, and percent distribution of people aged 25 or older in the civilian labor force, by educational attainment, 2012; numbers in thousands)

	number	participation rate	percent distribution
Total aged 25 or older	**133,690**	**65.4%**	**100.0%**
Not a high school graduate	11,328	45.5	8.5
High school graduate only	36,772	59.5	27.5
Some college	22,685	66.1	17.0
Associate's degree	14,675	73.4	11.0
Bachelor's degree or more	48,230	75.9	36.1

Source: Bureau of Labor Statistics, Labor Force Statistics from the Current Population Survey, Internet site http://www.bls.gov/cps/tables.htm#empstat

Table 7.63 Total Households by Number of Earners, 2012

(number and percent distribution of total households by number of earners per household, 2012; number of households in thousands)

	number	percent distribution
Total households	**121,084**	**100.0%**
No earners	28,569	23.6
One earner	45,578	37.6
Two or more earners	46,938	38.8
Two earners	37,943	31.3
Three earners	6,905	5.7
Four or more earners	2,089	1.7
Average number of earners per household	1.28	–

Note: "–" means not applicable.
Source: Bureau of the Census, 2012 Current Population Survey, Annual Social and Economic Supplement, Internet site http://www.census.gov/hhes/www/cpstables/032012/hhinc/toc.htm; calculations by New Strategist

Table 7.64 Labor Force Status of Total Married Couples, 2012

(number and percent distribution of married-couple family groups aged 20 or older by age of householder and labor force status of husband and wife, 2012; numbers in thousands)

	total	husband and/or wife in labor force			neither husband nor wife in labor force
		husband and wife	husband only	wife only	
Total married couples	**61,047**	**31,803**	**13,820**	**4,595**	**10,830**
Under age 25	1,247	653	491	52	51
Aged 25 to 29	3,576	2,217	1,118	149	91
Aged 30 to 34	5,482	3,618	1,564	195	105
Aged 35 to 39	5,727	3,803	1,616	203	104
Aged 40 to 44	6,622	4,593	1,583	257	189
Aged 45 to 54	13,822	9,335	3,071	834	582
Aged 55 to 64	12,431	6,188	2,726	1,625	1,891
Aged 65 to 74	7,751	1,208	1,288	1,059	4,197
Aged 75 or older	4,391	188	364	220	3,619
Total married couples	**100.0%**	**52.1%**	**22.6%**	**7.5%**	**17.7%**
Under age 25	100.0	52.4	39.4	4.2	4.1
Aged 25 to 29	100.0	62.0	31.3	4.2	2.5
Aged 30 to 34	100.0	66.0	28.5	3.6	1.9
Aged 35 to 39	100.0	66.4	28.2	3.5	1.8
Aged 40 to 44	100.0	69.4	23.9	3.9	2.9
Aged 45 to 54	100.0	67.5	22.2	6.0	4.2
Aged 55 to 64	100.0	49.8	21.9	13.1	15.2
Aged 65 to 74	100.0	15.6	16.6	13.7	54.1
Aged 75 or older	100.0	4.3	8.3	5.0	82.4

Source: Bureau of the Census, America's Families and Living Arrangements: 2012, Internet site http://www.census.gov/hhes/ families/data/cps2012.html; calculations by New Strategist

Table 7.65 Total Minimum Wage Workers by Sex, 2011

(number of employed wage and salary workers, number of workers paid hourly rates at or below minimum wage, and minimum wage workers as share of total, by sex, 2011; numbers in thousands)

		workers paid at or below minimum wage	
	total paid hourly rates	number	share of total
Total workers aged 16 or older	**73,926**	**3,828**	**5.2%**
Total men	36,457	1,433	3.9
Total women	37,469	2,395	6.4

Source: Bureau of Labor Statistics, Characteristics of Minimum Wage Workers: 2011, Internet site http://www.bls.gov/cps/minwage2011tbls.htm; calculations by New Strategist

Table 7.66 Union Representation of Total Workers by Sex, 2012

(number of total employed wage and salary workers aged 16 or older, number and percent represented by unions, median weekly earnings of those working full-time by union representation status, and index of union median to average median, by sex, 2012; number in thousands)

	total	men	women
Total employed	**127,577**	**65,898**	**61,679**
Number represented by unions	15,922	8,611	7,311
Percent represented by unions	12.5%	13.1%	11.9%
Median weekly earnings of full-time workers	**$768**	**$854**	**$691**
Represented by unions	933	990	865
Not represented by unions	742	821	663
Index, median weekly earnings of total workers represented by unions to average worker	**121**	**116**	**125**

Note: Workers represented by unions are either members of a labor union or workers who report no union affiliation but whose jobs are covered by a union or an employee association contract. The index is calculated by dividing median weekly earnings of workers represented by unions by median weekly earnings of the average worker and multiplying by 100.
Source: Bureau of Labor Statistics, Labor Force Statistics from the Current Population Survey, Internet site http://www.bls.gov/cps/tables.htm#empstat

Table 7.67 Labor Force Projections by Race and Hispanic Origin, 2010 and 2020

(number, percent distribution, and percent of people aged 16 or older in the civilian labor force by sex, race, and Hispanic origin, 2010 and 2020; percent change in number and percentage point change in rate 2010–20; numbers in thousands)

| | number | | percent change 2010–20 | percent distribution | | | participation rate | | |
	2010	2020		2010	2020	percentage point change 2010–20	2010	2020	percentage point change 2010–20
Total in labor force	**153,889**	**164,360**	**6.8%**	**100.0%**	**100.0%**	–	**64.7%**	**62.5%**	**–2.2**
Asian	7,248	9,430	30.1	4.7	5.7	1.0	64.7	63.1	–1.6
Black	17,862	19,676	10.2	11.6	12.0	0.4	62.2	60.3	–1.9
Hispanic	22,748	30,493	34.0	14.8	18.6	3.8	67.5	66.2	–1.3
Non-Hispanic white	103,947	102,371	–1.5	67.5	62.3	–5.3	64.6	62.0	–2.6
Other racial groups	3,694	4,738	28.3	2.4	2.9	0.5	63.2	61.4	–1.8
Men in labor force	**81,985**	**87,128**	**6.3**	**100.0**	**100.0**	–	**71.2**	**68.2**	**–3.0**
Asian	3,893	4,968	27.6	4.7	5.7	1.0	73.2	71.0	–2.2
Black	8,415	9,393	11.6	10.3	10.8	0.5	65.0	63.1	–1.9
Hispanic	13,511	17,859	32.2	16.5	20.5	4.0	77.8	75.9	–1.9
Non-Hispanic white	55,116	53,867	–2.3	67.2	61.8	–5.4	70.7	67.2	–3.5
Other racial groups	1,949	2,388	22.5	2.4	2.7	0.4	68.7	63.4	–5.3
Women in labor force	**71,904**	**77,232**	**7.4**	**100.0**	**100.0**	–	**58.6**	**57.1**	**–1.5**
Asian	3,355	4,462	33.0	4.7	5.8	1.1	57.0	56.1	–0.9
Black	9,447	10,283	8.8	13.1	13.3	0.2	59.9	57.9	–2.0
Hispanic	9,238	12,634	36.8	12.8	16.4	3.5	56.5	56.1	–0.4
Non-Hispanic white	48,831	48,504	–0.7	67.9	62.8	–5.1	58.9	57.2	–1.7
Other racial groups	1,746	2,350	34.6	2.4	3.0	0.6	58.0	59.5	1.5

Note: Numbers do not add to total because Hispanics may be of any race. Asians and blacks are those who identify themselves as being of the race alone. Non-Hispanic whites are those who identify themselves as being white alone and not Hispanic. "Other racial groups" are those of more than one race, American Indians, and Native Hawaiians. "–" means not applicable.
Source: Bureau of Labor Statistics, Labor Force Projections to 2020: A More Slowly Growing Workforce, Monthly Labor Review, January 2012, Internet site http://www.bls.gov/opub/mlr/2012/01/home.htm

Asians, Blacks, and Hispanics Account for a Large Share of Households

Because the Asian, black, and Hispanic populations are younger, on average, than the non-Hispanic white population, minorities account for a relatively large share of households headed by younger adults. Asians, blacks, Hispanics, and other minorities account for 46 percent of householders under age 25 and for at least one-third of householders between the ages of 25 and 50. In contrast, among householders aged 65 or older, minorities account for only 19 percent.

The minority share of households varies greatly by household type. Asians, blacks, Hispanics, and other minorities are more than 50 percent of the nation's female-headed families, but only 26 percent of married couples. Because minority households are more likely to include children, their household size is above average. Asians, blacks, Hispanics, and other minorities head most of the nation's households with six or more people. They head only 28 percent of single-person households and 24 percent of two-person households.

■ With immigration adding substantially to U.S. population growth each year, the minority share of households will grow rapidly.

Minorities are a large share of households headed by younger adults

(percent distribution of households headed by people under age 40 and aged 65 or older, by race and Hispanic origin of householder, 2012)

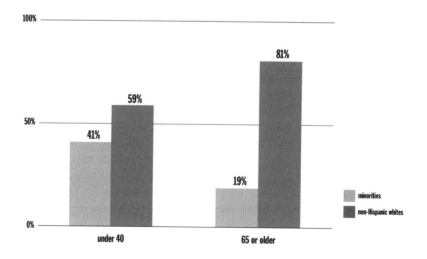

Table 7.68 Total Households by Age of Householder, 2012

(number and percent distribution of total households by age of householder, 2012, numbers in thousands)

	number	percent distribution
Total households	**121,084**	**100.0%**
Under age 25	6,180	5.1
Aged 25 to 29	9,208	7.6
Aged 30 to 34	10,638	8.8
Aged 35 to 39	10,111	8.4
Aged 40 to 44	11,129	9.2
Aged 45 to 49	11,763	9.7
Aged 50 to 54	12,433	10.3
Aged 55 to 59	12,037	9.9
Aged 60 to 64	10,742	8.9
Aged 65 or older	26,843	22.2

Source: Bureau of the Census, 2012 Current Population Survey, Internet site http://www.census.gov/hhes/www/income/data/incpovhlth/2011/dtables.html; calculations by New Strategist

Table 7.69 Households by Age, Race, and Hispanic Origin of Householder, 2012

(number of total households and percent distribution by race and Hispanic origin of householder, by age of householder, 2012; numbers in thousands)

	total		Asian	black	Hispanic	non-Hispanic white
	number	percent				
Total households	**121,084**	**100.0%**	**4.7%**	**13.4%**	**12.3%**	**69.0%**
Under age 25	6,180	100.0	6.6	18.1	20.8	54.5
Aged 25 to 29	9,208	100.0	6.0	15.2	17.6	61.1
Aged 30 to 34	10,638	100.0	6.5	15.3	18.2	59.5
Aged 35 to 39	10,111	100.0	7.1	14.9	18.2	59.5
Aged 40 to 44	11,129	100.0	5.5	15.0	16.0	63.3
Aged 45 to 49	11,763	100.0	5.3	13.8	13.6	66.7
Aged 50 to 54	12,433	100.0	4.1	13.7	10.8	70.3
Aged 55 to 59	12,037	100.0	3.9	13.4	9.0	72.8
Aged 60 to 64	10,742	100.0	3.6	12.1	7.9	75.6
Aged 65 or older	26,843	100.0	2.7	9.7	6.0	80.9

Note: Percentages do not sum to total because Asians and blacks are those who identify themselves as being of the race alone and those who identify themselves as being of the race in combination with other races, not all races are shown, and Hispanics may be of any race. Non-Hispanic whites are those who identify themselves as being white alone and not Hispanic.
Source: Bureau of the Census, 2012 Current Population Survey, Internet site http://www.census.gov/hhes/www/income/data/incpovhlth/2011/dtables.html; calculations by New Strategist

Table 7.70 Total Households by Household Type, 2012

(number and percent distribution of total households by household type, 2012; numbers in thousands)

	number	percent distribution
TOTAL HOUSEHOLDS	**121,084**	**100.0%**
Family households	**80,506**	**66.5**
Married couples	58,949	48.7
With children under age 18	25,114	20.7
Female householders, no spouse present	15,669	12.9
With children under age 18	10,380	8.6
Male householders, no spouse present	5,888	4.9
With children under age 18	2,982	2.5
Nonfamily households	**40,578**	**33.5**
Female householders	21,383	17.7
Living alone	18,354	15.2
Male householders	19,195	15.9
Living alone	14,835	12.3

Source: Bureau of the Census, Current Population Survey Annual Social and Economic Supplement, Internet site http://www.census.gov/hhes/www/income/data/incpovhlth/2011/index.html; calculations by New Strategist

Table 7.71 Households by Type, Race, and Hispanic Origin of Householder, 2012

(number of total households and percent distribution by race and Hispanic origin of householder, by household type, 2012; numbers in thousands)

	total		Asian	black	Hispanic	non-Hispanic white
	number	percent				
Total households	**121,084**	**100.0%**	**4.7%**	**13.4%**	**12.3%**	**69.0%**
Family households	**80,506**	**100.0**	**5.4**	**12.5**	**14.4**	**67.3**
Married couples	58,949	100.0	5.8	7.7	12.3	73.6
With children under age 18	25,114	100.0	7.3	9.3	18.6	64.7
Female householders, no spouse present	15,669	100.0	3.7	28.6	19.7	48.1
With children under age 18	10,380	100.0	2.9	30.9	22.7	43.8
Male householders, no spouse present	5,888	100.0	5.7	17.0	21.7	54.9
With children under age 18	2,982	100.0	4.0	17.2	24.3	53.6
Nonfamily households	**40,578**	**100.0**	**3.4**	**15.1**	**8.3**	**72.5**
Female householders	21,383	100.0	3.2	15.8	7.2	73.1
Living alone	18,354	100.0	2.9	16.6	6.8	73.0
Male householders	19,195	100.0	3.5	14.4	9.5	71.9
Living alone	14,835	100.0	3.2	16.0	8.5	71.7

Note: Numbers do not add to total because Hispanics may be of any race, not all races are shown, and some householders may be of more than one race. Asians and blacks are those who identify themselves as being of the race alone and those who identify themselves as being of the race in combination with other races. Non-Hispanic whites are those who identify themselves as being white alone and not Hispanic.
Source: Bureau of the Census, 2012 Current Population Survey Annual Social and Economic Supplement, Internet site http:// www.census.gov/hhes/www/cpstables/032012/hhinc/toc.htm; calculations by New Strategist

Table 7.72 Households by Age of Householder and Household Type, 2012

(number and percent distribution of households by age of householder and type of household, 2012; numbers in thousands)

| | | family households | | | nonfamily households | | | |
| | | | female householder no spouse present | male householder, no spouse present | female-headed | | male-headed | |
	total	married couples			total	living alone	total	living alone
Total households	**121,084**	**58,949**	**15,669**	**5,888**	**21,383**	**18,354**	**19,195**	**14,835**
Under age 25	6,180	1,058	1,455	819	1,427	724	1,421	654
Aged 25 to 34	19,846	8,658	3,420	1,432	2,551	1,758	3,784	2,323
Aged 35 to 44	21,241	11,954	3,672	1,157	1,653	1,319	2,805	2,137
Aged 45 to 54	24,195	13,299	3,137	1,112	2,977	2,500	3,671	3,052
Aged 55 to 64	22,779	12,093	2,013	795	4,141	3,697	3,736	3,206
Aged 65 or older	26,843	11,886	1,972	573	8,634	8,355	3,778	3,462

PERCENT DISTRIBUTION BY HOUSEHOLD TYPE

Total households	**100.0%**	**48.7%**	**12.9%**	**4.9%**	**17.7%**	**15.2%**	**15.9%**	**12.3%**
Under age 25	100.0	17.1	23.5	13.3	23.1	11.7	23.0	10.6
Aged 25 to 34	100.0	43.6	17.2	7.2	12.9	8.9	19.1	11.7
Aged 35 to 44	100.0	56.3	17.3	5.4	7.8	6.2	13.2	10.1
Aged 45 to 54	100.0	55.0	13.0	4.6	12.3	10.3	15.2	12.6
Aged 55 to 64	100.0	53.1	8.8	3.5	18.2	16.2	16.4	14.1
Aged 65 or older	100.0	44.3	7.3	2.1	32.2	31.1	14.1	12.9

PERCENT DISTRIBUTION BY AGE

Total households	**100.0%**	**100.0%**	**100.0%**	**100.0%**	**100.0%**	**100.0%**	**100.0%**	**100.0%**
Under age 25	5.1	1.8	9.3	13.9	6.7	3.9	7.4	4.4
Aged 25 to 34	16.4	14.7	21.8	24.3	11.9	9.6	19.7	15.7
Aged 35 to 44	17.5	20.3	23.4	19.6	7.7	7.2	14.6	14.4
Aged 45 to 54	20.0	22.6	20.0	18.9	13.9	13.6	19.1	20.6
Aged 55 to 64	18.8	20.5	12.8	13.5	19.4	20.1	19.5	21.6
Aged 65 or older	22.2	20.2	12.6	9.7	40.4	45.5	19.7	23.3

Source: Bureau of the Census, 2012 Current Population Survey Annual Social and Economic Supplement, Internet site http://www.census.gov/hhes/www/cpstables/032012/hhinc/toc.htm; calculations by New Strategist

Table 7.73 Total Households by Size, 2012

(number and percent distribution of total households by household size, 2012; number of households in thousands)

	number	percent distribution
Total households	**121,084**	**100.0%**
One person	33,188	27.4
Two people	40,983	33.8
Three people	19,241	15.9
Four people	16,049	13.3
Five people	7,271	6.0
Six people	2,734	2.3
Seven or more people	1,617	1.3
Average number of persons per household	2.55	–

Note: "–" means not applicable.
Source: Bureau of the Census, Current Population Survey Annual Social and Economic Supplement, Internet site http://www.census.gov/hhes/www/income/dinctabs.html; calculations by New Strategist

Table 7.74 Households by Size, Race, and Hispanic Origin of Householder, 2012

(number of total households and percent distribution by race and Hispanic origin of householder, by household size, 2012; numbers in thousands)

	total		Asian	black	Hispanic	non-Hispanic white
	number	percent				
Total households	**116,783**	**100.0%**	**4.7%**	**13.4%**	**12.3%**	**69.0%**
One person	32,167	100.0	3.1	16.3	7.6	72.4
Two people	38,737	100.0	3.9	10.7	8.3	76.3
Three people	18,522	100.0	6.1	14.4	15.2	64.1
Four people	15,865	100.0	7.3	12.1	18.1	62.1
Five people	7,332	100.0	6.2	13.4	24.7	55.2
Six people	2,694	100.0	6.1	15.1	28.4	50.0
Seven or more people	1,467	100.0	8.9	16.7	38.1	36.2

Note: Percentages do not sum to total because Asians and blacks are those who identify themselves as being of the race alone and those who identify themselves as being of the race in combination with other races, not all races are shown, and Hispanics may be of any race. Non-Hispanic whites are those who identify themselves as being white alone and not Hispanic.
Source: Bureau of the Census, Current Population Survey Annual Social and Economic Supplement, Internet site http://www.census.gov/hhes/www/income/dinctabs.html; calculations by New Strategist

Table 7.75 Total Households by Region, 2012

(number and percent distribution of total households by region of residence, 2012; number of households in thousands)

	number	percent distribution
Total households	**121,084**	**100.0%**
Northeast	21,774	18.0
Midwest	26,865	22.2
South	45,604	37.7
West	26,840	22.2

Source: Bureau of the Census, Current Population Survey Annual Social and Economic Supplement, Internet site http://www.census.gov/hhes/www/income/dinctabs.html; calculations by New Strategist

Table 7.76 Households by Region, Race, and Hispanic Origin of Householder, 2012

(number of total households and percent distribution by race and Hispanic origin of householder, by region of residence, 2012; numbers in thousands)

	total		Asian	black	Hispanic	non-Hispanic white
	number	percent				
Total households	**121,084**	**100.0%**	**4.7%**	**13.4%**	**12.3%**	**69.0%**
Northeast	21,774	100.0	5.4	12.6	10.4	72.8
Midwest	26,865	100.0	2.5	10.8	4.5	81.3
South	45,604	100.0	2.9	19.6	12.1	64.7
West	26,840	100.0	9.5	5.8	22.1	61.1

Note: Percentages do not sum to total because Asians and blacks are those who identify themselves as being of the race alone and those who identify themselves as being of the race in combination with other races, not all races are shown, and Hispanics may be of any race. Non-Hispanic whites are those who identify themselves as being white alone and not Hispanic.
Source: Bureau of the Census, Current Population Survey Annual Social and Economic Supplement, Internet site http://www.census.gov/hhes/www/income/dinctabs.html; calculations by New Strategist

Table 7.77 Total Households by Metropolitan Status, 2012

(number and percent distribution of total households by metropolitan status, 2012; number of households in thousands)

	number	percent distribution
Total households	**121,084**	**100.0%**
Inside metropolitan areas	101,526	83.8
Inside principal cities	40,616	33.5
Outside principal cities	60,910	50.3
Outside metropolitan areas	19,558	16.2

Source: Bureau of the Census, Current Population Survey Annual Social and Economic Supplement, Internet site http://www. census.gov/hhes/www/income/dinctabs.html; calculations by New Strategist

Table 7.78 Households by Metropolitan Status, Race, and Hispanic Origin of Householder, 2012

(number of total households and percent distribution by race and Hispanic origin of householder, by metropolitan status, 2012; numbers in thousands)

	total		Asian	black	Hispanic	non-Hispanic white
	number	percent				
Total households	**121,084**	**100.0%**	**4.7%**	**13.4%**	**12.3%**	**69.0%**
Inside metropolitan areas	101,526	100.0	5.5	14.3	13.6	66.4
Inside principal cities	40,616	100.0	7.2	20.5	18.1	54.4
Outside principal cities	60,910	100.0	4.3	10.2	10.7	74.4
Outside metropolitan areas	19,558	100.0	0.9	8.3	5.6	82.5

Note: Percentages do not sum to total because Asians and blacks are those who identify themselves as being of the race alone and those who identify themselves as being of the race in combination with other races, not all races are shown, and Hispanics may be of any race. Non-Hispanic whites are those who identify themselves as being white alone and not Hispanic.
Source: Bureau of the Census, Current Population Survey Annual Social and Economic Supplement, Internet site http://www .census.gov/hhes/www/income/dinctabs.html; calculations by New Strategist

Table 7.79 People Living Alone by Sex and Age, 2012

(total number of people aged 15 or older, number and percent living alone, and percent distribution of people who live alone, by sex and age, 2012; numbers in thousands)

	total	living alone		
		number	percent distribution	share of total
Total people	**247,696**	**33,189**	**100.0%**	**13.4%**
Under age 25	43,117	1,378	4.2	3.2
Aged 25 to 34	41,219	4,081	12.3	9.9
Aged 35 to 44	39,927	3,456	10.4	8.7
Aged 45 to 54	43,955	5,552	16.7	12.6
Aged 55 to 64	37,971	6,903	20.8	18.2
Aged 65 or older	41,507	11,817	35.6	28.5
Aged 65 to 74	23,383	5,198	15.7	22.2
Aged 75 or older	18,123	6,620	19.9	36.5
Total men	**119,946**	**14,835**	**100.0**	**12.4**
Under age 25	21,826	654	4.4	3.0
Aged 25 to 34	20,464	2,323	15.7	11.4
Aged 35 to 44	19,677	2,137	14.4	10.9
Aged 45 to 54	21,490	3,052	20.6	14.2
Aged 55 to 64	18,157	3,206	21.6	17.7
Aged 65 or older	18,332	3,462	23.3	18.9
Aged 65 to 74	10,980	1,829	12.3	16.7
Aged 75 or older	7,353	1,633	11.0	22.2
Total women	**127,751**	**18,354**	**100.0**	**14.4**
Under age 25	21,291	724	3.9	3.4
Aged 25 to 34	20,755	1,758	9.6	8.5
Aged 35 to 44	20,251	1,319	7.2	6.5
Aged 45 to 54	22,465	2,500	13.6	11.1
Aged 55 to 64	19,814	3,697	20.1	18.7
Aged 65 or older	23,174	8,355	45.5	36.1
Aged 65 to 74	12,404	3,369	18.4	27.2
Aged 75 or older	10,771	4,987	27.2	46.3

Source: Bureau of the Census, 2012 Current Population Survey Annual Social and Economic Supplement, Internet site http:// www.census.gov/hhes/www/cpstables/032012/hhinc/toc.htm; calculations by New Strategist

Table 7.80 Total Households by Age of Householder, Type of Household, and Presence of Children, 2012

(number and percent distribution of total households by age of householder, type of household, and presence of own children under age 18, 2012; numbers in thousands)

	all households		married couples		female-headed families		male-headed families	
	total	with children	total	with children	total	with children	total	with children
Total households	**121,084**	**34,989**	**58,949**	**23,704**	**15,669**	**8,869**	**5,888**	**2,415**
Under age 25	6,180	1,737	1,059	597	1,456	970	819	171
Aged 25 to 29	9,208	3,820	3,366	2,063	1,611	1,401	768	356
Aged 30 to 34	10,638	6,176	5,292	4,090	1,809	1,676	665	409
Aged 35 to 39	10,111	6,772	5,557	4,690	1,871	1,666	560	415
Aged 40 to 44	11,129	6,686	6,397	4,953	1,801	1,344	596	389
Aged 45 to 49	11,763	5,213	6,438	3,872	1,722	998	605	343
Aged 50 to 54	12,433	2,880	6,861	2,176	1,414	533	506	171
Aged 55 to 64	22,779	1,428	12,093	1,079	2,013	224	795	124
Aged 65 or older	26,843	277	11,886	183	1,972	57	573	37

PERCENT OF HOUSEHOLDS WITH CHILDREN BY TYPE

	all households		married couples		female-headed families		male-headed families	
Total households	**100.0%**	**28.9%**	**100.0%**	**40.2%**	**100.0%**	**56.6%**	**100.0%**	**41.0%**
Under age 25	100.0	28.1	100.0	56.4	100.0	66.6	100.0	20.9
Aged 25 to 29	100.0	41.5	100.0	61.3	100.0	87.0	100.0	46.4
Aged 30 to 34	100.0	58.1	100.0	77.3	100.0	92.6	100.0	61.5
Aged 35 to 39	100.0	67.0	100.0	84.4	100.0	89.0	100.0	74.1
Aged 40 to 44	100.0	60.1	100.0	77.4	100.0	74.6	100.0	65.3
Aged 45 to 49	100.0	44.3	100.0	60.1	100.0	58.0	100.0	56.7
Aged 50 to 54	100.0	23.2	100.0	31.7	100.0	37.7	100.0	33.8
Aged 55 to 64	100.0	6.3	100.0	8.9	100.0	11.1	100.0	15.6
Aged 65 or older	100.0	1.0	100.0	1.5	100.0	2.9	100.0	6.5

Source: Bureau of the Census, Current Population Survey Annual Social and Economic Supplement, America's Families and Living Arrangements: 2012, Detailed Tables, Internet site http://www.census.gov/hhes/families/data/cps2012.html; calculations by New Strategist

Table 7.81 Living Arrangements of Total Children, 2012

(number and percent distribution of total children under age 18 by living arrangement, 2012; numbers in thousands)

	number	percent distribution
TOTAL CHILDREN	**73,817**	**100.0%**
Living with two parents	**50,267**	**68.1**
Married parents	47,330	64.1
Unmarried parents	2,937	4.0
Biological mother and father	45,221	61.3
Married parents	42,691	57.8
Biological mother and stepfather	3,016	4.1
Biological father and stepmother	919	1.2
Biological mother and adoptive father	185	0.3
Biological father and adoptive mother	34	0.0
Adoptive mother and father	661	0.9
Other	231	0.3
Living with one parent	**20,916**	**28.3**
Mother only	17,991	24.4
Father only	2,924	4.0
Living with no parents	**2,634**	**3.6**
Grandparents	1,454	2.0
Other	1,180	1.6
At least one biological parent	**69,941**	**94.7**
At least one stepparent	**4,287**	**5.8**
At least one adoptive parent	**1,126**	**1.5**

Source: Bureau of the Census, Current Population Survey Annual Social and Economic Supplement, America's Families and Living Arrangements: 2012, Detailed Tables, Internet site http://www.census.gov/hhes/families/data/cps2012.html; calculations by New Strategist

Table 7.82 Marital Status of Total Men by Age, 2012

(number and percent distribution of total men aged 18 or older by age and marital status, 2012; numbers in thousands)

	total	never married	married, spouse present	married, spouse absent	separated	divorced	widowed
Total men	**113,213**	**34,471**	**61,039**	**1,730**	**2,421**	**10,688**	**2,864**
Aged 18 to 19	4,172	4,051	46	20	40	12	4
Aged 20 to 24	10,982	9,800	879	88	135	70	9
Aged 25 to 29	10,430	6,620	3,151	154	189	305	10
Aged 30 to 34	10,028	3,924	5,087	176	230	602	8
Aged 35 to 39	9,418	2,294	5,842	159	239	847	38
Aged 40 to 44	10,252	2,057	6,414	241	302	1,212	27
Aged 45 to 49	10,569	1,846	6,618	175	388	1,462	81
Aged 50 to 54	10,894	1,356	7,296	188	296	1,631	127
Aged 55 to 64	18,137	1,707	12,491	271	395	2,826	446
Aged 65 to 74	10,980	541	8,199	126	146	1,278	690
Aged 75 to 84	5,543	196	4,056	89	51	383	769
Aged 85 or older	1,809	79	961	43	10	61	656
Total men	**100.0%**	**30.4%**	**53.9%**	**1.5%**	**2.1%**	**9.4%**	**2.5%**
Aged 18 to 19	100.0	97.1	1.1	0.5	1.0	0.3	0.1
Aged 20 to 24	100.0	89.2	8.0	0.8	1.2	0.6	0.1
Aged 25 to 29	100.0	63.5	30.2	1.5	1.8	2.9	0.1
Aged 30 to 34	100.0	39.1	50.7	1.8	2.3	6.0	0.1
Aged 35 to 39	100.0	24.4	62.0	1.7	2.5	9.0	0.4
Aged 40 to 44	100.0	20.1	62.6	2.4	2.9	11.8	0.3
Aged 45 to 49	100.0	17.5	62.6	1.7	3.7	13.8	0.8
Aged 50 to 54	100.0	12.4	67.0	1.7	2.7	15.0	1.2
Aged 55 to 64	100.0	9.4	68.9	1.5	2.2	15.6	2.5
Aged 65 to 74	100.0	4.9	74.7	1.1	1.3	11.6	6.3
Aged 75 to 84	100.0	3.5	73.2	1.6	0.9	6.9	13.9
Aged 85 or older	100.0	4.4	53.1	2.4	0.6	3.4	36.3

Source: Bureau of the Census, Current Population Survey Annual Social and Economic Supplement, America's Families and Living Arrangements: 2012, Internet site http://www.census.gov/hhes/families/data/cps2012.html; calculations by New Strategist

Table 7.83 Marital Status of Total Women by Age, 2012

(number and percent distribution of total women aged 18 or older by age and marital status, 2012; numbers in thousands)

	total	never married	married, spouse present	married, spouse absent	separated	divorced	widowed
Total women	**121,385**	**30,061**	**61,021**	**1,764**	**3,141**	**14,208**	**11,190**
Aged 18 to 19	4,083	3,938	65	30	26	14	11
Aged 20 to 24	10,888	8,850	1,527	149	214	124	23
Aged 25 to 29	10,459	5,338	4,226	141	258	463	33
Aged 30 to 34	10,284	3,055	5,807	171	387	836	28
Aged 35 to 39	9,714	1,953	5,939	179	442	1,122	80
Aged 40 to 44	10,530	1,580	6,792	171	379	1,464	144
Aged 45 to 49	10,999	1,426	6,960	185	400	1,786	243
Aged 50 to 54	11,460	1,202	7,247	183	338	2,024	466
Aged 55 to 64	19,808	1,716	12,123	300	458	3,588	1,622
Aged 65 to 74	12,393	588	6,875	117	168	1,929	2,717
Aged 75 to 84	7,574	290	2,940	95	50	708	3,491
Aged 85 or older	3,193	125	521	43	21	152	2,332
Total women	**100.0%**	**24.8%**	**50.3%**	**1.5%**	**2.6%**	**11.7%**	**9.2%**
Aged 18 to 19	100.0	96.4	1.6	0.7	0.6	0.3	0.3
Aged 20 to 24	100.0	81.3	14.0	1.4	2.0	1.1	0.2
Aged 25 to 29	100.0	51.0	40.4	1.3	2.5	4.4	0.3
Aged 30 to 34	100.0	29.7	56.5	1.7	3.8	8.1	0.3
Aged 35 to 39	100.0	20.1	61.1	1.8	4.6	11.6	0.8
Aged 40 to 44	100.0	15.0	64.5	1.6	3.6	13.9	1.4
Aged 45 to 49	100.0	13.0	63.3	1.7	3.6	16.2	2.2
Aged 50 to 54	100.0	10.5	63.2	1.6	2.9	17.7	4.1
Aged 65 to 74	100.0	4.7	55.5	0.9	1.4	15.6	21.9
Aged 75 to 84	100.0	3.8	38.8	1.3	0.7	9.3	46.1
Aged 85 or older	100.0	3.9	16.3	1.3	0.7	4.8	73.0

Source: Bureau of the Census, Current Population Survey Annual Social and Economic Supplement, America's Families and Living Arrangements: 2012, Internet site http://www.census.gov/hhes/families/data/cps2012.html; calculations by New Strategist

Table 7.84 Race and Hispanic Origin Differences between Husband and Wife, 2012

(number and percent distribution of married-couple family groups by race and Hispanic origin differences between husband and wife, 2012; numbers in thousands)

	number	percent distribution
Total married-couple family groups	**61,047**	**100.0%**
Both white	41,996	68.8
Both Hispanic	6,730	11.0
Both black	3,860	6.3
Both other	3,616	5.9
Mixed race/Hispanic origin couples	4,507	7.4
Husband white, wife black	144	0.2
Husband white, wife Hispanic	1,098	1.8
Husband white, wife other	1,084	1.8
Husband black, wife white	315	0.5
Husband black, wife Hispanic	166	0.3
Husband black, wife other	85	0.1
Husband Hispanic, wife white	977	1.6
Husband Hispanic, wife black	36	0.1
Husband Hispanic, wife other	132	0.2
Husband other, wife white	644	1.1
Husband other, wife black	43	0.1
Husband other, wife Hispanic	121	0.2

Note: Whites, blacks, and "others" are non-Hispanic. "Others" include Asians and American Indians. Hispanics may be of any race. Married-couple family groups include married-couple householders and married couples living in households headed by others.
Source: Bureau of the Census, America's Families and Living Arrangements: 2012, Current Population Survey Annual Social and Economic Supplement; Internet site http://www.census.gov/hhes/families/data/cps2012.html; calculations by New Strategist

Table 7.85 Marital History of Men by Age, 2009

(number of men aged 15 or older and percent distribution by marital history and age, 2009; numbers in thousands)

	total	15–19	20–24	25–29	30–34	35–39	40–49	50–59	60–69	70+
TOTAL MEN, NUMBER	115,797	10,870	10,152	10,567	9,518	9,995	21,504	19,568	12,774	10,849
TOTAL MEN, PERCENT	100.0%	100.0%	100.0%	100.0%	100.0%	100.0%	100.0%	100.0%	100.0%	100.0%
Never married	33.0	98.0	87.5	59.7	35.6	23.5	16.4	10.8	4.6	3.4
Ever married	67.0	2.0	12.5	40.3	64.4	76.5	83.6	89.2	95.4	96.6
Married once	52.3	1.9	12.5	38.8	59.4	66.9	65.8	63.4	64.8	72.3
Still married	42.5	1.3	11.2	34.2	52.2	56.1	52.2	50.4	53.5	54.0
Married twice	11.6	0.1	0.0	1.5	4.8	8.7	14.8	20.0	22.1	18.9
Still married	9.0	0.1	0.0	1.3	4.0	7.4	11.3	15.5	17.5	13.2
Married three or more times	3.1	0.0	0.0	0.1	0.2	1.0	3.0	5.8	8.5	5.4
Still married	2.3	0.0	0.0	0.1	0.2	0.8	2.2	4.3	6.5	3.8
Ever divorced	20.5	0.3	0.8	5.0	10.5	17.9	28.5	35.7	36.5	23.4
Currently divorced	9.1	0.2	0.7	3.7	6.2	9.5	14.2	15.5	12.4	7.2
Ever widowed	3.6	0.4	0.1	0.3	0.2	0.5	1.3	2.5	6.4	22.6
Currently widowed	2.6	0.3	0.1	0.3	0.1	0.3	0.9	1.6	3.9	17.4

Source: Bureau of the Census, Number, Timing, and Duration of Marriages and Divorces: 2009, Current Population Reports P70-125, 2011, Internet site http://www.census.gov/hhes/socdemo/marriage/data/sipp/index.html; calculations by New Strategist

Table 7.86 Marital History of Women by Age, 2009

(number of women aged 15 or older and percent distribution by marital history and age, 2009; numbers in thousands)

	total	15–19	20–24	25–29	30–34	35–39	40–49	50–59	60–69	70+
TOTAL WOMEN, NUMBER	123,272	10,478	10,158	10,408	9,645	10,267	22,119	20,702	14,288	15,207
TOTAL WOMEN, PERCENT	100.0%	100.0%	100.0%	100.0%	100.0%	100.0%	100.0%	100.0%	100.0%	100.0%
Never married	27.2	97.5	77.3	46.8	26.7	17.3	13.0	9.1	6.0	4.3
Ever married	72.8	2.5	22.7	53.2	73.3	82.7	87.0	90.9	94.0	95.7
Married once	57.5	2.5	22.4	50.8	64.5	69.3	67.4	65.5	67.7	76.1
Still married	40.6	1.9	19.7	43.2	54.5	55.8	51.6	47.5	45.7	30.1
Married twice	12.1	0.1	0.3	2.3	8.0	11.6	15.8	19.5	20.1	15.2
Still married	7.9	0.6	0.2	2.0	6.9	9.1	11.3	13.4	13.2	5.2
Married three or more times	3.2	0.0	0.0	0.0	0.8	1.9	3.8	5.9	6.2	4.4
Still married	1.9	0.0	0.0	0.0	0.7	1.4	2.5	4.1	3.6	1.4
Ever divorced	22.4	0.2	1.8	7.3	15.6	22.7	31.0	37.3	34.5	21.4
Currently divorced	11.3	0.1	1.5	5.3	8.1	11.8	16.4	18.6	16.0	9.9
Ever widowed	10.0	0.3	0.1	0.2	0.6	1.4	2.6	6.5	17.0	51.2
Currently widowed	8.9	0.3	0.1	0.1	0.4	0.8	1.8	4.9	13.9	48.3

Source: Bureau of the Census, Number, Timing, and Duration of Marriages and Divorces: 2009, Current Population Reports P70-125, 2011, Internet site http://www.census.gov/hhes/socdemo/marriage/data/sipp/index.html; calculations by New Strategist

The United States Is Rapidly Becoming More Diverse

The U.S. population grew from 282 million in 2000 to 312 million in 2011, an increase of 10 percent. The non-Hispanic white share of the population fell from 69 to 63 percent during those years as minority populations grew much faster than the majority. Between 2000 and 2011, Hispanics (who may be of any race) surpassed blacks as the largest minority, growing to 52 million and accounting for 17 percent of the population. Blacks (alone or in combination) account for 14 percent of the population, and Asians (alone or in combination) for 6 percent.

The United States is becoming more diverse because of immigration. Between 2000 and 2009, more than 10 million immigrants came to the United States—a record high. The annual number of immigrants exceeded 1 million in 2010 and 2011.

Among regions, the West is the most diverse, with non-Hispanic whites accounting for only 52 percent of the population. Four states have minority majorities: California, Hawaii, New Mexico, and Texas, as well as the District of Columbia. Twenty-one percent of U.S. residents speak a language other than English at home. The 62 percent majority of those who speak a language other than English at home are Spanish speakers. In California, 44 percent of residents speak a language other than English at home.

■ The nation's growing diversity provides economic opportunity, but it also strains the political system.

Minorities account for more than one-third of Americans

(percent distribution of people by race and Hispanic origin, 2011)

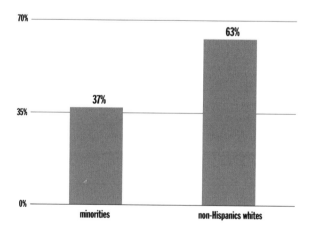

Table 7.87 Population by Race and Hispanic Origin, 2000 and 2010

(number of people by race and Hispanic origin, 2000 and 2010; numerical and percent change, 2000–10)

	2010		2000		change	
	number	percent distribution	number	percent distribution	numerical	percent
Total population	**308,745,538**	**100.0%**	**281,421,906**	**100.0%**	**27,323,632**	**9.7%**
Race alone						
American Indian	2,932,248	0.9	2,475,956	0.9	456,292	18.4
Asian	14,674,252	4.8	10,242,998	3.6	4,431,254	43.3
Black	38,929,319	12.6	34,658,190	12.3	4,271,129	12.3
Native Hawaiian	540,013	0.2	398,835	0.1	141,178	35.4
White	223,553,265	72.4	211,460,626	75.1	12,092,639	5.7
Other race	19,107,368	6.2	15,359,073	5.5	3,748,295	24.4
Two or more races	9,009,073	2.9	6,826,228	2.4	2,182,845	32.0
Race alone or in combination						
American Indian	5,220,579	1.7	4,225,058	1.5	995,521	23.6
Asian	17,320,856	5.6	12,006,894	4.3	5,313,962	44.3
Black	42,020,743	13.6	37,104,248	13.2	4,916,495	13.3
Native Hawaiian	1,225,195	0.4	906,785	0.3	318,410	35.1
White	231,040,398	74.8	231,434,388	82.2	–393,990	–0.2
Hispanic	50,477,594	16.3	35,305,818	12.5	15,171,776	43.0
Non-Hispanic white	196,817,552	63.7	194,552,774	69.1	2,264,778	1.2

Note: Numbers by race in combination do not add to total because they include those who identify themselves as being of the race alone and those who identify themselves as being of the race in combination with other races. Hispanics may be of any race. Non-Hispanic whites are those who identify themselves as being white alone and not Hispanic. Numbers are for April 1 of each year.
Source: Bureau of the Census, An Overview: Race and Hispanic Origin and the 2010 Census, 2010 Census Briefs, Internet site http://www.census.gov/2010census/data/2010-census-briefs.php; calculations by New Strategist

Table 7.88 Hispanics and Non-Hispanics by Race, 2010

(number and percent distribution of Hispanics and non-Hispanics by race, 2010; numbers in thousands)

	Hispanics		non-Hispanics	
	number	percent distribution	number	percent distribution
Total population	**50,477,594**	**100.0%**	**258,267,944**	**100.0%**
Race alone				
American Indian	685,150	1.4	2,247,098	0.9
Asian	209,128	0.4	14,465,124	5.6
Black	1,243,471	2.5	37,685,848	14.6
Native Hawaiian	58,437	0.1	481,576	0.2
White	26,735,713	53.0	196,817,552	76.2
Other race	18,503,103	36.7	604,265	0.2
Two or more races	3,042,592	6.0	5,966,481	2.3

Note: American Indians include Alaska Natives. Native Hawaiians include other Pacific Islanders.
Source: Bureau of the Census, An Overview: Race and Hispanic Origin and the 2010 Census, 2010 Census Briefs, Internet site http://www.census.gov/2010census/data/2010-census-briefs.php; calculations by New Strategist

Table 7.89 Total Population by Age, 2000 to 2011

(number of people by age, 2000 to 2011; percent change for selected years)

	2011	2010	2007	2000	percent change 2007–11	percent change 2000–11
Total people	**311,591,917**	**309,330,219**	**301,231,207**	**282,162,411**	**3.4%**	**10.4%**
Under age 5	20,162,058	20,192,942	20,125,962	19,178,293	0.2	5.1
Aged 5 to 9	20,334,196	20,332,370	19,714,611	20,463,852	3.1	–0.6
Aged 10 to 14	20,704,852	20,680,135	20,841,042	20,637,696	–0.7	0.3
Aged 15 to 19	21,644,043	21,980,141	22,067,816	20,294,955	–1.9	6.6
Aged 20 to 24	22,153,832	21,703,629	21,077,999	19,116,667	5.1	15.9
Aged 25 to 29	21,279,794	21,145,549	20,542,698	19,280,263	3.6	10.4
Aged 30 to 34	20,510,704	20,069,545	19,170,765	20,524,234	7.0	–0.1
Aged 35 to 39	19,594,309	20,078,157	20,963,891	22,650,852	–6.5	–13.5
Aged 40 to 44	21,033,645	20,903,642	21,832,339	22,517,991	–3.7	–6.6
Aged 45 to 49	22,158,005	22,634,608	22,799,761	20,219,527	-2.8	9.6
Aged 50 to 54	22,560,198	22,350,678	21,140,178	17,779,447	6.7	26.9
Aged 55 to 59	20,255,548	19,793,515	18,454,772	13,565,937	9.8	49.3
Aged 60 to 64	17,806,592	16,988,004	14,673,662	10,863,129	21.4	63.9
Aged 65 to 69	12,873,788	12,520,244	10,970,235	9,523,909	17.4	35.2
Aged 70 to 74	9,607,950	9,335,432	8,728,492	8,860,028	10.1	8.4
Aged 75 to 79	7,388,687	7,318,661	7,400,363	7,438,619	–0.2	–0.7
Aged 80 to 84	5,786,543	5,758,662	5,687,076	4,984,540	1.7	16.1
Aged 85 to 89	3,705,668	3,641,353	3,358,466	2,806,405	10.3	32.0
Aged 90 to 94	1,571,270	1,471,460	1,307,782	1,118,191	20.1	40.5
Aged 95 to 99	398,277	376,397	325,440	287,595	22.4	38.5
Aged 100 or older	61,958	55,095	47,857	50,281	29.5	23.2
Aged 18 to 24	31,064,709	30,764,659	29,808,025	27,315,274	4.2	13.7
Aged 18 or older	237,657,645	235,205,661	227,211,802	209,786,222	4.6	13.3
Aged 65 or older	41,394,141	40,477,304	37,825,711	35,069,568	9.4	18.0
Median age (years)	37.3	37.2	36.7	35.4	–	–

Note: Numbers are for July 1 of each year.
Source: Bureau of the Census, Population Estimates, Internet site http://www.census.gov/popest/index.html; calculations by New Strategist

Table 7.90 Total Population by Age, Race, and Hispanic Origin, 2011

(total number of people and percent distribution by age, race, and Hispanic origin, 2011)

	total		Asian	black	Hispanic	non-Hispanic white
	number	percent				
Total people	**311,591,917**	**100.0%**	**5.8%**	**14.1%**	**16.7%**	**63.4%**
Under age 5	20,162,058	100.0	6.9	18.4	25.8	50.3
Aged 5 to 9	20,334,196	100.0	6.6	17.2	24.1	52.8
Aged 10 to 14	20,704,852	100.0	6.0	17.3	22.4	54.8
Aged 15 to 19	21,644,043	100.0	5.7	17.6	21.2	55.7
Aged 20 to 24	22,153,832	100.0	6.4	16.6	20.2	57.1
Aged 25 to 29	21,279,794	100.0	7.0	14.8	20.5	57.9
Aged 30 to 34	20,510,704	100.0	7.2	14.6	20.7	57.7
Aged 35 to 39	19,594,309	100.0	7.6	14.1	20.1	58.3
Aged 40 to 44	21,033,645	100.0	6.5	13.6	17.0	62.7
Aged 45 to 49	22,158,005	100.0	5.6	13.4	14.2	66.5
Aged 50 to 54	22,560,198	100.0	5.0	12.8	11.4	70.3
Aged 55 to 59	20,255,548	100.0	4.8	11.9	9.8	73.0
Aged 60 to 64	17,806,592	100.0	4.5	10.7	8.3	75.8
Aged 65 to 69	12,873,788	100.0	4.3	9.8	7.9	77.5
Aged 70 to 74	9,607,950	100.0	4.2	9.6	7.7	78.0
Aged 75 to 79	7,388,687	100.0	3.9	9.0	7.2	79.4
Aged 80 to 84	5,786,543	100.0	3.4	7.8	6.5	82.1
Aged 85 or older	5,737,173	100.0	2.9	7.1	5.3	84.4
Aged 18 to 24	31,064,709	100.0	6.2	17.0	20.4	56.7
Aged 18 or older	237,657,645	100.0	5.7	13.0	14.6	66.6
Aged 65 or older	41,394,141	100.0	3.9	8.9	7.2	79.5

Note: Percentages do not sum to total because Asians and blacks are those who identify themselves as being of the race alone and those who identify themselves as being of the race in combination with other races, not all races are shown, and Hispanics may be of any race. Non-Hispanic whites are those who identify themselves as being white alone and not Hispanic.
Source: Bureau of the Census, Population Estimates, Internet site http://www.census.gov/popest/index.html; calculations by New Strategist

Table 7.91 Total Population by Age and Sex, 2011

(number of people by age and sex, and sex ratio by age, 2011)

	total	females	males	sex ratio
Total people	**311,591,917**	**158,301,098**	**153,290,819**	97
Under age 5	20,162,058	9,862,558	10,299,500	104
Aged 5 to 9	20,334,196	9,950,009	10,384,187	104
Aged 10 to 14	20,704,852	10,117,822	10,587,030	105
Aged 15 to 19	21,644,043	10,525,097	11,118,946	106
Aged 20 to 24	22,153,832	10,841,132	11,312,700	104
Aged 25 to 29	21,279,794	10,518,279	10,761,515	102
Aged 30 to 34	20,510,704	10,228,056	10,282,648	101
Aged 35 to 39	19,594,309	9,832,998	9,761,311	99
Aged 40 to 44	21,033,645	10,571,486	10,462,159	99
Aged 45 to 49	22,158,005	11,205,304	10,952,701	98
Aged 50 to 54	22,560,198	11,493,652	11,066,546	96
Aged 55 to 59	20,255,548	10,439,497	9,816,051	94
Aged 60 to 64	17,806,592	9,264,438	8,542,154	92
Aged 65 to 69	12,873,788	6,801,858	6,071,930	89
Aged 70 to 74	9,607,950	5,203,567	4,404,383	85
Aged 75 to 79	7,388,687	4,155,949	3,232,738	78
Aged 80 to 84	5,786,543	3,446,248	2,340,295	68
Aged 85 or older	5,737,173	3,843,148	1,894,025	49
Aged 18 to 24	31,064,709	15,167,425	15,897,284	105
Aged 18 or older	237,657,645	122,171,905	115,485,740	95
Aged 65 or older	41,394,141	23,450,770	17,943,371	77

Note: The sex ratio is the number of males divided by the number of females multiplied by 100.
Source: Bureau of the Census, Population Estimates, Internet site http://www.census.gov/popest/index.html; calculations by New Strategist

Table 7.92 Total Population Projections, 2012 to 2050

(number of people by age, 2012 to 2050, percent change, 2012–50; numbers in thousands)

	2012	2020	2030	2040	2050	percent change 2012–50
Total people	**314,004**	**333,896**	**358,471**	**380,016**	**399,803**	**27.3%**
Under age 5	20,274	21,808	22,252	23,004	24,115	18.9
Aged 5 to 9	20,457	21,307	22,451	22,886	23,983	17.2
Aged 10 to 14	20,639	20,616	22,365	22,893	23,682	14.7
Aged 15 to 19	21,326	20,806	21,946	23,174	23,642	10.9
Aged 20 to 24	22,554	21,651	21,940	23,863	24,463	8.5
Aged 25 to 29	21,375	23,366	22,712	24,151	25,493	19.3
Aged 30 to 34	20,901	22,906	23,340	23,924	25,949	24.1
Aged 35 to 39	19,479	21,869	24,423	24,002	25,513	31.0
Aged 40 to 44	21,017	20,361	23,403	24,000	24,655	17.3
Aged 45 to 49	21,678	20,008	21,935	24,595	24,262	11.9
Aged 50 to 54	22,572	20,467	20,083	23,176	23,866	5.7
Aged 55 to 59	20,769	21,747	19,393	21,384	24,094	16.0
Aged 60 to 64	17,808	21,017	19,454	19,242	22,348	25.5
Aged 65 or older	43,155	55,969	72,774	79,719	83,739	94.0

Source: Bureau of the Census, Population Projections, Internet site http://www.census.gov/population/projections/; calculations by New Strategist

Table 7.93 Total Population by Region, 2000 to 2011

(number and percent distribution of population by region, 2000 to 2011; percent change, 2000–11)

	2011	2010	2000	percent change 2000–11
Total population	**311,591,917**	**308,745,538**	**281,421,906**	**10.7%**
Northeast	55,521,598	55,317,240	53,594,378	3.6
Midwest	67,158,835	66,927,001	64,392,776	4.3
South	116,046,736	114,555,744	100,236,820	15.8
West	72,864,748	71,945,553	63,197,932	15.3

Note: Numbers in 2000 and 2010 are from the April 1 censuses; numbers in 2011 are estimates for July 1.
Source: Bureau of the Census, 2000 Census, 2010 Census, and Population Estimates, Internet site http://www.census.gov/popest/index.html; calculations by New Strategist

Table 7.94 Population by Region, Race, and Hispanic Origin, 2011

(total number of people and percent distribution by region, race, and Hispanic origin, 2011)

	total		Asian	black	Hispanic	non-Hispanic white
	number	percent				
Total people	**311,591,917**	**100.0%**	**5.8%**	**14.1%**	**16.7%**	**63.4%**
Northeast	55,521,598	100.0	6.5	14.0	13.0	68.5
Midwest	67,158,835	100.0	3.2	11.6	7.2	77.6
South	116,046,736	100.0	3.5	20.5	16.3	59.6
West	72,864,748	100.0	11.5	6.2	29.0	52.5

Note: Percentages do not sum to total because Asians and blacks are those who identify themselves as being of the race alone and those who identify themselves as being of the race in combination with other races, not all races are shown, and Hispanics may be of any race. Non-Hispanic whites are those who identify themselves as being white alone and not Hispanic.
Source: Bureau of the Census, Population Estimates, Internet site http://www.census.gov/popest/index.html; calculations by New Strategist

Table 7.95 Total Population by State, 2000 to 2011

(number of people by state, 2000 to 2011; percent change, 2000–11)

	2011	2010	2000	percent change 2000–11
Total people	**311,591,917**	**308,745,538**	**281,421,906**	**10.7%**
Alabama	4,802,740	4,779,736	4,447,100	8.0
Alaska	722,718	710,231	626,932	15.3
Arizona	6,482,505	6,392,017	5,130,632	26.3
Arkansas	2,937,979	2,915,918	2,673,400	9.9
California	37,691,912	37,253,956	33,871,648	11.3
Colorado	5,116,796	5,029,196	4,301,261	19.0
Connecticut	3,580,709	3,574,097	3,405,565	5.1
Delaware	907,135	897,934	783,600	15.8
District of Columbia	617,996	601,723	572,059	8.0
Florida	19,057,542	18,801,310	15,982,378	19.2
Georgia	9,815,210	9,687,653	8,186,453	19.9
Hawaii	1,374,810	1,360,301	1,211,537	13.5
Idaho	1,584,985	1,567,582	1,293,953	22.5
Illinois	12,869,257	12,830,632	12,419,293	3.6
Indiana	6,516,922	6,483,802	6,080,485	7.2
Iowa	3,062,309	3,046,355	2,926,324	4.6
Kansas	2,871,238	2,853,118	2,688,418	6.8
Kentucky	4,369,356	4,339,367	4,041,769	8.1
Louisiana	4,574,836	4,533,372	4,468,976	2.4
Maine	1,328,188	1,328,361	1,274,923	4.2
Maryland	5,828,289	5,773,552	5,296,486	10.0
Massachusetts	6,587,536	6,547,629	6,349,097	3.8
Michigan	9,876,187	9,883,640	9,938,444	–0.6
Minnesota	5,344,861	5,303,925	4,919,479	8.6
Mississippi	2,978,512	2,967,297	2,844,658	4.7
Missouri	6,010,688	5,988,927	5,595,211	7.4
Montana	998,199	989,415	902,195	10.6
Nebraska	1,842,641	1,826,341	1,711,263	7.7
Nevada	2,723,322	2,700,551	1,998,257	36.3
New Hampshire	1,318,194	1,316,470	1,235,786	6.7
New Jersey	8,821,155	8,791,894	8,414,350	4.8
New Mexico	2,082,224	2,059,179	1,819,046	14.5
New York	19,465,197	19,378,102	18,976,457	2.6
North Carolina	9,656,401	9,535,483	8,049,313	20.0
North Dakota	683,932	672,591	642,200	6.5
Ohio	11,544,951	11,536,504	11,353,140	1.7
Oklahoma	3,791,508	3,751,351	3,450,654	9.9
Oregon	3,871,859	3,831,074	3,421,399	13.2

	2011	2010	2000	percent change 2000–11
Pennsylvania	12,742,886	12,702,379	12,281,054	3.8%
South Carolina	4,679,230	4,625,364	4,012,012	16.6
South Dakota	824,082	814,180	754,844	9.2
Tennessee	6,403,353	6,346,105	5,689,283	12.6
Texas	25,674,681	25,145,561	20,851,820	23.1
Utah	2,817,222	2,763,885	2,233,169	26.2
Vermont	626,431	625,741	608,827	2.9
Virginia	8,096,604	8,001,024	7,078,515	14.4
Washington	6,830,038	6,724,540	5,894,121	15.9
West Virginia	1,855,364	1,852,994	1,808,344	2.6
Wisconsin	5,711,767	5,686,986	5,363,675	6.5
Wyoming	568,158	563,626	493,782	15.1

Source: Bureau of the Census, 2000 Census, 2010 Census, and Population Estimates, Internet site http://www.census.gov/popest/index.html; calculations by New Strategist

Table 7.96 Population by State, Race, and Hispanic Origin, 2011

(total number of people and percent distribution by state, race, and Hispanic origin, 2011)

	total number	total percent	Asian	black	Hispanic	non-Hispanic white
Total people	**311,591,917**	**100.0%**	**5.8%**	**14.1%**	**16.7%**	**63.4%**
Alabama	4,802,740	100.0	1.5	27.1	4.0	66.8
Alaska	722,718	100.0	7.3	5.0	5.8	63.7
Arizona	6,482,505	100.0	3.9	5.4	30.1	57.4
Arkansas	2,937,979	100.0	1.7	16.3	6.6	74.2
California	37,691,912	100.0	15.5	7.7	38.1	39.7
Colorado	5,116,796	100.0	3.9	5.3	20.9	69.7
Connecticut	3,580,709	100.0	4.6	12.3	13.8	70.9
Delaware	907,135	100.0	3.9	23.4	8.4	65.1
District of Columbia	617,996	100.0	4.7	52.2	9.5	35.3
Florida	19,057,542	100.0	3.2	17.5	22.9	57.5
Georgia	9,815,210	100.0	3.9	32.1	9.1	55.5
Hawaii	1,374,810	100.0	57.1	3.3	9.2	22.9
Idaho	1,584,985	100.0	2.0	1.2	11.5	83.6
Illinois	12,869,257	100.0	5.4	15.7	16.2	63.3
Indiana	6,516,922	100.0	2.1	10.4	6.2	81.3
Iowa	3,062,309	100.0	2.2	3.9	5.2	88.4
Kansas	2,871,238	100.0	3.1	7.4	10.8	77.8
Kentucky	4,369,356	100.0	1.5	8.9	3.2	86.1
Louisiana	4,574,836	100.0	2.0	33.2	4.4	60.1
Maine	1,328,188	100.0	1.4	1.7	1.4	94.3
Maryland	5,828,289	100.0	6.7	31.5	8.4	54.4
Massachusetts	6,587,536	100.0	6.3	8.8	9.9	76.4
Michigan	9,876,187	100.0	3.1	15.4	4.5	76.4
Minnesota	5,344,861	100.0	4.8	6.4	4.9	82.8
Mississippi	2,978,512	100.0	1.2	38.0	2.9	57.7
Missouri	6,010,688	100.0	2.1	12.6	3.7	80.8
Montana	998,199	100.0	1.1	1.0	3.1	87.5
Nebraska	1,842,641	100.0	2.4	5.6	9.5	81.8
Nevada	2,723,322	100.0	9.4	9.9	27.1	53.6
New Hampshire	1,318,194	100.0	2.7	1.8	2.9	92.2
New Jersey	8,821,155	100.0	9.4	15.7	18.1	58.9
New Mexico	2,082,224	100.0	2.2	3.2	46.7	40.2
New York	19,465,197	100.0	8.5	18.8	18.0	58.0
North Carolina	9,656,401	100.0	2.8	23.1	8.6	65.0
North Dakota	683,932	100.0	1.4	1.8	2.2	88.6
Ohio	11,544,951	100.0	2.1	13.6	3.2	81.0
Oklahoma	3,791,508	100.0	2.4	9.1	9.2	68.2
Oregon	3,871,859	100.0	5.1	2.8	12.0	78.1

	total		Asian	black	Hispanic	non-Hispanic white
	number	percent				
Pennsylvania	12,742,886	100.0%	3.3%	12.4%	5.9%	79.2%
Rhode Island	1,051,302	100.0	3.7	8.7	12.8	76.5
South Carolina	4,679,230	100.0	1.7	29.0	5.3	64.0
South Dakota	824,082	100.0	1.3	2.0	2.9	84.4
Tennessee	6,403,353	100.0	1.9	17.7	4.7	75.4
Texas	25,674,681	100.0	4.6	12.9	38.1	44.8
Utah	2,817,222	100.0	3.0	1.8	13.2	80.1
Vermont	626,431	100.0	1.8	1.6	1.6	94.2
Virginia	8,096,604	100.0	6.8	21.0	8.2	64.5
Washington	6,830,038	100.0	9.3	5.2	11.6	72.1
West Virginia	1,855,364	100.0	0.9	4.3	1.3	93.0
Wisconsin	5,711,767	100.0	2.8	7.3	6.1	83.1
Wyoming	568,158	100.0	1.3	1.6	9.1	85.5

Note: Percentages do not sum to total because Asians and blacks are those who identify themselves as being of the race alone and those who identify themselves as being of the race in combination with other races, not all races are shown, and Hispanics may be of any race. Non-Hispanic whites are those who identify themselves as being white alone and not Hispanic.
Source: Bureau of the Census, Population Estimates, Internet site http://www.census.gov/popest/index.html; calculations by New Strategist

Table 7.97 Population by Metropolitan Area, Race, and Hispanic Origin, 2010

(total number and percent distribution of people by race and Hispanic origin, by metropolitan area, 2010)

	total population number	total population percent	American Indian	Asian	black	Hispanic	non-Hispanic white
Abilene, TX	165,252	100.0%	0.7%	1.9%	8.5%	21.2%	68.2%
Akron, OH	703,200	100.0	0.2	2.4	13.2	1.5	82.4
Albany, GA	157,308	100.0	0.2	1.2	52.9	2.1	43.7
Albany–Schenectady–Troy, NY	870,716	100.0	0.2	3.8	9.1	4.1	82.9
Albuquerque, NM	887,077	100.0	5.9	2.8	3.6	46.7	42.2
Alexandria, LA	153,922	100.0	0.8	1.4	30.4	2.8	64.3
Allentown–Bethlehem–Easton, PA–NJ	821,173	100.0	0.3	3.0	6.1	13.0	78.6
Altoona, PA	127,089	100.0	0.1	0.8	2.4	1.0	95.6
Amarillo, TX	249,881	100.0	0.8	3.0	7.0	25.3	64.4
Ames, IA	89,542	100.0	0.2	6.7	3.1	3.0	86.9
Anchorage, AK	380,821	100.0	7.4	8.4	6.3	6.7	67.4
Anderson, IN	131,636	100.0	0.2	0.6	9.4	3.2	86.3
Anderson, SC	187,126	100.0	0.3	1.0	16.9	2.9	78.8
Ann Arbor, MI	344,791	100.0	0.3	9.1	14.3	4.0	72.1
Anniston–Oxford, AL	118,572	100.0	0.5	1.0	21.4	3.3	73.6
Appleton, WI	225,666	100.0	1.4	3.1	1.4	3.6	90.3
Asheville, NC	424,858	100.0	0.4	1.2	5.3	6.4	86.3
Athens–Clarke County, GA	192,541	100.0	0.2	3.8	20.3	8.0	67.8
Atlanta–Sandy Springs–Marietta, GA	5,268,860	100.0	0.3	5.5	33.6	10.4	50.7
Atlantic City–Hammonton, NJ	274,549	100.0	0.4	8.3	17.5	16.8	58.6
Auburn–Opelika, AL	140,247	100.0	0.3	3.1	23.4	3.3	69.8
Augusta–Richmond County, GA–SC	556,877	100.0	0.3	2.3	36.5	4.4	56.5
Austin–Round Rock–San Marcos, TX	1,716,289	100.0	0.8	5.7	8.3	31.4	54.7
Bakersfield–Delano, CA	839,631	100.0	1.5	5.2	6.7	49.2	38.6
Baltimore–Towson, MD	2,710,489	100.0	0.3	5.3	30.1	4.6	60.0
Bangor, ME	153,923	100.0	1.2	1.2	1.2	1.1	94.7
Barnstable Town, MA	215,888	100.0	0.6	1.4	2.8	2.2	91.4
Baton Rouge, LA	802,484	100.0	0.3	2.1	36.2	3.4	58.0
Battle Creek, MI	136,146	100.0	0.6	2.0	12.8	4.5	79.8
Bay City, MI	107,771	100.0	0.5	0.7	2.6	4.7	91.2
Beaumont–Port Arthur, TX	388,745	100.0	0.5	2.8	25.2	12.9	58.8
Bellingham, WA	201,140	100.0	2.8	5.0	1.7	7.8	81.9
Bend, OR	157,733	100.0	0.9	1.7	0.7	7.4	88.4
Billings, MT	158,050	100.0	3.8	1.0	1.2	4.5	88.7
Binghamton, NY	251,725	100.0	0.2	3.4	5.2	3.0	88.3
Birmingham–Hoover, AL	1,128,047	100.0	0.3	1.5	28.7	4.3	65.0
Bismarck, ND	108,779	100.0	4.0	0.6	0.9	1.3	92.5
Blacksburg–Christiansburg–Radford, VA	162,958	100.0	0.2	4.1	5.1	2.2	88.2
Bloomington, IN	192,714	100.0	0.3	4.5	3.2	2.4	89.3
Bloomington–Normal, IL	169,572	100.0	0.2	4.9	8.6	4.4	81.9
Boise City–Nampa, ID	616,561	100.0	0.9	2.7	1.4	12.6	81.9
Boston–Cambridge–Quincy, MA–NH	4,552,402	100.0	0.2	7.2	8.3	9.0	74.9

	total population		American Indian	Asian	black	Hispanic	non-Hispanic white
	number	percent					
Boulder, CO	294,567	100.0%	0.6%	5.3%	1.4%	13.3%	79.4%
Bowling Green, KY	125,953	100.0	0.3	2.9	9.3	4.2	83.0
Bremerton–Silverdale, WA	251,133	100.0	1.6	7.5	4.0	6.2	79.1
Bridgeport–Stamford–Norwalk, CT	916,829	100.0	0.3	5.3	11.8	16.9	66.2
Brownsville–Harlingen, TX	406,220	100.0	0.4	0.8	0.7	88.1	10.7
Brunswick, GA	112,370	100.0	0.3	1.2	24.3	5.1	69.0
Buffalo–Niagara Falls, NY	1,135,509	100.0	0.7	2.6	13.3	4.1	79.5
Burlington, NC	151,131	100.0	0.7	1.5	19.9	11.0	67.3
Burlington–South Burlington, VT	211,261	100.0	0.5	2.8	2.3	1.7	92.2
Canton–Massillon, OH	404,422	100.0	0.3	0.9	8.5	1.5	88.4
Cape Coral–Fort Myers, FL	618,754	100.0	0.4	1.8	9.1	18.3	71.0
Cape Girardeau–Jackson, MO–IL	96,275	100.0	0.3	1.2	9.5	1.8	86.8
Carson City, NV	55,274	100.0	2.4	3.0	2.3	21.3	70.7
Casper, WY	75,450	100.0	1.0	1.1	1.6	6.9	89.1
Cedar Rapids, IA	257,940	100.0	0.3	2.0	4.6	2.4	90.6
Champaign–Urbana, IL	231,891	100.0	0.3	8.7	12.0	4.8	74.3
Charleston, WV	304,284	100.0	0.2	1.0	5.8	0.8	91.8
Charleston–North Charleston–Summerville, SC	664,607	100.0	0.5	2.2	28.7	5.4	63.2
Charlotte–Gastonia–Rock Hill, NC–SC	1,758,038	100.0	0.5	3.6	25.1	9.8	61.2
Charlottesville, VA	201,559	100.0	0.3	4.7	13.6	4.8	76.6
Chattanooga, TN–GA	528,143	100.0	0.3	1.7	14.6	3.5	79.6
Cheyenne, WY	91,738	100.0	1.0	1.8	3.4	13.1	80.8
Chicago–Joliet–Naperville, IL–IN–WI	9,461,105	100.0	0.4	6.4	18.2	20.7	55.0
Chico, CA	220,000	100.0	2.0	5.2	2.4	14.1	75.2
Cincinnati–Middletown, OH–KY–IN	2,130,151	100.0	0.2	2.3	13.0	2.6	81.6
Clarksville, TN–KY	273,949	100.0	0.6	2.7	20.3	6.8	69.9
Cleveland, TN	115,788	100.0	0.3	1.0	4.4	4.2	89.7
Cleveland–Elyria–Mentor, OH	2,077,240	100.0	0.2	2.4	21.2	4.7	71.7
Coeur d'Alene, ID	138,494	100.0	1.3	1.3	0.7	3.8	92.0
College Station–Bryan, TX	228,660	100.0	0.5	5.1	12.5	22.5	59.8
Colorado Springs, CO	645,613	100.0	1.0	4.2	7.8	14.7	72.7
Columbia, MO	172,786	100.0	0.4	4.2	10.5	2.9	81.6
Columbia, SC	767,598	100.0	0.4	2.1	34.3	5.1	58.4
Columbus, GA–AL	294,865	100.0	0.4	2.4	41.9	5.7	50.0
Columbus, IN	76,794	100.0	0.3	3.7	2.5	6.2	87.0
Columbus, OH	1,836,536	100.0	0.2	3.7	16.3	3.6	75.9
Corpus Christi, TX	428,185	100.0	0.6	2.0	4.0	57.7	36.3
Corvallis, OR	85,579	100.0	0.7	6.7	1.5	6.4	83.6
Crestview–Fort Walton Beach–Destin, FL	180,822	100.0	0.6	4.6	10.7	6.8	77.1
Cumberland, MD–WV	103,299	100.0	0.1	0.8	7.5	1.2	90.0
Dallas–Fort Worth–Arlington, TX	6,371,773	100.0	0.7	6.0	15.9	27.5	50.2
Dalton, GA	142,227	100.0	0.6	1.3	3.5	26.5	68.5
Danville, IL	81,625	100.0	0.2	0.9	14.2	4.2	80.4
Danville, VA	106,561	100.0	0.2	0.7	33.3	2.4	63.2

| | total population | | American | | | | non-Hispanic |
	number	percent	Indian	Asian	black	Hispanic	white
Davenport–Moline–Rock Island, IA–IL	379,690	100.0%	0.3%	2.0%	8.3%	7.6%	81.9%
Dayton, OH	841,502	100.0	0.2	2.4	16.3	2.0	78.8
Decatur, AL	153,829	100.0	1.9	0.7	12.4	6.3	77.4
Decatur, IL	110,768	100.0	0.2	1.3	18.0	1.9	78.4
Deltona–Daytona Beach–Ormond Beach, FL	494,593	100.0	0.4	2.0	11.4	11.2	75.4
Denver–Aurora–Broomfield, CO	2,543,482	100.0	1.0	4.7	6.7	22.5	65.8
Des Moines–West Des Moines, IA	569,633	100.0	0.3	3.6	5.7	6.7	83.6
Detroit–Warren–Livonia, MI	4,296,250	100.0	0.3	3.9	23.8	3.9	67.9
Dothan, AL	145,639	100.0	0.5	0.9	23.9	3.0	71.5
Dover, DE	162,310	100.0	0.6	2.8	26.2	5.8	65.2
Dubuque, IA	93,653	100.0	0.2	1.2	3.3	1.9	92.9
Duluth, MN–WI	279,771	100.0	2.7	1.2	2.1	1.2	91.9
Durham–Chapel Hill, NC	504,357	100.0	0.5	5.0	28.2	11.3	55.3
Eau Claire, WI	161,151	100.0	0.5	2.9	1.7	1.6	93.0
El Centro, CA	174,528	100.0	1.8	2.4	3.8	80.4	13.7
Elizabethtown, KY	119,736	100.0	0.5	2.7	12.3	4.8	79.5
Elkhart–Goshen, IN	197,559	100.0	0.4	1.3	7.0	14.1	77.2
Elmira, NY	88,830	100.0	0.3	1.5	8.3	2.5	87.4
El Paso, TX	800,647	100.0	0.8	1.5	3.7	82.2	13.1
Erie, PA	280,566	100.0	0.2	1.4	8.5	3.4	86.5
Eugene–Springfield, OR	351,715	100.0	1.2	3.5	1.8	7.4	84.7
Evansville, IN–KY	358,676	100.0	0.2	1.3	7.3	1.9	88.9
Fairbanks, AK	97,581	100.0	7.0	4.3	6.1	5.8	74.1
Fargo, ND–MN	208,777	100.0	1.3	2.6	2.7	2.4	90.5
Farmington, NM	130,044	100.0	36.6	0.7	1.0	19.1	42.5
Fayetteville, NC	366,383	100.0	2.6	3.2	38.9	9.8	46.4
Fayetteville–Springdale–Rogers, AR–MO	463,204	100.0	1.5	2.8	2.4	14.9	76.3
Flagstaff, AZ	134,421	100.0	27.3	2.0	1.8	13.5	55.2
Flint, MI	425,790	100.0	0.5	1.3	22.1	3.0	72.7
Florence, SC	205,566	100.0	0.3	1.1	42.1	2.0	54.5
Florence–Muscle Shoals, AL	147,137	100.0	0.4	0.8	12.9	2.2	83.3
Fond du Lac, WI	101,633	100.0	0.5	1.4	1.8	4.3	91.9
Fort Collins–Loveland, CO	299,630	100.0	0.7	2.7	1.4	10.6	84.5
Fort Smith, AR–OK	298,592	100.0	6.3	2.6	4.3	8.2	76.0
Fort Wayne, IN	416,257	100.0	0.3	2.8	11.5	5.8	79.4
Fresno, CA	930,450	100.0	1.7	10.9	6.2	50.3	32.7
Gadsden, AL	104,430	100.0	0.4	0.8	15.8	3.3	79.3
Gainesville, FL	264,275	100.0	0.3	5.9	20.5	8.2	65.2
Gainesville, GA	179,684	100.0	0.5	2.1	8.0	26.1	63.6
Glens Falls, NY	128,923	100.0	0.2	0.8	2.4	2.0	94.3
Goldsboro, NC	122,623	100.0	0.4	1.8	32.6	9.9	55.6
Grand Forks, ND–MN	98,461	100.0	2.1	2.0	2.3	3.7	89.1
Grand Junction, CO	146,723	100.0	1.1	1.3	1.2	13.3	83.1
Grand Rapids–Wyoming, MI	774,160	100.0	0.5	2.4	9.4	8.4	79.5
Great Falls, MT	81,327	100.0	4.3	1.6	2.0	3.3	87.4

	total population		American				non-Hispanic
	number	percent	Indian	Asian	black	Hispanic	white
Greeley, CO	252,825	100.0%	1.1%	1.8%	1.4%	28.4%	67.6%
Green Bay, WI	306,241	100.0	2.4	2.6	2.5	6.2	86.1
Greensboro–High Point, NC	723,801	100.0	0.5	3.3	26.7	7.6	62.1
Greenville, NC	189,510	100.0	0.4	1.9	35.5	6.5	56.0
Greenville–Mauldin–Easley, SC	636,986	100.0	0.3	2.1	17.5	6.7	73.3
Gulfport–Biloxi, MS	248,820	100.0	0.5	3.0	20.3	4.7	71.3
Hagerstown–Martinsburg, MD–WV	269,140	100.0	0.2	1.5	9.5	3.4	85.1
Hanford–Corcoran, CA	152,982	100.0	1.7	5.1	8.3	50.9	35.2
Harrisburg–Carlisle, PA	549,475	100.0	0.2	3.4	11.7	4.7	80.5
Harrisonburg, VA	125,228	100.0	0.3	2.3	4.3	9.4	83.9
Hartford–West Hartford–East Hartford, CT	1,212,381	100.0	0.2	4.5	12.1	12.5	71.6
Hattiesburg, MS	142,842	100.0	0.2	1.0	29.0	2.8	66.9
Hickory–Lenoir–Morganton, NC	365,497	100.0	0.3	2.8	7.7	6.3	82.7
Hinesville–Fort Stewart, GA	77,917	100.0	0.6	2.8	41.8	10.2	45.7
Holland–Grand Haven, MI	263,801	100.0	0.4	3.1	2.1	8.6	85.7
Honolulu, HI	953,207	100.0	0.3	62.0	3.4	8.1	19.1
Hot Springs, AR	96,024	100.0	0.6	1.0	8.9	4.8	84.0
Houma–Bayou Cane–Thibodaux, LA	208,178	100.0	4.3	1.1	17.0	3.9	73.0
Houston–Sugar Land–Baytown, TX	5,946,800	100.0	0.6	7.2	18.0	35.3	39.7
Huntington–Ashland, WV–KY–OH	287,702	100.0	0.2	0.8	3.5	0.9	94.2
Huntsville, AL	417,593	100.0	0.7	2.8	22.7	4.8	68.6
Idaho Falls, ID	130,374	100.0	0.8	1.2	0.8	11.2	85.8
Indianapolis–Carmel, IN	1,756,241	100.0	0.3	2.8	16.1	6.2	74.6
Iowa City, IA	152,586	100.0	0.2	5.2	5.1	4.8	84.5
Ithaca, NY	101,564	100.0	0.4	9.8	5.3	4.2	80.2
Jackson, MI	160,248	100.0	0.4	1.0	9.5	3.0	85.9
Jackson, MS	539,057	100.0	0.2	1.2	48.2	2.1	48.3
Jackson, TN	115,425	100.0	0.2	1.1	33.1	3.2	62.3
Jacksonville, FL	1,345,596	100.0	0.4	4.3	22.9	6.9	65.8
Jacksonville, NC	177,772	100.0	0.7	3.2	17.7	10.1	68.9
Janesville, WI	160,331	100.0	0.3	1.4	6.1	7.6	84.5
Jefferson City, MO	149,807	100.0	0.4	1.1	8.3	2.1	87.7
Johnson City, TN	198,716	100.0	0.3	1.1	3.5	2.6	92.1
Johnstown, PA	143,679	100.0	0.1	0.7	4.5	1.4	93.3
Jonesboro, AR	121,026	100.0	0.3	1.1	12.7	4.0	81.5
Joplin, MO	175,518	100.0	1.8	1.4	2.3	6.0	86.6
Kalamazoo–Portage, MI	326,589	100.0	0.5	2.3	11.0	5.4	80.6
Kankakee–Bradley, IL	113,449	100.0	0.3	1.2	16.3	9.0	73.4
Kansas City, MO–KS	2,035,334	100.0	0.5	2.9	13.7	8.2	74.4
Kennewick–Pasco–Richland, WA	253,340	100.0	0.8	3.2	2.2	28.7	64.8
Killeen–Temple–Fort Hood, TX	405,300	100.0	0.8	3.9	22.0	20.3	54.0
Kingsport–Bristol–Bristol, TN–VA	309,544	100.0	0.2	0.6	2.4	1.3	95.0
Kingston, NY	182,493	100.0	0.3	2.2	7.5	8.7	81.7
Knoxville, TN	698,030	100.0	0.3	1.8	7.2	3.4	86.9
Kokomo, IN	98,688	100.0	0.3	1.1	7.1	2.6	88.6

	total population		American Indian	Asian	black	Hispanic	non-Hispanic white
	number	percent					
La Crosse, WI–MN	133,665	100.0%	0.4%	4.0%	2.0%	1.4%	91.9%
Lafayette, IN	201,789	100.0	0.2	5.9	4.3	7.0	82.4
Lafayette, LA	273,738	100.0	0.4	1.6	27.5	3.5	66.8
Lake Charles, LA	199,607	100.0	0.5	1.3	25.0	2.6	70.2
Lake Havasu City–Kingman, AZ	200,186	100.0	2.2	1.6	1.4	14.8	79.6
Lakeland–Winter Haven, FL	602,095	100.0	0.4	2.0	15.8	17.7	64.6
Lancaster, PA	519,445	100.0	0.2	2.2	4.7	8.6	84.9
Lansing–East Lansing, MI	464,036	100.0	0.5	4.4	10.7	6.2	78.3
Laredo, TX	250,304	100.0	0.4	0.7	0.6	95.7	3.3
Las Cruces, NM	209,233	100.0	1.5	1.6	2.3	65.7	30.1
Las Vegas–Paradise, NV	1,951,269	100.0	0.7	10.6	12.0	29.1	48.0
Lawrence, KS	110,826	100.0	2.7	4.7	5.4	5.1	81.7
Lawton, OK	124,098	100.0	5.9	3.7	20.3	11.2	58.9
Lebanon, PA	133,568	100.0	0.2	1.4	2.9	9.3	86.9
Lewiston, ID–WA	60,888	100.0	4.1	1.1	0.8	2.9	90.1
Lewiston–Auburn, ME	107,702	100.0	0.4	1.1	4.4	1.5	91.9
Lexington–Fayette, KY	472,099	100.0	0.2	2.8	12.0	5.9	79.0
Lima, OH	106,331	100.0	0.2	1.0	13.7	2.4	82.5
Lincoln, NE	302,157	100.0	0.7	3.9	4.6	5.6	85.0
Little Rock–North Little Rock–Conway, AR	699,757	100.0	0.5	1.9	23.0	4.8	69.6
Logan, UT–ID	125,442	100.0	0.6	2.2	0.9	9.6	86.1
Longview, TX	214,369	100.0	0.6	1.0	18.2	14.1	66.0
Longview, WA	102,410	100.0	1.5	2.2	1.2	7.8	85.8
Los Angeles–Long Beach–Santa Ana, CA	12,828,837	100.0	0.7	16.3	7.9	44.4	31.6
Louisville/Jefferson County, KY–IN	1,283,566	100.0	0.3	2.0	14.8	3.9	78.8
Lubbock, TX	284,890	100.0	0.7	2.5	8.1	32.3	57.0
Lynchburg, VA	252,634	100.0	0.4	1.6	18.6	2.1	77.1
Macon, GA	232,293	100.0	0.2	1.6	44.2	2.4	51.6
Madera–Chowchilla, CA	150,865	100.0	2.7	2.5	4.3	53.7	38.0
Madison, WI	568,593	100.0	0.4	4.8	5.7	5.4	83.7
Manchester–Nashua, NH	400,721	100.0	0.2	3.8	2.8	5.3	87.6
Manhattan, KS	127,081	100.0	0.7	4.6	10.7	7.7	76.2
Mankato–North Mankato, MN	96,740	100.0	0.3	2.2	3.1	2.9	91.3
Mansfield, OH	124,475	100.0	0.2	0.9	10.5	1.4	86.5
McAllen–Edinburg–Mission, TX	774,769	100.0	0.3	1.1	0.7	90.6	7.8
Medford, OR	203,206	100.0	1.2	1.9	1.3	10.7	83.7
Memphis, TN–MS–AR	1,316,100	100.0	0.3	2.2	46.4	5.0	46.2
Merced, CA	255,793	100.0	1.4	8.6	4.8	54.9	31.9
Miami–Fort Lauderdale–Pompano Beach, FL	5,564,635	100.0	0.3	2.8	22.1	41.6	34.8
Michigan City–La Porte, IN	111,467	100.0	0.3	0.8	12.0	5.5	81.4
Midland, TX	136,872	100.0	0.7	1.5	7.3	37.7	53.2
Milwaukee–Waukesha–West Allis, WI	1,555,908	100.0	0.5	3.5	17.9	9.5	69.0
Minneapolis–St. Paul–Bloomington, MN–WI	3,279,833	100.0	0.7	6.5	8.7	5.4	78.6
Missoula, MT	109,299	100.0	2.6	1.8	0.9	2.6	91.0
Mobile, AL	412,992	100.0	0.9	2.1	35.3	2.4	59.1

| | total population | | American | | | | non-Hispanic |
	number	percent	Indian	Asian	black	Hispanic	white
Modesto, CA	514,453	100.0%	1.1%	6.7%	3.8%	41.9%	46.7%
Monroe, LA	176,441	100.0	0.2	1.1	36.0	2.1	60.6
Monroe, MI	152,021	100.0	0.3	0.8	2.9	3.1	92.5
Montgomery, AL	374,536	100.0	0.3	1.9	43.2	3.2	51.4
Morgantown, WV	129,709	100.0	0.2	2.7	3.7	1.5	91.6
Morristown, TN	136,608	100.0	0.3	0.7	3.4	6.5	88.8
Mount Vernon–Anacortes, WA	116,901	100.0	2.2	2.6	1.2	16.9	76.7
Muncie, IN	117,671	100.0	0.3	1.3	8.1	1.8	88.1
Muskegon–Norton Shores, MI	172,188	100.0	0.8	0.9	15.9	4.8	77.3
Myrtle Beach–North Myrtle Beach–Conway, SC	269,291	100.0	0.5	1.4	14.4	6.2	77.3
Napa, CA	136,484	100.0	0.8	8.1	2.6	32.2	56.4
Naples–Marco Island, FL	321,520	100.0	0.3	1.5	7.1	25.9	65.7
Nashville–Davidson–Murfreesboro–Franklin, TN	1,589,934	100.0	0.3	2.8	16.1	6.6	74.0
New Haven–Milford, CT	862,477	100.0	0.3	4.0	14.1	15.0	67.5
New Orleans–Metairie–Kenner, LA	1,167,764	100.0	0.4	3.2	34.8	7.9	53.9
New York–Northern New Jersey–Long Island, NY–NJ–PA	18,897,109	100.0	0.5	10.9	19.1	22.9	48.9
Niles–Benton Harbor, MI	156,813	100.0	0.5	2.0	16.5	4.5	76.1
North Port–Bradenton–Sarasota, FL	702,281	100.0	0.3	1.8	7.3	11.1	79.6
Norwich–New London, CT	274,055	100.0	0.9	5.0	7.7	8.5	78.3
Ocala, FL	331,298	100.0	0.4	1.7	13.2	10.9	74.0
Ocean City, NJ	97,265	100.0	0.2	1.2	5.7	6.2	86.9
Odessa, TX	137,130	100.0	1.0	1.0	5.0	52.7	41.1
Ogden–Clearfield, UT	547,184	100.0	0.6	2.5	1.9	11.8	82.7
Oklahoma City, OK	1,252,987	100.0	4.1	3.5	12.0	11.3	67.4
Olympia, WA	252,264	100.0	1.4	7.2	4.1	7.1	78.9
Omaha–Council Bluffs, NE–IA	865,350	100.0	0.6	2.7	9.0	9.0	78.7
Orlando–Kissimmee–Sanford, FL	2,134,411	100.0	0.4	4.8	17.5	25.2	53.3
Oshkosh–Neenah, WI	166,994	100.0	0.6	2.7	2.4	3.5	90.7
Owensboro, KY	114,752	100.0	0.2	0.8	5.2	2.4	91.1
Oxnard–Thousand Oaks–Ventura, CA	823,318	100.0	1.0	8.4	2.5	40.3	48.7
Palm Bay–Melbourne–Titusville, FL	543,376	100.0	0.4	2.9	11.3	8.1	77.6
Palm Coast, FL	95,696	100.0	0.3	2.6	12.5	8.6	76.1
Panama City–Lynn Haven–Panama City Beach, FL	168,852	100.0	0.7	2.9	11.9	4.8	79.2
Parkersburg–Marietta–Vienna, WV–OH	162,056	100.0	0.2	0.7	1.7	0.8	96.0
Pascagoula, MS	162,246	100.0	0.4	2.4	20.4	4.2	72.5
Pensacola–Ferry Pass–Brent, FL	448,991	100.0	0.9	3.5	18.2	4.6	72.5
Peoria, IL	379,186	100.0	0.3	2.3	10.3	2.8	84.3
Philadelphia–Camden–Wilmington, PA–NJ–DE–MD	5,965,343	100.0	0.3	5.6	22.1	7.8	65.0
Phoenix–Mesa–Glendale, AZ	4,192,887	100.0	2.4	4.2	6.0	29.5	58.7
Pine Bluff, AR	100,258	100.0	0.3	0.8	48.4	1.8	48.6
Pittsburgh, PA	2,356,285	100.0	0.1	2.1	9.4	1.3	87.1

	total population		American Indian	Asian	black	Hispanic	non-Hispanic white
	number	percent					
Pittsfield, MA	131,219	100.0%	0.2%	1.6%	3.9%	3.5%	90.6%
Pocatello, ID	90,656	100.0	3.1	1.9	1.2	8.7	84.6
Portland–South Portland–Biddeford, ME	514,098	100.0	0.3	2.1	2.1	1.6	93.5
Portland–Vancouver–Hillsboro, OR–WA	2,226,009	100.0	0.9	7.2	3.9	10.9	76.3
Port St. Lucie, FL	424,107	100.0	0.5	1.8	15.4	15.1	67.8
Poughkeepsie–Newburgh–Middletown, NY	670,301	100.0	0.4	3.5	11.6	14.7	71.0
Prescott, AZ	211,033	100.0	1.7	1.3	1.0	13.6	82.0
Providence–New Bedford–Fall River, RI–MA	1,600,852	100.0	0.5	3.1	6.4	10.2	79.5
Provo–Orem, UT	526,810	100.0	0.6	2.2	0.9	10.7	84.3
Pueblo, CO	159,063	100.0	1.9	1.3	2.7	41.4	54.1
Punta Gorda, FL	159,978	100.0	0.3	1.6	6.4	5.8	86.0
Racine, WI	195,408	100.0	0.4	1.4	12.5	11.5	74.4
Raleigh–Cary, NC	1,130,490	100.0	0.5	5.1	21.3	10.1	63.4
Rapid City, SD	126,382	100.0	8.2	1.5	1.9	3.8	83.4
Reading, PA	411,442	100.0	0.3	1.7	6.1	16.4	76.9
Redding, CA	177,223	100.0	2.8	3.3	1.6	8.4	82.4
Reno–Sparks, NV	425,417	100.0	1.7	6.5	3.1	22.1	66.2
Richmond, VA	1,258,251	100.0	0.4	3.7	31.1	5.0	60.0
Riverside–San Bernardino–Ontario, CA	4,224,851	100.0	1.1	7.5	8.9	47.3	36.6
Roanoke, VA	308,707	100.0	0.2	2.0	13.9	3.1	80.6
Rochester, MN	186,011	100.0	0.2	5.0	4.6	4.1	85.9
Rochester, NY	1,054,323	100.0	0.3	3.0	12.9	6.1	78.2
Rockford, IL	349,431	100.0	0.3	2.6	11.9	12.3	73.0
Rocky Mount, NC	152,392	100.0	0.5	0.7	45.6	5.3	48.0
Rome, GA	96,317	100.0	0.4	1.6	15.0	9.3	73.7
Sacramento–Arden–Arcade–Roseville, CA	2,149,127	100.0	1.0	14.3	9.1	20.2	55.7
Saginaw–Saginaw Township North, MI	200,169	100.0	0.4	1.3	20.4	7.8	70.5
St. Cloud, MN	189,093	100.0	0.3	2.2	3.6	2.6	91.1
St. George, UT	138,115	100.0	1.4	1.3	1.0	9.8	85.6
St. Joseph, MO–KS	127,329	100.0	0.5	0.9	6.1	4.2	87.9
St. Louis, MO–IL	2,812,896	100.0	0.2	2.6	19.3	2.6	75.1
Salem, OR	390,738	100.0	1.7	2.8	1.6	21.9	71.0
Salinas, CA	415,057	100.0	1.3	8.1	4.0	55.4	32.9
Salisbury, MD	125,203	100.0	0.3	2.5	29.5	4.3	63.5
Salt Lake City, UT	1,124,197	100.0	0.9	4.0	2.1	16.6	74.9
San Angelo, TX	111,823	100.0	0.8	1.5	4.8	35.5	58.1
San Antonio–New Braunfels, TX	2,142,508	100.0	0.8	2.9	7.5	54.1	36.1
San Diego–Carlsbad–San Marcos, CA	3,095,313	100.0	0.9	13.2	6.3	32.0	48.5
Sandusky, OH	77,079	100.0	0.3	0.8	10.5	3.4	84.9
San Francisco–Oakland–Fremont, CA	4,335,391	100.0	0.6	26.0	9.7	21.7	42.4
San Jose–Sunnyvale–Santa Clara, CA	1,836,911	100.0	0.8	33.8	3.3	27.8	35.3
San Luis Obispo–Paso Robles, CA	269,637	100.0	0.9	4.5	2.6	20.8	71.1
Santa Barbara–Santa Maria–Goleta, CA	423,895	100.0	1.3	6.5	2.8	42.9	47.9
Santa Cruz–Watsonville, CA	262,382	100.0	0.9	6.0	1.8	32.0	59.6

	total population		American				non-Hispanic
	number	percent	Indian	Asian	black	Hispanic	white
Santa Fe, NM	144,170	100.0%	3.1%	1.7%	1.3%	50.6%	43.9%
Santa Rosa–Petaluma, CA	483,878	100.0	1.3	5.2	2.4	24.9	66.1
Savannah, GA	347,611	100.0	0.3	2.7	35.0	5.0	57.3
Scranton–Wilkes–Barre, PA	563,631	100.0	0.2	1.5	3.7	5.8	89.2
Seattle–Tacoma–Bellevue, WA	3,439,809	100.0	1.1	13.9	7.2	9.0	68.0
Sebastian–Vero Beach, FL	138,028	100.0	0.3	1.5	9.7	11.2	77.4
Sheboygan, WI	115,507	100.0	0.4	5.0	2.0	5.5	87.0
Sherman–Denison, TX	120,877	100.0	1.5	1.2	6.7	11.3	78.7
Shreveport–Bossier City, LA	398,604	100.0	0.5	1.6	39.7	3.5	54.7
Sioux City, IA–NE–SD	143,577	100.0	2.0	2.6	3.3	15.6	76.5
Sioux Falls, SD	228,261	100.0	2.0	1.7	3.8	3.4	88.7
South Bend–Mishawaka, IN–MI	319,224	100.0	0.5	2.1	13.1	6.6	77.5
Spartanburg, SC	284,307	100.0	0.3	2.3	21.5	5.9	70.1
Spokane, WA	471,221	100.0	1.5	3.2	2.8	4.5	86.7
Springfield, IL	210,170	100.0	0.2	1.9	12.5	1.7	83.4
Springfield, MA	692,942	100.0	0.3	3.0	8.0	15.4	74.5
Springfield, MO	436,712	100.0	0.7	1.6	2.9	2.7	91.5
Springfield, OH	138,333	100.0	0.3	0.9	10.4	2.8	85.3
State College, PA	153,990	100.0	0.1	5.9	3.6	2.4	87.9
Steubenville–Weirton, OH–WV	124,454	100.0	0.1	0.6	4.9	1.0	93.1
Stockton, CA	685,306	100.0	1.1	17.0	9.0	38.9	35.9
Sumter, SC	107,456	100.0	0.4	1.6	47.9	3.3	46.9
Syracuse, NY	662,577	100.0	0.7	2.8	9.4	3.4	83.8
Tallahassee, FL	367,413	100.0	0.3	2.9	33.5	5.8	57.7
Tampa–St. Petersburg–Clearwater, FL	2,783,243	100.0	0.4	3.6	13.0	16.2	67.5
Terre Haute, IN	172,425	100.0	0.3	1.4	5.9	1.9	90.2
Texarkana, TX–Texarkana, AR	136,027	100.0	0.7	0.9	25.3	5.2	67.7
Toledo, OH	651,429	100.0	0.3	1.8	14.9	5.8	77.4
Topeka, KS	233,870	100.0	1.5	1.4	8.4	8.8	79.7
Trenton–Ewing, NJ	366,513	100.0	0.3	9.8	21.4	15.1	54.5
Tucson, AZ	980,263	100.0	3.3	3.6	4.5	34.6	55.3
Tulsa, OK	937,478	100.0	8.3	2.2	9.8	8.4	67.8
Tuscaloosa, AL	219,461	100.0	0.3	1.3	34.3	2.8	61.2
Tyler, TX	209,714	100.0	0.5	1.5	18.7	17.2	62.1
Utica–Rome, NY	299,397	100.0	0.3	2.6	6.2	4.0	87.2
Valdosta, GA	139,588	100.0	0.4	1.8	34.9	5.5	57.4
Vallejo–Fairfield, CA	413,344	100.0	0.8	18.1	17.3	24.0	40.8
Victoria, TX	115,384	100.0	0.6	1.9	6.2	43.8	48.3
Vineland–Millville–Bridgeton, NJ	156,898	100.0	1.1	1.6	22.1	27.1	50.3
Virginia Beach–Norfolk–Newport News, VA–NC	1,671,683	100.0	0.4	4.6	33.1	5.4	57.2
Visalia–Porterville, CA	442,179	100.0	1.6	4.3	2.2	60.6	32.6
Waco, TX	234,906	100.0	0.6	1.8	15.7	23.6	58.9
Warner Robins, GA	139,900	100.0	0.3	3.4	29.9	6.1	60.5

	total population		American Indian	Asian	black	Hispanic	non-Hispanic white
	number	percent					
Washington–Arlington–Alexandria, DC–VA–MD–WV	5,582,170	100.0%	0.4%	10.7%	27.2%	13.8%	48.6%
Waterloo–Cedar Falls, IA	167,819	100.0	0.2	1.5	8.2	3.1	86.8
Wausau, WI	134,063	100.0	0.5	5.8	1.0	2.2	90.3
Wenatchee–East Wenatchee, WA	110,884	100.0	1.0	1.3	0.7	26.8	69.7
Wheeling, WV–OH	147,950	100.0	0.1	0.7	4.0	0.7	94.2
Wichita, KS	623,061	100.0	1.1	4.1	9.2	11.6	73.8
Wichita Falls, TX	151,306	100.0	1.0	2.4	10.1	15.2	71.5
Williamsport, PA	116,111	100.0	0.2	0.8	5.6	1.3	91.9
Wilmington, NC	362,315	100.0	0.6	1.3	15.1	5.4	77.6
Winchester, VA–WV	128,472	100.0	0.3	1.7	5.9	7.4	84.7
Winston–Salem, NC	477,717	100.0	0.4	1.8	21.3	10.3	66.5
Worcester, MA	798,552	100.0	0.2	4.6	5.1	9.4	80.7
Yakima, WA	243,231	100.0	4.3	1.7	1.5	45.0	47.7
York–Hanover, PA	434,972	100.0	0.2	1.6	6.8	5.6	86.2
Youngstown–Warren–Boardman, OH–PA	565,773	100.0	0.2	0.8	12.0	2.7	84.3
Yuba City, CA	166,892	100.0	1.8	13.0	3.8	27.1	54.0
Yuma, AZ	195,751	100.0	1.6	1.9	2.6	59.7	35.3

Note: Percentages do not sum to total because Asians and blacks are those who identify themselves as being of the race alone and those who identify themselves as being of the race in combination with other races, not all races are shown, and Hispanics may be of any race. Non-Hispanic whites are those who identify themselves as being white alone and not Hispanic. American Indians include Alaska Natives and are those who identify themselves as being of the race alone.
Source: Bureau of the Census, 2010 Census, Internet site http://factfinder2.census.gov/faces/nav/jsf/pages/index.xhtml; calculations by New Strategist

Table 7.98 Legal Immigration to the United States, 1900 to 2011

(number of legal immigrants granted permanent residence in the United States by single year, 2000 to 2011, and by decade, 1900 to 2010)

Single year	
2011	1,062,040
2010	1,042,625
2009	1,130,818
2008	1,107,126
2007	1,052,415
2006	1,266,129
2005	1,122,257
2004	957,883
2003	703,542
2002	1,059,356
2001	1,058,902
2000	841,002
Decade	
2000–09	10,299,430
1990–99	9,775,398
1980–89	6,244,379
1970–79	4,248,203
1960–69	3,213,749
1950–59	2,499,268
1940–49	856,608
1930–39	699,375
1920–29	4,295,510
1910–19	6,347,380
1900–09	8,202,388

Note: Immigrants are those granted legal permanent residence in the United States. They either arrive in the United States with immigrant visas issued abroad or adjust their status in the United States from temporary to permanent residence.
Source: Department of Homeland Security, 2011 Yearbook of Immigration Statistics, Internet site http://www.dhs.gov/ yearbook-immigration-statistics

Table 7.99 Immigrants by Country of Birth, 2011

(number and percent distribution of immigrants to the United States by world region and country of birth, 2011; for countries with at least 5,000 immigrants)

	number	percent distribution
IMMIGRANTS BY REGION		
Total	**1,062,040**	**100.0%**
Africa	100,374	9.5
Asia	451,593	42.5
Europe	83,850	7.9
North America	333,902	31.4
Oceania	4,980	0.5
South America	86,096	8.1
Unknown	1,245	0.1
IMMIGRANTS BY COUNTRY		
Total immigrants	**1,062,040**	**100.0**
Bangladesh	16,707	1.6
Bhutan	10,137	1.0
Brazil	11,763	1.1
Burma	16,518	1.6
Canada	12,800	1.2
China, People's Republic	87,016	8.2
Colombia	22,635	2.1
Cuba	36,452	3.4
Dominican Republic	46,109	4.3
Ecuador	11,103	1.0
Egypt	7,778	0.7
El Salvador	18,667	1.8
Ethiopia	13,793	1.3
Germany	6,125	0.6
Ghana	8,798	0.8
Guatemala	11,092	1.0
Guyana	6,599	0.6
Haiti	22,111	2.1
Honduras	6,133	0.6
India	69,013	6.5
Iran	14,822	1.4
Iraq	21,133	2.0
Jamaica	19,662	1.9
Japan	6,161	0.6
Kenya	7,762	0.7
Korea, South	22,824	2.1

	number	percent distribution
Mexico	143,446	13.5%
Nepal	10,166	1.0
Nigeria	11,824	1.1
Pakistan	15,546	1.5
Peru	14,064	1.3
Philippines	57,011	5.4
Poland	6,863	0.6
Russia	7,944	0.7
Taiwan	6,154	0.6
Thailand	9,962	0.9
Trinidad and Tobago	5,023	0.5
Ukraine	8,292	0.8
United Kingdom	11,572	1.1
Uzbekistan	5,056	0.5
Venezuela	9,183	0.9
Vietnam	34,157	3.2

Note: Immigrants are those granted legal permanent residence in the United States. They either arrive in the United States with immigrant visas issued abroad or adjust their status in the United States from temporary to permanent residence.
Source: Department of Homeland Security, 2011 Yearbook of Immigration Statistics, Internet site http://www.dhs.gov/yearbook-immigration-statistics

Table 7.100 Unauthorized Immigrant Population, 2000 and 2011

(number and percent distribution of unauthorized immigrants in the United States by country of birth and state of residence, 2000 and 2011; numerical and percent change, 2000–11; numbers in thousands)

	2011		2000		change, 2000–11	
	number	percent distribution	number	percent distribution	numerical	percent
COUNTRY OF BIRTH						
Total unauthorized immigrants	**11,510**	**100.0%**	**8,460**	**100.0%**	**3,050**	**36.1%**
Mexico	6,800	59.1	4,680	55.3	2,120	45.3
El Salvador	660	5.7	430	5.1	230	53.5
Guatemala	520	4.5	290	3.4	230	79.3
Honduras	380	3.3	160	1.9	220	137.5
China	280	2.4	190	2.2	90	47.4
Philippines	270	2.3	200	2.4	70	35.0
India	240	2.1	120	1.4	120	100.0
Korea	230	2.0	180	2.1	50	27.8
Ecuador	210	1.8	110	1.3	100	90.9
Vietnam	170	1.5	160	1.9	10	6.3
Other countries	1,750	15.2	1,940	22.9	−190	−9.8
STATE OF RESIDENCE						
Total unauthorized immigrants	**11,510**	**100.0**	**8,460**	**100.0**	**3,050**	**36.1**
California	2,830	24.6	2,510	29.7	320	12.7
Texas	1,790	15.6	1,090	12.9	700	64.2
Florida	740	6.4	800	9.5	−60	−7.5
New York	630	5.5	540	6.4	90	16.7
Illinois	550	4.8	440	5.2	110	25.0
Georgia	440	3.8	220	2.6	220	100.0
New Jersey	420	3.6	350	4.1	70	20.0
North Carolina	400	3.5	260	3.1	140	53.8
Arizona	360	3.1	330	3.9	30	9.1
Washington	260	2.3	170	2.0	90	52.9
Other states	3,100	26.9	1,750	20.7	1,350	77.1

Note: Percent change calculations are based on unrounded figures.
Source: Department of Homeland Security, Estimates of the Unauthorized Immigrant Population Residing in the United States: January 2011, Internet site http://www.dhs.gov/estimates-unauthorized-immigrant-population-residing-united-states-january-2011

Table 7.101 Language Spoken at Home, 2009–11

(number and percent of people aged 5 or older who speak a language other than English at home, and percent distribution by language spoken, 2009–11)

	number	percent distribution
Total people aged 5 or older	**289,077,942**	**100.0%**
English only at home	229,564,228	79.4
Language other than English at home	59,513,714	20.6
Language other than English at home	**59,513,714**	**100.0**
Spanish or Spanish Creole	36,957,894	62.1
Chinese	2,816,022	4.7
Tagalog	1,589,360	2.7
Vietnamese	1,371,252	2.3
French (including Patois, Cajun)	1,306,452	2.2
Korean	1,136,161	1.9
German	1,085,791	1.8
Arabic	878,458	1.5
Russian	871,629	1.5
African languages	845,237	1.4
Italian	727,453	1.2
French Creole	721,795	1.2
Portuguese or Portuguese Creole	693,830	1.2
Hindi	622,208	1.0
Polish	594,919	1.0
Japanese	444,324	0.7
Persian	393,947	0.7
Urdu	384,048	0.6
Gujarathi	358,635	0.6
Greek	308,034	0.5
Serbo–Croatian	271,820	0.5
Armenian	240,095	0.4
Mon–Khmer, Cambodian	216,492	0.4
Hmong	211,663	0.4
Hebrew	211,262	0.4
Navajo	169,451	0.3
Thai	156,532	0.3
Yiddish	154,129	0.3
Laotian	152,669	0.3
Scandinavian languages	130,338	0.2
Hungarian	90,499	0.2
Other language	3,401,315	5.7

Source: Bureau of the Census, 2009–11 American Community Survey 3-Year Estimates, Internet site Internet site http://factfinder2.census.gov/faces/nav/jsf/pages/index.xhtml; calculations by New Strategist

Table 7.102 Ability to Speak English, 2009–11

(number of people aged 5 or older who speak a language other than English at home, and number and percent who speak English less than "very well," 2009–11)

		speak English less than "very well"	
	total	number	percent
Total who speak a language other than English at home	**59,513,714**	**25,227,887**	**42.4%**
Spanish or Spanish Creole	36,957,894	16,505,878	44.7
Chinese	2,816,022	1,556,514	55.3
Tagalog	1,589,360	502,345	31.6
Vietnamese	1,371,252	828,229	60.4
French (including Patois, Cajun)	1,306,452	266,502	20.4
Korean	1,136,161	633,888	55.8
German	1,085,791	180,781	16.6
Arabic	878,458	323,920	36.9
Russian	871,629	425,072	48.8
African languages	845,237	270,140	32.0
Italian	727,453	199,630	27.4
French Creole	721,795	318,633	44.1
Portuguese or Portuguese Creole	693,830	277,093	39.9
Hindi	622,208	133,741	21.5
Polish	594,919	246,110	41.4
Japanese	444,324	192,211	43.3
Persian	393,947	148,200	37.6
Urdu	384,048	115,285	30.0
Gujarathi	358,635	130,103	36.3
Greek	308,034	77,398	25.1
Serbo–Croatian	271,820	105,717	38.9
Armenian	240,095	109,360	45.5
Mon–Khmer, Cambodian	216,492	111,537	51.5
Hmong	211,663	93,939	44.4
Hebrew	211,262	35,332	16.7
Navajo	169,451	37,587	22.2
Thai	156,532	83,853	53.6
Yiddish	154,129	51,215	33.2
Laotian	152,669	76,098	49.8
Scandinavian languages	130,338	13,613	10.4
Hungarian	90,499	27,501	30.4
Other language	3,401,315	1,150,462	33.8

Source: Bureau of the Census, 2009–11 American Community Survey 3-Year Estimates, Internet site Internet site http://factfinder2.census.gov/faces/nav/jsf/pages/index.xhtml; calculations by New Strategist

Table 7.103 People Who Speak a Language Other than English at Home, by State, 2009–11

(total number of people aged 5 or older and number and percent who speak a language other than English at home, by state, 2009–11)

	total people aged 5 or older	speak a language other than English at home	
		number	percent
United States	**288,553,996**	**59,513,714**	**20.6%**
Alabama	4,477,927	233,796	5.2
Alaska	658,127	109,153	16.6
Arizona	5,956,673	1,597,434	26.8
Arkansas	2,721,294	195,548	7.2
California	34,793,018	15,201,467	43.7
Colorado	4,702,519	793,312	16.9
Connecticut	3,372,311	716,460	21.2
Delaware	843,743	106,752	12.7
District of Columbia	571,129	81,228	14.2
Florida	17,774,767	4,853,544	27.3
Georgia	9,033,746	1,182,454	13.1
Hawaii	1,273,878	326,215	25.6
Idaho	1,449,701	149,807	10.3
Illinois	12,003,172	2,667,430	22.2
Indiana	6,057,433	489,033	8.1
Iowa	2,848,477	203,730	7.2
Kansas	2,651,027	291,529	11.0
Kentucky	4,063,448	197,152	4.9
Louisiana	4,223,687	372,640	8.8
Maine	1,260,061	86,457	6.9
Maryland	5,416,438	892,592	16.5
Massachusetts	6,187,386	1,340,198	21.7
Michigan	9,292,971	834,773	9.0
Minnesota	4,959,424	529,457	10.7
Mississippi	2,759,514	107,818	3.9
Missouri	5,602,736	345,389	6.2
Montana	930,061	43,922	4.7
Nebraska	1,697,746	174,430	10.3
Nevada	2,516,454	727,670	28.9
New Hampshire	1,247,618	97,527	7.8
New Jersey	8,253,094	2,455,117	29.7
New Mexico	1,917,278	696,102	36.3
New York	18,233,396	5,440,072	29.8
North Carolina	8,926,372	961,798	10.8
North Dakota	630,522	31,680	5.0
Ohio	10,821,383	713,670	6.6
Oklahoma	3,493,183	319,864	9.2

	total people aged 5 or older	speak a language other than English at home	
		number	percent
Oregon	3,603,503	532,109	14.8%
Pennsylvania	11,982,323	1,219,102	10.2
Rhode Island	995,269	210,681	21.2
South Carolina	4,333,308	293,357	6.8
South Dakota	757,925	51,680	6.8
Tennessee	5,949,415	390,291	6.6
Texas	23,304,988	8,075,535	34.7
Utah	2,509,875	359,922	14.3
Vermont	594,196	30,397	5.1
Virginia	7,508,820	1,103,960	14.7
Washington	6,307,524	1,145,519	18.2
West Virginia	1,749,410	41,646	2.4
Wisconsin	5,335,726	457,623	8.6
Wyoming	515,858	34,672	6.7

Note: Data for Wyoming are an ACS 5-year estimate, 2007–2011.
Source: Bureau of the Census, 2009–11 American Community Survey 3-Year Estimates, Internet site Internet site http://factfinder2.census.gov/faces/nav/jsf/pages/index.xhtml; calculations by New Strategist

Table 7.104 Time Use by Race and Hispanic Origin, 2011

(average hours per day spent in primary activities by people aged 15 or older by race and Hispanic origin, and index of race/Hispanic origin groups to total, by type of activity, 2011)

	total people	Asians	blacks	Hispanics
Total, all activities	**24.00 hrs.**	**24.00 hrs.**	**24.00 hrs.**	**24.00 hrs.**
Personal care activities	9.47	9.32	9.83	9.89
Sleeping	8.71	8.59	8.94	9.11
Grooming	0.69	0.68	0.82	0.73
Household activities	1.78	1.52	1.36	1.82
Housework	0.58	0.42	0.48	0.72
Food preparation and cleanup	0.56	0.74	0.50	0.68
Lawn, garden, and houseplants	0.19	0.10	0.12	0.12
Animals and pets	0.09	0.04	0.03	0.06
Household management	0.18	0.18	0.11	0.09
Caring for and helping household members	0.43	0.51	0.31	0.56
Caring for and helping household children	0.34	0.42	0.24	0.46
Caring for and helping people in other households	0.15	0.14	0.15	0.09
Working and work-related activities	3.29	3.79	2.86	3.10
Educational activities	0.44	0.65	0.58	0.66
Consumer purchases	0.37	0.35	0.32	0.39
Eating and drinking	1.12	1.36	0.85	1.09
Socializing, relaxing, and leisure	4.65	4.02	5.29	4.25
Socializing and communicating	0.61	0.54	0.67	0.62
Watching television	2.75	2.09	3.38	2.65
Playing games (including computer games)	0.22	0.17	0.21	0.14
Computer use for leisure	0.22	0.43	0.25	0.17
Reading	0.30	0.29	0.13	0.12
Sports, exercise, and recreation	0.34	0.38	0.27	0.35
Religious and spiritual activities	0.15	0.17	0.29	0.17
Volunteering	0.15	0.11	0.16	0.06
Telephone calls	0.10	0.12	0.17	0.07
Traveling	1.21	1.27	1.19	1.19

	total people	Asians	blacks	Hispanics
INDEX OF RACE/HISPANIC ORIGIN GROUP TO TOTAL				
Total, all activities	**100**	**100**	**100**	**100**
Personal care activities	100	98	104	104
Sleeping	100	99	103	105
Grooming	100	99	119	106
Household activities	100	85	76	102
Housework	100	72	83	124
Food preparation and cleanup	100	132	89	121
Lawn, garden, and houseplants	100	53	63	63
Animals and pets	100	44	33	67
Household management	100	100	61	50
Caring for and helping household members	100	119	72	130
Caring for and helping household children	100	124	71	135
Caring for and helping people in other households	100	93	100	60
Working and work-related activities	100	115	87	94
Educational activities	100	148	132	150
Consumer purchases	100	95	86	105
Eating and drinking	100	121	76	97
Socializing, relaxing, and leisure	100	86	114	91
Socializing and communicating	100	89	110	102
Watching television	100	76	123	96
Playing games (including computer games)	100	77	95	64
Computer use for leisure	100	195	114	77
Reading	100	97	43	40
Sports, exercise, and recreation	100	112	79	103
Religious and spiritual activities	100	113	193	113
Volunteering	100	73	107	40
Telephone calls	100	120	170	70
Traveling	100	105	98	98

Note: Hours per day do not add to 24.00 because not all activities are shown. Primary activities are those respondents identified as their main activity. Other activities done simultaneously are not included. The index is calculated by dividing time use of each race/Hispanic origin group by time use of the average person and multiplying by 100.
Source: Bureau of Labor Statistics, unpublished tables from the American Time Use Survey, Internet site http://www.bls.gov/tus/home.htm; calculations by New Strategist

Table 7.105 Time Use of Men by Race and Hispanic Origin, 2011

(average hours per day spent in primary activities by men aged 15 or older by race and Hispanic origin, and index of race/Hispanic origin groups to total, by type of activity, 2011)

	total men	Asian men	black men	Hispanic men
Total, all activities	**24.00 hrs.**	**24.00 hrs.**	**24.00 hrs.**	**24.00 hrs.**
Personal care activities	9.23	9.16	9.40	9.70
Sleeping	8.62	8.49	8.71	9.04
Grooming	0.56	0.61	0.64	0.64
Household activities	1.36	0.78	1.06	1.15
Housework	0.27	0.14	0.23	0.30
Food preparation and cleanup	0.31	0.28	0.26	0.29
Lawn, garden, and houseplants	0.26	0.11	0.20	0.18
Animals and pets	0.08	0.04	0.03	0.06
Household management	0.15	0.14	0.11	0.09
Caring for and helping household members	0.27	0.38	0.18	0.30
Caring for and helping household children	0.21	0.31	0.12	0.24
Caring for and helping people in other households	0.15	0.06	0.11	0.10
Working and work-related activities	3.89	4.61	3.00	3.71
Educational activities	0.46	0.73	0.62	0.74
Consumer purchases	0.31	0.34	0.30	0.35
Eating and drinking	1.16	1.33	0.93	1.11
Socializing, relaxing, and leisure	4.88	4.24	5.86	4.55
Socializing and communicating	0.57	0.54	0.78	0.59
Watching television	2.99	2.27	3.71	2.92
Playing games (including computer games)	0.28	0.22	0.32	0.23
Computer use for leisure	0.26	0.51	0.35	0.21
Reading	0.24	0.29	0.11	0.08
Sports, exercise, and recreation	0.43	0.45	0.42	0.05
Religious and spiritual activities	0.12	0.12	0.22	0.15
Volunteering	0.13	–	0.13	0.05
Telephone calls	0.06	0.12	0.13	0.06
Traveling	1.25	1.31	1.26	1.23

INDEX OF RACE/HISPANIC ORIGIN GROUP TO TOTAL	total men	Asian men	black men	Hispanic men
Total, all activities	**100**	**100**	**100**	**100**
Personal care activities	100	99	102	105
Sleeping	100	98	101	105
Grooming	100	109	114	114
Household activities	100	57	78	85
Housework	100	52	85	111
Food preparation and cleanup	100	90	84	94
Lawn, garden, and houseplants	100	42	77	69
Animals and pets	100	50	38	75
Household management	100	93	73	60
Caring for and helping household members	100	141	67	111
Caring for and helping household children	100	148	57	114
Caring for and helping people in other households	100	40	73	67
Working and work-related activities	100	119	77	95
Educational activities	100	159	135	161
Consumer purchases	100	110	97	113
Eating and drinking	100	115	80	96
Socializing, relaxing, and leisure	100	87	120	93
Socializing and communicating	100	95	137	104
Watching television	100	76	124	98
Playing games (including computer games)	100	79	114	82
Computer use for leisure	100	196	135	81
Reading	100	121	46	33
Sports, exercise, and recreation	100	105	98	12
Religious and spiritual activities	100	100	183	125
Volunteering	100	–	100	38
Telephone calls	100	200	217	100
Traveling	100	105	101	98

Note: Hours per day do not add to 24.00 because not all activities are shown. Primary activities are those respondents identified as their main activity. Other activities done simultaneously are not included. The index is calculated by dividing time use of men in each race/Hispanic origin group by time use of the average man and multiplying by 100. "–" means sample is too small to make a reliable estimate.
Source: Bureau of Labor Statistics, unpublished tables from the American Time Use Survey, Internet site http://www.bls.gov/tus/home.htm; calculations by New Strategist

Table 7.106 Time Use of Women by Race and Hispanic Origin, 2011

(average hours per day spent in primary activities by women aged 15 or older by race and Hispanic origin, and index of race/Hispanic origin groups to total, by type of activity, 2011)

	total women	Asian women	black women	Hispanic women
Total, all activities	**24.00 hrs.**	**24.00 hrs.**	**24.00 hrs.**	**24.00 hrs.**
Personal care activities	9.71	9.48	10.17	10.09
Sleeping	8.80	8.69	9.12	9.18
Grooming	0.82	0.75	0.96	0.82
Household activities	2.18	2.24	1.60	2.53
Housework	0.87	0.69	0.69	1.16
Food preparation and cleanup	0.79	1.18	0.70	1.09
Lawn, garden, and houseplants	0.13	0.09	0.05	0.07
Animals and pets	0.10	0.03	0.03	0.05
Household management	0.21	0.21	0.10	0.10
Caring for and helping household members	0.58	0.63	0.41	0.83
Caring for and helping household children	0.47	0.53	0.34	0.69
Caring for and helping people in other households	0.13	–	0.18	0.08
Working and work-related activities	2.73	3.01	2.74	2.45
Educational activities	0.42	–	0.55	0.57
Consumer purchases	0.43	0.36	0.34	0.43
Eating and drinking	1.09	1.38	0.78	1.07
Socializing, relaxing, and leisure	4.43	3.81	4.83	3.93
Socializing and communicating	0.66	0.54	0.58	0.66
Watching television	2.52	1.91	3.10	2.35
Playing games (including computer games)	0.16	–	0.12	0.05
Computer use for leisure	0.18	0.36	0.16	0.12
Reading	0.35	0.29	0.15	0.16
Sports, exercise, and recreation	0.25	0.31	0.14	0.19
Religious and spiritual activities	0.19	0.21	0.35	0.19
Volunteering	0.16	0.18	0.18	0.07
Telephone calls	0.13	0.12	0.20	0.08
Traveling	1.16	1.24	1.14	1.15

	total women	Asian women	black women	Hispanic women
INDEX OF RACE/HISPANIC ORIGIN GROUP TO TOTAL				
Total, all activities	**100**	**100**	**100**	**100**
Personal care activities	100	98	105	104
Sleeping	100	99	104	104
Grooming	100	91	117	100
Household activities	100	103	73	116
Housework	100	79	79	133
Food preparation and cleanup	100	149	89	138
Lawn, garden, and houseplants	100	69	38	54
Animals and pets	100	30	30	50
Household management	100	100	48	48
Caring for and helping household members	100	109	71	143
Caring for and helping household children	100	113	72	147
Caring for and helping people in other households	100	–	138	62
Working and work-related activities	100	110	100	90
Educational activities	100	–	131	136
Consumer purchases	100	84	79	100
Eating and drinking	100	127	72	98
Socializing, relaxing, and leisure	100	86	109	89
Socializing and communicating	100	82	88	100
Watching television	100	76	123	93
Playing games (including computer games)	100	–	75	31
Computer use for leisure	100	200	89	67
Reading	100	83	43	46
Sports, exercise, and recreation	100	124	56	76
Religious and spiritual activities	100	111	184	100
Volunteering	100	113	113	44
Telephone calls	100	92	154	62
Traveling	100	107	98	99

Note: Hours per day do not add to 24.00 because not all activities are shown. Primary activities are those respondents identified as their main activity. Other activities done simultaneously are not included. The index is calculated by dividing time use of women in each race/Hispanic origin group by time use of the average woman and multiplying by 100. "–" means sample is too small to make a reliable estimate.
Source: Bureau of Labor Statistics, unpublished tables from the American Time Use Survey, Internet site http://www.bls.gov/tus/home.htm; calculations by New Strategist

Spending Varies Greatly by Race and Hispanic Origin

Asian, black, Hispanic, and non-Hispanic white and "other" households spend differently for a variety of reasons. Different household compositions among the racial and ethnic groups determine the number of earners in the home and household incomes. Educational attainment also varies by race and ethnicity, with better-educated groups earning and spending more.

Asian households spend the most—21 percent more than the average household. Non-Hispanic white and other households (which also include Asians), spend 7 percent more than average. Black households spend 26 percent less than average, while the spending of Hispanic households is 15 percent below average.

By product and service category, spending varies greatly among the racial and ethnic groups. Hispanics and blacks account for 31 percent of the market for infants' clothes (the two groups overlap somewhat because some Hispanics are black). Hispanics and blacks account for 35 percent of the shoe market. Although Asians are the smallest minority examined by the Consumer Expenditure Survey, they account for a larger share of spending on public transportation than either blacks or Hispanics.

■ The racial and ethnic diversity of consumer markets is growing rapidly. Only by understanding the unique spending patterns of each group can businesses succeed in fulfilling consumer wants and needs.

Asians spend the most

(average annual spending of consumer units by race and Hispanic origin, 2011)

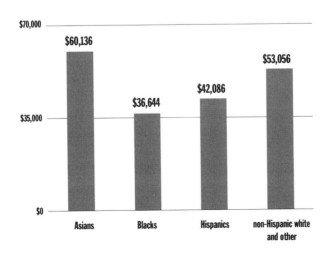

Table 7.107 Average Spending by Race and Hispanic Origin of Householder, 2011

(average annual spending of consumer units by product and service category and by race and Hispanic origin of consumer unit reference person, 2011)

	total consumer units	Asian	black	Hispanic	non-Hispanic white, other
Number of consumer units (000s)	122,287	5,048	15,118	15,222	92,163
Average number of persons per consumer unit	2.5	2.7	2.6	3.4	2.4
Average annual spending	$49,705	$60,136	$36,644	$42,086	$53,056
FOOD	6,458	8,163	4,743	6,373	6,743
Food at home	3,838	4,439	2,989	3,849	3,970
Cereals and bakery products	531	618	405	493	556
Cereals and cereal products	175	265	143	181	179
Bakery products	356	353	263	312	377
Meats, poultry, fish, and eggs	832	1,094	822	968	813
Beef	223	201	189	268	221
Pork	162	210	183	191	154
Other meats	123	92	86	110	130
Poultry	154	186	185	196	143
Fish and seafood	121	327	134	138	116
Eggs	50	77	46	66	48
Dairy products	407	337	246	388	435
Fresh milk and cream	150	161	98	163	156
Other dairy products	257	175	148	226	279
Fruits and vegetables	715	1,059	527	778	735
Fresh fruits	247	392	157	293	255
Fresh vegetables	224	415	145	241	234
Processed fruits	116	111	109	120	116
Processed vegetables	128	139	117	124	130
Other food at home	1,353	1,332	988	1,221	1,431
Sugar and other sweets	144	157	98	117	156
Fats and oils	110	115	94	122	110
Miscellaneous foods	690	678	502	580	737
Nonalcoholic beverages	361	324	280	370	373
Food prepared by consumer unit on trips	48	57	14	32	55
Food away from home	2,620	3,724	1,754	2,524	2,773
ALCOHOLIC BEVERAGES	456	311	199	281	525
HOUSING	16,803	20,834	13,985	15,648	17,449
Shelter	9,825	14,269	8,111	9,766	10,122
Owned dwellings	6,148	8,209	3,651	4,713	6,791
Mortgage interest and charges	3,184	4,348	2,151	2,814	3,412
Property taxes	1,845	2,523	930	1,202	2,100
Maintenance, repair, insurance, other expenses	1,120	1,338	570	697	1,278

	total consumer units	Asian	black	Hispanic	non-Hispanic white, other
Rented dwellings	$3,029	$4,843	$4,268	$4,806	$2,543
Other lodging	648	1,217	192	248	788
Utilities, fuels, and public services	**3,727**	**3,279**	**3,701**	**3,462**	**3,773**
Natural gas	420	436	429	350	429
Electricity	1,423	1,035	1,497	1,283	1,433
Fuel oil and other fuels	157	62	67	42	190
Telephone	1,226	1,229	1,242	1,288	1,214
Water and other public services	501	517	465	499	506
Household services	**1,122**	**1,593**	**810**	**755**	**1,233**
Personal services	398	808	307	319	426
Other household services	724	785	503	436	807
Housekeeping supplies	**615**	**393**	**426**	**536**	**656**
Laundry and cleaning supplies	145	108	155	195	136
Other household products	340	211	194	255	375
Postage and stationery	130	74	76	86	145
Household furnishings and equipment	**1,514**	**1,300**	**938**	**1,129**	**1,666**
Household textiles	109	69	52	73	124
Furniture	358	381	306	310	374
Floor coverings	20	11	10	7	24
Major appliances	194	153	152	128	211
Small appliances, misc. housewares	89	83	39	61	102
Miscellaneous household equipment	744	603	378	550	831
APPAREL AND RELATED SERVICES	**1,740**	**2,324**	**1,669**	**1,989**	**1,714**
Men and boys	**404**	**603**	**324**	**518**	**399**
Men, aged 16 or older	324	503	224	402	328
Boys, aged 2 to 15	80	100	99	116	71
Women and girls	**721**	**911**	**629**	**672**	**743**
Women, aged 16 or older	604	761	501	532	631
Girls, aged 2 to 15	117	150	128	140	112
Children under age 2	**68**	**109**	**77**	**91**	**63**
Footwear	**321**	**342**	**454**	**452**	**281**
Other apparel products and services	**226**	**359**	**185**	**256**	**227**
TRANSPORTATION	**8,293**	**10,281**	**5,944**	**7,520**	**8,798**
Vehicle purchases	**2,669**	**3,450**	**1,608**	**2,208**	**2,919**
Cars and trucks, new	1,265	2,342	634	691	1,464
Cars and trucks, used	1,339	1,100	959	1,511	1,373
Other vehicles	64	8	14	6	82
Gasoline and motor oil	**2,655**	**2,283**	**2,221**	**2,721**	**2,714**
Other vehicle expenses	**2,454**	**3,075**	**1,833**	**2,174**	**2,596**
Vehicle finance charges	233	168	194	215	242
Maintenance and repairs	805	717	587	638	867
Vehicle insurance	983	1,608	767	934	1,023

	total consumer units	Asian	black	Hispanic	non-Hispanic white, other
Vehicle rentals, leases, licenses, other charges	$433	$582	$285	$386	$464
Public transportation	516	1,473	283	417	570
HEALTH CARE	3,313	2,919	1,897	1,774	3,793
Health insurance	1,922	1,882	1,238	1,008	2,182
Medical services	768	667	300	453	896
Drugs	489	285	300	237	560
Medical supplies	134	84	59	75	155
ENTERTAINMENT	2,572	2,301	1,432	1,738	2,888
Fees and admissions	594	768	201	339	699
Audio and visual equipment and services	977	868	909	839	1,009
Pets, toys, and playground equipment	631	269	212	392	734
Other entertainment products and services	370	396	110	167	445
PERSONAL CARE PRODUCTS AND SERVICES	634	602	533	611	654
READING	115	111	48	46	138
EDUCATION	1,051	2,267	479	624	1,212
TOBACCO PRODUCTS AND SMOKING SUPPLIES	351	152	260	164	396
MISCELLANEOUS	775	696	521	476	864
CASH CONTRIBUTIONS	1,721	1,405	1,341	812	1,930
PERSONAL INSURANCE AND PENSIONS	5,424	7,771	3,593	4,030	5,951
Life and other personal insurance	317	337	250	115	361
Pensions and Social Security	5,106	7,434	3,344	3,915	5,590
PERSONAL TAXES	2,012	3,894	500	465	2,511
Federal income taxes	1,370	3,032	198	236	1,747
State and local income taxes	505	728	240	186	601
Other taxes	136	134	63	43	163
GIFTS FOR PEOPLE IN OTHER HOUSEHOLDS	1,037	1,120	495	585	1,198

Note: "Other" includes Alaska Natives, American Indians, Asians, Native Hawaiians, and other Pacific Islanders as well as those who report being of more than one race. The Bureau of Labor Statistics uses consumer unit rather than household as the sampling unit in the Consumer Expenditure Survey. For the definition of consumer unit, see the glossary. Spending by category does not add to total spending because gift spending is also included in the preceding product and service categories and personal taxes are not included in the total.
Source: Bureau of Labor Statistics, 2011 Consumer Expenditure Survey, Internet site http://www.bls.gov/cex/

Table 7.108 Indexed Spending by Race and Hispanic Origin of Householder, 2011

(indexed average annual spending of consumer units by product and service category and race and Hispanic origin of consumer unit reference person, 2011)

	total consumer units	Asian	black	Hispanic	non-Hispanic white, other
Average annual spending	$49,705	$60,136	$36,644	$42,086	$53,056
Indexed average annual spending	100	121	74	85	107
FOOD	100	126	73	99	104
Food at home	100	116	78	100	103
Cereals and bakery products	100	116	76	93	105
Cereals and cereal products	100	151	82	103	102
Bakery products	100	99	74	88	106
Meats, poultry, fish, and eggs	100	131	99	116	98
Beef	100	90	85	120	99
Pork	100	130	113	118	95
Other meats	100	75	70	89	106
Poultry	100	121	120	127	93
Fish and seafood	100	270	111	114	96
Eggs	100	154	92	132	96
Dairy products	100	83	60	95	107
Fresh milk and cream	100	107	65	109	104
Other dairy products	100	68	58	88	109
Fruits and vegetables	100	148	74	109	103
Fresh fruits	100	159	64	119	103
Fresh vegetables	100	185	65	108	104
Processed fruits	100	96	94	103	100
Processed vegetables	100	109	91	97	102
Other food at home	100	98	73	90	106
Sugar and other sweets	100	109	68	81	108
Fats and oils	100	105	85	111	100
Miscellaneous foods	100	98	73	84	107
Nonalcoholic beverages	100	90	78	102	103
Food prepared by consumer unit on trips	100	119	29	67	115
Food away from home	100	142	67	96	106
ALCOHOLIC BEVERAGES	100	68	44	62	115
HOUSING	100	124	83	93	104
Shelter	100	145	83	99	103
Owned dwellings	100	134	59	77	110
Mortgage interest and charges	100	137	68	88	107
Property taxes	100	137	50	65	114
Maintenance, repair, insurance, other expenses	100	119	51	62	114

	total consumer units	Asian	black	Hispanic	non-Hispanic white, other
Rented dwellings	100	160	141	159	84
Other lodging	100	188	30	38	122
Utilities, fuels, and public services	**100**	**88**	**99**	**93**	**101**
Natural gas	100	104	102	83	102
Electricity	100	73	105	90	101
Fuel oil and other fuels	100	39	43	27	121
Telephone	100	100	101	105	99
Water and other public services	100	103	93	100	101
Household services	**100**	**142**	**72**	**67**	**110**
Personal services	100	203	77	80	107
Other household services	100	108	69	60	111
Housekeeping supplies	**100**	**64**	**69**	**87**	**107**
Laundry and cleaning supplies	100	74	107	134	94
Other household products	100	62	57	75	110
Postage and stationery	100	57	58	66	112
Household furnishings and equipment	**100**	**86**	**62**	**75**	**110**
Household textiles	100	63	48	67	114
Furniture	100	106	85	87	104
Floor coverings	100	55	50	35	120
Major appliances	100	79	78	66	109
Small appliances, misc. housewares	100	93	44	69	115
Miscellaneous household equipment	100	81	51	74	112
APPAREL AND RELATED SERVICES	**100**	**134**	**96**	**114**	**99**
Men and boys	**100**	**149**	**80**	**128**	**99**
Men, aged 16 or older	100	155	69	124	101
Boys, aged 2 to 15	100	125	124	145	89
Women and girls	**100**	**126**	**87**	**93**	**103**
Women, aged 16 or older	100	126	83	88	104
Girls, aged 2 to 15	100	128	109	120	96
Children under age 2	**100**	**160**	**113**	**134**	**93**
Footwear	**100**	**107**	**141**	**141**	**88**
Other apparel products and services	**100**	**159**	**82**	**113**	**100**
TRANSPORTATION	**100**	**124**	**72**	**91**	**106**
Vehicle purchases	**100**	**129**	**60**	**83**	**109**
Cars and trucks, new	100	185	50	55	116
Cars and trucks, used	100	82	72	113	103
Other vehicles	100	13	22	9	128
Gasoline and motor oil	**100**	**86**	**84**	**102**	**102**
Other vehicle expenses	**100**	**125**	**75**	**89**	**106**
Vehicle finance charges	100	72	83	92	104
Maintenance and repairs	100	89	73	79	108
Vehicle insurance	100	164	78	95	104

	total consumer units	Asian	black	Hispanic	non-Hispanic white, other
Vehicle rentals, leases, licenses, other charges	100	134	66	89	107
Public transportation	**100**	**285**	**55**	**81**	**110**
HEALTH CARE	**100**	**88**	**57**	**54**	**114**
Health insurance	100	98	64	52	114
Medical services	100	87	39	59	117
Drugs	100	58	61	48	115
Medical supplies	100	63	44	56	116
ENTERTAINMENT	**100**	**89**	**56**	**68**	**112**
Fees and admissions	100	129	34	57	118
Audio and visual equipment and services	100	89	93	86	103
Pets, toys, and playground equipment	100	43	34	62	116
Other entertainment products and services	100	107	30	45	120
PERSONAL CARE PRODUCTS AND SERVICES	**100**	**95**	**84**	**96**	**103**
READING	**100**	**97**	**42**	**40**	**120**
EDUCATION	**100**	**216**	**46**	**59**	**115**
TOBACCO PRODUCTS AND SMOKING SUPPLIES	**100**	**43**	**74**	**47**	**113**
MISCELLANEOUS	**100**	**90**	**67**	**61**	**111**
CASH CONTRIBUTIONS	**100**	**82**	**78**	**47**	**112**
PERSONAL INSURANCE AND PENSIONS	**100**	**143**	**66**	**74**	**110**
Life and other personal insurance	100	106	79	36	114
Pensions and Social Security	100	146	65	77	109
PERSONAL TAXES	**100**	**194**	**25**	**23**	**125**
Federal income taxes	100	221	14	17	128
State and local income taxes	100	144	48	37	119
Other taxes	100	99	46	32	120
GIFTS FOR PEOPLE IN OTHER HOUSEHOLDS	**100**	**108**	**48**	**56**	**116**

Note: The index is calculated by dividing the spending of each race or Hispanic origin group by average spending and multiplying by 100. An index of 125 indicates spending by the race or Hispanic origin group that is 25 percent above average. An index of 75 indicates spending that is 25 percent below average. "Other" includes Alaska Natives, American Indians, Asians, Native Hawaiians, and other Pacific Islanders as well as those who report being of more than one race. The Bureau of Labor Statistics uses consumer unit rather than household as the sampling unit in the Consumer Expenditure Survey. For the definition of consumer unit, see the glossary.
Source: Calculations by New Strategist based on the Bureau of Labor Statistics' 2011 Consumer Expenditure Survey, Internet site http://www.bls.gov/cex/

Table 7.109 Market Shares by Race and Hispanic Origin of Householder, 2011

(percentage of total annual spending accounted for by race and Hispanic origin groups, by product and service category, 2011)

	total consumer units	Asian	black	Hispanic	non-Hispanic white, other
Share of consumer units	100.0%	4.1%	12.4%	12.4%	75.4%
Share of annual spending	100.0	5.0	9.1	10.5	80.4
FOOD	100.0	5.2	9.1	12.3	78.7
Food at home	100.0	4.8	9.6	12.5	78.0
Cereals and bakery products	100.0	4.8	9.4	11.6	78.9
Cereals and cereal products	100.0	6.3	10.1	12.9	77.1
Bakery products	100.0	4.1	9.1	10.9	79.8
Meats, poultry, fish, and eggs	100.0	5.4	12.2	14.5	73.6
Beef	100.0	3.7	10.5	15.0	74.7
Pork	100.0	5.4	14.0	14.7	71.6
Other meats	100.0	3.1	8.6	11.1	79.7
Poultry	100.0	5.0	14.9	15.8	70.0
Fish and seafood	100.0	11.2	13.7	14.2	72.3
Eggs	100.0	6.4	11.4	16.4	72.4
Dairy products	100.0	3.4	7.5	11.9	80.6
Fresh milk and cream	100.0	4.4	8.1	13.5	78.4
Other dairy products	100.0	2.8	7.1	10.9	81.8
Fruits and vegetables	100.0	6.1	9.1	13.5	77.5
Fresh fruits	100.0	6.6	7.9	14.8	77.8
Fresh vegetables	100.0	7.6	8.0	13.4	78.7
Processed fruits	100.0	4.0	11.6	12.9	75.4
Processed vegetables	100.0	4.5	11.3	12.1	76.5
Other food at home	100.0	4.1	9.0	11.2	79.7
Sugar and other sweets	100.0	4.5	8.4	10.1	81.6
Fats and oils	100.0	4.3	10.6	13.8	75.4
Miscellaneous foods	100.0	4.1	9.0	10.5	80.5
Nonalcoholic beverages	100.0	3.7	9.6	12.8	77.9
Food prepared by consumer unit on trips	100.0	4.9	3.6	8.3	86.4
Food away from home	100.0	5.9	8.3	12.0	79.8
ALCOHOLIC BEVERAGES	100.0	2.8	5.4	7.7	86.8
HOUSING	100.0	5.1	10.3	11.6	78.3
Shelter	100.0	6.0	10.2	12.4	77.6
Owned dwellings	100.0	5.5	7.3	9.5	83.2
Mortgage interest and charges	100.0	5.6	8.4	11.0	80.8
Property taxes	100.0	5.6	6.2	8.1	85.8
Maintenance, repair, insurance, other expenses	100.0	4.9	6.3	7.7	86.0

	total consumer units	Asian	black	Hispanic	non-Hispanic white, other
Rented dwellings	100.0%	6.6%	17.4%	19.8%	63.3%
Other lodging	100.0	7.8	3.7	4.8	91.6
Utilities, fuels, and public services	**100.0**	**3.6**	**12.3**	**11.6**	**76.3**
Natural gas	100.0	4.3	12.6	10.4	77.0
Electricity	100.0	3.0	13.0	11.2	75.9
Fuel oil and other fuels	100.0	1.6	5.3	3.3	91.2
Telephone	100.0	4.1	12.5	13.1	74.6
Water and other public services	100.0	4.3	11.5	12.4	76.1
Household services	**100.0**	**5.9**	**8.9**	**8.4**	**82.8**
Personal services	100.0	8.4	9.5	10.0	80.7
Other household services	100.0	4.5	8.6	7.5	84.0
Housekeeping supplies	**100.0**	**2.6**	**8.6**	**10.8**	**80.4**
Laundry and cleaning supplies	100.0	3.1	13.2	16.7	70.7
Other household products	100.0	2.6	7.1	9.3	83.1
Postage and stationery	100.0	2.3	7.2	8.2	84.1
Household furnishings and equipment	**100.0**	**3.5**	**7.7**	**9.3**	**82.9**
Household textiles	100.0	2.6	5.9	8.3	85.7
Furniture	100.0	4.4	10.6	10.8	78.7
Floor coverings	100.0	2.3	6.2	4.4	90.4
Major appliances	100.0	3.3	9.7	8.2	82.0
Small appliances, misc. housewares	100.0	3.8	5.4	8.5	86.4
Miscellaneous household equipment	100.0	3.3	6.3	9.2	84.2
APPAREL AND RELATED SERVICES	**100.0**	**5.5**	**11.9**	**14.2**	**74.2**
Men and boys	**100.0**	**6.2**	**9.9**	**16.0**	**74.4**
Men, aged 16 or older	100.0	6.4	8.5	15.4	76.3
Boys, aged 2 to 15	100.0	5.2	15.3	18.0	66.9
Women and girls	**100.0**	**5.2**	**10.8**	**11.6**	**77.7**
Women, aged 16 or older	100.0	5.2	10.3	11.0	78.7
Girls, aged 2 to 15	100.0	5.3	13.5	14.9	72.1
Children under age 2	**100.0**	**6.6**	**14.0**	**16.7**	**69.8**
Footwear	**100.0**	**4.4**	**17.5**	**17.5**	**66.0**
Other apparel products and services	**100.0**	**6.6**	**10.1**	**14.1**	**75.7**
TRANSPORTATION	**100.0**	**5.1**	**8.9**	**11.3**	**80.0**
Vehicle purchases	**100.0**	**5.3**	**7.4**	**10.3**	**82.4**
Cars and trucks, new	100.0	7.6	6.2	6.8	87.2
Cars and trucks, used	100.0	3.4	8.9	14.0	77.3
Other vehicles	100.0	0.5	2.7	1.2	96.6
Gasoline and motor oil	**100.0**	**3.5**	**10.3**	**12.8**	**77.0**
Other vehicle expenses	**100.0**	**5.2**	**9.2**	**11.0**	**79.7**
Vehicle finance charges	100.0	3.0	10.3	11.5	78.3
Maintenance and repairs	100.0	3.7	9.0	9.9	81.2

	total consumer units	Asian	black	Hispanic	non-Hispanic white, other
Vehicle insurance	100.0%	6.8%	9.6%	11.8%	78.4%
Vehicle rentals, leases, licenses, other charges	100.0	5.5	8.1	11.1	80.8
Public transportation	**100.0**	**11.8**	**6.8**	**10.1**	**83.3**
HEALTH CARE	**100.0**	**3.6**	**7.1**	**6.7**	**86.3**
Health insurance	100.0	4.0	8.0	6.5	85.6
Medical services	100.0	3.6	4.8	7.3	87.9
Drugs	100.0	2.4	7.6	6.0	86.3
Medical supplies	100.0	2.6	5.4	7.0	87.2
ENTERTAINMENT	**100.0**	**3.7**	**6.9**	**8.4**	**84.6**
Fees and admissions	100.0	5.3	4.2	7.1	88.7
Audio and visual equipment and services	100.0	3.7	11.5	10.7	77.8
Pets, toys, and playground equipment	100.0	1.8	4.2	7.7	87.7
Other entertainment products and services	100.0	4.4	3.7	5.6	90.6
PERSONAL CARE PRODUCTS AND SERVICES	**100.0**	**3.9**	**10.4**	**12.0**	**77.7**
READING	**100.0**	**4.0**	**5.2**	**5.0**	**90.4**
EDUCATION	**100.0**	**8.9**	**5.6**	**7.4**	**86.9**
TOBACCO PRODUCTS AND SMOKING SUPPLIES	**100.0**	**1.8**	**9.2**	**5.8**	**85.0**
MISCELLANEOUS	**100.0**	**3.7**	**8.3**	**7.6**	**84.0**
CASH CONTRIBUTIONS	**100.0**	**3.4**	**9.6**	**5.9**	**84.5**
PERSONAL INSURANCE AND PENSIONS	**100.0**	**5.9**	**8.2**	**9.2**	**82.7**
Life and other personal insurance	100.0	4.4	9.7	4.5	85.8
Pensions and Social Security	100.0	6.0	8.1	9.5	82.5
PERSONAL TAXES	**100.0**	**8.0**	**3.1**	**2.9**	**94.1**
Federal income taxes	100.0	9.1	1.8	2.1	96.1
State and local income taxes	100.0	6.0	5.9	4.6	89.7
Other taxes	100.0	4.1	5.7	3.9	90.3
GIFTS FOR PEOPLE IN OTHER HOUSEHOLDS	**100.0**	**4.5**	**5.9**	**7.0**	**87.1**

Note: Numbers do not add to total because some consumer units are included in more than one column. "Other" includes Alaska Natives, American Indians, Asians, Native Hawaiians, and other Pacific Islanders as well as those who report being of more than one race. The Bureau of Labor Statistics uses consumer unit rather than household as the sampling unit in the Consumer Expenditure Survey. For the definition of consumer unit, see the glossary.
Source: Calculations by New Strategist based on the Bureau of Labor Statistics' 2011 Consumer Expenditure Survey, Internet site http://www.bls.gov/cex/

Glossary

adjusted for inflation Income or a change in income that has been adjusted for the rise in the cost of living or the consumer price index.

age Classification by age is based on the age of the person at his/her last birthday.

American Community Survey The ACS is an on-going nationwide survey of 250,000 households per month, providing detailed demographic data at the community level. Designed to replace the census long-form questionnaire, the ACS includes more than 60 questions that formerly appeared on the long form, such as language spoken at home, income, and education. ACS data are available for the nation, regions, states, counties, metropolitan areas, and many places.

American Housing Survey The AHS collects national and metropolitan-level data on the nation's housing, including apartments, single-family homes, and mobile homes. The nationally representative survey, with a sample of 55,000 households, is conducted by the Census Bureau for the Department of Housing and Urban Development every other year.

American Indians In this book, American Indians include Alaska Natives (Eskimos and Aleuts). American Indians can identify themselves as being American Indian and no other race (called "American Indian alone") or as being American Indian in combination with one or more other races (called "American Indian in combination"). The combination of the two groups is termed "American Indian alone or in combination." In this book, the "American Indian alone" population is shown.

American Time Use Survey Under contract with the Bureau of Labor Statistics, the Census Bureau collects ATUS information, revealing how people spend their time. The ATUS sample is drawn from U.S. households that have completed their final month of interviews for the Current Population Survey. One individual from each selected household is chosen to participate in the ATUS. Respondents are interviewed by telephone about their time use on the previous day.

Asian The term "Asian" includes Native Hawaiians and other Pacific Islanders. Middle Eastern nations—such as Iran, Iraq, Israel, and Jordan—are considered part of the Asian world region. Therefore, immigrants from the Middle East are counted as Asians in the immigration tables. Asians can identify themselves as being Asian and no other race (called "Asian alone") or as being Asian in combination with one or more other races (called "Asian in combination"). The combination of the two groups is termed "Asian alone or in combination." In this book, the "Asian alone or in combination" population is shown whenever possible.

baby boom Americans born between 1946 and 1964.

baby bust Americans born between 1965 and 1976, also known as Generation X.

black The black racial category includes those who identified themselves as "black" or "African American." Blacks can identify themselves as being black and no other race (called "black alone") or as being black in combination with one or more other races (called "black in combination"). The combination of the two groups is termed "black alone or in combination." In this book, the "black alone or in combination" population is shown whenever possible.

Consumer Expenditure Survey The CEX is an ongoing study of the day-to-day spending of American households administered by the Bureau of Labor Statistics. The CEX includes an interview survey and a diary survey. The average spending figures shown are the integrated data from the diary and interview components of the survey. Two separate, nationally representative samples are used for the interview and diary surveys. For the interview survey, about 7,500 consumer units are interviewed on a rotating panel basis each quarter for five consecutive quarters. For the diary survey, 7,500 consumer units keep weekly diaries of spending for two consecutive weeks.

consumer unit *(on spending tables only)* For convenience, the terms consumer unit and households are used interchangeably in the spending sections of this book, although consumer units are somewhat different from the Census Bureau's households. A consumer unit includes all the related members of a household or any financially independent member of a household. A household may include more than one consumer unit.

Current Population Survey The CPS is a nationally representative survey of the civilian noninstitutional population aged 15 or older. It is taken monthly by the Census Bureau for the Bureau of Labor Statistics, collecting information from more than 50,000 households on employment and unemployment. In March of each year, the survey includes the Annual Social and Economic Supplement (formerly called the Annual Demographic Survey), which is the source of most national data on the characteristics of Americans, such as educational attainment, living arrangements, and incomes.

disability The National Health Interview Survey estimates the number of people aged 18 or older who have difficulty in physical functioning, probing whether respondents could perform nine activities by themselves without using special equipment. The categories are walking a quarter mile; standing for two hours; sitting for two hours; walking up 10 steps without resting; stooping, bending, kneeling; reaching over one's head; grasping or handling small objects; carrying a 10-pound object; and pushing/pulling a large object. Adults who reported that any of these activities was very difficult or they could not do it at all were defined as having physical difficulties.

dual-earner couple A married couple in which both the householder and the householder's spouse are in the labor force.

earnings A type of income, earnings is the amount of money a person receives from his or her job. *See also* Income.

employed All civilians who did any work as a paid employee or farmer/self-employed worker or who worked 15 hours or more as an unpaid farm worker or in a family-owned business during the reference period. All those who have jobs but who are temporarily absent from their jobs due to illness, bad weather, vacation, labor management dispute, or personal reasons are considered employed.

expenditure The transaction cost including excise and sales taxes of goods and services acquired during the survey period. The full cost of each purchase is recorded even though full payment may not have been made at the date of purchase. Average expenditure figures may be artificially low for infrequently purchased items such as cars because figures are calculated using all consumer units within a demographic segment rather than just purchasers. Expenditure estimates include money spent on gifts for others.

family A group of two or more people (one of whom is the householder) related by birth, marriage, or adoption and living in the same household.

family household A household maintained by a householder who lives with one or more people related to him or her by blood, marriage, or adoption.

female/male householder A woman or man who maintains a household without a spouse present. May head family or nonfamily household.

foreign-born population People who are not U.S. citizens at birth.

full-time employment Full-time is 35 or more hours of work per week during a majority of the weeks worked.

full-time, year-round Indicates 50 or more weeks of full-time employment during the previous calendar year.

General Social Survey The GSS is a biennial survey of the attitudes of Americans taken by the University of Chicago's National Opinion Research Center. NORC conducts the GSS through face-to-face interviews with an independently drawn, representative sample of 1,500 to 3,000 noninstitutionalized people aged 18 or older who live in the United States.

generation X Americans born between 1965 and 1976, also known as the baby-bust generation.

Hispanic Because Hispanic is an ethnic origin rather than a race, Hispanics may be of any race. While most Hispanics are white, there are black, Asian, American Indian, and even Native Hawaiian Hispanics.

household All the persons who occupy a housing unit. A household includes the related family members and all the unrelated persons, if any, such as lodgers, foster children, wards, or employees who share the housing unit. A person living alone is counted as a household. A group of unrelated people who share a housing unit as roommates or unmarried partners is also counted as a household. Households do not include group quarters such as college dormitories, prisons, or nursing homes.

household, race/ethnicity of Households are categorized according to the race or ethnicity of the householder only.

householder The householder is the person (or one of the persons) in whose name the housing unit is owned or rented or, if there is no such person, any adult member. With married couples, the householder may be either the husband or wife. The householder is the reference person for the household.

householder, age of The age of the householder is used to categorize households into age groups such as those used in this book. Married couples, for example, are classified according to the age of either the husband or wife, depending on which one identified him or herself as the householder.

housing unit A housing unit is a house, an apartment, a group of rooms, or a single room occupied or intended for occupancy as separate living quarters. Separate living quarters are those in which the occupants do not live and eat with any other persons in the structure and that have direct access from the outside of the building or through a common hall that is used or intended for use by the occupants of another unit or by the general public. The occupants may be a single family, one person living alone, two or more families living together, or any other group of related or unrelated persons who share living arrangements.

Housing Vacancy Survey The HVS is a supplement to the Current Population Survey, providing quarterly and annual data on rental and homeowner vacancy rates, characteristics of units available for occupancy, and homeownership rates by age, household type, region, state, and metropolitan area. The Current Population Survey sample includes 72,000 occupied housing units and 10,000 vacant units.

housing value The respondent's estimate of how much his or her house and lot would sell for if it were for sale.

immigrants Aliens admitted for legal permanent residence in the United States.

income Money received in the preceding calendar year by each person aged 15 or older from any of the following sources: earnings from longest job, earnings from jobs other than longest job, unemployment compensation, workers' compensation, Social Security, Supplemental Security income, public assistance, veterans' payments, survivor benefits, disability benefits, retirement pensions, interest, dividends, rents and royalties or estates and trusts, educational assistance, alimony, child support, financial assistance from outside the household, and other periodic income. Income is reported in several ways in this book. Household income is the combined income of all household members. Income of persons is all income accruing to a person from all sources. Earnings are the money a person receives from his or her job.

industry Refers to the industry in which a person worked longest in the preceding calendar year.

job tenure The length of time a person has been employed continuously by the same employer.

labor force The labor force tables in this book show the civilian labor force only. The labor force includes both the employed and the unemployed (people who are looking for work). People are counted as in the labor force if they were working or looking for work during the reference week in which the Census Bureau fields the Current Population Survey.

labor force participation rate The percent of the civilian noninstitutional population that is in the civilian labor force, which includes both the employed and the unemployed.

male householder *See* Female/Male Householder.

married-couple family group Married couples who may or may not be householders. Those who are householders are "married-couple households." Those who are not householders are married couples living in a household headed by someone else, such as a parent of the husband or wife. Because married-couple family groups include married-couple households, the number of married-couple family groups will always outnumber married-couple households.

married couples with or without children under age 18 Refers to married couples with or without own children under age 18 living in the same household. Couples without children under age 18 may be parents of grown children who live elsewhere, or they could be childless couples.

median The median is the amount that divides the population or households into two equal portions: one below and one above the median. Medians can be calculated for income, age, and many other characteristics.

median income The amount that divides the income distribution into two equal groups, half having incomes above the median, half having incomes below the median. The medians for households or families are based on all households or families. The median for persons are based on all persons aged 15 or older with income.

metropolitan statistical area, or MSA To be defined as an MSA, an area must include a city with 50,000 or more inhabitants, or a Census Bureau–defined urbanized area of at least 50,000 inhabitants and a total metropolitan population of at least 100,000 (75,000 in New England). The county (or counties) that contains the largest city becomes the "central county" (counties), along with any adjacent counties that have at least 50 percent of their population in the urbanized area surrounding the largest city. Additional "outlying counties" are included in the MSA if they meet specified requirements of commuting to the central counties and other selected requirements of metropolitan character (such as population density and percent urban). In New England, MSAs are defined in terms of cities and towns rather than counties. For this reason, the concept of New England County Metropolitan Area is used to define metropolitan areas in the New England division.

millennial generation Americans born between 1977 and 1994.

mobility status People are classified according to their mobility status on the basis of a comparison between their place of residence at the time of the March Current Population Survey and their place of residence in March of the previous year. Nonmovers are people living in the same house at the end of the period as at the beginning of the period. Movers are people living in a different house at the end of the period from that at the beginning of the period. Movers from abroad are either citizens or aliens whose place of residence is outside the United States at the beginning of the period, that is, in an outlying area under the jurisdiction of the United States or in a foreign country. The mobility status for children is fully allocated from the mother if she is in the household; otherwise it is allocated from the householder.

National Health and Nutrition Examination Survey The NHANES is a continuous survey of a representative sample of the U.S. civilian noninstitutionalized population. Respondents are interviewed at home about their health and nutrition, and the interview is followed up by a physical examination that measures such things as height and weight in mobile examination centers.

National Health Interview Survey The NHIS is a continuing nationwide sample survey of the civilian noninstitutional population of the United States conducted by the Census Bureau for the National Center for Health Statistics. In interviews each year, data are collected from more than 100,000 people about their illnesses, injuries, impairments, chronic and acute conditions, activity limitations, and use of health services.

Native Hawaiian and Other Pacific Islander The 2000 census identified this group for the first time as a separate racial category from Asians. In most survey data, however, the population is included with Asians.

nonfamily household A household maintained by a householder who lives alone or who lives with people to whom he or she is not related.

nonfamily householder A householder who lives alone or with nonrelatives.

non-Hispanic People who do not identify themselves as Hispanic are classified as non-Hispanic. Non-Hispanics may be of any race.

non-Hispanic white People who identify their race as white alone and who do not indicate their ethnicity as Hispanic.

nonmetropolitan area Counties that are not classified as metropolitan areas.

occupation Occupational classification is based on the kind of work a person did at his or her job during the previous calendar year. If a person changed jobs during the year, the data refer to the occupation of the job held the longest during that year.

occupied housing units A housing unit is classified as occupied if a person or group of people is living in it or if the occupants are only temporarily absent—on vacation, for example. By definition, the count of occupied housing units is the same as the count of households.

outside principal city The portion of a metropolitan county or counties that falls outside of the principal city or cities; generally regarded as the suburbs.

own children Own children are sons and daughters, including stepchildren and adopted children, of the householder. The totals include never-married children living away from home in college dormitories.

owner occupied A housing unit is "owner occupied" if the owner lives in the unit, even if it is mortgaged or not fully paid for. A cooperative or condominium unit is "owner occupied" only if the owner lives in it. All other occupied units are classified as "renter occupied."

part-time employment Part-time is less than 35 hours of work per week in a majority of the weeks worked during the year.

percent change The change (either positive or negative) in a measure that is expressed as a proportion of the starting measure. When median income changes from $20,000 to $25,000, for example, this is a 25 percent increase.

percentage point change The change (either positive or negative) in a value that is already expressed as a percentage. When a labor force participation rate changes from 70 percent to 75 percent, for example, this is a 5 percentage point increase.

poverty level The official income threshold below which families and people are classified as living in poverty. The threshold rises each year with inflation and varies depending on family size and age of householder.

principal city The largest city in a metropolitan area is called the principal or central city. The balance of the metropolitan area outside the principal or central city is regarded as the "suburbs."

proportion or share The value of a part expressed as a percentage of the whole. If there are 4 million people aged 25 and 3 million of them are white, then the white proportion is 75 percent.

race Race is self-reported and can be defined in three ways. The "race alone" population comprises people who identify themselves as being of only one race. The "race in combination" population comprises people who identify themselves as being of more than one race, such as white and black. The "race, alone or in combination" population includes both those who identify themselves as being of one race and those who identify themselves as being of more than one race.

regions The four major regions and nine census divisions of the United States are the state groupings as shown below:

Northeast:
—New England: Connecticut, Maine, Massachusetts, New Hampshire, Rhode Island, and Vermont
—Middle Atlantic: New Jersey, New York, and Pennsylvania

Midwest:
—East North Central: Illinois, Indiana, Michigan, Ohio, and Wisconsin
—West North Central: Iowa, Kansas, Minnesota, Missouri, Nebraska, North Dakota, and South Dakota

South:
—South Atlantic: Delaware, District of Columbia, Florida, Georgia, Maryland, North Carolina, South Carolina, Virginia, and West Virginia
—East South Central: Alabama, Kentucky, Mississippi, and Tennessee
—West South Central: Arkansas, Louisiana, Oklahoma, and Texas

West:
—Mountain: Arizona, Colorado, Idaho, Montana, Nevada, New Mexico, Utah, and Wyoming
—Pacific: Alaska, California, Hawaii, Oregon, and Washington

renter occupied *See* Owner Occupied.

rounding Percentages are rounded to the nearest tenth of a percent; therefore, the percentages in a distribution do not always add exactly to 100.0 percent. The totals, however, are always shown as 100.0. Moreover, individual figures are rounded to the nearest thousand without being adjusted to group totals, which are independently rounded; percentages are based on the unrounded numbers.

self-employment A person is categorized as self-employed if he or she was self-employed in the job held longest during the reference period. Persons who report self-employment from a second job are excluded, but those who report wage and salary income from a second job are included. Unpaid workers in family businesses are excluded. Self-employment statistics include only nonagricultural workers and exclude people who work for themselves in incorporated business.

sex ratio The number of men per 100 women.

suburbs *See* Outside Principal City.

Survey of Income and Program Participation
The Survey of Income and Program Participation is a continuous, monthly panel survey of up to 36,700 households conducted by the Census Bureau. It is designed to measure the effectiveness of existing federal, state, and local programs and to measure economic well-being, including wealth, asset ownership, and debt.

unemployed Unemployed people are those who, during the survey period, had no employment but were available and looking for work. Those who were laid off from their jobs and were waiting to be recalled are also classified as unemployed.

white The "white" racial category includes many Hispanics (who may be of any race) unless the term "non-Hispanic white" is used. In this book, the non-Hispanic white population is shown whenever possible.

Youth Risk Behavior Surveillance System The YRBSS was created by the Centers for Disease Control to monitor health risks being taken by young people at the national, state, and local level. The national survey is taken every two years based on a nationally representative sample of 16,000 students in 9th through 12th grade in public and private schools.

Bibliography

Bureau of Labor Statistics
   Internet site http://www.bls.gov/
   —American Time Use Survey, unpublished tables, Internet site http://www.bls.gov/tus/
   —Characteristics of Minimum Wage Workers, 2011, Internet site http://www.bls.gov/cps/minwage2011tbls.htm
   —Consumer Expenditure Survey, Internet site http://www.bls.gov/cex/home.htm
   —Current Population Survey, Internet site http://www.bls.gov/cps/tables.htm#empstat
   —Employee Tenure, Internet site http://www.bls.gov/news.release/tenure.toc.htm
   —Monthly Labor Review, "Labor Force Projections to 2020: A More Slowly Growing Workforce," January 2012, Internet site http://www.bls.gov/opub/mlr/2012/01/home.htm

Bureau of the Census
   Internet site http://www.census.gov/
   —2000 Census, American Factfinder, Internet site http://factfinder2.census.gov/faces/nav/jsf/pages/index.xhtml
   —2010 Census, American Factfinder, Internet site http://factfinder2.census.gov/faces/nav/jsf/pages/index.xhtml
   —American Community Survey, American Factfinder, Internet site http://factfinder2.census.gov/faces/nav/jsf/pages/index.xhtml
   —American Housing Survey, Internet site http://www.census.gov/housing/ahs/
   —The American Indian and Alaska Native Population: 2010, 2010 Census Brief, Internet site http://www.census.gov/2010census/data/2010-census-briefs.php
   —Current Population Survey, Annual Social and Economic Supplement, Internet site http://www.census.gov/hhes/www/income/data/
   —Educational Attainment, Annual Social and Economic Supplement, Internet site http://www.census.gov/hhes/socdemo/education/
   —Families and Living Arrangements, Current Population Survey Annual Social and Economic Supplement, Internet site http://www.census.gov/hhes/families/
   —Geographic Mobility/Migration, Current Population Survey Annual Social and Economic Supplement, Internet site http://www.census.gov/hhes/migration/
   —Health Insurance, Current Population Survey Annual Social and Economic Supplements, Internet site http://www.census.gov/hhes/www/cpstables/032012/health/toc.htm
   —The Hispanic Population: 2010, 2010 Census Brief, Internet site http://www.census.gov/2010census/data/2010-census-briefs.php
   —Historical Income Data, Current Population Survey Annual Social and Economic Supplements, Internet site http://www.census.gov/hhes/www/income/data/historical/index.html
   —Historical Poverty Tables, Current Population Survey Annual Social and Economic Supplements, Internet site http://www.census.gov/hhes/www/poverty/data/historical/index.html
   —Housing Vacancy Survey, Internet site http://www.census.gov/housing/hvs/
   —Income, Current Population Survey Annual Social and Economic Supplements, Internet site

http://www.census.gov/hhes/www/income/data/index.html

—Number, Timing, and Duration of Marriages and Divorces: 2009, Detailed Tables, Internet site http://www.census.gov/hhes/socdemo/marriage/data/sipp/2009/tables.html

—An Overview: Race and Hispanic Origin and the 2010 Census, 2010 Census Briefs, Internet site http://www.census.gov/2010census/data/2010-census-briefs.php

—Population Estimates, Internet site http://www.census.gov/popest/index.html

—Population Projections, Internet site http://www.census.gov/population/projections/

—Poverty, Current Population Survey Annual Social and Economic Supplements, Internet site http://www.census.gov/hhes/www/poverty/index.html

—School Enrollment, CPS October 2011, Detailed Tables, Internet site http://www.census.gov/hhes/school/data/cps/2011/tables.html

—Voting and Registration, Internet site http://www.census.gov/hhes/www/socdemo/voting/index.html

—Wealth and Asset Ownership, Survey of Income and Program Participation, Internet site http://www.census.gov/people/wealth/

Centers for Disease Control and Prevention

Internet site http://www.cdc.gov/

—Youth Risk Behavior Surveillance—United States, 2011, Mortality and Morbidity Weekly Report, Vol. 61, No. 4, 2012, Internet site http://www.cdc.gov/HealthyYouth/yrbs/index.htm

Department of Homeland Security

Internet site http://www.dhs.gov/

—Estimates of the Unauthorized Immigrant Population Residing in the United States: January 2011, Internet site http://www.dhs.gov/estimates-unauthorized-immigrant-population-residing-united-states-january-2011

—Yearbook of Immigration Statistics, Internet site http://www.dhs.gov/yearbook-immigration-statistics

National Center for Education Statistics

Internet site http://nces.ed.gov/

—The Condition of Education, Internet site http://nces.ed.gov/programs/coe/

—Digest of Education Statistics, Internet site http://nces.ed.gov/programs/digest/

National Center for Health Statistics

Internet site http://www.cdc.gov/nchs/

—Anthropometric Reference Data for Children and Adults: United States, 2007–2010, National Health Statistics Reports, Series 11, No. 252, 2012, Internet site http://www.cdc.gov/nchs/nhanes.htm

—Births: Final Data for 2010, National Vital Statistics Reports, Vol. 61, No. 1, 2012, Internet site http://www.cdc.gov/nchs/births.htm

—Births: Preliminary Data for 2011, National Vital Statistics Reports, Vol. 61, No. 5, 2012, Internet site http://www.cdc.gov/nchs/births.htm

—Deaths: Leading Causes for 2009, National Vital Statistics Reports, Vol. 61, No. 7, 2012, Internet site http://www.cdc.gov/nchs/deaths.htm

—Deaths: Preliminary Data for 2011, National Vital Statistics Reports, Vol. 61, No. 6, 2012,

Internet site http://www.cdc.gov/nchs/deaths.htm

—Health, United States, Internet site http://www.cdc.gov/nchs/hus.htm

—Summary Health Statistics for U.S. Adults: National Health Interview Survey, 2011, Series 10, No. 256, 2012, Internet site http://www.cdc.gov/nchs/nhis.htm

—Summary Health Statistics for U.S. Children: National Health Interview Survey, 2011, Series 10, No. 254, 2012, Internet site http://www.cdc.gov/nchs/nhis.htm

Survey Documentation and Analysis, Computer-assisted Survey Methods Program, University of California, Berkeley

Internet site http://sda.berkeley.edu/

—General Social Surveys, 1972–2012 Cumulative Data Files, Internet site http://sda.berkeley.edu/cgi-bin/hsda?harcsda+gss12

Index

401(k), as asset
    by Asians, 223–224
    by blacks, 355–356
    by Hispanics, 502–503
    by non-Hispanic whites, 628–629

ability to speak English, 742
accidents, as cause of death, 48, 122, 257, 395, 535, 657
ADHD. *See* Health conditions.
age
    of American Indians, 78–80
    of Asians, 187–190, 720
    of blacks, 327–330, 720
    of Hispanics, 467–470, 720
    of non-Hispanic whites, 603–606, 720
    of total population, 719–722
AIDS
    American Indians with, 47
    as cause of death, 257
    Asians with, 121
    blacks with, 256
    Hispanics with, 394
    non-Hispanic whites with, 534
alcoholic beverages, spending on. *See also*
        Drinking.
    by Asians, 218–220, 752–760
    by blacks, 350–352, 752–760
    by Hispanics, 497–499, 752–760
    by non-Hispanic whites, 622–624, 752–760
    by total, 752–760
Alzheimer's disease, as cause of death, 122, 535, 657
apparel, spending on
    by Asians, 218–220, 752–760
    by blacks, 350–352, 752–760
    by Hispanics, 497–499, 752–760
    by non-Hispanic whites, 622–624, 752–760
    total, 752–760
asset ownership
    by Asians, 223–224
    by blacks, 355–356
    by Hispanics, 502–503
    by non-Hispanic whites, 628–629
associate's degree. *See* Degrees earned.
asthma. *See* Health conditions.
attention deficit hyperactivity disorder (ADHD).
    See Health conditions.
attitude toward
    capital punishment, 25
    evolution, 18

    family income, 12–13
    financial situation, 13
    gay marriage, 23
    getting ahead, 11
    gun control, 26
    happiness, 9
    homosexuality, 22–23
    ideal number of children, 15
    life, exciting or dull, 10
    news sources, 24
    political, 24–25
    premarital sex, 22
    religion, 18–20
    science, 17
    sex roles, 16
    should government help the sick, 17
    social class, 12
    standard of living, 14–15
    trusting others, 10
    working mothers, 16

bachelor's degree. *See* Degrees earned.
bank accounts, as asset
    by Asians, 223–224
    by blacks, 355–356
    by Hispanics, 502–503
    by non-Hispanic whites, 628–629
bathrooms in home, 268–269, 404–405, 665
bedrooms in home, 268–269, 404–405, 665
Bible, belief in, 20
births
    American Indian, 40–43
    Asian, 112–115, 646–647, 649–650
    black, 247–250, 646–647, 649–650
    by age, 40, 112, 247, 380–382, 525–526, 645–647
    by birth order, 41, 113, 248, 382, 526, 648
    by ethnicity, 381, 385–388
    by marital status, 40, 112, 247, 382, 526, 646–647
    by state, 42–43, 114–115, 249–250, 383–388, 527–528, 649–650
    Hispanic, 380–388, 646–647, 649–650
    non-Hispanic white, 525–528, 646–647, 649–650
    total, 645–650
business debt
    of Asians, 225
    of blacks, 357
    of Hispanics, 504
    of non-Hispanic whites, 629
business equity, as asset
    of Asians, 223–224
    of blacks, 355–356
    of Hispanics, 502–503
    of non-Hispanic whites, 628–629